The Big Mac Book

Neil J. Salkind

CORPORATION
LEADING COMPUTER KNOWLEDGE

The Big Mac Book

Copyright© 1989 by Que® Corporation

Library of Congress Catalog No.: 89-62437

ISBN 0-88022-456-8

93 92 91 90 89   8 7 6 5 4 3 2 1

Interpretation of the printing code: the rightmost double-digit number is the year of the book's printing; the rightmost single-digit number, the number of the book's printing. For example, a printing code of 89-1 shows that the first printing of the book occurred in 1989.

The Big Mac Book is based on Macintosh System 6 and earlier, with added information about System 7.

Comparison charts were produced in Wingz on a Macintosh II and printed on a QMS-PS 810 printer.

D E D I C A T I O N

To my parents, Irene Helen Salkind and Harry Salkind, who
served as models of compassion and perseverance.
Ad Astra Per Asperum

Publishing Director

Lloyd J. Short

Acquisitions Editor

Karen A. Bluestein

Product Director

Karen A. Bluestein

Special Contributor

Barrie Sosinsky

Production Editor

Jeannine Freudenberger

Editors

Sara Allaei   Kelly D. Dobbs
Jo Anna Arnott   Joseph P. Goodwin
Fran Blauw   Gregory Robertson
Kelly Currie

Technical Editors

Barrie Sosinsky
Daniel Zoller

Editorial Assistant

Stacie Lamborne

Indexer

Sherry Massey

Book Design and Production

Dan Armstrong
David Kline
Lori A. Lyons
Jennifer Matthews
Mitzi Parsons
Cindy L. Phipps
Joe Ramon
Patricia Maupin Riggs
Dennis Sheehan
Louise Shinault
Mary Beth Wakefield

Composed in Garamond and Excellent No. 47
by Que Corporation

ABOUT THE AUTHOR

Neil J. Salkind

Neil J. Salkind lives among the rolling hills of eastern Kansas and has taught at the University of Kansas for 16 years, in the areas of child development and child and family policy analysis. He has written more than 20 computer books on various topics, including spreadsheets, word processing, and graphics. He has also published several college-level textbooks and written more than 100 papers dealing with children and families. He is currently editor of *Child Development Abstracts & Bibliography*.

When he's not on the third floor sitting at the Mac writing away, you can find him working on the Salkinds' old house, reading fiction, baking chocolate chip cookies, spending time with his family, or flying kites on the great plains.

CONTENTS AT A GLANCE

Part VI   Advanced Topics

TABLE OF CONTENTS

IV Deciding What To Buy

V   Networking and Communications

ACKNOWLEDGMENTS ▽

Y ou have all read the acknowledgments that come at the beginning of books—full of thanks for this person or that one and telling you, the reader, how a book (like this one) is the product of many people, and each deserves credit, and the book would not have been possible without Dick or Roz, and so on and so on. Some authors even thank the dog (and the kids for leaving them alone). Well, I won't thank the dog or the kids (because they didn't leave me alone), but it's true: no book is the product of only one person. And this book, especially, took long hours, commitment, and special attention from many people.

The person most responsible for the inception and the guidance I received throughout the preparation of the original manuscript is Karen Bluestein, Que's Acquisitions Editor and Product Director for this book. Karen does what few editors do anymore; she edits. Her suggestions and willingness to help whenever possible are deeply appreciated and place her apart from others who are more concerned with quantity than quality. My agent, Bill Gladstone, provided me with the opportunity, and as always, I am grateful for his support and encouragement.

The other member of the Que team who made the original manuscript (a euphemism for a first draft!) into a book is Jeannine Freudenberger. She took care of it all, from making sure that captions matched figures to gentle suggestions that this or that sentence makes no sense at all or that we (meaning me, of course) are running a little late, all the while keeping track of everything (which was an amazing feat in itself). Then there are the technical editors, who know more about the Macintosh than anyone would think possible. Daniel Zoller and Barrie Sosinsky are experts on the Mac and experts at teaching what they know. Their comments and guidance were invaluable, and I deeply appreciate their interest and kind words throughout the final revision.

Other people were also very helpful in the completion of the book. Bill Moore read through each chapter and provided helpful feedback as well as collected information for important charts. Chitra Thippivara and Peggy Billings spent endless hours typing the charts and the majority of the contents in the appendixes. To all of them, I owe a great deal of thanks.

I would also like to thank the numerous vendors of both software and hardware who sent me review copies of their products and information for possible inclusion in the book. Many efforts on their part went far beyond the call of duty to help educate me about the finer points of what their company can offer to Mac-dom, and I hope their products receive the support they deserve. I also made some new friends along the way, a wonderful side benefit.

In more ways than there is room to express here, I continue to learn and be dazzled by children, especially Sara, 13, and Micah, 5. They would enter my study unannounced and begin "fooling" with applications and games, every now and then discovering that, "Hey, Dad, did you know that when you do this you can..." and so on. (I usually didn't know it, by the way.) They are a delight, a constant source of inspiration, and the promise of how all "our" children can bring us toward a better world if we give them the chance. Finally, my wife, Leni, has figured out how to calm me down when deadlines get near and things seem out of sorts, while at the same time assuring me that the book will get done and it will actually appear in print! None of the efforts that went into this book would have been possible without her love and support.

TRADEMARK ACKNOWLEDGMENTS ▽

Que Corporation has made every effort to supply trademark information about company names, products, and services mentioned in this book. Trademarks indicated below were derived from various sources. Que Corporation cannot attest to the accuracy of this information.

Apple, AppleTalk, HyperCard, ImageWriter, Lisa, Mac, Macintosh, Macintosh Plus, Macintosh SE, Macintosh SE/30, MacPaint, MacWrite, and MacWrite II are registered trademarks and MultiFinder is a trademark of Apple Computer, Inc.

AT&T is a registered trademark of AT&T.

CompuServe is a registered trademark of H&R Block Incorporated.

DacEasy is a trademark of DAC Software Incorporated.

dBASE and FullWrite Professional are registered trademarks and Full Impact is a trademark of Ashton-Tate Corporation.

Freehand is a trademark and PageMaker is a registered trademark of Aldus Corporation.

Generic CADD is a trademark of Generic Software, Inc.

IBM PC is a registered trademark and IBM PC XT is a trademark of International Business Machines.

Lotus, 1-2-3, Symphony, and VisiCalc are registered trademarks of Lotus Development Corporation.

Managing Your Money is a registered trademark of MECA.

MCI Mail is a registered service mark of MCI Communications Corporation.

Microsoft is a registered trademark of Microsoft Corporation.

PostScript is a registered trademark of Adobe Systems Incorporated.

QuarkXPress is a trademark of Quark, Inc.

Quicken is a registered trademark of Intuit.

SideKick is a registered trademark of Borland International Incorporated.

SuperPaint is a trademark of Silicon Beach Software Incorporated

TeleNet is a registered trademark of GTE Telenet Communications Corporation.

UNIX is a trademark of AT&T.

Wingz is a trademark of Informix Software, Inc.

WordPerfect is a registered trademark of WordPerfect Corporation.

WorksPlus Spell is a trademark of Lundeen and Associates

WriteNow is a trademark licensed to T/Maker Company.

Xerox is registered and trademarked by Xerox Corporation

Trademarks of other products mentioned in this book are held by the companies producing them.

Introduction

Welcome to *The Big Mac Book*

Why a "big book" about something so exciting and "easy" to use as the Macintosh family of computers? Because the Mac and everything that surrounds it has grown by leaps and bounds over the past few years, and this growth doesn't look like it's going to stop for a long time. The people at Apple Computer, Inc., are hard at work designing better Macs and Macintosh peripherals, such as disk drives, scanners, and printers. Thousands of third-party developers are also designing and producing new software, hardware, and other goodies to match the demands of each of Apple's new products.

Where does all this growth leave you? Reading every periodical you can get your hands on or turning to one comprehensive source of information: *The Big Mac Book*. This book is for you, whether you just plugged in your Mac for the first time (Be careful!) or you're on the cutting edge (That's hi-tech talk!) of what's happening in the area of personal computers.

In this book you will find information about every aspect of the Macintosh, including

- The basics you need in order to get your Macintosh up and running

- Macintosh business applications and the latest reviews and comparison charts of word processors, spreadsheets, and databases

- Information for getting started in programming your Mac

- Information about desktop publishing and its potential application to your needs

- Instruction on how to select software and hardware

- Instructions for setting up your Macintosh system

- Good games and other "fun" Mac activities

- An introduction to HyperCard

- Information about upgrading your Macintosh

- Keeping your Mac (and everything around it) secure

- Networking and telecommunications

Whatever you do with the Mac, you will be able to find information about it in *The Big Mac Book*. In addition, extensive tables and appendixes provide information ranging from the closest user group for you to join to an extensive directory of products and where they are available.

Who Should Use This Book?

Just like the rest of us, when you first saw a Macintosh computer, you couldn't take your eyes off the screen—and the best display you had ever seen. The Mac's amazing graphics and truly user-friendly nature increased your interest and excitement, and you knew that this was the computer you had to have.

So here you are, reading *The Big Mac Book* for ideas, guidance, and information so that you can use your Macintosh to make your work and play more efficient and more enjoyable.

Whether you are a beginner who doesn't know the difference between an icon and an ImageWriter or an advanced Macintosh user who is interested in the latest desktop publishing applications, *The Big Mac Book* is just for you.

The book begins with a history of the development and production of the Macintosh computer (and a little about the Apple Computer, Inc.) and the way the Macintosh has moved to the forefront in personal computing, up through the designs and plans its producers have for the future of the Macintosh. For many people who do their computing at the office or at home, the Macintosh is the only tool they need for word processing, desktop publishing, data analysis, and even for just having fun.

No matter what types of experiences or what level of expertise you have with the Macintosh or with computing in general, you can pick up *The Big Mac Book*, open to any page, and begin learning about the

Macintosh world. And you can learn easily and quickly. The book is organized and written in a way that the information contained in any one of the 19 chapters can stand alone. Just turn to the chapter you want and read away—following the examples that are presented and illustrated with reproductions of actual Macintosh screens.

What's in This Book

Just like the Macintosh computer, *The Big Mac Book* is for everyone. If you are a beginning Mac user, you will find certain features of the book especially helpful, such as

- The Quick Start at the beginning of the book, which will get you up and running without delay

- The basic step-by-step approach that leads you through complex procedures

- Advice on buying software and hardware

- Information about user groups

- The Survival Guide at the end of the book, which gives you tips and steps for many basic tasks

For example, just a brief look at word processors for the Mac will reveal that FullWrite Professional, Word, WordPerfect, Write Now, and the old standby MacWrite (now MacWrite II) are only five among many programs that can do basically the same things. If you want to know what separates these word processors from one another, and if you are looking for that special feature (such as easily working with graphics or easy outlining), the information in Chapter 6 will take you where you want to go.

For you experts, there's plenty here as well, such as

- The basics of keeping your Mac healthy by doing your own maintenance at your convenience

- The fundamentals of programming with the Mac, plus using the Mac's resident programming tool, ResEdit

- Ideas for networking and communicating with the Mac

- An introduction to the worlds of graphics and desktop publishing

The Big Mac Book consists of 19 chapters organized into six major parts: "Quick Start," "Just the Basics," "Macintosh Applications," "Deciding What To Buy", "Networking and Communications," and "Advanced Topics." At the end of the book, you will find a "Survival Guide" and several appendixes with still more information.

The "Quick Start" gives you quick and clear instructions on everything from plugging in your Mac (Yes, some people forget to do it.) to printing your first document. Even if you're a Mac "star," you may want to read quickly through this section. It contains some time-saving hints you may have missed in your travels.

"Just the Basics" includes answers to the "everything you wanted to know about the Mac but were afraid to ask" questions. Here, you learn about working with the basics of the system, manipulating and storing information as files on disks, and printing. This section is required reading and strongly prescribed for all new Mac enthusiasts. You no longer have to go to 20 different magazines and 3 books to find out why your ImageWriter won't print or what PostScript means for you.

Part III, "Macintosh Applications," gets to the heart of what many personal computers users depend on for most of their computer-related activities. Here, word processing, spreadsheet, and database programs are discussed and compared so that you can see the similarities and differences among them. You see how the Mac's unique graphical interface allows you to establish a close relationship with the Mac because so many applications use the same menu structure and key combinations and offer the same features. You will also feel confident that whether you use the Excel or Wingz spreadsheet, or Word or WordPerfect for your word processing activities, you can pick up either one and you will already know the basics. This part of *The Big Mac Book* also covers applications such as accounting, project management, available integrated software, and training packages that teach you how to use all this software. You will even find information about games and other special kinds of applications.

Part IV, "Deciding What To Buy," gets to the heart of the matter. Do you know how to shop through the mail? Believe me, getting ripped off is almost easier than coming away satisfied, in spite of the price! What kinds of questions should you ask when you mail order? What about your needs next week? Next year? What about those discount, guaranteed-forever (your life or the disk's?) floppies. And let's not forget a discussion of all the different Macs that can now be yours and the different combinations of Macs and peripherals you can configure. All the answers will be yours.

"Networking and Communications" are the buzz words of the 1980s and 1990s. You will see how one office can have five Macs and yet only one printer. Need to write a business report or a term paper and you need to know the population of Tibet? No problem. Just go on-line with a variety of information services and what you need to get—you get. You even can talk to a friend across the street or FAX (send a facsimile) a document across the world, all based on your Mac's communications capabilities.

Once you have the basics down, you will find that you want more information, because what follows is more enjoyment and productivity with your Mac. You learn about Mac tools, like HyperCard; and you learn about doing your own programming and making your Mac work to its potential. These topics make the "Advanced Topics" section just what you may need to move beyond "just using" your Mac system. You also get a taste of programming with BASIC and PASCAL, two popular programming languages for the Mac.

The "Survival Guide" gives quick steps and tips for doing tasks that all users must perform. Finally, the appendixes contain a wealth of information—from interpretations of error codes to names and addresses of user groups, BBSs, and vendors of many Mac products.

How To Use This Book

Here are some hints to make reading and using *The Big Mac Book* more enjoyable and more profitable.

First, *don't try too read too much too soon*. The fast readers are not always the best ones. If you are new to the Mac, one of the great pleasures in learning about it is taking your time and allowing yourself the luxury of discovering new things (and even possibly making mistakes). Rushing leads to mistakes, which lead to frustration, and then no one gets anywhere.

Second, *don't be afraid to try new things*. You may be a beginner and have no experience with ResEdit, desktop publishing, scanners, or other "fancy" Macintosh tools and features, but don't worry—everyone starts at the beginning, and even the experts didn't know much when they first picked up their mouse. This book and your enthusiasm make a perfect combination to explore everything the Mac offers. Although you may not be able to purchase enough software to try everything you want, user groups and other clubs have available on-site programs that are often open to members.

Third, *work through the examples*. There's nothing like learning by doing, and even though people often think that watching (or reading) is enough, they find that they need to exercise their knowledge so that it becomes a part of a larger base of understanding.

Finally, even if you use the Mac in your daily business and control an empire of millions of dollars and thousands of employees, the Mac was born out of a strong desire to create a computer that's just plain fun. The recommendation here is to let nature take its course; don't rush or have unreasonable expectations and demand too much from yourself in too short a time; just *enjoy the Macintosh* and *The Big Mac Book*.

With all these caveats and more in hand, here comes the first part of *The Big Mac Book* and the Quick Start, which will have you up and running in no time. Good luck and have a ball.

Part I

Quick Start

Quick Start

Everyone has to start somewhere. This special Quick Start is written especially for people who aren't familiar with the Macintosh's basic functions and features. You can learn more about any of the topics covered by reading Part II of *The Big Mac Book*, "Just the Basics."

In this Quick Start, work through the steps, and before you know it, you will be doing things with your Mac you didn't think possible in such a short time.

Before Anything Else

Before you actually start working with your Macintosh, remember the following precautions:

- Save (in a dry place) all the original cartons in which your Macintosh and equipment were shipped. You may need this stuff to take your equipment in for service, to use the next time you move, or even (Heaven forbid!) to ship your equipment for repair. The original cartons are constructed especially to fit and protect your Mac. The equipment must be packed securely to ensure that it does not get damaged. You should be aware, however, that the word *Macintosh* on your boxes may tempt thieves.

- Fill out all the registration cards and mail them in—today. (Do this with all the new software and hardware you buy.) Sending in these cards is essential if you are to receive the updates and the service you paid for.

- Don't throw anything away—at least until you have finished setting up your computer, and everything is connected and working. The material always includes little parts, manuals, cords, and registration cards that can easily get lost.

Prepare the work space where your equipment will go *before* you start opening packages. Keep in mind the following points when you are setting up:

- The length of the power cord (about 6 feet) controls the distance from the outlet to your work area.

- You need adequate artificial lighting that will not reflect directly off the screen and cause eye strain.

- If possible, you need adequate natural lighting that is at your back so as not to cause glare off your Mac screen.

- Your work area must have enough space for printers, additional disk drives, and other computer supplies.

- Place the Mac screen as close to eye level as possible.

- Be sure that you have adequate room to set your keyboard and to maneuver the mouse (about a 9-by-11-inch area).

- Your work surface must be level and free from other dangers to your system, such as coffee makers (Spills can be fatal!), lunch bags, and wires and cables that can be accidentally unplugged.

Hooking Things Up

You are ready to hook things up and make those connections that make your Mac work.

First, take your equipment out of the boxes. You have a

- Macintosh computer (If you have a Mac II, you also need, or have, a separate monitor.)

- Keyboard

- Mouse

- Printer

You also will find in the various boxes a bunch of cables that you use to connect system components (such as keyboards, monitors, and so on). Many users also buy a surge protector, a device that helps protect your computer and data from unanticipated and potentially damaging electrical surges. Before you begin setting up, take some time to read the manuals that came with your equipment.

To connect the parts of your system to each other, follow these steps:

1. Place your Macintosh on the surface the computer will call "home." If you have a Mac II, place the monitor on top of the computer and allow room for the keyboard. (You may want to buy Apple's monitor stand to be sure that your monitor is secure.)

2. Place the keyboard in front of the computer.

3. Place the printer to the left or right of the computer, depending on your setup and how much room you have. Place all external disk drives to the right of the computer unit. *Don't place an external drive on the left side of the Mac computer.* That side of the computer contains components that emit a type of energy that can interfere with the workings of the drive.

4. Look at the back of your Mac, which should look like one of the drawings shown in figures QS1 through QS6, depending on your model.

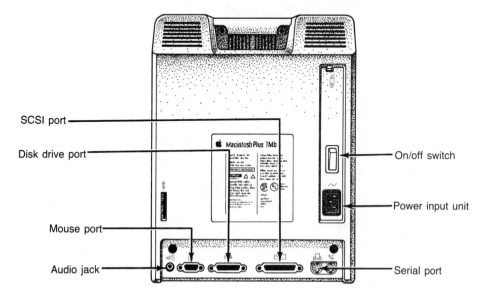

Fig. QS1. *The back of the Macintosh Plus.*

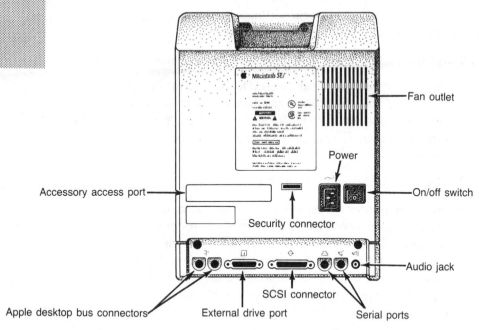

Fig. QS2. *The back of the Macintosh SE.*

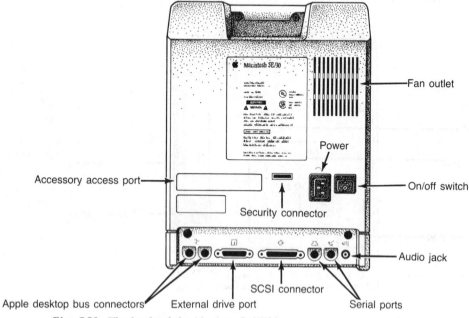

Fig. QS3. *The back of the Macintosh SE/30.*

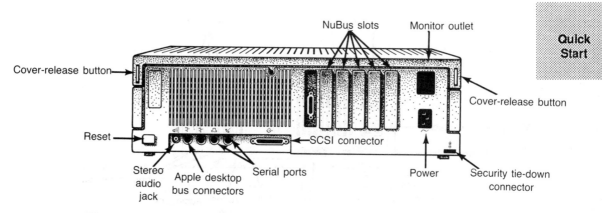

Fig. QS4. *The back of the Macintosh II.*

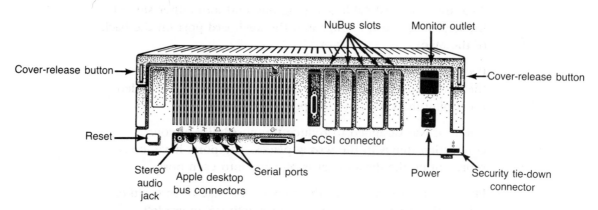

Fig. QS5. *The back of the Macintosh IIx.*

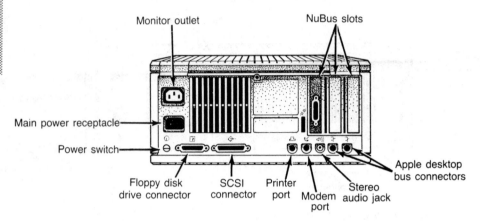

Fig. QS6. *The back of the Macintosh IIcx.*

5. Plug the power cord into your Macintosh computer right below the switch, which is on the left side of the machine.

6. Take the keyboard cable and plug one end into either side of the keyboard and the other into the keyboard port on the back of the Mac.

   People usually plug the keyboard cable into the same side of the keyboard as the hand they prefer to use. So right-handed users plug the cable into the port on the right.

   The Mac was designed to reduce the possibility of your connecting things in the wrong places. The ports have icons representing the device that is plugged into each port.

7. Plug the mouse cable into the back of the Mac or into either side of the keyboard, depending on whether you are left-handed or right-handed.

   A Mac II has more than one place to plug in the mouse, and you can plug it right into the main unit so that you can keep the mouse "tail" out of your way.

8. Plug the printer cable into your printer and then into the printer port on the back of the Macintosh.

   If you are using a laser printer, you may need additional cables. You may also need a switch box if you want to hook up more than one computer to the same printer or one computer to more than one printer. Consult your manuals, or ask your dealer for help with this hook-up.

If you have extras, such as external disk drives or (with some Macs) a separate monitor, follow these steps:

1. Place external drives to the right of the computer and plug the drive cable into the port with the floppy disk icon, in the back of the Mac.

2. If you have a Mac II, IIc, or IIcx, connect the monitor cable into the back of the Mac.

Finally, plug the three-pronged power cord into a grounded outlet or into a power strip with multiple outlets and surge protector, and you're ready to go. Now all that is left to do is to turn on your Mac.

Starting Your Macintosh

To turn on your Mac and display the opening screen, follow these steps:

1. Reach behind your computer and turn on the power switch. It is located on the back left side as you are facing the computer's front. On Mac IIs, the switch is on the right or on the keyboard.

   Three things happen:

   • You hear a pleasant beep telling you that your Mac is on.

   • The yellow plastic disk stabilizer inside your internal disk drive pops out. Save this disk stabilizer with the boxes and packing materials. It helps stabilize the drive's mechanical parts when the Mac is being shipped or moved. If you have a high-density drive or SuperDrive, like the ones that come with the Mac SE/30 and some Mac IIs, (1.44M), you don't have or need this plastic stabilizer. (More about this subject in Chapter 4.)

   • Your screen comes to life, and you see a cute little Macintosh with a smile welcoming you.

2. Place the Systems Tools Disk in the internal floppy drive. Insert the shiny metal part first. The disk should slide in easily and

"click" when it catches. If the disk does not slide in easily, you have it upside down. You soon see a smiling Mac icon. Shortly thereafter, you see the Mac opening screen.

If you have a hard disk that has been formatted, the computer will "boot up" automatically.

The opening Mac screen looks something like what you see in figure QS7. In the top right-hand corner is an *icon*, or a small picture, that represents the System disk you inserted into your internal drive.

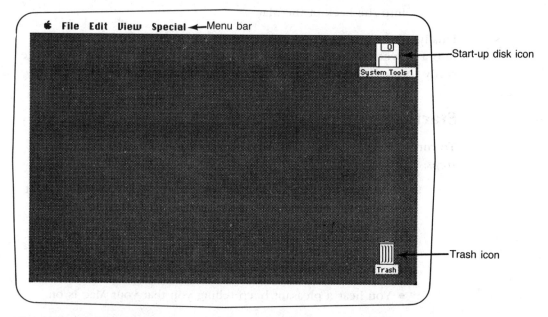

Fig. QS7. *The opening Macintosh screen.*

This opening screen represents what is called the *desktop*, which is created by Apple's Finder. If you have a hard disk, you will see a different icon located in the upper right corner of your opening screen; this icon represents the start-up disk.

Using the Mouse

The mouse (with its tail and all) is one of the vital connections between you and your computer and one of many different types of input devices. (The other vital connection is your keyboard.) The mouse is used to make selections on the desktop and to perform a variety of operations. In order to use the mouse efficiently, you need to learn and practice certain mouse techniques.

Practice moving the mouse around a solid surface. Just place your hand on the mouse and push it in different directions. You will see that as you move the mouse, the *mouse pointer*, or *cursor*, on the screen moves in the same direction as the mouse and in equivalent distances.

Place, or "point," the mouse pointer at the icon that represents the System disk. As you learn more about the Mac, you will use the mouse to point to and select icons before you perform an operation that affects that icon.

In figure QS8, you can see the mouse pointer placed on top of the System Tools icon. You are now using the mouse to point to this icon.

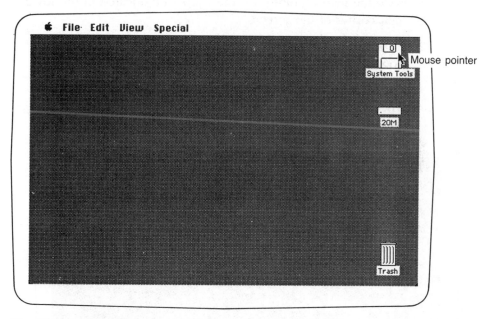

Fig. QS8. *Pointing to the System Tools icon.*

Three important mouse operations are clicking, dragging, and double-clicking. To *click*, you place the mouse pointer on an icon or other item and quickly press and release the mouse button once. To *drag*, you place mouse pointer on the item; then press the mouse button and hold it down while you move the item to a new location. When you release the mouse button, you have finished dragging. *Double-clicking* is two quick clicks. The interval between the clicks can be set through the Control Panel disk accessory, which you learn about in Chapter 2.

Place the mouse pointer on the System Tools icon (if the pointer is not already there). Now click the mouse button once. The icon reverses colors (goes from black to white). The icon is now *selected* (highlighted), and the next action you take will be applied to the disk that icon represents.

To *deselect* an icon, move the pointer off the icon and click again.

You move icons by dragging them. One reason for moving an icon is to rearrange the order of the file icons on your desktop. Follow these steps to drag an icon to another location:

1. Place the mouse pointer on the trash icon, located in the lower right corner of the screen.

2. Press the mouse button and with the button pressed, drag the icon to another location on the desktop.

3. Release the mouse button. Figures QS9 and QS10 show the process.

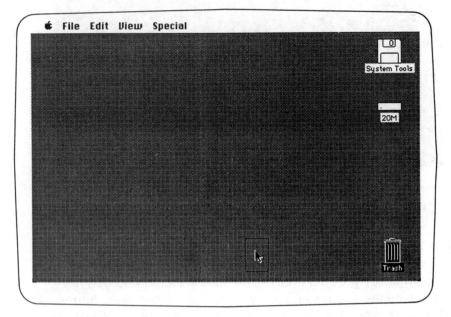

Fig. QS9. *Dragging the trash icon from one location on the screen to another.*

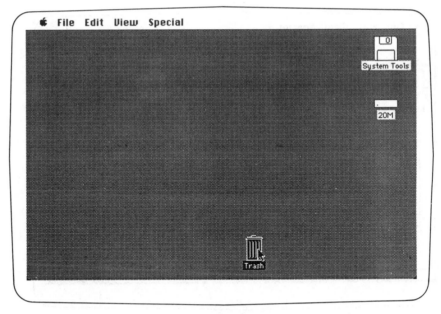

Fig. QS10. *Result of dragging the trash icon to another location.*

Opening a File

Now that you know how to move icons, you are ready to open a file.

1. Place the mouse pointer on the trash icon.

2. Click the mouse button twice in rapid succession. This action opens the file, creates a window, and reveals the file's contents (see fig. QS11). You have put nothing in the trash, and you can see that it contains no items.

Using the Macintosh Menus

Along the top of the opening screen is the *menu bar,* which lists a series of *menus.* Each menu contains various commands. Figure QS12 shows the different menus and their commands, which provide you with tools to do many things.

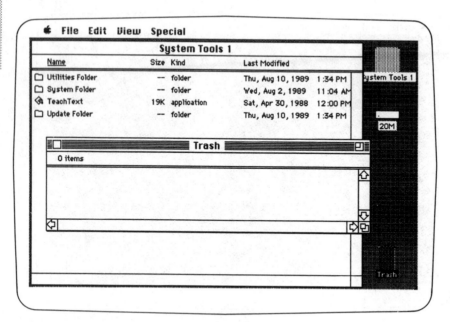

Fig. QS11. *Checking the contents of the trash.*

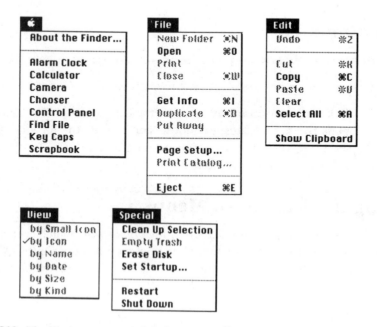

Fig. QS12. *The Finder menus and their commands.*

When working with menus, the menu items, or *commands*, that are dimmed are not active and have no effect if they are chosen.

To select a command from a menu, do the following:

1. Move the mouse pointer to the File menu title and press and hold down the mouse button to display the commands on the menu, as you see in figure QS13. As the cursor passes over each command, it is highlighted, but your selection is made only when you release the mouse button.

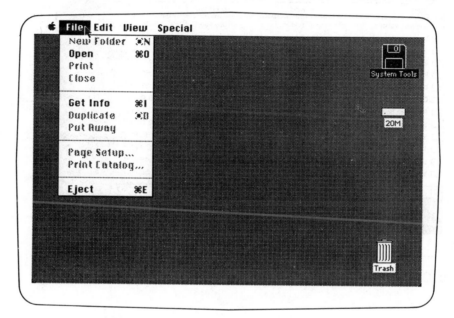

Fig. QS13. Displaying the File menu.

2. Press and hold the mouse button while you move the mouse pointer down to the command you want to choose. Then release the mouse button.

Working with Windows

When an icon representing a file is double-clicked and opened, the screen shows a *window*. A window is what you "look through" in order to work with a file's contents.

To open any window, double-click on the icon that represents the file you want to work with. Figure QS14 shows the results of clicking on the icon named 20M hard drive. The Mac displays names and information about some of the different files and folders on that hard disk. In figure QS14, you also see the various parts of the window labeled.

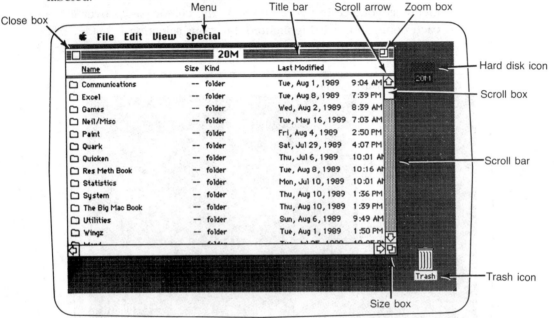

Fig. QS14. *Opening a window.*

To close a window, click on the *close box* located in the upper left corner of the screen. The window closes and "shrinks" back to the icon from which the window came.

To move a window, place the mouse pointer on the title bar and drag the window to its new location, as shown in figures QS15 and QS16. When you release the mouse button, the window is moved. One great Macintosh feature is that you can have more than one window open at once. However, only one window can be active. You can always tell the active window because it's the one with the horizontal lines in the title bar.

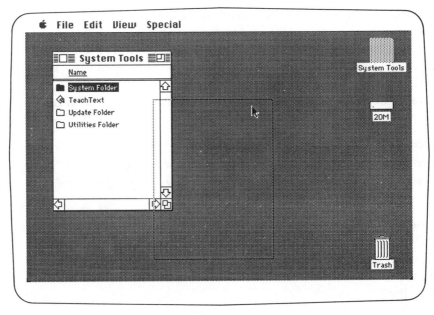

Fig. QS15. *Moving a window by dragging on the title bar.*

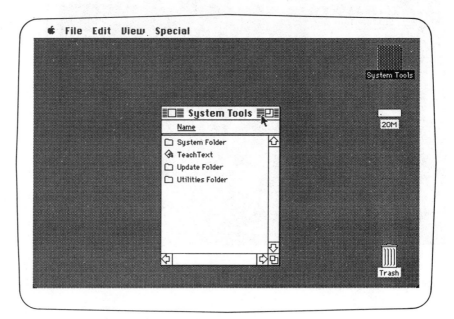

Fig. QS16. *The window in its new location.*

To change the size of a window to any size you want, drag the *size box*, located in the lower right corner of the window, as shown in figures QS17 and QS18. When you drag the size box to resize a window, the upper left corner of the window remains stationary. You can drag the size box in any direction to change the size of the window. When you release the mouse button, the window assumes the new size.

You also can change the size of a window by clicking the *zoom box*, located in the upper right corner of the window. Using the zoom box rather than the size box toggles the window between a larger window and the size you set.

Because not all the information contained in a document can fit on one screen (especially if you reduce the size of the window), you may have to *scroll* through the document's contents. Scrolling through a file means viewing a screenful at a time. As you scroll, you see different parts of the file.

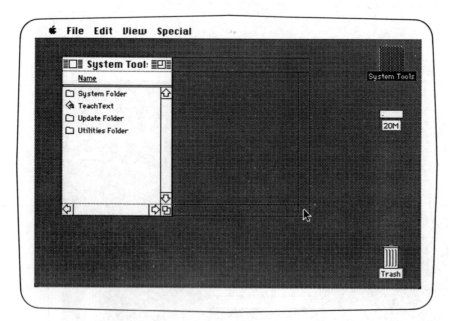

Fig. QS17. Resizing a window.

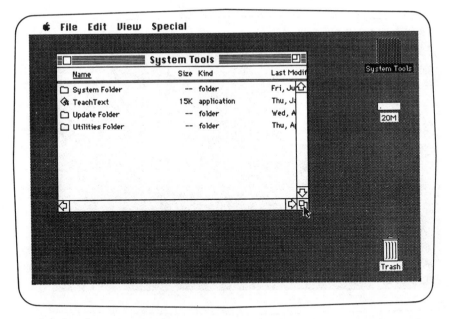

Fig. QS18. *A window that has been enlarged.*

To scroll through the contents of a window, follow these steps:

1. Place the mouse pointer on one of the *scroll arrows* at the ends of the horizontal or vertical scroll bars, as you see in figure QS19.

   Each time you click the scroll arrow, the content of the window changes, and the information in the window moves down one line.

2. Click the scroll bar above or below the scroll box. Each time you click, one new screen's worth of information is shown.

3. Place the mouse pointer in the *scroll box.* Drag the box up or down the vertical scroll bar, or to the right or left in the horizontal scroll bar. The information in the window shifts the same direction, in an amount relative to the distance you drag the scroll box. For example, if you drag the scroll box about halfway down the vertical scroll bar, you move to a point about halfway through the file. Let go of the mouse button at the place you want to stop.

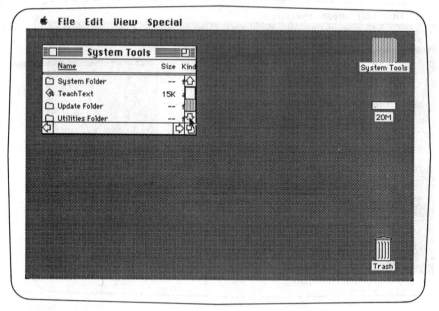

Fig. QS19. *Clicking on a scroll arrow.*

If you have only one window's worth of information, the scroll bars remain white. Otherwise, the scroll bars are gray.

You can open several windows at the same time. If you click a folder icon with one window already open, a second window opens. Figure QS20 shows you two windows. They were both resized and moved. Even though two windows are open, only one is active. (The active window is always the one that has the darkened lines across the title bar.) The second window always opens on top of the first. The window opens in the center of the screen if it is opening a new document; otherwise, the window opens in the same position it was when it was last closed.

When more than one window is open, click the one you want to be made active. If you can't see the window you want, resize the active window (using the size box) and move the other windows.

You can also move a window that is not active by holding down the Option key and dragging the window by its title bar. Using figure QS20 as an example, you hold down the Option key, move the mouse pointer to the 20M (the title of the inactive window), click and hold

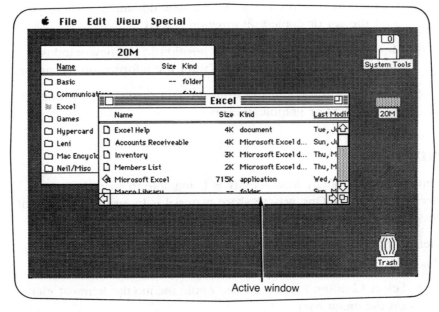

Active window

Fig. QS20. *Two open windows.*

down the mouse button; then you move the window without making it the active window.

Cutting, Copying, and Pasting

You will often need either to remove material from one window and place the material into another window (whether in the same document or in another application, such as from an accounting package to a word processor) or to copy the same information to more than one location. To accomplish either change, use Cut, Copy, and Paste commands, located on the Edit menu. Follow these steps:

1. Select the text or graphic you want to cut or copy by double-clicking it or dragging the mouse pointer over it.

2. Select Cut or Copy from the Edit menu.

Any information that is cut or copied is placed in the Clipboard, a kind of temporary storage area. The Clipboard can hold only one item at a time. When you cut or copy again, the old content is replaced.

3. Activate the window (or go to the new document) where you want the cut or copied information placed.

4. Move the mouse pointer to the position in the new window (or new document) where you want the information to appear.

5. Select the Paste command from the Edit menu, and the copied (or cut) text or graphic appears.

Printing

An important part of any Mac activity is being able to share your material with others. One way to share material is by printing a copy of a file.

To let your Macintosh computer know the type of printer you will be using, follow these steps:

1. Select Chooser, located on the Apple menu (the leftmost menu on the menu bar).

2. Select the icon representing the ImageWriter or the icon representing the LaserWriter, depending on what type of printer you will be using. You also need to click the name of the printer that appears in the dialog box on the right side of the screen. In figure QS21, the printer is named Silentwriter.

To print, select Print from the File menu. In the resulting Print dialog box, make your choices or accept the default values and click the OK button. You learn about the printing options that are available to you in Chapter 5 of *The Big Mac Book*.

When you print, you will see a dialog box similar to the one that you see in figure QS22 for printing with a LaserWriter Silentwriter printer. Dialog boxes appear throughout all Macintosh areas and require you to provide additional information so that the Mac can continue its work.

Quick
Start

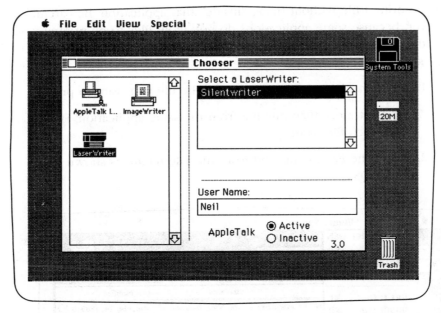

Fig. QS21. Selecting a printer in the Chooser.

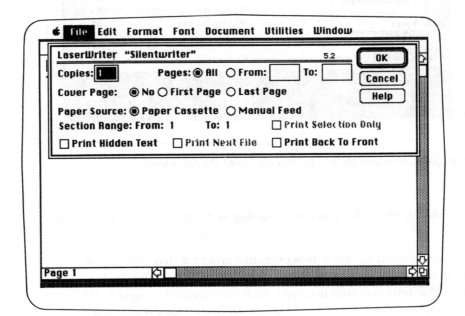

Fig. QS22. The LaserWriter Silentwriter Print dialog box.

You can print a file without being "inside" that application. Be careful, however, because some applications do not allow files to be printed from the desktop. To print a file from the Finder or desktop, follow these steps:

1. Highlight the icon that represents the file you want to print.

   To print more than one file from the same application, Shift-click each file name.

2. Select the Print command from the File menu, as shown in figure QS23.

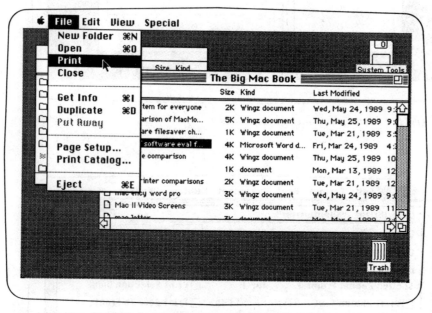

Fig. QS23. *Selecting the Print command from the File menu.*

The Mac displays the appropriate dialog box, and you can print from there.

For this method to work, however, the program that created the document must be on your disk. If you do not have the application, your Mac tells you that it cannot find the required program. This printing technique actually opens the program that created your document and tells that program to print the selected document. That program's Print dialog box is displayed, and the document is printed after you make your selections and click the OK button. After printing, that program automatically quits. This feature has been known to impress even the most die-hard MS-DOS users because they can't do this.

Ending a Work Session

To turn off your Mac safely and exit from the current application, follow these steps:

1. Select the Quit command to exit from the application.

   Or hold the down Option key and click one close box; all the other windows will close.

2. Select the Shut Down command on the Special menu on the desktop.

Even if you're very tempted, never just reach behind your Mac and turn it off when you are finished working. Your Macintosh needs to update files and do a little housekeeping so that the next time you boot up, things are in order and ready to go.

Even if you have never touched a Mac before, you should have mastered some of the fundamental skills by now. Dragging, cutting and pasting, and printing are techniques you use in almost every Macintosh activity. The next chapter helps you gain a perspective about where the Mac came from, where it is today, and where it will be tomorrow.

Part II

Just the Basics

Ready to go? If you're not, read through the Quick Start at the beginning of this book for an introduction to important techniques for using your Mac. Chapter 1 of *The Big Mac Book* introduces you in more detail to some of the important features of the Macintosh family of computers and prepares you for the parts that follow.

Chapter 2, "Getting Started," gets you started with detailed information about windows and some desk accessories and utilities that some people can't live (or work) without. You learn a little bit about how your Mac works and about the screen and keyboard.

Chapter 3, "The System, the Finder, and MultiFinder" introduces you to the ins and outs of the Macintosh operating system and teaches you skills to protect yourself against viruses, explains how to use MultiFinder, and gives some sample Macintosh configurations of systems and applications.

"Everything in its place and a place for everything" is the name of the storage game; information about file management, floppy disks, and hard disks is given in Chapter 4, "File Management and Storage."

Information on how to select and use a printer in order to produce beautiful hard copy can be found in Chapter 5, "Printing."

Beginners, especially, need to feel comfortable with the techniques described in these chapters. Because practicing these techniques is so easy, read this book while at your Mac, and work through the steps as they come. The only way you can feel comfortable and confident is to learn by doing.

Includes

How It All Began

Getting Started

The System, the Finder, and MultiFinder

File Management and Storage

Printing

How It All Began

In the Beginning...

Sound Biblical in nature? Sort of like a Cecile B. DeMille movie? Well, that comparison is not unlike the scope and the impact on the personal computing world of Apple Computer, Inc., and the Macintosh computer. Since the company's beginning in 1978 (and especially since the creation of the Mac in 1984), Apple has set a standard for a new way of working with computers, and the company continues to be a major influence on the design of hardware and software.

Let's go back to the beginning and see how Apple and the Mac started.

Apple Computer, Inc., literally was born out of the dreams of two people: Steve Jobs and Steve "Woz" Wozniak. Woz was the whiz kid with an appetite to learn all he could about computers, and Jobs was the person who was going to (and did) put it all together. The rest, as they say, is history. Both college dropouts (Jobs from Reed College in Oregon and Wozniak from the University of Colorado), the two men spent some time exploring career and lifestyle alternatives. In fact, their experiences outside the more traditional world of college probably had a significant impact on Apple's becoming an incubator of ideas, where people were free to think broadly about the future of computing.

Wozniak and Jobs eventually ended up in what is now known as Silicon Valley and, of course, founded Apple Computer, Inc. The Silicon Valley area, located in northern California not far from San Francisco, was already a stockpile of electronics manufacturers with factories filled with technicians. The raw material for the revolution that would occur was already in place.

Jobs' and Wozniak's introduction during the early 1970s led to a collaboration and, under Wozniak's direction, the building of the Apple I, which was seen as simply a plaything and the result of Wozniak's lifelong ambition to build his own computer. In his desire, Woz had contacted such companies as Hewlett-Packard (for whom he worked at that time), but they weren't interested in the idea and saw no potential in what they saw as a limited market.

Before the two entrepreneurs knew it, they were in the computer business. For a little under $700, anyone could (and many did) own this "garage computer creation." The Apple I led to the Apple II, and things really began to take off. The infrastructure that was already established in Silicon Valley employed thousands of people, many wanting to be part of an upstart company that seemed to offer the freedom to explore new ideas and financial goals.

But success also presented difficulties, mostly on the side of management and growth. Clearly, what the fledgling Apple Computer, Inc., needed was a skilled manager who also understood the emerging field of personal computers. The person who filled this role was Armas Clifford "Mike" Markkula, a 33-year-old retired multimillionaire, who was so intrigued by the two Steves' plans that he agreed to come on board as the chief executive in 1977. With Markkula's money invested in the firm, Apple incorporated and went public in 1977, for about $25.00 a share. In 1983, Apple sold more than $1 billion worth of personal computers and their hardware. Markkula really got things going when he encouraged Wozniak to quit his job at Hewlett-Packard and go full time with Apple so that his creative energies could be devoted fully to the new products that future needs would demand.

Wozniak left Hewlett-Packard. Then Jobs, in a move that would contribute to his downfall five years later, hired John Sculley away from Pepsi-Cola. Apple Computer, Inc., became a haven for the counterculture computer wizard; with the success of the Apple II and the peripherals and software that helped create an even more successful market came plans for and the realization of the development of an entirely new type of computer: the Macintosh.

The Beginning of the Macintosh Revolution

If you could have looked in on the group of 15 or so people who were in charge of creating the first Macintosh, you would have seen a mixture of young, committed, and passionate people who dreamed of creating a computer unlike any other the world had seen.

In some ways, the Lisa computer was the prototype for the Mac and the beginning of that dream. The Mac was a vision for Jobs, and he saw it as the people's computer, not unlike the Volkswagen of the 50s and 60s was seen as transportation for the masses. The Lisa was also Apple's hope to capture a large portion of the business world's computer needs. The Lisa was a powerful $10,000 computer, which was reviewed positively in the computer press, and the first computers were shipped around April of 1983—with great expectations. The Lisa was much like the Macintosh—with terrific graphics and that now familiar, easy-to-use mouse.

Although what the Lisa was then was in part due to the hard and creative work of many people at Apple, the Lisa was also a product of earlier research done at the Xerox Corporation's Palo Alto Research Center during the 1970s. There computer engineers from all over the country developed the first computer with a graphical interface, which Jobs saw on a visit. The only problem was that, for whatever reason, the developers did not have the vision that Jobs had, and the technology never really went anywhere. Some people left Xerox to work for Apple and to head up the Lisa project, and the bells and whistles developed at Xerox—most notably the mouse and the graphical interface—slowly worked their way into the new Apple products.

The Lisa was a little slow, but what probably hurt sales most was the big price tag. Ten thousand dollars for the then unexplored world of personal computing applications caused many businesses to pull back. The result? Anticipated sales of 10,000 turned into actual sales of about 6,500, and the IBM PC (and the introduction of Lotus' best-selling 1-2-3 spreadsheet) started to take the business world by storm. The crest that Apple had been on for the preceding five years was beginning to fall. Apple had never been well established in the business community, and the battle looked like it would be even harder than anticipated, and indeed it was. Sales fell considerably; without the continued sales of the Apple II, there would not have been any Apple Computer, Inc., at all.

Think of a place where anything you want to do is either within reach or, with the help of the people around you, can be reached. People who truly love and are committed to their work know that this place is any place their work takes them. For the small group of people responsible for the Mac, this world soon became the Macintosh building on Apple's campus. Here they could find fresh fruit juice available at all times, masseuses offering back rubs to tired engineers, concert pianists to release tension, and an atmosphere of sharing and cooperation. For many of the people who worked on the Mac in those early days, the place was what the hippies during the 1960s would have called Nirvana. Work went on, all hours of the day and night; the competition within the Mac group was healthy and encouraged unique solutions to problems that had seemed insoluble the day before.

The Lisa project, which Jobs originally wanted to direct, didn't go very well because of personal conflicts and vague management goals. The Macintosh project, however, which Jobs did direct, became an inspiration for everyone to produce a computer that could do much of what the Lisa was touted for but with less power and at a much lower cost. Jobs' intent, which probably led to the "Computer for the rest of us" slogan, was to create something that everyone could afford and easily learn how to use—in other words, a computer and software that were really user-friendly. This machine was to be the computer you could set up within 10 minutes after you took it out of the box and begin using in another 5 minutes. For most Mac users, these goals seem to have been met, although increasingly sophisticated and demanding (even for the Mac) software can at times require more than the user's intuition and good design of the computer.

To increase the new machine's attractiveness to consumers and to third-party software (and eventually hardware) developers, the designers intended the Macintosh to be the people's machine, much like the Volkswagen—one design and one configuration of the peripherals. In this way, add-ons could be shared freely, and one standard for software design and implementation could evolve. In fact, the standard Mac was so standard that the original Mac could not be opened without the use of a special tool kit, because the developers believed that the owner would have no need to go inside the machine and add anything. "What you see is what you get and what you will get" seemed an apt way to describe the possibility of expanding the computer. In fact, the Mac could not be expanded. In the early days, what came with your machine came with everyone's. For the time, this 128K (now just enough for the smallest word processing application) machine seemed to be it. This philosophy, however, soon had to change because the market demanded expanding the Mac's capability through add-ons as well as through the designs of the various generations of Macs that have taken place.

The time for change came in 1984. The $2,495 Macintosh computer was ready to be sold to the public, and along with the tremendous accomplishments of the team who developed the Mac, came an advertising campaign to match. John Sculley had a good deal of experience with retail sales, but nothing could match what was dreamed up by the media people who handled the Apple account. To this day, people still talk about the commercial that cost more than one-half million dollars to make and more than one and one-half million to show on Super Bowl Sunday in 1984, trying to communicate the message that the Mac was unlike anything you had ever seen before. The cost was about $27,000 per second of air time! Although there was some doubt and trepidation about the content and presentation of the commercial (It showed a high tech world being challenged by a young woman wielding a sledge hammer!), the commercial turned out to be a rousing success, both commercially (It got Apple the attention they wanted.) and artistically (It was acclaimed and panned by media folks around the country.).

The Mac has gone on to become the most successful (both financially and in popularity) personal computer of all time, creating a "cult" of users unmatched by any other corporate product. While the company still experiences growing pains, and had to deal with an almost fatal financial mess with too much inventory in the early 1980s, Apple and its Mac continue to lead the way in futuristic and easily accessible products.

The Macintosh Family of Computers

The original Macintosh computer was introduced to the computing world in 1984, and since then seven models have been introduced. How have they changed? You can look at figure 1.1 and get some idea about the technical improvements that have taken place; but more to the point is what those improvements mean in terms of your being able to use the machine to accomplish what you want. Even a cursory examination of the information in the table tells you that Steve Jobs was wrong when he thought that the technology would be limited enough to offer only a plain-vanilla mode.

Here are just some of the improvements and what they mean:

- *An Open Mac.* With the introduction of Macintosh models that have expansion slots, or places where additional computer boards and such can be placed, the opportunities to connect all types of enhancements are greater than ever. As you can see in figure 1.1, several Macs come with expansion slots.

- *A Faster Mac.* The speed of a computer depends on the speed of the central processing unit (CPU), which is measured in megahertz, as well as the I/O or Input/Output architecture. Computers have gotten faster with the latest machines. (The Macintosh IIcx running at more than twice the speed of the earlier ones and a screaming 25 megahertz, is soon to come.) The new IIcx is slated to be released the end of September; it will be called the Macintosh IIci, and will have a clock speed of 25MHz, built-in 8-bit video, and 2M bps LocalTalk. A new IIx level of machine will be introduced in the first quarter of 1990, and it will have a clock speed if 33MHz.

- *A Cheaper Mac.* Late in 1988, Apple raised prices on all products, but the increase was met with such negative publicity that the company not only relented but lowered prices. In addition, there is talk of an entry-level Mac at about $1,000. Although it might not seem like there are other computers out there as competition for the Mac, other manufacturers are constant threats to market takeovers for powerful workstations and versatile low-end machines. It is a powerful industry trend to have graphical user interface (GUI) on most of the new computers being made, making the Mac less unique as time goes by.

- *A More Useful Mac.* The Macintosh is a unique machine in many ways, but it is unique in a very special way. With its new 1.44M SuperDrive, it can even use software developed for other operating systems. In addition, the development and availability of programs on everything from naming presidents to dissecting a frog have blossomed to the point that keeping track of all the programs is nearly impossible.

	Original Mac	Mac 512K	Mac 512KE	Mac Plus	Mac SE	Mac SE/30	Mac II	Mac IIx	Mac IIcx	Mac IIci
Processor	Motorola 68000	Motorola 68000	Motorola 68000	Motorola 68000	Motorola 68000	Motorola 68030	Motorola 68020	Motorola 68030	Motorola 68030	Motorola 68030
Processor Speed	7.8336 MHz	7.8336 MHz	7.8336 MHz	7.8336 MHz	7.8336 MHz	15.6672 MHz	15.6672 MHz	15.6672 MHz	15.6672 MHz	25 MHz
Memory (Standard)	128K	512K	512K	1M	1M	1M	1M	1M	1M	1M
Memory (Maximum Using 1M SIMMs)				4M	4M	8M	8M	8M	8M	8M
PMMU (Paged Memory Management Unit)	no	no	no	no	no	Standard	Optional	Standard	Standard	Standard
Who Changes ROMS	Dealer	Dealer	Dealer	Dealer	Dealer	User	Dealer	User	User	User
Coprocessor	no	no	no	no	no	68882	68881	68882	68882	68882/68852
Expansion slots	None	None	None	None	1 for optional Accessory cards	1 for optional Accessory cards	1 for video card; 5 for optional Accessory cards	1 for video card; 5 for optional Accessory cards	1 for video card; 3 for optional Accessory cards	1 built-in video card; 3 for optional Accessory cards
Disk Drives (Min. Configuration) (All internal)	1-400K floppy	1-400K floppy	1-800K floppy	1-800K floppy	2-1.44M floppies	1-1.44M floppy; 1 hard drive	1-800K floppy; 1 hard drive	1-1.44M floppy; 1 hard drive	1-1.44M floppy; 1 hard drive	1-1.44M floppy; 1 hard drive
Optional Disk Drives (All external except as noted)	1-400K floppy	1-400K floppy	1-800K floppy; 1 hard drive with SCSI port only	1-800K floppy; up to 7 hard drives	1-1.44M floppy; 1 internal hard drive; up to 7 hard drives	1-1.44M floppy; 1 internal hard drive; up to 6 hard drives	1-800K internal floppy; up to 6 hard drives	1-1.44M internal floppy; up to 6 hard drives	1-1.44M floppy; up to 6 hard drives	1-1.44M floppy; up to 6 hard drives
Disk Formats It Can Read										
Apple II GS (Pro DOS)	no	no	no	no	yes	yes	no	yes	yes	yes
MS-DOS	no	no	no	no	yes	yes	no	yes	yes	yes
OS2	no	no	no	no	yes	yes	no	yes	yes	yes
Supports LocalTalk	no	no	no	yes	yes	yes	yes	yes	yes	yes
Video	9" diagonal	9" diagonal	9" diagonal	9" diagonal	9" diagonal	9" diagonal	External (Color capability)	External (Color capability)	External (Color capability)	External (Color capability)
Resolution	512 x 342 pixels	512 x 342 pixels	512 x 342 pixels	512 x 342 pixels	512 x 342 pixels	512 x 342 pixels				
Ports	2 serial; Audio output; Keyboard & mouse	2 serial; Audio output; Keyboard & mouse	2 serial; Audio output; Keyboard & mouse	2 serial; SCSI; Audio output; Keyboard & mouse	2 serial; SCSI; Audio output; 2 Apple Desktop Bus	2 serial; SCSI; Stereo audio output; 2 Apple Desktop Bus	2 serial; SCSI; Stereo audio output; 2 Apple Desktop Bus	2 serial; SCSI; Stereo audio output; 2 Apple Desktop Bus	2 serial; SCSI; Stereo audio output; 2 Apple Desktop Bus	2 serial; SCSI; Stereo audio output; 2 Apple Desktop Bus
Dimensions (inches)	13.5 x 9.7 x 10.9	13.5 x 9.7 x 10.9	13.5 x 9.7 x 10.9	13.5 x 9.7 x 10.9	13.6 x 9.6 x 10.9	13.6 x 9.6 x 10.9	5.5 x 18.7 x 14.4	5.5 x 18.7 x 14.4	5.5 x 11.9 x 14.4	5.5 x 13.7 x 14.4
Weight	16 lbs.	16 lbs.	16 lbs.	16.5 lbs.	17-21 lbs.	21.5 lbs.	24 lbs.	24-26 lbs.	14 lbs.	24-26 lbs.
Apple Suggested Retail Price	Discontinued	Discontinued	Discontinued†	$1,799	$2,869 w/20M HD - $3,469 w/40M HD - $4,069	$4,369 w/40M HD - $4,669 w/80M HD - $6,569	$4,869 w/40M HD - $6,169 w/80M HD - $7,369	$4,669 w/40M HD - $5,369 w/80M HD - $7,069	$5,269 w/40M HD, 8M RAM - $7,369 w/80M HD, 8M RAM - $7,669	$5,369
Street Price (New)	$495	$595	$895	$1,299	$2,250	$2,999	$3,400	$4,675	$3,295	n/a
Used Price (Sun Remarketing)	$495	$595	$895	$1,095	$1,995 (2 floppies) $2,495 (20M)	None available	$3,600-$7,000	n/a	n/a	n/a

Fig. 1.1. *A Comparison of Different Macintosh Computers.*

1

How It Began

For example, programs once used only on MS-DOS machines now are successfully being "ported" to the Mac. The programs include the word processing giant WordPerfect and the database dBASE and, in the future, 1-2-3 and Ventura. In addition, the ease of connecting the Mac to other Macs and peripherals has made it more attractive to small and large businesses.

- *A More Visible Mac.* For years, the computers manufactured by Apple have been the ones most often seen in the public elementary and junior high schools in this country. At the higher levels (high school and college), Apple has taken second place to IBM. The same situation is even more prevalent in the business world. As a result of an aggressive campaign targeted at higher education and business, however, Macintoshes are showing up everywhere. Apple now provides excellent discounts to members of the faculty at institutions of higher learning and offers large equipment grants to help increase the computers' presence on campus. In 1988, Apple shipped more Macs than IBM shipped PCs. However, because of PC clones, there are about 12 PCs to every Mac in use.

What's Available?

At this writing, Apple is offering six Macintosh computers, listed here from the low end (in price and power) to the top of the line. For your information, the first Macs were the Mac 128K, the Mac 512, and then the 512E (an expanded version of the 512) and even a "Fat" Mac along the way. The Macs offered now are

- The Macintosh Plus

- The Macintosh SE

- The Macintosh SE/30

- The Macintosh II

- The Macintosh IIx

- The Macintosh IIcx

The following paragraphs describe the models' basic features and differences. More details about these different computers and their capabilities can be found in Chapter 13, "Buying Software," and Chapter 14, "Buying Hardware." Right now, you will be given just enough information to help you make a decision about which Mac you need.

The Mac Plus

The Mac Plus is the entry-level computer that does almost everything a Mac fan—especially a beginner—can want. Mac Plus is slower than the rest and has some limitations such as lack of a hard disk and limited memory, with 1M of RAM (which can be expanded to 4 megabytes), but Mac Plus is the ideal place to begin.

This machine is the standby for thousands and thousands of Mac users, and you can do a great deal with it, including word processing, desktop publishing, graphics, and more. You have to pay a great deal more to move up, and whether the money buys you that much worth in increased utility and value is sometimes questionable.

The Mac Plus is especially cost-effective if you need to set up several Macs, and their use is not too memory intensive, meaning that you don't need to use all the available memory all the time. For example, this machine is not the machine for large-number crunching or computer-aided design, but Mac Plus is just what you need to do word processing or to use as a "dumb" terminal (one that does no computing, but acts as an input and output source) to a file server or another Mac that hands out the information you want to work with.

These days, everything you buy can be purchased for less than the list price. (As Woody Allen said, "Never buy retail.") The specifics of buying software and hardware are covered in Chapters 13 and 14. In this book, the phrase *street cost* represents what you can usually get the product for through a mail-order or discount house—most often 15 percent to 25 percent below what you would otherwise pay. The costs for the Mac Plus are

Retail Cost: $1,799

Street Cost: $1,299

The Mac SE

About 20 percent faster than the Plus, the Mac SE has an expansion slot (which the Plus does not have) so that you can use various speed-up and video options. These qualities set the SE apart from the entry-level machine just described. The Mac SE also has plenty of room inside for an internal drive and one Apple desktop bus.

Retail Cost: $2,869

Street Cost: $2,250

The Mac SE/30

The SE/30 is a recent addition, which combines the best of the SE and the Plus with some features of the higher-end Macs. Most notably, the SE/30 has a faster 68030 central processor, which enables you to speed your work greatly. The more complex the work, the faster the computer goes. For example, most SE/30 applications run about four times faster than applications on a plain SE.

Another major advantage is the new 1.44M 3.5-inch internal disk drive (called the SuperDrive) that comes with the computer, allowing the use of high density 1.44M large-capacity floppy disks (see Chapter 4 for a complete discussion of this topic). This drive is capable of working with programs and data created using different operating systems, such as MS-DOS. Now we're moving!

Retail Cost: $4,369

Street Cost: $2,999

The Mac II

The "bottom" of the high-end Macs, this computer can display color and has six expansion slots for adding memory, a math coprocessor to help speed up mathematical operations, video capability, communications, stereo sound, and more. This model is the general workhorse of the high-end Macs. Although the Mac II is still available, it will be discontinued because the more advanced Mac IIs have much more to offer at a price that is not much higher.

Retail Cost: $4,869

Street Cost: $3,400

The Mac IIx

Newer on the scene, the big advantage the Mac IIx has over the SE/30 and the Mac II is an even faster internal processor and a coprocessor that acts like a helping hand when numbers, instructions, and the size of a data set get to be too much at once. Like the SE/30, the IIx can use the new high density disks and (given the correct software) can read disks created from other systems.

Retail Cost: $5,269

Street Cost: $4,675

The Mac IIcx

The first thing you notice about the Mac IIcx is the size of the unit where the central processing takes place. The CPU is noticeably smaller than the other Mac IIs and can fit under your monitor (unless you have a two-page display model). The CPU is the ultimate Mac (for today anyway) and has the speed and power you want if you want the top of the line. This is the most popular high-end Mac and costs a little more than a Mac II.

The Mac IIcx is all the power you will get from the Macintosh people right now because the Mac IIcx is their most powerful machine; however, the introduction of the Mac IIcxi is coming in early 1990.

Retail Cost: $4,669

Street Cost: $3,295

What's To Come

There is a great deal of activity at Apple with new ideas and designs constantly being tossed around, and even a few reaching the marketplace. Next on Apple's list is a "cheaper" Mac, which would sell for under $1,000. This is clearly an effort on the part of Apple to get their Macs into the hands of future Mac buyers: students! Even closer to reality is a Mac laptop (see Chapter 14).

Which One To Buy

If you bought this book and don't even have a Mac yet, that's OK, and you're allowed to browse. But how in the world can you decide which model to buy? In this discussion, let's leave out the whole topic on where you buy your Macintosh. You can get tons of advice and information about that in Chapter 14.

For now, the two factors you should keep in mind are price and your needs. The best advice is to

- Read as much as you can about the Macintosh in general, especially in the area in which you intend to use it.

- Find out about what types of software you will be using and what the system requirements are for this software. For example, if you want simple drawing tools like MacPaint (or even more advanced ones like SuperPaint), you can stick with the low-end machines. If you plan to use one of the more advanced computer-assisted design packages, you need a machine that is more powerful and that can work with these programs more efficiently. Otherwise, you will find yourself staring at your screen waiting for things to happen. (They eventually will, but at great expense to that part of you that tells you to be patient.) Or sometimes the application you're using will crash because of memory limitations.

- Always keep in mind your intent. If you're a graphics designer, color is essential, and so you need one of the Mac II line of computers. If you're buying a Mac for your children to become familiar with, for an occasional game for you, and even for access to some sophisticated software, the Plus may be your best choice.

- Try out the machines and the keyboards. See whether the screen is large enough, or do you need to consider a full-page monitor?

 What about cost? the space you have to put your new Mac? a printer? the memory you need?

Here's a list of questions that you should try to answer before you go out shopping; finish those you cannot answer with the information you gain on your shopping expedition. These questions will help you make some decision about which of the many Mac models would be best for you.

- What do you plan to do with your Macintosh?

- What types (word processing, graphics, page layout, etc.) of software do you intend to buy?

- Do you need a specific model Macintosh to run the software or will the software work on any Mac?

- How much money do you have available for the complete system purchase?

- If Apple introduces a new System (which is supposed to happen every six months), will you be interested in incorporating that System into your setup?

- What's the most important feature to you? Speed? Expandability? Reliability?

- Do you need color?

- What kind of printing will you be doing? Drafts? Finished work? Envelopes? Mailing labels?

- How much printing will you be doing?

- How much disk storage do you need? What will you be saving, and for how long?

- How much money can you afford to spend to back up your data? Tape drives? Backup hard disks?

- What kind of storage device do you need? Hard disk? Write once-read many?

- Will you be on a network and have access to other files?

- Do you plan on doing any telecommunicating, and will you need a modem? What speed and with what features?

- Will you be working primarily with text and numbers, graphics, or both?

- Will you need full-page capabilities?

Where are things going from here? That depends on what Apple and other companies develop and sell and what Mac consumers demand. Regardless of what's next, really exciting changes are taking place almost daily. When the first 128K Mac came out, many saw it as a toy. Now it's used to help produce the "Day in the Life" (United States, Soviet Union, California, and so on) series, to produce text and graphics for *Newsweek* and *USA Today*, to help design and launch rockets carrying satellites, to help medical research to image parts of the body that previously were inaccessible without surgery, and even to run supercomputers. In fact, the world's most powerful supercomputer, the Cray II, was designed using a Mac, and Apple used a Cray to design its Macs!

Where are things going from here? Anywhere you want . . .

Getting Started

If you're reading this chapter, you probably have already done the Quick Start at the beginning of *The Big Mac Book*. I'm assuming that your Mac is all set up and that you have the opening screen on your monitor.

This chapter takes you further into understanding some Mac basics, elaborates on what you did in the Quick Start, tells a little about how your Mac works, and opens some new and exciting doors by introducing you to "those always available when you need them" desk accessories.

Inside Your Macintosh

All computers work in basically the same way. Information goes in (input); the computer works with the information, following a set of instructions contained in the computer (operating system); and the information in a new form (analyzed data, a spreadsheet, a graphic) is displayed (output). Conventionally, the input is accomplished through a keyboard, the instructions are carried out by the *central processing unit*, or the CPU, and the output is displayed on the screen; but this process does not always have to be the case. You can enter data with a touch-sensitive tablet, and you can have output appear as printed copy, be printed on a plotter, or be written to a disk.

How Your Mac Remembers

The Macintosh operates according to a set of instructions called *the System*, which is discussed in Chapter 3. The System requires space for storing itself and for operating.

When you build a house, you need sufficient room in which to move the lumber and tools around. In the same way, the Mac needs internal room to store the System and to work with the information you provide. This internal space, or memory, is called *random-access memory* (RAM). Random-access memory is the location where your Macintosh does its figuring and scratch pad work. This memory is called random access because the computer can go at any time to any place on the storage medium (silicon chips) and find the needed instruction or information. Anything that is stored in RAM disappears when you turn off your computer.

You run out of room when you have too little RAM to work with all the applications or hardware devices you want. Your computer displays the out-of-memory message when you don't have enough RAM (see fig. 2.1). This message means that there's just not the space in RAM to accommodate all the necessary directions.

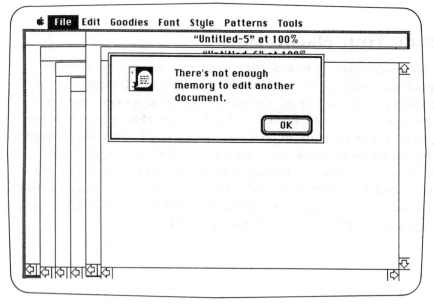

Fig. 2.1. The out-of-memory message.

Another kind of important memory is *read-only memory* (ROM). ROM permanently stores certain types of information, such as the instructions for operating your disk drives and monitors and instructions for how the machine starts. These permanent instructions are etched on the silicon chips inside your Mac, and the only way to change these instructions is to change the chip.

You may ask why not include the System itself on a ROM chip? The best reason is that Systems for the Mac are constantly changing (about every six months). If the System were stored in ROM, changing it would be very expensive. The way the Macintosh is currently designed, all you need to do is load another System from a floppy.

How Your Mac Uses Information

The information computers use comes, at its most basic levels, as bits and bytes. A *bit* is the smallest piece of information a computer can work with, and a bit is usually coded (at the system level) as a 1 or a 0, meaning, respectively, that the bit is either on or off. A *byte* is a set of bits that represents information, such as a letter, a number, or a punctuation mark. An eight-bit processor, for example, has eight spaces in which a 1 or 0 can appear. The letter *H* is represented by the following combination:

0 1 0 0 1 0 0 0

Each piece of information—from the % sign to the letter *Z*—can be translated into what is called an *ASCII* (pronounced as-key) character. (ASCII stands for American Standard Code for Information Interchange.) All computers use this universal code so that they can share information. When you hear people talk about sharing a text file, they are referring to an ASCII file. Because there are no ASCII codes for underlining or tabs (these are application specific), only the character values are transmitted; any computer and most applications can understand what these values mean. You can imagine how much storage is needed to save documents, when so many different values in sequence need to be represented.

One distinction among different models of the Macintosh is how many bits in one byte the machine can handle. Currently, the upper limit is 32 bits. Different-sized bytes (or chunks of information that can be used once) account for the difference in the speed with which the central processor works.

Understanding the Desktop

It must have been a stroke of genius or a stroke of common sense or both. The Mac designers tried to think of how they could design a computer as close as possible to the "real life" work and play world of potential users.

What the designers came up with is the *desktop*, a method of organizing and displaying the workings of the Macintosh, that is similar to the organization of your own desktop in your home or office. Before I talk more about what the desktop is and how it functions, let's first see what happens when you turn on your Mac and display the desktop on the opening screen.

Your Macintosh Comes Alive

When you turn on your Mac, you see a little smiling Mac (see fig. 2.2). (Be sure that your System disk is in the internal drive if you're working on floppies. The internal drive is the drive that is part of your Mac's main unit.)

As soon as power comes to the Mac, several important procedures, which you never see, begin. First, a program that is "hard wired" and part of your Macintosh's read-only memory (ROM) sends a signal to the main central processing unit (the Mac's brains). This signal tells the computer to start a program called Boot. Boot, in turn, looks for a file called System in the System folder. System contains the operating instructions, which present the displays you see on the opening desktop and also provide the tools you need to perform such tasks as cutting, copying, pasting, and printing. These instructions are in the System folder and are loaded into the Mac's memory every time you start the computer. In System 6.0 (the current version), the System folder shows a Mac icon on it. Some people refer to this as the "blessed" folder. Your System folder can be on your hard disk or on a floppy, but you can have only one System file on your boot disk or else you will get crashes and errors.

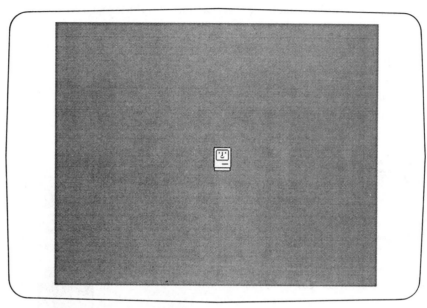

Fig. 2.2. The opening Macintosh screen.

All this activity takes place quickly, and before you know it, you're seeing a Mac window. Like any other window, this one can be closed, resized, and moved.

What's on the Desktop?

If any one characteristic separates the Mac from all other personal computers, that characteristic is the *desktop*: the image that appears on the Macintosh screen after the System files are loaded. What an impressive sight: an easily understandable set of symbols and a well-designed and inviting environment in which to work. The symbols are called icons. An *icon* is a graphical representation of an element, such as a folder, a file, or a disk. In the Mac environment, icons are frequently the way these elements are represented.

You can work at the desktop, just as if you were working at your desk. So let's take a little tour of the desktop and learn what each desktop offering can do for you.

First, you see the gray area that is the desktop itself. This area is the *work area*, where you "take" files out of folders, work with them, and put them back into the same (or another) folder for safekeeping.

In the desktop window itself, you see a set of folders that represent the way the files are stored (see fig. 2.3). Here, you can see that files are grouped by category (Neil/Misc) and by program (Excel or Word). Right below the title bar, you see additional information about the window's contents, such as the number of items it holds (15), the number of K the items are taking on the disk (18,037—almost full!), and the amount of free space (983K).

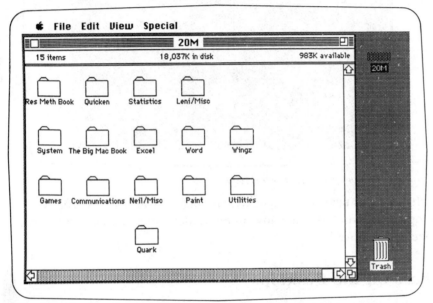

Fig. 2.3. *The Macintosh desktop.*

The disk that contains the start-up, or System, files is the dominant, or start-up, disk; and that icon is always in the upper right corner. Finally, you see the trash can in the lower right corner.

Just to show you how different a desktop can look, figure 2.4 shows you a desktop for one of the folders (Manuscripts, which was stored in the folder Neil/Misc) after the Manuscripts folder has been opened. Here you can see a variety of icons and note how the differently designed icons represent the applications used in their development. Just in this window alone, there are a Word, a Wingz, and a MacPaint file. The different designs of these icons give a quick, handy way to identify files.

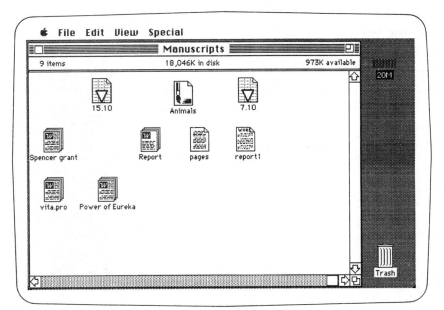

Fig. 2.4. The desktop for an opened folder.

Some of the true meaning of the Mac's use of icons comes through when you view a window filled with icons, as shown in figure 2.5. Here you can see an interesting collection of icons and the files they represent. Notice the scroll for the W2Script folder. People who design programs and icons to go with them usually try to create a graphic that reflects the content of the file the icon represents. MacPaint icons appear as small palettes, for example. The icon that represents the SuperPaint application consists of a compass (for drawing) and a brush (for painting), indicating that the program has both capabilities.

Just as on a regular desktop, you have a selection of tools. The most obvious is the *trash can*; its icon is shown in the lower right corner of the screen. Do you want to throw something away? Just drag the item over to the trash icon, and the item is gone (well almost, anyway). When you want to empty your trash can, select the Empty Trash command from the Special menu. Once you select this command, whatever was thrown away really is gone forever.

You also have the selection of menus that are available on the *opening menu*, which runs across the top of the desktop. Although all Macintosh programs have menus, the one you see on the opening desktop is the opening menu, which provides access to other menus for

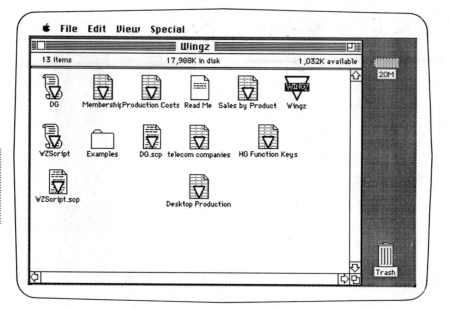

Fig. 2.5. Viewing files by icon.

operations like cutting and pasting, printing a file, emptying the trash can, and preparing a disk for use with your Macintosh.

You find more tools under one of these special menus. The left most menu, called the Apple menu (indicated by the little Apple), contains several standard tools that help you get through your Mac work sessions. For example, at any time, you can move to the Calculator and use this desk accessory to perform mathematical calculations. Or you can use the Alarm Clock, which sounds and tells you that it's time to go downstairs and check the bread rising or to stop working.

Using the Mouse

The mouse is your direct connection with your Mac. Although you can use keyboard commands for many of the same activities, most users consider the mouse faster or more accurate (for drawing and graphics, for example). The mouse's actions are represented on the screen by the mouse pointer, which takes on one of the many shapes shown in table 2.1. The shape alone should give you some clues as to what your Mac is doing.

The most important element about the mouse is what you can do with it. The second most important feature is the different shapes the mouse pointer can assume and what the different pointers do.

The mouse pointer helps you perform several activities:

- Select an area on the desktop in order to perform an operation

- Select a location in a document to add or delete characters

- Provide a visual cue, informing you "where you are" on the desktop

- Perform a variety of different functions, as listed in table 2.1

2

Getting Started

The Mouse Pointer

On the basic desktop, the mouse pointer always appears as an arrow pointing toward the upper left corner of the screen. When you are in a specific application, however, the mouse pointer takes on many different forms, depending on the function. Some of most frequently seen shapes and their applications are given in table 2.1. You can alter the mouse pointer or any icon by using a Mac tool called ResEdit (discussed elsewhere in this chapter).

As you can see, different programs share the same pointer shapes. This sharing is another example of how the relatively high level of standard procedures and symbols (or icons) makes moving from one program to another within a Mac environment a reasonable task.

Mouse Techniques

The first and most important mouse technique is *selecting*. You must always select an object, such as a file icon, before you can do anything to it. Selection is usually done by placing the mouse pointer on an icon and clicking once. To click, you quickly press and release the mouse button. The color of the icon changes (or reverses) to indicate that it has been selected. In figure 2.6, you can see that the icon representing SuperPaint is selected, but none of the others are. To select more than one icon (or file or application) at a time, Shift-click—just hold down the Shift key as you click the icons.

Table 2.1
Macintosh Pointer Shapes

Shape	Use
General Pointer Shapes	
▲	Pointing, dragging, and selecting
I	Dealing with text
|	Insertion point for inserting text
⌚	I'm busy—don't bother to enter anything
Pointer Shapes in Spreadsheets	
✛	Adjusting the height of a row (Excel, Wingz)
◀�▶	Adjusting the width of a column (Full Impact)
⚲	Magnifying a section of a worksheet (Excel)
▮▮	Creating a graph (Wingz)
Pointer Shapes in Word Processors	
GO	Going to a specific page (WordPerfect)
Pointer Shapes in Paint and Graphics Programs	
▱	Erasing an image or part of an image (SuperPaint)
⇕	Perspective (Super 3D)
◣◥	Zoom controls (MacDraw II)
♄	Lassoing text or graphics (SuperPaint)

Another important technique is *dragging*. You drag objects (such as icons and windows) on the desktop to move them from one location on the screen (or within a window) to another.

To drag an icon, position the mouse pointer on the icon, press and hold the mouse button; then, keeping the button pressed, move the mouse pointer to the position where you want the icon located. When you release the button, the icon moves. In figures 2.7 and 2.8, the SuperPaint icon is being moved from one position in the window to

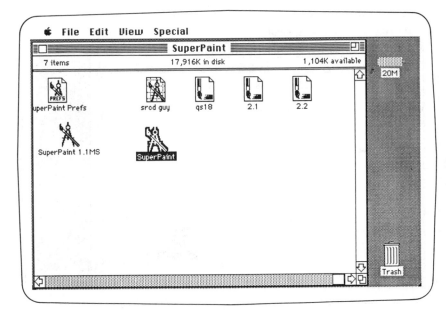

Fig. 2.6. Selecting an icon.

another. Notice that the icon is selected (changes color) when it is dragged.

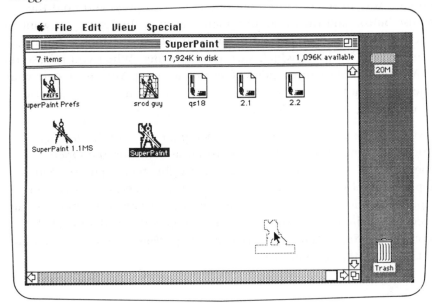

Fig. 2.7. Dragging an icon from one position on the desktop to another.

2

Getting
Started

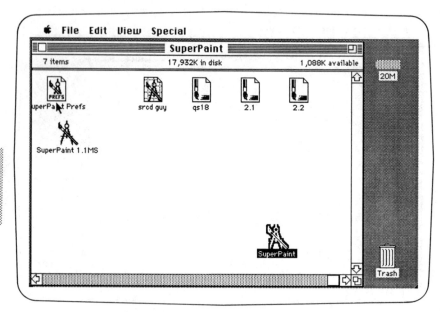

Fig. 2.8. *The SuperPaint icon in its new position.*

Another way to select more than one icon is to press and hold the mouse button and then drag the pointer around the icons you want to select. When you do this (and before you release the mouse button), you create a *marquee*, which surrounds the files. When you release the mouse button, the "surrounded" files are selected. You must start your selection on a blank area of the window, not on an icon. Otherwise, you will drag only the selected icon.

Last on the list of important mouse techniques is *double-clicking*. Double-clicking produces the same result as selecting the Open command (⌘-O) on the File menu. To use this technique to open an application, place the mouse pointer on an icon, and click twice in rapid succession. Double-clicking is the primary way you open, or gain access to, a file or an application. For example, if you double-click the icon labeled SuperPaint, the application SuperPaint opens, and you are ready to use this graphics tool.

Using Windows

To make life even easier, *windows* are used to display the contents of a file or a folder. Windows help you keep files and folders separate from one another. Have you ever put an important "real" (as in paper) document into the wrong stack and then been frantic until you found the paper? The organizational structure of the Macintosh minimizes this kind of error because the Mac allows you to maintain separate files and folders as containers in which to store information. Windows then can be opened or closed, and you can view several open windows at the same time.

A *window* is a separate work space with its own title bar. You use and manipulate windows to work with individual files or folders. Creating a window is like selecting a new station on your TV; the material is self-contained and independent from any of the other information (or channels) available.

Windows have their own menu bars, depending on what you're looking at. For example, in figure 2.9, you can see the opening window for Quark XPress. Notice how this window differs from the opening window of the word processor Word in figure 2.10, and yet how the two windows have many items in common.

In no time at all, you can master the basics of windows, and users at all levels find windows an irreplaceable convenience.

In the Quick Start, you learned various skills to help you get acquainted with windows. In this section of this chapter, you add to those skills.

Viewing Files through the Window

The window also contains a great deal of information that you will not see unless you alter the way the information is presented. You select the way you want to view files in the window through the View menu. The options are to view the collection of files by Small Icon; Icon; Name of the file; Date the file was last modified; Size (in Ks, or thousands of bits); and Kind (application, document, and so on).

For example, in figure 2.11 you can see how the window lists each file on the disk (or in the folder) by name, with information about the size of the file, its kind, and the date the file was last modified. When files are listed by name, they always appear in alphabetical or numerical

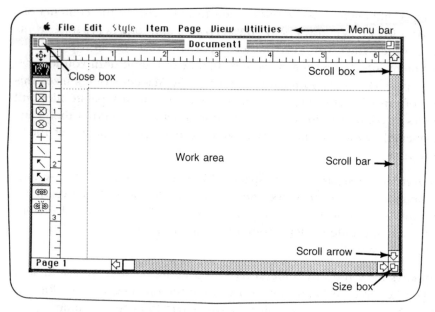

Fig. 2.9. *The opening window for QuarkXPress.*

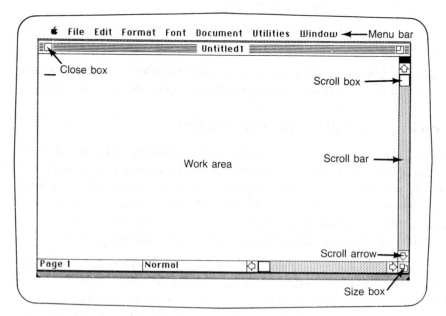

Fig. 2.10. *The opening window for Microsoft Word.*

ascending order (from A to Z or from 1 to 10). If you have a group of files numbered from 1 through 30, the listing by name is 1, 10, 11, 12, 13, 14, 15, 16, 17, 18, 19, 2, 20, and so forth. If you insert a space before single-digit names, however, the files will be listed in correct numerical order.

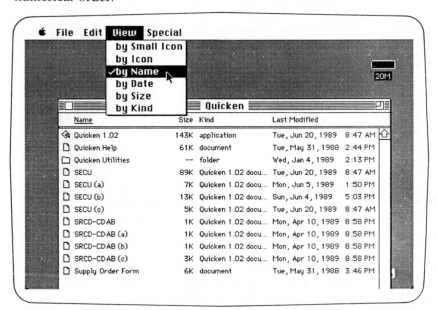

Fig. 2.11. Viewing files by name.

An alternative to viewing files by name is to view them by date (see fig. 2.12). The same information for each file is given in the same order, but the files and folders are listed by date, beginning with the most recent file. The heading Last Modified is underlined to show you the way the file names are listed. The major advantage of this way of viewing the contents of a window is that you can see when files were last altered. Viewing by date is a handy tool to use when you want to back up only the files that have been altered on a particular day.

Which way to view? The decision depends on what you want to see. In general, viewing by name is most convenient because you have all the information you may need, and you can easily find a particular file by name. Although viewing files by small icon or icon is informative and pleasing to the eye, the view takes up a great deal of space on the screen. If you want to see more information, the alternatives of viewing by name, date, kind, and size work well.

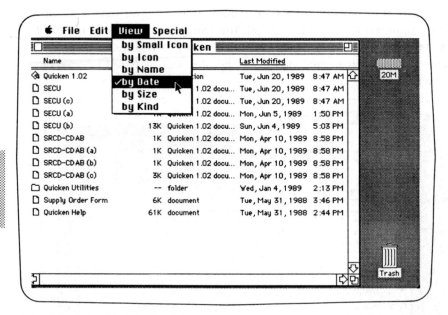

Fig. 2.12. *Viewing files by date.*

You can also view icons by group or by color (if you have a color monitor). For example, you can display together all the icons for a particular application or for a group of related files. You select colors by using the color and monitor resources in the Control Panel. Every element on the desktop can be colored, and you can find some interesting combinations, which can be helpful for organizing your desktop.

Working with Multiple Windows

The Macintosh allows you to have as many windows open on your desktop as the application you are using and the memory in your Mac can support. For example, Works allows you to open 14 at one time—and then runs out of memory to keep any more images active. In figure 2.13, four SuperPaint windows are open, but none has been resized or moved. Each window is automatically named Untitled - 1, Untitled - 2, and so on. In figure 2.14, the windows have been resized and moved so that each one can be worked with individually while the others are still in view.

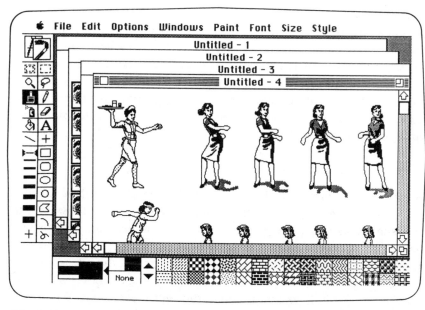

Fig. 2.13. *Several overlapping windows that are automatically titled.*

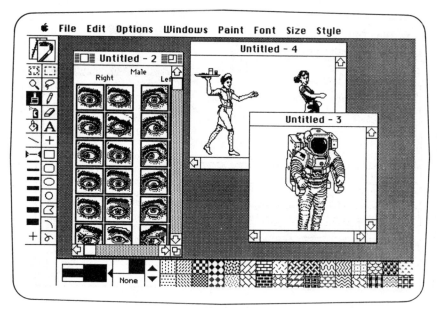

Fig. 2.14. *Resizing and moving several windows on the screen.*

Even if you do not resize windows, you can activate one at a time by just clicking any part of the window you want to activate. The only difficulty is that some windows may "cover" others, and you can't access a window that is completely covered by another window. In this case, you have to resize or move windows so that you can see the one you want to work on. In addition, many applications have a Window menu, which allows you to activate any one of many different open windows. Remember, the active window is the one with the horizontal lines in the title bar. It is the window in which any action you take (open, close, and so on) will occur.

As explained in Part III, "Macintosh Applications," many Macintosh application programs come with a tiling feature, which allows you to view simultaneously all the open windows. One program that provides tools to work with windows is Wingz. In figure 2.15 four windows are open at the same time. This example demonstrates the advantage of having a large-screen monitor on which you can see more of a window at a time. The windows are arranged through the Arrange Windows command on the Window menu, as shown. You can also see in this figure that one of the file names listed at the bottom of the Window menu is checked. The checked file is in the active window.

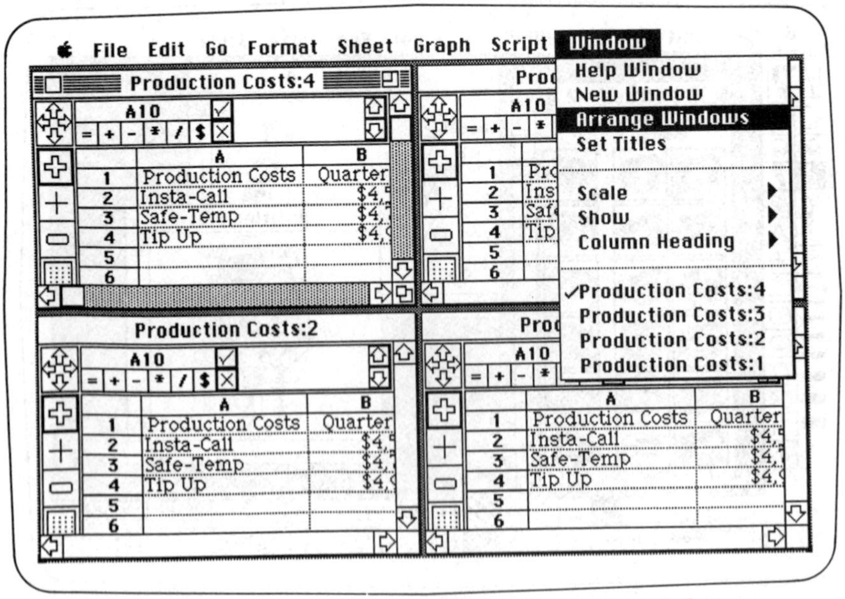

Fig. 2.15. Opening several windows and using the command that arranges all the open windows.

At times, you will want to close all the windows on the desktop. You can, of course, click the close box for each open window or select the Close command from the File menu, and each window will close. An alternative is to hold down the Option key and click the active window shut. All the windows close, and you are left with a nice, clean, empty desktop. This practice is a good way to end a Mac work session because you will be starting next time with a clean slate. Your Mac won't have to take the time to rebuild the desktop the next time you boot up.

Here's another window tip. If you want to move a window on the desktop when the window is not active, press the Option key and then drag the window by its title bar.

2

Getting
Started

Scrolling through Windows

Most of the windows that you have seen up to now have one "screenful" of information. The one Mac screen cannot hold all the information contained in every document, however. You need to *scroll* through most files to see everything.

To scroll through a file screen-by-screen, place the mouse pointer either below or above the scroll box in the scroll bar. Each time you click, you move one screen's worth. Click the horizontal scroll bar to shift the screen's contents to the left or right. Click the vertical scroll bar, to shift the screen's contents up or down.

To scroll through a file line-by-line, click on the arrow in the scroll bar.

To move a large amount of space, click and then drag the scroll box a proportionate distance in the direction you want to move. For example, if you have a 20-page document and you want to move to the middle, drag the scroll box about halfway down the scroll bar.

Working with the Window's Contents

If you choose to view the window's contents by Small Icon or by Icon, you may run into what you see in figure 2.16, where icons overlap. This overlapping certainly doesn't help you work more efficiently.

To rearrange the icons in a window, select the Clean Up Window command from the Special menu. The icons are arranged on an invisible grid so that they do not overlap (see fig. 2.17). The icons may

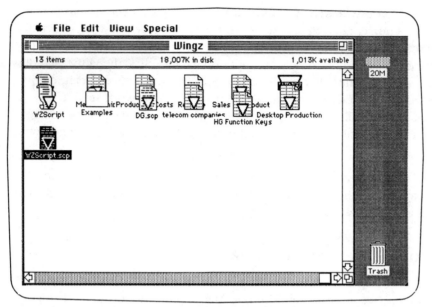

Fig. 2.16. Overlapping icons make seeing what's on the screen difficult.

not fit on the same screen (especially if you have a large number), but you view them by icon in order to get a quick overview of the types of files contained on a disk. You also can scroll to see icons that will not fit on the screen.

Getting Information about a Specific File

Sometimes you must know the particulars about a specific file, such as its date of creation, version number, and more. You can get this information for any file, regardless of how it is viewed, by first selecting the file (click the icon that represents the file) and then by selecting the Get Info command on the File menu.

This command reveals the Info window, which you see in figure 2.18, full of important information. You see

- Kind of file

- Size

- Location of the file

- Date the file was created

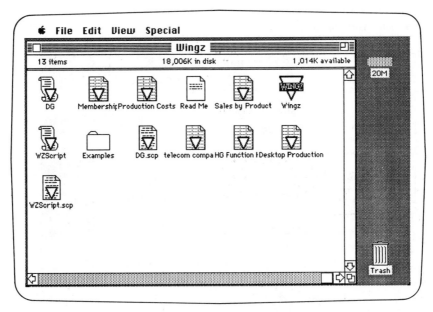

Fig. 2.17. *"Cleaning up" a window of selected icons.*

- Date the file was last modified

- Additional information, which sometimes, but not always, contains the version number

You can modify the information in the Info window simply by entering new information, such as notes to yourself or other users. However, you can enter information only if the file is not locked, and you will not be able to get the version number, if available, if the file or application is in use. Finally, you are allowed to enter or change information only in the information window.

You also will notice in the upper right corner of the Info window a small box labeled Locked. An X in this box means that the file cannot be altered. You also can tell whether a file is locked without opening the Info window. Select the file from the desktop (click the icon once) and move the mouse pointer to the name of that file. If the pointer shape changes into an I-beam, the file is not locked. If the pointer remains an arrow, the file is locked. To unlock a file just click the Locked box to remove the X.

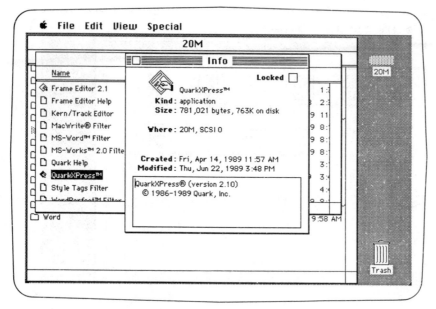

Fig. 2.18. The Info window.

You can compare several files by opening more than one Info window at the same time.

The Info box is particularly important when you are using MultiFinder because it is here that you can adjust the amount of memory that an application uses. By controlling the amount of memory used, you can fine tune your system to have the maximum number of applications available simultaneously.

Understanding the Menus

Across the top of the screen you see five menus on the menu bar: the Apple [🍎], File, Edit, View, and Special menus (see fig. 2.19). Each menu has listed "underneath" it a set of menu commands, sometimes called *menu options*. Each menu is part of the Finder and provides many different tools. You view a menu by clicking the name and dragging down. Figure 2.20 shows the menus.

The Apple menu lists the desk accessories. These small applications are always available within almost every Macintosh application through the Apple menu. For example, suppose that you are writing a letter using

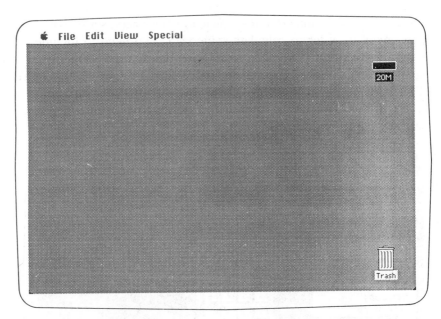

Fig. 2.19. The opening menus on the menu bar.

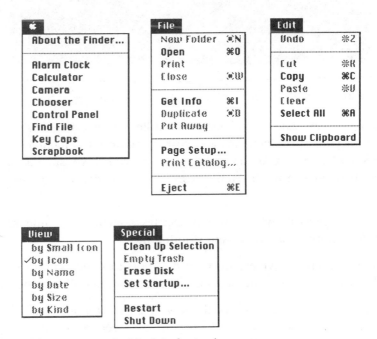

Fig. 2.20. The menus on the Macintosh opening menu.

WordPerfect; you can select the Calculator desk accessory from the Apple menu in order to calculate some value you need to include in the letter. Or you may want to store a frequently used image, such as a logo, in the Scrapbook, another desk accessory. In figure 2.21, you see a list of some desk accessories besides those that appear on your screen. In this list, some new desk accessories have been added, and some standard ones deleted.

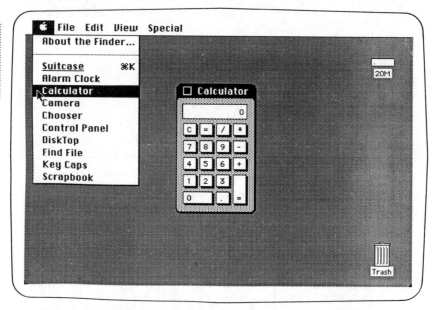

Fig. 2.21. *An Apple menu of available desk accessories.*

After you have used your Mac for a while, you will begin to customize it to fit your specific needs, and customization often includes deleting desk accessories (DAs) and adding DAs of your own, such as specially designed calculators or even a word processor that can be used as a DA.

The File menu allows you to perform tasks, such as opening, saving, getting information about, and printing files.

The Edit menu provides you with the tools to select, cut, or copy information within a file or to move data from one file to another.

The View menu lets you decide how you want to view the contents of a Macintosh window or a disk, as you have seen. You can view files by Name, by Date, or by Small or Large Icon.

Finally, the Special menu lets you rearrange the contents of the monitor screen and turn off your Macintosh (Shut Down) safely at the end of a session. The Set Startup command lets you select the Finder or MultiFinder, with or without a special application. This subject is discussed in detail in the next chapter.

On several menus, you may have noticed symbols to the right of the commands. These symbols and letters are *keyboard equivalents*. You can use keyboard equivalents to select the command instead of using the mouse. For example, an almost universal key combination to open files is ⌘-O. To use this keyboard equivalent, you press and hold the Command (⌘) key while you press the O. Once you become familiar with these key combinations, the speed with which you can select certain commands really increases.

2

Getting Started

Using Dialog Boxes and Alert Boxes

User friendly is a phrase that's been thrown around so much that we now even have user-friendly refrigerators! A large part of the reason that the Mac is considered user friendly is its interactive capability. The Mac waits for you to supply needed information at various points in your work. The Mac is also very forgiving of your mistakes and tries to prevent you from mishaps, like accidentally deleting a file, by giving you some kind of warning message. Apple requires the software developers to adhere to a set of strict rules. As a result, all applications for the Mac work in similar ways. One element of the Mac's user friendliness is the consistent use of icons; another is the use of dialog boxes.

A *dialog box* is the Mac's way of asking you for additional information while you are working within a Macintosh application, such as a word processor or a graphics program. For example, in figure 2.22, you can see a dialog box for printing. When you select the Print command from the File menu, your Mac (or the application you are working in) needs additional information before the program can continue. Dialog boxes come in different shapes and sizes, but each one requires you to make some kind of a response. Dialog boxes also almost always contain an OK button, which you click when your options have been selected and a Cancel button to cancel your choices. Any button with a bold double line around it, like the OK button, usually can be activated by pressing the Return key. You usually can cancel a choice by pressing ⌘-period.

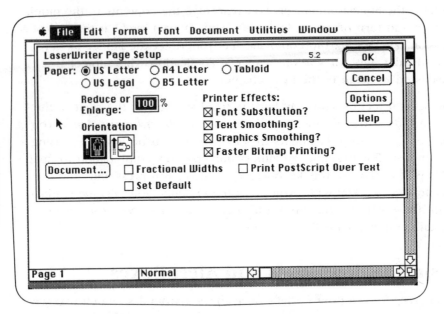

Fig. 2.22. *A typical Macintosh dialog box.*

Let's look a little more closely at the dialog box shown in figure 2.22, which prepares a Word document for printing. First, you notice that the box has a title (LaserWriter Page Setup), which gives you some idea what the dialog box does. The dialog box contains two kinds of *buttons*—round buttons and oval command buttons. Dialog boxes may also contain square check boxes and text boxes.

You can chose only one type of round or oval command button at a time because these options are mutually exclusive. For example, you cannot have paper sizes that are both US Letter and US Legal simultaneously. Check boxes can be chosen in any combination. You can click as many as you want, as shown in figure 2.22. After you click these buttons and then click the OK button, the selected changes will be in effect. Finally, there are text boxes, such as Reduce or Enlarge or Resolution, in which you provide text or numerical information.

Some oval command buttons are followed by an ellipsis (as Document...). Clicking that button leads you to another dialog box. Oval command buttons usually place into effect the choices you made with buttons and check boxes.

Another oval button shows up in many dialog boxes: the Options button, usually located near the OK and the Cancel buttons. This button does what it says; the Options button provides you with additional options (see fig. 2.23, which shows the options available for printing). You will find other buttons on various dialog boxes, such as Help (for getting help), Eject (for ejecting the current disk), and Disk (for changing disk drives).

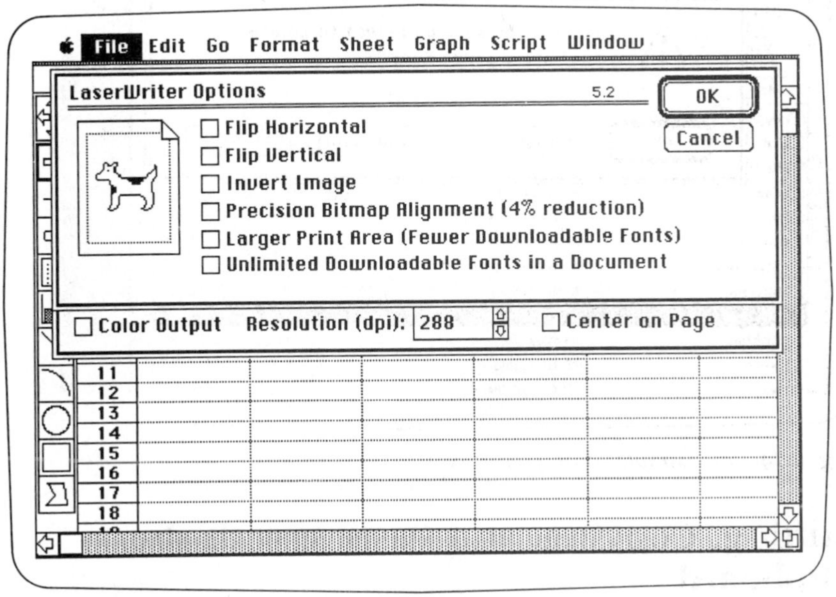

Fig. 2.23. *Other options available for the LaserWriter printer.*

Some dialog boxes have only an OK command button. These boxes are for informational purposes only. For instance, when you switch from a LaserWriter printer to a non-networked ImageWriter printer, the dialog box indicates that you should make sure that certain connections are correct. Your only option is to click the OK button.

Although Apple has tried to set some conventions for the structure of dialog boxes, not all applications follow these conventions.

A second fixture on the Mac scene is the *alert box*, which gives you a message warning you that you are about to do something risky or irrevocable and which you may not want to do. (Or at least, you need to think about the procedure before you do it.) For example, in figure 2.24, the desk accessory DiskTop is asking the user to be sure that he or she wants this file deleted. Most programs have several alert boxes to help you avoid making irreversible errors.

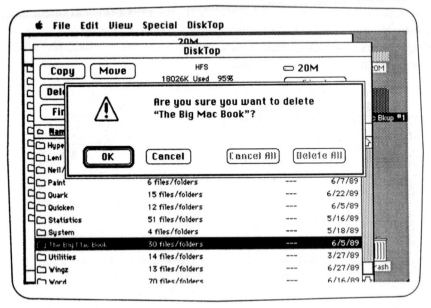

Fig. 2.24. An example of an alert box.

Cutting, Copying, and Pasting with the Clipboard

A major universal Mac feature is the capability to cut or copy text and graphics from one part of a file and transfer the item into another file in the same application or to another application. Suppose, for example, that you are using a spreadsheet program. You have certain information that you want to copy from Worksheet 1 to Worksheet 2. Using simple Mac menu commands (or their keystroke equivalents), you can accomplish this move easily.

Copying and Pasting

Figures 2.25. 2.26, and 2.27 show a sequence of copying text from one Excel file and placing that text into another. Here are the steps that apply to all Copy (or Cut) and Paste operations:

1. Open the document containing the text you want to copy.

2. Select the text you want to copy by dragging the mouse pointer over the text, which will be highlighted.

3. Select Copy from the Edit menu (see fig. 2.25).

4. Open the document into which you want to copy the text. You now have two windows open on your screen.

5. Move and resize the windows so that you can see both of them.

6. Click the window into which you want to copy the text.

7. Select the position in the new document where you want the information to appear by placing the cursor in that location and clicking once.

8. Select the Paste command from the File menu (see fig. 2.26).

The copied (or cut) text appears at the new location (see fig. 2.27).

Here's how the process works. When you select Copy (or Cut) from the Edit menu, the Mac automatically stores the cut material in what is called the Clipboard, which acts as a buffer. A *buffer* is a temporary storage place in RAM. When information is stored in the Clipboard, the

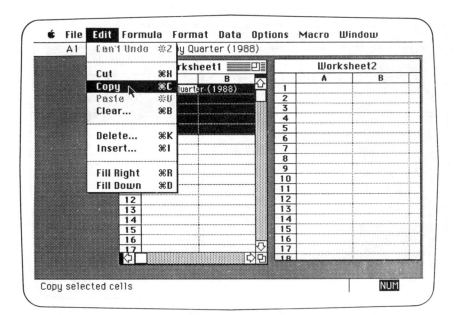

Fig. 2.25. *Selecting the Copy command.*

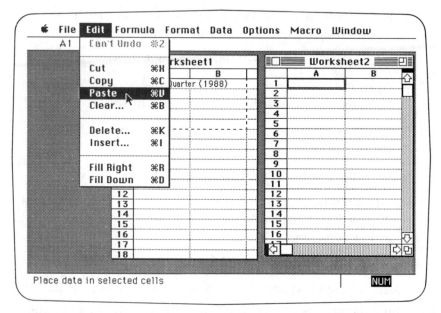

Fig. 2.26. Selecting the Paste command after two windows have been opened.

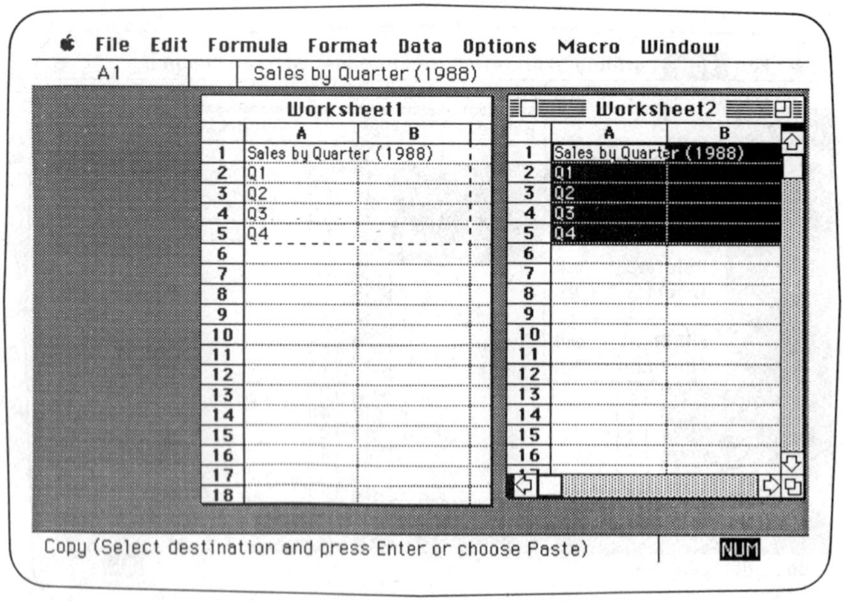

Fig. 2.27. Text has been copied to another window.

Edit menu's Paste command (usually ⌘-V) places a copy of the stored text or graphic at the cursor's current location.

Using the Clipboard

Where do text or graphics that are cut or copied from one document go while waiting to be pasted? That's right, into the Clipboard, the special Macintosh buffer that was just mentioned.

The Clipboard is the storage area in your Mac's memory where the contents of the cut or copied information resides until it is pasted. If the amount of information you want to place in the Clipboard is too large for the memory of your Macintosh, the information is stored temporarily as part of the file named Clipboard File, which is located on the current start-up disk or in the folder that holds the System file. If you don't have a Clipboard File in your System folder, don't worry. You Mac will create the file the first time you cut or copy something.

Most Macintosh applications have some kind of Clipboard command, which allows you to view the contents of the material in the Clipboard. For example, in figure 2.28, you can see how the Show Clipboard command on the Window menu in Microsoft Word 4.0 opens a window showing the contents of the Clipboard. This information can then be inserted into any document. You may want to view the contents of the Clipboard for various reasons. First, you may simply forget what's in there and not want to replace the material with something else. Second, you may want to reuse some of the same information and paste it into more than one location.

While working with the Clipboard, keep the following points in mind:

- The Clipboard can hold only one item at a time, and that item disappears when your Mac is turned off! (That's because all Clipboard information is stored in RAM—the part of your Mac's memory that is not permanent.)

- Once something is cut or copied, that text or graphic replaces whatever is in the Clipboard. That's why the people at Apple bring you the Scrapbook (discussed in a later section of this chapter).

2

Getting Started

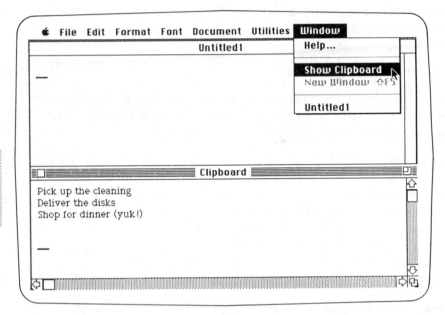

Fig. 2.28. Viewing the contents of the Clipboard.

Comparing Cut and Copy

What's the difference between the Cut and Copy commands? In both cases, whatever you cut or copy goes into the Clipboard. In the case of Cut, the material is removed from the original document. In the case of Copy, the information remains as part of the original document but also appears in the one to which the information is being copied.

Here are a few points to remember about the cut and paste features:

- Only one selected portion of text or selected graphic can be in the Clipboard at any one time. If you copy something into the Clipboard and then copy something else, the contents consist of the most recently cut or copied information. Some programs, however, such as MultiClip from Olduvai, allow you to append text or graphics to whatever is already in the Clipboard.

- Once something is cut or copied into the Clipboard, the text or graphic remains there until it is replaced. You usually can paste copied information into a variety of places. (With some applications, you can paste the material only once.)

- You can cut or copy from one application (such as a word processor) and then paste the information into another application (such as a spreadsheet). When you do this, you must be sure that the applications are compatible.

One great benefit of using the Mac is that you can use keyboard commands to accomplish the same things that the mouse can do. In the case of Cut, Copy, and Paste, all the following commands work well and are fast:

To Cut, use the ⌘-X key combination.

To Copy, use the ⌘-C key combination.

To Paste, use the ⌘-V key combination.

In some applications, such as WordPerfect, you can use the keyboard to select text.

Working with Desk Accessories

A *desk accessory* (DA) is a mini-applications tool that you install in your System by using the Font/DA Mover. The DA automatically becomes part of your active System and is always available. Using a DA is as simple as selecting it from the Apple (⌘) menu, located on the left side of the menu bar on the opening screen.

A DA can be a great time-saver. Because DAs are part of the System file, they are always ready to be used; but because they are resident, DAs take up valuable memory space. The only major limitation then on using DAs is that you are limited to 15 on the ⌘ menu. If you want to install more DAs, you will have to use one of the DA managers discussed later in this chapter (such as Suitcase II or Master Juggler).

When the Macintosh was first developed, the set of desk accessories available consisted of those that you see listed in figure 2.29. (These DAs are still on each System disk.) Like everything else with the Mac, the number and diversity of DAs have increased tremendously, and they perform many tasks to make your computing activities easier and more efficient. The DAs that come with your Mac add features such as an alarm clock, a calendar, and a fast file-finder.

2
Getting
Started

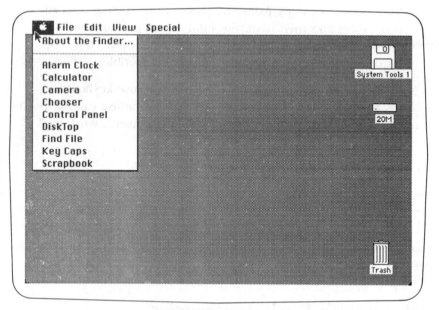

Fig. 2.29. *DAs listed on the* ⬛ *menu.*

There for the Asking

Following are brief descriptions of the start-up DAs and what they do. Remember, these DAs are available every time you start your Macintosh. If you want to use others, you will have to install them by using Font/DA Mover. More about that subject elsewhere in this chapter.

Any DA listed on the Apple menu can be selected by selecting the Apple menu and then dragging down with the mouse until that DA is highlighted. When you release the mouse, the DA appears on your screen, often in a window, and becomes active. The DAs regularly available on the Apple menu are Alarm Clock, Calculator, Chooser, Control Panel, Find File, Key Caps, and Scrapbook.

Alarm Clock

Alarm Clock displays a clock on your screen when you select Alarm Clock from the Apple menu. Alarm Clock reveals all its information when the small lever on the right side is clicked (see fig. 2.30).

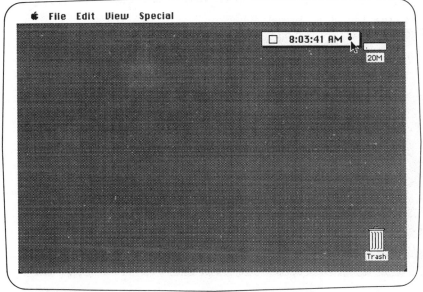

Fig. 2.30. *The Alarm Clock DA.*

The Alarm Clock provides the following information (see fig. 2.31):

- The time (as set by your Macintosh system clock) appears in the top panel.

- The date appears in the middle panel.

- The three icons in the bottom panel are used to reset the time, date, and alarm time.

To reset any of these items, follow these steps:

1. Click the appropriate icon. For example, to reset the time, click the alarm clock icon.

2. Click the time, date, or alarm setting as it appears in the middle panel. When you do this, you see a small set of arrows appear to the right of the current setting.

3. Click the up arrow to advance the time, date, or alarm setting.

   Click the down arrow to move the setting back.

   Or click the value you want to change (such as the 8 in

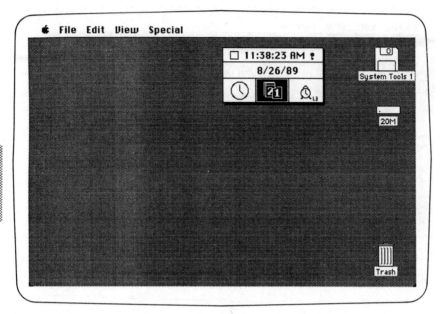

Fig. 2.31. The information displayed by the Alarm Clock DA.

8:58.01 AM) and then type the new number, such as 9, so that
the time is reset.

4. Click the close box to save the new settings.

You can also move the Alarm Clock to a new location by dragging the
top panel of the Alarm Clock window.

When Alarm Clock is active, you can copy and paste the time or date
to another application by selecting the appropriate information in the
lower panel and then cutting and pasting the data into the new
location. The Alarm Clock sound is a nice little beep. If your Mac is not
turned on when the alarm time is passed, you get the beep when you
turn on the computer.

Calculator

Suppose that you're in the middle of an application, and you need to
figure out what 56 times 43 is (2,408). You can use a spreadsheet
program and create a formula, or you can use the Calculator DA (see
fig. 2.32).

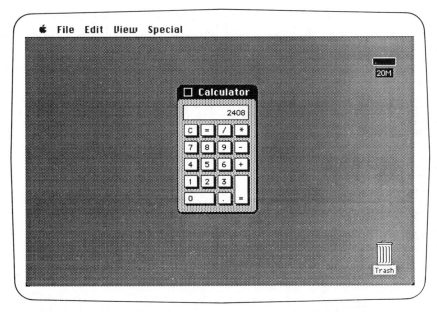

Fig. 2.32. *The Calculator.*

Much like using any other calculator, using Calculator involves selecting the keys with the mouse or entering the values from the keyboard. If you enter the values from the keyboard, you must press the equal sign (=) or Enter, not the Return key, to get the final answer.

For example, to divide 300 by 2, work through the following simple steps. Use either the mouse or keyboard to enter values and operators.

1. Enter the value *300.*

2. Enter the operator /.

3. Enter the value *15.*

4. Click on the = sign or press the equal sign on the keyboard or press the Enter key.

Calculator performs the calculation and displays the answer.

One of the best things about Calculator is that you can easily cut and paste the result of the calculation into your current document. To do this, just select the Cut or Copy command from the File menu, and the values in the Calculator window are placed in the Clipboard. You then can go to any document, click an insertion point, and when you select the Paste option, the calculated value is inserted. You have to add the dollar sign (see fig. 2.33).

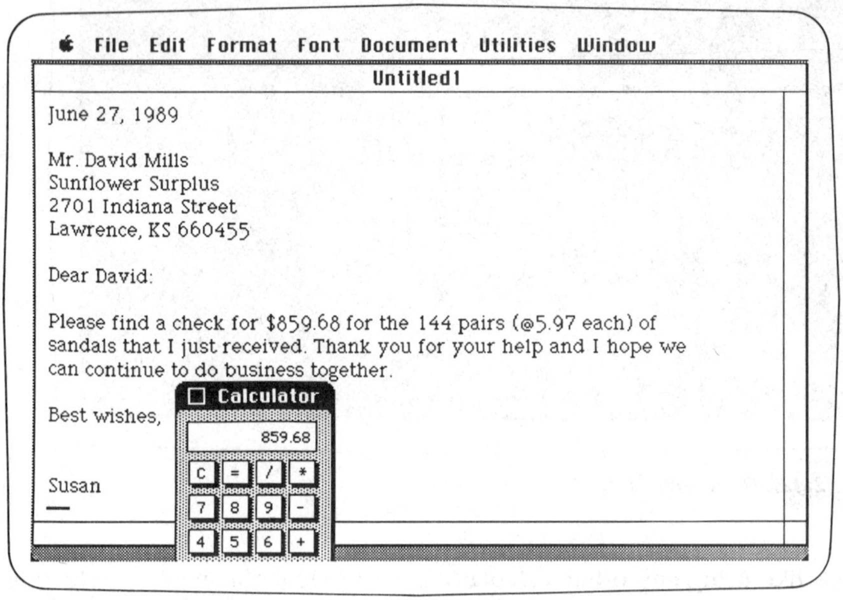

Fig. 2.33. *Pasting a value from the Calculator DA.*

Chooser

Chooser is a DA that many new Mac users ignore because the name is not as descriptive as the names of other DAs. Chooser is extremely important, however, because you select the type of printer you are going to use through this DA (see fig. 2.34).

After you select Chooser from the Apple menu, you need to indicate which type of printer (or other output device) you will be using: an ImageWriter (or some other dot-matrix printer) or a laser printer (Apple or some other brand). You also use Chooser if you have different AppleTalk zones set up for use with a network (more about that in Chapter 15).

You need to use Chooser at these times:

- When you use the Mac to print for the first time in a session

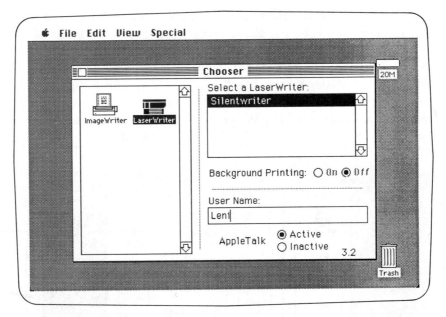

Fig. 2.34. *The Chooser window.*

- When you change from one type of printer (such as a dot-matrix printer) to another type of printer (such as a laser printer)

- When you change the port, where the printer is connected

- When you want to select a device (a printer, for example) on the AppleTalk network

- When you want to select a device (such as a modem) in a different AppleTalk zone

When you want to change printers or select a device, highlight (select by clicking) the icon that represents the device in the Chooser window. For example, to select a laser printer (as in fig. 2.34), select (highlight) the icon representing the printer; then highlight the name of the printer.

Control Panel

The Control Panel is especially fun to work with because it provides you with the opportunity to change many of your Macintosh's default

2

Getting
Started

settings, such as the screen background, pattern of the screen, speaker volume, the time, the date, the alarm, and even the responsiveness of the keyboard (see fig. 2.35). Each icon in the left scroll box is a Control Panel Device (CDEV), and these devices give you a set of Control options for your System file. If you have a System setting you want to save (and prevent others from changing), you can remove the Control Panel by using Font/DA Mover, and your settings are safe.

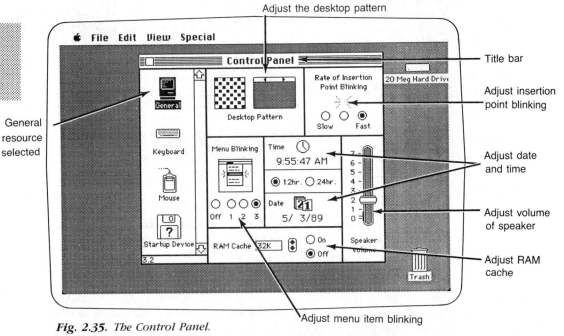

Fig. 2.35. *The Control Panel.*

You can determine the use of the different panels on the Control Panel by the way they look and what they do. For example, you can change the pattern of the desktop by clicking a small right or left arrow above the little window on the right in the Desktop Pattern panel. You can even customize the way the opening desktop appears by changing the pattern in the window on the left in that panel. Whatever changes you make in the desktop pattern are normally made when you click the pattern window in the Control Panel and then in the entire desktop when you restart your Mac.

Besides changing the pattern of the desktop, you also can change

- The rate at which the insertion point blinks (helpful if you have a hard time finding it in a great deal of text)

- The number of times menu items blink when selected

- The system time, 12- or 24-hour time scale, and the date

- The speaker volume (from no sound, 0, to a fairly loud 7)

- The RAM cache, an area in RAM that can hold information so that if it needs to be accessed again, your Mac does not need to go back to the location where the information is stored. A RAM cache can be a real time-saver.

You can change other aspects of your Mac's operating world by selecting and adjusting such things as the keyboard repeat rate (how fast keys repeat when pressed), the distance you need to move the mouse before the mouse pointer moves, and the speed with which you have to double-click the mouse for it to select an icon. You make these changes by selecting one of the icons in the left panel of the Control Panel. For example, if you want to set the double-click speed so that you must click rapidly, select the mouse icon. You will see the screen in figure 2.36; select the right-hand button in the bottom panel.

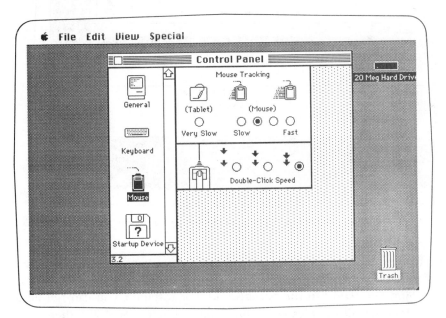

Fig. 2.36. *Selecting a new double-click speed from the Control Panel.*

2
Getting
Started

Find File

As you continue working with your Mac, you undoubtedly will find a time when you have saved a file and can't remember its location. Find File comes to the rescue. This DA searches through the disk or folder you designate and locates the file for you (if it is there).

And you don't even have to tell Find File everything for it to find your file. For example, in figure 2.37, you can see the Find File DA and the string of characters entered to find a file named System. The entry is *sys*, so Find File searches and finds any file name that contains those characters and tells you the file's size, date created, and date last modified. When you click the name of the found file, the location appears at the bottom right of the Find File window.

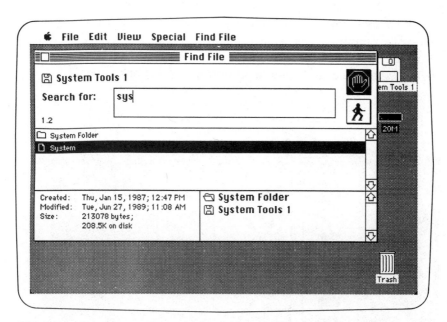

Fig. 2.37. Find File locating all files with the letters sys *in the name.*

One of the nicest features of the Find File DA is that you can continue to work with an application (such as a spreadsheet or word processor) while Find File works in the background. For instance, you can tell Find File to look for all the files containing the characters *SCREEN*; then select and double-click an application icon. While you are working in the application, Find File continues to search for the specified files.

Key Caps

One reason the Macintosh has become so popular is the ease with which you can change fonts. (A font is a set of characters of a particular design; see Chapters 5 and 10 for more information about fonts.) Key Caps provides a preview of the fonts that are part of the System file. After you select a font family from the Key Caps menu, you can select fonts from a list of all the fonts installed on the System. The Key Caps on-screen keyboard then shows you how each character in the font appears. For example, if the font named Chicago is selected, you see the characters on the keyboard as they will appear in a Mac document.

Key Caps lets you view the font's special characters. To see the special characters, press the Option key; press the Option-Shift key combination to see another set of special characters. The keyboard of special characters you see in figure 2.38 is the result of pressing the Option key when the Chicago font is selected.

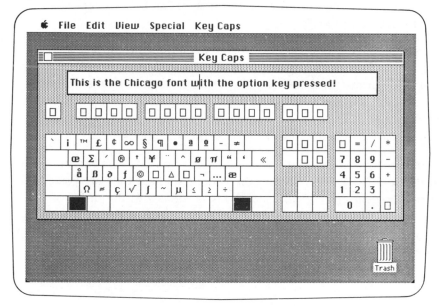

Fig. 2.38. Chicago font displayed with the Option key pressed.

As you enter characters (either using the mouse or the keyboard), they appear at the top of the Key Caps window so that you can view combinations. For example, the Option-8 combination produces a bullet, and the Option-5 combination produces the infinity sign.

Scrapbook

Let's say that you're trying to complete a job which requires in more than one document the same text or graphic, such as a company logo. You may be working in the same application (perhaps the Word or WordPerfect word processor) or in more than one document in different applications (such as the Excel spreadsheet and the PageMaker desktop publishing program). If you want to use the same information more than once, store it in the Scrapbook—a type of permanent Clipboard.

The Scrapbook is a separate file stored in the System folder. In the Scrapbook, you can collect graphic images or text to be used at a later time. You access the Scrapbook from the Apple menu, as you access any other DA.

Unlike the Clipboard, the Scrapbook allows you to store things for use at a later time. When your Mac is turned off, the information in the Clipboard disappears, but information in the Scrapbook is retained as part of the System file.

For example, figure 2.39 shows you the Scrapbook window displaying the second of three text or graphics screens in the Scrapbook. You can scroll through the Scrapbook as you scroll through any other window. You can drag the horizontal scroll box to the left or the right to see the Scrapbook entries, or you can click one of the scroll arrows to move to the preceding or next entry in the Scrapbook.

The images or text (also called objects) that you copy or cut and paste into the Scrapbook are stored in the order in which they are pasted. The most recent entry in the Scrapbook is the last in the order of images and text entries made. You can control that order as you paste, however. Just use the scroll arrow or scroll box and go to the entry before which you want the new entry placed. Then paste the new object in. It will appear before whatever is currently on your Scrapbook screen.

To add a picture or text to the Scrapbook, follow these steps:

1. Open the application, MacPaint, for example, containing the picture or text that you want to store in the Scrapbook.

2. Select the item you want.

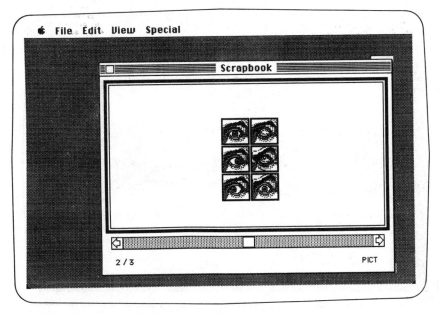

Fig. 2.39. The Scrapbook window.

3. Choose the Cut or Copy command from the Edit menu.

4. Select Scrapbook from the Apple menu. You see the Scrapbook window.

5. Select the Paste command from the Edit menu.

   You have placed the picture or text in the Scrapbook, as you see in figure 2.40.

When you want to use a picture or text from the Scrapbook, follow these steps.

1. Select Scrapbook from the Apple menu.

2. Click the scroll arrows or the gray scroll area to scroll to the text or graphic you want to select.

3. Select Copy from the Edit menu.

4. Open the application or document into which you want to insert the text or picture from the Scrapbook, and click an insertion point.

Fig. 2.40. *A graphic in the Scrapbook.*

5. Select Paste from the Edit menu. The object appears in your document.

Now save the document, and go about the business of finishing it. The procedure is that easy.

Font/DA Mover

When the first Macs came out, people found the DAs to be wonderful tools. There was, however, one problem. Apple did not provide a utility for adding or removing DAs or moving them from one system to another. This omission meant that you were more or less stuck with what you had. This situation was fine if what you had was all you needed. But often you have more DAs than you need, and they take up valuable memory. Also, as you will see, you may want to add new desk accessories to your System file.

You're no longer stuck with what you have. Today you have Font/DA Mover, which allows you to move DAs and fonts from one System file to another and to add DAs to your heart's content (up to the magic number 15, that is, unless you have a Font/DA manager, which I discuss next). Fonts and desk accessories are represented by the Suitcase icons you see in figure 2.41. The Font/DA Mover is the little truck icon.

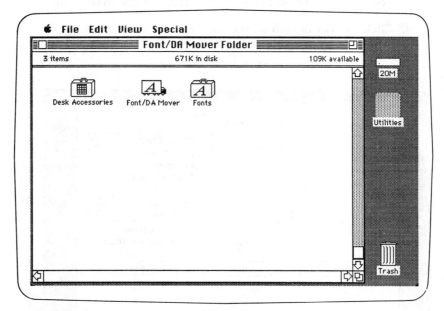

Fig. 2.41. *The contents of Font/DA Mover folder.*

Your System folder contains a ton of resources that your Mac uses to perform a variety of different tasks. A resource is a System file that allows the System to communicate with output devices, such as printers, and pointing devices like the mouse.

Just a hint of the future. The new releases of the Macintosh System (System 7) will not require a Font/DA mover. Instead, you will be able simply to drag DAs and fonts from one folder to another to install them. What a glorious feature!

To use Font/DA mover, work through the following steps. Here the DA DiskTop is copied to the System file from the floppy disk on which the DA is supplied. The first example is for those who don't have a hard disk.

1. Place the Utilities disk into your floppy disk drive. (The Utilities disk is usually disk #2 of the two utilities disks that come with your Mac.)

2. Open the Font/DA folder to reveal the Fonts and DA files and the Font/DA Mover icon.

3. Double-click the Font/DA Mover icon.

   You see a list of all the fonts currently in the System file.

4. Click the DA button to see the DAs currently available, as shown in figure 2.42.

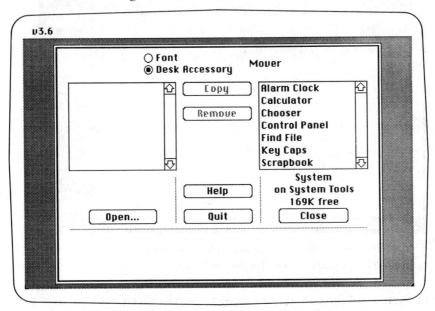

○ Font
● Desk Accessory   Mover

| Copy |
| Remove |

Alarm Clock
Calculator
Chooser
Control Panel
Find File
Key Caps
Scrapbook

| Help |
| Open... | Quit |

System
on System Tools
169K free

| Close |

v3.6

Fig. 2.42. *The Font/DA Mover screen listing the current DAs.*

If you want to go right to the listing of desk accessories from clicking the Font/DA Mover icon, press the Option key while double-clicking the Font/DA Mover icon.

You can see from the message under the list of DAs that this set of DAs is in the System file on the System Tools disk and that 169,000 bytes of disk space are unused. This information gives you some idea of the number and size of the DAs you can add.

5. Place the disk containing the DA you want to copy to your System into your other floppy disk drive.

   If you have only one drive, you have to exchange disks when your Macintosh prompts you to do so. You click the Eject button in the Open File dialog box (displayed when you click the Open button).

Your Mac reads the DAs on the new disk and lists them in the left-hand window (see in fig. 2.43).

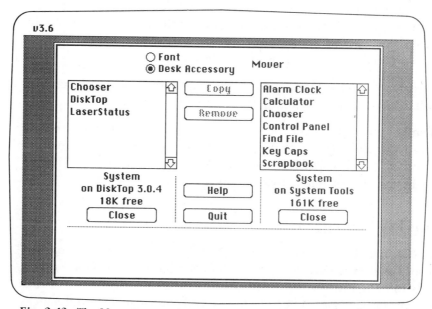

○ Font
◉ Desk Accessory   Mover

Chooser		Copy	Alarm Clock
DiskTop			Calculator
LaserStatus		Remove	Chooser
			Control Panel
			Find File
			Key Caps
			Scrapbook

System
on DiskTop 3.0.4   Help
18K free
Close   Quit

System
on System Tools
161K free
Close

Fig. 2.43. *The Mac opens and reads the list of DAs or fonts.*

6. In the left window, click the word DiskTop to highlight it. The two middle dimmed buttons, Copy and Remove, become active.

7. Click the Copy button.

Arrows in the Copy button point toward the System file where the DA will be installed. You know that the DA is installed when your mouse pointer stops being a watch and returns to its familiar arrow shape and you see the DA installed in its "new home" on the System you copied it to.

Under the left-hand window, you can see information about DiskTop, including the version number and size.

If you have a hard disk, you do not have to do any disk swapping because Font/DA Mover is already in the Utilities folder, ready to go. You do, of course, have to insert the disk containing the new DA into a floppy disk drive so that the DA can be transferred. Then you go through the same series of steps that you follow with a floppy disk.

2
Getting
Started

That's the procedure for installing any DA in any System file. If you want to remove a DA (or a font) from a System file, click the Remove button rather than the Copy button. You may want to remove a DA from the system to free up space or to keep the number of DAs down to 15, which is your limit unless you have one of the DA extenders, which are discussed elsewhere in this chapter.

Warning: You must leave at least one DA installed or the System will crash. I recommend leaving the Control Panel and the Chooser.

When you first open Font/DA Mover, the list of available fonts is shown. Instead of waiting to select the Desk Accessory button, hold down the Option key when you select the Font/DA Mover. Keep the key down and the list of DAs, rather than the list of Fonts, will appear.

Font/DA Managers

The Mac was designed with a limit of 15 DAs in any one System file. (Who would ever have thought you might need or want more?) But who's to deny that obvious challenge? Along came a series of DAs that help you manage DAs. With products like Font/DA Juggler and Suitcase II, you can have as many fonts and DAs in a System file as you want. The font DAs are not installed in the System files but stay in their own Suitcase II or Juggler folder, so valuable RAM is not being used. Both of these DA managers are installed as DAs on the System you intend to use them with.

Both DAs are installed by just dragging their icons on the desktop and placing them in the System folder. You have to restart your Mac to activate them.

Suitcase is a special type of file called an INIT file, which is short for initialization file; *initialization* is what happens when you turn on your Mac. A file like Suitcase is part of the resources in the System file and hence becomes part of the instructions that operate the Mac. When you start your Mac, it looks first for INIT files and then runs these programs. After Suitcase starts, it looks for designated files that are marked as Fonts or as DAs and opens them, thereby making them available to you at any time through the use of the Apple menu.

Once Suitcase is installed, you see it on your Apple menu as the first item. You then select Suitcase by using the mouse pointer or the

Option-K key combination. If you are using an application that uses the Option-K key combination, don't worry—Suitcase allows the application to take precedence.

Now here's the neat part of using these Font/DA managers. You can store in separate files as many fonts or DAs as you want. The most immediate implication of this is that you can create separate files of fonts and DAs and access the files only as needed. For example, you can have a special file that stores DAs for desktop publishing or for computer-aided design applications. What about a separate file of fonts containing symbols for architects? Or another file containing specialized fonts for use in equations?

Suitcase also comes with Pyro! a visually appealing screen saver that automatically blacks out your monitor if it is left unattended for a certain period of time. The program replaces the display with a moving fireworks display, which on the Mac II in color is incredible. A screen saver prevents the image on the screen from "burning" into the phosphor coating on the back of your screen. If one image remains too long in one position, there is the danger that the image can be burned in.

You have a number of DAs (which are free). But what about all those wonderful others out there that can become as important a part of your Mac as your keyboard. Here's just a sample.

Ten Terrific DAs

Hundreds and hundreds of DAs are available to do everything from computing loan payments to displaying the time in the title bar to playing poker. Although many of these DAs are wonderful, just as many are duds; so you have to be careful about what you choose and when you choose to use it.

What follows is a brief description of 10 DAs. (Actually, there are more, but who could resist the "Ten Terrific" heading?) I think you may find these DAs interesting. First, these DAs work. Second, they are helpful because they do a limited number of things very well, the original purpose of a DA. But don't fool yourself. Trying to find just the right set of DAs is like trying to find the perfect outfit for the interview. The process can take hours and hours, and even then you may not be satisfied.

If you want more information about these DAs, consult the Vendor Guide and Product Listings in the back of this book. Here you can find the name and address of the person who manufacturers and/or sells the DA. Don't stop with this list. Keep looking. Because great ideas (evolution, gravity, splitting the atom) usually don't occur to only one person, exactly what you need is probably out there somewhere.

One of those great ideas that for some reason nobody else thought of is Post-It notes, those handy stick-on (but don't stick) memos. **Comments 2.0** (Deneba Software) provides a kind of electronic Post-It note. You attach a note to a cell in a spreadsheet or a word or phrase in a word processing document by simply selecting Note from the Apple menu. You manage all the notes in the file with the Note Manager, and you can even create a timed note, which appears at a specified date and time.

No matter how well organized you are, keeping files organized is always a task. Having to return to the Finder each time you want to copy or delete a file can be an inconvenience. Here's where **DiskTop** (CE Software) takes over. A mini-Finder in DA form, DiskTop allows you to copy, move, delete, rename, find, and get additional information on files, all from within the application, as you can see in figure 2.44. **Disk Tools Plus** (Electronic Arts) is another Finder-like DA that gets high marks.

For those of you who are heavily involved in desktop publishing or graphic design, **SmartScrap** and **The Clipper** (both from Solutions International) are two DAs you may not want to be without. SmartScrap allows you to create and access multiple Scrapbooks so that you can organize graphics and text passages, as well as use SmartScrap's table of contents to avoid having to go page-by-page through an entire Scrapbook to find what you are looking for.

The Clipper provides you with tools to crop a graphic from within the Clipboard so that the graphic fits the space provided for it in the document (see fig. 2.45). The proportions of the graphic are maintained, and the resizing can be done either visually or precisely by entering exact numbers.

Paint programs are popular Macintosh applications that are often used to create graphics, which are then inserted into other documents, such as text. What happens if you want to touch up a graphic after it has been inserted? **DeskPaint** (Zedcor) is a full-featured paint-tool desk

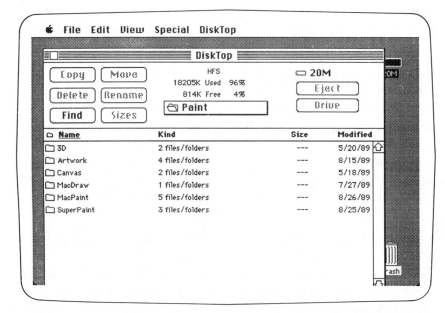

Fig. 2.44. *The DiskTop working window.*

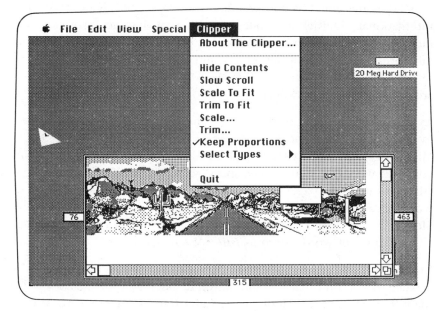

Fig. 2.45. *A graphic clipped using The Clipper.*

accessory. With DeskPaint, you just go to the Apple menu, select DeskPaint and the paint tools you need, and go to work. DeskPaint is so complete that you can even use it as a stand-alone paint tool.

Here's one of those do-everything DAs from CE Software. **MOCKPACKAGE** contains five different and useful DAs, including MockWrite (a text editor almost as sophisticated as the early word processing programs), MockPrinter (a spooler that allows you to continue working while you are printing), MockTerminal (a communications package), MockChart (a chart and graph producer), and LaserStatus (a general DA for keeping up with your laser printer's activities). The advantage is that with the one product you can get just about everything you need in terms of DA help.

Anyone need help in organizing your life? Anyone not? **QuickDex** (Greene, Inc.) is a kind of on-screen Rolodex, which helps you keep track of names, addresses, and phone numbers, and also lets you print these items and search through them for a particular entry. QuickDex doesn't "know" that *Ed Morris* is any different from *swimwear*, so the program can be used for keeping track of inventory or any relatively simple database operation.

This DA is the grandma and grandpa of them all: **SideKick** by Borland International. SideKick now offers 10 different desk accessories, including a communications package, a phone log, a minicalendar, a minispreadsheet (with 1,000 cells), and a report generator. By the test of time and popularity alone, this DA is a time-saver and a good all-around assistant for a variety of Macintosh activities.

As you and your Mac grow, you will find it easy to "misplace" a file every now and then and not be able to find it. **Gofer** (from Microlytics—the same people who bring you all kinds of DAs that help you with words) conducts high-speed searches through 1 megabyte (that's around 600 pages) of text in less than 1 minute and locates a word, phrase, or whatever you specify. Gofer works with any type of file—word processor, spreadsheet, or database— and can be used with combinations of words, such as *Bill AND Texas*.

I can't resist adding just one more to make the number an "even eleven." If you find that the simple Apple calculator DA just doesn't fit the bill anymore, take a look at the **Calculator Construction Set** (from Dubl-Click Software). Here's where you can amaze your techy friends into thinking you're a mathematical genius. The program comes with literally every tool that you need to perform mathematical calculations.

OK, so I went over by one. How about an even dozen? A new DA called **CanOpener** (Abbot Systems) is amazingly handy. CanOpener allows you access to all your Macintosh documents, regardless of the application used to create the document. This fact means that you can take a graphic from SuperPaint, store the graphic, access it, and then paste it into Microsoft Word without leaving Word. You can manage a library of images, text, and sound as well as append objects to other documents. In figure 2.46, you see a graphic being viewed through CanOpener. This program is a powerful DA that acts more like a desktop manager. This accessory also has a neat "working" icon like the little watch handles that go around, only this one is a spinning can opener working on a can. CanOpener also comes as a full application on the same disk as the DA.

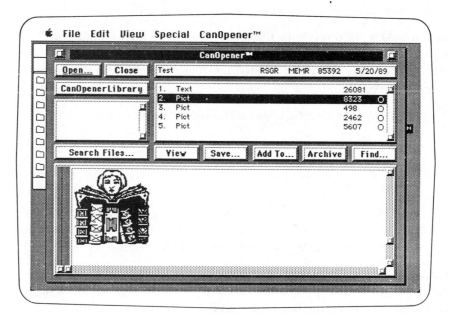

Fig. 2.46. *The CanOpener operating screen.*

Customizing Your System

If you don't want to buy any of these DAs, or any of the other Font/DA Managers, you can create a customized System file that contains just the Fonts and DAs you need and start your Mac with that file each time. For example, you can have separate folders or floppy disks with systems customized for

- Word processing

- Spreadsheets

- Graphics

- Computer-assisted design

Within each System file on these disks, you place the DAs that do the things you need when operating under a specific application. If you are using a hard disk, start the System with the floppy disk, and then click to your hard disk drive to access the application.

You can add a DA directly to the application for which that DA is intended. This method is another way to avoid loading your System file with DAs you may not want to have resident at all times but want only when it is needed.

To attach a DA to a specific application, follow these steps:

1. Open the application into which you want to paste the DA, by using the Font/DA Mover.

2. Select Copy.

Now this DA is available only when you are using that application. This technique is a terrific way to use task-specific DAs and not to have your DA list cluttered with DAs you don't need all the time.

So much for DAs. We have talked a good deal about how to get started with your Macintosh and covered such important topics as the desktop, the mouse, windows, menus, dialog boxes, and important desk accessories.

We even touched a bit on some Macintosh applications just to give you a touch for what's up ahead. In Chapter 3, you learn more about the System and the Finder and are introduced to the world of Apple's multitasking environment, MultiFinder.

The System, the Finder, and MultiFinder

Like any other tool, computers need instructions in order to operate. In general, the more sophisticated these instructions, the more power and utility your computer has. Fortunately, the System and the Finder, which come on your System Tools disks, provide a great deal of this power and distinguish the Mac from other popular personal computers by its graphical interface.

In this chapter, you learn what's in the System folder and how its contents determine a great deal of the way your Mac operates. An important part of the System folder is the Finder, the software that is responsible for the desktop presentation discussed in Chapter 2 and for your being able to access and manage files and disks. Another important tool in your System folder is MultiFinder, a System file that provides you with the tools to switch instantly between applications while still managing disks and files. You also learn about CDEVs and INITs, and you will find suggestions for avoiding the dreaded computer viruses.

The information in this chapter is based on Version 6.02 of the System (referred to as System 6) and Version 6.1 of the Finder, but most of what is discussed applies to any System from Version 4.2 on and to Finder Version 6.0.

Why the different System and Finder versions? In a word, progress. Apple has come out with some noticeable improvements in the efficiency with which the System operates and the options it provides. These improved versions are given new version numbers. Major changes in systems (and other software) are usually distinguished by changes in the digit preceding the decimal (4.0, 5.0, 6.0, and so on).

Minor changes are indicated by changes in the numbers following the decimal (6.01, 6.02, and so on).

As you will see in this chapter, the upcoming System 7.0 will make your Macintosh life even easier. The disadvantage of introducing new systems is that software designed for a previous version of the System may not be fully compatible with the newer version. Fortunately, you can always reinstall a previous System version if your application or DA doesn't run.

Exploring the System Folder

Your Macintosh operates the way it does because of a complex set of operating instructions, which are contained in files in the System folder. In particular, several different types of System files reside in this folder. All these System files have different types of assigned jobs, which are described in this chapter.

Basically the System folder contains the information that tells the Mac how to

- Construct the desktop and control its appearance and operation

- Allocate memory as needed

- Keep track of file locations

- Load and run programs

- Print text in one of the available fonts, styles, and sizes

- Save and open files

The files in the System folder are what make the Mac what it is, because without this folder your Mac is useless. The System folder must be part of the start-up disk (or the "boot-up" routine). You may have the System folder and its files stored on a hard disk, or you may boot from a floppy disk on which the System folder is stored.

As you can see in figure 3.1, different icons represent various types of System files. The following text describes the different files located on the four disks that make up the System and Utilities folders for System 6—what each one looks like and what it does. Table 3.1 gives a list of these files.

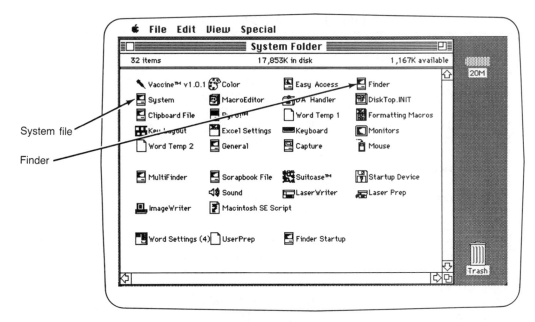

System file

Finder

Fig. 3.1. *The contents of the System folder viewed by Small Icon.*

3
System
& Finder

Table 3.1
Contents of System and Utilities Folders

File Name	Version	Type
System Tools		
Apple HD Setup	2.00	Application
Backgrounder	1.10	System Document (print spooler)
Clipboard File	4.20	System file
Color	3.30	CDEV
DA Handler	1.10	MultiFinder file
Easy Access	1.00	INIT
Finder	6.10	Finder
General	3.30	CDEV
Installer	2.60	Application
Installer Scripts	----	Folder
Key Layout	2.20	Keycaps DA file
Keyboard	3.30	CDEV
Macintosh II Script	6.00	Installer document
Macintosh Plus Script	6.00	Installer document
Macintosh SE Script	6.00	Installer document

Table 3.1—*continued*

File Name	Version	Type
Monitors	3.30	CDEV
Mouse	3.30	CDEV
MultiFinder	6.00	MultiFinder
Read Me	----	TeachText Document
Scrapbook File	2.30	System file
Setup Folder	----	CDEV
Sound	3.00	CDEV
Startup Device	3.30	CDEV
System	6.02	System
System Folder	----	Folder
Teach Text	1.20	Application

Utilities Disk 1

File Name	Version	Type
Access	----	AppleShare DA
Privileges	----	
Apple HD SC	2.00	
Setup	2.00	Application
AppleShare	1.10	INIT
Script	1.10	Installer document
Clipboard File	4.20	System file
Color	3.30	CDEV
Disk First Aid	1.40	Application
Easy Access	1.00	INIT file
Finder	6.00	Finder
General	3.30	CDEV
HD Backup	1.10	Application
Installer	2.60	Application
Key Layout	2.20	Keycaps DA file
Keyboard	3.30	CDEV
Minimum Mac II Script	6.00	Installer document
Minimum Mac Plus Script	6.00	Installer document
Minumum Mac SE Script	6.00	Installer document
Monitors	3.30	CDEV
Mouse	3.30	CDEV
Responder	1.00	AppleTalk file
Scrapbook File	2.30	System file
Sound	3.30	CDEV
Special Installer Scripts	----	Folder
Startup Device	3.30	CDEV
System Folder	----	Folder

File Name	Version	Type

Utilities Disk 2

File Name	Version	Type
Apple File dd Apple File Exchange	1.10	Application
Apple File Exchange Folder	----	Folder
CloseView	1.00	CDEV
CDA-RFT/Mac Write	----	Apple File Exchange Document
Desk Accessories	----	Font/DA Mover document
Fonts	----	Font/DA Mover document
Font\DA Mover	3.80	Application
Font\DA Mover Folder	----	Folder
MacroMaker	12.00	INIT
MacroMaker Folder	----	Folder
MacroMaker Help	1.00	MacroMaker document
Macros	----	MacroMaker document
Map	1.00	CDEV

Print Tools

File Name	Version	Type
AppleTalk Imagewriter	2.70	Printer driver
ImageWriter	2.70	Printer driver
Laser Prep	5.20	LaserWriter Prolog Document
LaserWriter	5.20	Printer driver
LaserWriter IISC	1.00	Printer driver
PrintMonitor	1.20	Application

3
System & Finder

System Files

System files include the System file itself and the Finder, both of which are labeled in figure 3.1. The icons for the System and the Finder files look like small Macintosh computers, as do the icons for several other System files, such as MultiFinder and the Clipboard (a temporary storage location). Only one System file should be on the start-up disk (either hard or floppy). More than one System file will cause System crashes. Because many applications come with a System folder and System files, be careful to copy only the files you want to your hard disk. Do not copy any of the application's system files.

The System folder also includes a variety of other files that perform different functions. Desk accessories (DAs) and font files are stored as part of the System folder. You can see in figure 3.2 how the System folder is marked with a special Mac icon to help you distinguish it from other folders.

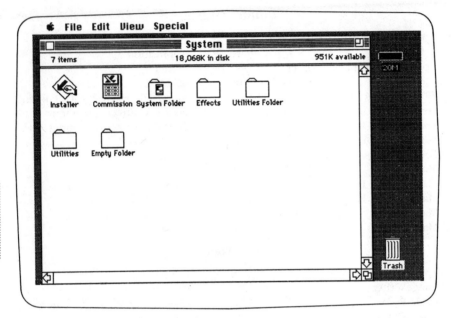

Fig. 3.2. *The System folder's special marking.*

Another set of short programs contained in the System folder are the FKEYS, which are invoked by pressing the ⌘ and Shift keys in combination with a number (1 through 9). With FKEYS, you define short programs to perform specific tasks and so save yourself the time of having to enter all the keystrokes. Apple has already defined several FKEYS as follows:

⌘-Shift-1 ejects a floppy disk from the internal drive.

⌘-Shift-2 ejects a floppy disk from the external drive.

⌘-Shift-3 creates and saves as a MacPaint file whatever is on the screen.

⌘-Shift-4 prints the contents of the active window (on an ImageWriter but not on a LaserWriter). This printout is called a screen dump. If you hold down the Caps Lock key when you press ⌘-Shift-3, you get a screen dump of the entire screen rather than just the active window.

If you have an extended keyboard or a third-party (other manufacturer) keyboard, you have actual F keys along the top of the keyboard. Although Apple has defined keys F1 through F4, you can use FKEY installation programs, such as FKEY Install (from Dreams of the Phoenix), to configure keys F5 through F12 or F15, depending on the type of keyboard you have. You can also use these tools to reprogram keys F1 through F4. Some applications (such as Excel) have other uses specified for the F1 through F4 keys.

If you use the key combination ⌘-Shift-3 to create MacPaint files, you need to be aware of two peculiarities:

> First, the key combination saves the first file as Screen 0, the second as Screen 1, and so on, up to Screen 9. After you get past Screen 9, you have to go back and rename the MacPaint files so that you can continue capturing screens. If you try to continue to capture screens, you hear the beep, but no file is created.
>
> Second, this key combination saves these files in the folder where the System is active. As a result, you can have two files named Screen 0 stored in different folders.

A good practice is to rename MacPaint screen files periodically as you are creating them. Use a DA like DiskTop and rename the files before file names get so confusing that you cannot distinguish one from the other without opening the file and examining it. Also remember that a screen shot takes up many K, or actual space on the disk, and your floppy (or even your hard disk) can fill up quickly. Unfortunately, you won't get a message to that effect. Instead, you will have to keep your eye on available space and juggle files accordingly.

CDEVs

Control panel devices (CDEVs) are utilities that are set, invoked, and controlled through the use of the Control Panel. CDEVs are controlled by clicking the appropriate icon in the left scrolling window of the Control Panel. The CDEVs that come with your Macintosh are the General, Keyboard, and Mouse CDEVs. (Refer to Chapter 2 for more information about CDEVs.)

The General CDEV controls the desktop pattern, the rate the insertion point blinks, the rate the selected menu items blink, the time and date,

3

System
& Finder

the volume level, and the amount of RAM you allocate to the RAM cache (see fig. 3.3). Because all these settings are preserved in RAM, access to them is fast.

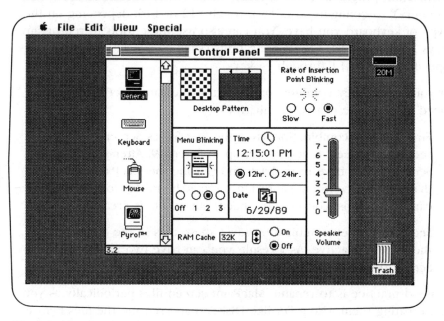

Fig. 3.3. *The General CDEV and what it controls.*

One setting on the General CDEV panel may be of interest to you: the RAM cache (pronounced "cash"). The RAM cache is a portion of the Mac's memory reserved for information normally stored on a disk. A RAM cache speeds processing because your Mac does not have to return to the disk each time it needs a certain instruction but instead already has it accessible in RAM. As you may suspect, the larger the cache, the faster your Mac can work because it needs to spend less time going back and forth. On the other hand, the more RAM you allocate to the cache, the less you have available for other purposes. If you set the cache, the change becomes effective only after you restart your Mac.

Some applications, like FullWrite (from Ashton-Tate) are so memory intensive that I suggest that you turn the cache off altogether if your machine has less than 1M of RAM. The RAM cache also interferes with some other programs, especially those that do constant disk read/write,

such as the virtual memory INIT Virtual (by Connectix) and with
certain hardware configurations. When using one of these programs,
you may need to turn off your cache. A cache setting of 32K is
considered standard, and 64K is considered the maximum.

The Keyboard CDEV controls the rate that a key will repeat when held
down and the length of time between the repetitions (see fig. 3.4).

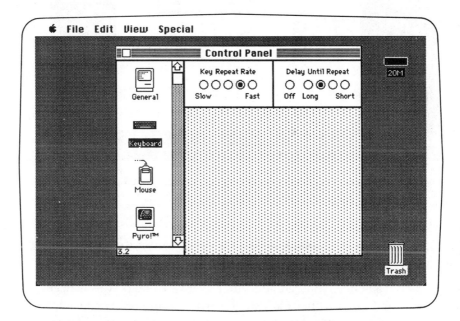

Fig. 3.4. The Keyboard CDEV and what it controls.

The Mouse CDEV controls how the mouse pointer "tracks," or mimics,
the movements of the mouse pointing device (whether you use a
mouse or draw on a tablet with a special stylus). If you set Mouse
Tracking on Slow, the mouse pointer moves an equivalent distance as
the mouse moves. If set on Fast, the mouse pointer moves farther on
the screen than the mouse is moved. This setting is ideal when you
have limited space in which to move the mouse. You can also control
the length of time between clicks for a double-click (see fig. 3.5).

If you are a beginner, set the mouse at a slower speed and choose the
slow double-click response time until you become comfortable with the
mouse. Once you're an expert, you can zoom the mouse around on
your desktop. But even if you are an expert, you will find that some

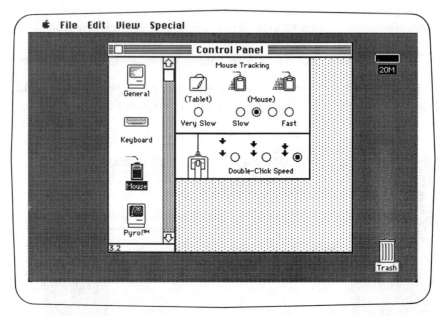

Fig. 3.5. *The Mouse CDEV and what it controls.*

applications, such as graphics, are much easier to use if you slow down the mouse.

At your convenience, you can add other CDEVs to help you manage your Mac (and often to have a little fun while doing it). For example, the public domain CDEV Moire Screen Saver (by John Lim of Australia) automatically places a moving three-dimensional geometric pattern on your screen after you have left your machine unattended. This device is a "screen saver" because it prevents the image on the monitor from being burned into the coating of phosphorus material on the inside of the screen.

Another CDEV is Berkeley Systems' Stepping Out, a nifty monitor extender that allows your 9-inch Mac screen to act like a 20-inch screen, or larger. Stepping Out creates what is called a virtual page. In computerese, the word *virtual* means "it seems like it's there, but it really isn't." You don't have a 20-inch monitor, but it seems that way. You can read more about this CDEV in Chapter 14. You can get sound CDEVs, graphics CDEVs, and more; what they have in common is that they are all placed in the System folder, become active when you boot up, and are set and controlled through the Control Panel. For example, when the CDEV Vaccine is installed in the System folder, the Vaccine icon appears on the Control Panel (see fig. 3.6).

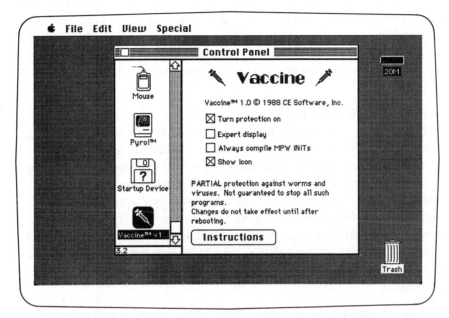

Fig. 3.6. *The CDEV Vaccine on the Control Panel.*

To install a CDEV, you simple drag the icon that represents the CDEV into the System folder. Many CDEVs do not become active until you restart your machine and give the CDEV a chance to become part of the System. Others become active as soon as they are highlighted in the Control Panel. The one big advantage of a CDEV is that it can be installed in the System folder and be available for use at start-up. Unlike DAs, you are not limited to 15.

INITs

INITs, or initialization files, are also placed in the System folder and become active when you start your machine. INITs are system files that are automatically loaded after your System adds their names into the memory of your Macintosh. INITs are executed on start-up. If you have several INITs, they are loaded into your System based on what is referred to as an ASCII ordering scheme. (ASCII is a numerical system used to represent every character available.)

Although INITs can be a blessing, there's a catch. (Isn't there always?) Different INITs (and CDEVs) may not be compatible with one another, or an INIT may affect the way another program on the system runs (or doesn't run!). In this case, the solution is trial and error: keep removing INITs and restarting your machine. This method is tedious, but it may be your only choice. To lessen the trial part, add only one INIT at a time and try different applications to see whether everything is as it should be.

Another way to work with conflicting INITs is to use a tool like INITPicker (from Microseeds Publishing) or AASK (from CE Software). These INITs help you manage other INITs. INITPicker gives you two important and time-saving capabilities. First, you can control the order in which INITs are loaded when you boot up. Because you have control over this sequence, you can see which INITs are causing trouble. Sometimes, simply changing their order resolves the conflict. Second, when you start your Mac, you can specify which INITs should be skipped (turned off) or ignored. (An INIT may not be needed for a particular project.) This capability simplifies the trial-and-error part of using INITs.

Don't forget: an INIT is loaded automatically at start-up and takes up precious RAM that could be going to processing power. If you have more INITs in the System folder than memory can handle, your Macintosh and everything "in it" will come to a screeching halt. In any case, the more INITs in the folder, the slower your Mac runs.

Finally, among other available resources are resources that "drive" your printer or other output devices, such as a plotter, so that Mac signals can be converted into output. These icons look like little printers or plotters and must be in the System folder or on the start-up disk for you to be able to change from one device to another through the use of the Chooser (discussed in Chapter 2).

System Files on Floppy Disk Systems

People who have a dual floppy disk system rather than a hard drive have a limited amount of space to allocate to System files. These users need to store as much as they can on the start-up disk, which contains the System files, so that they can be sure that they have the tools they need to perform the tasks they want. The rules for conserving space are pretty straightforward:

- Be sure that you keep on the start-up disk the essentials, such as the System file, the Finder, and the printer driver you will be using.

- Use the Font/DA mover to remove all the fonts or desk accessories you will not be using. (See Chapter 2 for more information about DAs.) Fonts take up a great deal of space, and many desk accessories, such as Calculator and Alarm Clock, may not be necessary to you.

- Create for each application a separate start-up disk that contains the files you need for that application. For example, if you are working with an accounting program, you may want the Calculator DA to remain on the disk while eliminating many of the others. If you are composing long documents, one of the many mini-word processors may take a front seat at the expense of losing some other DAs. You can also move these programs back to the System disk if necessary.

- Streamline your applications so that they include only the files you need to make things work. For example, you may want to delete special files that convert last year's MacInTax format to this year's, especially if this year is the first year you're using the program. The essential files take you some time to identify because many applications create temporary files (such as Word Temp 1 for MicroSoft Word) that are also stored in the System folder. These temporary files, which are created by your applications, are critical to the application's working correctly.

3
System & Finder

In general, the only files you need for booting up are the System file and the Finder file. To produce output with your Mac, you also need a file that acts as a driver for your printer (or drivers for any other output devices) and various CDEVs (called Keyboard, Monitors, and so on) in order to make the adjustments you want through the Control Panel.

Even though you boot up with a System file on a specific disk (floppy or hard), you can specify another disk that contains a System file to be the System, or the dominant, disk. This technique is useful for several reasons. It allows you to access DAs on another System or to switch to a version of the System that is compatible with the software you want to use.

To specify a different disk (with a System on it), follow these steps:

1. Open the System file on the disk you want to be the dominant, or the controlling, System.

2. Press ⌘-Option.

3. Double-click the Finder or the MultiFinder that is in the System folder containing the System you want to be in control.

Remember, the disk that contains the System in control is represented by the icon in the upper right corner of your screen. When you change the dominant disk, the icon for the disk containing the new System is displayed in the upper right corner.

Avoiding Viruses

If you think a fever of 102, aches and pains, and that terrible feeling of the flu is bad, just wait until you have encountered your first computer virus. A real virus works by attaching itself to a healthy cell and fooling the cell into thinking that its new job is to produce virus clones. A computer virus works in much the same way. A virus duplicates itself through active applications that are copied or messages that are passed from user to user.

Then the virus goes on to its second function in life, which is to do whatever the developer of the virus designed it to do: simply duplicate itself, crash the System, erase specific sectors on a hard disk, lock users out, and more. For example, the Universal Message of Peace virus appeared on thousands of Mac screens on March 2, 1988. Last year this same virus invaded copies of Aldus FreeHand, and thousands of copies went out the door before the problem was spotted. Although this virus was not fatal, it had no business being there. After all, one's system is a private place, which only the owner has any right to modify.

A Trojan Horse is a virus that does not reproduce itself. It just comes out and does its job at inopportune times. The primary difference between a Trojan Horse and a virus is that a Trojan Horse is meant to be destructive but does not reproduce, and a virus is not always (but may be) destructive and does reproduce itself.

Fortunately, Apple's Virus Rx comes on your System disk as an application and is free. (Well, almost—you did pay for the System software.) In any case, this vaccine lists files with warning labels as "Dangerous", "Fatal", or "Altered" if something suspicious crops up.

Before a virus hits, you can take some steps that will help you prevent disaster:

- Use one of the products designed to detect and eliminate viruses. Some of these products are described in this chapter.

- Use software that is available only through normal distribution channels, such as reputable manufacturers, because most manufacturers now take great care to prevent viruses from invading their media. Some public domain companies screen as well (Ask).

- If you are in doubt, don't copy or allow to be copied disks with applications or systems that might be infected, and the only way you can tell is through the use of some type of vaccine program.

- Be especially cautious about sharing "new finds" that are on networks, which, by definition, share programs, applications, and data files (and viruses).

3

System & Finder

Vaccines, programs that fight viruses (perhaps the most accurately named category of software ever) are often installed as CDEVs, such as (you guessed it) Vaccine from CE Software (also available as a shareware DA). When you boot up, you see a little icon reminding you that the program is working, and then through the Control Panel you set certain options (again see fig. 3.6).

Several commercial and shareware products check to see whether one or more of the major known viruses is lurking in the background ready to invade your Macintosh system. Among them are

- Vaccine (from CE Software), a free CDEV

- Ferret 1.1 (from Larry Nedry), an application that removes certain types of viruses and then attempts to repair any damage that may have been done

- KillScores (from Mac Pack/Apple Corps), which does the same as Ferret 1.1 and repairs the System and the Finder

- 1st Aid (from 1st Aid Software), a popular tool for recovering damaged files (comes with extensive documentation)

- Interferon 3.0 (from Vision Fund), a shareware application that checks for damage after it has been done

- Virex (from HJC Software) offers an effective virus catcher and destroyer as well as toll-free hotline support for registered users and product updates to help fight new viruses that may appear.

- Perhaps the best vaccine yet is AntiToxin (from Mainstay), which does what no other vaccine to date can do: both prevent infections from setting in (using an INIT) and eradicate any infections that may be present. Updates will arrive at registered users' doorsteps as new viruses are discovered and "cured."

Virex and Antitoxin are commercial programs. The other products are free, except Interferon, which asks for a donation to a charitable organization. You can find the addresses in the Vendor Guide.

Does every user hate viruses? Almost. Then why are they here? For some unknown reason, some computer users think that destroying other people's hard work and livelihood is fun. Viruses are not a prank but a serious threat to what is generally known as an open community.

Using the Finder

Finder may be the most important program in the System folder because Finder controls the appearance and operation of the desktop; yet Finder is not part of the operating system itself. Finder is the tool that allows you to move icons from one folder to another, delete them, and perform the many desktop operations. It's of interest that many other computer manufacturers are interested in offering a graphical interface like that of the Mac.

The Finder is responsible for the following jobs:

- Managing documents and applications

- Ejecting disks

- Initializing and erasing disks

- Opening, closing, copying, moving, renaming, and trashing

- Organizing documents, applications, and folders on the desktop

- Providing information in the Info box

- Starting and turning off your Macintosh

Updating the System File and Finder

The safest and most efficient way to update the System and the Finder files is to install them on your hard disk (or another floppy) by using the Installer, which comes on your Mac Tools. As the Mac operating system becomes more and more complex, a reliable tool that will help you stay current with new System changes is invaluable.

To install the Macintosh System tools, follow these steps:

1. Select the Shut Down command from the Special menu and turn off your computer.

2. Place a copy of the Macintosh System Tools disk into one of your external floppy drives. Remember, don't use the original! Use a backup.

3. Turn on your Mac.

4. Open the System Tools disk and open the folder named Installer (again see fig. 3.2). Installer may be in a folder named Utilities or in one called Setup.

5. Open the folder and select the Installer for your Mac model, as shown, for example, in figure 3.7.

6. Select the drive in which you want to install tools.

7. Click the Install button and wait. Soon the Finder, the System, and other important files are transferred.

3

System & Finder

Warning: Keep in mind that you must have only one System on a disk; otherwise, you are more than likely to get a System crash at some point or another because your Macintosh can have only one master at a time giving out the important operating instructions. Because many Macintosh applications (such as Word and Excel), come with System files, inadvertently allowing an additional System to slip in where it does not belong is easy.

Just because you don't have the latest version of the System or Finder, you have little reason to despair. When Apple releases a new System,

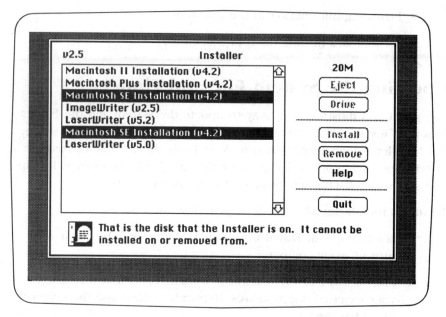

Fig. 3.7. Choosing the Installer Script for your Macintosh model.

you can get these tools into your Mac's "hands" by several different means.

First, you always get a new System from your Apple dealer when you buy a new computer. By the time you read this book, System software should no longer be in short supply, so what you need should be in your new box of goodies. The request through the card can take up to 16 weeks to fill, so when you buy your new Mac, have the dealer make you a copy of the latest System as a condition of the sale.

If you are not buying a new System, your Apple dealer should allow you to copy the System from a master disk to disks you supply. After all, to have people stay current is in the dealer's best interests because new software is often based on the newest System. However, don't expect too much. Your Mac dealer is not required to make these copies, and although Apple encourages dealers to do so, this service is up to the dealer's discretion. If your dealer does provide this service, don't forget to take along a set of blank formatted disks to use in making copies.

If these first two possibilities fail, you can always buy the latest System and associated files from your dealer. Buying the System is the only way to get the latest manuals. The current price for the System is $49.00, and you may be able to bargain the dealer down a bit. Don't look for a better price in the newspaper or from the many mail order houses that abound. The System is sold only through Apple or through Apple dealers.

Second, user groups often have copies of the latest System available for copying, or you can download the System from one of the many bulletin boards that offer the service (see Appendix D, "Directory of Bulletin Boards and On-Line Services"). Note that anyone who distributes System software must be licensed by Apple; duplication without a licensing agreement is illegal.

Portal Communications (408/973-9111) offers the latest versions of MultiFinder, Clipboard Color, DA Handler, Scrapbook, Keyboard, Finder, and the System. All these programs can be downloaded. CompuServe offers the same programs to subscribers. As explained in Chapter 16, you need communications software and a modem to download these programs. Although you may not think all these services and purchases are worth the expense, these purchases equip you for future adventures in telecommunications, an important and vital part of the Mac world.

3

System & Finder

Using MultiFinder

Ever try to rub the top of your head in a circle, while at the same time patting your tummy? Tough, but not impossible. You can probably do both one at a time, but both at the same time is a bit more difficult. That's what multitasking through the use of the Mac's MultiFinder is all about; doing more than one task at the same time. You already know about multitasking on a less ambitious level. Every time you select and use a desk accessory, such as Calculator, you are actually running one program "on top" of another. (Hence, this capability is called *multitasking*.)

But in spite of what you hear, MultiFinder is not truly multitasking. MultiFinder lets you have several applications active, but you cannot have operations (other than printing) going in both applications simultaneously. MultiFinder replaces Switcher, an early program done by Andy Hertzfeld (one of the original "Mackers"). Switcher allowed you to switch from one application to another; but memory limitations really didn't make Switcher practical, and it has been replaced with MultiFinder.

MultiFinder is a System file, like the System and Finder files. Like the original Finder, MultiFinder is a separate file, located in your System folder. MultiFinder is not available as a separate application on its own disk; you purchase it with the System. The System also offers you several new tools, and—most important—some of the applications you will read about in *The Big Mac Book* will not work without the most current System (which is 6 as of this writing, but soon will be 7.0, which is discussed later in this chapter).

Who needs MultiFinder? Anyone who wants to switch between applications quickly and easily. Certainly not everyone who uses a Mac needs MultiFinder. But before you know it, with your new-found applications and the ease with which they simplify your business and personal life, you may want to have your Mac doing more than one thing at one time. Let's look at a few examples.

> Lew runs an accounting firm, and every April he is inundated with tons of tax returns to prepare. He uses the menu-driven program MacInTax to complete the forms after all the relevant data is entered. While MacInTax is computing the values, Lew uses MultiFinder to switch to FullWrite Professional to compose a cover letter to the client. Although MacInTax is finished with the tax return before Lew is finished with his letter, he saves a considerable amount of time completing each client's material.

> The Mac often takes a "long time" to complete certain tasks: for example, updating complex drawings in files completed by a computer-assisted design package like Generic CADD (discussed in Chapter 11). John uses such a program to help produce drawings for his architectural firm. While drawings are being "redrawn" on the screen, he also uses several HyperCard applications to update information about the project, including costs for preparation of drawings, next steps in the design process, and so on.

> Joan runs a financial consulting firm that regularly prints prognostications about the markets. She uses MultiFinder to search an entire database to find a particular client's portfolio while she works on some "what if" predictions in her spreadsheet.

How MultiFinder Works

Let's assume that you are in Joan's shoes and you're using FileMaker II to search for the financial records for Frank Ryan. While you're doing this search, you're using Excel to perform a simple user-designed financial function that will compute the tax advantages of moving Frank's office out of his home. Here's what MultiFinder does and how it works.

Each software application Joan is using is called a *task* (that's why the operation is often called multitasking). Each task is being executed at what appears to be the same time. But because your Mac is limited to processing only one instruction at a time (unlike supercomputers that can process millions simultaneously), MultiFinder's real job is to allocate both tasks to the central processing unit of the Macintosh so that both can get done.

The beauty in MultiFinder is how it switches back and forth from application to application and gets both jobs done. This switching takes place so fast that to human eyes and other senses, the tasks look as if they are taking place simultaneously. This switching is not really multitasking, but it is simultaneous in the sense that two tasks are being completed during the same period of time—but not, strictly speaking, at the same moment in time. Keep in mind, however, that the more applications you run under MultiFinder, the slower everything works.

What You Need for MultiFinder

You must have System Version 6 and Finder Version 5 for MultiFinder to work, and you need a minimum of 1M of RAM. (The first personal computers had 48K—21 times smaller!) With only 1M of RAM, however, you are limited in what you can do because you simply don't have enough room to hold all the operating instructions for all the applications. If you want to use more than one large application (such as Word and Excel or PageMaker and WordPerfect), you need 2M.

The reason for this requirement is that a large part of the first megabyte of memory in your Mac goes to the System and Finder. Along with most applications, System and Finder can take up a good part of that available RAM. Any added program requires more space. For example, to use Word and Wingz with System 6, you need at least

3
System
& Finder

1.5M, and that's without considering any additional DAs or fonts that may already be part of your System.

Elsewhere in this chapter, I talk more about memory restrictions with MultiFinder and suggest ways you can try to get around these restrictions.

How To Use MultiFinder

Using MultiFinder is a simple and straightforward procedure. Basically, you change to the Finder screen, and select MultiFinder under the Startup command on the Special menu on the opening screen. After configuring MultiFinder to fit your needs, you restart your Mac, and then open applications as you need them.

As much fun as using MultiFinder can be, keep these two points in mind:

First, if you don't need MultiFinder, don't use it. If you are working with only one application, you don't need the power of MultiFinder. At best, processing slows; and at worst, you can get confused as to what you're actually trying to accomplish.

Second, don't be greedy and open more files than you will be working with. For example, HyperCard alone takes almost 1M of RAM; HyperCard and MultiFinder together require 2M even to get started! As another example, there's no shame in using WordPerfect and QuarkXPress under MultiFinder without adding SuperPaint. Do your text and page layout first, and then get into SuperPaint.

You also may not need MultiFinder at all. If all you want is to be able to switch quickly from application to application, you may want to use an INIT called On Cue (from Icon Simulations). On Cue is an application that is added to your System folder. As you can see in figure 3.8, you can configure On Cue so that you can switch from application to application with one click, for example, from Wingz to HyperCard. When you start your Mac, On Cue automatically makes available the applications you have indicated in the On Cue setup routine. In this example, HyperCard, MacLink Plus, Wingz, and Word 4.0 can be easily navigated through. Remember, On Cue is not in any way a multitasking tool, but it can be convenient. As with any other INIT or CDEV, however, you may have conflicts with other programs.

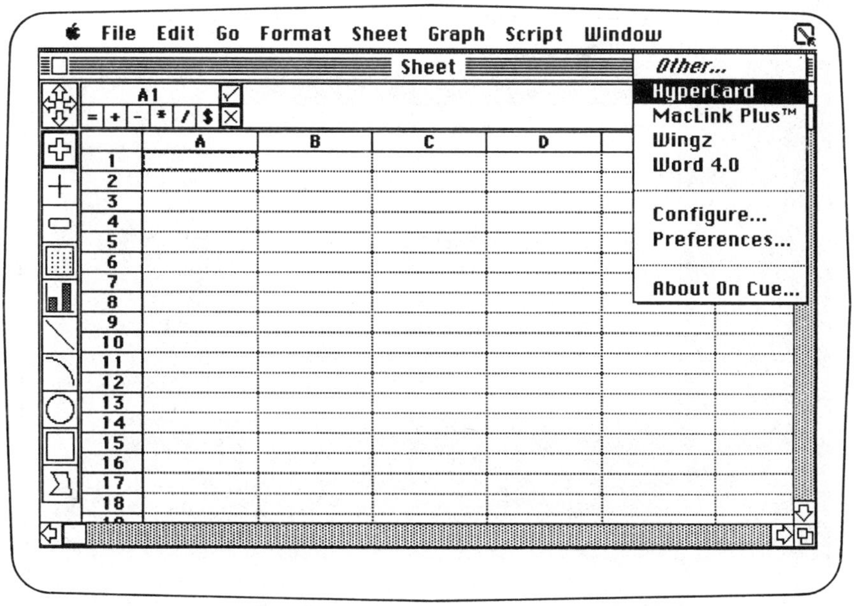

Fig. 3.8. *The On Cue menu configured for various applications.*

On the other hand, if you have 8M of RAM, take advantage of all this memory and use MultiFinder to increase your efficiency. Otherwise, you will be hard pressed to justify why you purchased so much RAM in the first place.

How To Install MultiFinder

Because using MultiFinder depends so heavily on the size of the applications you will be using, be sure to start with small applications (such as MacPaint) and practice using MultiFinder so that you can get a feel for what it does.

Here are the basic steps in getting MultiFinder up and running:

1. To set up MultiFinder, select the Set Startup command from the Special menu. You will see the Set Startup window for MultiFinder, as shown in figure 3.9.

2. Click the radio button labeled MultiFinder.

3. Click OK.

    MultiFinder will be installed the next time you start your Mac.

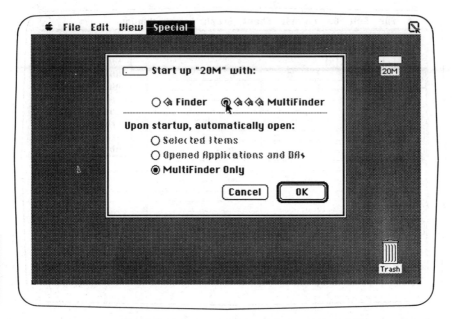

Fig. 3.9. *The Finder/MultiFinder Set Startup window.*

4. Select the Restart command from the Special menu to load MultiFinder.

When your Mac starts, MultiFinder is installed, and you see a small MultiFinder icon in the upper right corner of your screen, indicating that MultiFinder is active and ready to go (see fig. 3.10).

Using MultiFinder for the first time is a great deal like using your Mac for the first time. Switching between applications is almost unbelievably easy, and you will soon realize that MultiFinder is another "Mac thing" that you can't live without. Multifinder really can be that important. In figure 3.11, you see the Apple menu after SuperPaint and Word have both been opened under MultiFinder.

How To Navigate with MultiFinder

When you have MultiFinder installed, you have several ways to select applications.

First, you can simply select the application from the Apple menu, which lists the applications available through MultiFinder. For many people,

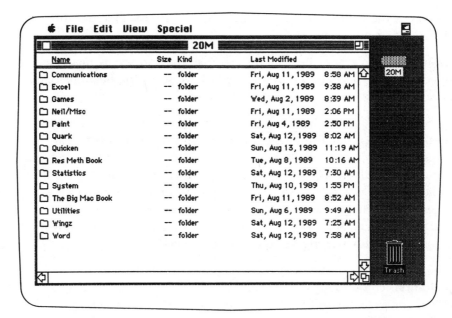

Fig. 3.10. *The MultiFinder icon.*

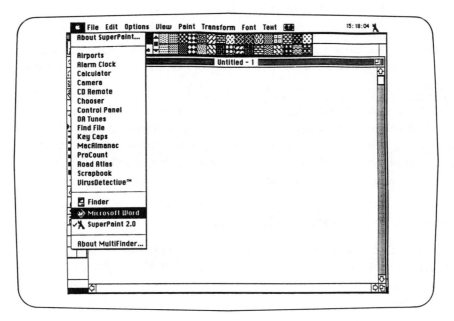

Fig. 3.11. *Apple menu with SuperPaint and Word opened under MultiFinder.*

this way is the easiest and most logical way to access an application while another one is active.

Second, you can resize the windows so that you can see as many applications as you have windows. If you have many applications open, however, your screen can get quite crowded.

The alternative to this dilemma is, of course, a big full-page monitor like the Radius 19-inch full-page monitor. With it, some really neat things begin to happen. First, you can see quite a few windows because they are all available. Next—and this fact is incredible—adding another monitor allows you to isolate certain windows on the extra monitor. For example, with a few clicks and drags, you can have Word all by itself, while Excel, SuperPaint, and an accounting program are shown on the other monitor waiting to be called into service.

Third, you can go to the next active application by clicking the application icon located in the upper right corner of the MultiFinder screen. For example, in figure 3.11, you can see that the current application is SuperPaint. If you are working in SuperPaint and want to switch to the next application, just click the SuperPaint icon. You can click the icon as often as necessary; by doing so, you scroll through the set of options located on the Apple menu.

Remember, when you use Finder, you have to leave one application before you can launch another. MultiFinder, on the other hand, is as fast as selecting a DA; you go right to the application you want and it's there.

Both Finder and MultiFinder provide a tool to select applications. The significant difference between the two is that MultiFinder allows you to select an application while another is still active and to perform work in one application while working in another. For example, you can be sorting in one application while you are drawing in another.

How To Print with MultiFinder

Even though MultiFinder is not truly a multitasking tool, it can be a marvelous time-saver, especially in printing. With MultiFinder, you can do background printing on a LaserWriter while you are working in an application.

To print in the background, follow these steps:

1. Select the LaserPrinter icon from the Chooser. Background printing is automatically turned on when you are in MultiFinder.

2. If you haven't already, select the LaserWriter icon appropriate for your printer.

3. Close the Chooser window and you're ready to go.

Printing is fast because part of your Mac's memory is devoted to that task.

Once you select background printing, a small Apple program called Printer Monitor becomes available so that you can control many of the procedures during printing. For example, you can examine the status of a document that is being printed or determine when it will print (before or after other applications).

The Printer Monitor screen offers you a good deal of information and several different options. First, Printer Monitor tells you what document is being printed. Second, Printer Monitor tells you what documents are waiting to be printed and the order in which they are to be printed. Third, Printer Monitor tells you the status of the document that is currently being printed. Documents are printed in the order in which you select them with the Print command from within the application you are using. If you want to change the order in which the documents are to be printed, just drag the document name to a different place in the sequence. Quick and easy.

You set the time that you want a document to be printed by clicking the Set Print Time button. You are then greeted by a dialog box that asks you to set the time you want the document to begin printing. (You set the time in much the same way you set the Mac Alarm Clock.)

How To Conserve Memory with MultiFinder

What's good about MultiFinder? It gives you multitasking, easy switching between applications, and increased efficiency, and that's only for starters. What's bad? Using more than one application within MultiFinder eats up memory like young kids eat popcorn at the movies

3
System & Finder

on Saturday afternoon. MultiFinder is a memory-intensive tool, and because your Mac never seems to come with enough memory (only 1M for the Mac Plus), you can count on needing more memory if you want to use MultiFinder. More memory costs more! Chapter 19 discusses increasing memory in your Mac and some of the costs involved.

If you try to load too many applications into MultiFinder, you get the message that not enough memory is available (see fig. 3.12). You can try certain actions to get around the problem. For example, suppose that you want to operate both Word and SuperPaint under MultiFinder; but when you start to open SuperPaint, you get the insufficient-memory message. The first and most obvious remedy is to adjust the amount of memory used by the applications you are running. To adjust the memory allocation, follow these steps:

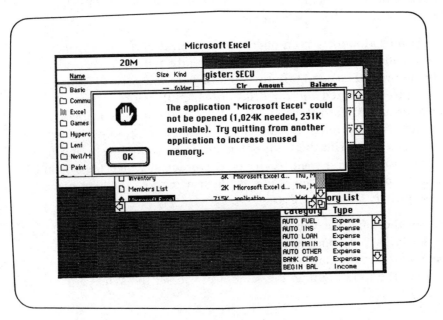

Fig. 3.12. *MultiFinder's insufficient-memory message.*

1. Select the icon for the application you want to use and then select the Get Info command from the File menu (or use the ⌘-I key combination).

2. As you can see in figure 3.13, the Info window shows you the amount of memory suggested to run this application and the amount of memory allocated. You can decrease the amount of application memory. You can adjust that amount until you get things to work as you want, but if you go below the required amount of memory, eventually the application will not work; you will get unexpected results and system crashes.

Adjusting memory allocation can be a tricky process and should be attempted only after you have some experience with MultiFinder and are well aware of your application's memory requirements.

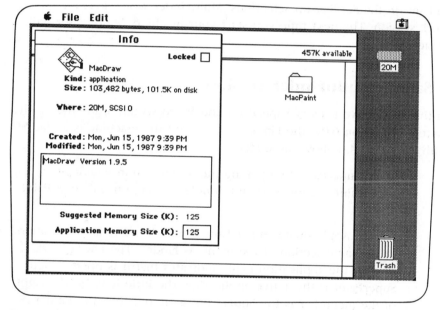

Fig. 3.13. *Determining the memory needs of an application.*

You can keep adjusting and squeezing more and more in. If you run into memory problems after you have made all the adjustments you can, you need more memory or need to adjust your computer's limitations.

Running low on room (or RAM) means that DAs are going to be hard to use because they take up their own chunk of memory. To get around this problem, press the Option key when you select a DA. This procedure allocates application memory, not MultiFinder memory. You can run out of this memory also, of course, so use your DAs wisely.

Another way to conserve memory is to work without MultiFinder. You can turn off, or disable, MultiFinder two ways.

First, you can deselect MultiFinder at the Set Startup command on the Special menu. You just need to select Finder instead of MultiFinder and restart your Mac so that the change goes into effect.

Second, if you want to keep the installation of MultiFinder intact but bypass its installation just for the specific session, hold down the Option key while you are starting your Mac. Although MultiFinder is still set on the Set Startup selections, MultiFinder won't start for this work session. The next time you start your machine, MultiFinder will be active.

A Sample MultiFinder Session

In this session, you select SuperPaint and Word within MultiFinder. The System is Version 6.02, the Finder is V5.0, and the machine is a Mac SE with 2M of RAM. Follow these steps:

1. Open SuperPaint by opening the folder within which SuperPaint is contained and double-clicking on the SuperPaint icon.

   On the Apple menu, SuperPaint is now listed as an application, in the same section of the menu as Finder. The check mark next to the application name indicates that it is open. When SuperPaint is the active application, the little icon on the right of the menu bar is the SuperPaint icon, not the MultiFinder icon.

2. Go back to the Apple menu and select the Finder (which is really MultiFinder). You need to return here to open another application.

3. Open Word by double-clicking the Word icon. The SuperPaint icon on the menu bar is replaced by the Word icon.

On the Apple menu, the applications available under MultiFinder are Finder, Word, and SuperPaint (see fig. 3.14). To switch from one to the other, select the application by clicking the title of the application on the Apple menu or the small icon in the upper right corner of the screen.

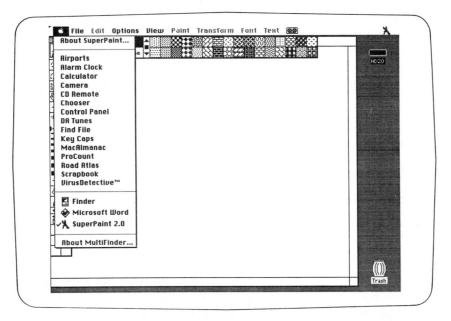

Fig. 3.14. *The "active" applications operating under MultiFinder.*

You can also shrink the current window and launch an application directly from the desktop, an even faster method. Also, clicking the icon in the upper right corner, toggles between the active applications. For example, to go from Word to SuperPaint, just click the SuperPaint icon.

Easy, quick, and a dream if you need to switch back and forth between applications. For example, suppose that as part of your business you need to prepare a large directory of names and addresses. To prepare the directory, you need to sort a set of names and addresses in Word. You also want to create a logo for the directory. You want to work on the logo in SuperPaint while the address list is being sorted in Word. The solution—using MultiFinder, begin the sorting process. Then open SuperPaint and begin to work on the logo. You can't see Word doing the sort, but it is working, nevertheless.

Customizing Start-up with MultiFinder

After you have some experience with MultiFinder and the applications, DAs, and other Mac files you want to work with, you may want to change the Set Startup command so that you can load a chosen set of applications and DAs, tailored to your needs. (There's no sense performing this step unless you regularly use a standard set of applications, such as Word, FileMaker II, Wingz, and Super 3D.) Follow these steps, beginning at the desktop level:

1. Shift-click all the applications you want to become active when MultiFinder is started.

2. Select Set Startup from the Special menu.

3. Select MultiFinder and Selected Items.

4. Click OK.

5. Select Restart from the Special menu.

Your Mac reboots, making MultiFinder active, and launches all the applications you have specified. MultiFinder can be confusing at first, but when you realize its benefits, you will not work without it.

Determining Your System and Finder Combination

Ever since the Macintosh computer was introduced, the System folder has been undergoing extensive modifications. In some cases, new files are added so that new hardware developments (such as laser printers and plotters) can function properly. In fact, Apple tries to update periodically the System file (and several of the other files within the System folder).

Unfortunately, as already mentioned, not all software applications work with all versions of the System file and the Finder. Not only that, not all versions of the System files and Finder are entirely compatible with all machines. Check to determine what versions of these important files you must have before you purchase software. Refer to figure 3.15 to make sure that you have the correct combination of System and Finder files. And before you buy, always ask what versions of the System and Finder are required to run the software you're considering.

System	Finder	128 Mac	512K, 512KE	Plus	SE	II
2.00	4.10	*				
3.20	5.30		*	ok		
4.00	5.40		ok	ok	ok	ok
4.10	5.55		ok	ok	ok	ok
4.20	6.00			*		
6.03	6.10			*	*	*
*=best combo						

Fig. 3.15. *Recommended System and Finder combinations.*

The best way to customize your Mac, of course, is to try to load the applications you want to use and follow the guidelines given for trimming memory requirements application-by-application until you find a combination that fits.

What's Next?

Apple is hard at work on a new System, which is being field tested now with a release date of sometime in the spring of 1990. Code named "Big Bang" (where do they get these names?), System 7.0 sends shivers through everyone because implementing a new System has major implications for the whole world of Mac users.

First, and perhaps most important, you will need 2M of RAM to run System 7. That's a great deal of money just to get the machine up and running. Second, some versions of software you now use will need to be updated. Third, for developers (those people who bring us all the wonderful software we use), a whole new set of operating rules need to be incorporated into their designs; DAs, INITs and full-program applications may need to be changed.

The press and periodicals are abuzz with excitement about this new system, and here are some of the features (for better or worse) that have been discussed. Whether they are realized or not, we will have to wait (and pay?) and see.

- Increased RAM requirements

  System 6 takes up almost a whole floppy disk right now. How could anything that is supposed to be more powerful and offer more new features take up less room?

3
System & Finder

- A new Finder

  This program is really going to be a change. The new Finder will offer such things as E-mail capabilities (see Chapter 16) with a mail-box icon on the opening screen; faster access to large numbers of files; and additional ways of viewing and organizing files, like the new trash can, which will be a folder. When you want to empty the trash can (with its own directory) you will treat it as you do any folder full of files. In addition, a new feature, using aliases, supports the use of icons that reference other files or folders.

  In addition to all these features will be an integrated Help system, very fast search tools (10 times faster than Find File), a Sleep command for saving the screen and reducing power consumption, an icon editor, and increased macro-making and macro-using capabilities.

- Virtual memory

  The new System will use virtual memory to create additional memory and dedicate unused RAM for such functions as creating an electronic hard drive.

- DAs

  Almost everyone uses DAs, and the new System will continue to support their use. (But don't be too confident about versions after 7.0.) With the new System, DAs will be installed by dragging them into the System folder, rather than by using the Font/DA mover. The DAs can then be launched from the System folder by double-clicking. As you might suspect, DAs will be treated more and more like full applications, and DAs will become applications that are quickly accessible.

You're now familiar with a good many of the technical details of the Mac. The System and Finder provide the framework within which you create documents of all kinds. To learn how those materials are saved, let's turn to a discussion of disk management and storage media, including floppy and hard disks, and the new world of CD ROM.

4

File Management and Storage

Welcome to the world of information management and media: SCSI, floppy disks, densities, hard drives, access times, formatting, tape backups, sectors, tracks, and more. Probably the most significant breakthrough in information management that computers have brought us is the capability of saving and sharing information— without using paper. Computers store information on flexible plastic disks (called floppy disks) or on rigid metal or glass disks (called hard disks), both coated with a magnetic substance that can record the electromagnetic signals.

This chapter discusses different types of storage media, focusing on floppy disks, hard disks, and optical storage devices, such as CD-ROM (Compact Disk Read-Only Memory) and WORM (Write Once Read Many times). You also learn about managing the files on your disks and making backups.

4
Files

Using Macintosh Floppy Disks

The letters, reports, and computerized drawings you produce, as well as scores from the games you play, all have to be stored somewhere. The medium most frequently used for the storage of Macintosh files is a floppy disk, a small circular cutout of plastic material (often mylar) that is coated with a magnetic material, such as iron oxide. With both floppy and hard disks, the electrical impulses (or the information) generated by the read/write heads in your disk drives are stored as magnetic domains that can be recorded (written) or played back (read) by applying another magnetic field and generating current. In the basic language that computers use, your Mac sends these impulses as 1s or

0s, high-current or low-current levels, using a binary (off/on) system of communications, which you learn more about in Chapter 16.

Although some floppy disks come in soft or flexible covers, the disk you use with your Mac is contained in a rigid case. The combination of convenient size (small enough to fit into a shirt pocket) and protective covering makes transporting your disks safe and easy. The capacity and the size of the disk that the Mac works with have changed as well. First, the 3.5-inch disk could be formatted for 400K worth of information, then 800K, and now 1.44M, or 1,400K, with the new SuperDrive in all SE and higher machines. If you add the SuperDrive's capacity to read DOS formatted 360K and 720M and 1.44M disks, the versatility of the Mac becomes apparent.

Understanding the Floppy Disk's Structure

From the outside, you can see that a Macintosh floppy disk comes in a plastic case with a protective metal door. When you insert the disk into the drive, the door opens, providing the read/write heads access to the disk. In the corner of the disk is a small cutout with a tab that enables you to access files on the disk but not to alter them.

When this little *write-protect* tab is pushed back, leaving the hole open, the disk is locked, or protected. You can read the files on the disk, but you cannot write to the disk, save information, or alter the disk's contents in any way. If you try to change its name, the cursor remains an arrow over the name, and a lock is displayed in the disk window. You should get into the habit of locking your original application disks (the ones that came right out of the box) to avoid accidentally blitzing part of a file. When the hole is closed, the disk can be modified.

Figure 4.1 illustrates how a floppy disk looks with its insides exposed. On the inside, you find a circular disk made of the same material as an audio cassette tape. A lining on the inside helps keep the disk free of contaminants that can destroy your data. As the disk turns (at about 300 revolutions per minute), the disk lining picks up very small particles of dust and debris. If the disk is used excessively, these particles can build up and just like scratches on a record, affect performance. Therefore, making more than one backup copy of files stored on your floppy disks is a good idea. (Backups are explained later in this chapter.)

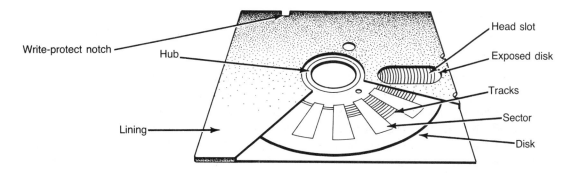

Fig. 4.1. *Diagram of the inside of a floppy disk.*

Many different sizes of floppy disks are available, but the disks you use with your Mac are 3.5 inches square and can hold up to 800K of information. A *K* (for kilobyte) represents 1,024 bytes, or individual units of information; the number of bytes is 2^{10}, or 1,024 (the 2 is for the number of values that can be assumed—on = 1 or off = 0). A double-spaced page containing 33 lines of text with 65 characters per line would be about 2,145 bytes, or approximately 2K. At this rate, a standard 800K floppy disk could hold 400 pages of text. But because other information also needs to be recorded on a disk (the title of the disk, disk markings, disk directory, and so forth), an 800K floppy disk actually holds about 783K of your data, or around 390 pages, depending, of course, on how the pages are formatted (double-spaced, and so on).

Understanding High-Density Floppy Disks

New on the Mac scene are high-density floppy disks that can hold millions of bytes. Apple now has a 1.44 million-byte drive, called a SuperDrive, that uses high-density floppy disks capable of storing more than three times as much data as a 5.25-inch flexible floppy disk used in IBM PCs. Here are the differences between the low- and high-density Mac disks:

- Single-sided disks can hold 400K (that's 400,000 bytes of information), equivalent to about 200 pages of text. Double-sided disks can hold twice as much—800K, or a little under 400 pages of text.

4

Files

- High-density double-sided disks hold 1.44 megabytes (that's 1,440,000 bytes), or around 800 pages of text and cost about $4 each.

  High-density disks look different from low-density disks. The most prominent difference is that they have another hole in the upper corner opposite the write-protect hole. The new high-density drives use a light beam; if the beam can shine through that corner of the disk, the computer knows that it's a high-density disk.

The Macintosh IIcx, IIx, and SE/30 come equipped with these new Floppy Drive High Density SuperDrives (FDHD), and the Macintosh II can be modified to accept the SuperDrive. Apple now also has an external model that sells for about $625, but you can use it only with the IIcx, IIx, and the SE/30. These SuperDrives can also read 400K and 800K disks formatted on double-density drives.

You need to be aware of two differences with the new high-density disks and drives. First, the disks are not manufactured in the same way as double-density disks and cannot be formatted in double-density drives. (The next section discusses formatting.) Second, double-density drives come with a plastic stabilizer that pops out when you turn on your Mac for the first time. This plastic stabilizer keeps the ceramic heads in the drive from being damaged while the computer is being transported. High-density drives don't come with this stabilizer, and to avoid damage, you shouldn't place a stabilizer in the drive.

What's really on the inside of these little disk marvels (be they low or high density) and how you work with them is an entirely different matter. Let's turn to that now.

Initializing Floppy Disks

When you buy a floppy disk, it is blank and unreadable. To help you understand what initializing a disk does, imagine that your blank disk is analogous to a parking lot with no painted stripes to mark parking spaces—that's how your disk appears to your Mac before you *format*, or *initialize*, it. Let's say that cars are like pieces of information: with no marked parking spaces, they have no place to park. After you complete the initialization process (painting parking spaces), the information (like the cars) has a place to "park." If the disk is new, the initialization process adds "parking slots" so that information can be recorded and stored. If the disk has already been used, initialization tows away the cars (erases any old information), erases the lines, and repaints the lot to ready it for more cars (information).

Initialization is the first step you take to prepare a disk for storing information. If you haven't initialized a new disk, your Mac prompts you to do so.

Caution: NEVER initialize an application disk, or you will erase all information from the disk, including the program itself.

You should initialize a disk under two conditions. First, a new disk must be initialized in order to accept data. When you place a new disk into one of your drives, you see a message asking you whether you want to format (or initialize) one or both sides (see fig. 4.2). Click the Two-Sided option. Your Mac formats the disk and then displays a dialog box prompting you to supply a title.

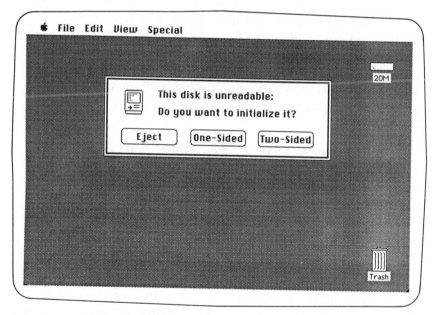

4

Files

Fig. 4.2. Initializing, or formatting, a disk.

The second condition under which you should initialize occurs when you have a used disk and no longer need the information on the disk, or when you want to destroy the data on the disk. In either case, you want to clean off the disk to make it "new" again. To initialize a disk used on the Mac before, follow these instructions:

1. Place the disk in your internal disk drive.

2. Select the icon representing that disk.

3. Select the Erase Disk command from the Special menu.

4. Your Macintosh displays a dialog box asking you whether you want to erase the disk. Click Yes (or press Return), or click Cancel if you want to abort the initialization process.

When the initialization process is complete, your Mac asks you through a dialog box to name the disk. You can use up to 31 characters (but no colons) in any combination. Use a descriptive name to help you remember the contents of the disk. If you want to change the name of the disk after you have assigned it a name through the dialog box, you need to do it on the Finder. The easiest way is to select the icon that represents the disk is by clicking it once. When it is highlighted, anything that you type replaces the current name. If you want to insert or delete only part of the name, move the cursor to the area underneath the disk icon where the name is actually written and click once. The cursor takes the shape of an I-beam, and you can use it to place the insertion point where you want. Now you can backspace and delete or insert text.

When you initialize a disk, those "parking stripes" don't get put down just anywhere. A formatted disk is organized into *sectors* and 80 *tracks*, as shown in figure 4.3. Each sector is like a slice of pie, and the tracks divide the disk into concentric circles. As you can see, each sector contains the same amount of information, but some tracks contain more sectors than others. A formatted high-density disk contains twice as many tracks and thus can hold twice as much information.

When your Mac saves information on a floppy disk, the Mac records the physical location where the file is stored on the disk. Your Mac operating system takes these *addresses* and constructs a *directory* of the file names, called the desktop file, which is what you see when you view the files under the View menu on the desktop. This directory is an invisible file that is created on each disk and stores the addresses to the files on the disk and the associated icons. The directory, normally

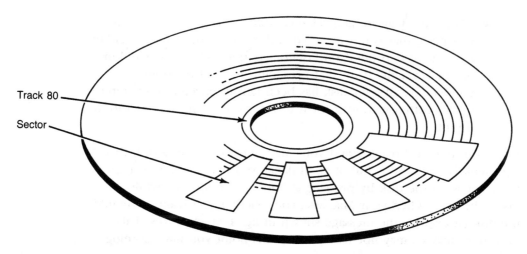

Fig. 4.3. *A disk divided into sectors and tracks.*

Track 80

Sector

with no icon showing, uses several tracks for storage. Each time you add information to a disk by saving a file, your Mac adds the name the file is saved under to the directory.

When you select a file to work with, your Mac finds the name in the directory, notes the address, goes to that location on the disk, and reads the necessary information. When you erase the file, you don't actually erase anything more than the address or location of that file on the disk; that file can be restored, as you will learn about later in this chapter and in Chapter 19.

Salvaging Unreadable Disks

The time may come when you try to initialize a disk, and it refuses to do so, or you place a disk you have used before in your drive, and the Mac gives you a message that it cannot read the disk. If the disk is new, you can take it back to the dealer for a replacement or refund. If the disk is not new and has valuable data on it, you cannot try to recover a file if the Mac isn't even reading the directory. Before you panic, try one or both of these homespun solutions:

- Find another Mac. The problem may be your drive, not your disk.

4

Files

- Wait and try again later. Like Goldilocks, your disk wants to be in a place that is not too cold and not too hot. If it is in either extreme, it expands (too hot) or contracts (too cold) and may not be readable. It needs to reacclimate itself to room temperature. If your disk has been left in extreme temperature or has gotten wet, wait for it to return to room temperature or dry off.

If you run into real trouble and your Mac refuses to read a disk that you think is fine (and is full of good data), you may be able to recover whatever is on the disk by pressing ⌘ and the Option key while you insert the disk. When your Mac asks you whether you want to rebuild the disk (it displays the message shown in fig. 4.4), click Yes. This procedure may or may not work, but at this point you have nothing to lose.

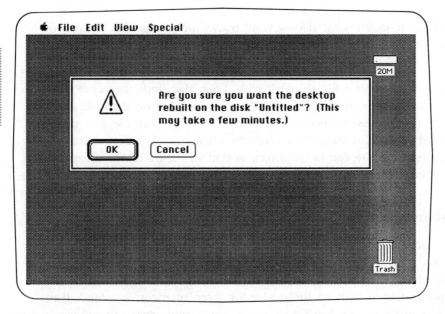

Fig. 4.4. *Trying to salvage a disk.*

One commercial product that may help you recover information or "repair" a disk before it is unreadable (or even after) is 1stAid Kit from 1stAid Software. The program is easy to use, and the 300-page manual is well-written and comprehensive. It teaches you about not only the product but also the Mac's hierarchical filing system and a good deal about your Mac in general. The kit costs $99.95. SUM (from Symantec) is also excellent for helping you rebuild or salvage an unreadable disk.

Ejecting Disks

You can eject a disk from a drive in several ways. The simplest way is to drag the disk icon from its location in the desktop to the trash can. The icon disappears from the desktop screen and the disk is ejected. This method is preferred because it also clears the desktop of information about the disk you are ejecting. Just be careful not to drag a file icon to the trash can, or you can (almost) say good-bye to all the information on that file. It's "almost" good-bye, because you can recover a trashed file by opening the trash can and copying the file back to another disk. The trash can, however, is automatically emptied when you select Empty Trash from the Special desktop menu, shut down your Mac, or launch another application. Then the information on that file really is gone. Another safe method is to highlight the disk icon and then select the Eject command from the File menu, but this technique leaves the icon dimmed on the desktop.

You also can use one of the following key combinations to eject a disk:

- ⌘-Shift-1 ejects the disk in the internal drive.

- ⌘-Shift-2 ejects the disk in the external drive.

- ⌘-E ejects the selected disk.

One shortcoming of using a key combination is that the disk icon remains visible on the desktop, taking up space and cluttering your workspace. Your Mac is also likely to delay your work by asking you to reinsert the disk for housekeeping purposes. Icons that are left on the desktop when you shut down are stored as names in the directory, which slows the operation of your Mac a bit. For those of you with one disk drive, however, it is necessary to keep these icons on the desktop, because you need the icon to copy or transfer files from one floppy to another.

You can usually find an Eject option in most of the applications that you use, such as the one shown in figure 4.5 from the tax preparation software MacInTax. Ejecting a disk in this manner also leaves the dimmed icon on your desktop.

4

Files

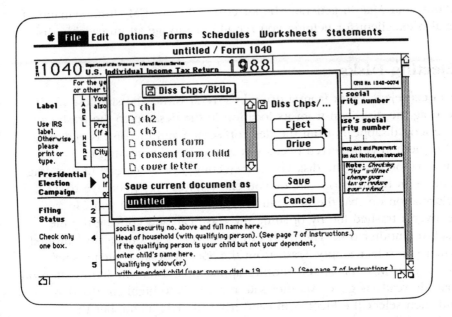

Fig. 4.5. The Eject button.

You can also forcibly eject a disk by pushing the straight portion of a
paper clip into the tiny hole to the right of the floppy disk drive
"door." This technique may become necessary if your Mac "freezes up"
and does not eject the disk from the drive, but it is not very safe
because the workings of the drive are delicate, to say the least. Try this
method only if nothing else works. You may need to have your drive
serviced if ejecting disks becomes a problem.

Caring for Your Floppy Disks

Caring for your floppy disks properly is extremely important, so here
are six—not ten—commandments that you should follow:

1. Keep your disks away from all heat sources. The plastic disk
   melts at a very low temperature—160° Fahrenheit. If your disk
   melts, no one will be able to recover the data for you.

2. Keep your disks away from magnetic fields, such as magnets or
   magnetic paper clip holders. The rays emitted from screening
   machines at airports and other security checkpoints are not

harmful, but metal detectors are absolutely deadly because they have electromagnetic properties that will erase your computer disks. Don't carry your disks through the metal detector.

Other sources of potential problems, believe it or not, are your color TV and your telephone (but not your modem because it doesn't ring). Both have magnetic elements that are strong enough to render your disk damaged at best and useless at worst.

3. Store your backup disks in a safe place. Many users, especially those who use computers in their business activities, keep one backup disk on site and another at a different location. The likelihood that both will be destroyed is very low.

4. Keep the outside of the floppy disk case clean. If removing a label leaves a glue residue, use lighter fluid or nail polish remover to clean the disk. You can also use a wax pencil, crayon, or permanent marker to write on the disk, forgetting about labels altogether.

5. Keep your disks (and your other computer equipment, for that matter) away from food, coffee, dog biscuits, and cigarette smoke. The plastic material inside a floppy disk is very thin, and the read/write head must make contact with the disk in order to transfer or read data. Even a smoke particle that is 25 ten thousandths (.00025) of an inch thick can damage the disk or the read/write head.

6. Keep your disks protected from dust by storing them in a closed container. If you have a little child around the house, shoe boxes for tots' shoes make great containers. You can also buy nice disk storage containers from the dealers listed in the Vendor Guide. Data International Wares has a wide selection of storage containers ranging from a single disk holder to a wall-mounted model that holds 250 disks.

If you do damage a disk or the rigid plastic holder it spins in, try one or both of these possible solutions:

- If the case is visibly damaged (cracked or smashed), try to copy it onto another disk as soon as possible; it just may copy. If it doesn't, gently pry the case open and, grasping the disk by the

4

Files

edges only, place it into a new case. Take great care not to get any fingerprints on the disk.

- If the disk itself gets wet or soiled and you cannot get your Mac to read your files, try this. (It may sound crazy, but if you cannot access your data, anything is worth a try.) Gently pry the mylar disk out of its case and wash it in warm, soapy water. Rinse the disk in clear water and let it *air dry* on a clean surface (towels may leave lint on the disk). When dry, place the disk back in its case and try again to read it. Be sure to take great care not to get any fingerprints on the disk.

Buying Floppy Disks

Besides knowing how floppy disks work and how you should handle them, you also need to know where and how to buy them. Because most Mac owners use 3.5-inch double-sided disks, this discussion focuses on disks of this size, with just a few comments about the new FDHD disks.

Floppy disks always have two sides, which are coated during the manufacturing process. They are tested and certified error-free, as your friendly disk manufacturer will tell you. (Sony disks are particularly good, with only one defective disk per thousand.) If one of the two sides is defective (it failed a test in which information was written on it and then read from it), the disk is sold as a single-sided disk. Many users buy these single-sided disks and format them as double-sided, assuming that they can be used as double-sided disks if the format takes. The advantage is that single-sided disks cost less than double-sided ones, but this procedure is not recommended because your data on the second side may suddenly become unreadable.

The price of floppy disks is related to several factors: the amount of data they can hold (the more they hold, the more expensive they are); the quality of the disks (determined by the manufacturing process); and availability (a shortage in 1988 of 3.5-inch disks pushed prices up). You can buy your floppy disks from a local dealer or through the mail, or through one of many discount stores (such as K Mart or Wal-Mart). You can buy a name brand (such as Sony or Memorex) or a generic. Chapter 14 discusses these options in more detail.

The advantages of buying disks from a dealer are few, especially when not much can go wrong with the product. Even if one becomes unreadable, throwing it out will not make much of a dent in your budget. On the other hand, supporting your local dealer is never a bad idea; if your Mac breaks down, you may get the same kind of treatment you have given the dealer. A dealer will also give you replacement disks if one fails, although a replacement is little consolation for losing your data.

Buying mail order has one big advantage: price. For example, a box of 10 3.5-inch double-sided floppy disks in the Kansas City area costs around $23.95 for Maxell or 3M disks, whereas national mail order companies advertise the same disks from $15.95 to $18.95 for a box of 10. If you buy disks in large quantities, the price is even lower. However, you have to pay for the shipping, and if you need disks immediately, you obviously cannot wait for a mail order to arrive. Nevertheless, you may need as many as 25 floppy disks to back up the contents of a 20-megabyte hard disk, so mail order can be a good way to obtain quantities of "extra" disks for such purposes.

You also need to decide whether to buy generic (unlabeled) or name brand disks. Generic disks are often made by large manufacturers and sold without labels for much less than the name brands. The best way to find out whether they are safe is to ask your dealer or the company you are buying them from. If they tell you, "They're made by a large manufacturer, and we cannot release the name," don't buy them. If they tell you the manufacturer, you have to make your own decision. Some disk manufacturers such as Sony or Maxell simply have a better reputation for quality than others. Generic disks are cheaper (about 80 cents each), but they are often sold without disk labels or boxes.

4
Files

The FDHD (Floppy Drive High Density) disks are new, and the price is a bit steep (about $3.50 each for Sony FDHDs). However, FDHDs hold almost twice as much as a double-sided floppy disk. If you have a high-density drive, your work habits will probably determine the type of disks you use. If you create very long documents consisting of many files and you want to have the entire document on one disk, high-density disks may be for you. The 1.44M storage space on high-density disks also is helpful when you have to back up large quantities of data, especially with the new larger systems.

Whether you buy name brand or generic disks, from your dealer or through the mail, the bottom line is the quality of the disks. MEMCON of Omaha, Nebraska, produces an annual report on the results of rigorous tests on floppy disks conducted according to standards of the American National Standards Institute (ANSI). The report states that C.Itoh, Sony, TDK, and IBM are the most reliable. These brands are also the most expensive, but when you have spent 50 hours entering data on a colossal worksheet that is due to the boss at 4 p.m. this afternoon, you don't want to risk a disk crash. Of course, even these name brand disks do crash on rare occasions, so *always* make backup copies of your work.

Using Hard Disks

If you have ever had to wait several minutes for an application program to load from a floppy disk, if you have had to swap disks while using a large application that takes up more than one floppy disk, or if you have more data than you could ever hope to organize on all your disks, then you should consider obtaining a hard disk for your Macintosh. In fact, it's uncommon to find even the "lowly" Mac Plus without an external hard drive attached. Even more interesting is that when hard drives were first offered, they came with a 10M capacity, which very quickly moved up to 20M and then 40M, and now you can purchase them as large as 600M, as you learn more about later.

Understanding Hard Disks

Hard disks store and access data much faster than floppy disks do, and they provide much more storage space. If you use applications requiring large amounts of storage, such as graphics or spreadsheets, you may find that a hard disk is a necessity. Making the decision to buy a hard disk even easier, competition has reduced the prices of hard disks by more than 50 percent. Five years ago a 20M hard drive for the Mac cost more than $1,000; today, you can get the same model for less than $400. Furthermore, an increasing number of hard disks now match the capacity of the technologically more advanced optical storage devices. For example, CMS Enhancements markets the Platynim series of hard disks storing 291M and 584M, and the HAMMER600 hard disk from FWB, Inc., has a storage capacity of 600M.

A Brief History of Hard Disks

The need for a better data-handling capacity quickly became apparent as personal computers grew in popularity. Floppy disks simply are not adequate to handle and store the large amounts of data being processed by personal computer users. Mainframe computer facilities first used hard disk technology when they switched from tape to disk packs (large plastic cases of coated aluminum platters). These disk packs greatly increased the speed with which mainframes could access and utilize information stored on the platters.

IBM developed the technology for the hard disk drive, then named a Winchester (after the Winchester 30-30 rifle because it used two 30M disks). In the early 1980s, the manufacturing cost of hard drives dropped as demand for them in personal computers increased, and manufacturers began offering hard disk drives as options on personal computers. The hard disk drive is now standard on the Macintosh SE models.

In order for a hard disk drive to function, the computer originally had to have a *controller card*, which enabled the drive to communicate with the computer's operating system. Early Macs had no such card. The time spent designing the controller cards for the Mac explains the high cost of the first hard disk drives, which often sold for more than $2,000 despite their relatively small capacity of about 10 million bytes. Today Apple's hard disks for the Mac have storage capabilities of 350M (about 180,000 pages of text at 500 pages per megabyte of storage), and third-party disks are sold in capacities of up to 600M.

An alternative to controller cards came when Apple adapted a special type of interface to Macintosh computers. This interface, known as SCSI (Small Computer Systems Interface) and pronounced "scuzzy," enables data to be transferred from the hard disk to the computer and back again fast enough to eliminate traffic jams along the way. The SCSI has become an industry standard for connections between disk drives and other peripherals, and Macs are now equipped with a SCSI port, where the external hard disk drives are connected.

How a Hard Disk Works

As you know, a floppy disk is made of a flexible, coated plastic material. In contrast, a hard disk is a thin platter (or platters) of metal or glass.

4

Files

Whereas floppy disks spin in hundreds of revolutions per minute, a hard disk can spin at 3,600 rpm. It spins continuously, not just when it is being accessed, as a floppy disk does. At this speed, a great deal of data can be transferred very quickly, and you don't have to wait for the disk to get moving to access information. Another reason for the speed is that it generates a cushion of air upon which the platter "floats" and prevents the head from actually touching the disk surface.

When you turn on your computer and your hard disk begins to spin, the following sequence of events takes place. The computer tries to locate a System file. If you have a hard drive and start your Mac with one of the System Tools floppy disks that came with your Mac, your Mac finds this disk and starts up the System. If your Mac does not locate a System disk, the computer turns to the hard disk for a System folder containing the System file and the information your Mac needs to start up.

The computer's "starting itself" is called *booting* for technical and folksy reasons. When your Mac starts, it "pulls itself up by its own boot straps." Technically, certain tracks on the hard disk provide the computer with the information about the disk that it needs to start operations. When your Mac has this information, the hard disk icon appears on the desktop, and you are ready to work with its contents.

Hard disk speeds are measured in four ways: the speed at which the computer can find the information it is looking for, called *average access time* or *seek time*; the speed at which the hard disk can transfer this data from the disk to the computer's memory, called *transfer time*; the speed with which the read/write heads can jump from track to track when a file is spread across more than one track (which is often); and the *interleave ratio*. Average access and seek time are measured in milliseconds (thousandths of a second). One great advantage of hard disks over earlier methods of storing information, notably tapes, is that the hard drive does not search sequentially, as tapes must, through each file from the beginning of the directory on down in order to find a specific file. Instead, a hard disk drive uses a random-access method that searches much more efficiently and quickly.

The speed at which a hard disk can transfer information to or from the computer's central processor (CPU), which holds all instructions on what to do with the data, is related to how efficiently the information is read, or the *interleave factor*. This ratio is a measure of how much data is read per revolution of the disk. A ratio of 1:1 indicates that each sector on the hard disk is read as it passes the read/write head. If the ratio is 2:1, every other sector is read, and so on. The higher the ratio, the more times the disk has to spin in order for all the data to be read. The more times it spins, the longer it takes to read the data. Macintosh II computers have an interleave factor of 1:1.

Types of Hard Disk Drives

Three types of hard disk drives are available: internal, external, and removable drives.

The *internal* hard disk drive is a drive placed inside your Macintosh housing. The obvious advantage here is that the drive takes up no desk space. The great disadvantage of internal drives is that they must be placed inside the computers. Few users are brave enough to open a new Mac and to put in a drive, voiding the warranty in the process. If you are not one of the brave, you can have a technician install a hard disk for you for about $35 per hour. One advantage is that internal drives are cheaper.

If you have an internal hard drive, the hard disk icon should appear on-screen when you turn on your Mac (see fig. 4.6). You are now ready to begin work.

External hard drives are freestanding units that are placed under, next to, or even on the back of your Macintosh computer, as is the Jasmine backpack line of hard drives. You usually just need to plug in these external drives, and they are ready to use. External drives will also show up as an icon on the desktop. External drives are connected directly through the SCSI port on the back of your Mac. It's as simple as plugging an electrical cord into an outlet. As you saw in Chapter 1, it's tough to make a mistake. First, the SCSI port is clearly marked on the back of the Mac, and second, this is the only place the hard drive cable will fit!

Finally, a new class of hard storage devices are removable, enabling you to take the data storage unit (but not the drive) with you. Although these disks are technically not "hard" because they are made out of materials similar to floppy disks, they can store a great deal of information and access it quickly. For example, Syquest drives use 44M floppy-type disks and are fast and reliable.

4

Files

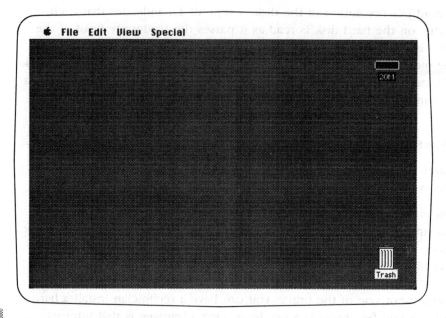

Fig. 4.6. The hard disk icon.

The primary advantage of the removable disk technology is increased security; no one can read your data if it isn't in the computer. Another advantage of this technology is that you can have separate disks for different purposes: one for office records, another for one year's budget reports, and so on. The only disadvantage is expense. These data cartridges can cost up to $120 each, but, on the other hand, you will never run out of storage space. Like hard disks, removable disks come in many sizes: 10, 20, 30, and 45 megabytes.

When you buy a hard disk, decide the maximum capacity you will need, and then double that capacity to determine the size you should buy. Filling up a hard disk is much easier than you can imagine.

Connecting External Hard Drives

Because hard disk drives for the Mac have been so carefully designed, connecting your external drive is easy. Make sure that your Mac is turned off, and then simply plug in the cable that came with the hard disk or that you purchased from your dealer. You plug the cable into the SCSI port in the back of your Mac (see Chapter 2 for more information). Now restart your Mac.

You also can connect more than one hard drive in a *chain* of drives (sometimes called a daisy chain). This chain may contain up to seven devices, including an internal hard drive. Your Mac differentiates these drives by the address (from 0 to 7), which you assign using software provided by the manufacturer (unless the manufacturer or your dealer has already set the addresses). Some devices can be set using a rotary switch on the back of the drive. A good rule of thumb might be that if it is not abundantly clear how you assign a number (if one has not been assigned), then do not buy the hardware. Generally, the higher the number of the address, the closer the drive (or other peripheral) is physically to the computer. Thus, your Mac's original internal drive always has the address 7, and your internal hard drive, if you have one, has the address 6. To make assigning addresses simpler, some drives have toggle switches for changing the address.

You can run into all kinds of problems if two devices have the same address. If this problem occurs, the disks most likely will not mount properly; a less likely scenario is that the directories on both disks may be destroyed, rendering the data unreadable because the computer cannot find it. (The computer needs the information in the directory to know where to look for the file.)

4

Files

The first and final links in the chain of drives require a *terminator,* a resistor that tells the system where the end of the chain is. If the drive at the end of the daisy chain is not "terminated," the information at the end of the chain bumps into itself and loses its integrity. Thus, if you want to add an external drive to your system, it must be terminated, as most drives are. But if you want to add another external drive, you need to buy a drive that is not terminated or that has an external termination switch (such as the Mass Micro Data Pak, the Everex EMAC 20DL, or the MacBottom HD21). "Determinating" the drive yourself is another option, but this procedure involves opening the case and disabling electronic components and is not recommended for the average Mac user. Also, the total combined length of all the SCSI cables has to be less than six feet with no single cable being more than three feet.

Chaining devices together is at best difficult. Some devices do not work together, and others may work but affect the performance of the other devices. You will probably need to experiment a great deal to find the proper sequence of your different devices (drives, printers, CD-ROMs, scanners, and so on) so that they all function properly.

Using Hard Disk Optimizers

Your hard disk stores data in sectors, in much the same way as a floppy disk does. If one sector is not large enough to contain all the information in one file, the computer stores the data wherever the drive can find the space, often in a sector completely removed from the sector containing the rest of the file.

When you use your hard disk frequently, adding new files, reading and resaving old files, deleting files, and so on, the files tend to be split and stored at different places on the disk. When you choose to open a file, the system has to locate all these pieces and rebuild the entire file, a process that can take a considerable amount of time, depending on how large and how fragmented the file is.

To keep your disk from becoming too cluttered, you can rebuild the desktop about once a month by holding down the Option and ⌘ key when you start your Mac. The Finder reorganizes itself and clears out unnecessary files; however, you lose all the information you have in the Get Info boxes (such as notes to colleagues). This procedure helps clean up your disk but does not speed up the operation of the hard disk drive.

You can also use a disk *optimizer*, software such as Optimizer (part of PC Tools from Central Point Software) or DiskExpress (from ALSoft). Figure 4.7 shows Optimizer's opening screen. Both programs reunite fragmented files, taking all the pieces of a file and placing them in contiguous (or adjacent) blocks so that each file is in only one area of the disk. DiskExpress, one of the most highly recommended utilities, also prioritizes files and overwrites deleted data with logical 0s to create free space. Another utility, SUM (from Symantec) rebuilds the desktop as well. You also can defragment the disk manually (if you have the time it takes) by doing the following:

1. Copying all of the files on your hard disk to floppy disks.

2. Reformatting your hard disk (just don't erase or trash all the files).

3. Copying the system back to your nice clean disk.

4. Copying all the applications files to your disk.

5. Copying all the data files.

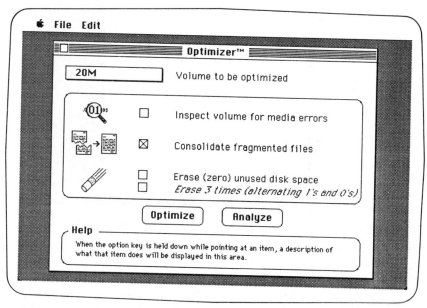

Fig. 4.7. Unfragmenting a disk using Optimizer from PC Tools.

Using Hard Disk Software

A variety of software programs are available to help you organize your folders and files efficiently on your hard disk. One such program, MacTree Plus (from Go Technology) is superb.

MacTree is best at helping you organize and view your folder and files in a vertical or horizontal format (see fig. 4.8). You can then move through levels of the hierarchy. Using menu commands, you can move, erase, rename, find, and copy files quickly, and you can view a document without first launching its application. MacTree Plus is available in English, German, Japanese, and French and comes with a hard disk backup utility. Another benefit of using MacTree Plus is that it can print a file directory; having a hard copy of your file directory is never a bad idea.

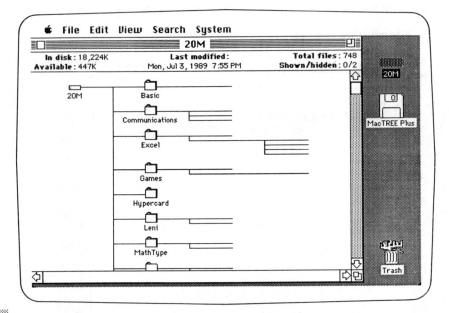

Fig. 4.8. MacTree Plus's horizontal display format.

Hundreds of programs are available to help you work more efficiently and easily with your hard disk. Some of these programs are DAs (desk accessories), which become resident when you boot up your Mac; others are programs that must be run from the desktop.

One type of program merely helps you locate specific files by name, date of creation, or type. For example, Findswell (from Working Software) and HFS Navigator provide the *path* through the HFS system for the file name you enter. Findswell appears inside standard file Open and Save dialog boxes, just where you need it.

Other programs, such as DiskTop (from CE Software) and Desk Tools (from Electronic Arts), actually act as finders, enabling you to search for a file, copy it, rename it, move it, delete it, and more, all while you are working in another application. If you have ever had to work with a great many files and have to return to the Finder to rename them, you can appreciate the time and trouble these programs can save you.

Buying a Hard Disk Drive

When you are ready to buy a hard disk drive, you should keep the following questions in mind:

- *Does the drive automatically "park" the read/write heads when you turn it off?* When your hard disk drive is turned off, the read/write heads should lift off the platter to a secure resting place so that they cannot damage any data. You should buy a drive that parks its read/write heads automatically; otherwise, you will have to use software. Incidentally, you should have the heads parked when you move your hard drive, or the head may "crash" on the platter, destroying valuable data.

- *How much storage space do you need?* If you write small documents and don't use many different applications, a 40M drive should be sufficient. However, if you work on large projects with large applications (such as FullWrite or PageMaker), get as much storage as you can afford. An 80M drive may run a small business, but if you require complex graphics, get as much storage as you can.

- *Does the drive have an external switch for changing the SCSI address?* If you plan to add additional hard disk drives to your system, you should have an external switch.

- *What kind of support does the manufacturer offer?* Many companies provide toll-free numbers you can call with your questions. Some even offer you a loaner if your machine needs to be sent in for repair. Inquire by calling the company and discussing the policy with a customer service representative.

- *How reliable is the drive?* The best way to answer this question is to ask other Mac owners who have hard disk drives. You can also get information about hard disk drives from magazine reviews, user groups, bulletin boards (see Chapter 16), and even your local repair shop.

- *What software comes with the drive?* Some companies, such as Jasmine, offer a disk full of public domain software, including games, file management routines, and print spoolers that enable you to work on one document while your Mac is printing out another. You can get the same programs free from bulletin

4

Files

boards, but having it all on your hard disk when you buy it is convenient and saves you the time you would take to collect it all.

- *What options does the drive have?* Some drives come with extra outlets, switches for controlling other peripherals (such as a printer), and lights indicating when the drive is on. You need to determine which, if any, of these options are important to you.

- *What does the drive look and sound like?* Appearance and noise factors are primarily subjective judgments, but we all have our prejudices that determine, in part, our buying preferences.

Many users judge the value of a hard disk drive by the number of dollars it costs per megabyte. For example, a Jasmine Direct Drive 80 lists for $1,399—$17.49 per megabyte. A Warp 9 Photon 80 sells for $17.29 per megabyte. In this comparison, the price difference is minimal, so you should consider other factors in choosing between the two. Figure 4.9 gives the retail price and per megabyte cost of a number of hard disk drives. Keep in mind that these are retail prices; Chapters 13 and 14 discuss a number of alternatives to buying retail. Apple drives, made by other manufacturers (currently Quantum), are generally good, but they tend to be overly expensive.

Before buying a hard disk drive and spending a considerable amount of money, get as much information as you can. Ask other Mac users, read computer magazines and newsletters, and visit a number of dealers to see what they have. You cannot "sample" all the drives available, but you can learn about the different features that they have.

Managing Your Disk Files

To get the most out of your Mac, you need to keep your files in good working order, organized so that you can find what you need easily. This section explains how Macintosh files are organized and provides guidelines for managing your files efficiently.

Manufacturer	Type	Size (in M)	Cost	$ per M
Aristotle Ind	Portable	20	$549	$27.45
Cache Systems	External	30	$559	$18.63
	External	45	$629	$13.98
	External	60	$729	$12.15
	External	80	$849	$10.61
	External	150	$1,499	$9.99
	Internal	30	$425	$14.17
	Internal	45	$499	$11.09
CMS	External	20	$559	$27.95
	External	30	$599	$19.97
	External	45	$749	$16.64
	External	60	$829	$13.82
	External	80	$1,189	$14.86
	External	140	$1,895	$13.54
Cutting Edge	External	20	$439	$21.95
	External	30	$499	$16.63
	External	40	$559	$13.98
	External	65	$649	$9.98
	External	80	$749	$9.36
	Internal	30	$469	$15.63
	Internal	45	$645	$14.33
	Removable	44	$1,100	$25.00
Dolphin Sys Tech	External	20	$549	$27.45
	External	30	$599	$19.97
	External	40	$769	$19.23
	External	60	$819	$13.65
	External	80	$1,179	$14.74
	Tape Backup	150	$1,439	$9.59
	Removable	44	$1,195	$27.16
Ehman	External	20	$399	$19.95
	External	30	$449	$14.97
	External	45	$529	$11.76
	External	65	$579	$8.91
	External	80	$679	$8.49
	Internal	20	$329	$16.45
	Internal	30	$379	$12.63
	Internal	45	$449	$9.98
	Internal	65	$499	$7.68
	Internal	80	$599	$7.49
	Removable	44	$849	$19.30
HardPac Mac	Portable	40	$799	$19.98
	Portable	80	$1,195	$14.94
Jasmine	External	20	$649	$32.45
	External	40	$799	$19.98
	External	80	$1,099	$13.74
	External	100	$1,299	$12.99
	External	160	$2,899	$18.12
LaCie	External	32	$519	$16.22
	External	42	$699	$16.64

4
Files

Fig. 4.9. *Comparison of prices of hard disk drives.*

Manufacturer	Type	Size (in M)	Cost	$ per M
	External	70	$799	$11.41
	External	84	$999	$11.89
	External	111	$1,199	$10.80
	External	142	$1,499	$10.56
	External	177	$1,799	$10.16
	External	613	$3,199	$5.22
MacBest	External	20	$499	$24.95
	External	30	$549	$18.30
	External	45	$599	$13.31
	External	60	$729	$12.15
	External	80	$849	$10.61
	External	90	$939	$10.43
	External	173	$1,749	$10.11
	Internal	20	$399	$19.95
	Internal	30	$449	$14.97
	Internal	45	$499	$11.09
MicroNet	External	20	$499	$24.95
	External	30	$579	$19.30
	External	60	$739	$12.32
	External	173	$1,649	$9.53
	External	620	$3,899	$6.29
Microtech	External	20	$520	$26.00
	External	40	$649	$16.23
	External	80	$1,019	$12.74
	External	100	$1,099	$10.99
	External	150	$1,469	$9.79
	Internal	40	$569	$14.23
	Internal	80	$919	$11.49
	Internal	100	$999	$9.99
	Internal	150	$1,399	$9.33
	Internal	320	$2,699	$8.43
	Removable	45	$1,059	$23.53
PCPC MacBottom	External	21	$779	$37.10
	External	32	$829	$25.91
	External	45	$979	$21.76
PLI Turbo	External	30	$625	$20.83
	External	50	$819	$16.38
	Removable	40	$1,299	$32.48
Quantum	External	40	$699	$17.48
	External	80	$949	$11.86
	External	105	$1,099	$10.47
	Internal	40	$599	$14.98
	Internal	80	$889	$11.11
	Internal	105	$999	$9.51

Fig. 4.9. Comparison of prices of hard disk drives.

Understanding the Hierarchical Filing System (HFS)

The Macintosh operating system, using the Hierarchical Filing System, or HFS, enables you to create and store files in *folders*, represented on your Mac desktop as icons that look like ordinary manila file folders. Desktops can contain many folders, each folder containing many files. For example, figure 4.10 shows a desktop with 17 folders. To view the contents of a folder, double-click that folder icon. Figure 4.11 shows the Hypercard folder open, revealing more folders and some files. You can have files in folders and folders in other folders, but you cannot have folders in files.

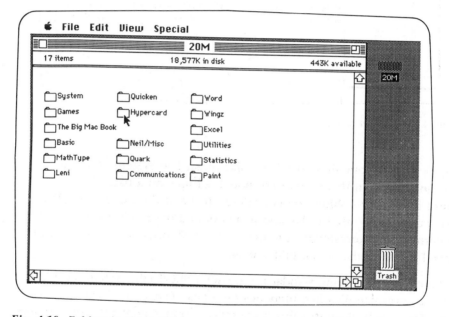

Fig. 4.10. *Folders in the desktop.*

4

Files

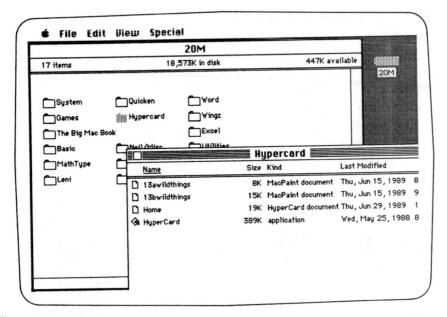

Fig. 4.11. Files in a folder.

Apple's early computers used the Macintosh File System (MFS) to organize files. In this structured model, all files on a hard disk were read in a linear fashion and considered to be at the same level. This system is rarely used today and is mentioned here only for your information. Interestingly, a folder that is MFS organized has an extra pixel inside of the actual folder icon.

The current operating standard, the Hierarchical File System, enables you to organize files like branches on a tree. Figure 4.12 (created using MacTree Plus) illustrates this hierarchical arrangement with two folders in the root directory and three files in Folder A.

The HFS system has two major advantages:

- You can have more than one file with the same name as long as they are in different folders. Your Mac sees no conflict with two files in separate folders having the same name.

- You can organize related files (and related folders) into groups to make working with a hard disk much easier. For example, you can place all word processing files in one folder and all database files in another.

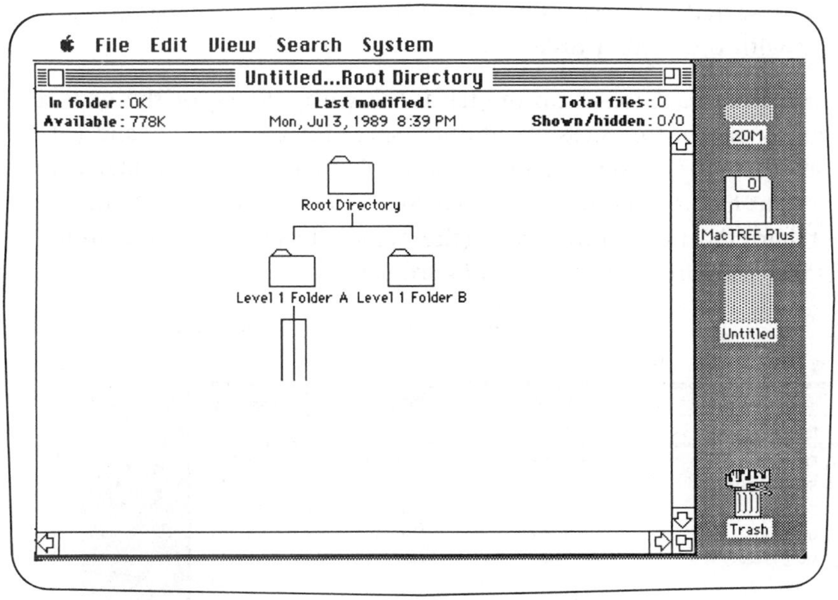

Fig. 4.12. *A hierarchy of files.*

Organizing Files on Your Hard Disk

When you start a new Mac, your hard disk is most likely ready for use and the System already installed in a folder. If so, the folder will have a Macintosh icon; if not, create a new folder, name it *System Folder*, and use the Install program to copy all the System files from the floppy System disks into this folder (see Chapter 3).

You will no doubt change the organization of your hard disk as your needs change and you add applications and files to your System. This discussion assumes that you are first starting out and creating a new "tree" of files and folders. To illustrate the process, assume that you own the following software:

- Microsoft Word
- MacWrite II
- Excel
- Quicken

- Assorted utilities, such as PC Tools, and the tools that come with the System disks

Basically, you want to set up the hard disk with folders for the general categories of word processing, utilities, spreadsheets, finance, and (of course) the System. Remember, if you don't have a System folder (or the System file) on the desktop, your Mac doesn't know where to look to get started. The *root directory* (the highest level) in this hierarchy looks like the directory shown in figure 4.13.

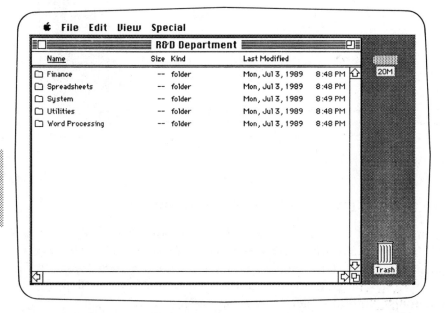

Fig. 4.13. *The root level for the hard disk named 20M.*

To create a folder while at the desktop, just select the New Folder command from the File menu and type a new name for the folder labeled Empty Folder. When you open an empty folder by double-clicking the folder icon, you see that the folder contains no files or folders because you haven't added anything yet. Use the New Folder command to create folders named Word and MacWrite. (These folders will contain all the files for these programs.) You can then add the appropriate files by dragging them into the folder.

Your organization will be something like this:

- All Word application files, folders, and document files in the folder called Word

- All MacWrite application files, folders, and document files in the folder called MacWrite

- All system files in the folder named System Folder

- Any other utilities in the folder named Utilities

Some users choose not to place the actual documents they create using a particular application in the same folder as the application itself. Where you place your document files is really a matter of personal preference and work habits, but here's one suggestion from an anonymous Mac expert:

- A folder for each application (Word, PageMaker, Excel, for example) or a folder for each category (Word Processors, Utilities, and so on).

- A folder in the root directory named Data.

- A folder in the Data Folder for each project.

This system keeps all the data in one location and greatly simplifies the process of making backups.

Each folder or file in the HFS system has a *path*, or a description of the location of the file in the HFS "tree." For example, a file stored in the WordPerfect folder would have the path 20M:R&D Department:Word Processing:Letters:Gordon. In figure 4.14, you see the entire structure of the sample HFS with this path just before you open the Gordon file.

The following guidelines will help you organize your hard disk:

- The principles of working with disks, files, and folders (naming them, dragging them to the trash can, and so on), discussed in the earlier sections on floppy disks, apply equally to hard disks.

- Work with and fine-tune your hard disk organization until it does what you want. Move and rename files and folders whenever doing so will improve the organization of your hard disk.

4

Files

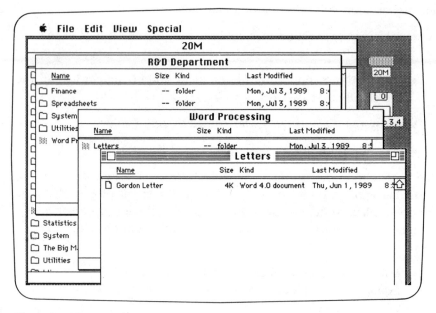

Fig. 4.14. The HFS structure of a part of a hard disk.

- Don't create files at the root level. The root level is the first level in the directory, the one that first appears on your Mac screen. Having only folders at this level enables you to get a quick look at the contents of the entire hard disk.

- Try to limit the number of files in a folder to 20 or fewer so that you can see them all at a glance when you view by name, date, or kind.

- Keep the organization as simple as possible. If you have 200 folders at the root level, you're in trouble. The less clutter you have, the more efficiently you can work with your disk.

- If you have a special application, such as a word processing program, that you use frequently, and you do not want to have to set the Start Up option to call it, simply move that icon from its folder to the desktop (see fig. 4.15). Each time you boot up, you can just click the program's icon to launch the application. In this example, you can then double-click the Microsoft Excel icon to start up the application.

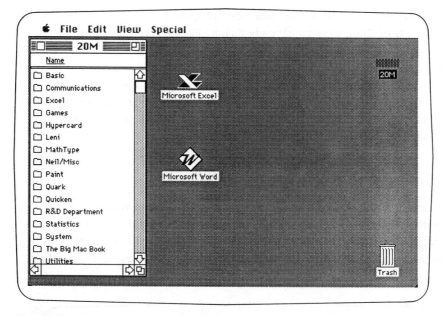

Fig. 4.15. *Moving icons for frequently used applications to the desktop.*

Naming and Renaming Files

The unit of storage that your Mac works with is a *file*, defined as a set of information stored under a unique name. You usually create and save files within specific applications such as Excel, Word, SuperPaint, and PageMaker (for more information, see Chapter 2).

You assign a name to a file when you create it for the first time within an application. You can name a file anything you want (using up to 31 characters) and include any character except a colon (:). Keep the following two guidelines in mind:

- Keep file names as short as possible. The less information you have on-screen, the easier it is to work with.

- Use descriptive names that you can distinguish from one another. For example, don't name one file *letter1* and another *letter2*. You will soon not be able to tell them apart. Instead, use *peggy/ltr* or *roger/ltr*.

4

Files

If you try to use a file name that already exists, your Mac tells you in an alert box, That name is already taken. Please use a different name. A file keeps the name you assign it until you change it. To change a file name, just click the icon or the name of the file (while you are in the desktop) and type the new name. You can edit file names by placing the I-beam cursor where you want the editing to begin in the name bar, clicking, and then entering the title information that you want to include, or just by typing a completely new title.

Deleting and Recovering Files

To delete a file, select it and drag it to the trash can icon on the desktop. Figure 4.16 shows a Word file named '89 Qtr 1 Sales Report being dragged to the trash can for disposal. When you place the file in the trash can, the trash can bulges a little to show you that something is in it. The file is no longer in its original window.

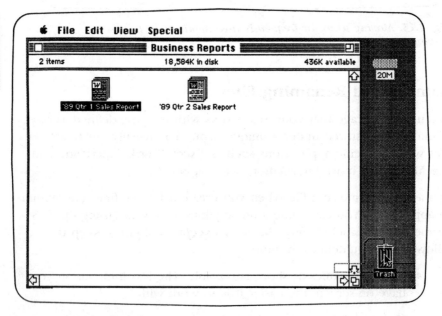

Fig. 4.16. *Deleting a file by dragging the icon to the trash can.*

Although you place the file in the trash can, it is not gone until you "take it to the dump." To see the file, open the trash can by double-clicking it (see fig. 4.17). Your file icon appears, with the file still intact. To use the file again, simply drag its icon back to its original window, or select the icon and then select the Put Away command from the File menu. As long as the file in the trash can is selected, the Put Away command returns it to its original window.

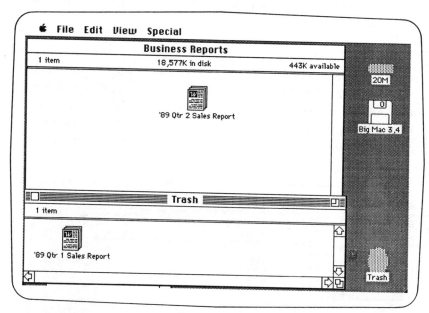

Fig. 4.17. *Opening the trash can.*

You certainly don't want to keep putting your deleted files into the trash can and never dispose of them completely. When you want to empty the trash can, select the Empty Trash Can command from the Special menu on the desktop. Files remain in the trash can until you do one of several things: empty it (the disk or folder from where they came keeps the space "open"), shut down the system, start a new application, eject the disk by dragging the on-screen icon to the trash, or copy a new file to the disk that the deleted file is on. So if you want to delete a file, drag it to the trash can and empty the trash as soon as possible. If you have your doubts, try to avoid any activity that automatically empties the trash can, or just don't put any files that you are unsure of into the trash can.

If you inadvertently empty the trash and want to recover a file, some special utilities are available that can help you get the file back. Chapter 19 discusses these utilities and the file recovery process.

Duplicating Files

Duplicating a file (making an exact copy of the file on the same disk) is a snap. Just highlight the file and select the Duplicate command on the File menu (or press the ⌘-D key combination). You get an exact copy of the file, named

Copy of [*filename*].

Figure 4.18 shows a duplicate of the file '89 Qtr 2 Sales Report named Copy of '89 Qtr 2 Sales Report; a duplicate of Copy of '89 Qtr 2 Sales Report would be named Copy of Copy of '89 Qtr 2 Sales Report. If you try to keep going, your Mac continues to make copies until the name exceeds 31 characters, at which time an alert box tells you to edit the name.

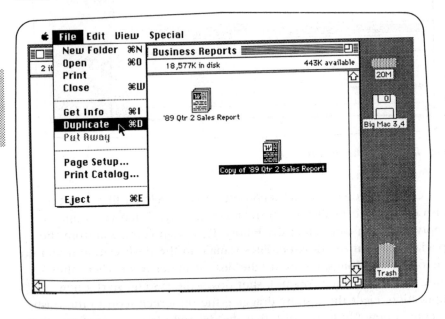

Fig. 4.18. *Creating a duplicate of a file.*

Duplicating a file on the same disk can save you time when you want to alter part of a file without losing the original, and you don't want to enter the information all over again. For example, you may have written a letter and want to send the same letter with a slight modification to another person. Just copy the file and then rename it; you then have a duplicate that you can modify as you want.

Copying Files

Copying a file is like duplicating a file, with one major difference. When you *duplicate* a file, you copy it onto the same disk, but when you *copy* a file, you copy it from one disk to another. To copy a file from one disk to another disk, or to a folder, just select the file icon and drag the file to its destination. When you do, you see a message box with a progress bar telling you what is being read and copied.

If you want to copy more than one file, while holding the Shift key down, select the files you want to copy. Next, drag the entire set of highlighted files over to the disk on which you want the files to be copied (see fig. 4.19). Notice that when a number of files are highlighted, you need to drag only one to carry the whole set over. An important distinction needs to be made between copying and moving. If you want to change the location of the file so that it is no longer in its original folder, this is called *moving*. The Mac assumes that when you drag a file to another location on the same disk that you meant to *move* the file, not *copy* the file. The file is actually moved, and this action will eliminate unintentional duplicate files on your disks. However, when moving a file from one disk to another, the Mac assumes that you want to copy the file and will leave the source file in place. If you no longer want the source to be where it was, you will then have to delete it.

4
Files

Making File and Disk Backups

Unfortunately, many users realize the importance of backing up files and disks *after* they have lost a file they have spent hours, days, or even months creating. You should get into the habit of backing up your files at the end of each work session so that you are not the one with the missing 342-page dissertation.

Backing Up Files on a Floppy Disk System

You can copy any file from one disk to another simply by dragging the icon representing the disk to which you want to copy from the *source*

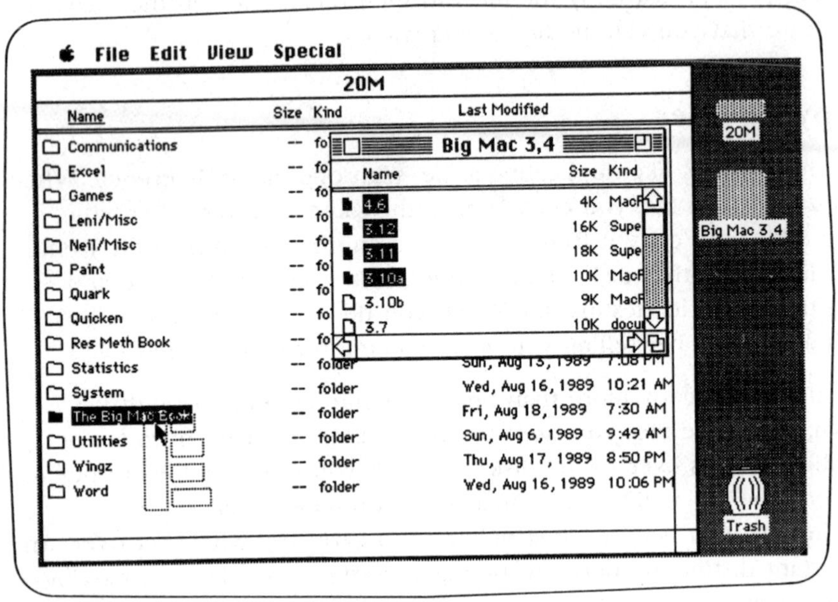

Fig. 4.19. Copying multiple files.

to the *target*. The source is the file you want to copy, and the target is the disk you are copying it to.

To back up an entire disk, drag the icon representing the disk you want to copy to the destination disk. When you do this, your Mac asks you whether you want to replace the entire contents of the *target* disk with the contents of the *source* disk, substituting the appropriate names. When you see this message, take a moment to make sure that you no longer need the contents of the target disk. The "Copied the Wrong Disk Hall of Fame" is filled with people who acted too quickly. Remember, copying the contents of an entire disk to a target disk erases all of the contents of the target disk before copying takes place.

When you're ready, click OK (or press Return), and your Mac copies all the files and folders on the source disk to the target disk. If any files or folders on the target disk have the same name as any on the source disk, your Mac asks whether you want to replace them. Because you are presumedly backing up those files, you should click Yes.

As it copies, your Mac provides a message, telling you that it is copying, showing its progress, and alerting you when it is finished.

The following is a step-by-step guide for backing up, but because this procedure selects the files to be backed up by date, it backs up only what you have worked on today. If you do not have two floppy disk drives, your Mac instructs you to switch disks back and forth as necessary.

1. Return to the desktop and open the disk with the files you want to back up.

2. Select By Date from the View menu.

3. Select the files you want to back up from the list that you worked on that day. If you want to back up more than one file, press Shift while you select the files. Release the Shift key.

4. Pressing and holding the mouse button, drag the file(s) to the target disk.

Your day's work is backed up. If you need to back up other files, you must identify them individually.

Backing Up Files on Your Hard Disk

Although you may go through your Mac routines carefully and think that you would never inadvertently lose or erase a file, you can never be sure that an accident will not happen to you. Almost all users lose important information at one time or another because they have failed to back up their files. Like insurance, backup copies enable you to continue working when disasters strike—disasters caused by power failures, system crashes, or human error (for example, when you mistakenly erase a file).

To minimize the amount of data you lose to such disasters, you should back up to a floppy disk the work you complete each day. You can also back up to another hard disk, but few users have more than one hard disk. After you back up, you have a copy of the file on the hard disk and on a floppy disk. You may also want to make a second copy of the floppy disk and store it in a physically separate location to minimize the chances of an accident damaging both copies of the file. It's probably sufficient for individuals to back up their files onto floppy disks every so often (no less than once a week for a thorough back up and daily for what you worked on that day). Businesses and others who handle very large amounts of data could probably use the large capacity and speed of tape backups, which can back up about 10M in 10 minutes. Although tapes and tape drives are expensive (about $1,000), they save time and are highly reliable.

If one or more sectors on your hard disk are damaged so that they are unreadable, you may have to reformat your disk. Reformatting the disk erases the contents, marks off the bad sectors, and places new tracks on the disk. You can then use your backup files to restore your hard disk.

Using Different Types of Backups

You can choose from a number of different backup methods for creating your backups. The simplest, fastest method is to back up individual files. At the end of each work session, make a backup copy of the files that you have worked with during that session. One way to remember the files you have worked with is to view them on-screen by date. Copy these files to a floppy disk and label the disk as a backup with the names of the files.

You can also do a *global* backup of your entire hard disk, backing up the full set of folders and files. Good backup software (discussed in the next section) stores the entire contents of the hard disk on several different floppy disks while maintaining the original disk organization. You can, of course, do a complete backup yourself, without using backup software. Just select all the files in each folder and copy them to floppy disks, or use a commercial program (such as FastBack II from Fifth Generation, DiskFit from SuperMac, HFS Backup from PcPc, or Apple's own HD Backup) to compress the files so that they fit on fewer floppy disks. This practice is a good weekly habit to get into to make sure that you catch any files you may have missed when backing up individual files.

Finally, you can back up in an *incremental* fashion, backing up files that have been modified or added since a certain date. This is the method that most people prefer, because it only backs up those files that have been changed. Why back up 60M of files when they are backed up already, and they have not been changed since the last backup?

Some users never do a complete backup but get in the habit of backing up each file as they finish with it. The method you choose for backing up depends on how often you work with your files, how much time you are willing to spend backing up, and how much data you are willing to lose in the event of a crash.

Using Backup Software

Many of the hard disk drives listed in figure 4.9 come with their own software for backing up files. For example, the software included with the Everex 20-megabyte disk drive provides most of the options described in the preceding section. You can back up individual files and do global or incremental backups. All Apple hard disk drives also come with the HD Backup software on the utility disk; it provides the basic tools for backing up what you need.

All backup packages have a Restore command that you can use to copy the backup files back to the hard disk. When this particular software backs up, it changes the nature of the file structure (so that more information can be saved in the same space). Most backup programs also calculate the number of disks you need to do your backup, prompt you when to insert a new floppy disk, and number the disks so that you have some idea how the backup is organized.

Besides the software that comes with your hard disk, other commercial products that provide backup tools are available. FastBack II is notably the fastest backup utility; DiskFit and PC BackUp (from PC Tools by Central Point Software) also get high marks for speed, and DiskFit even stores the file in Mac format. Figure 4.20 illustrates how the PC BackUp screen keeps track of the percentage of data that has been backed up. PC BackUp also comes with options for on-line help, incremental and file backups, and more. Of the available programs, HFS Backup is probably the most flexible. Backup software prices range from $50 to $100; you also can obtain many backup programs through shareware on bulletin boards or shareware networks.

Making Tape Backups

Tape backups are an alternative to using floppy disks as your primary backup medium. A tape backup device is, in effect, a tape recorder that can quickly back up large amounts of data.

Tape backups have two advantages over floppy disk backups. First, they are very fast—many can store 20M of data in 10 minutes. Second, you

4

Files

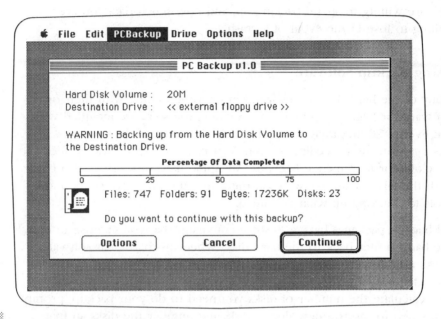

Fig. 4.20. *The PC BackUp screen.*

need only one or two tape cassettes as opposed to approximately 20 floppy disks to back up a full 20M drive. You can even schedule timed backups while you sleep because you don't have to sit at the computer swapping disks, as you must with floppy disks. Another type of tape is digital audiotape (DAT); one tape can hold a gigabyte (1,000 megabytes) of data.

The primary disadvantage of tape backups is the price. Tape drives cost between $650 and $1,500 (an amount that can buy many floppy disks). If you do consider buying a tape drive for backing up, be sure to confirm its compatibility with your existing hard drive. Because both are SCSI devices, you should not have a problem, but check with the manufacturers of your drive and the tape backup unit just to make sure. An alternative to a tape backup unit is a combination tape drive and hard disk in one unit. Because they come as a unit, they are compatible, making you well-equipped for efficient backing up. However, if one part of the combination unit becomes inoperative, the other part also becomes inoperative.

Finally, the JukeBox is back. The 125-gigabyte JukeBox from Summus Computer Systems sells for $49,995 and contains 54 tapes. Each tape holds 2.3 gigabytes for a total of 125 billion bytes, around 625 million pages of text. Although this may seem like overkill for your Macintosh Plus, large networks of 50 computers could very well use this amount of storage space.

Using Optical Storage Devices

Remember when you used to go to the library to find out how many hairs are on the average person's head, or how many red blood cells are produced in one day, or how large Asia is? You'd use the encyclopedia. Now, right through your Mac, you can access storage media that contain the contents of thousands and thousands of pages—all ripe for your perusal!

For example, the directory of *one* CD-ROM (Compact Disk Read-Only Memory) costs $100 and was put together by the Berkeley User's Group. This small plastic disk contains the following:

- 250 DAs

- 250 games

- 500 HyperCard stacks

- 1,000 pictures

- 500 Fonts

- 100 graphics packages

- 200 Mac II programs

- 100 sounds

- 200 utilities

- 30 telecommunications programs

- 50 educational programs

The CD-ROM can hold at least 550M of data, equivalent to 700 double-sided floppy disks, 1,500,000 pages of text, or 3,000 reams of paper. But remember, these disks have a read-only memory (ROM), so you can read off these marvels but not write to them. In other words, you cannot alter the contents of a file. You may wonder how a compact disk (the same kind that your Red Ryders In The Sky, The Who, or

4

Files

Brandenberg Concerti are recorded on) can hold so much information. Tiny lasers record the data as infinitesimal pits on the surface of the disk; the size of the pit determines the value (1 or 0) of the information. The variety of information offered on CD-ROMs is increasing, and turning to a CD-ROM as we do now to encyclopedias and other reference works will soon be an everyday matter.

Better yet, CD-ROMs and other optical storage devices are not damaged by crashes, coffee spills, or dirt. They are not indestructible, but they are much tougher than floppy and hard disk drives.

In spite of how gloriously receptive these disks are for storage, they have not caught on very fast. One reason is that they (and the drives) are expensive, selling for about $1,000. Another reason is that you can only read from them and not write to them, which makes them impractical for everyday storage needs. Finally, there just aren't that many of these disks available. Things may be changing, however. Industry leader MicroSoft will shortly offer MicroSoft Office on a CD-ROM consisting of Excel, Word, Mail, and Chart, all for $1,000. What a deal.

Another type of optical drive, Write Once Read Many (WORM) differs from a CD-ROM disk in one important way: you can write to a WORM disk. When you do this, you can erase the information, but you cannot use the erased part again. WORM disks are ideal for recording information that you want to archive or save for a long period of time.

Some companies (such as Kodak) are working on erasable optical disks, and several have just appeared on the market. For example, a 600M Sony erasable optical drive sells for about $6,000. Prices will drop over time. These drives tend to be slow, with 35- to 70-millisecond seek times, two to six times slower than fast hard drives. As an aside, the NeXT machine (from Steve Jobs, whom you remember from Chapter 1 as one of Apple's founders) has a magneto optical drive, a cross between a magnetic and an optical disk.

Optical disk technology is very new; only a few companies are manufacturing CD-ROMs. One manufacturer, of course, is Apple, which offers a 748M CD-ROM drive for about $1,200. Summus offers the LightDisk-650 for about $4,000 along with a GigaTape backup system, which has a capacity of 1,200M, or 1.2 billion bytes of information.

If you want to buy a WORM, Corel (from Corel Systems) offers a variety of WORM models that are ready to use when you plug in the cables. Although they are expensive, ($4,200 for the 800M drive), you should have no more storage problems (for a while) when you hook one up to your Mac. Compared to hard disks, the 800M drive at about $4,000 costs about $15 per megabyte, quite competitive with other storage tools. Removable cartridges cost about $160 each. Pinnacle also offers a WORM with removable cartridges, providing a huge storage capacity with some measure of security.

So you spend the price of a Yugo on an optical drive. What is available to read? The following is just a glimpse of what you can look forward to opening up when your CD-ROM or WORM drive is in place:

- *The Timetable of Science and Innovation* (from XIPHIAS) with more than 6,000 entries on scientific discoveries and technological innovations

- Also from XIPHIAS, the *National Directory*, a guide to North American business, government, and industrial institutions

- A set of storyboards, animation tools, and color presentation tools from MacroMind

- The 9th edition of the *Merriam Webster Collegiate Dictionary* (from Highlighted Data) containing graphics and sound

- *Books in Print* (from Bowker Electronic Publishing)

- *Groliers Encyclopedia*

The future should bring decreased prices and much more information available on optical devices. CD-ROM drives may soon be as affordable as the compact disk players you use to listen to your favorite music.

Chapter Summary

This chapter has familiarized you with the options you have for storing data and the related hardware. You also learned about file organization on your Mac. Chapter 5 discusses printing with the Mac so that you can produce hard copies of your work after you have safely stored it.

How you store things (and how you organize what you store) is a critical part of becoming a good Mac user. Perhaps the best first step that you can take when just starting is to think about what it is you will be storing (as best you can) and how you want to organize those files and folders. Live clean and back up!

Printing

Almost everyone who uses a personal computer has to print hard copy at one time or another. If you use your Macintosh primarily for desktop publishing, design, or the preparation of business documents, a printer is an essential part of your system. Although you can view the contents of a file on the monitor, a well-designed, tangible document is indispensable for communicating your ideas to others.

Many different types of printers are available, and this chapter can help you decide which printer will best fit your needs. Although Apple originally designed the Mac so that only the ImageWriter printer was compatible, you now can select from a large assortment of Macintosh printers. Providing even more options, interface cards and other tools enable you to use non-Mac printers with your Macintosh.

5

Printing

This chapter introduces you to the different types of printing technology available and then discusses the various types of printers. You learn about fonts and the special characters you can produce with your Mac and printer. The final section of the chapter introduces you to programming languages, which give you the power to design and use special effects on your laser printer.

Getting Started

No matter what type of printer you have or what you are printing, you need to take care of several steps before you begin to print.

First, make sure that you have the appropriate *printer driver* in your System folder. The printer driver is software that acts as the translator between your Mac and printer.

185

Second, select the printer you want to use through the Chooser on the Apple menu. Failing to select the appropriate printer often is the one problem that keeps users, especially newcomers to the Mac, from successfully printing.

To begin the printing process, select the Print command from the File menu in the application (or use a key combination such as ⌘-P). When you do so, your screen displays a Print dialog box that, when completed, provides your Macintosh with the information it needs to complete the printing process.

Unfortunately, not all applications use the same key combination (SuperPaint uses ⌘-semicolon, for example). This lack of standardization is especially regrettable because much of the Mac's popularity stems from the standardization and transferability of commands and techniques from one application to another. However, you always can reassign a keystroke by using a macro program.

Depending on the application and the type of printer you are using, you see different options in the dialog box. For example, figure 5.1 shows the Print dialog box for WordPerfect, which has several alternatives and is similar to the dialog boxes for many other Mac applications. On the other hand, the Print dialog box for the Quicken accounting package looks quite different and is designed specifically for that application (see fig. 5.2). No matter what application you are using, examine the dialog box before you print so that you can take advantage of the features offered by the application.

To print a file, complete the following steps:

1. Open the file (although you can print from the desktop, as discussed in Chapter 2).

2. Select the Print command from the File menu.

3. Click OK in the Print dialog box (see fig. 5.1). In this dialog box, you also set the number of copies you want printed, the range of pages, and so on.

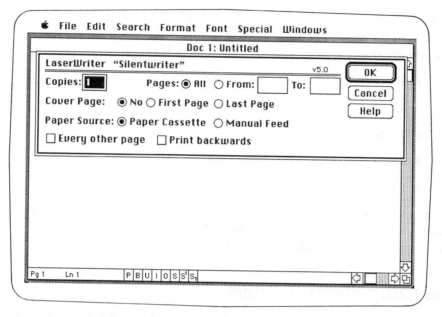

Fig. 5.1. *The WordPerfect Print dialog box.*

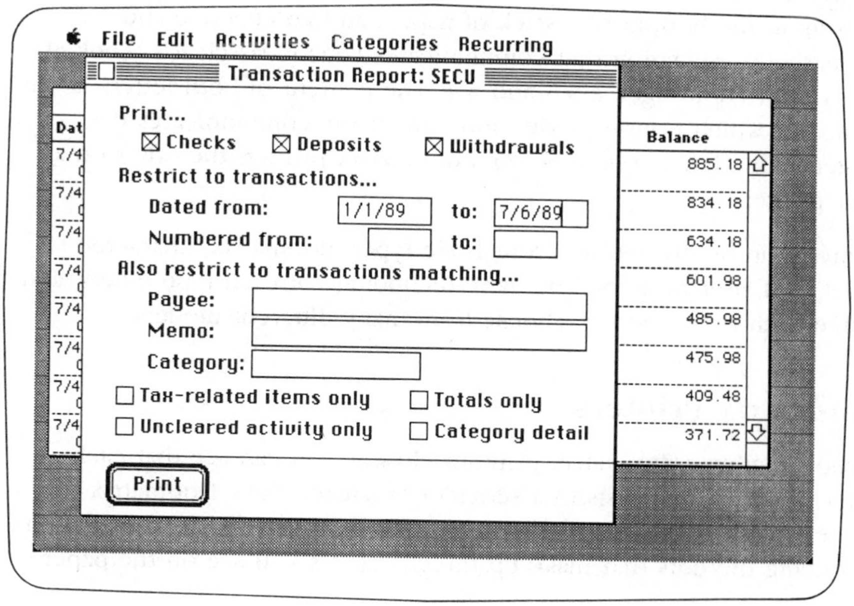

5
Printing

Fig. 5.2. *The Quicken Print dialog box.*

Almost every Macintosh application offers you a variety of printing options in the same type of Print dialog box as the one shown in figure 5.1. These options enable you to specify the following:

- The number of copies you want to print

- The range of pages to print

- A cover page

- The source of the paper (manual or cassette)

- Page preview

Many applications offer another set of options enabling you to reverse images when printing (black becomes white and white becomes black) or change the position of text (invert, rotate, and so on).

Learning about Printers

One important decision is the type of printer to buy. Of the various types of printers available, each type uses a different technology to produce different results. Sometimes these differences are negligible, but sometimes they can make the difference between a document that ends up at the bottom of a stack of papers and an effective and persuasive presentation that communicates your ideas clearly. Look at the two letters in figures 5.3 and 5.4. The content of both letters is the same, but which printing style more effectively communicates the content? One letter was done on a dot-matrix printer, the other on a laser printer.

Printers can be divided into four basic types: dot-matrix, character, inkjet, and laser printers. The basic technology of each type differs, and within each type, you can choose from many different models.

Dot-Matrix Printers

If you examine a dot-matrix printout closely, you can see that each letter or graphic consists of a series of organized dots. Dot-matrix printers work exactly as their name implies. Print wires strike a ribbon, producing the dots that make up the characters you see on the paper.

Delphi Associates
POB 1425
Lincoln. ME 12345

August 8, 1989

Dr. Reva Williams
Joy Associates
Williams, MA 12345

Dear Reva:

I'm pleased to write and tell you that the contract has been signed and we can begin the planning stage of the project as soon as possible.

On behalf of the entire team at Delphi, welcome, and I look forward to hearing from you.

Sincerely,

Paul Laffs, President

Fig. 5.3. *A letter printed on a dot-matrix printer.*

Delphi Associates
POB 1425
Lincoln, ME 12345

August 8, 1989

Dr. Reva Williams
Joy Associates
Williams, MA 12345

Dear Reva:

I'm pleased to write and tell you that the contract has been signed and we can begin the planning stage of the project as soon as possible.

On behalf of the entire team at Delphi, welcome, and I look forward to hearing from you.

Sincerely,

Paul Laffs, President

Fig. 5.4. *A letter printed on a laser printer.*

5
Printing

The impression is made by a set of small *print pins*, or *print wires*, that are part of the print head. These print wires remain inside the print head until your Mac sends a graphic or text code to the print head indicating which combination of wires should be "fired." When fired, the wires protrude from the print head, hit the ribbon, and make an impression on the paper, as shown in figure 5.5. Each wire is the same size and shape and produces a clean, uniform mark on the paper. The higher the number of wires in the print head, the higher the quality of the printout.

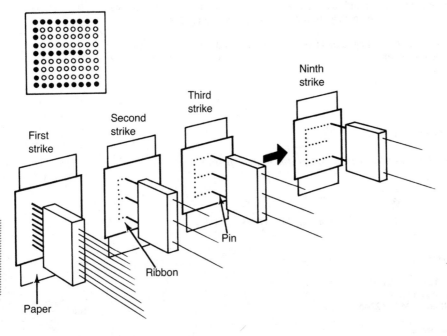

Fig. 5.5. *How a dot-matrix print head creates an image.*

For example, the first dot-matrix printers had 35 pin wires (5 horizontal rows and 7 vertical rows). Today's top-of-the-line dot-matrix printers have 24 horizontal and 24 vertical rows of pin wires, allowing for more precise printing (but also more wear because these printers use finer pins).

Figure 5.5 shows you how a dot-matrix printer produces text as the print head moves across the paper. The print head does not create a character all at once; instead, the print head creates only the upper part of the character and moves on to the next character—moving back and forth across the entire line. You can see the individual dots that make up the collective image of a character. In a conventional dot-matrix printer, each pin creates one part of the character and then moves to the next position one character at a time.

Another type of dot-matrix printer, the Near Letter Quality (or NLQ) printer, creates an image using the same technology—but with one difference. Instead of advancing the paper so that space is left between the dots, the NLQ printer advances the paper only a small fraction of a space so that the dots touch one another. As a result of these incremental passes, the character almost appears to be a continuous stream of ink. Some printers, including the ImageWriter II in Best mode, double-strike the character with a slight offset to accomplish the same result.

Dot-matrix printers print anywhere from 50 to 250 characters per second, depending on the quality of output that you desire. The higher the quality, the more "hits" the printer head has to make and the higher the quality of the finished product.

Thermal printers, which also are dot-matrix printers, use dots, but no wires, to make an image. The print head contains dots heated to burn an impression on paper coated with a heat-sensitive material. The paper turns darker to reveal characters where it is heated. Remarkably, the dots on the print head get hot and cool quickly enough to avoid any misprints because of overheated heads. This thermal printing technology is used mostly in portable printers like the Diconix (which weighs 8 pounds and is 12 by 6 inches).

5
Printing

A significant advantage of thermal printers is that they do not have many moving parts, and therefore, rarely break down. Thermal printers, however, are slow, and the paper often comes in a roll not easily cut into regular sheets. Because of the paper's coating, it does not have the feel of "real" paper.

Character Printers

Character printers, as the name suggests, print one character at a time when a die (impression device located on the print head) strikes the paper. You may have heard about or used a *daisywheel* printer, a common character printer given this name because the element that strikes the paper is round with the individual characters located at the ends of "petals." As the computer sends instructions, the daisywheel rotates to the appropriate character. A hammer then strikes the character, producing a fully formed character. One wheel can hold up to 96 characters, and you change the font or size of the character by changing the wheel.

A daisywheel printer can print from 10 to 60 characters per second when it operates in a bidirectional mode—the wheel moving across the paper from left to right and then back again, printing in both directions. Although character printers are becoming less popular, their print quality is as good as a typewriter's, making them suitable for many small businesses that do not produce large quantities of output or require great speed.

Inkjet Printers

Inkjet printers are relatively new, but recent advances in their reliability and the quality of their output have increased their popularity. An inkjet printer actually paints the image of a character by spraying ink through a small nozzle. The latest models spray droplets of ink where they are needed, and they dry quickly. Inkjet printers can be an inexpensive substitute for laser printers because they print very quickly (up to 10 times faster than dot-matrix printers) and can produce very attractive graphics.

New on the scene is the Hewlett-Packard DeskJet, the cousin of the successful DeskJet for DOS-based machines. This fast inkjet printer for the Mac prints about 6 pages per minute and provides high-quality output, approaching that of a laser printer at 300 dpi. The DeskJet for the Mac sells for about $1,200.

Laser Printers

Laser printers often are the preferred printer for several reasons: the quality of their output is outstanding; they are very fast (some produce up to 15 pages per minute), and in contrast to the noisy dot-matrix printers, they are very quiet. Having a laser printer is like having your own printing press. Laser technology has helped create a revolution in computer printouts.

Once only for the high-roller (the original LaserWriter cost $7,000), laser printers are now within the reach of almost anyone. You can buy Apple's basic laser printer, the LaserWriter SC, or one of many other laser printers, such as the GCC PLP (Personal LaserPrinter), for around $2,500. GCC Technologies also makes a three-pound dot-matrix 192 dpi printer for the Mac—just right for the upcoming Mac laptop (see Chapter 14 for more information). Laser technology is becoming more affordable and sophisticated in the features it offers, enabling users to take advantage of increasingly sophisticated software applications.

Laser printers are glorified photocopying machines, working on almost the same principle. They bear no resemblance to impact printers (except that both produce hard copy) and have extremely high resolution, up to 300 dpi (with 600 and 800 dpi printers on the way). Printers with a resolution of 300 dpi use about 6,000,000 dots for one page. These dots are very small and are printed close together, making a denser image than dot-matrix printers can achieve. As a result, you avoid the jagged characters produced by a dot-matrix printer. Figure 5.6 illustrates the sharp image a laser printer can produce.

Laser printers produce beautiful images

5
Printing

Fig. 5.6. *The sharp image produced by a laser printer.*

As mentioned earlier, laser printers work on the same principle as photocopying machines. Both contain a Light Amplification by the Stimulated Emission of Radiation (LASER) system and are cousins to the lasers used in industrial, medical, and military applications—as well as the entrapment methods used by Ghostbusters.

The following is a step-by-step description of the relatively simple process by which a laser printer produces a page of characters or graphics. The process begins when the signal (a "blueprint" for the page to be printed) is transmitted from the computer to the printer, where it is translated and then printed.

1. The smooth metal drum rotating inside the laser printer is electronically cleaned (or neutralized from the last printing) and then charged (positively or negatively), using a charging corona wire. The drum is magnetized, ready to attract materials of the opposite charge.

2. The drum, now charged, is exposed to light from the laser beam. Through the use of a mirror, the beam hits the drum at a precise angle, creating the image on the drum.

3. The parts of the drum exposed to the laser become demagnetized, leaving a charged image of the signal that is part of your document.

4. As the magnetized drum turns, the magnetized surface picks up a thin coating of toner wherever the light strikes the drum. This toner is a mixture of carbon, metal shavings, and plastic dust. Where the drum has been charged, the material sticks to the drum.

5. The drum continues to revolve into position for transferring the image to paper.

6. As the paper moves through the feeder, it is charged by another corona wire that does not charge the paper but transfers the charge. The opposite charges of the drum and the paper cause the magnetized toner to transfer from the drum to the paper.

7. Finally, the paper passes through a *fuser* that uses pressure and heat to melt the plastic dust, fusing the image onto the paper. You now have a laser-produced printout.

A comparison of some of the characteristics of Apple's family of LaserWriters is shown in figure 5.7.

Plotters

The Mac can create images on paper in many ways, and a device other than a printer may be just what you need if you use computer-assisted design applications (see Chapter 11 for a discussion of these software packages).

	LaserWriter	LaserWriter Plus	LaserWriter IISC	LaserWriter IINT	LaserWriter IINTX
Processor	68000	68000	68000	68000	68020
Processor Speed	12MHz	12MHz	7.45 MHz	12 MHz	16.67 MHz
RAM	1.5M	1.5M	1M	2M	2M
Primary Connection	AppleTalk	AppleTalk	SCSI	AppleTalk	AppleTalk
Imaging Language	PostScript	PostScript	QuickDraw	PostScript	PostScript
Max. Pages Per Minute	8	8	8	8	8
Type of Fonts	Bit-mapped	Bit-mapped	Bit-mapped	Outline	Outline
Font Location	ROM	ROM	Mac	Printer	Printer
Built-in Fonts	4	11	0	35	35
Hard Disk Font Storage	no	no	no	no	no
Requires Hard Disk on Mac	no	no	no	no	Optional
Networkable	yes	yes	no	yes	yes
Resolution (dpi)	300	300	300	300	300
Engine Life in Pages	100,000	300,000	300,000	300,000	300,000
Expendable Components	Drum-toner cartridge	Drum-toner cartridge	Drum-toner cartridge	Drum-toner cartridge	Drum-toner cartridge
Pages Between Replacement	3,000	3,000	4,000	4,000	4,000
Price for Replacement	$130	$130	$130	$130	$130
Weight (lbs.)	55	55	45	45	45
List Price	Not Available	Not Available	$2,799	$4,599	$6,599

Fig. 5.7. *LaserWriter characteristics compared.*

A plotter uses a pen or a set of pens to produce line drawings, usually for special jobs that require very large paper sizes (for example, 2 by 3 feet), such as construction drawings or blueprints, and particularly Computer-Aided Design/Computer-Aided Manufacturing (CAD/CAM). Because the line produced by a plotter is not interrupted, the lines are smoother and more precise than output from a dot-matrix printer. The plotter can use multiple pens simultaneously; you tell the plotter which pen to use to draw which lines, symbols, designs, or charts. The color of the printout varies according to the colors of the pens that you use.

5
Printing

Two advantages that plotters have over printers are the size of the document they can produce and the number of colors in which they can print (limited only by the number of pens and the color of the ink in the cartridges). In some applications, such as computer-aided manufacturing, you can create a drawing the size of the actual product to be fabricated and then use the paper as a pattern. This practice is used with great success in the airline manufacturing industry.

Plotters are expensive but serve a specific purpose. Several models are available for Macintosh users, some manufactured by Hewlett-Packard and some by Toshiba.

Print Spoolers and Buffers

When your computer prints, it uses a great deal of its memory to transfer signals to the printer, and the computer often cannot perform any other functions while printing. If you try to enter text or change to another application while the computer is sending signals to the printer, your Macintosh does not respond.

No matter how fast your printer is, sometimes it is not fast enough. For example, a 20-page, double-spaced document can take 15 minutes to print at high quality on a dot-matrix printer. A *print spooler* is software that tells the computer to send the file to be printed to a disk until the printer is ready for it (or until you tell it to print). When you use a spooler, the file waits on the disk, not in RAM, and you can continue to work on another project as the file prints.

Print spoolers are sold by many software companies and are even part of some applications, such as MicroSoft Excel. Some printers also have built-in spoolers. Many spoolers are quite remarkable in what they can do. For example, the Grappler Spooler (from Orange Micro) can have up to 1,000 documents waiting to be printed. Because the Grappler Spooler loads as a CDEV device, it is easy to work with and always available.

Hardware solutions to this problem are called *print buffers*. They are actual equipment enhancements to your Macintosh, that enable you to store the unprinted document in the buffer until the printer is ready. You can even print two different documents on two different printers at the same time. Spoolers and buffers accomplish the same task, but buffers tend to be more expensive (about $150 for the MacBuffer from Ergotron) because they are hardware. The cost of obtaining a spooler is minimal, especially when one is built into an application program. Several shareware organizations and user groups also provide spoolers at no cost.

Using Typesetters

You get more than one and one-half million dots-per-square-inch resolution when you print your Mac files using a high-performance typesetter produced by a company such as Linotronic, Varityper, or Compugraphics. These typesetters produce visually striking graphics. Figure 5.8 compares a printout at 72 dpi from an ImageWriter, at 300 dpi from a LaserWriter, and at 1,270 dpi from a Linotronic. As you can see, the text and graphics from the typesetter are crisper, better suited for serious desktop publishing work.

WHAT'S   NEW?   Draft ImageWriter printer at 72x80 dpi

WHAT'S NEW?   ImageWriter printer at 144x160 dpi (2 passes)

WHAT'S NEXT?   Laser printer at 300 dpi

WHAT'S NEXT?   Linotronic at 1,270 dpi

Fig. 5.8. *A comparison of several grades of printing.*

5
Printing

Because typesetters are very expensive, starting at $25,000, they are impractical for all but professional printers. If you need to have files printed at this high level of resolution, you have several options. You can go to a commercial shop that specializes in printing on high-quality imagesetters. The usual charge is $10 to $15 per page. You probably will not use this service for a term paper, but you may want to use it for an original wedding invitation. (The printer produces a plate and then reproduces your invitations using offset printing.)

You also can mail your disks or send your files via modem to firms that charge less because of lower overhead costs. Finally, many universities have art and design programs that use typesetters and may charge as little as $2.50 to $5 per page for the same quality that you get from a commercial printer. Because you often have to be a student or a faculty member to take advantage of this service, register for one credit of independent study and save yourself a few hundred dollars in printing costs.

Determining Print Quality

Perhaps the most important criterion for choosing a printer is the quality of the output, which is usually related to price. Designing and constructing equipment that produces high-quality output simply costs more. The print quality of a $450 ImageWriter is lower than that of a $4,000 laser printer and even lower than the print quality of a $50,000 Linotronic printer.

Figure 5.8 shows examples of different types of printing using a variety of printers designed to work with the Mac. You can see for yourself the difference in quality.

Although cost and quality are related, cost is a poor criterion for determining the quality of a printer. For judging the quality of a printout, a standardized measure of print quality is better than an arbitrary dollar figure. A printer's quality is best measured by the number of dots per inch (dpi) that the printer produces or the resolution with which the printer prints.

For example, the ImageWriter produces approximately 72 dpi horizontally and 80 dpi vertically in its Draft mode (see fig. 5.8). The next level up, Faster, provides an easier-to-read, denser image. The Best option produces an even more distinct image. Looking at the LaserWriter output, you see that 300 dpi produces attractive copy. Finally, commercially produced output is well over 1,000 dpi, with Linotronics operating at 1,270 or 2,540 dpi, which is as good as actual typesetting.

Using Macintosh Fonts

Your choice of fonts—their size, style, and weight—and the appearance of the words on a page is like a painter's choice of shapes, brush strokes, and textures. Your finished document is more than words, and knowing something about the world of type will make your document more effective.

The word *font* traditionally has meant a set of characters of a particular design; a *typeface*, therefore, has represented a specific font, such as Helvetica, Garamond, or Palatino. This definition is not true in the Mac world. Here, every different modification of a typeface is a font. Helvetica Bold, therefore, is a separate font from Helvetica Italic. I do not know why Macintosh designers made this distinction, but I have followed the Macintosh convention in this book. (Apple used the Chicago font in the design of most of its windows, dialog boxes, and other text that appears on-screen.)

Major Characteristics of Fonts

Type talks to the reader, and the shape of the type conveys a message. Figure 5.9 illustrates how type can convey a formal message or one that is contemporary and upbeat. You need to be able to distinguish clearly among the fonts you often use and to determine the font that is best for the job at hand. The following information gives you the basic tools to make distinctions between font styles and appropriate uses.

Your words are important, but the font that you express them with can be just as important. While the words here are the same, look at the different message that is conveyed.

YOUR WORDS ARE IMPORTANT, BUT THE FONT THAT YOU EXPRESS THEM WITH CAN BE JUST AS IMPORTANT. WHILE THE WORDS HERE ARE THE SAME. LOOK AT THE DIFFERENT MESSAGE THAT IS CONVEYED.

Your words are important, but the font that you express them with can be just as important. While the words here are the same, look at the different message that is conveyed.

Your words are important, but the font that you express them with can be just as important. While the words here are the same, look at the different message that is conveyed.

Fig. 5.9. *How the typeface affects the message.*

A *type character* consists of different components as shown in figure 5.10. Characters are positioned on an imaginary line called the *baseline*. The height of an uppercase character is called the *cap height*. Lowercase characters have an *x-height*. The part of the character that extends below the baseline is called a *descender* and the part that extends above the baseline is called an *ascender*.

Fig. 5.10. *The components of type characters.*

Fonts can be divided into categories based on different sets of characteristics, including size, weight, width and angle, family, and style. One of the most obvious differences among fonts is whether they are serif or sans serif (see fig. 5.11). *Serifs* are the little crossbars added to the ends of letters, as in Times or Palatino. Serif type often is the first choice for the body of text because the serifs help break up the monotony, and the text is easier to read. *Sans serif* text, such as Helvetica or Avant Garde (especially when a heavy weight is used), adds a quality of boldness terrific for headlines. You can hardly go wrong with this combination of copy and headline fonts.

This is Times, a serif font.

This is Helvetica, a sans-serif font.

Fig. 5.11. *A comparison of serif and sans serif Macintosh fonts.*

Type size usually is expressed in the standard printer's measures of picas and points; 6 picas equal an inch, and 12 points equal a pica. For example, an 18-point character is 1.5 picas or 0.25 inch high. Most applications enable you to set type size in inches, picas, or points, but the most frequently used measuring unit is points, such as 10/12 (10 on 12), meaning 10-point characters with the baselines spaced 12 points apart. The distance between baselines (from baseline to baseline) is known as *leading*. You can get some idea of how many lines of type will fit into how much space by using the chart in figure 5.12. The logic is pretty straightforward. If an inch is 72 points, a 12-point letter takes up 6 lines. This handy chart can help you in your planning. For example, if you have one inch of column space, you can fit 6 lines of 12-point type.

Keep in mind that the amount of space used between baselines is somewhat arbitrary. Commercial printers generally want to use about 120 percent of the font's size, but you should use whatever looks right to you and works well with the font you have chosen.

Type weight refers to the heaviness of the letters. For example, you can see the contrast between Helvetica Condensed and Helvetica Condensed Bold in figure 5.13. The lighter the type and its arrangement on the page, the more delicate and less obtrusive the type appears. Heavy types, like Cooper, really make the point but often have to stand alone because anything else around them gets swamped.

Changing the *type angle* adds an interesting dimension to the way a font appears. Many applications enable you to rotate or slant text to a specified degree. For example, choosing to rotate text 90 degrees turns the text on its side for printing in horizontal mode. Keep in mind, however, that italicized type is a style all its own and should not be thought of as an angled text. Slanting characters often distorts their proportions.

Type style refers to the boldface, outline, italic, and so on, style options, which you see on many Macintosh applications. Some different styles have been added to more recent applications, however, so that you also can choose superscript, condensed, shadow, and others. Most of these styles are available on the Style menu or as part of the Font menu. As a result, you do not have to go outside of the application for special effects.

5
Printing

Column Depth in Inches	Type Size in Points										
	6	7	8	9	10	11	12	15	18	24	30
0.25	3	3	2	2	2	2	2	1	1	1	1
0.50	6	5	5	4	4	3	3	2	2	2	1
0.75	9	8	7	6	5	5	5	4	3	2	2
1	12	10	9	8	7	7	6	5	4	3	2
2	24	21	18	16	14	13	12	10	8	6	5
3	36	31	27	24	22	20	18	14	12	9	7
4	48	41	36	32	29	26	24	19	16	12	10
5	60	51	45	40	36	33	30	24	20	15	12
6	72	62	54	48	43	39	36	29	24	18	14
7	84	72	63	56	50	46	42	34	28	21	17
8	96	82	72	64	58	52	48	38	32	24	19
9	108	93	81	72	65	59	54	43	36	27	22
10	120	103	90	80	72	65	60	48	40	30	24
11	132	113	99	88	79	72	66	53	44	33	26
12	144	123	108	96	86	79	72	58	48	36	29
13	156	134	117	104	94	85	78	62	52	39	31
14	168	144	126	112	101	92	84	67	56	42	34
15	180	154	135	120	108	98	90	72	60	45	36
16	192	165	144	128	115	105	96	77	64	48	38
17	204	175	153	136	122	111	102	82	68	51	41
18	216	185	162	144	130	118	108	86	72	54	43
19	228	195	171	152	137	124	114	91	76	57	46
20	240	206	180	160	144	131	120	96	80	60	48
21	252	216	189	168	151	137	126	101	84	63	50
22	264	226	198	176	158	144	132	106	88	66	53
23	276	237	207	184	166	151	138	110	92	69	55
24	288	247	216	192	173	157	144	115	96	72	58
25	300	257	225	200	180	164	150	120	100	75	60
26	312	267	234	208	187	170	156	125	104	78	62
27	324	278	243	216	194	177	162	130	108	81	65
28	336	288	252	224	202	183	168	134	112	84	67

(Cell entries equal the number of lines per column-inch.)

Fig. 5.12. *Computing lines for a given space.*

Helvetica Condensed

Helvetica Condensed Bold

Fig. 5.13. *The contrast between Helvetica Condensed and Helvetica Condensed Bold.*

Bit-Mapped versus Laser Fonts

Fonts are divided into two basic types: bit-mapped (also called screen fonts) and laser fonts.

Each square inch on a Mac monitor contains a grid of about 72-by-72 pixels. (A *pixel* is a picture element—a measure of the monitor's resolution.) *Bit-mapped fonts* are created by the software's filling in a pattern of these squares on the grid. In effect, the font designer creates a map of what pixels are to be darkened. After the darkened pixels are arranged to form a particular character, that image is stored as a character in the font. In figure 5.14, the *D* from the popular Venice font is shown as a bit-mapped character.

If an image has the same resolution as shown by the monitor, printers can process an image's pattern as whole numbers. Because the standard Mac monitor is 72 by 72 (or 5,184 pixels), reducing the page size to 96 percent (5,184/96)—by using the Page Setup command on many applications—gives you a whole number. Your output, therefore, will be cleaner, but not free, of the dreaded jaggies.

Bit-mapped characters often have a jagged appearance on-screen. One way to get rid of the jaggies is by using tools like FontSizer (from U.S. MicroLabs). FontSizer is a utility that enables you to build a screen font in any size or style without worrying about the accuracy of the printer's scaling capability. This really is WYSIWYG (What You See Is What You Get). (In many applications programs, WYSIWYG view shows the document on-screen as it will be printed, without accompanying icons or rulers.)

5

Printing

Laser fonts are stored as mathematical equations outlining the general shape of the font. Because the computer (or printer) needs to store only one outline (and then can adjust the outline for size), a laser font takes much less room than the space necessary to store every "bit" of information that goes into the map describing one bit-mapped character.

Coming with the next version of the System (Version 7) will be Apple's own font-outline technology. This technology will make the screen fonts a much more accurate representation of what you actually get when you print.

Fig. 5.14. *A bit-mapped character.*

Products are available to help you work with fonts so that they appear more true on-screen. Some of these products also accomplish other effects. FontSizer from U.S. Micro Labs resizes the font inside the printer and reflects the change on your monitor. Because your screen resolution is far more limited than your laser printer resolution (which is 300 dpi or 90,000 dots per square inch), many fonts appear ragged on-screen. FontSizer builds an NFNT (or new font) bit map that accurately reflects what the image looks like when printed.

FontSizer also can set kerning and leading so that you get an even more accurate picture of what the final result will look like.

Special Fonts and Characters

Although the alphabet has only 26 letters, more than 5 times that number (190) different characters can be used for different effects in setting type and creating a document. The following paragraphs contain some examples of different type characters and a brief description of their uses.

If you use conventional keys to create quotation marks, you get funny-looking marks in some cases, especially for the closing single quotation mark. As you can see in table 5.1, however, you can use specific key combinations to produce curly quotation marks. Curly quotes, however, do not work in spreadsheet formulas or HyperCard.

Table 5.1
Producing Curly Quotation Marks

To get	to look like this	use these keys
Opening double	"	Option-[
Closing double	"	Shift-Option-[
Opening single	'	Option-]
Closing single	'	Shift-Option-]

A ligature occurs when two or more letters are joined together, such as fl and œ (which are also known as diphthongs). You can use the Mac key combinations to produce dipthongs, or you can just reduce the amount of space between the letters through kerning.

Some special characters also can be produced easily. In the following list, you can see the combination of keys that produce different characters and accents.

Â	Shift-Option-R
Ê	Shift-Option-T
Ï	Shift-Option-F
Ë	Shift-Option-U

Reference marks are used to indicate that additional text material is tied to a certain word or sentence in the main body of text. A footnote is marked by a reference mark, usually a superscripted number. Good reference-generating software automatically assigns numbers, enables you to change the reference format, and keeps the footnotes on the same page if you want.

5

Printing

Bullets, boxes, and dingbats are all special type characters used to set off phrases or sentences, as in the following, where a bullet is used in the creation of a list:

- 30-day no-hassle returns

- Nationwide service

- Free 800 support number

You can create bullets, boxes, and dingbats in a variety of ways. Most of these characters are font-based, but you can create some of them by using simple key combinations, such as Option-8 for a bullet. For other characters, you need a font that includes these character options, such as bullets and boxes from Casey's Page Mill (see fig. 5.15). If you get too frustrated, you always can create an open (o) or a closed (●) bullet with the lowercase letter *o* and then fill the letter in.

•••••••••••• These bullets were formed using the Option+8 key combination.

Here are some of the bullets and boxes offered by Casey's Page Mill:

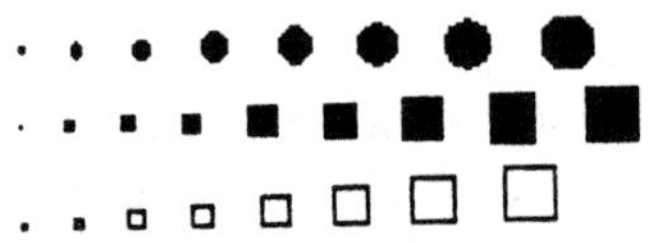

· · • ● ⬢ ● ●
· · ■ ■ ■ ■ ■
· · ▫ ▫ ◻ □ □ ☐

Fig. 5.15. Some bullets and boxes produced by Casey's Page Mill.

The registered trademark symbol (®) that often follows the name of a product is produced by the key combination, Option-R. This ease is the case for almost every symbol you use, unless you have a special application need. Table 5.2 shows the key combinations to produce special characters in Courier. Remember to use your Key Caps DA when you want to hunt for a special character.

The majority of people never even know that the Option and the Shift-Option key combinations can produce so many different special characters and symbols. Users quickly learn that everything they need is at their fingertips.

Hundreds (if not thousands) of fonts are available for the Macintosh. Figure 5.16, shows over 100 fonts (besides the ones that you usually see on your Font menu). Now, more than 20 companies are manufacturing PostScript fonts alone. The following section presents general guidelines for selecting a font. Keep things simple, and your productions will turn out fine.

If you want a terrific overview of many of the available fonts, you can spend $54 and get MacTography's PostScript Typeface Sampler. This loose-leaf collection provides samples of most Macintosh fonts.

Table 5.2
Special Characters Available in Courier

Key Pressed	Option-key Produces	Shift-Option-key Produces
a	å	Å
b	∫	ı
c	ç	Ç
d	∂	Î
e	´	‰
f	ƒ	Ï
g	©	Ì
h	˙	Ó
i	ˆ	È
j	∆	Ô
k	˚	
l	¬	Ò
m	µ	˝
n	˜	˘
o	ø	Ø
p	π	Π
q	œ	Œ
r	®	Â
s	ß	Í
t	†	Ê
u	¨	Ë
v	√	◊
w	∑	„
x	≈	Û
y	¥	Á
z	Ω	Û
1	¡	⁄
2	™	¤
3	£	‹
4	¢	›
5	∞	fi
6	§	fl
7	¶	‡
8	•	°
9	ª	·
0	º	‚
-	–	—
=	≠	±
[	"	"
]	'	'
;	…	Ú
'	æ	Æ
,	≤	¯
.	≥	˘
/	÷	¿
`	`	Ÿ

From World Class Fonts by Dubl-Click:

Underwood SPC 12 SPC point. SPCSPC ICON SO- SPCSPC The SPC quick SPC fox SPC jumped SPC the SPC lazy SPC dog.

Berekely 12 point. The quick fox jumped the lazy dog. The quick fox jumped

Greenbay 18 point. The quick fox jumped

Hollywood 12 point. HOLLYWOOD The quick fox jumped the lazy

Liverpool 18 point. LOVE The quick fox jumped the

Stanford 12 point. The

Woodstock 12 Point. The Quick fox jumped the lazy dog.

Boca Raton 24 point. The quick

DAKAR 24 POINT.

FRANKFURT 18 POINT. THE QUICK FOX

NEW ORLEANS 24

Ascii SP City SP12. SP SP The SP quick SP fox SP jumped SP the SP lazy SP dog.

Hex SP City SP12. SP SP The SP quick SP fox SP jumped SP the SP lazy SP dog. SP SP The

Cupertino 12 point. The quick fox jumped the

SCOTTSDALE 12 POINT. THE QUICK FOX JUMPED

Tempe 12 point.

Santa Fe 12 point. The quick fox jumped the lazy dog.

Sydney 12 point. The quick fox jumped the lazy dog.

Carmel 24 point. The quick fox

Istanbul 12 point. The quick fox jumped the lazy dog. The quick

Kawasaki 12 point. The quick fox jumped the lazy

Tel Aviv 12 point. האדרל'פסמצדלחן'עבקגגבנש1234567890

Gorky 12 point. фисвуапршолдьтщзйкыегмцчня1234567890фисвуапрш

Novgorod 12 point. фисвуапршолдьтщзйкыегмцчня1234567890фисвуа

Stalingrad 12 point. фисвуапршолдьтщзйкыегмцчня1234567890

Moscow 12 point. абцдефгжийклмнопщрстуввшхыз1234567890

Norilsk 12 point. абцдефгжийклмнопщрстуввшхыз1234567890-ч

Melbourne 12 point. The quick fox jumped the lazy dog.

Cape Canaveral 12 point. The quick fox jumped the lazy dog.

Detroit 24 point. The quick fox

Fig. 5.16. More than 100 of the fonts available for the Mac.

Las Vegas 12 point. The quick fox jumped the lazy dog.

Prague 18 point. The quick fox jumped the lazy dog.

Muleshoe 12 point. The quick fox jumped the lazy dog. The quick fox jumped the lazy

Borders 1 24 point.

Borders 2 24 point.

Borders 3 24 point.

Boston 12 point. The quick fox jumped the lazy dog. The quick

Washington DC 12 point. The quick fox jumped

Austin 9 point. The quick fox jumped the lazy dog. The quick fox jumped the lazy dog. The quick fox

BABYLON 12 POINT. THE QUICK FOX JUMPED OVER THE LAZY DOG. THE QUICK FOX JUMPED THE LAZY DOG. THE QUICK FOX JUMPED

Reno 9 point. The quick fox jumped the lazy dog. The quick fox jumped the lazy dog. The quick fox

Dallas 12 point. The quick fox jumped the lazy dog. The quick

Laredo 12 point. The quick fox jumped the lazy dog.

Nuevo Laredo 9 point. The quick fox jumped the lazy

Camelot 18 point. The quick fox jump

luxembourg 14 point. The quick fox jumped the lazy dog. The quick fox jumped the

London 24 point. The quick fox jump

Manchester 24 point. The quick fox

Arlington 12 point. The quick fox jumped the lazy dog. The quick fox

New York Headline 24 point.

Rome 18 point. The quick fox jumped

Florence 12 point. The quick fox jumped the lazy dog.

Athena 12 point. αβψδεφγηιξκλμνοπQρστθωςχυζ 1234567890-=

Sparta 12 point. αβψδεφγηιξκλμνοπQρστθωςχυζ 1234567890-=

Chicago 24 point. The quick fox

Manhattan 12 point. The quick fox jumped the lazy dog.

Venice 12 point. The quick fox jumped the lazy dog.

Stuttgart 12 point. The quick fox jumped the lazy dog.

STUTTGART CAPS 12 POINT. THE QUICK FOX JUMPED THE LAZY DOG.

Saigon 12 point. The quick fox jumped the lazy dog.

Fig. 5.16. *More than 100 of the fonts available for the Mac.*

5
Printing

San Diego 24 point. ⚓ The quick fox

Montreal 12 point. ✪ The quick fox jumped the lazy dog. ✪✪✪✪

Paris Headlines 24 point.

Sunnyvale 12 point. ✧ ✧ The quick fox jumped the lazy dog. ✧ ✧
Sunnyvale Caps 12 point. ✧ ✧ The quick fox jumped the lazy dog. ✧ ✧

Sunnyvale Headlines 24 point.

Paris 12 point. ✪✪ The quick fox jumped the lazy dog. ✪✪
Paris Caps 12 point. ▲▲▲ The quick fox jumped the lazy dog. ▲▲▲

Nazareth 24 point. ⚒ 🔔 ♡ ✝ 🌴 📖 ⚗ 🐑 ✗ ⛪
Odessa 24 point. ŸŸ The quick fox jumped the lazy dog. The quick fox jumped the lazy dog.

Postal City A 18 point. 🏤🏤 The quick fox jumped

POSTAL CITY B 18 POINT. 🏤 🏤 THE QUICK FOX

Albuquerque 12. ✿ The quick fox jumped the lazy dog.

BOISE 18 POINT. ◯◯ THE QUICK FOX SPED

CALDWELL 12 POINT. ❀❀❀❀ THE QUICK FOX JUMPED THE LAZY DOG. THE QUICK FOX
NAMPA 9 POINT. 🌷🌷🌷🌷 THE QUICK FOX JUMPED THE LAZY DOG. THE QUICK FOX JUMPED
POCATELLO 12 POINT. ☠☠☠ THE QUICK FOX JUMPED THE LAZY DOG. THEN....

TWIN FALLS 24. ✍ THE QUICK FOX

Malibu 12 point. ♀♀ The quick fox jumped the lazy dog. ♀

Monterey 24 point. 🪑 *The quick fox*

Tokyo 12 point. 🐎 The quick fox jumped the lazy

Canton 12 point. ✿✿ The quick fox jumped the lazy dog. The quick fox
Hong Kong 12 point. ✿✿ The quick fox jumped the lazy dog. The quick fox
Osaka 12 point. ✿✿ THE QUICK FOX JUMPED THE LAZY DOG.
Peking 9 point. ♥♥ the quick fox jumped the lazy dog. The quick fox jumped the
Copenhagen 12 point ●●● The quick fox jumped the lazy dog. The quick fox jumped the
Helsinki 12 point. ♥♥ The quick fox jumped the lazy dog. The quick fox jumped the lazy dog.
Oslo 9 point. ❯❯❯ The quick fox jumped the lazy dog. The quick fox jumped the
Stockholm 12 point. ✪✪ The quick fox jumped the lazy dog. The quick

Hartford 24 point. 🦌 🦌 The quick

Fig. 5.16. *More than 100 of the fonts available for the Mac.*

Obispo 24 point.

From Fluent Fonts:

ARCHITECTURE 24 POINT

Art Nouveau 18 point. The quick fox

ASCII 18 point. The quick
65 83 67 73 73 49 56 112 111 105 110 116 46 217 84 104 101 113 117 105 99 107

Astro bio 12 point.

Astrology 12 point.

Berkshire 18 point. The quick fox jumped the lazy dog. The quick

Berlin 18 point. The quick fox jumped the lazy

Bodoni 12 point. The quick fox jumped the lazy dog. The quick

Borderline 18 point.

BoxBorder 18 point.

Calligraphy 12 point. The quick fox jumped the lazy dog. The quick fox

Canterbury 24 point.

China 24 point.

CHUBBY 18 POINT. THE QUICK FOX JUMPED

Chubby Shadow 24 point.

Calligraphy Laser 24 point. The quick fox jumped the lazy dog. The

Regency Script 24 point. The quick fox jumped the lazy dog. The quick

From Casey's Page Mill:

Bullet 14 point.

5
Printing

Fig. 5.16. *More than 100 of the fonts available for the Mac.*

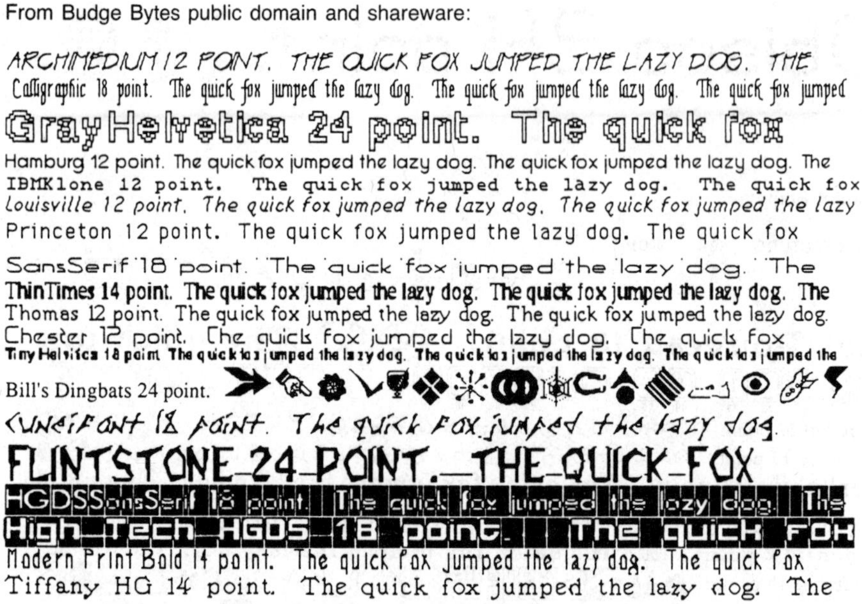

From Budge Bytes public domain and shareware:

ARCHIMEDIUM 12 POINT. THE QUICK FOX JUMPED THE LAZY DOG. THE

Calligraphic 18 point. The quick fox jumped the lazy dog. The quick fox jumped the lazy dog. The quick fox jumped

GrayHelvetica 24 point. The quick fox

Hamburg 12 point. The quick fox jumped the lazy dog. The quick fox jumped the lazy dog. The

IBMKlone 12 point. The quick fox jumped the lazy dog. The quick fox

Louisville 12 point. The quick fox jumped the lazy dog. The quick fox jumped the lazy

Princeton 12 point. The quick fox jumped the lazy dog. The quick fox

SansSerif 18 point. The quick fox jumped the lazy dog. The

ThinTimes 14 point. The quick fox jumped the lazy dog. The quick fox jumped the lazy dog. The

Thomas 12 point. The quick fox jumped the lazy dog. The quick fox jumped the lazy dog.

Chester 12 point. The quick fox jumped the lazy dog. The quick fox

Tiny Helvitica 18 point The quick fox jumped the lazy dog. The quick fox jumped the lazy dog. The quick fox jumped the

Bill's Dingbats 24 point. ➤➤ ✆✺❦✦✿❄❂◉◖◗Ｃ♠━━┅♙◉ ✿✄

CUNEIFONT 18 point. The quick fox jumped the lazy dog.

FLINTSTONE 24 POINT. THE QUICK FOX

HGDSSansSerif 18 point. The quick fox jumped the lazy dog. The

High Tech HGDS 18 point. The quick fox

Modern Print Bold 14 point. The quick fox jumped the lazy dog. The quick fox

Tiffany HG 14 point. The quick fox jumped the lazy dog. The

Fig. 5.16. *More than 100 of the fonts available for the Mac.*

One very important point to remember about fonts has to do with font ID numbers. When a new font is developed, it must be assigned an ID number so that the new font can be accessed and used. These numbers range from 0 to 255. The numbers 0 through 127 have been reserved by Apple for the fonts supplied with the Mac, and the rest of the font-developing world has the other 138 numbers. The problem, as you might expect, occurs when these numbers get used up or when two manufacturers develop different fonts and assign the same number. Remember that each typeface style combination is a font; for example, Courier and Courier Bold are two different fonts.

The solution? Although you can change a font's ID number, the best strategy is to keep sets of fonts by the same manufacturer on the same disk or in the same folder. If fonts are physically separate from other manufacturer's products, the chances for confusion are minimized.

As a better solution, you can use font/DA utilities, such as Font/DA Juggler and Suitcase, to renumber fonts when a conflict occurs.

The best news, however, is that Apple has changed the number of available fonts. The numbers now go up to 32,768, and even you do not need that many. Apple also is providing a range of numbers to developers to lessen still further the likelihood of conflict.

Selecting and Mixing Fonts

You have seen all these fonts. Now how do you make a decision as to which one to use and in what combination with other fonts? The following are some general guidelines to help you make those decisions:

- Use a serif font for text and a sans serif font for headers. This tried-and-true combination almost always works well.

- Fit the font to the text to do your best job of getting the message across. Each font has a set of characteristics and a feel all its own. Some are bigger than life and just yell out "read me!" and others are more refined and quiet.

- Do not work with more than two families of fonts. If you use Helvetica and Times, don't add a third.

- Experiment. The beauty of the Mac is that you can change the font of an entire selection through a few mouse moves. Don't leave the changes on-screen. Print them and compare them. Print and leave them while you get a cup of coffee or search bulletin boards for more fonts. After a break, you will better be able to judge whether the fonts you selected do the required job.

5
Printing

Figure 5.17 gives some suggestions about which fonts can be mixed. Keep in mind that selecting fonts to mix is a project-by-project decision and must be evaluated in light of the message you are trying to convey. (You cannot go wrong if you stick to one font.)

Modifying Fonts

If you really get into working with Mac fonts, sooner or later you will want to modify what already exists or create your own fonts. If you have the right tools, either of these activities is easier than you might think. (You can use ResEdit, the Mac's resource editor covered in Chapter 18.) Altsys Corporation makes two products that help you accomplish these goals. You can edit and create PostScript fonts with Fontographer and bit-mapped fonts with Fontastic Plus.

	Bodoni	Bookman	Courier	Garamond	Helvetica	New York	Optima	Palatino
Bodoni	1							
Bookman	1	1						
Courier	2	2	2					
Garamond	3	3	2	1				
Helvetica	1	1	2	1	1			
New York	2	2	2	2	1	1		
Optima	1	2	2	1	2	1	1	
Palatino	3	3	2	1	1	1	1	1
Schoolbook	2	3	2	3	1	1	1	3
Times	3	2	2	2	1	1	1	2

1 = goes well together
2 = may be acceptable
3 = don't use

Fig. 5.17. Mixing fonts for better or worse.

Fontographer (Version 2.4.1) is a graphics editor designed to work with PostScript fonts and other images. As you can see in figure 5.18, the program displays an outline of a character. Then, you can use Fontographer's drawing tools to change the outline until you get the effect you want. In addition, Fontographer enables you to do the following:

- Assign a graphic image to a key or combination of keys

- Trace the outline of scanned images

- Use Bezier-curve tools for the flexible creation of curves. Bezier curves (named after Pierre Bezier) are mathematically derived using four control points.

- Create logos and clip art

- Scale, rotate, stretch, and distort fonts as they are being built

Fontographer is a terrific tool for making those little (or big) changes to make a font look exactly as you want. Fontographer does not do actual designing, but the program executes changes for you in a simple and straightforward manner.

Fontastic Plus (Version 2.0) is similar to Fontographer, but Fontastic Plus operates on bit-mapped images that can be up to 127 points in height. This program is not nearly as powerful as Fontographer but does an excellent job of helping you manage fonts and achieve excellent results on QuickDraw printers (a welcome assist).

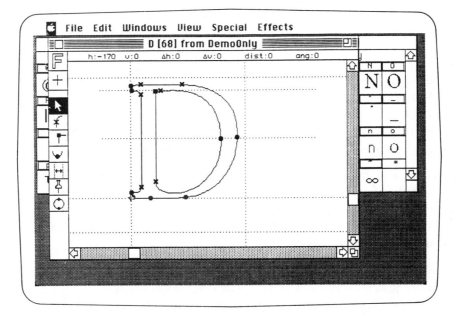

Fig. 5.18. *Using Fontographer to edit a PostScript font.*

One other tool from Altsys deserves a mention. The Art Importer (formerly known as KeyMaster) provides tools to create PostScript fonts based on art work.

Using Laser Printer Languages

Obviously, laser printers have become so popular because they produce clear, readable images that approach typeset quality. At the same time, they offer a variety of fonts, styles, and sizes, usually limited only by the printer's internal memory. Different laser printers handle fonts in different ways, however, and a basic understanding of laser printer languages is necessary to understand the capabilities of Apple's various laser printers.

Some laser printers use QuickDraw, a language that provides a specific series of fonts as a predesigned set. For example, the LaserWriter II SC has four fonts of various sizes and prints these fonts beautifully. If you try to vary from Helvetica 12 point to Helvetica 13 point, however, the results may not be satisfactory. Because Helvetica 13 point is not one of the SC's resident fonts, the SC has to approximate the new font size. At times, this approximation may be acceptable; often it is not.

Note: Even the IINT and IINTX fail to produce great printed output all the time because of the use of different types of fonts. If you use the resident fonts, the result is superb. Downloadable PostScript fonts and fonts designed especially for laser printers also give you excellent copy. If you use a bit-mapped font, however, you may be disappointed in the results. You may find severe jaggies and fonts that look terrible.

In most cases, however, computers and printers do not store the actual fonts or the shapes of the characters themselves. Instead, they use a *page description language* (PDL) to store the directions for drawing the fonts or graphics, and the laser printer actually constructs fonts of the size and style you specify.

PostScript, the most popular PDL, has become almost synonymous with the more general term, PDL, which more accurately reflects its technology. PostScript describes the shape of the character to be printed as a mathematical formula that defines an outline to be drawn and then filled in. PostScript uses no "predetermined" shapes, and different characters need not be stored in different fonts and sizes. Instead, PostScript waits for a command to draw a character or graphic and then sends a message to the printer telling the printer how to draw that particular character or graphic. This command telling "what to draw" (located in your printer's ROM) is in QuickDraw terms, and the PDL, PostScript, translates that command for the printer.

The primary advantage of PostScript is that you actually can program your printer for many special effects, as Chapter 10 describes. PostScript is expensive, however. Its developers, Adobe Systems, receive a royalty that raises the price of every laser printer incorporating PostScript by about $1,000. PostScript's capabilities are discussed in more detail in the following sections.

Using PostScript Tools

Of the page description languages (PDLs) available, PostScript is the one most often included in the ROMs (or the controller boards) of laser printers. As with any other programming language, you enter a set of commands. With other programming languages, such as BASIC, you create a program to perform a certain task (for example, totaling a column of numbers), but with PostScript your commands result in a visual image printed on your LaserWriter or a photo-typesetting machine.

PostScript and other PDLs, such as UltraScript and Impress, were developed to take advantage of laser printers' extensive capabilities. Adobe, the leading developer and manufacturer of fonts (and PostScript), licenses printer manufacturers who embed the fonts and PostScript into the printer's ROM. Other manufacturers sell the PDL as a separate software product, but these products have been less successful. Other manufacturers already have introduced PDLs as part of the printers' ROMs, giving Adobe some competition. Early indications show that you may save some money, but clones are not always 100 percent compatible. If you do lightweight graphics, using a clone probably is OK for your purposes, but if graphics are your business, you should buy the real McCoy.

Creating Fonts in PostScript

PostScript has two capabilities that enable you to be as creative as your imagination allows:

- PostScript considers anything on-screen to be a graphic, whether it is a font or an image.

- Variables such as the type size and type style (italic, bold, and so on) are user-defined.

Because of this flexibility, you can use PostScript to produce many special effects. If each letter in a PostScript alphabet had to be stored as an individual entry rather than as the set of directions that PostScript follows, the amount of storage necessary would be impractical. For this reason, the number and type of fonts and styles on QuickDraw printers are limited.

The beauty of PostScript is that it uses a mathematical equation to represent an outline of the image you create. Instead of outlines, non-PostScript devices use *bit maps* to store the individual dots making up a letter according to its actual size and shape. In contrast, one simple PostScript command identifies the font, another the size, and so on. The commands and procedures for creating a set of characters are stored, not the actual characters themselves. This flexible, powerful strategy

5

Printing

enables you to create a theoretically infinite number of sizes and shapes. Some laser printers do limit the size of fonts to 127 points, but other laser printers have no such limits. With System 7, you have no limit as to the number of sizes or the absolute size that you can produce.

PostScript fonts often are part of the printer's ROM, and different printers come with a different selection of fonts. For example, the NEC LC-890 comes with a set of 35 resident fonts represented by 6 families (New Century, Helvetica, and others). Remember that a font is defined as a separate design, width, and style, such as ITC Bookman Light Italic.

To use additional fonts, you can download them from a disk to the printer to make them temporarily resident. Your printer's memory, however, is limited and may run out of space, in which case you get a message to that effect. Your printer probably can hold two or three downloaded fonts, which should be enough for any job. If this number is not enough, remove the fonts you are not using to make room for others. The next section discusses downloading in more detail.

You also can add more memory (discussed in Chapter 19) by attaching a hard disk through an SCSI port. This technique works on the Apple IINTX LaserWriter, giving you the storage capability that you need to have many different fonts available at the same time. Before you spend your hard-earned money on additional memory or fonts, read the discussion of fonts in this chapter to help you determine your needs.

Downloading Fonts

Of the hundreds of fonts available for downloading, some are expensive (Univers sells for $370), but others are not high priced (Carta, a group of map symbols, sells for $95). Each set of fonts has its own special uses and effects.

You can download fonts in two ways. One method is to use an *automatic sequence* that your Mac puts into effect as the printing process begins. You sit back and let your Mac (and the fonts) do the work for you. When the printing job is finished, your Mac removes the fonts from the printer's memory, leaving room for the next font. This method works well when you want to change fonts for the next printing job but is not very efficient if you want to use the same font again.

You also can use a utility included on the font disk to load the font into the printer. This manual method loads the font only once, not every time the printer needs to use it, as the automatic method does. You save time, but if you are dealing with different fonts in the same document, the automatic method may be easier. If you plan to print several documents using the same fonts, however, you should use the utility to download.

Printing with a PostScript Printer

This section discusses the actual printing process that takes place when you send a document to your PostScript printer. Because PostScript is a language that designs the format of a printed page instead of affecting the on-screen appearance of a document, you cannot see PostScript changes on-screen. To view the changes, you have to print your document, unless you have a utility like LaserTalk, discussed later in this chapter.

If your PostScript printer does not contain the equations for a particular font on your Mac, your printer cannot draw the font from scratch, so it approximates the font based on other available information. For example, New York may be printed as Times and Geneva as Helvetica. While printing, your screen displays a message that bit maps are being created for the unavailable fonts. If you select the Font Substitution option from the Page Setup menu (available from the File menu), your Mac substitutes a font instead of approximating. Figure 5.19 illustrates the difference in quality between printing with and without the Font Substitution option selected.

5
Printing

Your LaserWriter helps you improve the job that it does by providing you with the Font Substitution and Smoothing options from Aldus FreeHand on the Page Setup dialog box shown in figure 5.20.

Programming with PostScript

Computer buffs of great renown tremble, ace programmers shake, and techno-wizards have fallen at the thought of programming in PostScript. But never fear; you actually can program in PostScript by using a host of utilities now available to help you along the way.

This is New York with font substitution.

This is Geneva with font substitution.

This is Monaco with font substitution...

This is New York without font substitution.

This is Geneva without font substitution.

This is Monaco without font substitution...

Fig. 5.19. Printing with and without the Font Substitution option selected.

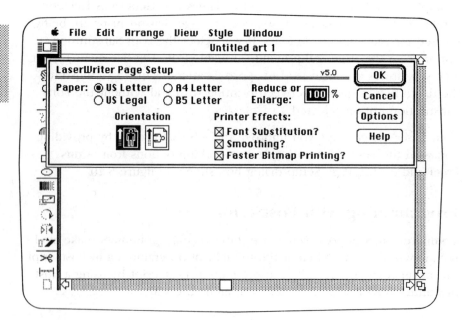

Fig. 5.20. The Page Setup dialog box for Aldus FreeHand.

The following is a simple example of the steps you take to create and print a PostScript file. This graphic was created using Aldus FreeHand, one of the few graphics applications that allows PostScript-printer interaction. The end product is a circle of stars filled in with a light gray pattern.

1. Using the FreeHand circle tool, draw the simple graphic shown in figure 5.21.

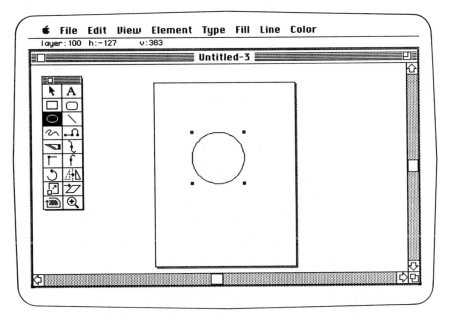

Fig. 5.21. *A simple circle graphic drawn in FreeHand.*

2. Name the procedure, which is a set of programming commands, *circle*, and press the Tab key to move into the procedure box.

3. Select the PostScript command from the Fill menu and enter the following instructions:

    inside 125 256 noise

   This line tells PostScript to create a gray shade using 125 as the low value and 256 as the high value. Click OK.

4. Select the 40% Gray command from the Fill menu.

5. To create a procedure to produce the circle of stars, first select PostScript from the Line menu and enter the following command:

   {stars} 10 10 10 0 newrope

   The numbers in the command represent the pattern, width, height, and spacing.

6. Now apply this procedure to the circle in the graphic after the circle is selected.

7. You have produced the graphic shown in figure 5.22, although you will not see the actual changes until you print the figure.

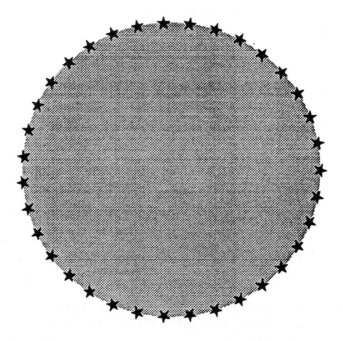

Fig. 5.22. A graphic produced from two simple PostScript procedures.

Some applications actually show you what your PostScript code will look like. Aldus is not one of them. As color 32-bit QuickDraw and Apple's outlined fonts become more common, you will see more applications displaying what your printer can print.

Using PostScript Utilities

Several PostScript utilities help you use PostScript to your advantage. If you are not familiar with PostScript and don't want to take the time to learn the program, these utilities and stand-alone applications may be just what you need. Most of these utilities translate the effect you want to achieve into PostScript code just as compilers take a BASIC command and translate the command into the 1s and 0s of the computer's assembly language.

The first, and perhaps the best, of these PostScript utilities is LaserTalk (from Emerald City Software), a programming tool that enables you to interact with the PostScript language commands in your laser printer's memory. When you open the window that lists the PostScript procedures, you begin entering the PostScript code that you want your printer to follow. LaserTalk is especially good for beginners because it provides feedback each step of the way. If the printer does not understand the command you enter, you get a message. If you don't get a message, you can continue with the next command. While you are working, you can consult the status box, which keeps you informed of the amount of memory still available, the current file name, and much more. The *PostScript Language Reference Manual* (published by Addison-Wesley) also can help you to use PostScript.

With applications such as FreeHand, you cannot see the images that you create on-screen. However, LaserTalk and other similar utilities provide on-screen a reasonably faithful reproduction of what will print (see fig. 5.23). You also can browse through dictionaries of PostScript files and use the built-in debugger to determine why your listing does not work. LaserTalk is copy-protected, but when you register your copy with the company, you get an unprotected version.

5
Printing

Postility (from PostCraft International) is another utility that increases your power as a PostScript programmer. This utility offers many of the same features as LaserTalk and some special menu items that cut down the tedium of PostScript programming. For example, the Insert Font command on the Special menu enables you to insert a specific font with a particular style (such as Times Roman Bold) through menu selections instead of through complicated PostScript commands like /*(fontname) findfont...*. If you change fonts several times within a procedure, you will appreciate this convenience.

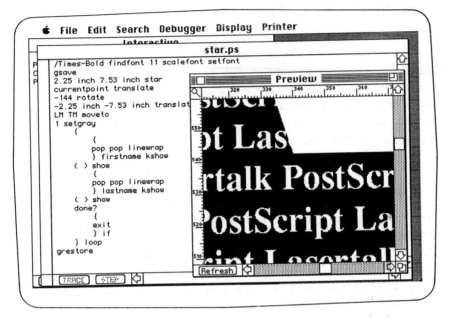

Fig. 5.23. A LaserTalk screen displaying a graphic altered using PostScript commands.

Using PostScript Applications

One PostScript application that can produce outstanding graphics is Cricket Draw (from Cricket Software). This drawing program has two features of interest to PostScript users. First, Cricket Draw enables you to view the results of your work on your monitor without having to print the graphic. Second, because you can see the graphic on-screen, you also can print it on an ImageWriter, although the resolution is not nearly as crisp as with a laser printer.

Aldus FreeHand and Adobe Illustrator also offer a large selection of predesigned techniques, often called procedures, for creating different patterns. For example, figure 5.24 shows 10 different patterns you can create with procedures. They are

- Triangles

- Balls

- Swirls

- Romans

- Crepes

- Right diagonals

- Solid Lines

- Snowflakes

- Waves

- Checkers

The procedures can be applied easily in any combination to any selected shape.

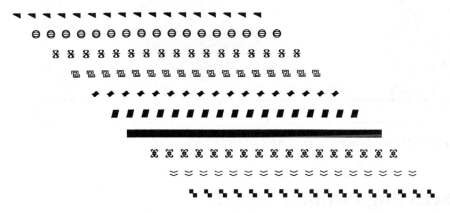

Fig. 5.24. *Ten FreeHand patterns.*

Sharing PostScript Files

You can create a PostScript file through applications like FreeHand under one condition: that the program in which the PostScript file was created can be saved as an Encapsulated PostScript file. A variety of programs accept this file format, including QuarkXpress and Aldus PageMaker, two applications that make good use of graphics created using PostScript. Keep in mind, however, that Encapsulated PostScript files take up a great deal of space because each includes a great deal of information about and instructions for printing. For example, when you save a file in FreeHand, it attaches the extension EPS to the file name and saves the file as an Encapsulated PostScript file. Figure 5.25 shows a Quark document that has imported an EPS file.

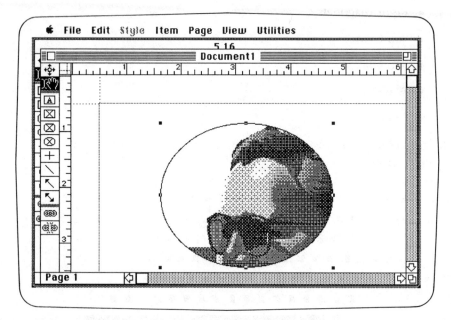

Fig. 5.25. *Transferring a PostScript file to another application.*

Selecting Printing Supplies

The type of paper you use affects the overall quality of the job as well as the expense. High-quality paper not only allows for a clearer impression but holds up better under use. Ribbons also affect the quality of your final copy. This section discusses some of the options you have in purchasing these consumable items. As with any other computer product, buying locally or mailing away for your supplies have their own merits. Chapter 14 provides a complete discussion of the pros and cons of ordering supplies through the mail.

Paper

The most common type of computer paper for dot-matrix printers is called *fan-fold* or *continuous feed* because it consists of thousands of continuous sheets of paper that fold like a fan. Little holes along the detachable edges fit into the printer's sprockets to provide a smooth trip through the printer. Although the sheets are attached to one another, each sheet is perforated so that it can be separated cleanly. Some users find that these perforations don't separate cleanly enough, giving a ragged appearance to the paper. If this happens, try tearing fewer sheets at once or fold the edge over and tear it against a smooth edge.

Several manufacturers produce continuous forms perforated with a laser so that when separated, the edges are smooth. This paper is more expensive, but if you use a dot-matrix printer for correspondence or other final drafts, you want your finished job to be well-trimmed. You can buy continuous-feed paper in many quantities, from a small package of 100 sheets (usually packaged by your computer store and sold for a few bucks) up to 3,500 sheets (for about $35).

Besides the way paper is packaged, you also need to consider the weight of the paper, identified by the weight in pounds of 1 ream, or 500 sheets of paper. For example, 500 sheets of 20# 8.5-by-11-inch fan-fold paper weighs 20 pounds. Although you don't want your paper to be too flimsy (15# is about the lower limit), paper that is too heavy also may jam your printer. The ImageWriter II has a spring-loaded adjustment to correct for the thickness of the paper to avoid problems with jamming.

Several companies (such as NEBS Business Forms) produce personalized stationery and business forms of all kinds on continuous forms, so that you can print your correspondence using your dot-matrix printer. These companies also produce envelopes that are pin-fed and inserted as a continuous set in dot-matrix printers. Laser printers use single-sheet paper almost exclusively, except for standard 9.5-by-4-inch business envelopes.

5

Printing

Single-sheet paper usually comes cut in sheets 8.5 by 11 inches in a package of 1 ream (500 sheets). However, you can purchase paper in a variety of other sizes to use for different printing jobs. The standard sizes and their dimensions are shown in the following list:

- Letter   8.5 by 11 inches

- Legal   8.5 by 14 inches

- A4   approximately 11.75 by 8.25 inches

- B5   approximately 10 by 7.5 inches
- Mini   8.5 by 5.5 inches

A4 and B5 are European sizes.

Depending on the type of Macintosh application you use, you will see one or more of these choices in the Page Setup dialog box. Figure 5.26 shows the Page Setup dialog box for the desktop publishing program QuarkXpress, and figure 5.27 shows PageMaker's Page Setup dialog box. Most good application programs enable you to choose a custom size in the Page Setup dialog box. The page sizes available depend on your printer.

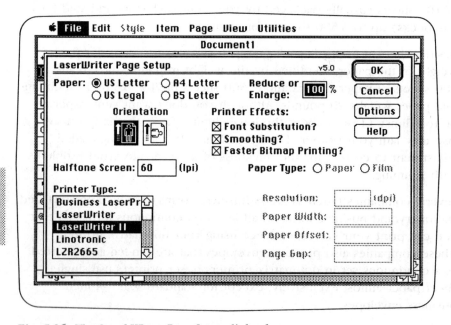

Fig. 5.26. The QuarkXPress Page Setup dialog box.

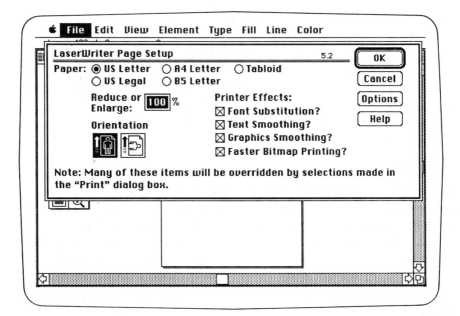

Fig. 5.27. *The PageMaker Page Setup dialog box.*

A major advantage that dot-matrix and character printers have over other nonimpact printers (such as inkjet and laser printers) is that they can produce multiple forms; businesses that need to produce such forms really have no other choice. Carbon paper is now being replaced with *no-carbon-required* (NCR) paper. This paper is coated on the back to create a copy of the image that the pin wires or daisywheel produces. Although NCR paper is more convenient, it is also more expensive to use.

If you need to print on materials other than paper, such as transparencies, check with someone who has experience or buy only materials manufactured especially for such printing operations. Just any piece of plastic does not make a decent overhead transparency. The plastic must be treated so that the ink takes well and is permanent after printed on the sheet. One way to create a transparency and not risk having the ink smear is to print and photocopy the hard copy onto a plastic sheet. If you use the right materials (which you can buy at most office supplies stores), you should have no problem printing on transparencies.

5

Printing

Finally, you can purchase mailing labels on continuous-feed paper. One of the problems with impact printers, however, is that preglued labels can get caught on the printers' inside parts if you try to roll the labels backwards. You may have to send your printer out for repair. (This warning applies primarily to ImageWriters and only when the labels are rolled backwards.) If you use preglued labels, be sure that they are recommended by your printer's manufacturer.

Ribbons

Ribbons for your dot-matrix printer come in two varieties: a loop of cloth (usually nylon) or a strip of carbon-coated plastic. You can use the cloth ribbon until you can no longer tolerate the faintness of the printout. The carbon-coated ribbon makes a very sharp, clear image but can be used only once because the printing process removes the carbon from the ribbon. Although this type of ribbon produces high-quality printouts, a carbon-coated ribbon is rarely used in impact printers.

When you need a new ribbon, you have several options. You can buy a ribbon from your local dealer—but be careful. Many companies manufacture generic ribbons for dot-matrix printers like the ImageWriter; the ribbon is not an Apple-supplied original and may not have the same quality. If you want to be safe, pay the extra few bucks and buy an Apple ribbon, available through your Apple dealer. Most veteran dot-matrix printer owners who have purchased generic ribbons have at least one horror story to tell about the ribbon breaking in the middle of a long document.

Your second option is to re-ink your existing cloth ribbons using a kit such as the one offered for around $40 by Bede-Tech. Cloth ribbons do not wear out quickly; the ink simply gets used up. Re-inking is neither difficult nor messy and works quite well. More information about these re-inkers is provided in Chapter 19. Do not just keep re-inking without examining the condition of the ribbon itself. Too much use can lead to a weakening of the ribbon fabric and eventually to fraying. The threads can get caught in the print head and bend or jam the pins. The expense of a $7.50 ribbon pales in comparison to a $100 print head.

Printer Mufflers

At best, dot-matrix and daisywheel impact printers are very noisy. In fact, they are so loud that many offices place their printers in an different location from the computers.

One way to solve this problem is to use a *printer muffler*, a box made of soundproof material into which you put the printer to absorb some of its clickity-clack. Commercially available mufflers can be expensive (about $150), but you can build one yourself from a sturdy carton and some insulation material. Remember to leave a place for the paper to feed in and out, and cover the insulation so that the fibers don't get into your printer.

To make a printer muffler, complete the following steps:

1. Find a box at least as large as the box your printer came in, preferably larger. Don't use your printer box; you will need it if you move.

2. Cut slots in the top and the back for paper to feed into and out of as it passes through the printer.

3. Glue insulation or packaging material to the inside surfaces of the box. Choose your glue carefully—many glues "melt" the popular polyinsulations. (Liquid Nails works well.)

4. Place the box over your printer and print away. The denser the insulation you use, the more sound will be absorbed.

5
Printing

Caring for Your Laser Printer

Your laser printer does not require a great deal of maintenance other than keeping surfaces clean and free of dust and following common-sense rules, such as not placing a cup of coffee on top of the printer.

You do need to be careful when you change toner cartridges or drums, however, more for your sake than for the printer's. Some of the printer's working parts, such as the fuser, can get extremely hot. Besides unplugging the printer, take care not to touch those parts hot enough to burn (they are usually marked inside the computer).

If you start to get messy pages—the black no longer stands out from the white—you may need to clean your printer. The following instructions are not specific to any one laser printer; they are general guidelines. Read your manual carefully to familiarize yourself with the parts of your printer before you begin. (You may want to have a technician clean the printer for you.)

1. Remember to unplug the printer and avoid touching hot surfaces.

2. When you replace the toner, tap the sides of the toner cartridge or the bottle so that it will empty more completely.

3. If you have a paper separator belt, make sure that it, or any of the springs attached to it, is not stretched out. If necessary, replace the belt according to the manufacturer's instructions.

4. Use rubbing alcohol, cotton swabs, and lint-free cloths for cleaning.

5. Wipe down all surfaces with excess toner on them, but don't wipe down the drum.

6. The corona wires, high-voltage wires used in the process of transferring the image from the drum to the paper, usually need cleaning when your laser printer is not producing clear images. These wires are very thin and usually run horizontally across the width of the drum. They are not easy to find and even harder to clean. Be very careful and work slowly using a cotton swab and alcohol until you have removed all the toner.

7. Drums are a separate, replaceable element and must not be exposed to light for more than a minute. Before you begin cleaning, remove the drum and place it in a safe, dark place. You can use the case the drum came in for storage.

Chapter Summary

No matter how many hours you spend slaving over a keyboard, your work does not boil down to much unless you can communicate it with others. The way you most often communicate ideas and information is through a printed document.

You currently have several choices in the world of Mac printing, and even more choices will soon be available. You can begin with a relatively inexpensive dot-matrix printer and move up to a powerful PostScript printer with the storage capacity for many resident fonts. Even if you are a writer whose words fall like elegant prose on the paper, no one will notice if you print with a frayed ribbon or a damaged drum on your laser printer. Marshall McLuhan probably did not have a Mac, printing, fonts, and everything that has been discussed in this chapter in mind when he said that the medium is the message, but these words seem to ring truer and truer as printing technology becomes more sophisticated, less expensive, and more within your reach.

5
Printing

Part III

Macintosh Applications

The thousands of applications programs that are available for the Macintosh computer form the heart of what the Mac is all about for millions of people. True to the spirit behind the Macintosh development, popular applications, such as word processors and spreadsheets, fit the needs of the user. These applications can help you write the briefest one-sentence memo or a full-length screen play, design an aircraft, or do movie animation.

This section discusses the major Macintosh applications, explains what they can (and cannot) do, and makes a comparison of their features. You should look at the comparison closely before you make any buying decisions.

Includes

Word Processors

Electronic Ledgers: Working with Spreadsheets

Working with Databases

Integrated Software and Financial Programs

Desktop Publishing

Graphics

The Macintosh at Home

Word Processors

A *word processor* is a fancy electronic paper and pencil that allows you to create and manipulate text. In many ways, word processing on any computer goes to the heart of what the personal computer revolution is all about—increasing people's productivity. Word processors have saved uncounted hours of retyping. They decrease production time of a report or a manuscript, and they enable you to exert great control over what your documents look like when they are finished.

Word processors come in all shapes and sizes. They range from the DA word processor, to specialized word processors designed to produce mathematical formulas, to the full-fledged workhorses that have become the mainstay of many businesses. Currently, the most popular full-fledged word processors include Word (the market leader), FullWrite, WordPerfect, and WriteNow. In this chapter, I discuss these word processors, as well as some others, and provide you with recommendations for which one might be best suited to your needs. You also will find a chart comparing the features of the leading word processors.

With prices ranging from $50 up to $500, almost everyone can find a program that will fit his or her budget. Price is not the best guide to the usefulness or ease of learning of a word processor. MacWrite, which costs only $125, compares favorably with Word, which retails for $395. Both programs do an excellent job of managing text and files, but Word has some extras such as a terrific table-construction tool and the SuperPaint painting and drawing program, and Word also creates tables of contents and indexes very efficiently. If these features are important to you, you may want to pay the extra amount.

6

**Word
Processors**

237

In this chapter, you learn not only about the capabilities of these programs, but also about how the most basic features of all word processors work, including entering, editing, and deleting text; formatting pages; printing; using such special features as a spell checker and a thesaurus; merging to generate form letters; and constructing tables.

Generating Documents

Although a word processor's most general function is to manipulate text, this task can be further broken down into five steps: entering text, saving text, editing text, accessing stored text, and outputting text. All word processors, whether they be the most basic memo-writing tool or the most advanced and complex programs, can do these five things.

The first task in using any word processor is to enter the information you want to work with. As you are probably aware, the most frequently used input device is the keyboard, but there are others as well. For example, you can use a drawing tablet that has been "taught" to recognize your handwriting, or you can use voice-recognition software to enter your text by "talking" to your computer. You can even use the $9,000 DataGlove, a glove you wear that enters information by reflecting the way the glove moves.

Once the text has been entered, the next step in the process is to *edit* as you see fit. This involves a variety of different operations ranging from the simple insertion of new text to checking the spelling or even correcting the grammar of your document. Many utilities exist to automate these operations. You always should save your document when you finish your editing.

After you have edited your text, you will probably want to *save* it as a file so that it will be available later if you want to use the same information again (such as in a form letter) or if you want to continuing editing the file. Many people save at regular intervals while they edit to make sure that their documents are safe as they go along. If your document isn't saved to disk, you don't "own" it. What's on the screen exists only in volatile memory (RAM)—when you shut off your computer, the memory holding your document loses its contents. Therefore, to keep a copy, you must save your work to disk.

During your next session, in order to work with the same text you worked on before and saved, you must retrieve, or *open*, the saved file.

Finally, the last step in the process is the *printing* of the document so that you have a permanent copy to share with others or keep for your own files.

Looking at the Process

The best way to illustrate what a word processor can do is to explain the various steps in a typical work session. For this example, I will discuss the procedures involved in using Microsoft Word 4.0 to write an article.

The first step is to create a new file. Choosing the New command on the File menu produces the opening window you see in figure 6.1. Once you have opened the file, you are free to use your Mac as a typewriter and enter your text (see fig. 6.2). You can see that the file has not been named yet. Word provides the name Untitled1 for your first new document.

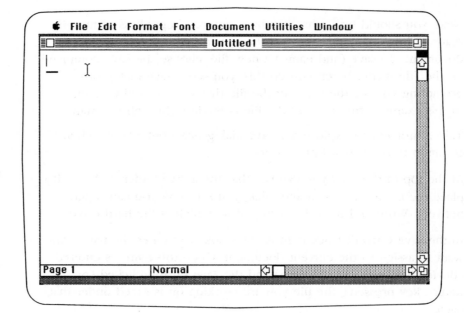

Fig. 6.1. *Creating a new file.*

6
Word
Processors

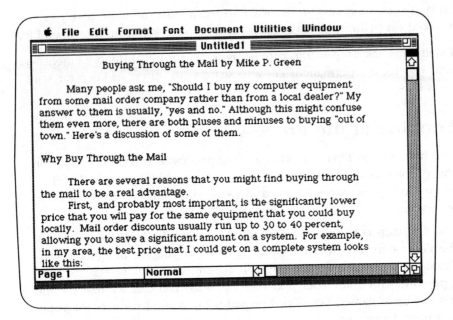

Fig. 6.2. Entered text in a new file.

Next, you should save what you have entered, regardless of how it reads or how many mistakes you have made while typing your document. To save (and name) a new file, choose the Save command on the File menu. When you do this, you see a Save dialog box prompting you for the name of the file that you created (see fig. 6.3). In this example, the name of the file is Buying Through the Mail.

Take a moment to explore the Save dialog box contents, which are common to other word processors.

At the top of the box, you can see that the active folder is Word. If you place the mouse on Word and click, you see how you can toggle between Word and the other active disk, which is the hard drive.

In the Save Current Document As text box, you enter the name you want to assign to the current document. Once this name is entered (Buying Through... in this case) and the Save button clicked (or the Return key pressed), the file you are working on is saved under that name.

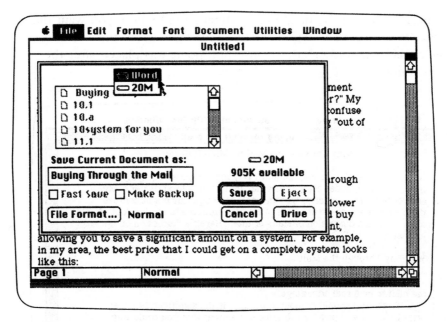

Fig. 6.3. *Naming a new file.*

You use four buttons (Save, Cancel, Eject, and Drive, respectively) to save the file under the name you assign, cancel the save operation and return to your document, eject the disk whose files are listed in the list box, or change the drive so that the listing of a disk in another drive or a hard drive is revealed in the list box.

Above those buttons is the icon that indicates the hard disk that the current active folder is a part of and the amount of free space on that drive (905K). Other things you see on the screen, such as File Format (which allows you to save the file under other formats), Fast Save, and Make Backup, are part of Word's system.

Now that the file is saved, you can recall (open) it to be edited at your leisure.

Macintosh word processors offer many features, from the most basic insertion of a space up through the use of a spell checker and thesaurus, to help you with your writing.

Suppose, for example, that you want to add a sentence at the end of the first paragraph in figure 6.2. Place the *insertion point* (which is a vertical line about the height of a capital letter) where you want the sentence to begin and type your text (see fig. 6.4). In this example, before the text was added, the insertion point was placed after the word *some*.

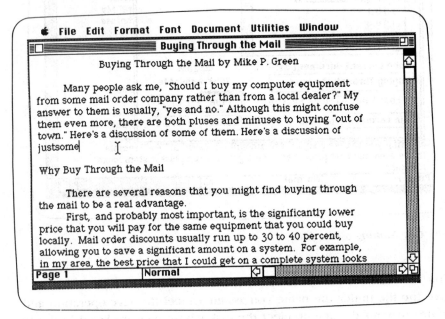

Fig. 6.4. Placing the insertion point to insert a sentence.

The insertion point is not the cursor. When you open a new word processing document, the insertion point appears in the upper right corner (again see fig. 6.1). The horizontal line you see below the insertion point indicates the end of the file.

The insertion point marks where any text that you enter (via the keyboard or any other input device) will be placed. The cursor is an I-beam that moves as you move the mouse. If you want to change the location of the insertion point, move the I-beam to that location and click once. The insertion point moves to location, and any text you enter will appear there.

You may have noticed, however, that in adding the sentence, the words *just* and *some* run together. To insert a space, put the I-beam cursor between the letters, click to place your insertion point, and then press the space bar.

If you don't like the sentence, you can delete it easily by selecting it and then pressing the Backspace key. You select text by click-dragging through all the text you want to select. To click-drag through text, place the I-beam at the beginning of the text you want to select. Click the mouse button and hold it down. Then drag over the text you want to select, highlighting it. If you wanted to move the sentence to another location in your document, you can select the sentence, choose the Cut or Copy command from the Edit menu, place the insertion point in the new location, and choose the Paste command from the File menu.

Different word processors have different selection capabilities. Almost all allow you to select just one word by double-clicking that word. Others go beyond that. WordPerfect, for example, allows you to select sentences or paragraphs using menu or keyboard combinations. The QuarkXPress word processor allows you to select a line, sentence, or paragraph, depending on the number of clicks you make. Word allows you to select an entire document by moving the cursor to the left until it turns into an arrow that points to the upper right, and then pressing the ⌘ key and clicking once.

The document will look better if it is dressed up a bit. To make the title boldface, select the title, and choose the Bold command from the Format menu or use the keyboard equivalent Shift-⌘-B (see fig. 6.5). Next, select the entire document and choose the Character command on the Format menu to change the font from New York to Times. Remember that in order for any changes to be permanent and part of the file, you must save the file after the changes are made. Now you're ready to print.

The final job is to print the document. Choose the Print command on the File menu, and the final document is printed (see fig. 6.6).

Starting the printing process is identical in all Macintosh applications. Be sure that you have selected the appropriate printer driver by using the Chooser DA. Keep in mind that you will print what you see on the screen, not what has been stored. So if you make changes to the

6
Word
Processors

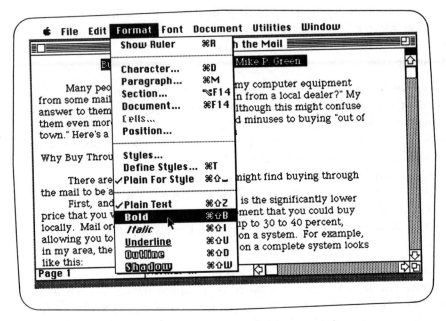

Fig. 6.5. *To make text boldface, choose the Bold command.*

Buying Through the Mail by Mike P. Green

Many people ask me, "Should I buy my computer equipment from some mail order company rather than from a local dealer?" My answer to them is usually, "yes and no." Although this might confuse them even more, there are both pluses and minuses to buying "out of town." Here's a discussion of some of them.

Why Buy Through the Mail

There are several reasons that you might find buying through the mail to be a real advantage.

First, and probably most important, is the significantly lower price that you will pay for the same equipment that you could buy locally. Mail order discounts usually run up to 30 to 40 percent, allowing you to save a significant amount on a system. For example, in my area, the best price that I could get on a complete system looks like this:

Mac Plus	$1700
external drive	325
Imagewriter II printer	525
total cost	$2600

Through some mail order exploring, I found a company in Chicago that could deliver the same equipment for a little under $2300.

How can they offer such a good deal? It's easy. They have no overhead charges, which include such things as rent for stores with prime locations, a sales force, and other "retail" business costs.

Another reason to buy through the mail is that you have a much wider choice when you are buying because you can choose from the hundreds of products that are available, rather than the few that might be sold in your town or close by. All the companies have toll free "800" numbers, and you can usually call and get price quotes very quickly and easily. (more) ▷▷

Fig. 6.6. *The finished document.*

document and then print it, the changes will be on the printed copy, but not stored in the file until you also change the file.

Using File Functions

Most of the commands necessary to perform the functions just described are located on the File and Edit menus. In figure 6.7, for example, you can see the File menus for some of the most popular Mac word processors—Word 4.0, WordPerfect 1.01, MacWrite II, WriteNow 2.0, FullWrite, and Nisus.

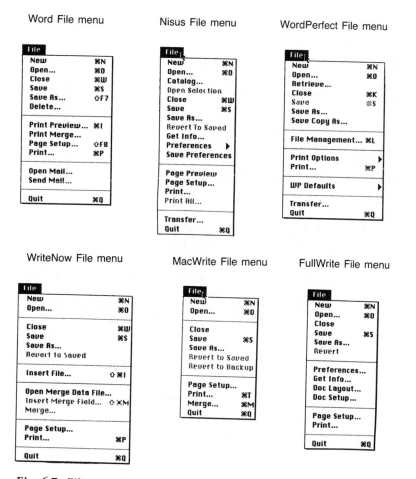

Fig. 6.7. File menus from the various programs.

Opening Documents

Word processors would not be much good if all you could do was to save a file but not recall it for later use. Once you have saved your file, it's easy to access it the next time you are ready to work on it. Choose the Open command from the File menu (or use the ⌘-O key combination) and choose the file by name (see fig. 6.8). Normally, files that can't be opened by your word processor will appear dimmed. One trick you can use to select the file that you want to open is to enter the first few characters in the file name as soon as you select the Open command. Your word processor will highlight the name of the file that matches those characters.

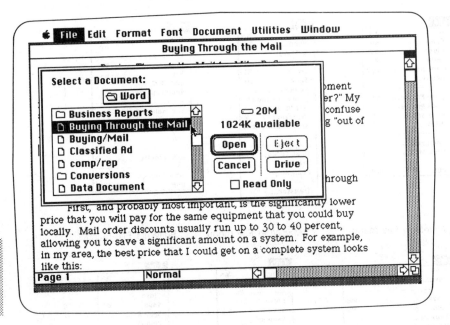

Fig. 6.8. *Choose your file by name.*

Another command on the File menu, New (⌘-N), can sometimes confuse beginning word processor users. Select New when you want to begin an entirely new document and not when you want to recall one that has already been saved. A new document is initially called Untitled1 if it's the first new document to be opened in that work session. Otherwise, it is assigned titles such as Untitled2, Untitled3, and so forth. You can open as many untitled new documents as your computer's memory will allow.

Saving Documents

One of the basic steps in word processing (and most other Macintosh applications as well) is saving a document as a file, as you saw earlier in this chapter. It's one of the essential steps. There are some other components to the save process that you should be aware of.

First, on the File menu, you can select the Save As command. This command allows you to save the active document under a different name. For example, let's say that you create a letter and you want to modify it slightly depending on whom you are sending it to. The original letter could be saved as LETTER/MAIN. You could make a few changes to the letter and save this version as LETTER/MODIFIED. If you use the Save command to save a file that has already been named and saved, your word processor will save it under the existing name. To save the same document under a different name, you must use the Save As command.

Some word processors offer nice features that go along with the save process. For example, in figure 6.9, you see how WordPerfect enables you to set an automatic backup feature so that WordPerfect will save your document every five minutes and make a backup of your file under a different name. You can imagine how handy this can be if you accidentally delete a file, or a drive crash destroys your original as you work.

Look at the Nisus Saving Files Preferences box in figure 6.10. You can create a backup of a file (with the same file name and .BAK extension), save after a certain number of keystrokes, and save to two disks at once. You check the Secondary Disk Save box shown in figure 6.10 and specify where to have Nisus save your document to two places at once. For us absent-minded folks, that's reason enough to choose this word processor.

WriteNow has a Save/Compact command, which saves your file in the smallest form possible, deleting any spaces that might have been created when you edited or deleted characters during your work. WriteNow also has a Revert to Saved file command, which you use

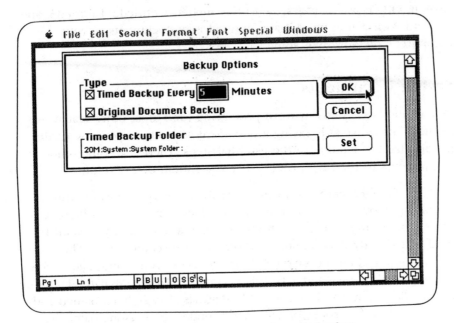

Fig. 6.9. *WordPerfect enables you to set an automatic backup feature.*

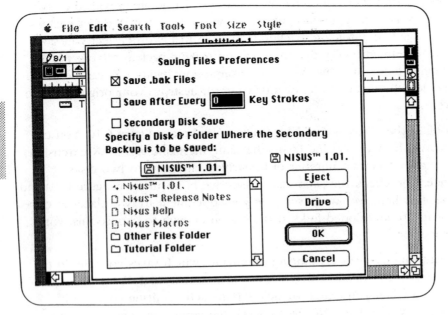

Fig. 6.10. *The Nisus Saving Files Preferences box.*

after you have made changes but before you save the file again. Select the Revert to Saved command to return you to the last saved version of the file.

Editing Functions

The capability to edit and manipulate your text is probably the most important feature of a word processor—it is the nitty gritty of word processing. This section discusses the features that affect the way you edit your documents. In MacWrite, for example, you can insert the date into the text with an Edit menu command, and in WordPerfect, you can manage files without returning to the desktop.

Deleting Text

How delightful it would be if we all were perfect, but that isn't the case. When you make errors, you need a way to edit your text and make changes.

Here's some text with a simple error—the wrong form of the word *too* was used.

We were going too meet at the airport, but my plane was late.

The easiest way to correct this type of error is to use the mouse and place the insertion point to the right of the extra *o*, and then backspace (see fig. 6.11). It's that easy.

If you want to delete a large amount of text, you select the unwanted text and press the Del or Backspace key.

If you make an error and delete something you really meant to save, you can use the Undo command, usually located on the Edit menu. Undo reverses the results of your last keystrokes and restores the deleted text.

Undo works beautifully, and in some word processors, such as Nisus (from Paragon), you can set the number of levels of undo (Nisus allows up to 32,767 levels of undo!) You could undo a deletion even after 10 different operations have been completed.

6
Word
Processors

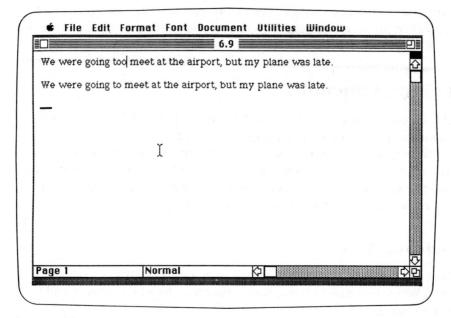

Fig. 6.11. *Using the insertion point to edit a document.*

Keep in mind that every deletion that is saved through the use of Undo takes up precious memory and deprives you of operating speed. If you use Nisus, keep the number of undo levels low.

Inserting Text

In addition to the times when you need to delete text, there certainly will be times when you need to insert text.

Any text that you enter always begins appearing at the location of the vertical insertion point. You move the insertion point by moving the I-beam to where you want to insert text and clicking.

Moving Text

Moving text is perhaps one of the most useful features of a word processor. When you move text, you use the Cut, Copy, and Paste commands located on the Edit menu. When you select text, the highlighted area is called a *block*. These commands place the block on the Clipboard.

Some word processors make it easier to select text and create blocks than others. WordPerfect, for example, allows you to select by sentence, paragraph, page, column, or even the entire document. You also can use WordPerfect to select a block of text by placing the I-beam beam at the beginning of the block and then moving it to the end of the block and clicking the mouse button with the Shift key held down.

In figure 6.12, you see one item (*Deposit check*) being cut (⌘-X) from the list of things that need to be done this week. In figure 6.13, you see the insertion point positioned to insert the item in the *Things to do today* list using the Paste command (⌘-V) on the Edit menu. In figure 6.14, you see the results.

You can paste as many different things as you like, keeping in mind that the Clipboard can store only one item at a time. Once the second item is cut, the first is no longer available. If you want to store items on a more permanent basis, you must use the Scrapbook.

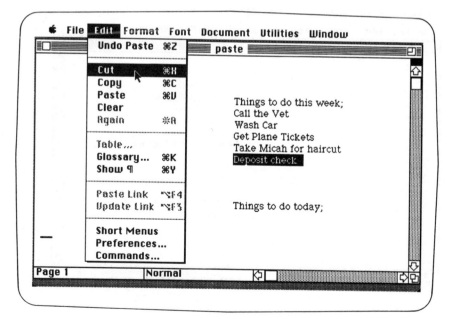

6

Word Processors

Fig. 6.12. *The* Deposit check *item has been selected to cut.*

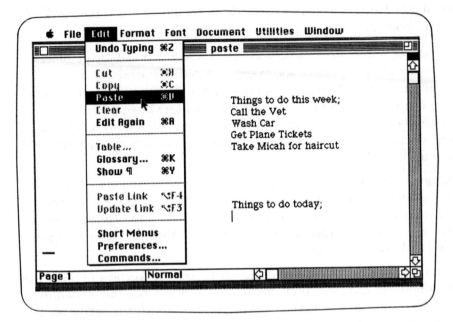

Fig. 6.13. *Choosing Paste.*

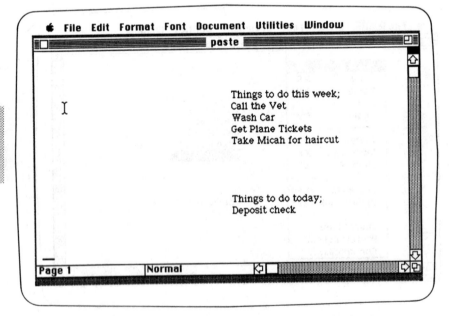

Fig. 6.14. *The* Deposit check *item has been moved to the second list.*

In some applications, including all the word processors discussed in this chapter, you can paste the same Clipboard contents over and over again by selecting the Paste command or using the ⌘-V key combination.

As you remember from Chapter 2, the Clipboard is a temporary storage place for text and graphics. When you select the Copy or Cut command from the Edit menu, the cut or copied material is automatically placed into the Clipboard. All word processors have this Clipboard feature because it is part of the Mac operating system and not really a separate feature of the word processor itself. Once something has been cut or copied, the only way to get it out of the Clipboard is by using the Paste command on the Edit menu.

You can cut, copy, and paste any amount of text, but beware: you should always save your document before you do any extensive cutting and pasting. Or better yet, work on a copy of your original document. Saving your document can help you recover from such errors as pasting material in the wrong place, or cutting two blocks of material and then discovering that the first one is gone forever because the buffer can hold only one thing at a time. Also, there is a limit to how much text a buffer can hold. If you exceed the limit, you will get a not enough memory to complete operation message. How much text can the buffer hold? It depends on the memory capacity of your Macintosh, the size of your application, and, of course, how much you are storing on the Clipboard.

Searching For and Replacing Text

The search and the search and replace features come in handy, particularly when you are dealing with a long document.

The search feature (also called find) allows you to "hunt" throughout a document for a string of characters. The search and replace feature can save you much typing time. Suppose, for example, that you are writing a report. Instead of entering the full phrase *economic advantages of lower tax rates*, you could enter the letters *ETX*. When you have finished typing your report, you can use the search and replace feature to replace each occurrence of *ETX* with the full phrase.

Often word processors make it possible for you to search for an item capitalized in a specific way, or you can search for the word regardless

6

Word
Processors

of whether it is upper- or lowercase. What this means is that you can search for just *CAT*, just *cat*, just *Cat*, or any occurrence of the three letters no matter how they are capitalized.

In figure 6.15, for example, you can see how Word allows you to search for whole words, or to match or not to match upper- and lowercase letters. Some word processors also enable you to search and change by attribute. For example, the Find/Change box in the QuarkXPress word processor shown in figure 6.16, shows you how to change text from a certain font size and type (Helvetica 12 point) to another size and type (Chicago 10 point).

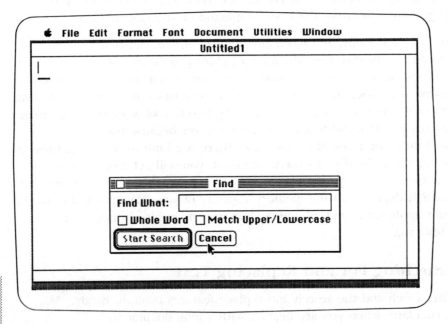

Fig. 6.15. *The Word Find box.*

Easy? Yes. Dangerous? Maybe. Here's why. The key to a successful search and replace operation is to make sure that you have chosen a unique set of characters for the search. Suppose that you want to change the word *to* to *too*. If you instructed the program to search for all occurrences of the word *to* and replace it with *too*, you would end

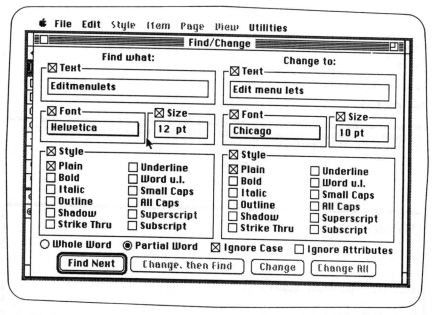

Fig. 6.16. *The QuarkXPress Find/Change box.*

up with words such as *toold*, *toown*, *toook*, and so forth. Obviously not what you intended!

Formatting Functions

How documents look is often as important as the message they contain. No, the medium is not the message, but it sure can make the difference between a message that is received with pleasure and one that is just tolerated. The memos in figure 6.17 were both created with Word 4.0. Which one would you rather receive? Good spacing, wisely chosen fonts, and other formatting can make your documents stand out from the crowd.

Setting Margins and Tabs

You can change the top, bottom, left, and right margins of your documents to achieve the effect you want. With most Mac word processors, you use increments along a ruler to help you change the

6

Word Processors

Plain memo

Memo

8/15/89

To: All department heads

From: K.B., Boss!

Let's get the lead out and get ready for the upcoming sales. Remember, all of the items need to be repriced and tagged and the inventory has to be completed by the 5th. Now for the serious stuff. The party at my house begins at 8 PM. See you then!

Improved memo

Memo

8/15/89

To: All department heads

From: K.B., Boss!

Let's get the lead out and get ready for the upcoming sales. Remember, all of the items need to be repriced and tagged and the inventory has to be completed by the 5th. Now for the serious stuff. *The party at my house begins at 8 PM. See you then!*

Fig. 6.17. You can use the formatting features to make the memo more readable and attractive.

margins. In figure 6.18, you can see two paragraphs. The top paragraph uses the default margin settings, and the bottom paragraph has margin settings of .5 inch for the left margin and 3.5 inches for the right margin. In this example, the margins were adjusted by dragging the small triangles on the ruler. In figure 6.19, you can see a dialog box that can be used for more precise adjustments.

Note, however, that the adjustments are for the entire document and not for just one paragraph as in figure 6.18. Word processors usually allow you to set a default margin setting for the entire document and then change the settings for lines or paragraphs as you see fit.

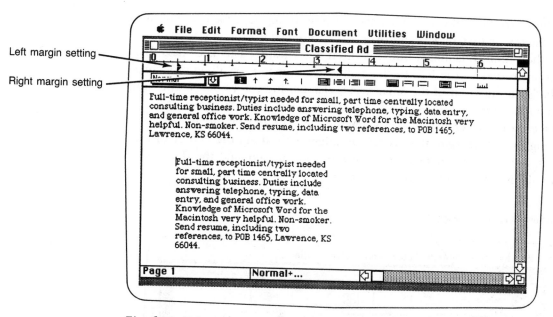

Fig. 6.18. *Using both default and set margins.*

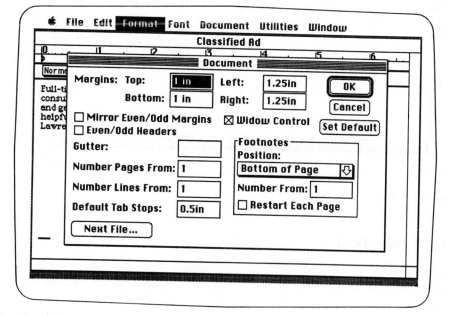

Fig. 6.19. *Use the Document dialog box to adjust margins more precisely.*

Where would we be without tabs? Imagine trying to construct columns of figures or text by spacing over again and again! Not only is that method time-consuming, but it is often inaccurate. Nisus uses tabs that can align text to the left, to the right, in the center, or along a decimal. That's the function of the small triangular tab indicators below the Edit menu in figure 6.20. To set these tabs, drag the tab indicator to the place on the ruler where you want the tab. The left tab aligns text along the left margin, the center tab aligns text along the center of the text, the right tab aligns text along the right margin, and the decimal tab aligns text along the decimal point.

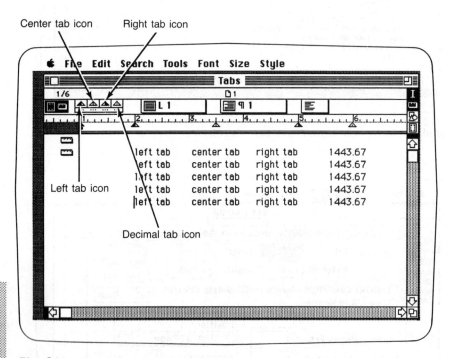

Fig. 6.20. Nisus tab settings.

Justifying Text

Depending on your needs, text can be aligned or *justified* in several ways. The text in most books is fully justified, which means that all the text is spaced so that each line is as long as all the other lines.

Text can also be left-justified, right-justified, centered, or fully justified. It just depends on what you want to do.

You can see four sample paragraphs in figure 6.21 showing these types of justification. Which one should you use? Most documents are left-justified because we have learned to read documents that have a straight left edge and that's where our eyes are trained to start or to return to after we finish a line. A fully justified document can look very attractive, but often unnatural spaces are forced into lines to make all the lines even. These spaces can be compensated for by spacing changes, but the trouble is often not worth the effect. Center justification is useful for titles and other heading information. Right-justification is rarely, if ever, used because it is hard to read.

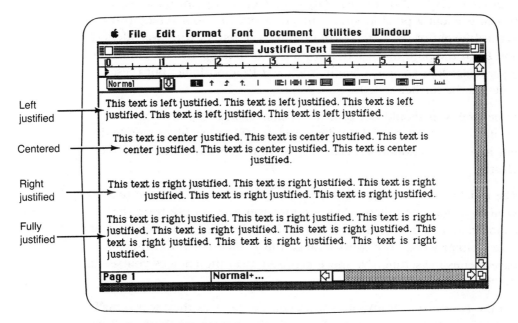

Fig. 6.21. *Four different types of justification.*

Most documents should either be ragged right (left-justified) or fully justified. Often, however, full justification produces awkward-looking lines. On some word processors, such as WordPerfect, you can adjust spacing the between letters (called *kerning*) as well as between words (called *tracking*). See Chapter 10 for a full discussion.

Using Fonts, Sizes, and Styles

The Macintosh can offer you almost unlimited choices when it comes to using fonts. A font is a family of characters, numbers, and symbols that have the same characteristics. Examples of these families are Times Roman, Helvetica, Cooper, Palatino, Geneva, and Zapf Chancery Dingbats. Fonts are discussed in Chapter 5.

Fonts come in different styles (such as underline or boldface) and sizes ranging in most word processing applications from 1 to 127 points (the most common point sizes are from 6 to 12 points). A *point* is approximately 1/72 of an inch. (By coincidence, a point on a Macintosh screen is about a pixel in size.) The point size of a font refers to the vertical height of the letters, from the tops of letters with ascenders (*b* and *h*) to the bottoms of letters with descenders (*p* and *q*). Sometimes a particular font style is a family, such as I Palatino Italic, but these fonts can be further styled.

In general, you should not print fonts smaller than 4 points on a laser printer or 6 points on a dot-matrix printer. These machines simple do not have the resolution at such small sizes to reproduce the character clearly.

The usual way to change fonts, styles, and sizes is to select the text you want to change, and then select the font you want to use from the appropriate menu. WordPerfect offers the style, font, and size all on one menu. Other word processors arrange things differently, but they all have menus for setting size more precisely than the choices you see in the figure.

On the Font menu, MacWrite shows you the fonts as they will actually look when printed (see fig. 6.22). No doubt about what things will look like here. Select the Font menu, and you get a good look at what something will look like when it is in your document. This feature is an enormous help to people who are always trying different combinations of fonts.

WordPerfect has letters representing style changes at the bottom of the screen. If you want to make text bold, select it, and click the B. The same is true for Plain, Underline, Italic, Outline, Superscript, and Subscript. FullWrite has what it calls "walk-down menus," in which you can select fonts and attributes with keyboard combinations, bypassing the mouse and increasing your selection speed.

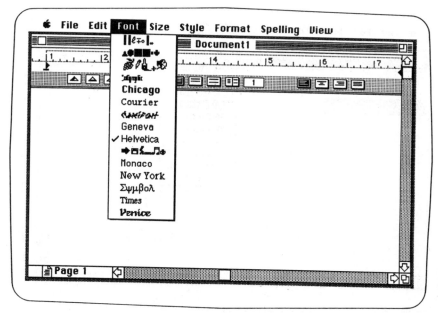

Fig. 6.22. MacWrite fonts are displayed as they will appear.

WriteNow has Larger and Smaller commands on the FontSize menu, which you can use to increase or decrease the size of the font in 1-point increments (see fig. 6.23). To do this, you select the text, and then choose this command.

In Word, you highlight the text you want to resize, and then select the Character command on the Format menu and specify the size of the font you want to use.

This feature is a convenient way to increase or decrease the size of text without having to leave the screen. Nisus enables you to do the same thing with its Increase and Decrease commands located on the Size menu.

Notice that, in figure 6.23, some font sizes are outlined while others are not. The ones that are outlined are fonts that have been installed by your application program working in conjunction with the printer and are readily available. The others can be selected and used, but the clarity and resolution is not likely to be as good because your Mac has to build these fonts based on the model it selects from those that are already installed.

6

Word
Processors

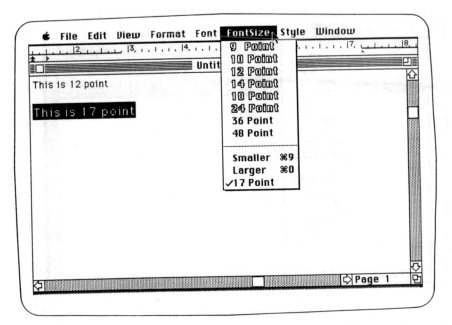

Fig. 6.23. *The WriteNow Fontsize menu with the Smaller and Larger commands.*

Beware of font junk, however. That's when the need to use every font feature the Mac offers becomes overwhelming. Choose just one or two fonts per document to avoid the distraction of too many fonts competing for attention on a page.

Adjusting Line Spacing

Just as you can change the way lines align, so you change the line spacing. All word processors offer you an easy way to change from single- to double- (and sometimes triple-) spacing. Some of the programs also offer a dialog box from which you can adjust spacing precisely. In the Nisus dialog box you see in figure 6.24, the spacing is adjustable and is set at 30 points or 2.5 lines for a 12-point font. Typically, business forms (and typewriters) use a 6-lines-per-inch setting.

In this figure, you can see the L (30) indicator just above the Line Spacing dialog box. This is an alternative way to space lines.

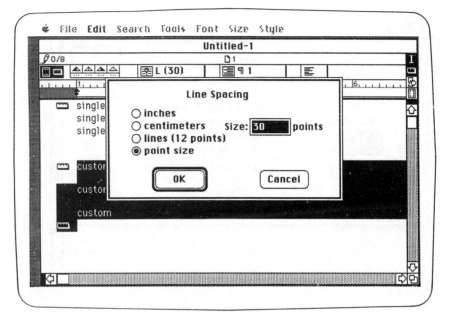

Fig. 6.24. *The Nisus Line Spacing box.*

Working with Pages

In addition to changing line width and spacing, working with different fonts, and searching and replacing text, you can also make changes to the entire page by using a Page Setup command. This command is often located on the File menu.

As you can see from the dialog box shown in figure 6.25, you can make changes in the orientation of the printed copy, and you can also enlarge or reduce your final output. You can enlarge an image up to 400 percent or reduce it to as much as 25 percent of its original size.

Some people enter text larger than they want it and then reduce it, thereby increasing the density of the image on the printed page, although this method takes some trial and error to get it right. When 12-point text is reduced 25 percent, it prints as 9-point text, but it is more dense and blacker than regular 9-point type. But sometimes laser fonts don't scale well. Scalable fonts are a feature of System 7.0.

6

Word Processors

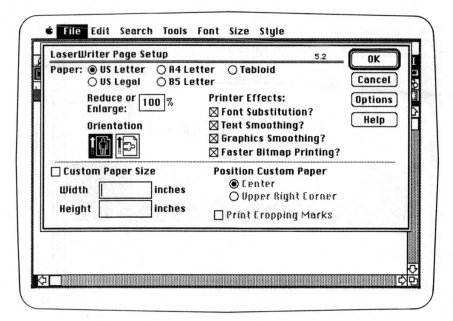

Fig. 6.25. Use the Page Setup dialog box to change your document's orientation.

Another common feature is page orientation. In the Page Setup dialog box, you can find the *Portrait* option (which prints the page in a vertical direction), and the *Landscape* option (which prints the page in a horizontal direction). Figures 6.26 and 6.27 show examples of these orientations. The choice is as much aesthetic as practical, although if you want to keep long lines of type together, Landscape may be best. You can have either of the two orientations in a document, but not both.

Most of the special tasks that printers can do are listed on the Page SetUp menus or in the Print dialog boxes.

One feature that most word processors have in common is Print Preview. With Print Preview, you can see what the pages of a document will look like when they are printed. Figure 6.28 shows Word facing pages as they will appear in print. Notice the printer icon on the left edge of the page. Clicking this icon directs the computer to send the document to the printer. This feature helps you save a step if what you see on-screen is what you want printed.

Buying Through the Mail by Mike P. Green

Many people ask me, "Should I buy my computer equipment from some mail order company rather than from a local dealer?" My answer to them is usually, "yes and no." Although this might confuse them even more, there are both pluses and minuses to buying "out of town." Here's a discussion of some of them.

Why Buy Through the Mail

There are several reasons that you might find buying through the mail to be a real advantage.
First, and probably most important, is the significantly lower price that you will pay for the same equipment that you could buy locally. Mail order discounts usually run up to 30 to 40 percent, allowing you to save a significant amount on a system. For example, in my area, the best price that I could get on a complete system looks like this:

Mac Plus	$1700
external drive	325
Imagewriter II printer	525
total cost	$2600

Fig. 6.26. *Portrait orientation.*

Buying Through the Mail by Mike P. Green

Many people ask me, "Should I buy my computer equipment from some mail order company rather than from a local dealer?" My answer to them is usually, "yes and no." Although this might confuse them even more, there are both pluses and minuses to buying "out of town." Here's a discussion of some of them.

Why Buy Through the Mail

There are several reasons that you might find buying through the mail to be a real advantage.
First, and probably most important, is the significantly lower price that you will pay for the same equipment that you could buy locally. Mail order discounts usually run up to 30 to 40 percent, allowing you to save a significant amount on a system. For example, in my area, the best price that I could get on a complete system looks like this:

Mac Plus	$1700
external drive	325
Imagewriter II printer	525
total cost	$2600

Fig. 6.27. *Landscape orientation.*

6
Word
Processors

The icon with the parallel vertical lines is a margin icon, which you use to set margins. You can switch from a one-page to a two-page display by clicking the third icon.

With many word processors, however, you can look but not touch (edit) while in the preview mode. Certain programs, such as Microsoft Word, allow you to change margins and view two pages at once while in the preview mode.

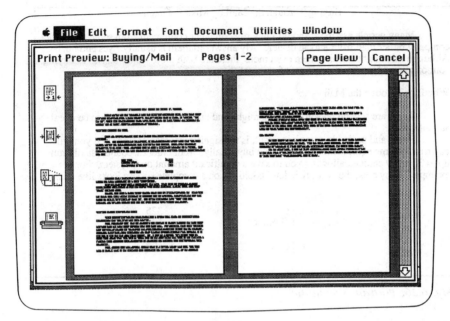

Fig. 6.28. Using Word's Print Preview feature to see facing pages of a document.

But others do indeed offer some interesting and outstanding features. For example, Nisus allows you to retain the time and date the document was created rather than updating it automatically, and enables you to print absolute page numbers (within a section, for example) without concern for the number of pages in an entire document.

Word prints hidden text, which can consist of notes and such, as well as markers that are used to create tables of contents and indexes. WriteNow enables you to print in forward or reverse (so do WordPerfect and several others) and also to print odd, even, or both pages by number. This feature is handy for printing on special forms. But without a doubt, FullWrite is the granddaddy of print options, as you can see in figure 6.29.

You can print collated copies, print labels, print on both sides (after you turn the paper over, of course), and more. One of the neatest features of FullWrite is the capability to print a background picture with your document. You simply select the picture and indicate whether you want it to print on the first page only, or on every page.

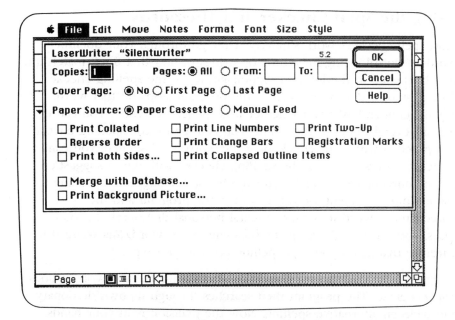

Fig. 6.29. FullWrite offers many different options for printing.

Remember that you have to select the printer you want to use through the Chooser DA on the Apple menu. Unless you do that, your Macintosh will tell you that it can't find your printer and then nothing gets done.

Understanding Special Functions

All word processors are capable of performing the editing and formatting functions already described, but there are some special features that really add power and versatility to your word processing chores.

Although these features may not be for everyone, they certainly can make performing highly specialized tasks much easier, and they save time as well.

6

Word
Processors

Using the Spell Checker and Thesaurus

Most spell checkers work similarly. They go through your document word-by-word looking for words or strings of text that don't match the text contained in the internal dictionary. When the spelling checker finds a word it doesn't recognize, the program stops on that word, highlights it, and asks you whether it is spelled correctly. You can do one of several things at this point. You can ignore the spelling checker and proceed with your check, or if the word is misspelled, you can correct it yourself. Often, the spelling checker will offer a suggestion for the unrecognized word. You can choose the suggested spelling to use in your document, or you can have the program add the unrecognized word to a supplemental personal dictionary. In some cases, you can even look up the meaning of the word. MacWrite II has a feature that alerts you to a spelling error as you type.

In figure 6.30, you can see how WordPerfect highlights a word it does not recognize. The program then searches through its own dictionary and picks an alternative spelling. Now the decision is in your hands. Like many other word processors, WordPerfect also gives you a word count when it is finished checking your spelling—something that Word has as a separate menu command (it's new to Version 4.0).

Yes, spelling checkers are great, but there's one hitch. They don't actually check your spelling as much as they do your typing. In other words, you may be spelling the word correctly, but using it improperly. For example, if you type *We went too the movies*, there is no spell checker that will tell you that *too* should be spelled *to*. You are also not likely to get much help if you don't know how to spell a word. For example, if you don't know how to spell the word *predicament*, and you type *purrdikamint*, you might be out of "luk."

You need not rely on only your built-in spell checker. Spelling Coach (from Deneba) and WordFinder (from Microlytics) are two examples of add-ons that work quite well. Both are DAs, making them very convenient. Spelling Coach includes standard legal and medical dictionaries to expand its usefulness.

Along with a spell checker comes a thesaurus, a tool that helps you find that word that's on the tip of your tongue, such as the thesaurus from Nisus (see fig 6.31). You highlight the word that you want to find a substitute for (*heartfelt*) and then select the Thesaurus tool from the

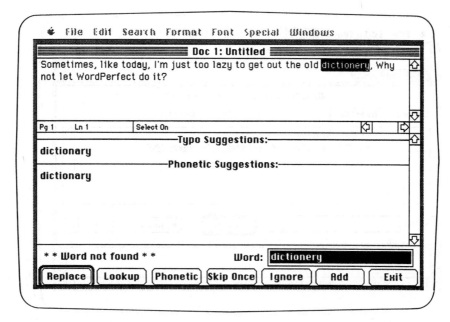

Fig. 6.30. *The WordPerfect spell checker highlights words it doesn't recognize.*

Tools menu. In a flash, you see a definition of the word along with the substitutes that the word processor suggests. Double-click the word you want to use as the substitute.

Merging

What a life-saver the merge feature is. Imagine having to write 2,000 personalized letters. Wouldn't it be much better if you could write just one letter and then merge the letter with a file of those addresses? This method is certainly more efficient.

That's exactly what the merge feature allows you to do. You create a main document (a letter or contract, for example) into which other information will be merged. Then you create a data document that contains the information to be merged into the main document. In figure 6.32, for example, you see the main document, which will be used with a data document appearing in another window.

6

Word
Processors

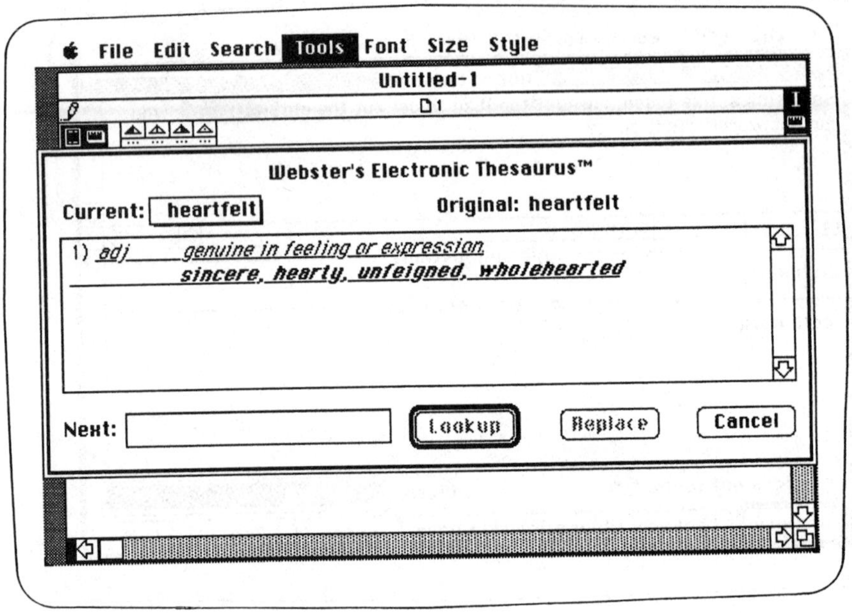

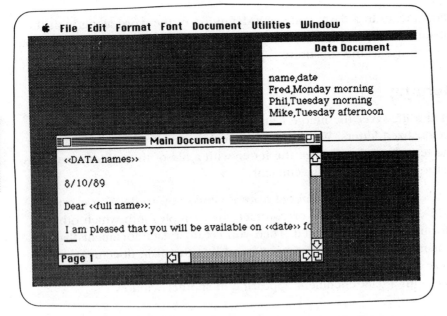

Fig. 6.31. The Nisus thesaurus at work.

Fig. 6.32. A main document and a data document used with the merge feature.

The ‹‹DATA names›› line at the beginning of the main document tells Word to look for the information in the document saved under the file name names. When you choose the Print Merge command from the File menu, your form letters are printed.

The merge feature, which is available on all these word processors except MacWrite and Nisus, has more uses than you can imagine. You can use this tool for many different applications, such as:

- Modifying letters containing the same basic structure but different information

- Maintaining mailing lists

- Using the conditional features offered by such programs as Word to select files with certain characteristics and print one document for them and another type document for those without those characteristics

- Advertising and marketing research

You can use established databases to read in a set of names and addresses to use with your own letter or form. Commands such as Create Merge File (found in Word) allow you to export this information in a quick and useful way.

In addition to simple data fields, you can do some conditional logic in Word with commands like ‹‹if...›› and ‹‹then...›› embedded in the text.

You are by no means limited to print merging only letters. You can use this feature for documents, such as direct mail advertisements where certain factors are varied to see their effects, or contracts with client-dependent clauses.

6
Word
Processors

Sorting

Although sorting is a sophisticated feature of databases (see Chapter 8), most word processors offer simple sort functions.

With the Sort command, you can sort lists of items alphabetically or numerically, and some programs can sort in ascending and descending order.

In figure 6.33, you can see an unsorted and a sorted list in FullWrite. The Sort command (found on the Edit menu in FullWrite) sorts on the first character it encounters and "brings along" all the other information that goes with that word (such as the first name, in this case). With FullWrite, you can sort in alphabetical (the default) or numerical order and in ascending (the default) or descending order. FullWrite will sort paragraphs as well as as set of individual lines within a paragraph.

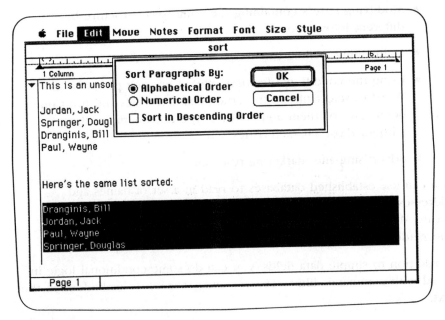

Fig. 6.33. *A simple sort using FullWrite.*

Using Glossaries

A glossary is a word processing feature that lets you store text or graphics, which you can then insert into a document with little effort. For example, you might store a stationery heading logo or a paragraph from a contract. Whenever you need the insert, you just go to the glossary and pick what you need.

Some word processors, like Word, automatically store the date as a glossary entry. To insert the date, you just click the glossary entry named "date."

For example, in figure 6.34, you can see the Glossary dialog window. To enter the date (as has been done in the upper left corner of this new document), you just double-click. What you see are the formats of the glossary entry for dates in the abbreviated, long, and short forms.

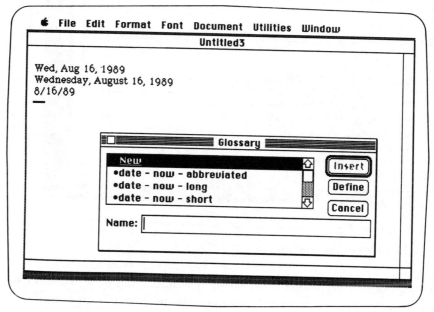

Fig. 6.34. *Word's Glossary window.*

You also can create your own glossary entry by highlighting the text or graphic, selecting the Glossary box, assigning the entry a name, and clicking the Define button. Next time you go to the Glossary box, the entry is there, ready to be double-clicked and inserted into your document.

Making Document Comparisons

Word comes with a nifty feature, called DocuComp (from Advanced Software) that compares two documents and produces a line-by-line comparison as shown in figure 6.35. The changes or differences are underlined.

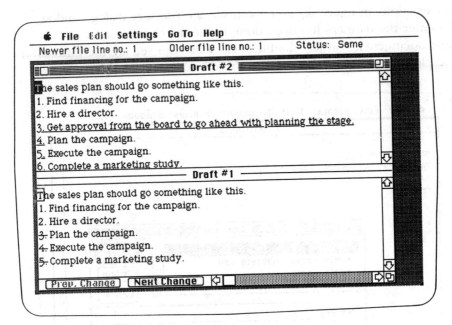

Fig. 6.35. *A DocuComp comparison.*

Although this utility comes with Word, it is not a part of Word and can be used to compare any two documents. DocuComp is a great tool when more than one person works on the same document and has comments. Then the final draft can be put together with each person's additions added.

If you do anything with direct mail, or if you send many letters and combine them with other information, you can't get along without this feature. Nisus has this same capability built into the program.

A more advanced comparison tool is MarkUp (from MainStay). With this "group editing" tool, several people can enter comments, strike outs, corrections, and annotation, and they can highlight text in the same document. MarkUp keeps a record of who does what and what changes were made. You can see in figure 6.36 the wide selection of tools that can be used.

MarkUp is an independent product that can be used with any document, including all the word processors discussed in this chapter.

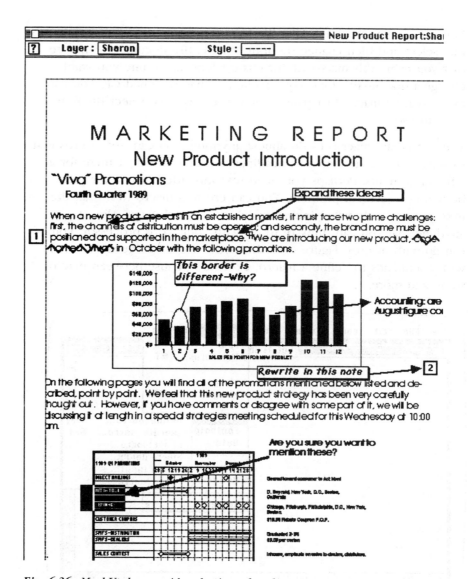

Fig. 6.36. *MarkUp has a wide selection of tools.*

6

Word
Processors

Understanding Macros

Some word processors (Nisus, Word, WordPerfect) have macro
features, which many users believe is the most useful feature. A macro
is a set of stored keystrokes that acts just like a tape recorder. You
record what you want the macro to do, and then you can play the
macro back.

You can, for example, tell WordPerfect to memorize a set of keystrokes that select and then change the font of an entire document. Suppose that you name this macro CF for change font. Each time you want to change a document's font, you invoke the macro named CF. You can even create a macro that pauses for you to insert or select the font you want to use.

You can create macros to do almost anything. You can use macros first to select all your document's headings and then to select them for a table of contents. Perhaps you need text formatted just so for your paste-up project. No problem. You can create a macro to format the text into two columns 2 inches wide on an 8-inch page. Almost anything that you can think of to do with your word processor, you can do with macros. Figure 6.37 shows the WordPerfect Macro menu with commands to define a macro, execute it, pause between macro steps, and more.

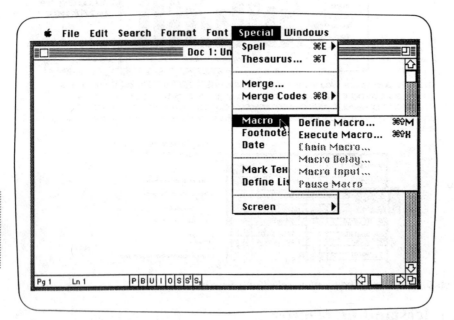

Fig. 6.37. WordPerfect's Macro menu.

Not all word processors come with macro features, and some (like Works) have add-on utilities (like WorksPlus) that can be purchased. WordPerfect and Nisus, for example, have built-in macro functions, and

Word has an add-on INIT called AutoMac III 2.1 (from Genesis Micro Software). When you install AutoMac, you see a small tape-cassette icon on your screen, which indicates that the utility is active and ready to record your keystrokes. AutoMac comes with Word, but can also be used with any other Mac application.

Another easy-to-use and popular macro program is QuicKeys (from CE Software). You install this utility in your System folder. QuicKeys provides tremendous flexibility in the design and use of macros. Part of its ease of use lies in the Define menu, which contains commands for defining keystrokes, such as mouse movement, sequences of keystrokes, date and time operations, and FKEYS. Among the special commands are shut down, choose second window, read keys from disk, and more.

One of the most attractive features of macro generators, such as QuicKeys, is that you can do just about anything you can imagine in designing and executing macros. QuicKeys is a keyboard enhancer program that you can purchase to enable you to take advantage of the many option keys on your keyboard. (See Chapter 14 for a more complete discussion of keyboard enhancers.)

But the winner is this category is Nisus, which comes with a library of already written macros. All ready to go, they can make your word processing life easier by doing such things as

- Count paragraphs
- Count sentences
- Search for phone numbers
- Remove blank lines
- Select last two lines of a paragraph
- Insert "smart quotes" (the curvy kind, not the straight ones) plus much more.

Creating Tables of Contents and Indexes

It is a great time-saver when a word processor can generate a table of contents or an index, which all the word processors except WriteNow and MacWrite can do.

6
Word
Processors

To create a table of contents or index, you mark the text that you want to be included and then tell the word processor what level of entry for a table of contents or what type of index entry you want. Once you do this for all the text you want entered, you generate the table of contents and it is placed at the beginning of your document.

Figure 6.38 shows some text marked with Word .c. header codes to show the level of headline entry in the table of contents. Figure 6.39 shows the table of contents that Word generated. In Word, you can designate up to nine levels of entries. In WordPerfect, you select the text and use the Mark Text command to assign it to a table of contents or an index. This process is a bit less cumbersome than Word's.

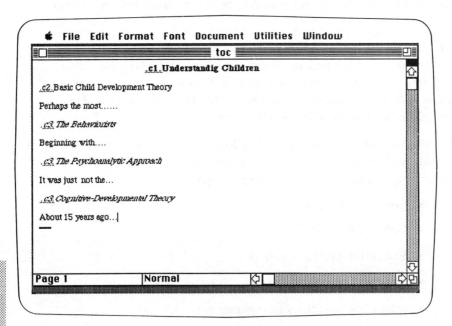

***Fig. 6.38.** Marking text for a table of contents in Word.*

You will notice that all the page numbers for this sample table of contents are 1s. This is because all the headings appeared on page 1.

Want to speed things up? You can create a macro that automatically marks your text for a specific table of contents level (such as 1, 2, or 3).

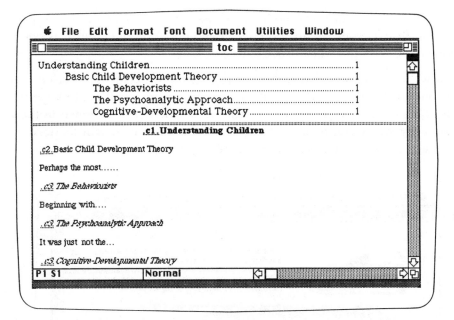

Fig. 6.39. *A Word table of contents.*

Using Graphics

It was only a matter of time until graphics became integrated with word processing. Now many desktop publishing programs, such as QuarkXPress and PageMaker, offer both. The stand-alone graphics packages and word processors, however, do these tasks better.

For the most part, you can create a graphic by using one of the many available paint programs, and then insert it into an already existing document. You can then use the cut, copy, and paste operations quite effectively.

Graphics are inserted just like any other piece of information that is cut or copied from another source. You simply cut or copy the graphic from its home location, go to the document in which you want to insert the graphic, and then paste it. If you do much cutting and pasting of graphics, you will find that DAs, such as SmartScrap, the Clipper, and the Curator, will be a tremendous help in allowing you to view things before they are pasted.

SuperPaint 2.1, which is a modified version of SuperPaint 2.0 (from Silicon Beach) comes with Word as an additional product, but it is not integrated with the word processor.

FullWrite includes a draw feature as part of the program. You create graphics using the toolkit, and then you place your graphic into your document. Figure 6.40 shows a picture of a shoe that was drawn in the picture window and then used in a FullWrite document. WordPerfect 2.0 also comes with an integrated graphics package.

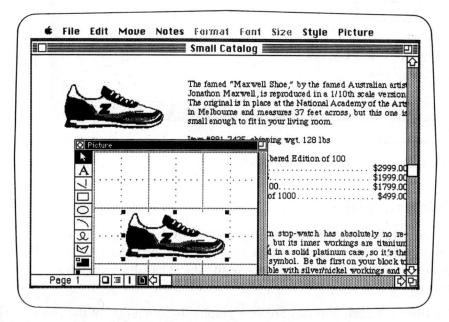

Fig. 6.40. *Integrating text and graphics with FullWrite.*

Assessing Word Processor Compatibility

Suppose that you create a document at home in Microsoft Word 4.0, and then you want to use WordPerfect to work on it at the office. What are your options? The comparison chart in figure 6.41 shows you which word processors are compatible, but don't get carried away. For the most part, no word processor can perfectly reproduce all the options that others can create. The routines used to create these marvelous writing tools are too complex to be easily and successfully shared.

	FullWrite	MacWrite	Nisus	Word	WordPerfect	WriteNow
Version	1.1	II	1.00	4.00	1.0.2	2.00
Document Size Limit	Disk space limits	Disk space limits	RAM limits	Disk space limits	Memory dependent	Disk space limits
Memory Required	1M	512K	1M	512K	600K	Min 200K (Rec 400K)
Size of Basic Application	750k	78K	540K	350K	317K	102K
Suggested Retail Price	$395	$125	$395	$395	$395	$195
Street Price	$269	$99	$255	$255	$185	$109
Characters and Fonts						
Condensed	yes	no	yes	yes	yes	yes
Extended	yes	no	yes	yes	yes	yes
Largest Font Size		500 pt		127 pt	127 pt	127 pt
Small Caps	yes	no	yes	yes	no	Case change
Smallest Font Size		9 pt		2 pt	1 pt	4 pt
Strike-Through	yes	yes	yes	yes	yes	no
Subscript	yes	yes	yes	yes	yes	yes
Superscript	yes	yes	yes	yes	yes	yes
Files It Can Read						
MacWrite	yes	yes	yes	yes	yes	yes
Microsoft Word	yes	no	yes	yes	yes 3.0	yes
Text Only	yes	yes	yes	yes	yes	yes
Text with Line Breaks	yes	yes	yes	yes	yes	yes
Files It Can Write						
MacWrite	yes	yes	yes	yes	no	no
Microsoft Word	no	yes	yes	yes	yes 3.0	yes
Text Only	yes	yes	yes	yes	yes	yes
Text with Line Breaks	yes	no	yes	yes	no	yes
Pages						
Automatic Repagination	yes	yes	yes	no	yes	yes
Insert Page Breaks	yes	yes	yes	yes	yes	yes
Page Preview	yes	no	yes	yes	yes	no
See Page Breaks	yes	yes	yes	yes	yes	yes
Rulers						
Measures (e.g. pica, in., etc.)	pica, pt., cm., in.	pica, pt., cm.	pica, pt., cm.	pica, pt., cm.	in., cm., pt.	in., cm.
Windows						
Maximum Number of Open Windows	RAM limit	7	RAM limit	22.00	RAM limit	RAM limit
Multiple Windows to a Document	yes	no	yes	yes	no	no
Split Window	yes	no	yes	yes	no	no
Tiling of Windows	yes	no	yes	yes	no	no
Zoom Window	yes	no	yes	yes	In page preview	yes
Searching						
Glossary or Library	yes	no	yes	yes	no	no
Go to Page	yes	yes	yes	yes	no	no
Search and Replace by Attribute	yes	no	yes	no	yes	yes
Search by Block	yes	no	yes	yes	yes	no
Search by Reveal/Hidden Code	yes	no	yes	yes	no	no
Search by Wild Card	yes	no	yes	yes	yes	yes
Wild Card Find	yes	no	yes	yes	yes	yes
Footnotes						
At End of Page	yes	yes	no	yes	yes	
At End of Document	yes	yes	no	yes	yes	yes
Automatic Numbering	yes	yes	no	yes	yes	yes
Formatting						
Alter Default Format	yes	yes	yes	yes	yes	yes
Change Case	yes	no	yes	yes	yes	yes
Copy Paragraph Formats	yes	yes	yes	yes	yes	yes
Global Change Size/Style	yes	yes	yes	yes	yes	yes
Page No., Time/Date Stamps		In headers/footers		Anywhere	Anywhere	Anywhere
Style Sheets	yes	no	no	yes	no	no
Max. No. of Columns	16	1	8	100	24	4

Fig. 6.41. *A comparison chart of popular word processors.*

	FullWrite	MacWrite	Nisus	Word	WordPerfect	WriteNow
Graphics						
Create Sidebars	yes	no	no	no	no	no
Export Graphics	yes	no	yes		no	
Graphics Tools	yes	no	yes	yes	no	no
Import via Clipboard	yes	yes	yes	yes	yes	yes
Max. Size of Header/Footer (% of Page)	100%	33%	100%	100%	100%	25%
Odd/Even Pages Options	yes	no	yes	yes	yes	yes
Runarounds	yes		yes	no	no	In 90 deg. increments
Page Layout Features						
Kerning	yes	no	no	no	yes	no
Leading	yes	yes	yes	1-432 pts	1-127 pts	1-99 pts
Maximum Number of Columns	16	1	8	100	24	4
Tracking	yes	no	yes	yes	no	no
Variable Width	no	n/a	no	no	yes	no
Spelling Help						
Number of Root Words in Thesaurus	220,000	10,000	40,000	10,000	10,000	10,000
Number of Words in Dictionary	100,000	100,000	80,000	130,000	115,000	110,000
Spelling Checker	yes	yes	yes	yes	yes	yes
Other Features						
Attach Notes	yes	no	yes	no	no	no
Automatic Counting of Words, Lines, etc.	yes	no	yes	no	yes	yes
Automatic Hyphenaton	yes	no	no	yes	yes	no
Glossary	yes	no	yes	yes	yes	no
Index Generation	yes	no	yes	yes	yes	no
Levels of Undo	1	1	Unlimited	1	1	1
Macro Editor	no	no	yes	no	no	no
Macros	no	no	yes	no	yes	no
Mail Merge	yes	yes	no	yes	yes	yes
Math	no	no	no	yes	no	no
Math Characters and Equation Generation	no	no	no	yes	no	no
MultiFinder Compatible	yes	yes	yes	yes	yes	yes
On-line Help	yes	yes	yes	yes	yes	no
Outlining	yes	no	no	yes	yes	nno
Show Nonprinting Characters	yes	no	yes	yes	yes	yes
Sorting	yes	no	yes	yes	no	no
Table of Contents Generation	yes	no	yes	yes	yes	no
Revision Marking	yes	no	no	no	yes	no
Style Sheets	yes	yes	no	yes	With macros	Equivalent

Fig. 6.41. *A comparison chart of popular word processors.*

The best way to transfer text from one word processor to another is by using the Text Format command available in all the word processors discussed here. The Text, or ASCII, command translates characters into their original values and completely removes all the fancies that you may have inserted, such as page breaks, font styles, special codes, and so on. ASCII (American Standard Code for Information Interchange) is a code that represents the most basic format for transmitting information. You get what's important, but you also lose a good deal of work that you may have invested in formatting the document.

Some word processors can save in other formats as well. Word, for example, can save in RTF (Rich Text Formatting) format, which preserves many of the control codes for formatting and such. The question is, how well will other applications accept and incorporate this kind of format so that sharing becomes easier? What if the word processor that you are using cannot read the text you are importing? You will probably get a message telling you that the file is in an unreadable format. This problem will rarely happen when you are reading a text file, but will, for example, if you try to use WordPerfect to read a Word file. WordPerfect has just not yet caught up with some of the other word processors, which can import and export much more easily. Perhaps Version 2.0 will be able to do some of these things.

Use the Word File Format options shown in figure 6.42 to save your file as a text-only file. Unless you use RTF, text files are saved without their control or formatting codes, so anything fancy (such as underlining and bold) will not transfer (a good reason to keep a hard copy of your work). But your text will be intact, and you can go from there.

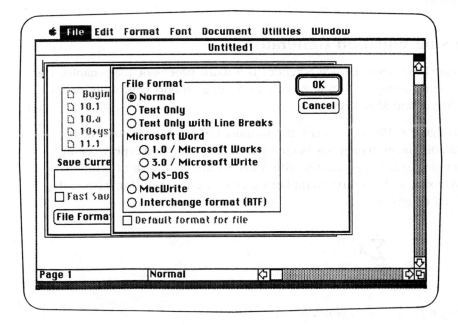

Fig. 6.42. *Word File format options.*

Various options are usually available for file conversion. The Text Only command saves the file to a standard ASCII text file, and the text is considered one line until the program encounters the Return key character. The Text Only with Line Breaks option inserts a Return character at every place that the text wraps (meets the right margin) in the original document.

Some programs, such as Word and WriteNow (Version 2.0) can save files in Rich Text Format (RTF). This capability means that other programs can read these files without losing any of the formatting codes and characteristics. If you have to "split" word processors at home and the office, you may want to look for this feature.

Using Specialized Word Processors

Any of the word processors discussed in this chapter can probably meet most of your needs. You may, however, need special capabilities these programs don't have. There are several special-function word processors available that may take care of the problem. These are not full-fledged word processors in the same sense as the ones already discussed.

Using Equation Generators

MathType (from Design Science) is a word processor that enables you to enter complex formulas without fooling around with fonts or the Option and Shift keys.

In figure 6.43, you can see the formula for the computation of the sample mean, which has been entered into the MathType working window. MathType comes with a macro utility, a strip of often-used symbols, and over 100 templates that you can set up for frequently used equations.

$$\bar{X} = \frac{\sum_{i=1}^{n} X_i}{n}$$

Fig. 6.43. A formula generated with MathType.

This program is easy to use and is handy if you need to incorporate mathematical expressions into your documents. MathType can run as either a DA or an application, and it provides on-line help and keyboard and mouse access to all symbols. Expressionist (from Allan Bonadio Associates) is another equation generator that works with virtually any Macintosh word processor.

Both MathType (as an application) and Expressionist (as an independent DA and an application) are useful and easy to use as word processors to generate mathematical and scientific symbols. They are both good deals, but Expressionist is smaller (only about 100K compared to about 200K) and has an easier-to-use interface and more logically arranged symbols. Expressionist has a Change button represented by a Yin Yang symbol, that allows you to change the structure of a formula quickly and a convert-to-text feature that enables you to switch from Expressionist to a word processing format.

Using Desk Accessories

With a word processing desk accessory (DA), you can edit a document without actually working within the application in which the document was created.

Vantage (from Preferred Publishers) is perhaps the most comprehensive of these DAs. It is a desk accessory that allows you to access and manipulate text created with other applications, and it contains a dictionary, macro capability, an undo command, an icon grabber that allows you to capture icons and move them to the Clipboard, and more. In addition, you can open up to 16 windows simultaneously, sort, reverse the order of lines, form paragraphs, and convert spaces to tabs; the feature list goes on and on.

Vantage can be used in conjunction with mainframe computers, so you can dial your local Cray Computer, download a file to work on, and remain on-line with the Cray.

Vantage uses more than 130K, which is a great deal for a DA, and is fairly expensive for a desk accessory ($99.95), but the program offers many features.

6
Word
Processors

ExpressWrite (from Exodus) is a DA that is particularly well suited for letters and correspondence. It uses about 113K. In fact, as you can see on the opening screen shown in figure 6.44, there is even an envelope icon to place text into the correct position for printing. Although ExpressWrite is not a full-fledged word processor, it has features (such as the envelope printer) that make it quite handy.

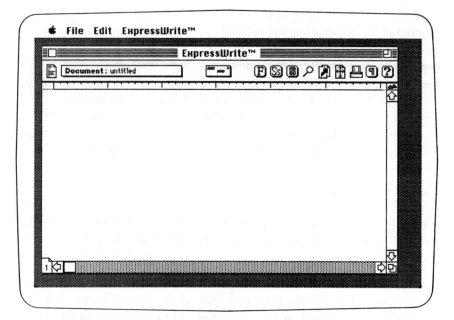

Fig. 6.44. The ExpressWrite DA has an envelope icon to help you place your text correctly.

Using Guide

A word processor in a class by itself because there aren't any others like it available, is Guide from Owl International.

Guide is a HyperText application, that, much like HyperCard, allows you to relate text-based ideas to one another.

You use Guide much like your everyday word processor. But that's where the similarity ends. Guide allows you to create "hot spots" that are linked to other text or graphics in the same or in another document.

Suppose that you are preparing an on-screen document for people to read to find out about your company. Using a HyperText application, you could identify a series of words or phrases that are "hot," such as profits, plant location, and so forth. If the user double-clicks "plant locations," a map of all plant locations appears on the screen. Once any one point on the map is clicked, a nice picture of the plant and a drawing of the interior is displayed. At any time, the user can return to the report. Guide is not relational in the sense that when one document is changed the ones that are related to it are changed as well. Documents are linked but aren't members of the same family.

Guide takes some getting used to, and it is intended for the person who wants to explore relational word processing and idea development.

Choosing a Word Processor

The comparison chart shown in figure 6.41 will help you to see the comparative advantages and disadvantages of the various programs.

When you're ready to buy a word processor, you should keep the following points in mind:

- If at all possible, try the package before you buy it. See whether your local dealer has different packages, or perhaps your local user group can help. The T/Maker company includes a sample copy of WriteNow with each full copy of the program, so you can ask a friend or a dealer for a copy of the sample to help you decide.

- Know what you need before you start looking. Use the comparison chart presented in this chapter so that you will be looking for only those programs that fit your needs. Don't pay for those "bells and whistles" that you will never use.

- Read reviews of the different word processors in the popular magazines to learn what others think about a particular package.

- Be sure to consider such factors as how easy the program is to use and the amount of memory it requires (FullWrite takes almost 1M versus WriteNow which takes 102K).

- Keep in mind that there are integrated packages, notably Microsoft Works, that include a word processor, a spreadsheet, a database, and communications software, all at a relatively low price. The word processors included in the integrated packages may not have the power of the high-end programs, but one of them may certainly fit your needs.

Finally, keep in mind what you already know. If you are a WordPerfect user on a DOS machine, then maybe you should consider WordPerfect for the Mac. The same goes for Word. Besides being familiar with the

6
Word
Processors

general command structure, you will also find that most Macintosh word processors have easy-to-use transfer utilities so that you can go from Mac to DOS and back again.

The Big Mac Recommendation

Do you want to write a memo? Or a letter to the Editor? How about some haiku? Any of the word processors discussed in this chapter will do just fine for short documents, including letters and simple reports.

If you are a recent convert from an MS-DOS system and you are used to Microsoft Word, for example, then you may want to use Word for the Mac because the transfer will be easy and so many of the commands will be familiar.

If you are used to WordPerfect DOS, you may want to switch to WordPerfect Mac. WordPerfect's toll-free number and excellent support is always a big plus.

Although FullWrite offers tremendous built-in graphics capability and some exciting desktop publishing tools, its size can be daunting, and the program often is very slow, especially if you are limited to 1 megabyte of RAM. Ashton-Tate offers 90 days free support; thereafter you must pay for additional support at sizable additional expense.

Although Nisus has much to offer, it is relatively new program, and it is fairly expensive ($395). It is a good word processor and should be considered if you need a full-featured word processor.

MacWrite II and WriteNow are more reasonably priced programs. They are quite acceptable, and they are especially easy to learn. Both of these programs are good middle-of-the-road choices.

CHAPTER 7

Electronic Ledgers: Working with Spreadsheets

Imagine the "old days." You work for an accounting firm and it's time to balance the books. You take out your trusty 16-column pad and your number 2 pencils, roll up your sleeves, adjust your visor, and start the tedious task of balancing the books. Five hours later, when the numbers don't quite agree, you're still adding this column to that, trying to find your error.

These days, no business, whether a small "mom and pop" kite shop or a multinational heavy equipment manufacturer, does its bookkeeping, invoicing, and inventory tracking without the help of computers. In many, if not most, businesses, the tool of choice (after a word processor) is a spreadsheet, which is a kind of electronic ledger used to help manage and organize information and to generate graphical representation of that data.

In this chapter, you will learn what spreadsheets are and how they work; what some of their special features are, including functions, formulas, and graphing; and where you can buy one if you are interested.

What Is a Spreadsheet?

A spreadsheet is an electronic ledger with which you organize information into worksheets that consist of rows and columns. A spreadsheet is the actual application program, such as Wingz or Excel, and a worksheet is the file or document that you prepare with a spreadsheet. Just as you do with other Macintosh applications, you can create a worksheet and then save it for later editing or output. A

289

spreadsheet program consists basically of four components: a worksheet, graphics features, a database, and macros.

The worksheet enables you to work with and manipulate numbers and text by providing you with a "grid" of rows and columns. You can enter numbers or text into the intersections of these rows and columns (called cells) and then perform a variety of operations on the information, such as sorting, mathematical calculations, and more. The graphics feature enables you to represent numerical data in the form of a chart or graph, and the best spreadsheet programs have graphing capability that rivals the best graphics programs. The most popular programs offer, for example, pie, line, area, column, and bar graphs, among others. The database component of a spreadsheet allows you to organize data in the form of records and then use the information in the records to search for and select particular records, based on the information they contain. Macros work with spreadsheets as they do with word processors: they automate keystroke and mouse operations. By using macros, you can do things such as open a worksheet, go to a specific location, enter a particular formula, reformat the worksheet, and then exit the spreadsheet.

What Spreadsheets Do

Although word processing programs are the most frequently used applications, spreadsheets are almost irreplaceable to the business community. Just some of the reasons for this popularity can be seen in what spreadsheets can do. Among the many uses of a spreadsheet program are the following:

- Create a monthly budget for all your income and expenses and then compute the difference between the two values, as shown in figure 7.1

- Perform what-if calculations to test numerical hypotheses and do break-even calculations

- Use the built-in functions to figure the monthly principal and interest payments on a loan

- Produce graphs (even three-dimensional with some spreadsheets), such as a graph of employee ownership as a function of years on the job, as shown in figure 7.2

 File   Edit   Formula   Format   Data   Options   Macro   Window

C18

	A	B	C	D	E
1	Budget for July, 1989				
2					
3	Category	Budgeted	Spent	Difference	
4	Rent	$350	$350	$0	
5	Food	$400	$389	$11	
6	Entertainment	$100	$131	($31)	
7	Car	$350	$341	$9	
8	Insurance	$37	$37	$0	
9	Misc	$150	$179	($29)	
10					
11	Total	$500	$529	($29)	
12					
13					
14					
15					
16					
17					
18					

Ready

Fig. 7.1. *A monthly budget with actual and budgeted amounts.*

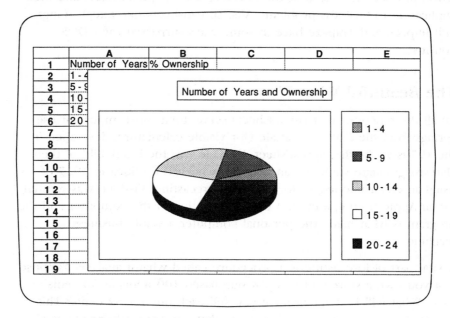

Fig. 7.2. *A three-dimensional graph.*

7
Spread-
sheets

- Create a database of clients and search through the file to find names of those who have an interest in a new product

- Design organizational charts that relate different levels of a structure (and people) to one another

- Make gridlike sheets that take advantage of the horizontal and vertical lines for the preparation of tables and schedules

All these possibilities and more, and the spreadsheet is as easy to work with as any other Mac application.

Spreadsheets are fast and extremely reliable. They do not make mistakes and are perfect for the person who has always been afraid of math, yet needs to work with large sets of numbers. In fact, spreadsheets are perfect for people who are hesitant to tackle big number jobs. Spreadsheets are logically organized and will give you the wrong results only if you give them the wrong information.

Mac spreadsheets are especially nice because they take advantage of Macintosh's friendly graphical interface and use the mouse to help speed up your work and increase your efficiency. Although the IBM world has been far ahead in the development of spreadsheets and their application to business problems, Mac spreadsheets like Excel, Wingz, Full Impact, and Trapeze have in some ways surpassed their DOS cousins.

The Beautiful What If

Of all the functions that spreadsheets serve, their most important use springs from the days of VisiCalc (for visible calculator), developed in the 1970s as the first spreadsheet. VisiCalc was the brainchild of then Harvard graduate student Dan Bricklin, who had the idea in 1977 of using an electronic ledger for business forecasting. VisiCalc was written for an Apple II computer, and the combination of the computer and the program is what made the personal computer a viable business machine.

A vital part of forecasting is a procedure called what-if analysis. Suppose that you own a store and you just purchased 100 items at 50 cents each. What will be your profit if you sell each one for 52 cents? This example is an easy one, right? Imagine that you have 300 products to sell at prices that vary according to season and the number of each product that you purchase, and that you also must figure in tax rates and other variables. A spreadsheet can assign values to each variable and be set up in such a way that any one variable can be changed and you see the effects of that change on all variables. Calculations become easy and neat.

The power in a spreadsheet program lies in its capability to recalculate all entries when only one entry is changed. You can have the spreadsheet do it manually (when you indicate) or automatically (each time the spreadsheet is updated). This capability means that you can look at the effects on several different variables when you change only one. This power applies to the change of one number in a simple list and the effect it has on the total, as well as to a large spreadsheet that contains hundreds of variables all dependent on one another. In both cases, the power of the spreadsheet is easy to see because the spreadsheet saves endless hours recalculating values.

Suppose that you have a spreadsheet of thousands of cells. You change one (critical) value. All the other values are adjusted automatically to conform to the change. You can see that a spreadsheet can save you many hours of work.

Using Worksheets

To show you some of the ins and outs of a spreadsheet, let's use the leading Macintosh spreadsheet, Excel, to create a simple loan analysis, as shown in figure 7.3.

Any loan analysis takes into account the amount of money being borrowed, the interest rate, and the period of time for which the money is loaned. In figure 7.3, you can see how the *monthly* payment (which is why interest is divided by 12) is calculated using one of Excel's financial functions (shown in the formula bar at the top of the spreadsheet), which are predesigned computation tools in which you substitute certain values in the equation. Here, the interest rate, number of months of the loan, and the amount borrowed are entered in columns called Interest Rate, Period, and Value, respectively. The formula determines the amounts of the payments (parentheses usually mean a negative number because a payment is a negative transaction). You can see that as the period of the loan changes (the number of months decreases), the payment increases.

7
Spread-
sheets

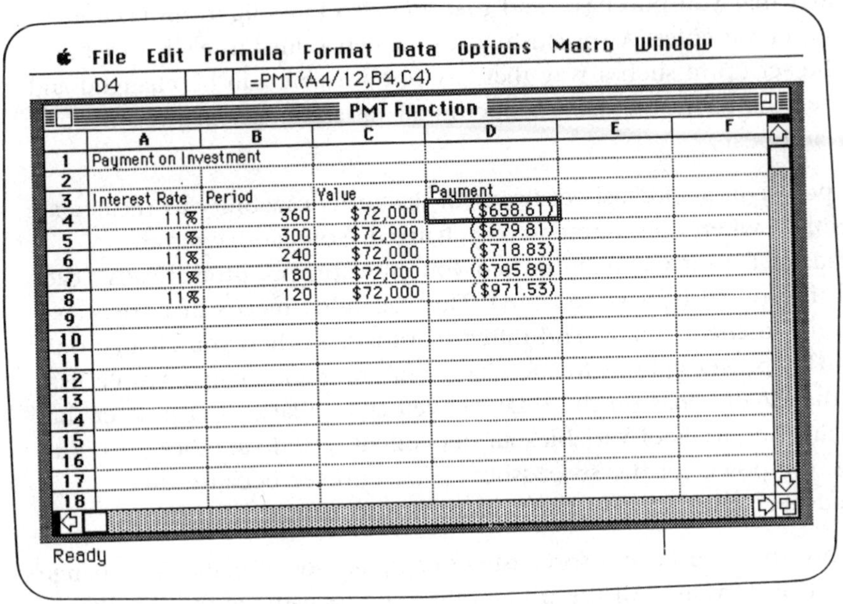

Fig. 7.3. *Using a spreadsheet for loan analysis.*

This example uses the what-if capabilities of Excel to manipulate one factor and see the results immediately. This capability is not magic, just a terrific tool.

Understanding the Worksheet Screen

A blank worksheet, like the Excel worksheet you see in figure 7.4, consists of many separate features.

The most obvious component of any worksheet is the large number of squares, or *cells*, making up the grid. The grid is composed of rows, designated by numbers, and columns, designated by letters of the alphabet. Each cell has an address, which is determined by intersection of a row and a column. These rows and columns also have headings. In figure 7.3, you can see how the cell address B4 (representing column B and row 4) holds the value 360.

Different spreadsheet programs hold different numbers of cells. For example, an Excel 2.2 worksheet can contain as many as 16,384 rows and 256 columns (for a total of 4,194,304 cells), and Informix's Wingz 1.0 can contain up to 32,768 rows and 32,768 columns for a total of

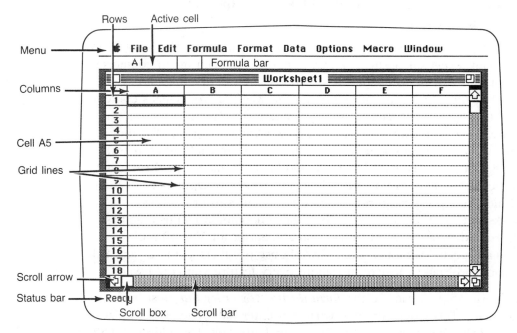

Fig. 7.4. *An Excel opening worksheet screen.*

more than one billion (that's a thousand million) cells. Impressed by the size of these spreadsheets? Don't be. Your Mac isn't large (or smart) enough right now to handle a worksheet with so many cells anyway, but Wingz does portend what the future may be bringing.

There are some real advantages of large worksheets, but some disadvantages as well. On the plus side, you can contain whole units of information on one sheet, such as a month's schedule or a year's budget. This capability saves you the work of going other places to find information. Large worksheets also have some significant disadvantages, however. First, the larger a worksheet gets, the more slowly it performs calculations. You cannot see the difference between a worksheet with 10 rows and 10 columns and one with 20 rows and 20 columns, but you can see a difference if the larger worksheet has 100 rows and 100 columns and continues to get bigger. Navigating a large worksheet can be trying for the beginner, and probably you will see a reduction in calculating speed as a spreadsheet grows larger, especially if you have many formulas and calculations to do. Spreadsheets are smart programs, however, and in general can handle large amounts of data. Large

7
Spread-
sheets

worksheets seem easier to work with as your experience and confidence increases.

You will notice the usual menu names across the top of the window in the blank Excel spreadsheet shown in figure 7.4. Each menu contains commands that perform specific functions, such as opening and saving files (on the File menu) and changing the way the worksheet's contents look (on the Format menu). If you compare this menu to the one in figure 7.5, which shows a blank Wingz worksheet, you see that they have some things in common, yet they differ from each other as well. For example, the File, Edit, Format, and Window menus perform many of the same functions you read about in Chapter 6. Options is a catch-all menu for everything from displaying formulas to protecting worksheets from outside eyes. The other uncommon menus (such as Macro and Data for Excel, and Graph and Script for Wingz) are product-specific, although such powerhouse products as these (and Full Impact and Trapeze) share just about every feature you could want.

In figure 7.5, you can see the *formula bar* (or *entry bar*) just below the menu. This space is where what you enter data. The entry is placed in the cell when you press the Return or Enter key. The address for the active cell (or the intersection of a row and a column) such as A56 or BC231 always shows in the left side of the formula bar. The active cell is the one that is selected. As you will see elsewhere in this chapter, you can select one cell or a group of cells (called a *range* of cells). You will also notice the check and the X boxes on the formula bar. The X box can be clicked to cancel any entry before it is entered, and the check box can be clicked to enter data. Most spreadsheet programs also have some kind of protect mechanism that enables you to lock the values in a cell so that they cannot be inadvertently changed.

In figure 7.5, you see the Wingz opening screen; it has a more elaborate set of symbols on its formula bar than what you see in figure 7.4, which is the Excel opening screen. The program has operators ($=$, $+$, $-$, $*$, $/$, $) for doing arithmetic in the creation of formulas, as well as a navigation tool for moving around the worksheet quickly and easily. You will also notice the Tool Box, which is part of the Wingz opening screen. Excel has these tools, but they are often hidden within menus. I will talk about this subject more later in this chapter.

Another spreadsheet program that goes beyond just row and column headings on the opening screen is Full Impact (from Ashton-Tate). As

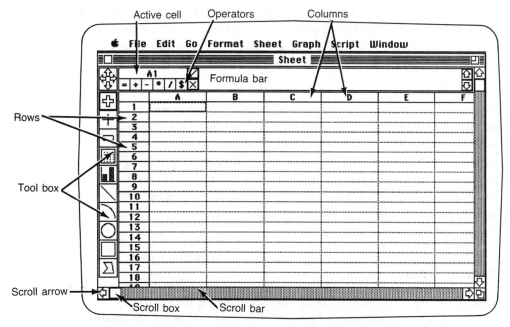

Fig. 7.5. *The Wingz opening screen with the Tool Box.*

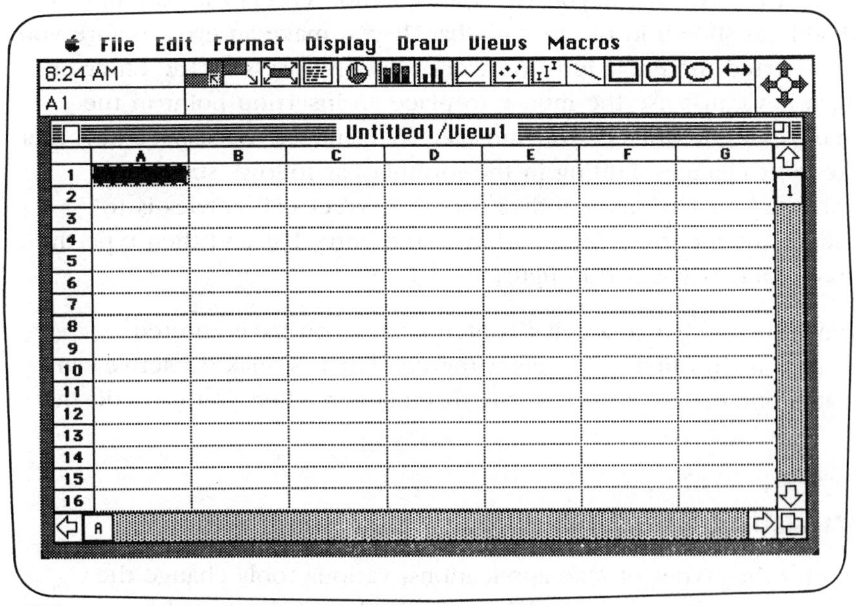

Fig. 7.6. *The Full Impact opening screen with the icon bar for creating graphs.*

7

Spread-sheets

you can see in figure 7.6, Full Impact has a row of icons across the top of the screen. (The spreadsheet actually has three rows of icons, but you can see only one at a time.) These icons can be modified to fit your particular needs. The icon bar shown in figure 7.6 is for the creation of graphs.

At the bottom of the screen, you see messages as you work. For example, when you first begin creating a worksheet, you may see the message Enter, indicating that the application is waiting for you to enter information. When you are editing a cell entry, the message may be Edit; and when you are creating a macro, the message may be Recording. The content of these messages depends, of course, on your specific application, but in general you can look to the lower left corner of the screen for some help.

Entering Data

Entering data into a worksheet is as easy as entering data into a document in a word processor. Just type the data and press the Return key, or move the mouse pointer to the next cell, or use one of the direction keys on the keyboard—each method enters the data into the cell address shown in the formula bar. If you make an error before you have inserted the entry into the worksheet (by pressing the Enter or Return key), just use the mouse to place an insertion point in the formula bar, and correct your mistake by using the Backspace key; then make your changes. Editing in the formula bar follows standard Macintosh conventions. Another way to correct cell entries is to highlight the incorrect information in the entry bar and then type the correct data, as you see in figure 7.7.

If you want to change a cell's contents after you have entered information, you first must select the cell (that is, make it active) so that its contents are shown in the formula bar. Then you can edit the cell.

Formatting Cell Contents

As with other types of Mac applications, various tools change the appearance of the information you are displaying. In spreadsheets, some of the changes you can make match the power and versatility of many word processors, where alignment, fonts, presence of grid lines, and

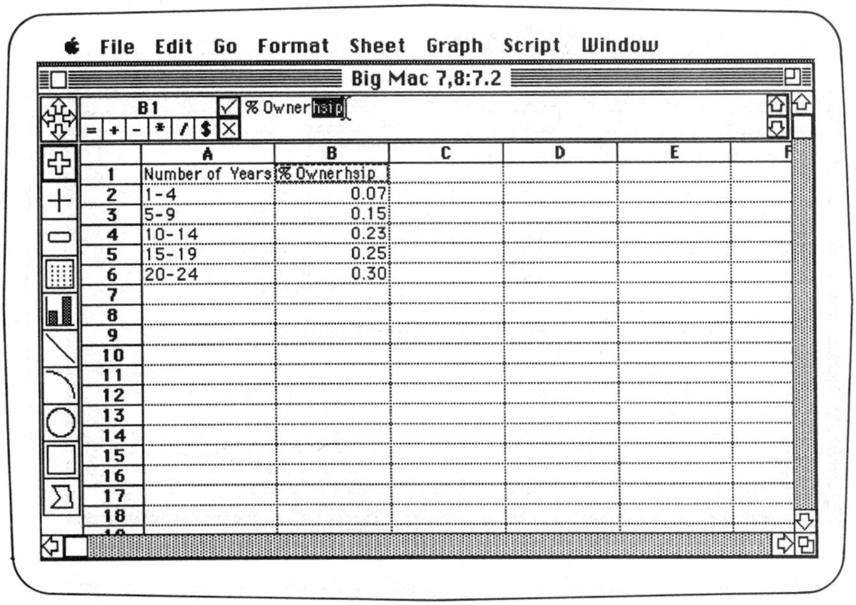

Fig. 7.7. Highlighting incorrect information to replace it.

more are under your control. Maybe that's why a good deal of spreadsheet work has nothing to do with numbers; worksheets are also used to construct charts (as was done with all the charts in this book). Spreadsheets provide the same types of formatting options as do word processors, and in some cases, you can do even more.

Aligning Cell Entries

You have great variety in the ways you choose to align cell contents. For example, in figure 7.8 you can see the dialog box Excel provides, with the five alignment choices; on the same screen, you can see how each choice appears. As with other Macintosh applications, you first highlight the cell entries you want aligned and then select the type of alignment you want under the appropriate menu. The Left, Right, and Center options do what they say. The default General option aligns text on the left margin and numbers on the right. The Fill option will repeat a value within a cell until it is full. If cells are blank to the right of the active cell and are also formatted by the Fill option, repetition continues in those cells. These formatting choices are specific to Excel 2.2; other spreadsheets have similar options.

7
Spread-
sheets

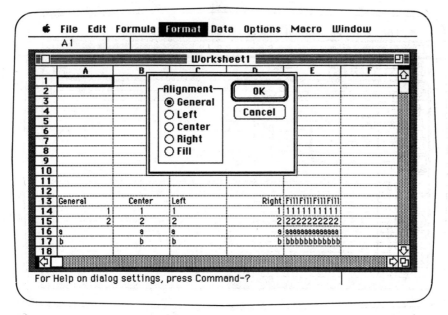

Fig. 7.8. *Excel's alignment options.*

You will find that column headings look best centered and that the General format option, which places text to the left and numbers to the right, will suit most of your needs—except when you have particular design requirements, such as using your worksheet to design an organizational chart in which you want all the text centered.

Formatting Numbers

Most spreadsheets offer a large variety of formats for numbers (such as $7,390.82, 7390, or $7,390), and not just in the way that the values appear in the worksheet but—just as important—in what the values represent. For example, in figure 7.9, you can see the Format menu from Wingz and the choices under the Numbers submenu. Figure 7.10 shows the Format Number dialog box in Excel.

Your choices on the Format Number menu range from straight Currency ($32,067) to D-Mon-YY (19-MAR-88) to a format you can custom define, such as 0003.26 or 3.26000-82 for special inventory or tracking purposes.

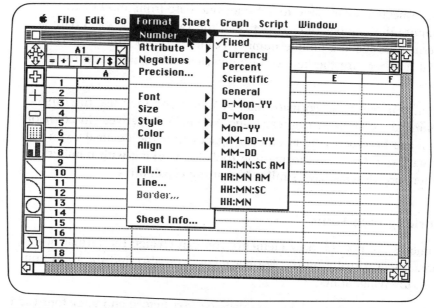

Fig. 7.9. *One set of formatting options for numbers.*

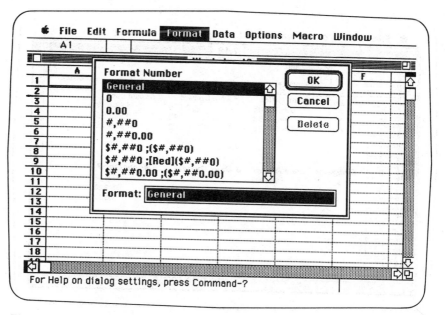

Fig. 7.10. *The Format Number dialog box in Excel.*

Spreadsheets also are able to subtract one date from another to compute the number of days between the two because each date is internally assigned a unique number (called a *serial number*). These serial numbers are the key to the numerical calculations regarding dates.

When you select the Format menu in Wingz and then use the other commands, such as Attributes (using commas), Negatives (in color or not), and Precision (the number of spaces after the decimal), you end up with some powerful formatting tools for working with numbers. Other spreadsheets have similar formatting capabilities.

Working with Fonts

Numbers are not the only elements you can change the format of in a spreadsheet. Usually on the Format menu, you also find the tools you need to change fonts.

For example, in figure 7.11, you can see text before and after font (and some other format) changes. The lower set of cells is in the New York

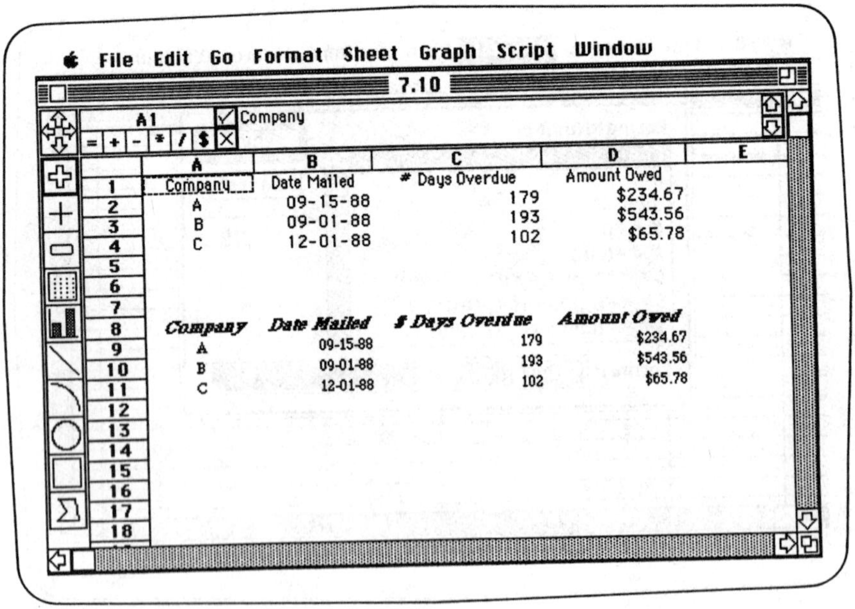

Fig. 7.11. Changing the style of text.

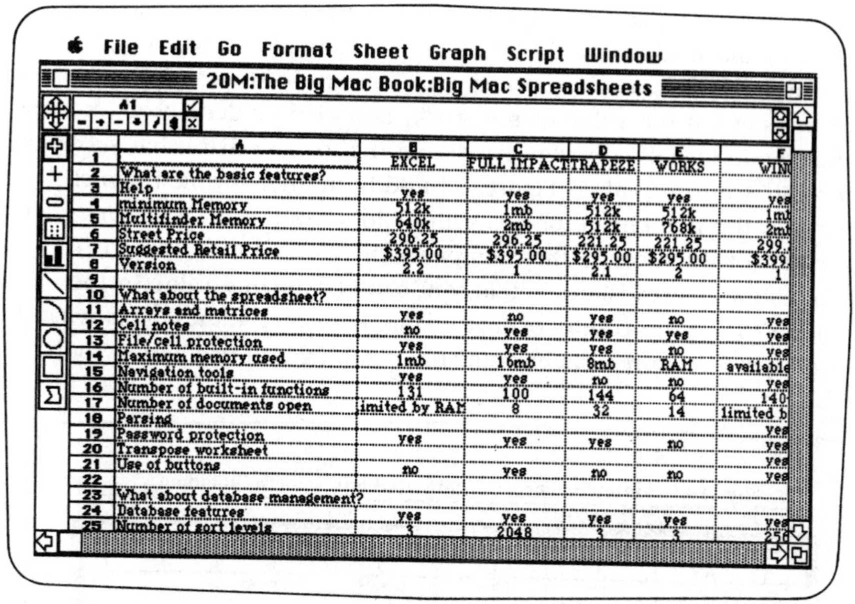

Fig. 7.12. Using Wingz to create a comparison chart.

font (selected from the Font command on the Format menu), with the headings centered and in bold italic. The last column was formatted by selecting the Currency option. You may also notice that the grid lines have been removed from the worksheet so that you can see the changes more clearly.

Figure 7.12 shows a spreadsheet comparison chart being created with Wingz.

Fonts are fun, but remember the old *font junk* from the last chapter on word processing. You can easily make the same mistake here. Use formatting changes for emphasis, but be careful not to overdo formatting. Visual disasters pop up all too often.

Using Formulas

Formulas (and functions, discussed elsewhere) are the true workhorses of any spreadsheet program. By using a formula, you can manipulate information to meet your specific needs.

7
Spread-
sheets

A formula is an equation you write; the formula contains various cell addresses and mathematical operators. For example, in figure 7.13, you can see the open and close prices for a variety of stocks. If you want to find the amount the value of the stock increased or decreased, you can use a simple formula (as you can see in the formula bar) that subtracts one value from the other. Figure 7.14 adds another formula, which computes the percentage of this gain or loss from the buying price and the result of the formula that computes the gain or loss. What is so useful about a spreadsheet is that you can change any value in the equation to see the results of that change on other values. This what-if capability makes spreadsheets valuable planning and prediction tools.

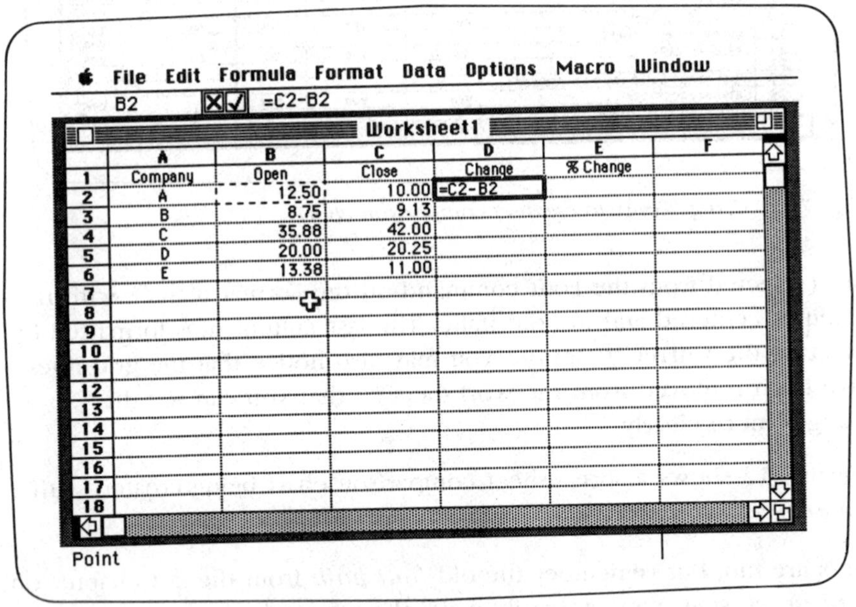

Fig. 7.13. A formula to find the change in stock prices.

Take a look at the formula in the formula bar in figure 7.14. First, Wingz "knows" that the entry is a formula because it begins with an equal sign. The formula then uses some cell addresses and performs a specific operation. In this case, the formula subtracts the value in cell B2 from the value in cell C2 and divides the result by the value in B2. Notice that the formula does not subtract the specific values (10 from 12.5) but works with any values in these cell addresses.

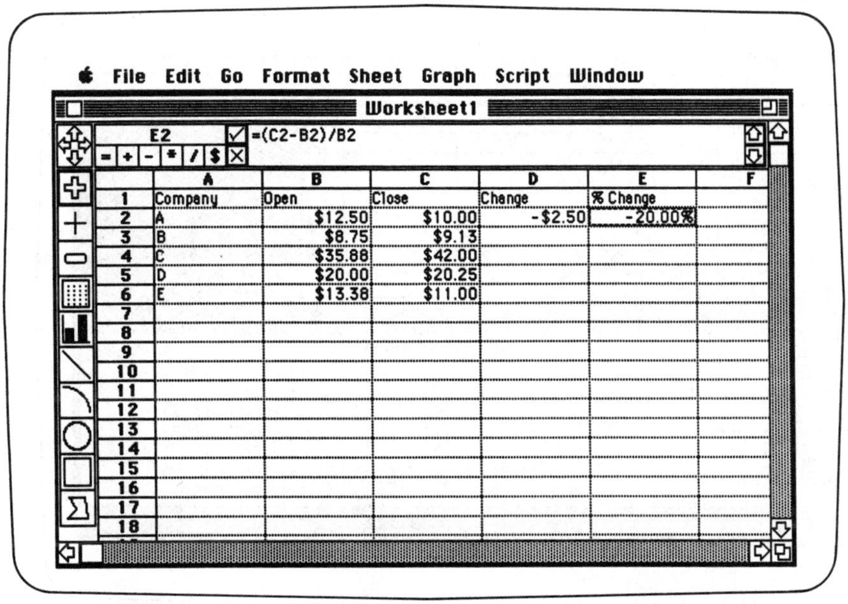
File Edit Go Format Sheet Graph Script Window
Worksheet1
E2
=(C2-B2)/B2
= + - * / $
A B C D E F
1 Company Open Close Change % Change
2 A $12.50 $10.00 -$2.50 -20.00%
3 B $8.75 $9.13
4 C $35.88 $42.00
5 D $20.00 $20.25
6 E $13.38 $11.00

Fig. 7.14. A formula to compute the percentage change in stock prices.

To give you an idea of what formulas can do, figure 7.15 shows you a set on an Excel worksheet used to compute various types of test scores. In this figure you see both the results of the formulas and the formulas in the cells themselves. Spreadsheets usually have an option for showing formulas, which in Excel is on the Options menu.

Entering Formulas

One convenient feature of many spreadsheets is that when you are writing a formula and want to refer to a particular cell address (such as C2 or B2), you just need to click that cell to enter the address in the formula. When using Excel, clicking another cell places the addition operator in the equation before it. An especially nice Wingz feature is that on the formula bar, you can click any one of the five mathematical operators (=, +, −, *, /) needed in your formula rather than having to use keyboard entries. Full Impact has a similar shortcut tool, which is displayed when you begin a cell entry with an equal sign, as you see in figure 7.16. Full Impact has an Undo command right on the worksheet. You also can see several statistical symbols representing summation and

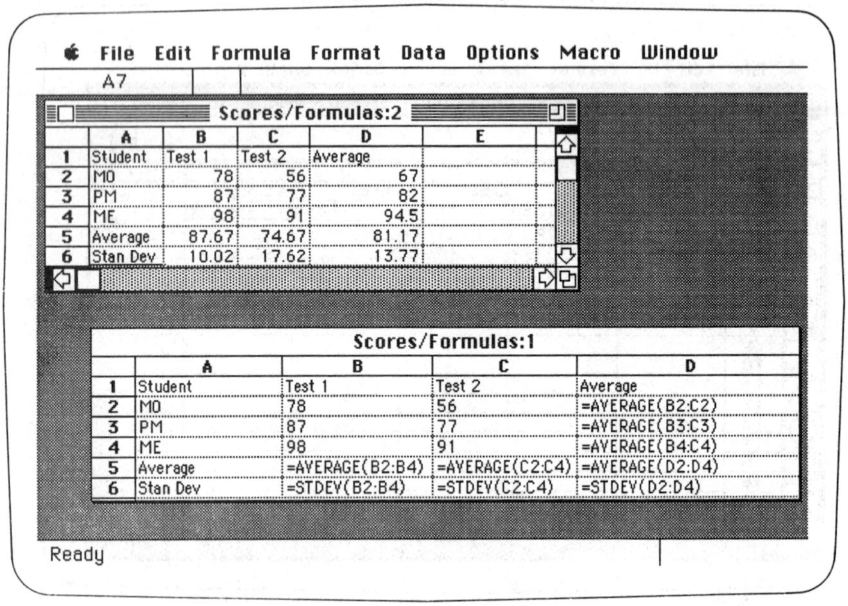

Fig. 7.15. The formulas used to make calculations.

square root operations, making Full Impact useful for complicated calculations.

You are almost unlimited in your options to use formulas. They can be simple or complex, depending on your purpose. You are however, limited in the size of the formula—usually no more than 255 characters in a formula—so you need to be creative and break apart very complex formulas so that they fit in the formula bar (entry box).

Copying Formulas

You have used a formula, as shown in figures 7.13 and 7.14, to compute a value and return that value to the cell address in which the formula is located. To finish the worksheet shown in figure 7.14, the values in the rest of columns D and E need to be computed.

One way to perform this computation is to enter the formulas into every cell in these columns. Another way is to highlight the column and use Copy Down or Copy Right (sometimes called Fill Down and Fill Right) to copy the formula. The reason that spreadsheets can

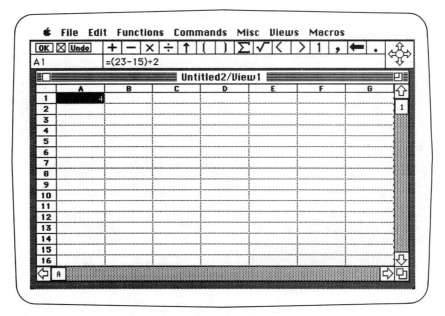

Fig. 7.16. *Using Full Impact's on-screen options to create a formula.*

perform this task is that they consider the relative, and not the absolute, position of cells in the worksheet, unless you specify otherwise. *Absolute* means that the cell address that is referenced in the formula does not change as the position of the formula does. *Relative* means that cell addresses change relative to the position of the formula. It's like the difference between saying "the house is on the northwest corner" (absolute position) and "the house is on the left" (relative to where you are standing). For example, if you want to find the difference in the buy and sell prices for the remaining stocks shown in figure 7.17, you can use Copy Down (on the Edit menu). The spreadsheet knows to subtract whatever is two columns to the left from whatever is in the cell one column to the left, regardless of where you are in relation to the column from which the original reference was established. Figure 7.17 shows the results.

Using Functions

A function is a special kind of formula. A function is predesigned so that all you need to do is plug in the values (or the cell addresses of the values) and you're ready to go. Spreadsheets offer many different

7
Spread-
sheets

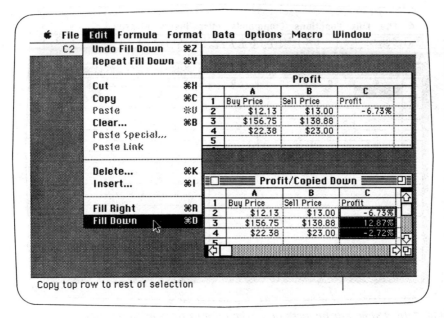

Fig. 7.17. *Copying formulas down a column.*

types of functions. For example, Excel offers more than 130, Wingz more than 150, and Full Impact more than 90 in areas such as business, date and time, and statistics. Functions are incredible time-savers and allow you to compute sophisticated values quickly and easily.

Take the amortization computation chart shown in figure 7.18, which demonstrates the Excel function PMT. Here, the function was entered by using the Paste Function command on the Format menu.

All functions have a syntax, which requires special values placed in a special order. The syntax for the PMT function is

= PMT(rate,nper,pv,fv,type)

PMT (the function) is the payment due on a loan.

The arguments and their meanings are as follows:

rate is the interest rate.

nper is the number of periods.

pv is the present value of the loan.

fv is the future value of the loan.

type is the type of loan.

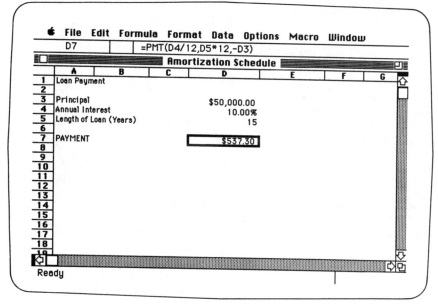

Fig. 7.18. *Example of the use of a function in Excel 2.2.*

Do you think that you may have a difficult time remembering all the functions and what they do—let alone what each one requires for input? To make using functions easier, some spreadsheets, such as Excel, allow you to paste the function's arguments into the cell so that you can see what's required, as shown in figures 7.19 and 7.20. Here the function AVERAGE, which computes the average of a set of scores, has been selected under the Paste Arguments command. The formula appears in the formula bar (see fig. 7.20). This feature allows you to pick up almost any function and at least know what arguments are needed to make the function work. As you can see, the function was pasted into a cell. Now the range of cells needs to be entered and the Return or Enter key pressed, which results in the average of the range of scores.

The big challenge of functions is to understand enough about your needs to identify which of the many functions can be of assistance to you. And to understand functions, you have to use your spreadsheet

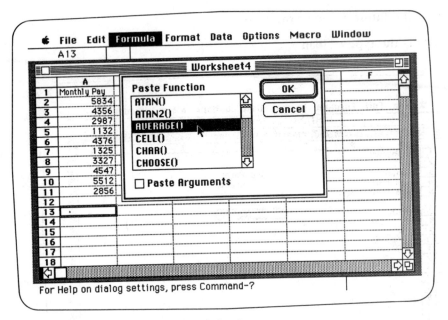

Fig. 7.19. *Excel's Paste Function dialog box.*

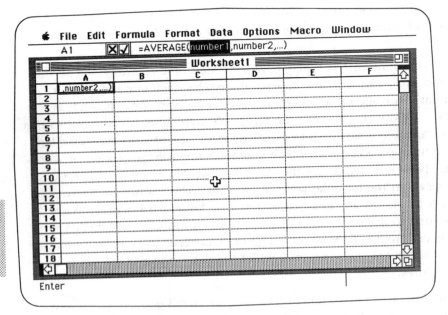

Fig. 7.20. *A function pasted into a cell.*

program for every possible task you can think of and practice with it all the time. Read the manual and get acquainted with the functions. For example, an overlooked function that all spreadsheets have is DATE, used to compute the number of days between two dates. This function is handy for billing, scheduling jobs, and so forth; but many people don't use the feature because they don't know that it exists.

Table 7.1 gives a sample of some of the functions that you will find in spreadsheets such as Wingz, Excel, Full Impact, and Works. Notice that the functions may be named differently, but they serve the same purpose.

Table 7.1
Useful Spreadsheet Functions

The Function	What the Function Does
AVERAGE (Excel, Works)	Computes the average
AVG (Wingz, Full Impact)	Computes the average
MIRR (Excel, Works)	Computes the internal rate of return
PMT (Excel, Wingz, Full Impact)	Computes payment
Sqrt (Works)	Computes the square root
SQRT (Excel, Wingz, Full Impact)	Computes the square root

Working with Graphs

Graphs (called charts in many spreadsheet programs) are indispensable for making data in a worksheet more understandable. They can add pizzazz to a presentation and make otherwise confusing information crystal clear.

Spreadsheets offer a variety of graph types. Figure 7.21 shows a menu listing some of Excel's 15 available graph types. Wingz offers you 20 different types of graphs, more than enough even for the most picky graph person and more than any other spreadsheet available. Full Impact offers 7 graph types.

7
Spread-sheets

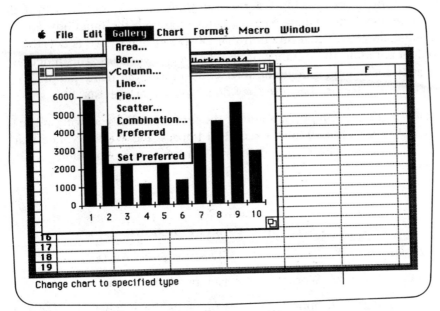

Fig. 7.21. *Some of the graphing options available on Excel.*

But what to use when? There are some rules you can go by, but for the most part, what looks right to you may be best. For example, when you are representing sales over time, a line graph is best. When you are dealing with categorical information, such as percentage of sales by category, a pie graph is best. You can see one of the "slices" of the pie "exploded" for emphasis in the pie graph in figure 7.22.

Most Macintosh spreadsheet applications offer graphing capabilities that are very easy to use. The general steps in creating any graph are defining or highlighting the area of the data that will be used for making the graph and then selecting the graphing (or charting) command either through a menu or with a tool, such as the Chart tool on the Wingz Tool Box. When this procedure is finished, the application automatically generates a graph. After the graph is generated, you can add legends, rescale axes, and change fonts through a set of new graph-specific menus that appear at the top of the window.

Figure 7.23 shows a samples of the different graphs that Excel can generate using data from figure 7.1. You select the type of graph from the Graph Gallery.

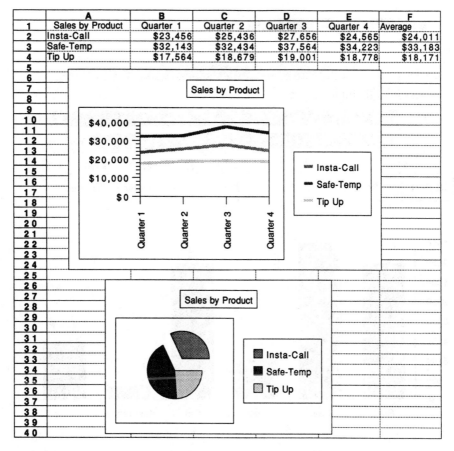

	A	B	C	D	E	F
1	Sales by Product	Quarter 1	Quarter 2	Quarter 3	Quarter 4	Average
2	Insta-Call	$23,456	$25,436	$27,656	$24,565	$24,011
3	Safe-Temp	$32,143	$32,434	$37,564	$34,223	$33,183
4	Tip Up	$17,564	$18,679	$19,001	$18,778	$18,171

Fig. 7.22. A line and a pie graph.

Creating a Graph

In figure 7.23, you can see how Excel uses the budget data to create a column graph. To create that graph, highlight the data and then select the New command from the File menu. A dialog box with three choices (Worksheet, Macro, and Chart) appears. Select Chart. Voila! A column graph, the default graph type, appears.

Other spreadsheet programs, such as Wingz, require the same steps, but with some programs (such as Wingz and Full Impact), you select a Chart tool after the data is highlighted. Formatting and changes in the way the information is presented can then be made.

7
Spread-
sheets

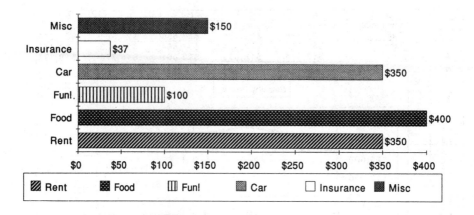

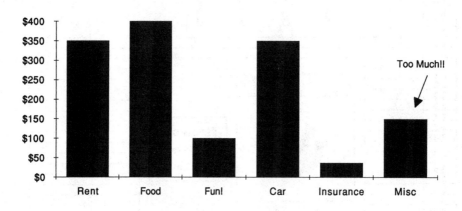

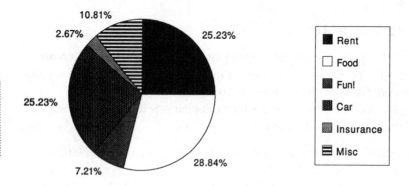

Fig. 7.23. A column, a bar, and a pie graph.

Adding Text

Graphs or charts by themselves contribute greatly to our understanding of a set of data. Yet you can even improve on the high-quality visuals produced by programs such as Excel, Wingz, Full Impact, and Trapeze by using text added to the graph in the form of legends, titles, notes, and more.

Graphs are easy to customize beyond the type of graph you want to use. Let's say, for example, that you want to point out a particular quarter of sales as being exceptional by attaching text to the graph. You also can add an arrow to this Excel graph to emphasize the point, as shown in figure 7.24.

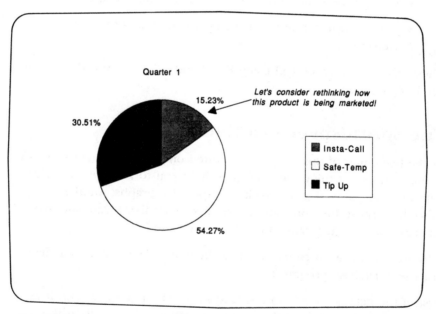

Fig. 7.24. Adding text to an Excel graph.

Excel allows you to add text to any place on a graph by entering the text and then using the mouse to position the text where you want it. You enter the text from the keyboard, and when you press the Return key, the text appears in the middle of your screen. You then can drag the text wherever you want it to be placed. As you will see, you also can change the font and its size and style just as you can with the other major spreadsheets.

7

Spread-
sheets

Formatting Graphs

After a graph is finished, you can fancy it up by using some of the formatting tools that are available, usually on the Format menu. For example, just some of the things that you can do are

- Change the patterns used to represent different series of data

- Enclose added text, titles, and other information in boxes to highlight it

- Remove (or add) boxes around certain parts of the graph

- Create three-dimensional effects

- Change the scale of the x- or y-axis for more emphasis

- Emphasize the title by changing the style and font (to Helvetica)

These effects were achieved using Excel and Wingz in the graphs you see in figure 7.25.

The Spreadsheet as a Database

At the beginning of this chapter, I pointed out how a spreadsheet can do many different things, among them help you to arrange and work with numbers as well as to produce impressive graphs. Another valuable purpose the application serves is to act like a database, where records (and not just values) can be manipulated.

Why would you want to use a spreadsheet as a database, rather than just use a database program?

First, if the data is already in a spreadsheet, why not work with it as it stands rather than transfer the data to a database? Especially if the operations you need to perform are relatively simple, such as finding and extracting records, rather than relational activities (which you learn about in the next chapter), working in the spreadsheet is more convenient.

Second—and this reason may be a bit of a lazy response—you may not want to go to the trouble (or the expense) of learning a database program if your spreadsheet can do all that you need.

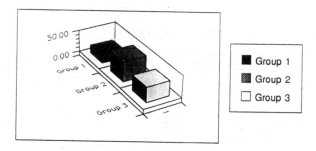

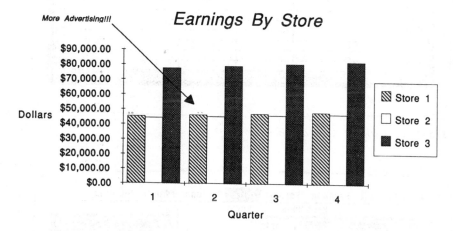

Fig. 7.25. *A 3-D Wingz graph and an Excel graph with text and an arrow added.*

Creating a Database

In figure 7.26, you see an Excel spreadsheet used as a database. The records (one each for five people) are organized by fields (Last Name, First Name, Age, Gender, and Years at the company). A record consists of a set of fields and corresponds to a row in the spreadsheet. Fields are the columns of the spreadsheet.

Databases are usually established by first entering and selecting the data (including the column labels) and then selecting a Database command on the appropriate menu. In the case of Excel, the menu is the Data menu and the command is Set Database (see fig. 7.27). Once this command is selected, the database is automatically defined.

7

**Spread-
sheets**

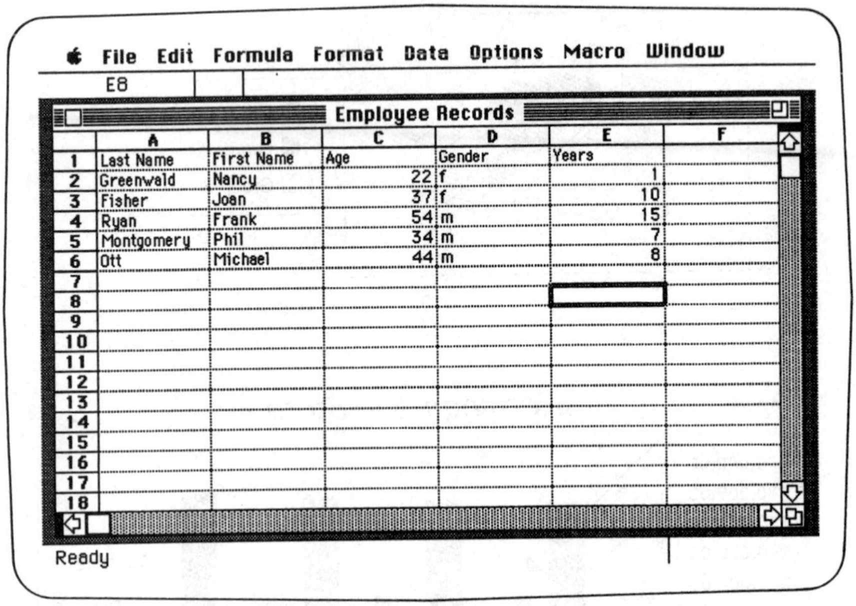

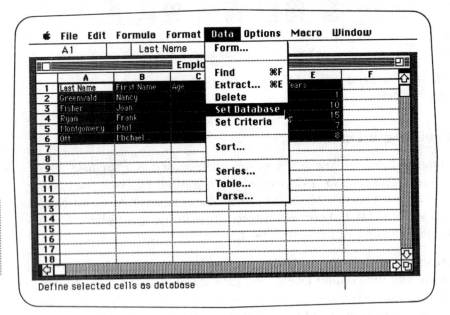

Fig. 7.26. *A simple Excel database.*

Fig. 7.27. *Defining a database after selecting the cells in the worksheet.*

Until the database is defined, you cannot perform any type of database operations. Any time new records are added to the database, it must be redefined.

Sorting

Sorting is an often-used tool that is not limited to databases. In figure 7.28, the records that are part of the Employee Records database have been sorted alphabetically (after being highlighted) by selecting the Sort command from the Data menu. Most databases automatically sort on the first field (in this case, Last Name), but most can sort on any field, or they can "nest" sorts within fields if you want. For example, you can sort Years at the company within Gender.

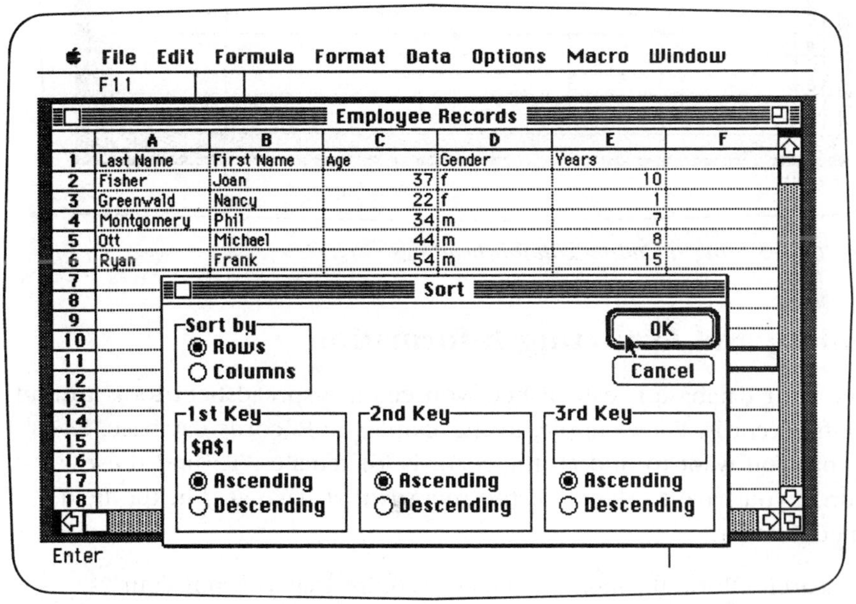

Fig. 7.28. *Sorted records and the dialog box for choosing sort criteria.*

When you highlight information in a database, be sure that you highlight only what you need to use. For example, if you are sorting a column, you do not want to sort the column heading. But if you are defining the database, you must select column headings, because you will need these headings if you want to find and extract information. For example, figure 7.29 shows the same database you see in figure

7

**Spread-
sheets**

7.28, sorted with column headings included. If you make a mistake, use Undo to return to the previous state.

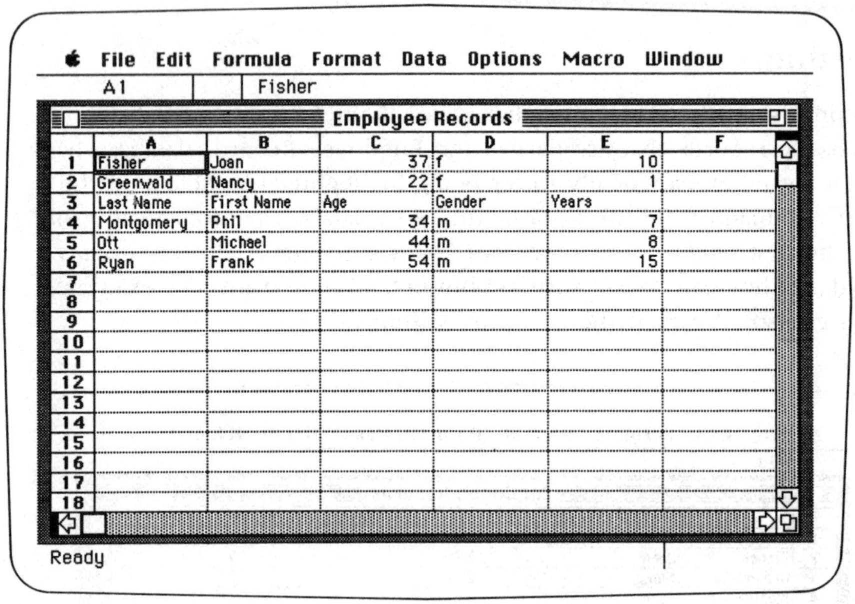

Fig. 7.29. *Sorting including column headings.*

Finding and Extracting Information

Once your database is established, you can use spreadsheet tools to find specific records. For example, in the Employee Records database, let's say that you want to find all the records for females. To find these records, you have to select all the records that have an *f* in the field named Gender.

Any search efforts through a database require that you tell your database what the criteria are for the search. In this case, you add a criterion in another location on the spreadsheet, as you see in figure 7.30. In the same figure, you can see that we have selected the criterion range and then designated it as the criterion for searching through or extracting records. A criterion can be thought of as a filter through which you pass the data. Data is allowed to pass through if it meets certain conditions (such as listing the first name as Joan (expressed as = "Joan") or listing time as more than 5 years (expressed as = Years>5). A criterion can be located anywhere on the worksheet. The criteria range consists of a name (such as female) and some values (such as *f*), as you see in the formula bar in figure 7.30. Once this criterion is entered, you can see how Excel returns a TRUE statement in cell A9, indicating that for cell D2, an *f* is present.

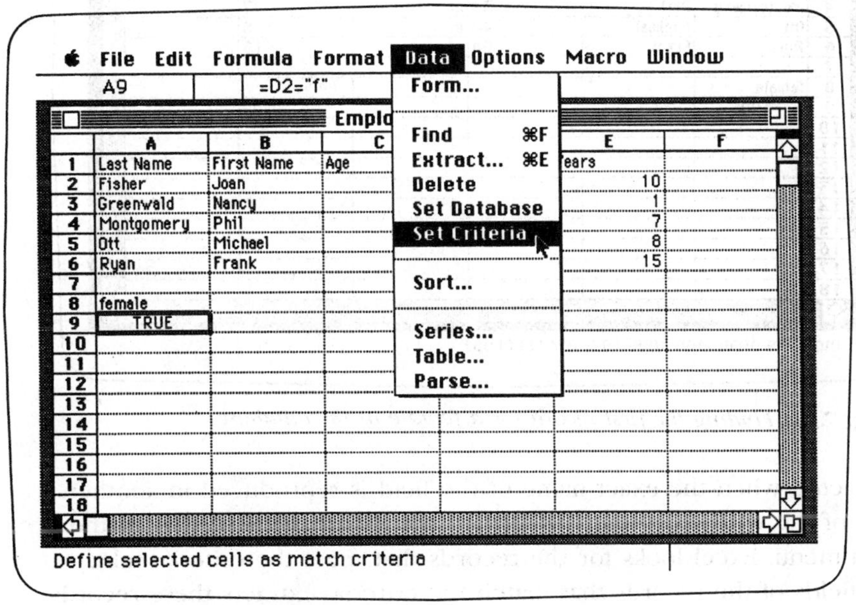

Fig. 7.30. Selecting and defining a criterion range in a database.

Once the criteria are designated and the Find command is selected, Excel highlights all the records that have an *f* in the field called Gender, which in this case happens to be the first record (see fig. 7.31). The highlighting begins with the first occurrence.

You can combine criteria as well. For example, what if you are looking for all men who have worked for the company for more than 10 years. You use two criteria: Gender being equal to *m* and Years more than 10 (written as a formula =E2>10). Excel will then select the records that fit the criteria.

Finally, in figure 7.32, a new field is defined where records that meet the criteria can be extracted, and as you see, the two records that meet the criteria of being female are reproduced in the extract range. Data is

7
Spread-
sheets

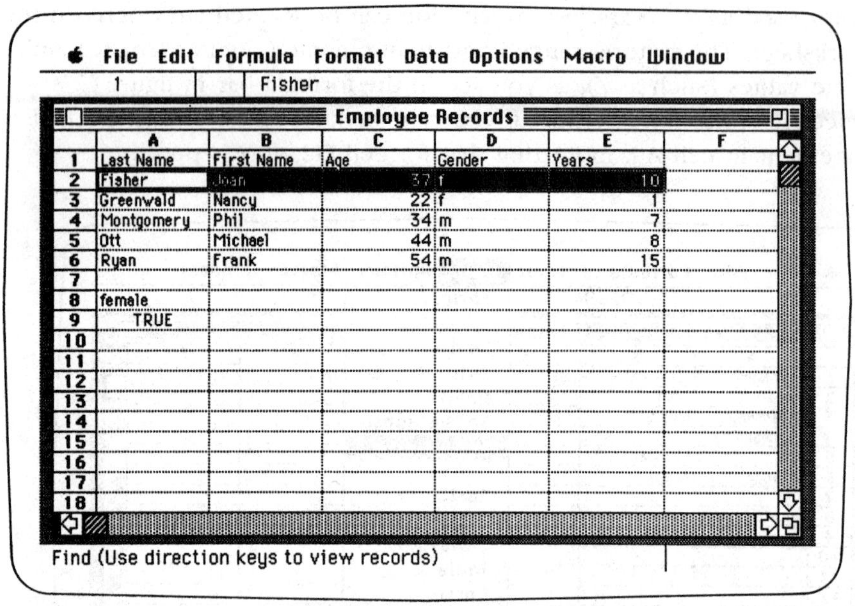

Fig. 7.31. Finding the first record for a female in the database.

extracted when the exact name of the field is reproduced in another part of the worksheet and the Extract command is selected from the Data menu. Excel looks for the records that meet the criteria, selects the fields of the records that match the criteria, extracts these records, and places them in the area you have previously defined in the worksheet. Just imagine hunting through 2,000 records trying to find the book reviewer with an expertise in chocolate cakes and having that record pop up almost immediately. Amazing!

Macros, Programming Languages, and Databases

As spreadsheet users' demands for more flexibility have increased, the designers of spreadsheets have tried to meet these needs by including "languages," which you can use to have spreadsheets perform specific tasks.

For example, the designers of Wingz developed HyperScript, a language that allows you to use commands to have Wingz perform certain functions. In figure 7.33, you see a script that automatically labels rows

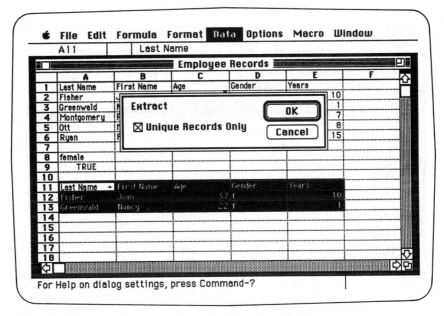

Fig. 7.32. *Extracting information based on the criteria range.*

A, B, and C with the names of the three months in the first quarter. This example is simple but can easily be expanded to construct any format you want to use. The command *Put "January" into A1* is an example of a HyperScript command. This simple example saves you the time of having to reenter the information each time you start a new worksheet that needs it. But what about more complex applications? How about a macro or a script that automatically takes the day's income from different stores, adds them to a main accounting worksheet, and then updates each store's individual worksheet records? All these things can be done with the touch of a button on a script.

A more complex Wingz example can be see in figure 7.34, where buttons have been created. When you click a button, you move to another worksheet or area of the worksheet. Once these buttons are clicked, they provide additional information. These buttons can provide information because each is tied to its own script. For example, when the button Production Costs is clicked, it displays the Production Costs worksheet (see fig. 7.35). Likewise, you can return to the original sheet by clicking the Return to Sales button.

7

Spread-sheets

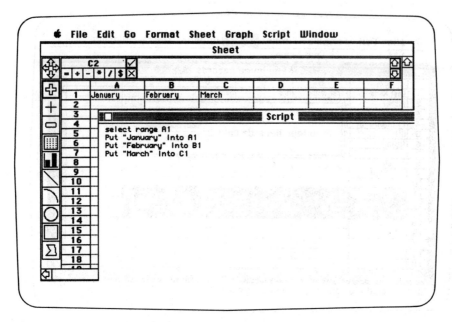

Fig. 7.33. *A simple Wingz script.*

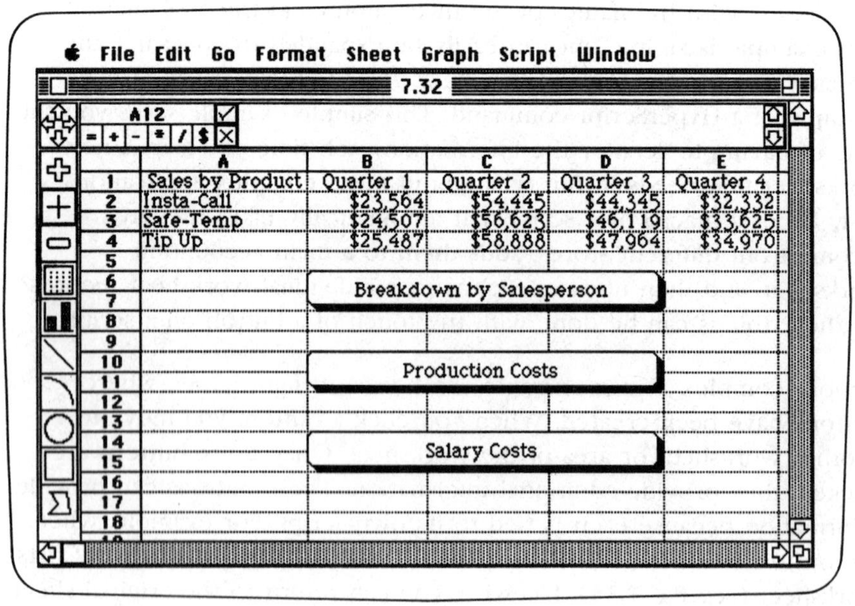

Fig. 7.34. *A Wingz worksheet with buttons linked to other worksheets.*

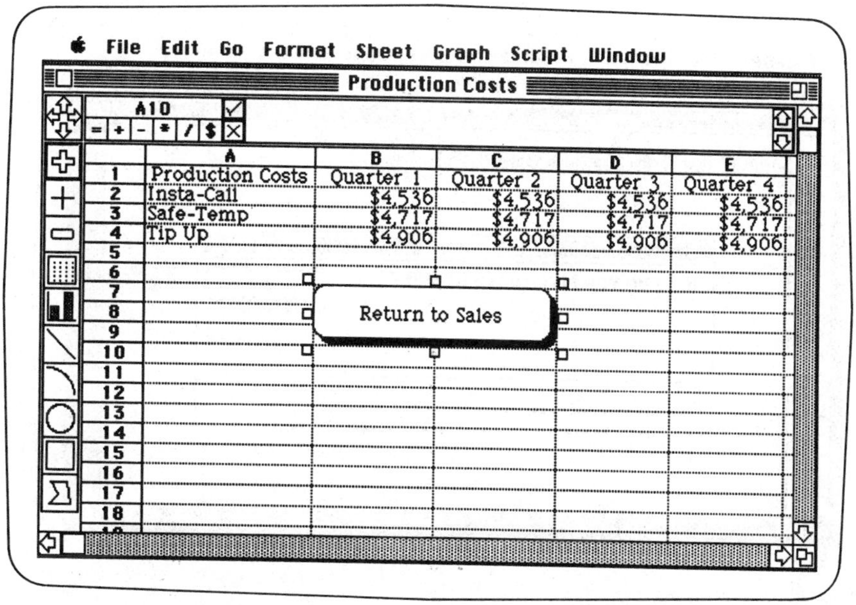

Fig. 7.35. *The worksheet displayed by the Production Costs button.*

Using a language like HyperScript is the same as using macros, where keystrokes and other operations are recorded and can be invoked as needed. Although languages like HyperScript may look a bit intimidating, they can be used to maximize the efficiency of your spreadsheet activities. For example, you can have a note pop up when a new user signs on and clicks the Any Message? button. Using languages or macros successfully just takes some experimentation and willingness to fool around a little until the technique works.

Excel also has a comprehensive macro command language that allows you to customize a worksheet to fit some very specific needs. For example, the prompt you see in figure 7.36 was created by entering the prompt's text into a macro sheet and then running the macro. While these kinds of operations are more advanced, all it takes is the commitment to use them and practice. You will be amazed at what you can do.

7
Spread-sheets

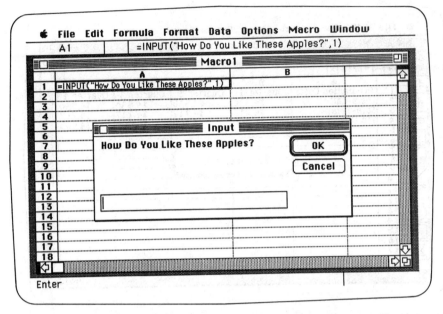

Fig. 7.36. Using Excel's INPUT statement to create a prompt.

Compatibility among Spreadsheets

Like word processing files, worksheet files can be transferred from one spreadsheet application to another, but you may be limited by the export capability of the program itself.

Because 1-2-3 for DOS is so popular, most Macintosh applications allow you to make this transfer. You can always, of course, save a spreadsheet as a text file and then transfer the file to another application.

Most often, changing the format of a worksheet file consists of selecting a command from the File menu. In the case of Excel, the Save As command leads you to the file formats you see in figure 7.37. With the worksheet active, selecting any one of those file formats saves the file in the new format. The file is now ready to be "read" by another application, depending on the format that application can read.

One of the problems you can encounter in any file transfer is that functions and formulas may not always stay intact. That is, although the cell entries may transfer, the actual contents of the cell may not. Make

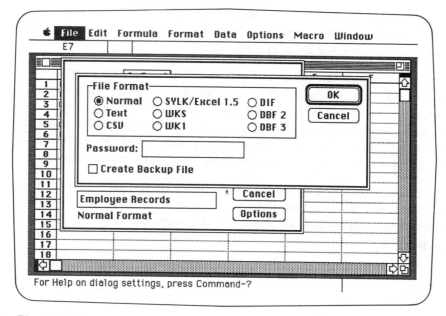

Fig. 7.37. Excel options for saving a file under a new format.

a practice of testing a newly transferred spreadsheet to ensure that it works properly.

Excel for the Mac and Excel for DOS machines are remarkably similar. Microsoft, the developer of Excel, provided a file format that allows you to go directly from one (Excel 2.2 for the Mac) to the other (Excel 1.5 for DOS systems) and preserve most, if not all, of the formula and function entries.

The Big Mac Recommendation

Perhaps the most important factor in your choice of a spreadsheet program is that more than 70 percent of people using a spreadsheet on the Mac use Excel. This fact means that Excel has more support, more articles written about it in popular periodicals like *MacUser* and *MacWorld*, more available add-ons (such as task-specific spreadsheet utilities), and more competition for sales (meaning lower prices for you). On the other hand, Wingz (which is very new as of this writing) offers graphics capability that Excel can't touch, plus a programming language that can be very useful for personalizing applications and

7

Spread-
sheets

making the program highly user-responsive. Also, if you are affiliated with an educational institution, the Wingz price is $89.00, an amazing reduction from the list price of $399.00.

Look at the comparison table in figure 7.38 to get an idea of what features different programs offer. You cannot go wrong with a market leader like Excel, because with so many other users, transferring programs may not involve much difficulty. On the other hand, products like Wingz and Trapeze offer some useful features such as graphics and the use of blocks (Trapeze), which doesn't constrain you to grids.

This brief introduction to spreadsheets has given you information to help you make an informed decision about which one to buy. Now it's time to move on to find out about the electronic file cabinet—the database.

	Excel	Full Impact	Trapeze	Wingz	Works
What are the Basic Features?					
Version	2.2	1	2.1	1	2
Minimum Memory	512K	1M	512K	1M	512K
MultiFinder Memory	640K	2M	512K	2M	768K
Suggested Retail Price	$395.00	$395.00	$295.00	$399.00	$295.00
Street Price	$296.25	$296.25	$221.25	$299.25	$221.25
Help	yes	yes	yes	yes	yes
What about the Spreadsheet?					
Arrays and Matrixes	yes	no	yes	yes	no
Cell Notes	no	yes	yes	yes	yes
File/Cell Protection	yes	yes	yes	yes	no
Maximum Memory Used	1M	16M	8M	**	RAM
Navigation Tools	yes	yes	no	yes	no
Number of Built-in Functions	131	100	144	140+	64
Number of Documents Open	*	8	32	*	14
Parsing					
Password Protection	no	no	no	yes	no
Transpose Worksheet	yes	yes	yes	yes	no
Use of Buttons	no	no	no	yes	no
	no	yes	no	yes	no
*Limited by RAM					
**Available RAM					
What about Database Management?					
Database Features	yes	yes	yes	yes	yes
Number of Sort Levels	3	2,048	3	256	3
How Does It Handle Macros?					
Custom Menus/Dialog Boxes	yes	no	no	yes	no
Definable Functions	yes	yes	no	yes	no
Macro Editor	yes	yes	no	yes	no
Macro Language	yes	yes	no	yes	no
Macro Recorder	yes	yes	no	yes	yes
Single Key Macros	yes	yes	no	yes	yes
What about Graphics and Screen Displays?					
3-D Graphs	no	no	no	yes	no
Attached Text	yes	yes	yes	yes	yes
Cell Notes	no	yes	yes	yes	yes
Graph Rotation	no	no	no	yes	no
Drawing Tools	no	yes	no	yes	yes
Logarithmic Scaling	yes	yes	yes	yes	yes
Mix Data/Graphics/Text on Page	no	yes	yes	yes	yes
Multiple Fonts Per Worksheet	no	yes	yes	yes	no
Number of Graph Types	7	7	10	20	5
Number of Colors	8	8	8	8	8
Perspective	no	no	no	yes	no
Reduce/Enlarge Views	yes	yes	yes	yes	yes
Built-in Display Formats	19	44	25	14	17
What Other Files is It Compatible With?					
dBASE II, III+	no	yes	no	no	no
DIF	no	yes	no	yes	no
Lotus 1-2-3	no	yes	no	yes	no
PICT	no	yes	yes	yes	yes
SYLK	yes	Import	yes	yes	yes
	yes	yes	no	yes	yes

Fig. 7.38. *Checklist for determining your spreadsheet's capabilities.*

7
Spread-
sheets

8

Working with Databases

Names, addresses, purchase records, buying habits, dates of last sales, and more. This is just part of the information that we are responsible for keeping track of. Fortunately, there are now software tools called database management systems (sometimes abbreviated DBMS) that can help. These management systems range from the simple to the very sophisticated. The database is the last of the "big three" (word processor, spreadsheet, database) applications; although there are many other applications (see Chapter 9), the databases are workhorses of the Mac business and home worlds.

Although you can easily keep track of large data sets using a spreadsheet, a database has one major advantage. It treats each independent collection of data (called a record) as an independent unit, and you have great flexibility as to what you want to do with that unit as to formatting, searching, sorting, and manipulating. You know all that junk mail you get at home and the office asking you to buy that lot in the Sun Belt for only $49? Hats off to the database management systems those companies use.

Defining a Database

A *database* is a listing of information organized into functionally related files that allow for easy manipulation and retrieval. Your telephone book, for example, is a database of names, addresses, and telephone numbers. It is organized by name. Your real estate agent has a list of properties organized by address, which is the same information as in your telephone book, but arranged in a different way.

8

Data-
bases

331

The word *database* refers to the data itself, and the database management system is the tool that binds or organizes the data. Although database management systems (such as Fourth Dimension, Foxbase+/Mac, Borland's Reflex, Odesta's Double Helix, Claris's FileMaker II, Ashton-Tate's dBASE, and others) differ from one another, they can be organized in such a way as to serve very specific purposes.

The database form is a skeleton into which information from a particular record can be incorporated. For example, using Reflex's language, or template (see fig. 8.1), you can use the database management system to select only those clients whose bills are over 30 days due and print the form you see in figure 8.1, with all relevant client information ready to be mailed.

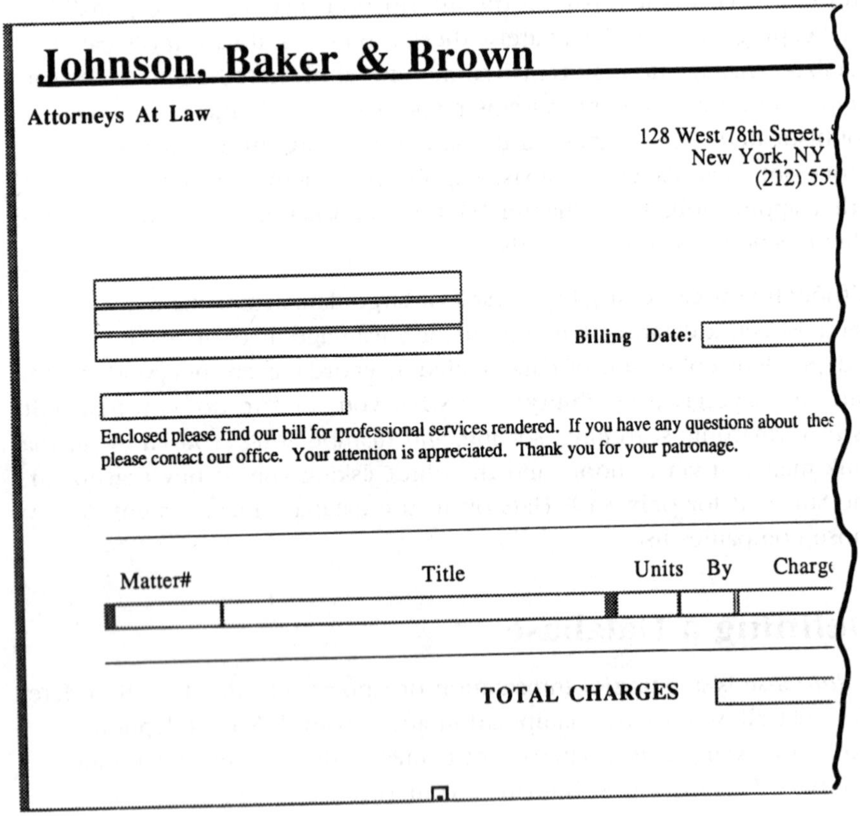

Johnson, Baker & Brown

Attorneys At Law

128 West 78th Street,
New York, NY
(212) 55

Billing Date:

Enclosed please find our bill for professional services rendered. If you have any questions about thes
please contact our office. Your attention is appreciated. Thank you for your patronage.

Matter# Title Units By Charg

TOTAL CHARGES

Fig. 8.1. A billing form created with Reflex Plus.

Understanding Files, Records, and Fields

A database management system allows you to organize information in a logical fashion so that you can manipulate it as needed. All databases are organized into three different levels: fields, records, and files. A field is an individual piece of data, such as a last name, a first name, an address, sales for a year, or the name of a student. A record is a collection of fields such as the last name, first name, and address of a client. A file is a collection of records. Each record is manipulated as an individual unit, and this is what distinguishes a database from a spreadsheet.

Suppose that a kite shop owner needs to keep track of the following information:

Account Number
Name
Street Address
City
State
ZIP Code
Phone Number
Type of kite preferred
Date of last purchase

Each of these pieces of information, called entries, will be organized by fields. A *field* is a unique piece of information.

A set of fields makes up a *record.*

In this example, there are eight different fields. A *calculated field* is one in which the contents are a function of some operation involving two other fields (balance due multiplied by some interest rate, for example).

Sound like a spreadsheet? Calculated fields are not that different, especially when you realize that you need to use a formula (called a *procedure* in some database management systems) to create these calculated fields.

In the kite shop example, the entries in the eight different fields for one customer make up a single record. In turn, a set of records make up a *file.*

8
Data-
bases

It is not necessary that all the fields in a record contain information. In figure 8.2, you can see the format for a record from the database for the Things That Fly kite shop. This record was created using Dbase Mac from Ashton-Tate.

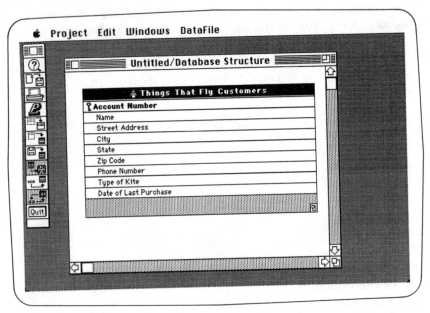

Fig. 8.2. *A record form from a newly designed database.*

Some database management systems, such as Double Helix II (from Odesta), use different terminology. These systems call files *relations*, and they call a set of relations a *collection*.

The essence of a database is that it can take the information that is contained in fields and records and manipulate it in a variety of ways, such as sorting, extracting some information to be used in another file, setting criteria to identify certain records based on certain parameters, and so on.

Database management systems can hold enormous amounts of data. Take, for example, 4th Dimension from Acius. It can hold 16 million records consisting of 99 files, an unlimited number of links between the files, 511 fields per file, 511 subfiles, and 511 sub-subfields. A tremendous amount of information!

Defining a Good Database

What are some questions you should ask about a database?

If it is relational, it should allow you to integrate existing data files easily to save you the trouble of re-entering information. For example, you might run a business where you have several different files that contain information about clients.

Wouldn't it be nice if all you needed was the account number on the record in each of the files rather than name, address, phone number, and so on, on each record in each of the different files. Efficient databases enable you to relate information from one file to another so that you need not duplicate.

Another consideration is how easily the data is imported to and exported from other applications. Suppose that you have taken over a business whose mailing list was created with Microsoft Works, and you want to import it to your new database management system application. You surely would save time if the 6,000 records were in a form that your database application could understand.

Does the database you're considering work with graphics easily? In figure 8.3 you can see a Panorama (from ProVUE) record that includes a graphic of the type of glassware you should use when you mix a cocktail. You can see in Panorama's tool box (located on the left side of fig. 8.3) that there are some tools for working with graphics. More and more databases are beginning to have this capability.

Does the database allow for sufficient security so that people who are not authorized cannot gain access to the system? This is most often done through the use of a password, which is similar to the method used with the spreadsheet and word processing programs that are discussed in earlier chapters.

If relational, how easily do the databases reduce data redundancy? What this means is that the same information need not be present on a variety of files for you to be able to access and integrate what you need. This capability saves time because there's less information to process and it also reduces complexity.

Does the database come with a supply of templates and predesigned forms so that you can get started right away? Even better, can you customize these for your own purposes? Panorama (from ProVUE), for

8

Data-bases

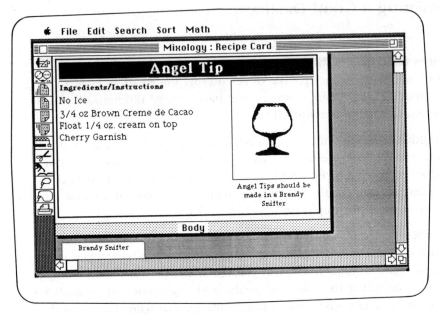

Fig. 8.3. Integrating graphics into a database.

example, provides a cookbook of tables or templates (so you can just enter data into a ready-designed form), boxes, and notebook forms that are ready for your personal imprint.

In figures 8.4 and 8.5, you can see some templates from the flat file database, Panorama. Here you can use these templates to create a box with a caption and paste it into your database—an easy way to jazz up your organization of data.

Does your database allow you to edit and add records easily after the database file has already been created? Sometimes you will need to add an additional field after the definition stage, and a good database management system allows you to add the information without disrupting the organization of the existing records in the file. In figure 8.6, for example, you can see an established database created using FileMaker II (from Claris). Adding a new field means using the Field option on the Layouts menu located on the left side of the database screen.

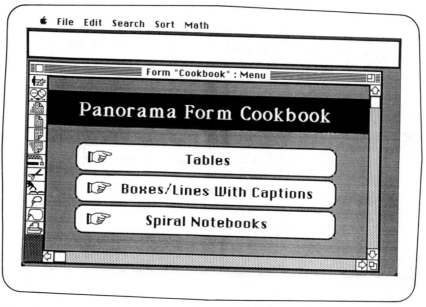

Fig. 8.4. *Using templates in the design of a database.*

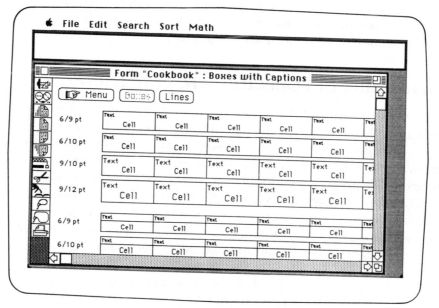

Fig. 8.5. *Using a template to create a data entry table.*

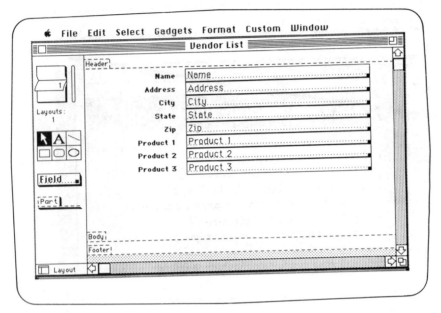

Fig. 8.6. *Adding a new field to an established database.*

A good database allows for the easy formatting of both input and output files, which eases data entry and allows you to match your database reports to other documents that you might be preparing.

What Kinds of Databases Are Out There?

We have already learned that a database is a list of information which you want to keep track of. There are different types of databases to help you keep track of your information according to how you want it. The two types I will cover are the flat file and the relational file databases. The names refer to how your information can be handled. Flat files consist of just one file that you can work with at a time. With relational files, you can work with more than one file at a time—in essence, relating one file to another. Flat files have been around longer than relational files. As with most things, the newer something is, the more powerful and flexible it becomes; relational files are more powerful and flexible than flat files and most stand-alone databases are relational in nature today. Let's also not forget that more powerful often translates into more difficult to learn and to use, as well as more expensive. So what type of database is right for you? It depends on your requirements. Let's look at the two types now.

Flat File Databases

A flat file database is just that: a flat file. What does a flat file look like and why is it called flat? It is a single file with no links or connections to any other file. Consider the standard office manila file folder with a bunch of invoices in it. The individual items on each invoice would be considered fields, each invoice would then be a record, and the manila file folder would be your actual database file. Sounds pretty easy, eh? Flat files tend to be less complicated and, in general, easier to use than relational files (see fig. 8.7).

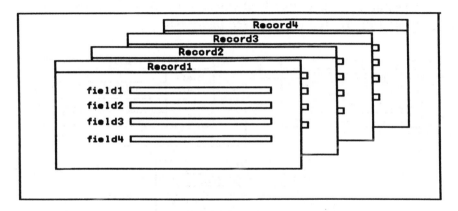

Fig. 8.7. A flat file.

There are two types of flat file databases. And you thought this was going to be simple. The two types of flat file databases are memory-resident and disk-based. A memory-resident database keeps your data file in RAM memory (that's why we call it memory-resident), thus speeding up the operations you perform on your data. Disk-based databases tend to range from slower to much slower than memory-resident files, because they are always reading and writing from your disk. There is a benefit to disk-based files, however. You can have very large data files with disk-based files, but with a memory-resident database you are limited in file size to what your available RAM can hold.

The Microsoft Works database is a memory-resident database, and FileMaker II from Claris is a disk-based database. Both are quite good flat file databases (at least I like them). They are easy to use and quick to set up. With FileMaker II, you can even have a picture as a field! Imagine your household inventory or even your sales catalog showing the items as well as describing them.

Relational File Databases

Unlike a flat file database, a relational database has more than one flat data file that has one or more fields linked together so that you can update or add new information in more than one data file at the same time. In order for this linking to take place, you need to have a *key field*. A key field is a field that is identical in the files and is used to keep track of the related records (see figure 8.8).

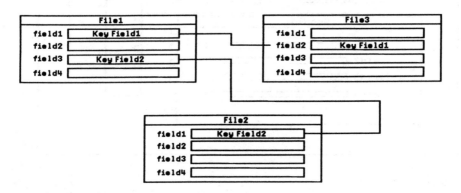

Fig. 8.8. A relational file.

There are a number of reasons why you would choose a relational database over a flat file database. The main reason is, of course, that you can relate files to one another. Other reasons are the flexibility that relational databases offer. Generally, they provide a scripting language with which you can create a program to help automate the database and even to provide special menus for the user. One powerful relational database is 4th Dimension, from Acius. It is big, flexible, powerful, and yes, it is complex. It is not as easy to use as any of the flat file databases that I know of, but it can do about everything except wash your car. In addition to doing the standard database functions, 4th

Dimension can access your mainframe database, download the data, perform complex mathematical analysis on that data, and then give you your results in a graphical format. What price is there to pay for this kind of power? Speed. 4th Dimension is one of the slower databases, but Guy is fixing that in subsequent releases. Foxbase+/Mac from Fox Software is considered one of the fastest databases available. Its reporting features are lacking, but not for long. Fox is updating its database to include better and more complete report-generating features.

With the power and expense of these relational databases, it would be nice if they could be put onto a network where everybody could make use of them. Some can—Oracle, for example (and of course 4th Dimension). It is a relational database that is considered to be multiuser. This means that more than one person can use the database at one time. The only constraint is that if you are using the same data file as another user on the network, the first one to open that file is the only one who has write priviledges. That is, no one else who opens the file after the first person will be able to save his or her changes to the file. This is generally not a problem on a networked database, because the data files are usually for information retrieval only; you don't want just anybody changing (messing up) your database program.

Designing a Database

Many people make a good living designing databases. However, a database is not easy to design even if you have had some experience. You must be sure that you have organized your information in such a way that it is easy for you to understand and to see how you can examine the relationships between things.

When designing your first or fiftieth database, follow these steps and you will find the task gets easier as you gain insight into how to avoid mishaps along the way.

List the information that you want to include in the database. Be sure that you have included all the information that you might want to use such as first name, last name, street address, city, state, ZIP, and so on. Although you can add more later, it is better to include it now.

8
Data-
bases

Keep in mind, however, that the more you add at any time, the larger the database becomes and the more processing power your program and machine need to work in an efficient manner.

Use graph paper (or a spreadsheet) to create a table or rows that will include each field you want in your database as well as the order in which the fields will appear. This plan helps you to organize your database better, because you can check the appearance to make sure that your data is logically organized. For example, City should follow Street Address. Fields that are used only occasionally should be listed last. Although the Mac is a visual machine by nature, and all good databases "walk" you through the process of creating a database form, a little advanced planning never hurt the process.

Create as many tables as you will have files that you want to relate to one another. When you have these tables established, you should be able to see the relationships among parts of various files. Use as many fields as you will need, but not so many that things become confusing and unmanageable. Too few fields and you can't "break" down the information to do what you need. Too many fields and you can be overwhelmed with managing all the information. You want it "just right." This means enough fields so that you can get what you need out of the database. For example, if you need to sort by preference for size, don't place size information in a field called preference which would include color as well. Create a field called size so it has a unique place in the database. Also, use specific terms for field names.

For example, Michael runs a large book store, where he keeps track of his customer's preferences. He could organize a database with the following fields;

Field	Example
Name	Linda Frankel
Address	4401 Widge Way, Queens, NY 12345
Preference	Mystery

On the other hand, a more complete organization (that requires more fields) could be as follows;

Field	Example
Last Name	Frankel
First Name	Linda

Address   4401 Widge Way, Queens, NY 12345
Preference   Mystery
First Authors Paretsky
Second Author Andrews
Editions   First American

In this example, it's not important for Michael to separate street address and city, but it is important to have more information so that he can search for the author that is preferred (even first and second preference), as well as the type of edition the customer may be interested in.

Avoid entering the same data in more than one file or in more than one place in a file. Data redundancy is a waste of space and your energy in entering all that unnecessary information.

Last but not least, each of the files that will be linked or related to one another should have a common field that can be used to connect files to one another. This way, the common characteristic of each data file can be used as a connecting link. You will see how files can be linked to one another in the following sections.

Creating a Database

Let's go through the steps used to create the database for the Things That Fly kite store. Although this database may appear to be simple in form, these general steps are similar regardless of the database management system that you are using. In general, the only two steps are designing the form (including all the fields you want to use) and adding the records that will make up the file. After that, the power of the database takes over.

The first step involves opening and naming a new file within which records will be stored. Database management systems require you to identify what is called a *key field*, the one field that uniquely distinguishes records from one another.

In this example, the customer's account number will be used. You would not use type of kite preferred because many people probably prefer the same kind, and this entry would not distinguish customers from one another. What you see in figure 8.9 is dBASE's opening screen

8
Data-
bases

for creating a key field. Data in a database can take many forms such as text, numbers, time, and others. You can see in figure 8.9 that the default data type is text. This will change if new fields (such as phone numbers, ZIP code, or date of last purchase) become key fields.

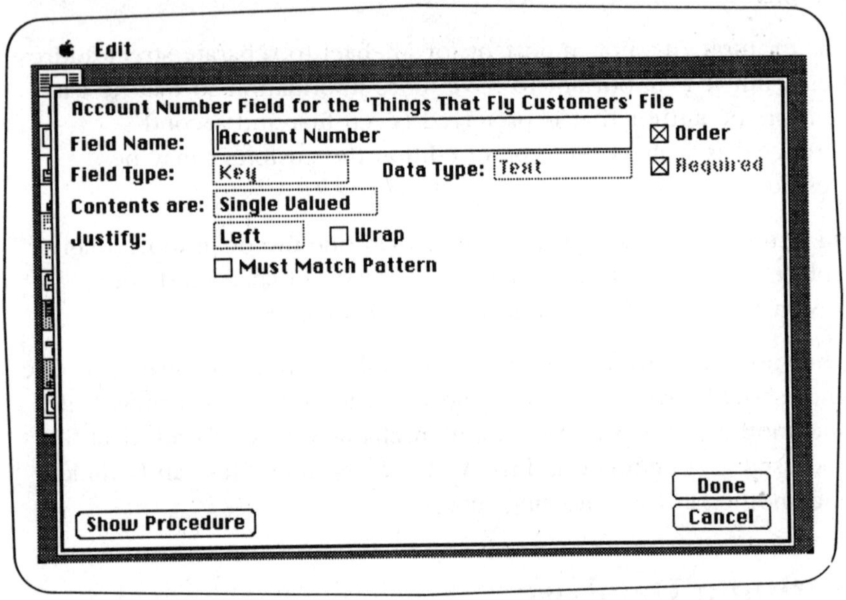

Fig. 8.9. *The dBASE screen for creating a key field.*

The next step is to create all the other fields that will be used in the database.

After the data form that you will be using has been created, you enter the actual contents of the records into each of the fields. Remember that a database is organized to enable you to access information when you want it and in the form that you need. A client's name in this case is not an important piece of information because it will not be used for searching or any other organization task, so the entire name is included in one field. If you want to sort by last name, the database would have to be reorganized by adding a new field. Although almost all databases enable you to add fields as you work, it's much better to have a clear idea of what you want to include in the field as you work.

After you have completed creating records within the form that you designed, your database is finished, and you can begin using it to search for particular records, create custom applications, and make reports.

Looking at Relationships

The primary job of relational database management systems is to make your information management life easier. This goal is accomplished by letting you relate files to one another through a variety of links.

The best way to do this is to look at a series of files and how they are related to each other. Sample files from Borland's Reflex Plus are used to illustrate this example.

Reflex Plus, like other database management programs, offers a Database Overview function so that you can view the relationships among the various files that are linked together. In figure 8.10, you can see the relationship among four files. Each of these files can stand alone as a type of flat files database, because each one contains information that is organized into fields. When they are linked, they become relational in nature.

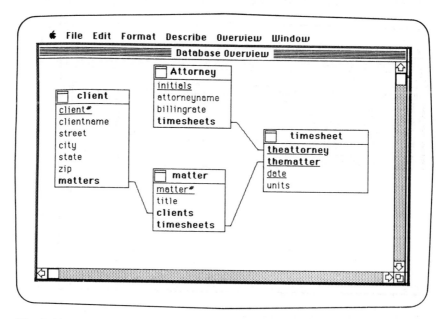

Fig. 8.10. Relationships between files.

You can see in figure 8.10 that within each of the four files (Attorney, Timesheet, Matter, and Client) there is a listing of fields. The underlined fields are key fields. The Client #, for example, is the key field in the file named Client, and the Matter # field is the key field in the file named Matter.

The boldface field names are the fields that form the links between files. The fields named Timesheets and Matter form the link between the Matter and Timesheet files, for example. You can see that there is no link between the files named Attorney and Client (the designer felt that this would not be a path along which information would be passed). All the information can be passed easily through the links that are already established.

Let's begin looking at relationships with the file named Attorney (see fig. 8.11). The figure shows the file name as AttorneyEntry because it is the entry form for that file. The fields that make up this file are Initials, Attorney Name, Billing Rate, and Units Billed. You can see how this file is a separate and independent database in its own right. Attorney JB bills at $300 per hour (units) and has billed 150 units for the month.

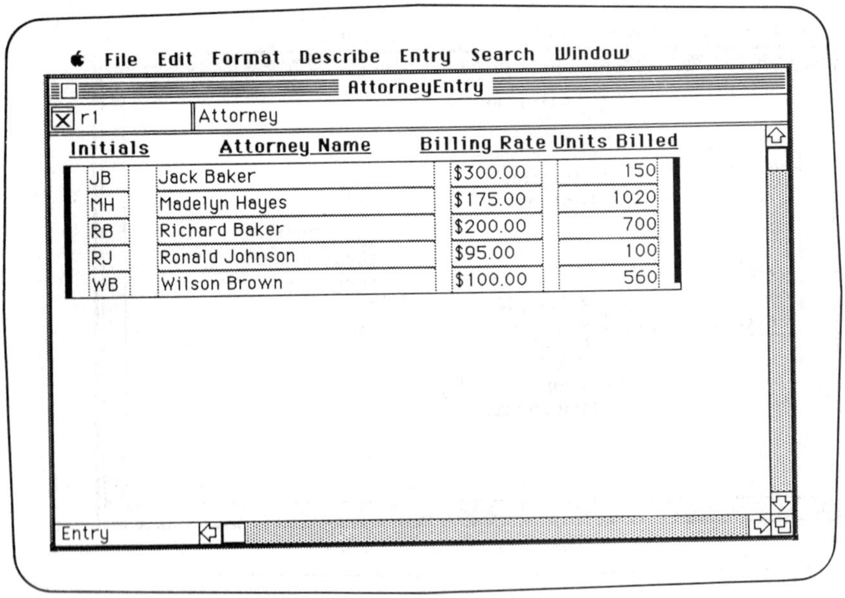

Fig. 8.11. The AttorneyEntry file.

You can follow the links and go to the Timesheet file (see fig. 8.12). There, you can discover attorney JB's current case number (the Matter #) and the total amount billed.

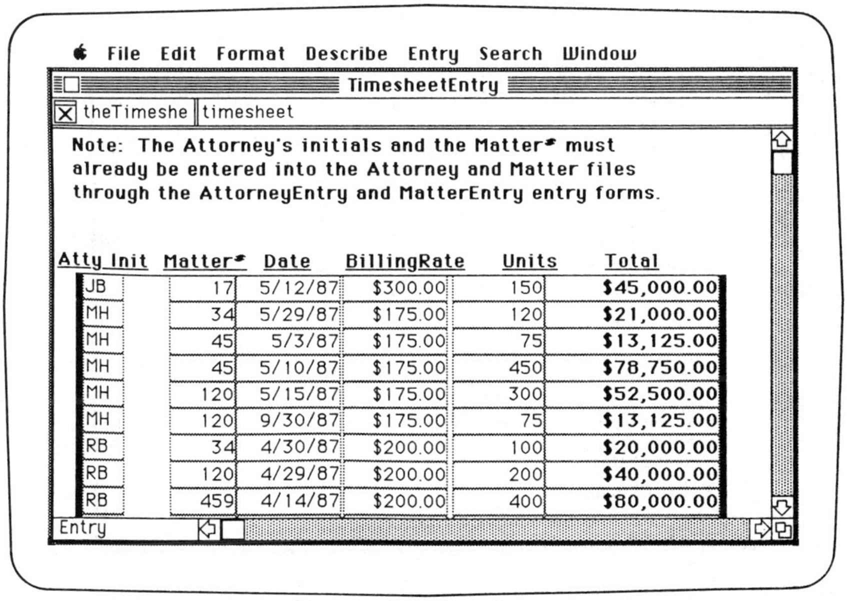

Fig. 8.12. *The TimesheetEntry form.*

The next link is between the Matter# (in the Matter file) and the information about the case. The link is from the Timesheet file to the Matter file. In figure 8.13, you can see the detailed information belonging to case #17. The Matter file is linked to the Client file (see fig. 8.14) through the Clients and Timesheets fields.

Each of these four separate files was created using Reflex Plus, and each was then linked using the appropriate database function. *Links* are associations between two database files. When links are made, individual fields (not files) are connected.

Even though a relational database management system can at times be difficult to use, Reflex Plus and Dbase Mac have the simplest method of linking fields in files; just use the mouse to draw a line between the different fields (and hence the files).

Through an examination of the contents of these separate files, you can easily trace how the links were designed and see how different information can be shared between different files.

8
Data-
bases

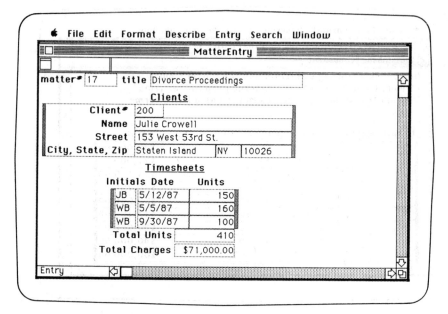

Fig. 8.13. *The MatterEntry form.*

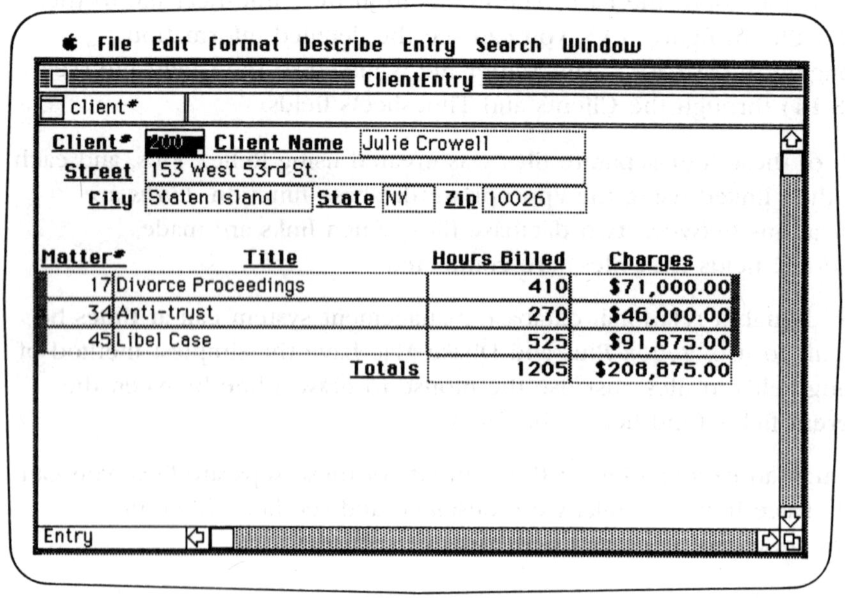

Fig. 8.14. *The ClientEntry form.*

Understanding HyperCard

In Chapter 17, you will learn about HyperCard, Apple's application, which strongly resembles a database in that each card can be thought of as a record and you have fields of information. Whether you know about HyperCard, you can read these few paragraphs about its use as a database management system. It has many of the features of many databases, such as searches and sorts. It can prepare reports, find things (very quickly), sort, and even relate stacks (HyperCard's word for files) to one another. To get the relational component, you have to know something about *scripting*, but that's not difficult to get started with. HyperCard is free with a newly purchased Macintosh or for only $49 if you buy it as a separate item.

Perhaps the feature that is most attractive about using HyperCard as a database management system is that you can easily create and manipulate graphics in data records.

If you want to add more power to HyperCard's database management capability, there are commercially available stacks that can help you import and export data, perform complex sorting, and more. StackWare (from Heizer Software) has such stacks (which are really sets of scripts that save you the programming time) available, and the price (from $6 to $30) can't be beat.

Using DA Databases

An alternative to a full-fledged database management system application is the use of a DA such as QuickDex (from Greene, Inc.), which is shown in figure 8.15.

QuickDEX is billed as a "random data organizer" that can be used to organize and quickly retrieve information. (How about a search through 1,000 cards in less than 2 seconds?) If that information is a telephone number (and if you have a modem), QuickDEX will even dial for you. If you don't have a modem, you can hold the telephone receiver to the Mac speaker and let the tones do the dialing for you. This feature is not a database management system function, but it sure adds a nice convenience.

As with any database management system, you add records (in the form of cards) and can then search through these to find the information

8
Data-
bases

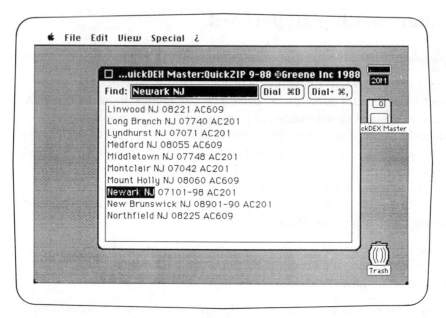

Fig. 8.15. A QuickDEX screen.

you need, to add, to delete, or to print. Cards are stored as decks. The PrintDEX utility allows for a high degree of report design flexibility for a DA, including the Rolodex format and many others.

One of PrintDEX's neatest features is a ZIP code directory called QuickZIP. With QuickZIP, you enter the name of the city, and you will see the ZIP code and the area code highlighted, as shown in figure 8.16.

Another database DA is DAtabase Version 1.1 (from Preferred Publishers; see fig. 8.17), which contains several different modules including a tutorial. DAtabase enables you to create a complete database; for flat file databases, DAtabase may be all you need. DAtabase contains some neat features, such as

- complete and friendly graphic interface

- phone dialing capability

- HyperCard-like design options for designing backgrounds and linking cards

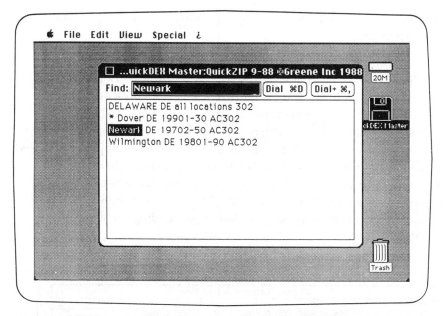

Fig. 8.16. *You can find ZIP codes quickly with QuickZIP.*

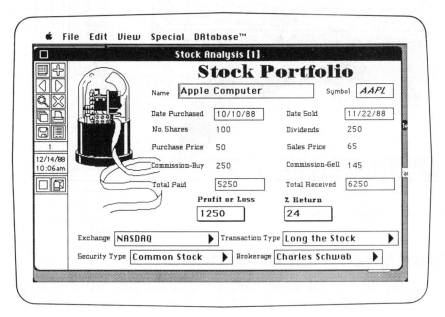

Fig. 8.17. *The opening screen for a stock analysis database accessed with DAtabase.*

8

Data-bases

However, DAtabase has no scripting capability, which distinguishes it from HyperCard.

An interesting approach to data management is Filevision (from Marvelin Corporation). Filevision is sold as a business tool. It differs from other accounting packages in that it enables you to work with information presented as pictures as well as numbers. At heart, Filevision is a database, and it has capabilities for sorting, adding records, and more. Filevision's drawing features, for example, were used to create a housing plan in which you click buttons indicating the house model to produce a floor plan of a particular house: a visual database. Another example is the map database you see in figure 8.18, which provides demographic information, depending on what button you click.

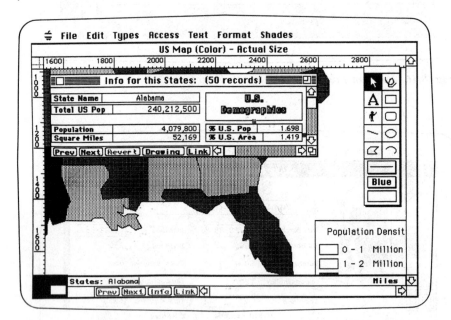

Fig. 8.18. A Filevision screen.

Using Specialized Databases

It shouldn't come as any surprise that many people have the need for a particular data management tool and don't want to fuss with creating their own database management system.

EndNote (from Niles Associates) is an example. EndNote's special job is to store and manage bibliographic references. For many of you, this may not be a top priority, but for many others (such as researchers, lawyers, and academic types) this is what much of their work consists of, and to have a tool so helpful is a blessing. EndNote comes as a DA and as a full-blown application. Maybe everyone likes something, but bibliographic management tasks are something that no one likes.

Figure 8.19 shows 12 references available on a sample EndNote library, and how a reference appears when selected. You can see the complete reference ready to be modified as the user chooses.

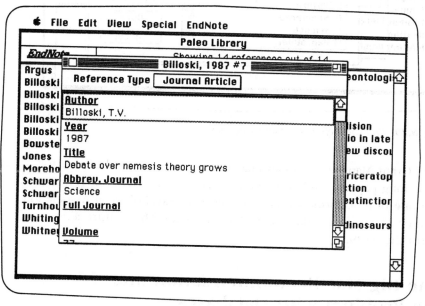

Fig. 8.19. *An EndNote Library reference.*

Figure 8.20 shows you the choices you have for categorizing references when you go to the Reference Type option.

Another specialized database from Niles is Grant Manager, which is a checkbook-like database and spreadsheet combination that helps you manage private and federal grants by keeping track of accounts, payments, and other types of important grant-related activities. When the month (or year) is over, you can print a record of all transactions.

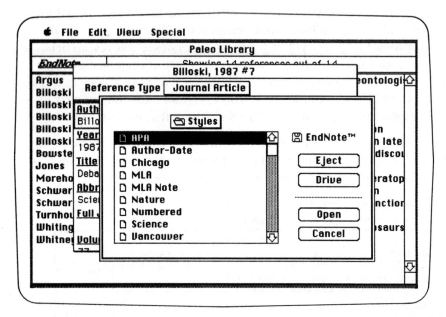

Fig. 8.20. *EndNote reference type categories.*

With Grant Manager, you can manage up to 32,000 references (for those long papers), and you can automatically format your references into one of nine formats (such as American Psychological Association style or *The Chicago Manual of Style* format). This feature alone is worth the $129.

The Big Mac Recommendation and the Problem with Databases

Databases are the newest and the least used of the big three Mac applications (word processing, spreadsheets, and databases). In 1988, for example, only $15 million worth of database products were sold compared to hundreds of millions of dollars for the other applications. Why the hesitation? Excel has been such a market leader that many people have used it or Works as their database.

Although some people prefer the ease of setting up with FileMaker II and the easy linking with Reflex Plus, not any of these or the other major hitters (Panorama, 4th Dimension, Dbase Mac, or Double Helix, among others) have gained an inroad into the user or the business community. Another problem is that because databases have not been around a very long time, there isn't even an established base of users, especially in the business world.

So what should you do? Look at the summary table in figure 8.21 to get some idea about the comparison between major database applications. Then, with this application, more than any other, really try before you buy, and talk to others who have database needs. Ask them what they want their database to do that it cannot do, and use the summary chart to find a database with the features that appeal to you.

	FoxBase+/Mac	4th Dimension	dBASE Mac	FileMaker II	Reflex Plus	Double Helix II
Version	2	2	1.01	1	1.01	51
Document Size Limit	1 billion records	32,000 chars.	Avail. Disk Space	Avail. Disk Space	Avail. Disk Space	Unlimited
Memory Required	1M	1M	512K	512K	512K	1M
Suggested Retail Price	$495	$795	$495	$299	$279	$595
Street Price	$205	$389	$329	$229	$189	$339
Size of Basic Application	800K	905K	800K	384K	350K	
Relational Capabilities	yes	yes	yes	no	yes	yes
What Can It Do with Text?						
Condensed	yes	yes	no	yes	no	If installed
Extended	yes	yes	no	yes	no	If installed
Largest Font Size	Largest installed	72	127	72	Largest installed	Largest installed
Small Caps	yes	yes	no	yes	no	If installed
Smallest Font Size	Smallest installed	3	4	6	Smallest installed	Smallest installed
Strike-through	yes	yes	no	yes	no	If installed
Subscript	no	yes	no	yes	no	If installed
Superscript	no	yes	no	yes	no	If installed
What Files Can It Read?						
DIF	no	yes	yes	no	no	yes
SYLK	no	yes	yes	yes	no	yes
Text Only	yes	yes	yes	yes	yes	yes
Others	dBASE III		Jazz, MS File, Multiplan, Omnis 3, OverVUE, PFS	Merged files		
What Files Can It Write To?						
DIF	no	yes	yes	no	no	yes
SYLK	no	yes	yes	yes	no	yes
Text Only	yes	yes	yes	yes	yes	yes
Others	dBASE III					
What Functions Does It Offer?						
Math Functions	yes	yes*	yes*	yes*	yes	yes
Text Functions	yes	yes*	yes*	yes*	yes	yes
Date/Time Functions	yes	yes*	yes*	yes*	yes	yes
Financial Functions	yes*	yes*	yes*	yes*	yes	yes
Statistical Functions	yes*	yes*	yes*	yes*	yes	yes
*Available or Programmable						
What About Windows?						
Max. Number of Open Windows	9	8	16	8	15	Unlimited
Multiple Windows to a Document	yes	yes	yes	yes	yes	yes
What Does It Do For Footnotes?						
At End of Page	yes	no	no	yes	no	yes
At End of Document	yes	no	no	no	no	no
Automatic Numbering	yes	no	no	no	no	no
How Does It Handle Graphics?						
Page Preview	yes	yes	yes	yes	no	

Fig. 8.21. *A summary chart of the various database programs.*

	FoxBase+/Mac	4th Dimension	dBASE Mac	FileMaker II	Reflex Plus	Double Helix II
Report Summaries	yes	yes	yes	yes	yes	yes
Calculated Fields	yes	yes	yes	yes	yes	yes
Picture Fields	yes	yes	yes	yes	yes	yes
Import Pictures	yes	yes	yes	yes	yes	yes
Produce Charts	no	yes	no	no	no	no
Edit Pictures	no	no	Scaling	no	no	no
Other Features						
Mail Merge to Other Programs	yes	yes	yes	yes	yes	yes
Automatic Counting of Words, Lines, etc.	no	Programmable	Programmable	no	no	no
Macros	yes	yes	yes	yes	no	no
Macro Editor	yes	yes	yes	yes	no	no
Templates	yes	Available at cost	yes	yes	yes	yes
On-line Help	yes	yes	yes	yes	yes	yes
Sample Files	yes	yes	yes	yes	yes	yes
Specific Other Features	Arrays				Not	
	Code generator				Programmable	
	Compiler					
	Trace window					
	Debug window					
	Report writer					

Fig. 8.21. *A summary chart of the various database programs.*

9

Integrated Software and Financial Programs

You may not believe it, but many people never pick up a word processor or a spreadsheet; they just don't need them in their line of work. Many Mac users can do all their work with a word processor, a spreadsheet, or a database. Others, however, need to go beyond these applications toward the completion of more specific types of tasks such as accounting, tax preparation, the statistical analysis of data, and project management, among others.

This chapter introduces you to these applications and shows you what you should look for in these special task tools. It also gives you some information about different training options, if you decide to look for outside help in learning these and other applications.

Integrated Software

Often you will not need the three most powerful types of software—word processors, databases, and spreadsheets. Instead, you may want some features of each in an integrated package. The most important characteristic that distinguishes an integrated package from other software is that the sharing of information between modules in the package is "seamless." That's a computerese term that means you can easily go from one module to another without worrying about file formats, memory restrictions, menu changes, and general compatibility. The screen in figure 9.1 shows the interface for Microsoft Works 2.00, from which you can select one of four program options.

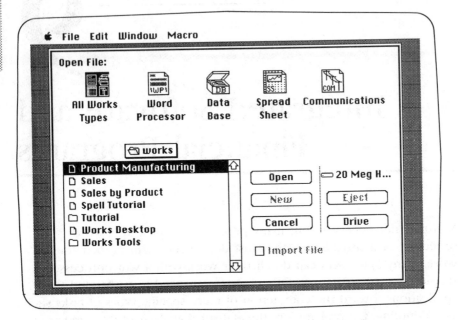

Fig. 9.1. *The opening Works screen.*

For example, you can create a database file that consists of names and addresses and then, with very little trouble, incorporate those records into personalized letters by using a print-merge feature. Other programs sometimes can communicate easily with one another, but integrated packages are designed especially for that purpose. Most Macintosh integrated software packages, like Works, communicate well. One of the added benefits of Works is that it maintains file compatibility with other Microsoft products, such as Excel and Word. Most users find that Works is a good introduction to the more powerful Microsoft programs.

Works: A Typical Integrated Package

Because Works is the leading product of its kind, I use it as an example of the various software capabilities that I discuss in this section of the chapter.

In the past, other products such as Jazz and Modern Jazz have been introduced as integrated projects, but late release dates and many "bugs" (computerese for problems in the program) caused their abrupt failure in the marketplace.

Works offers four modules. These modules and some of their features are the following:

- Word processor

  Standard editing and file features, such as cut and paste

  Spell checker

  An object-oriented draw layer to draw lines, circles, boxes, and graphics and include them in the text

  Automatic reformatting and pagination

  Easy insertion of graphics (a particularly strong feature because many "full fledged" word processing and desktop publishing programs do not allow easy inclusion of graphics)

  An efficient well-designed low- to mid-level word processor modeled on Word

- Spreadsheet

  Formulas—more than 60 of Excel's most useful functions in mathematics, statistics, trigonometry, logic, and finance, as well as formulas for date and time and special operations

  Creation of line, bar, stack, and combination graphs

  Cell notes to bring attention to a particular part of the worksheet

  An object-oriented draw layer identical to the one in the word processor

  A mid-level spreadsheet modeled on Excel

- Database

  Capability to create records and perform such basic database functions as sorting and selecting

  Various formats for reporting database information

  A mid-level version of Microsoft's File or Multiplan database

- Communications

  Full communications capability to share data with other computers, including on-line information services, other Macs,

DOS-based machines, and even mainframes. Works provides the conduit through which you communicate.

Direct dialing from the database with saved phone books and settings

Hayes modem compatibility

The word processor, database, and spreadsheet share such features as fully functioning macros, a macro editor, and a print preview function.

Works can copy information from one module to another with little effort. In fact, (depending on memory) you can have up to 14 different windows open at the same time to make things even easier, although it's somewhat doubtful that you could "manage" that many at once. The most common way of transferring information among documents is the familiar cut-copy-paste routine using the Clipboard (see Chapter 2).

Transferring Data from the Database to the Word Processor

Suppose that you have your list of customers in the Works database and want to use that same list as part of the word processor file. What do you do? That's the beauty of an integrated package where applications are constructed in a way that transferring data from one module to the other is simple and accurate.

Figure 9.2 shows the results of the Show Form command, where the database is defined and then built by the addition of information to each field. Figure 9.3 shows the database with five records (each having five fields) already entered, saved, and displayed using the Show List command. You will notice that Works tells you that you are looking at a database by putting (DB) in the title bar of the window. This database can be searched, sorted, and worked with like any other.

Let's assume that you have written a letter with the word processing module and you want to include the information in the database in that letter. Figure 9.4 shows that both the database and the word processing files are open, with the database material selected in order to be transferred. Figure 9.5 shows the letter that was created with the word-processed text after the records from the database have been copied into it.

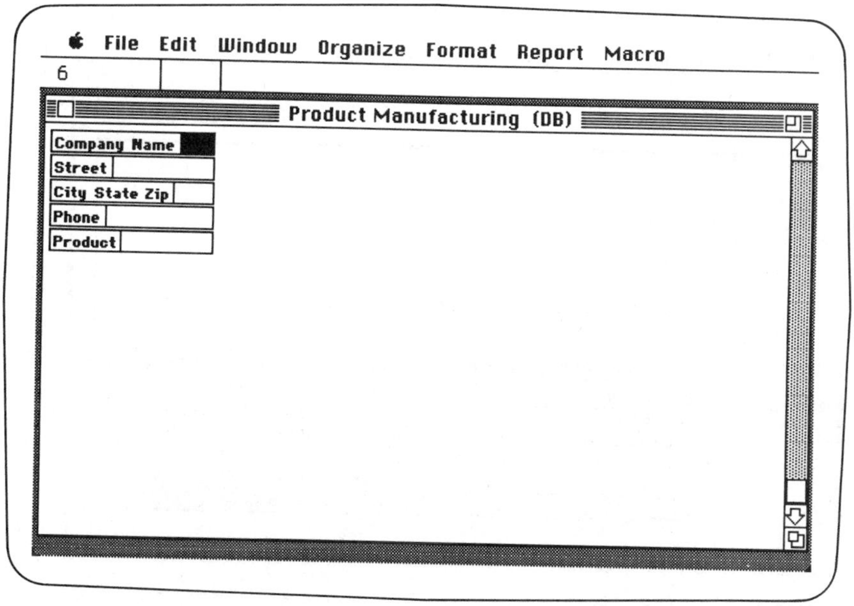

Fig. 9.2. The Works database forms window.

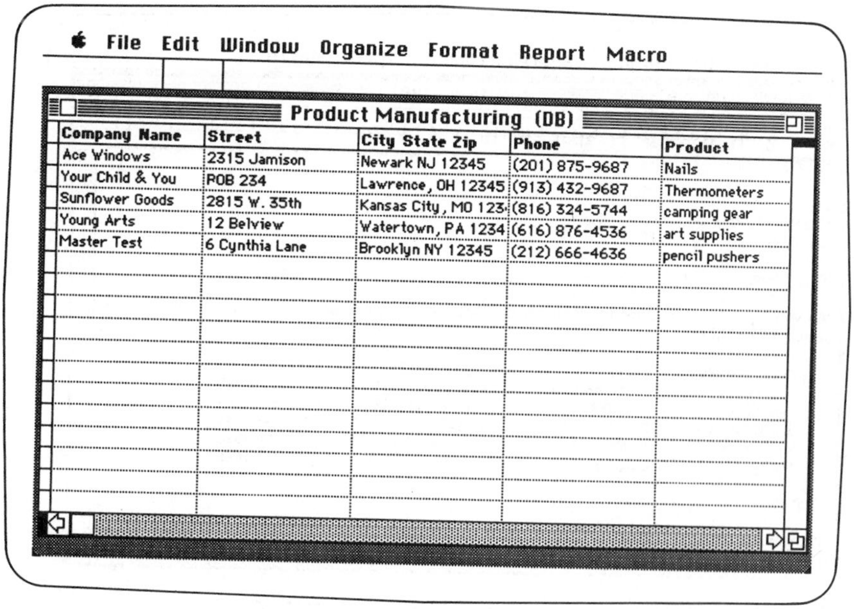

Fig. 9.3. A simple database in Works with five records and five fields.

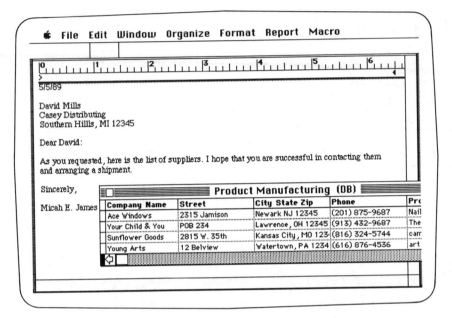

Fig. 9.4. *Preparing to import the database information into a letter.*

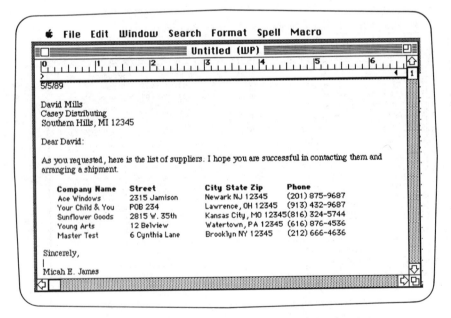

Fig. 9.5. *The letter after the database material has been imported.*

This operation is a simple copy and paste. Not having to leave one module to enter another makes the procedure much easier and is a real benefit of any integrated package. This sharing is not a substitute for MultiFinder, which enables you to run different applications simultaneously. The integrated nature of Works, however, enables you to share information between Works modules with ease.

Transferring Data from the Spreadsheet to the Database

Figure 9.6 shows a Works spreadsheet. The rows and columns contain data describing the sales of certain products over a five-year period. When you transfer data from a worksheet to a database, each column in the worksheet becomes a field in the database, and each row becomes a record; the data then can be worked with, as can any database information. In this case, only the data on products 1 and 2 is being imported, so only columns A, B, and C will be selected.

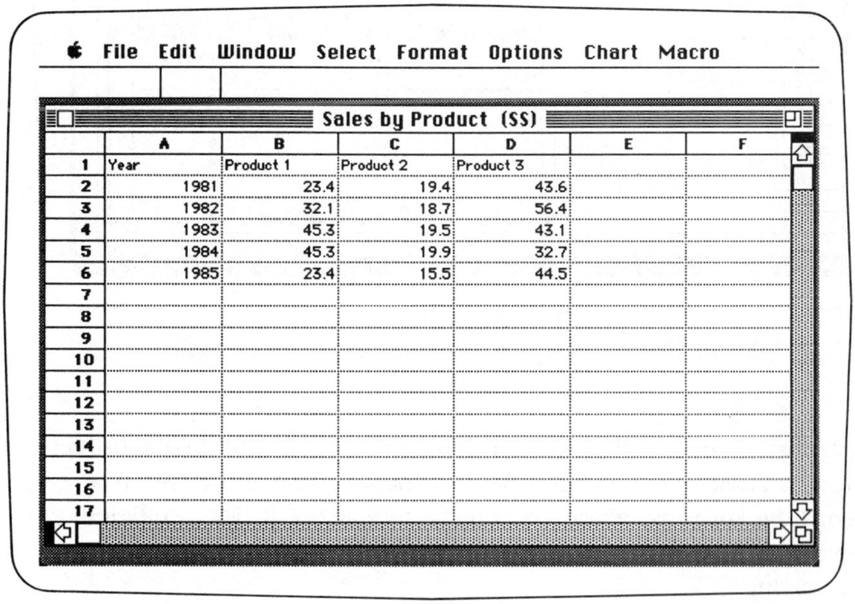

🍎 File Edit Window Select Format Options Chart Macro

Sales by Product (SS)

	A	B	C	D	E	F
1	Year	Product 1	Product 2	Product 3		
2	1981	23.4	19.4	43.6		
3	1982	32.1	18.7	56.4		
4	1983	45.3	19.5	43.1		
5	1984	45.3	19.9	32.7		
6	1985	23.4	15.5	44.5		
7						
8						
9						
10						
11						
12						
13						
14						
15						
16						
17						

Fig. 9.6. *A Works spreadsheet file.*

To transfer data into a database, however, first you must create a database form with sufficient room to receive the data to be transferred. Then when you paste in the data you have copied, the information falls into place, as figure 9.7 shows. Although the data is arranged in rows and columns for both modules, you can perform operations on the database that you cannot do with the spreadsheet; you can generate reports and merge data with other documents to produce personalized forms. You also can define number formats (Works calls these *attributes*) identically in both modules.

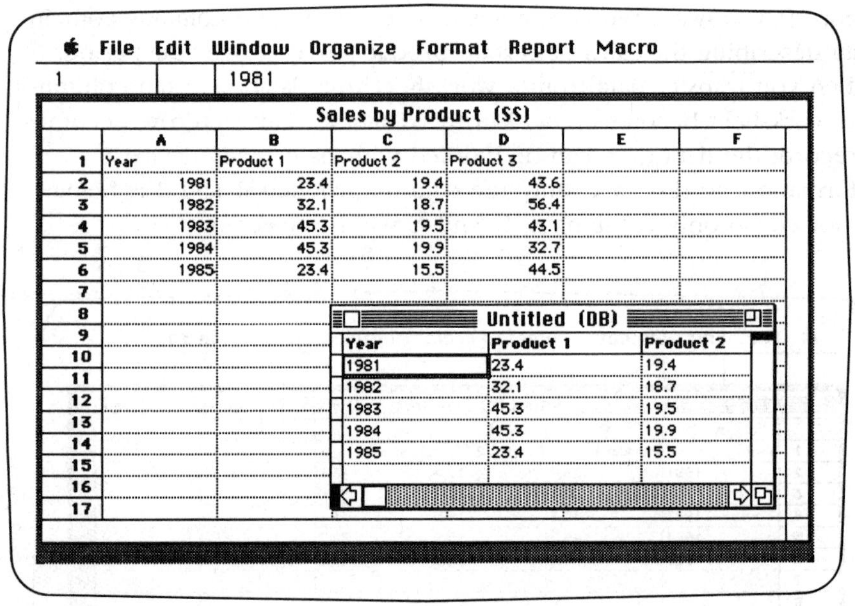

File Edit Window Organize Format Report Macro

1 | 1981

Sales by Product (SS)

	A	B	C	D	E	F
1	Year	Product 1	Product 2	Product 3		
2	1981	23.4	19.4	43.6		
3	1982	32.1	18.7	56.4		
4	1983	45.3	19.5	43.1		
5	1984	45.3	19.9	32.7		
6	1985	23.4	15.5	44.5		
7						

Untitled (DB)

Year	Product 1	Product 2
1981	23.4	19.4
1982	32.1	18.7
1983	45.3	19.5
1984	45.3	19.9
1985	23.4	15.5

Fig. 9.7. Data transferred from a Works spreadsheet to a database.

Once again, you should note the relationship between a spreadsheet and a database: a column is a field in the database and a row is a record. Be sure that when you create a database, it has a sufficient number of fields to hold the number of columns that you are transferring.

Importing Files from Other Products into Works

Works imports files from many other products, especially such Microsoft products as Word and Excel. Works also imports MacWrite files. Unfortunately, Works is limited to importing data from the earlier versions of other programs. For example, Works can import Word files only from Version 1.05 or earlier. Word 4, however, enables you to save files in Works (Word 1.0) and Word 3.0 format.

To avoid this limitation, you can create a text file with your software (such as MacWrite, Word, Wingz, or Full Impact) and then open the text file in Works. You will lose some information (such as format and font), but you will not have to type the entire document again.

Another alternative is to save the file in DIF (Data Interchange Format) or 1-2-3 format if possible, where formulas remain intact, which does not happen when a file is saved as straight text.

Works Add-Ons

As with every other Mac application, Works has add-ons that increase its usefulness. Lundeen & Associates, who were involved in the development of Works, are the manufacturers of WorksPlus Spell and WorksPlus command.

WorksPlus Spell

What does WorksPlus Spell offer that Works Spell lacks?

- WorksPlus Spell counts words.

- WorksPlus Spell remembers what has been checked, so the program doesn't have to stop and query you when it encounters a misspelled or mistyped word a second time.

- WorksPlus Spell lets you use glossary terms, short blocks of text that you use over again and want to enter quickly.

- WorksPlus Spell is fast: more than 350 words a minute—15 times faster than the Works spell checker.

- WorksPlus Spell checks your spelling interactively as you type, if you wish. A beep tells you that the word is *pieces,* not *peices.*

(But the program cannot tell you when your typographic error has resulted in another word; for example, WorksPlus Spell does not beep if you type *form* when you meant *from.*)

- WorksPlus Spell enables you to view and edit the contents of the dictionary.

WorksPlus Spell offers a variety of nice options and can be a great help in polishing documents. Keep in mind, however, that any spell checker is merely a utility that checks spelling (and perhaps performs other functions). A spelling program does not teach you how to spell (although if you constantly misspell certain words, these misspellings should decrease eventually, because of sheer exposure to the correct spelling), and it does not tell you which spelling of a particular word you should use. For that, you need to go back to those weekly lists.

WorksPlus Command

Works has a macro feature, but WorksPlus Command goes beyond that level of performance. WorksPlus Command enables you to create programs in the WorksPlus Command macro language. WorksPlus Command also has some built-in macros for different Works modules. Among these are the following:

- For all Works tools—dialing a phone number, converting text, and saving all open files

- For the database or the spreadsheet—searching and replacing data and transforming values

- For the word processor—creating multicolumn documents, defining and using styles, resizing and repositioning pictures, and generating tables of contents and indexes

- For the database—filling data down a column and importing a database from another program

For example, suppose that you are working with a database of potential customers, and you want to call them all to try to persuade them to buy their supplies from you. Normally, to get out of a database, you need to call up your communications software, and then enter the number to dial. With WorksPlus Command, you can use the built-in macro called DialPhone. This macro is invoked by the ⌘-Shift-D key combination; the phone number in the database (one that is selected) will be dialed. This macro can save time when you have more than a few calls to place.

The new version of Command (2.0) also allows you to resize pictures, add recorded macros to the Command menu for easy selection, and play macros back in any application (not just Works).

Accounting Packages

Businesses of all sizes, as well as individuals, use general accounting software, tax management software, and checkbook accounting software to manage information. Whatever the task, business people, academics, and scientists find themselves dealing with numbers and needing to manipulate numerical information. With the Mac and some of the available software I will discuss later, description and calculation become easy.

Accounting is the process of measuring economic information and using it to help make decisions about budgets, payments, and financial planning. Most of the accounting software that is available for the Macintosh helps people with the everyday job of running a business. Some programs, like SBT (from SBT Corporation), handle many different functions, such as general ledger, accounts payable, and sales order processing; others, like Quicken from Intuit, serve a single purpose, such as balancing checkbooks. Many of these programs are configured to use spreadsheets or databases as their "engines." For example, SBT modules run on Foxbase+/Mac, a dBASE clone.

Before you shop for accounting assistance, you must determine your needs. If you are the owner of a business with frequent and complex financial transactions, you may need to seek additional assistance from an accountant to find out what program will fit your needs best. If you own a small business or you simply want some help with your taxes, what your friends use and like may be adequate. Among the basics that almost all business users need are the following:

- A *general ledger* program contains of a set of accounts and keeps track of transactions in them as the transactions occur. It also reconciles each account activity with overall balances and is the basis of a business's balance sheet.

- *Accounts receivable* and *accounts payable* features give the business manager information about what is coming in and what is going out, as well as whose accounts are overdue and by what amount.

- *Payroll* records such data as hours worked, overtime, hourly rate, Social Security and other tax information, and the generation of checks.

When you consider accounting, tax preparation, and other such software, keep in mind that the program does not "know" whether what you enter into it is valid. Financial and statistical applications give the saying "garbage in = garbage out" its meaning.

A Complete Accounting Library

The best way to get an idea of what a comprehensive accounting package can do is to examine the capabilities of a popular accounting package.

The SBT Database Accounting Library (Mac/Series Six Plus) was written using the dBASE database system and consists of 14 modules that are linked together. You can see how some of these modules are linked in figure 9.8. SBT is relational. For example, the balance due on an account can appear in several different modules, even though you enter the information about the account only once. (See Chapter 8 for a discussion of what *relational* means in data management.) SBT provides the source code and other development tools so that you can develop programs to meet your specific needs.

SBT's modules perform a variety of functions.

- The dLedger module gives you information about journal transactions and helps manage balance sheets and income statements. Figure 9.9 shows an SBT general ledger. This module can compute more than 20 different business ratios.

- The dInvoice/dStatements module keeps track of inventory and produces sales analysis and accounts payable and accounts receivable reports.

- The dPayables module writes checks and keeps track of business expenses.

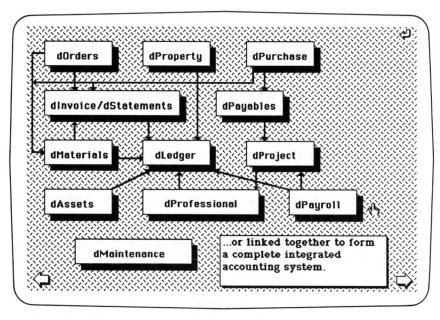

Fig. 9.8. *Linking modules of an accounting package.*

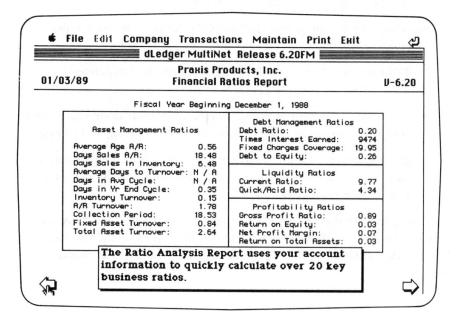

Fig. 9.9. *Financial ratios computed by SBT Mac/Six Plus modules.*

- dOrders tracks inventory and maintains sales orders. Because modules are linked (as in a relational database), dOrders enables you to create an invoice automatically when a product is shipped.

- dPurchase updates vendor and inventory account balances.

- dPayroll makes it easier to compute different types of payroll checks—for example, for employees who are hourly, those who are salaried, and those who are on commission. This module also generates W-2 forms and other IRS documents.

- dAssets can help you profit from the depreciation of equipment and other assets, and traces loan activity.

- dProject is one of the what-if modules of SBT. It examines how changes in categories can affect overall budgets.

- By tracking the use and cost of materials, dMaterials helps forecast the costs of manufacturing.

- dProfessional helps manage a business (mostly for professionals) by providing billing and accounts receivable capability, as well as reporting on how time is being spent.

- dProperty can help you manage everything from your office building to apartments and commercial real estate.

- dMaintenance helps you keep up with the maintenance schedule of equipment you sell or lease.

- dScanner reads information generated from bar code readers to help speed up such tasks as inventory, purchasing, and billing.

- dMenu/Backup is a file management system that helps manage files (move, delete, back up, and so on) and ensure against the loss of important data.

You purchase only the SBT modules that fit your needs. For example, for basic accounting, dInvoice/dStatements, dPayables, dPayroll, and dLedger are sufficient. If your company grows, you can add modules easily.

9

Other Accounting Packages

There are other accounting programs that offer many of the same features as the SBT library, such as Great Plains Software. Like SBT, Great Plains has the following features:

- General ledger
- Accounts payable
- Accounts receivable
- Payroll
- Inventory
- Purchase order
- Order entry
- Job cost
- Printers Ink
- Executive Advisor
- Network Manager

Great Plains also has some other features that are well worth noting. Especially interesting is the Executive Advisor, which analyzes business performance in tables or graphs. This module also includes 70 business ratios to help you to understand your current financial position and to decide about adjustments that you might need to make. Printers Ink is used to estimate printing costs and to track jobs from inception through completion. Printers Ink also produces schedules and invoices.

Great Plains also offers a Network Manager that has various levels of security and file protection and enables several people to use different Great Plains modules simultaneously. This networking arrangement is an attractive alternative to large, more powerful computers that would otherwise be needed for several people to access the software at the same time.

Insight Expert from Layered has many of the same capabilities as SBT and Great Plains. These modules are easy to use. Figure 9.10 shows an opening screen where the customer's logo has been clicked and the screen for the first customer is displayed (from a database of customers). When you click ITEM CARD, you see a description of items in the inventory and various important information about stock numbers and the like (see fig. 9.11). Insight Expert includes sets of templates for constructing entry forms and control logs to assist in tracking expenses.

The modules are accompanied by a complete training package that takes you from setting up to using the programs. Several different companies offer a variety of printed forms for use with Insight Expert. Layered has established a network of CPA firms and consultants who are trained to implement the Expert system for businesses. The cost of this service depends on the installer and his or her hourly rates.

Unlike some programs, which were originally created for DOS systems, Insight Expert was originally designed for the Macintosh. Thus, it has such features as multiple windows and uses double-clicking to add entries to a field.

Layered also offers a new mid-range accounting product called At Once, which is a bundled program of modules (you do not buy the modules individually). At Once includes general ledger, accounts receivable, accounts payable, and payroll, and at $395 it is a good place to start.

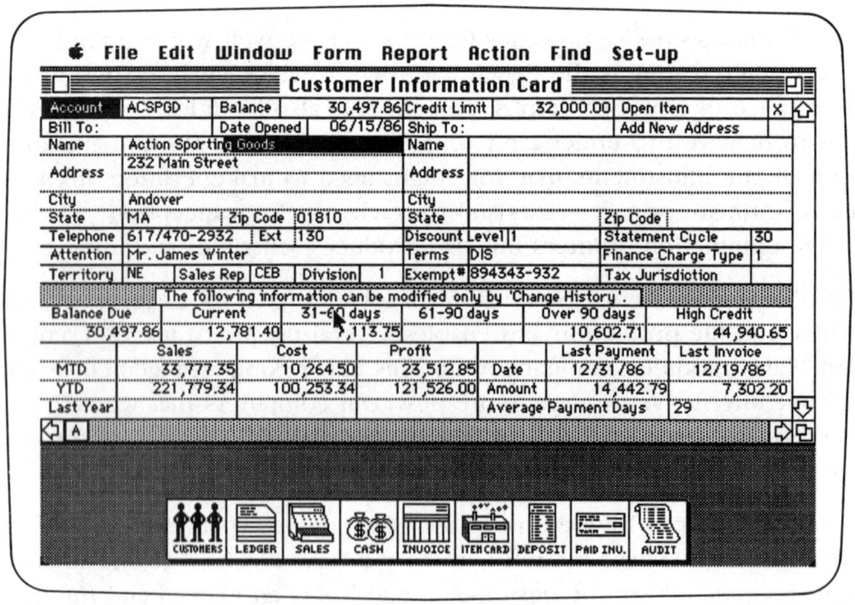

Fig. 9.10. *Selecting customers from the Insight database.*

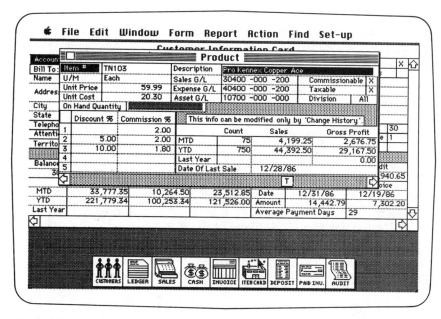

Fig. 9.11. *Selecting an item (a product) to work with.*

Another popular program, SuperMOM, or Super Mail Order Manager, (from National Tele-Press), is often compared to general ledger programs, but it can do much more. SuperMOM has the general ledger and accounting features, but it specializes in helping manage mail order business by offering such features as the following:

- Customer tracking by group and marketing efforts

- A variety of shipping charge methods

- Preparation of shipping manifests

- Inquiry tracking

The Tele-Press people offer exceptional support. They will even help you customize SuperMOM to meet your requirements. Figure 9.12, for example, shows an address file for a customer, including information about dates catalogs were sent, pricing, tax codes, and sales people involved.

This highly specialized vertical-market tool (dealing with products in various ranges for various worksheets) contains the standard material

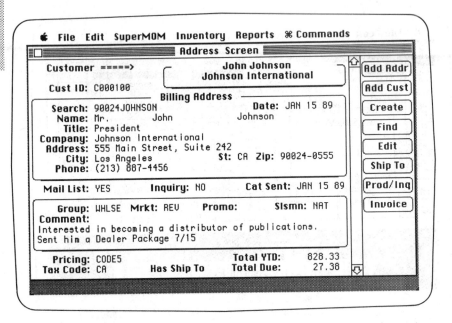

Fig. 9.12. *A sample screen from SuperMOM showing direct mail information.*

for accounting combined with a powerful marketing tool and is recommended for people in the catalog and direct mail business.

ShopKeeper (from ShopKeeper Software) is a less elaborate accounting system that is designed for ease of use and is especially suited for smaller businesses. Although ShopKeeper does not consist of linked modules, it does a nice job of keeping track of inventory. This program prepares bids and billing and other accounting "regulars," such as accounts payable and accounts receivable. ShopKeeper can do floor planning (for sales per square foot, for example); produce mailing labels; and read bar codes, which can be incorporated into point-of-sale management. ShopKeeper even reminds you to back up your file when you quit the present session. You can order specially designed checks and forms that ShopKeeper can print for you.

DacEasy (from Dac Software) combines home and business accounting features. DacEasy is easy to learn and is organized by menu, by the source, or by the type of the transaction. The program features a Bank menu, a Credit Card menu, an Invoice menu, an Accounting menu, and a Reports menu. When you sign on and set up accounts, you choose between personal and business accounts, allowing you access to DacEasy's listings of categories for such transactions as assets, liabilities, revenues, equity, and expenses.

Other accounting packages you may want to investigate include Rags to Riches, BPI General Accounting, Strictly Business, Simply Accounting, and Back to Basics Accounting. You may also want to look into Aatrix modules, Accountant Inc., CheckMark, MultiLedger Payroll, Flexware Accounting System, or In-House Accountant, M.D.A.

Forecasting and Planning Programs

Much of the material in this chapter discusses how to organize business information after it is generated. What about predicting outcomes on the basis of previous sales or employee information? Or designing a business plan?

Tim Berry of Palo Alto Software has designed a set of forecasting and planning tools that enable you to make predictions based on previous sales or employee information, as well as to design a business plan.

For example, Forecaster allows you to make a forecast not by using numbers, but by drawing a line (by clicking points along a scale) and having the program fit the numbers to it. Figure 9.13 shows a line drawn using the cursor; the values of the points are shown in the Forecast data window. You may enter information by number rather than by using the cursor, if you prefer.

The Business Plan Toolkit (from Palo Alto Software) is compatible with Excel (which you need to run many of Business Plan Toolkit's features) as well as almost all popular word processors. This planning tool helps you design a business plan and then use it in forecasting. Business Plan Toolkit is easy to use. As you can see in figure 9.14, a HyperCard Stack is used to generate a business plan (see Chapter 17 for more information about HyperCard). Through this stack, you answer questions about business plan categories, such as the example in figure 9.15. Some of the categories used are

- Executive summary

- Mission (goals of the company)

- Company history

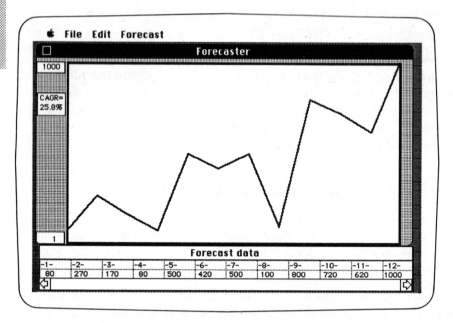

Fig. 9.13. *Using Forecaster to draw a forecasting line.*

- Company locations and facilities

- Product description and features

- Present and future products

- Market analysis

- Financial plan

- *Pro forma* cash flow

After you enter the answers to the questions, you simply create a text file and put all the information in it as you do in an actual business plan.

The Sales Marketing Forecasting Toolkit is designed around Excel and comes with Excel templates and macros for producing forecasts by customer polls, market share, the chain method, and several other techniques.

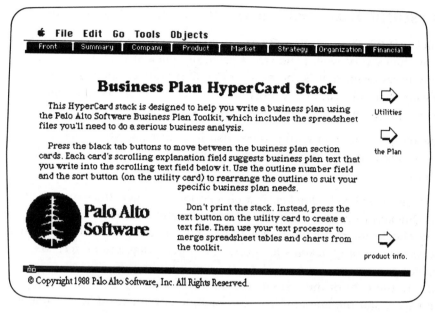

Fig. 9.14. *Generating a business plan using the Business Plan Toolkit.*

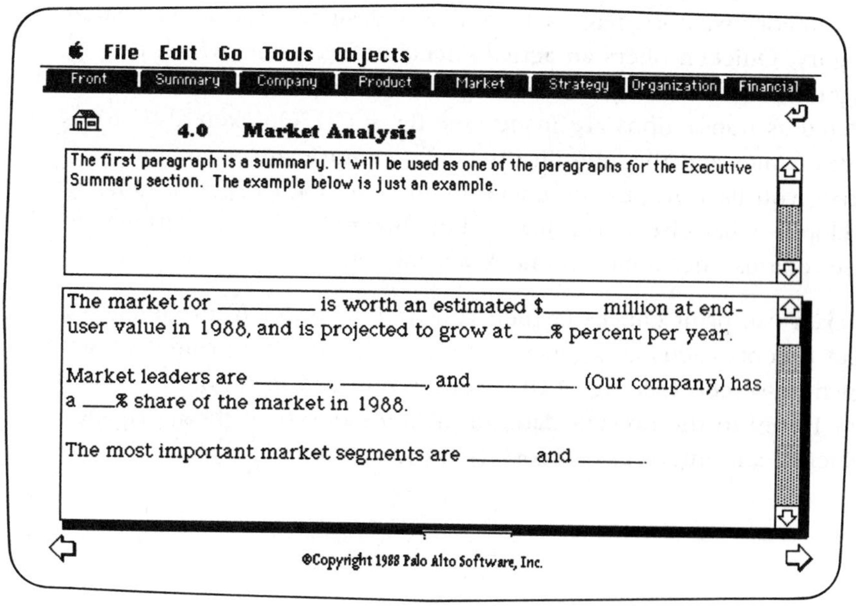

Fig. 9.15. *Questions for generating a business plan.*

Personal Business and Financial Programs

Quicken 1.02, from Intuit Software, is an inexpensive program that does a few things very well. (The street price of Quicken is about $32, and many users claim that is the best money they've ever spent.) It is unlikely that you can find a more intuitive and easy-to-use personal finance program.

Quicken presents you with screens that look just like your real checkbook ledger or the checks that you need to write and print every month.

At its simplest level, Quicken is a checkbook manager. But you can also use Quicken to generate reports of tax deductible items, write and print checks for recurring transactions, and track expenses. Figure 9.16 shows several of Quicken's features. The Enter Transactions screen enables you to enter checks, deposits, and withdrawals. You also can indicate the date of the transaction, an associated number (for a check), the payee, and the amount. You can include any memo that you might want to attach as well.

Figure 9.16 also shows the Category List (which you change as needed), from which the Tax Fed category has been selected. When this category was originally set up, it was designated as a tax-related category. Quicken offers an actual checkbook register, which the program maintains for you, allowing you to keep a balance that is updated as transactions are made (see fig. 9.17). Quicken also stores payees names and the amount due and can automate payment. Of course, you have to put the check in an envelope (a special Quicken envelope—what else?) and mail it, but this method is far better than those tedious once-a-month check-writing blues.

Quicken can print checks (which you have to order from Quicken for about 8 cents each) and generate reports that can be printed or simply shown on-screen (see fig. 9.18). Here, a transaction report is generated from 1/1/89 to the present date for all transactions in the mortgage (principal and interest) category (paid to Columbia Savings).

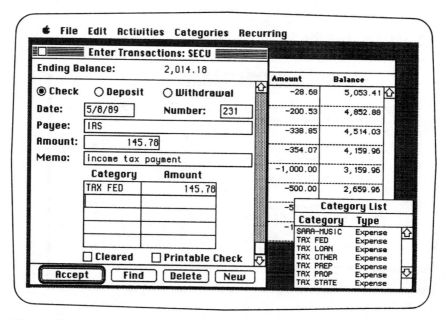

Fig. 9.16. Some Quicken windows.

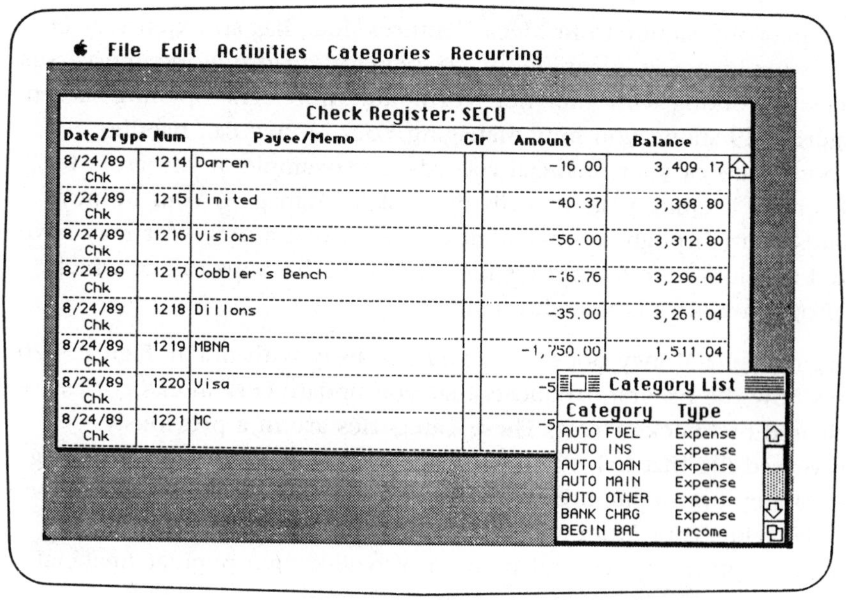

Fig. 9.17. The Quicken check register.

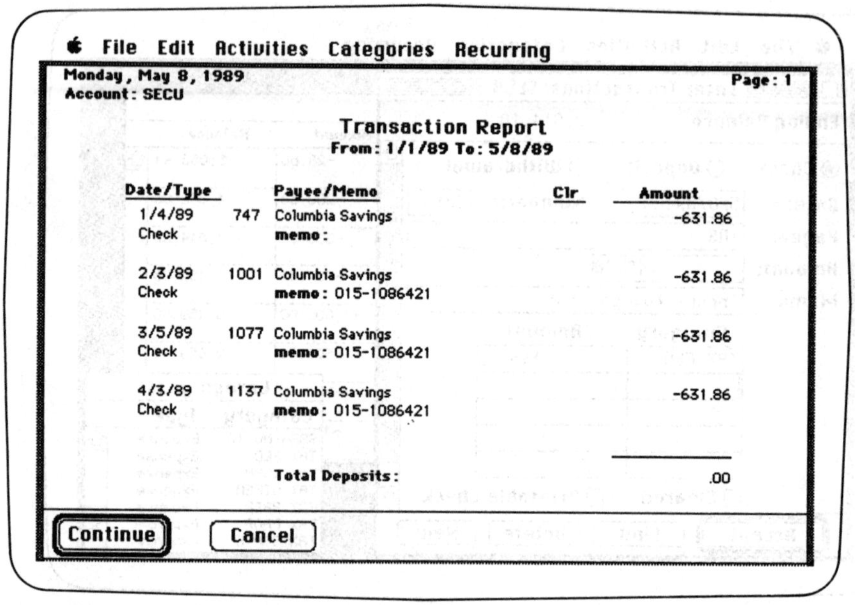

Fig. 9.18. A Quicken transaction report.

You can also export a Quicken file to an Excel spreadsheet.

Managing Your Money from Meca Ventures, Inc., has an extensive set of features for investing, planning for tax benefits, analyzing income versus expenses, working with your net worth, and more. The opening screen in figure 9.19 shows you how Managing Your Money can handle different facets of your financial records. For example, if you are a bit negligent in keeping your records up to date, Managing Your Money reminds you (through an on-screen message) that a new year may have started and it is time to transfer files and make backups (all of which the program will walk you through).

Managing Your Money doesn't let you get away with much. Figure 9.20 shows how the program requests that you update certain categories (indicated by check marks). These categories are in a previously constructed file that helps you estimate your year-end taxes. Managing Your Money even computes the tax values you may (or may not) owe. The Managing Your Money manual is outstanding, and this program seems to capture the wit and wisdom of well-known popular financial writer Andrew Tobias in an easy-to-use program.

Fig. 9.19. *The Managing Your Money opening screen.*

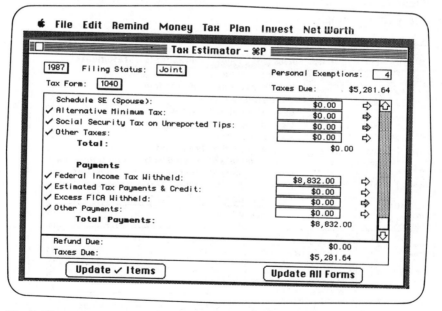

Fig. 9.20. *Managing Your Money automatically updates previous records as it performs such functions as estimating income tax payments.*

Tax Preparation

MacInTax, from Softview, is one of several programs that can help you prepare your tax returns. MacInTax forms look just like Internal Revenue Service forms. MacIntax even prints the forms exactly as they would appear if you had completed the actual IRS forms, and the IRS will accept the signed printed output.

MacInTax is a large, well-thought-out spreadsheet program that links many different smaller spreadsheets (representing tax schedules) to produce one final accounting. Figure 9.21 shows a MacInTax screen, including a copy of an actual tax form. You can access any one of more than 70 schedules from this main screen. As you enter data on a schedule or the main form, all the information is tied together into the bottom line. This means that any information you enter into any of the schedules or forms is automatically entered into any other form that might list that schedule as a source of input. Programs like MacInTax are a group of very well designed worksheets that are all "linked" to one another. They are not independent of each other; what happens in one affects the others. The MacInTax package also comes with an excellent *Federal Tax Highlights* book, produced by the accounting firm of Arthur Young.

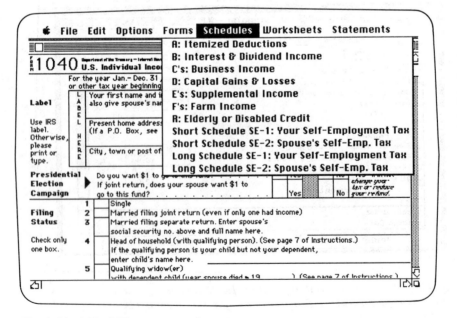

Fig. 9.21. *A MacInTax screen and menu.*

For the simple 1040 EZ form, nothing beats a program like MacInTax. After you get your W-2 form, you can complete your taxes easily in less time than it takes to print the return. On the other hand, if you have a complicated and detailed tax situation, MacInTax can certainly handle the numbers—but do you know what numbers go where? Perhaps, but don't assume that if you use a computerized tax-generation system your decisions as to what items are deductible will be acceptable to the IRS automatically. The IRS accepts what is allowed by the tax law, not necessarily what your Mac can generate.

Last warning! These programs can only be slick, fun, and easy to impress your spouse, if you enter the correct numbers in the correct categories. In other words, programs like Quicken, EZTax, or Managing Your Money will enable you to deduct the costs of ice cream for the kids. How you respond to your friendly IRS agent is another story. Perhaps the first time around, have your return checked by a tax accountant so that you can save yourself quite a headache.

Spreadsheets as Financial Tools

Even though there are specific programs for accounting and other financial uses, don't forget what your spreadsheet can offer you. Be it Excel, Wingz, Full Impact, or Works, by using the built-in functions, you can easily program the spreadsheet to produce the exact type of output you need. With their ease of programming (Excel) and scripting features (Wingz), spreadsheets can be especially useful for business owners.

You have already seen in this section how certain products are designed specifically to be used with spreadsheets like Excel. Here are some examples of other accounting activities, which can be performed with spreadsheets.

Figure 9.22 shows an Excel worksheet—Balance Sheet and Ratio Analyses—for the four quarters of a business year. This worksheet was relatively easy to construct with only a few formulas. Even what seem like complicated computations can be executed with simple planning. The payroll ledger in figure 9.23 shows the total amount due after calculating overtime and tax contributions (using simple formulas).

Balance Sheet/Ratio Analysis

	A	B	C	D	E	F	G	H
1	BALANCE SHEET AND RATIO ANALYSES							
2								
3					J&R Manufacturing			
4					101-598 W.57th Street			
5					Seattle, WA 12345			
6					(314)-878-2400			
7								
8				Quarter 1	Quarter 2	Quarter 3	Quarter 4	Total
9	ASSETS							
10								
11	Cash			$899,354	$1,876,453	$987,096	$994,097	$4,757,000
12	Market Securities			$298,576	$372,645	$172,645	$253,456	$1,097,322
13	Bonds			$98,465	$101,987	$100,987	$99,067	$400,506
14	Treasury			$20,000	$40,000	$30,000	$20,000	$110,000
15	Accounts Receivable			$286,756	$354,676	$325,676	$298,765	$1,265,873
16	Inventory Value			$789,465	$867,543	$657,486	$657,887	$2,972,381
17	Prepayments/Taxes			$150,987	$104,987	$135,768	$107,987	$499,729
18								
19	Total Current Assets			$2,543,603	$3,718,291	$2,409,658	$2,431,259	$11,102,811
20								
21	Equipment			$645,978	$645,978	$645,978	$645,978	$2,583,912
22	Property			$1,500,000	$1,500,000	$1,500,000	$1,500,000	$6,000,000
23	Depreciation			($62,800)	($67,196)	($71,900)	($76,933)	($278,828)
24								
25	Total Fixed Assets			$2,083,178	$2,078,782	$2,074,078	$2,069,045	$8,305,084
26								
27	TOTAL ASSETS			$4,626,781	$5,797,073	$4,483,736	$4,500,304	$19,407,895
28								
29	LIABILITIES							
30	Notes Payable			$65,748	$67,345	$90,867	$87,456	$311,416
31	Employee's Retirement			$2,345,756	$2,978,654	$2,876,456	$2,313,453	$10,514,319
32	Taxes On Income			$89,675	$78,454	$84,567	$91,243	$343,939
33	Wages			$213,453	$241,234	$231,456	$243,453	$929,596
34	Mortgage			$5,968	$5,968	$5,968	$5,968	$23,872
35	Loans			$87,456	$65,375	$54,768	$45,654	$253,253
36	Long Term Debt			$354,674	$453,123	$543,234	$453,654	$1,804,685
37								
38	TOTAL LIABILITIES			$3,162,730	$3,890,153	$3,887,316	$3,240,881	$14,181,080
39								
40	STOCKHOLDER'S EQUITY							
41	Common Stock			$1,134,222	$187,657	$165,467	$176,789	$1,664,135
42								
43	TOTAL EQUITY			$1,134,222	$1,875,641	$1,654,345	$1,231,232	$5,895,440
44								
45	TOTAL LIABILITIES AND EQUITY			$4,296,952	$5,765,794	$5,541,661	$4,472,113	$20,076,520
46								
47	RATIOS							
48	Current Ratio			1.46	1.49	1.15	1.39	1.37
49	(Assets/Liabilities)							
50	Equity Ratio			0.25	0.32	0.37	0.27	0.30
51	(Equity/Assets)							
52	Debt/Equity Ratio			2.79	2.07	2.35	2.63	2.46
53	(Liabilities/Equity)							

Fig. 9.22. *Using a spreadsheet for calculating a balance sheet.*

Payroll Ledger

	A	B	C	D	E	F	G	H	I	J	K	L	M	N
1	PAYROLL LEDGER													
2														
3	FICA value		0.08											
4	State Tax		0.00											
5	Overtime Rate		1.50											
6														
7	Name	# Ded	FIT	Hourly	Hours	Over-	Over-	Base	Total	FICA	FIT	State	Total	Total
8			Rate	Wage	Worked	time	Time ($)	Salary	Wages			Tax	Deduction	Payment
9														
10	J.K.	2	0.33	$11.50	51	11	$189.75	$586.50	$776.25	$44.05	$193.55	$32.26	$269.85	$316.65
11	H.G.	2	0.15	$7.50	42	2	$22.50	$315.00	$337.50	$23.66	$47.25	$17.33	$88.23	$226.77
12	W.B.	1	0.15	$8.50	45	5	$63.75	$382.50	$446.25	$28.73	$57.38	$21.04	$107.14	$275.36
13	R.T.	4	0.15	$8.00	41	1	$12.00	$328.00	$340.00	$24.63	$49.20	$18.04	$91.87	$236.13
14	I.O.	2	0.28	$8.50	42	2	$25.50	$357.00	$382.50	$26.81	$99.96	$19.64	$146.41	$210.59
15	F.D.	2	0.28	$7.50	44	4	$45.00	$330.00	$375.00	$24.78	$92.40	$18.15	$135.33	$194.67
16	W.E.	1	0.28	$11.00	48	8	$132.00	$528.00	$660.00	$39.65	$147.84	$29.04	$216.53	$311.47
17	H.T.	2	0.28	$12.00	40	0	$0.00	$480.00	$480.00	$36.05	$134.40	$26.40	$196.85	$283.15
18	W.Q.	2	0.28	$10.00	50	10	$150.00	$500.00	$650.00	$37.55	$140.00	$27.50	$205.05	$294.95
19	T.F.	0	0.28	$8.50	44	4	$51.00	$374.00	$425.00	$28.09	$104.72	$20.57	$153.38	$220.62
20														
21			TOTALS		447			4181.00		313.99	1066.69	229.96	1610.64	2570.36
22														
23														
24														
25														
26														
27														
28														
29														
30														
31														
32														
33														
34														
35														
36														

Fig. 9.23. *Using a spreadsheet to calculate wages due.*

Some developers have combined the power of spreadsheets with specific user demands to create spreadsheet-dependent templates for such tasks such as the preparation of taxes. One of these companies, EZ Ware Corporation, produces EZTax-Prep 1040 and EZTax-Plan Business for the preparation of federal income tax returns. EZ Ware runs under Excel.

These products contain all the formulas and categories needed to complete the returns. You simply enter the numbers in the appropriate places. EZTax-Plan has some nice features. It prepares your present schedule of taxes, and it can help you plan for the future by predicting what your taxes will be for the next 45 years. Perhaps EZTax-Plan's most valuable feature is its side-by-side comparison of different tax strategies, where you can finally see the advantages of giving nephew Bruce that $1,000 or keeping it for yourself.

EZWare includes such extras as a guide to the Tax Reform Act of 1986, free first upgrades, and an increasing number of software packages that will prepare certain state returns. EZWare also includes acetate templates to help prepare batches of returns (for the professional return preparers). The 1989 version will work with Excel 2.2 (which is the latest release of Excel from Microsoft) as well as older versions.

Statistical Analysis Programs

In the old days (which few of us remember) mainframes (and the personal computers of that era, which were handheld calculators) were used almost exclusively to "crunch" numbers, that is, to take data, manipulate it, and process it. Suppose, for example, that a manager is interested in the relationship between sales in dollars and the number of hours of sales training. Back then, the manager had a punch card for each sales person; on that card were entered the values for the two variables being examined. Today, you can use simple and quick statistical analysis programs on the Mac and have your answer in a fraction of the time.

The statistical analysis, or "number crunching," software that is available today is simply incredible. The capabilities of such programs as Systat and Statview 512 mimic the capability of mainframes today. And in some cases, these programs exceed the mainframe's features because of the control you have.

Systat offers three levels of programs: MyStat (free), FastStat ($195), and Systat ($395). Systat can handle the most complex operations. You can get Mystat free by sending the company a letter of request; the company hopes that later you will buy FastStat or Systat.

What's a Good Statistics Program?

The answer to this question depends on your needs, but any statistics program should have the following features:

- Easy transferability of data between applications. For example, you can create your data file using Wingz, save it as a text file, and easily import it into MyStat (from Systat).

- Ease of use. Most users of statistical analysis programs know what they want to do, so the options should be easily available.

- Graphic output. Even the most simple data becomes more powerful when it is illustrated. Histograms, stem and leaf charts, box charts, and other charts and graphs should be available as well.

- Data transformation. Many times, data needs to be transformed or recoded to make it more easily understood. A good statistics program should be capable of assigning weights, recoding, or transforming special types of standardized scores.

- Output that can be easily understood, including probability levels that are associated with the results. No more searching through tables of significance levels; they're all right there in the output.

Most programs begin with some kind of data screen like the ones shown in figure 9.24 (created using FastStat from Systat) and in figure 9.25 (created with StatView 512+). On the data screen, you enter the data you want to use and then go on to choose from a variety of dialog boxes the type of analysis you want to work with.

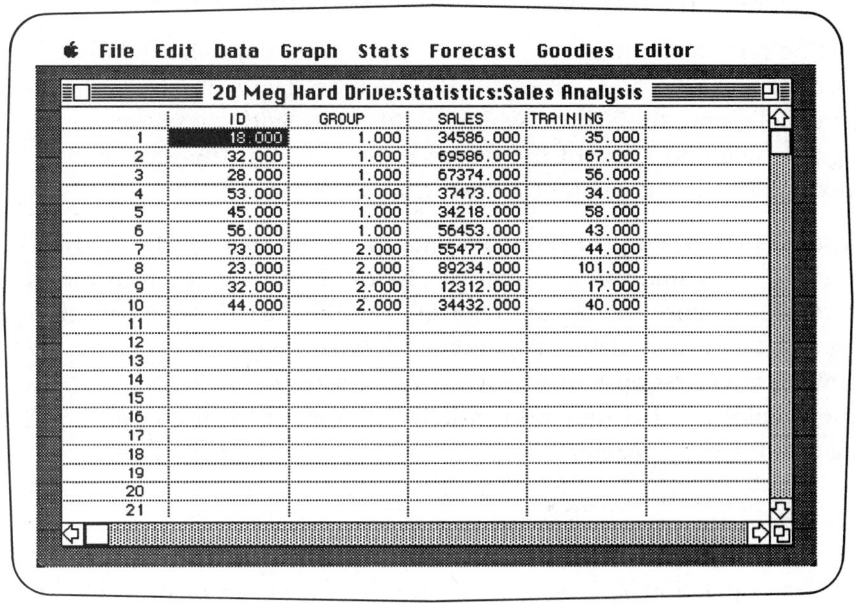

File Edit Data Graph Stats Forecast Goodies Editor

20 Meg Hard Drive:Statistics:Sales Analysis

	ID	GROUP	SALES	TRAINING
1	18.000	1.000	34586.000	35.000
2	32.000	1.000	69586.000	67.000
3	28.000	1.000	67374.000	56.000
4	53.000	1.000	37473.000	34.000
5	45.000	1.000	34218.000	58.000
6	56.000	1.000	56453.000	43.000
7	73.000	2.000	55477.000	44.000
8	23.000	2.000	89234.000	101.000
9	32.000	2.000	12312.000	17.000
10	44.000	2.000	34432.000	40.000

Fig. 9.24. A FastStat data screen with 10 cases and four variables.

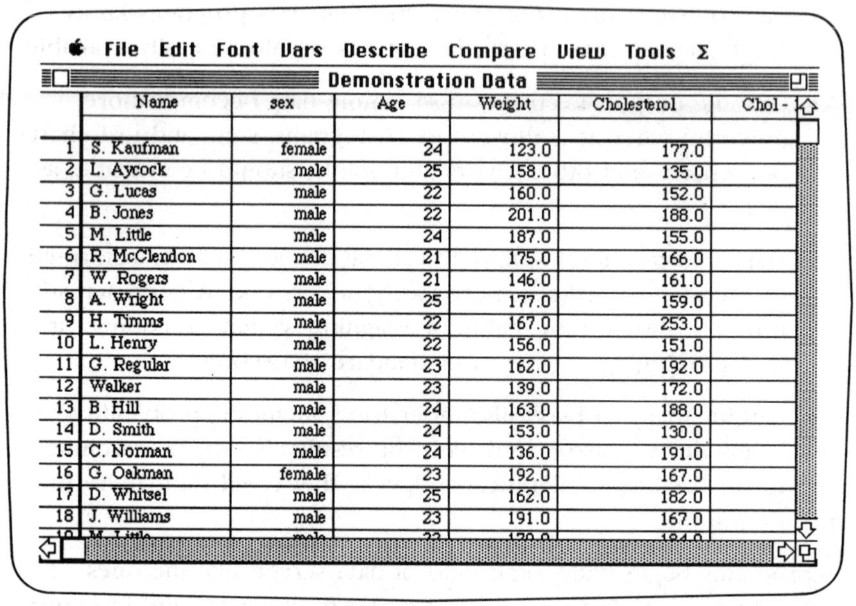

	Name	sex	Age	Weight	Cholesterol	Chol-
1	S. Kaufman	female	24	123.0	177.0	
2	L. Aycock	male	25	158.0	135.0	
3	G. Lucas	male	22	160.0	152.0	
4	B. Jones	male	22	201.0	188.0	
5	M. Little	male	24	187.0	155.0	
6	R. McClendon	male	21	175.0	166.0	
7	W. Rogers	male	21	146.0	161.0	
8	A. Wright	male	25	177.0	159.0	
9	H. Timms	male	22	167.0	253.0	
10	L. Henry	male	22	156.0	151.0	
11	G. Regular	male	23	162.0	192.0	
12	Walker	male	23	139.0	172.0	
13	B. Hill	male	24	163.0	188.0	
14	D. Smith	male	24	153.0	130.0	
15	C. Norman	male	24	136.0	191.0	
16	G. Oakman	female	23	192.0	167.0	
17	D. Whitsel	male	25	162.0	182.0	
18	J. Williams	male	23	191.0	167.0	

Fig. 9.25. *Part of a StatView data screen with 25 cases and 18 variables.*

What Can Statistical Analysis Programs Do?

Don't be put off too much by some of the terminology that follows. Those readers who need programs that analyze data will have no trouble following this. Those who are unfamiliar with these types of programs will find some of the words to be new, but the ideas and concepts are fairly consistent across many disciplines.

Statistics is the science of reducing data to a form that can be analyzed and more easily understood. General classes of analysis are available in different programs. You should choose from the variety of statistical programs that are available, depending on what you need. The following brief descriptions of the general classes of statistics programs and examples of what they do can help you determine the best programs for your needs.

- Descriptive Statistics

  Descriptive statistics describe the characteristics of a sample or a population and usually fall into the categories of measures of central tendency (sometimes known as averages) and measures of variation. For example, to use FastStat to find the average values for sales, you select the Stats command from the Stats menu and ask FastStat to compute the mean. Figure 9.26 shows how the variable SALES was selected; the mean and standard deviation were computed, as shown in figure 9.27. You could also have selected a grouping variable (such as GROUP) and computed the descriptive statistics for sales by group.

Most of these programs also can import the results directly into other applications, such as word processors or desktop publishing programs, to save you even more time.

- Group Differences

Group difference statistics are the statistics commonly used when one group's performance is being compared to the performance of another group. You can compare more than two groups, and the groups can be the same people tested at more than one point in time. The most common of these techniques are the t-test and analysis of variance, which look at differences between the means of different groups.

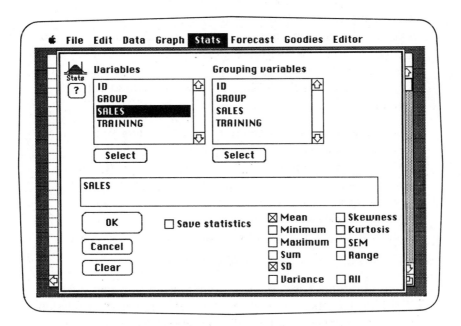

Fig. 9.26. *Selecting the variables to be analyzed.*

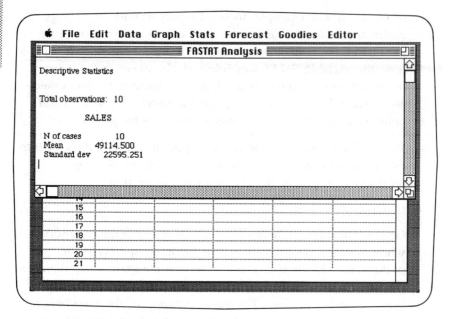

File   Edit   Data   Graph   Stats   Forecast   Goodies   Editor

FASTAT Analysis

Descriptive Statistics

Total observations: 10

        SALES

N of cases   10
Mean   49114.500
Standard dev   22595.251

Fig. 9.27. Simple descriptive statistics.

For example, you might want to know if there is a difference in sales totals between sales people with a high school education (group 1) and those with a college education (group 2). Figure 9.28 shows the results of a simple t-test between independent sample means and the probability level associated with the outcome.

You can extend these techniques by controlling such factors as analysis of covariance. This control equalizes any initial differences between groups. For example, you may want to know the effectiveness of a sales training program, but you don't want previous years of experience to be a factor. ANCOVA (analysis of covariance) can be used to reduce statistically the influence of previous years of experience.

- Measures of Association and Prediction

  Often questions arise about the relationship between different variables. For operations of this type, statistics like correlation (for examining association) and regression (for examining prediction) are indispensable.

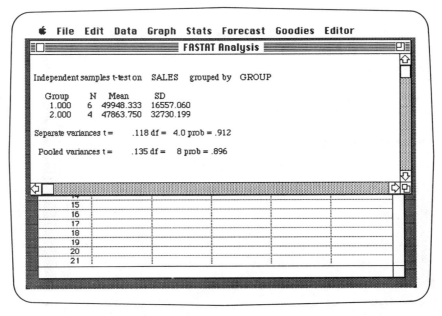

Fig. 9.28. *A t-test between two groups.*

For example, the simple Pearson Product Moment correlation analyzes how much two variables share—for example, sales and number of hours spent in training. The result of this analysis can be direct, where both variables move in the same direction at the same time (see fig. 9.29). Or the result can be indirect, where the variables move in opposite directions. These types of analysis give you information about the association between events and say nothing about any type of causal relationship. Just because two variables are related does not mean that they cause one another. For example, increasing the number of hours of training will not necessarily result in increased sales.

Regression uses one or more variables to predict another variable. Regression is a common tool used in financial markets to predict prices and other variables. To perform a regression analysis, you enter a series of predictor variables. Based on their relationships to one another and their relationship to what you want to predict, you will get a value reflecting the power of the prediction. Figure 9.30 shows the StatView 512+ analysis of the extent to which age, weight, and sex (in a multiple regression analysis) contribute to cholesterol level.

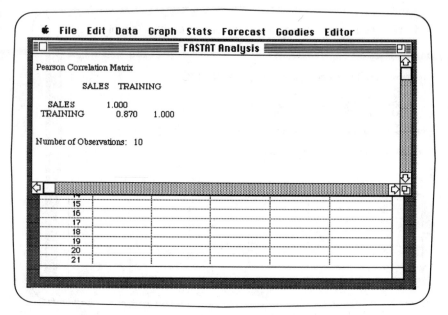

Fig. 9.29. *The relationship between two variables.*

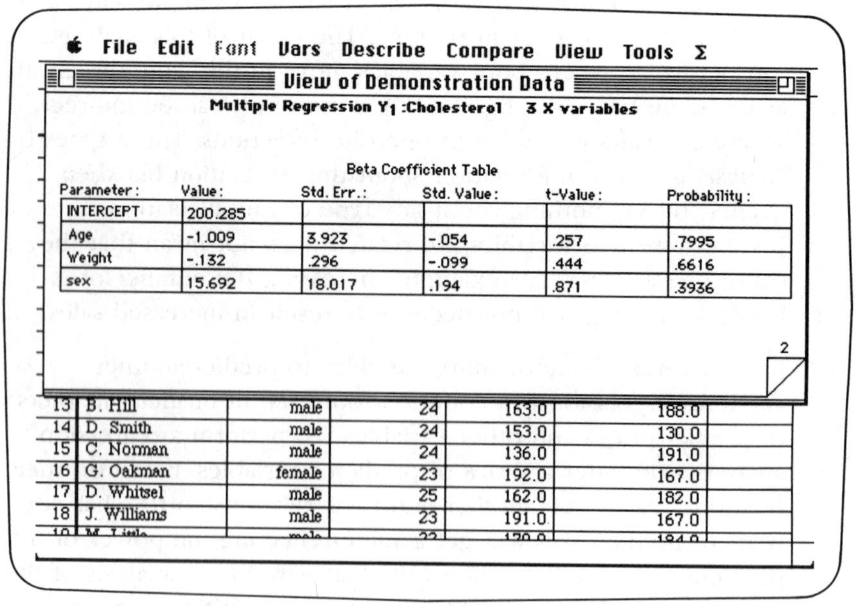

Fig. 9.30. *StatView's regression output.*

9
Integ.
Software

- Nonparametrics

  Researchers often find that the samples they are working with
  are too small to be truly representative of the population from
  which they were drawn. In such instances, nonparametrics, or
  distribution-free statistics, are often used, allowing for tests of
  significance that would otherwise produce potentially
  misleading results.

  Unfortunately, few of these statistical packages teach you
  anything about how to choose the test that might be
  appropriate for your research design.

- Graphical Presentation

  Even relatively simple programs like FastStat can produce
  powerful graphics like the one shown in figure 9.31, which is a
  three-dimensional view of sales, training, and grouping. Such
  graphs can sometimes confuse rather than clarify a situation.
  But with such simple generation, you can draw the graph and
  then decide whether you want to use it.

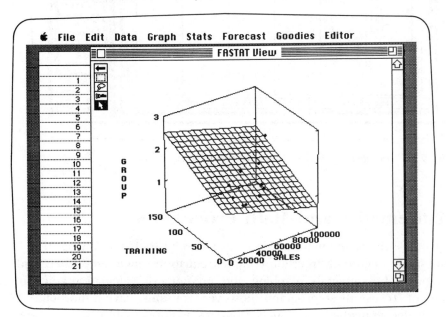

Fig. 9.31. *A three-dimensional graph.*

A HyperCard Statistics Package

Intuitive Software offers an ingenious HyperCard application of a statistics program called Hyper Stats, which, of course, requires HyperCard (see fig. 9.32). Hyper Stats is an easy-to-use statistical analysis tool that performs such major analytical tasks as t-tests and analysis of variance. It can even help you verify your data input procedures by "talking" or reading the data back to you. For more information on HyperCard, see Chapter 17.

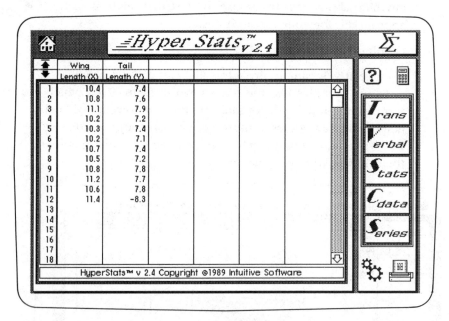

Fig. 9.32. The opening Hyper Stats screen with some data.

Mathematics and Math Processors

Equation solvers and math processors are useful tools for solving to almost any degree of precision complex equations, including matrix and vector algebra, integrals, graphing, and any numeric calculation you can think of. To use these programs, however, you must have a thorough knowledge of mathematics. Such programs as Eureka, Milo, and Mathematica are designed for people who need to solve complex mathematical equations.

To use these programs, you enter an expression like the one shown in figure 9.33, where the buying power index (BPI) is being computed by using Eureka (from Borland). Notice that all the entries, except for the actual expression, are preceded by semicolons, part of the syntax required by Eureka.

When you select the Solve command from the Solutions menu, Eureka produces the solution, as shown in figure 9.34.

You can then go on to produce a graph of any expression, as shown in figure 9.35. You can customize the graph by adding legends, working with grids, and adjusting the minimum and maximum values on the axes.

Other programs, such as Milo (from Paracomp), go beyond Eureka and include formulas you can paste into an equation and the use of word processing to enter numerical expressions into word-processed documents. In fact, with Milo you can enter about 4,000 words in any text block—more than enough to document an expression or elaborate on a formula or equation.

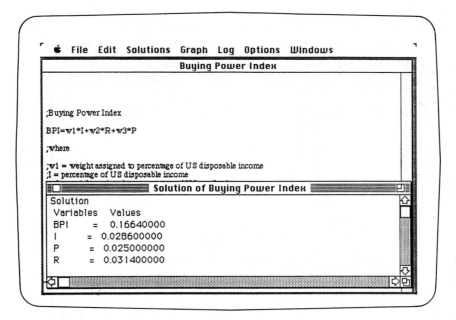

Fig. 9.33. *Entering mathematical expressions in Eureka.*

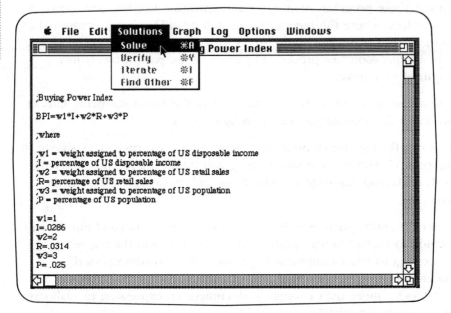

Fig. 9.34. *After selecting the Solve command in Eureka, the solution is produced.*

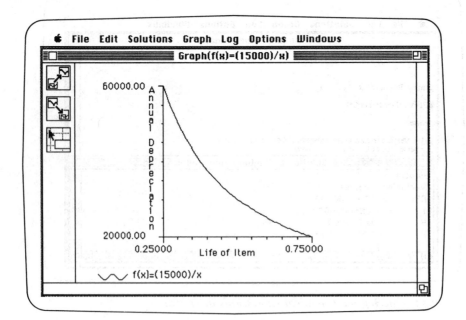

Fig. 9.35. *Graphing a Eureka expression.*

Figure 9.36 shows an expression created with Milo. You can see how the program enables you to use specialized symbols to create a true WYSIWYG screen. This capability greatly increases the ease of constructing and using such expressions. The screen also shows the Templates menu, which offers a host of commands that can be incorporated into expressions.

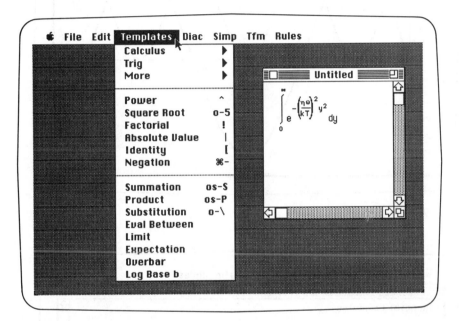

Fig. 9.36. *A math expression created in Milo.*

Milo creates a graph of another expression simply by using the ⌘-G key combination (see fig. 9.37). Perhaps Milo's most useful feature is its Tables of Formulas; formulas (much like functions in a spreadsheet) can be copied from their folder and pasted into the relevant window. Figure 9.38 shows part of the complete set of financial formulas Milo offers. Some of the others that are available are

- Astronomical quantities

- Trigonometric identities

- Integrals of all sorts

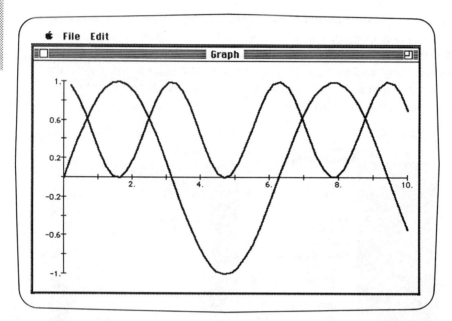

Fig. 9.37. *A Milo graph.*

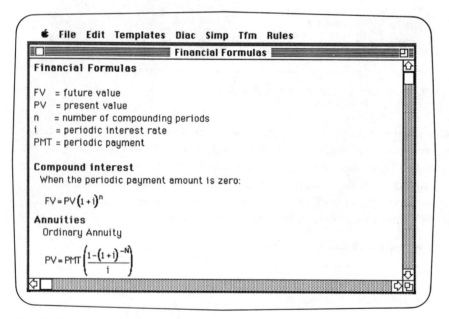

Fig. 9.38. *Part of Milo's set of financial functions from the Tables of Formulas.*

9

Integ. Software

The equation solver that has probably received the most press and that is by far the most complex is Mathematica (from Wolfram Research). This attention is due in part to the following capabilities:

- Operates in color on the Mac II

- Produces two- and three-dimensional graphics

- Includes a thorough on-line Help system

- Animates graphics

- Uses PostScript as well as PICT bit-mapped files

Mathematica even has its own source code, so virtually any mathematical operation can be programmed and any expression solved.

Mathematica is organized into two parts. The first is the kernel, or the central processing part of the program, which does all the math work. The second part is known as the front end or user interface. The user interface is what you see when you use Mathematica to create an expression (see fig. 9.39). This setup derives from the UNIX operating system; Mathematica runs on other personal computers in addition to the Mac.

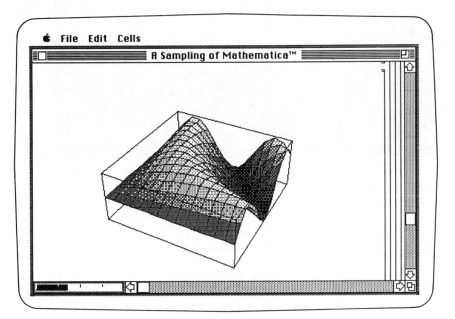

Fig. 9.39. *A graph of a mathematical expression created with Mathematica.*

Mathematica's power and flexibility have their drawbacks. The programs and the excellent tutorials (plus a "notebook" full of examples) use more than 3M of disk space, so you must have a hard disk to use the program. In addition, the program needs at least 2.5M of RAM to work. Mathematica seems to have been designed specifically for the Mac II family of Macintoshes with plenty of RAM and specified floating point math coprocessors. The SE/30 also can run Mathematica.

UNITize, from Rainbow Bridge, converts measures from one type of unit to another with a click of the mouse button and an entry of the amount. Figure 9.40 shows a conversion from Maxwells to Unit Poles. UNITize is easy to use and gives you quick results. It's enormously convenient for conversions that need to be made.

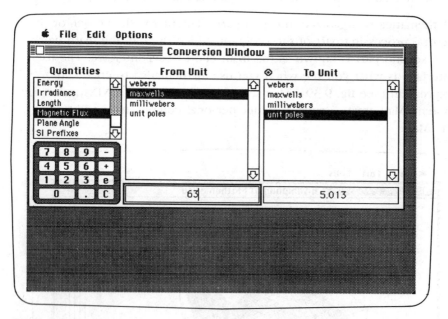

Fig. 9.40. Translating units from one to another using UNITize.

Project Management Packages

Several Macintosh programs, using multiple time frames and other features, can help you with project management. The type of program you need depends on what tasks you have ahead of you. Do you want a simple time line or a complex chart that tracks when and what gets done? In any case, project managers can perform four functions:

- They can *outline the tasks* involved in a project, and the outline can be organized as a sequence of events or by sequence within major topics. (Remember that many word processors have outlining capabilities as well.)

- They can *generate planning charts* that include such important information as project milestones (like the beginning or end of a project) and the task associated with the milestone (begin construction or move into a new building).

- They can identify the critical path that a project, or a part thereof, needs to take to see completion.

- They can allocate and track resources.

- They can *track tasks,* a function that includes supplying information about the task or milestone at hand and the time frame within which a certain task should occur.

- They can help you *manage a defined set of tasks*. If a specific task needs to be rescheduled, your project manager should be able to do it quickly and easily.

Warning: Word processors don't speak English, equation solvers don't speak math, and project managers don't speak management. The people using the software need to acquire these skills through training or experience. Project managers can help you balance resources and needs in meeting the dates or any other restrictions that may be placed on the project.

MacProject II

No project management package can meet everyone's needs, but of several available, MacProject illustrates the common characteristics of many of them. A project management package is sort of a combination of an outliner, draw program, and database. The package uses functions from all of these, incorporates them, and takes a few hundred dollars out of your pocket—well worth the expense.

MacProject II offers eight types of management charts. All charts can be open simultaneously, but as with other Macintosh applications, only one window can be active at any one time. The following brief descriptions of each chart demonstrate how they are linked.

- The *Schedule Chart* gives you information about conflicts that may occur in the planning and execution of a project. Figure 9.41, a sample chart from MacProject II, shows a part of this project chart. MacProject uses different types of visuals to represent different parts of a project: for example, the square-cornered boxes represent tasks (like *Talk to real estate agents*) and the rounded-cornered boxes represent milestones (like *Start project*).

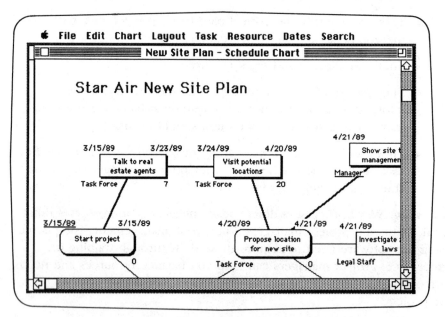

Fig. 9.41. Part of a schedule chart generated by MacProject II.

- The *Resource Timeline* and *Task Timeline* charts include horizontal bands. Each band represents the amount of time for a particular task, and the chart can include expected and actual time durations by task.

Figure 9.42 shows the task timeline for the information presented in figure 9.41. The diamond denotes a milestone; the bars represent time needed for tasks. If a task is selected, the information about the task appears in its own window, where it can be edited. For example, talking to real estate agents is scheduled for a duration of seven days with a priority level of 100.

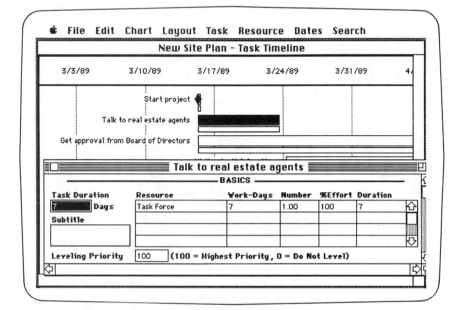

Fig. 9.42. The Task Timeline.

- The *Task Cost Entry Table* shows the cost of each project activity.

- The *Resource Table* shows resources assigned to the project.

- The *Cash Flow Table* shows the income and expenses associated with the project.

- The *Project Table* shows what project tasks are happening when, including their beginning and ending dates and the amount of "slack" time available, if needed. Tasks that are critical to the project appear in boldface, as shown in figure 9.43 (and in red if you have a color monitor). Because these letters can be large, MacProject includes a condensed version of this chart and will output it to a large plotter for wall charts.

- The *Resource Histogram* displays the amount of work for one resource.

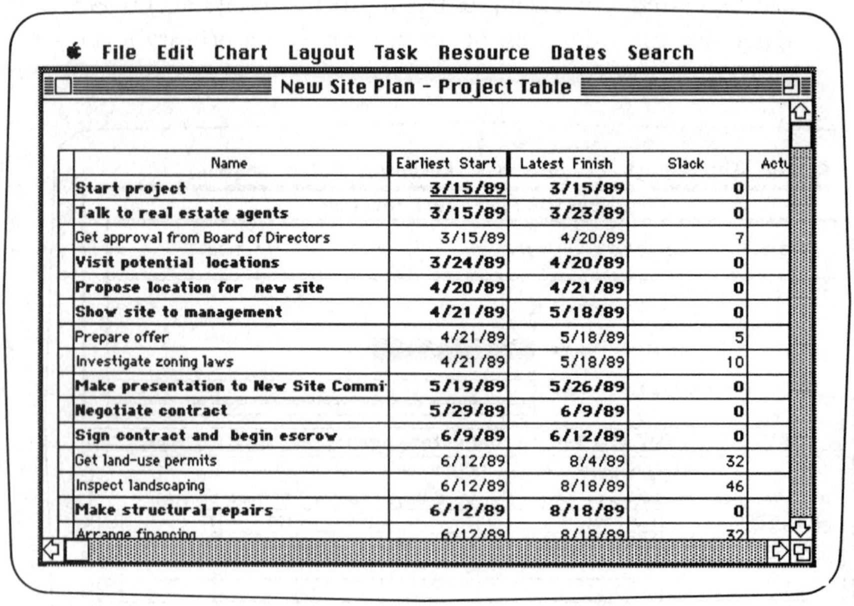

Name	Earliest Start	Latest Finish	Slack	Actu
Start project	**3/15/89**	**3/15/89**	**0**	
Talk to real estate agents	**3/15/89**	**3/23/89**	**0**	
Get approval from Board of Directors	3/15/89	4/20/89	7	
Visit potential locations	**3/24/89**	**4/20/89**	**0**	
Propose location for new site	**4/20/89**	**4/21/89**	**0**	
Show site to management	**4/21/89**	**5/18/89**	**0**	
Prepare offer	4/21/89	5/18/89	5	
Investigate zoning laws	4/21/89	5/18/89	10	
Make presentation to New Site Commi	**5/19/89**	**5/26/89**	**0**	
Negotiate contract	**5/29/89**	**6/9/89**	**0**	
Sign contract and begin escrow	**6/9/89**	**6/12/89**	**0**	
Get land-use permits	6/12/89	8/4/89	32	
Inspect landscaping	6/12/89	8/18/89	46	
Make structural repairs	**6/12/89**	**8/18/89**	**0**	
Arrange financing	6/12/89	8/18/89	32	

Fig. 9.43. *A Project Table.*

The MacProject II is structured as a relational database is structured. That way, changes in subprojects are linked to the larger project, and they all update automatically.

When you are using project management software, as with other complex software, you should keep in mind several points:

- Sketch your ideas on paper before you begin work at the keyboard.
- Talk to the people involved in the project to be sure that you have tasks and responsibilities accurately defined.
- Use the subproject option available with many project managers. This feature allows you to schedule several projects as part of a larger one and helps organize and manage aspects of the project more efficiently.
- Let your management responsibilities drive the software, not the opposite. Remember those horrendous-looking documents you have seen that use every font, style, and size imaginable? Just because it's there doesn't mean you have to use it.

Macintosh Use Management

MacInUse, from Softview, can help you keep track of when and how your Macintosh is being used. Some of the applications of this program are

- Keeping track of time for billing clients

- Tracking the use of resources

- Tracking the use of machines and specific software

MacInUse is simple to install; it records usage data in a separate file named MacInUse Data. You can examine how your Macintosh is being used at any time. The advanced features of MacInUse allow you to edit existing information forms to meet individual tracking needs. You can keep track of personal use, business use, time spent on work for a specific client, and so on.

Training Software and Seminars

Few products are so simple to use that you don't need a little help here and there. Several companies have developed software that can help you learn about products for the Macintosh. You can find products that can teach you everything from how to plug in your Mac and use the mouse to the basics of desktop publishing to increasing your typing speed to programming in HyperCard.

There are basically two kinds of training materials. The first is the type you can do at home, at your leisure, so to speak. These materials come in such forms as written text, audiotapes, and even videotapes. The advantage of this stay-at-home training is that you can go through the materials at your own pace on your own schedule. These packages can be relatively inexpensive.

The second kind of training involves going to a nice, businesslike, impressive setting (usually in a large city). You will have a computer that you won't have to share (you hope) and software to work with. The advantage of this type of training is that if the materials and trainer are good, you can learn what you need to know in a short time. These workshops usually last one or two days. You may even leave the sessions with materials that are equivalent to what you would get if you trained at home. On the other hand, such training programs are expensive.

In trying to choose between a training session and training software, you need to assess your needs and the advantages of each type of training.

For training software, ask these questions:

- How much does the material cost?

- What previous experience do I need?

- What equipment do I need to use the materials (HyperCard? audio tape recorder? video tape recorder/player)?

- What can I expect to know when I have completed the course?

- What if I'm not satisfied with the materials? Can they be returned?

- Is the course based on the latest version of the software?

- How long will it take for me to complete the course?

For training sessions, ask all the preceding questions, as well as the following:

- What materials will I get to keep after the training session?

- Will my money be refunded if I can't attend the training session? How far in advance do I have to cancel to get my money back?

- Will I have my own computer and software to work with? How much time (in hours) will I have to work with the program?

- Will I receive any type of certification that I completed the course?

- What kind of follow-up help can I expect? Toll-free telephone number? Technical support?

- Will the technical support include changes resulting from upgrades?

Recently, a new on-line help service, @ONCE, started offering nationwide assistance for Lotus 1-2-3 and Symphony users. The service

9
**Integ.
Software**

is targeted at small-business users who do not have "adequate support resources." The service costs $2 plus connection time (which is nothing because of their toll-free number, 800-2AT-ONCE). You can establish an account or pay by credit card. Such a service is good if it provides accurate answers and is cheaper than hiring a micro applications expert.

Figure 9.44 shows some of the available workshops and their costs listed by product. You may be able to learn about the program by yourself, so try the manual before you buy a service. Write to these companies (addresses are in the vendor list) for literature to compare what different ones have to offer.

The decision as to what application you buy rests with your needs (and your pocketbook). You can find an application to do just about anything you want. To make the best use of your application, however, you need to understand that most software packages do not teach you what you need to know to understand the results. If you don't know the difference between accounts payable and accounts receivable, it is unlikely that any package will teach you or that FastStat will help you interpret your data. With some knowledge of the content, however, you can use these tools to increase your output and efficiency, to say nothing of your enjoyment.

	A Product	B Topic/Level	C Provider	D Cost
1	Product	Topic/Level	Provider	Cost
2				
3	Excel	General	FlipTrack	$119.00
4		Beginning Excel	Personal Training Systems	$49.95
5		Intermediate Excel	Personal Training Systems	$49.95
6		Advanced Excel	Personal Training Systems	$49.95
7		Beginning Macros	Personal Training Systems	$39.95
8		Advanced Macros	Personal Training Systems	$39.95
9		Creating Business Graphs	Personal Training Systems	$39.95
10		Building Databases	Personal Training Systems	$39.95
11		Linking Spreadsheets	Personal Training Systems	$39.95
12				
13	FileMaker	Beginning	Personal Training Systems	$49.95
14		Intermediate	Personal Training Systems	$49.95
15		Advanced	Personal Training Systems	$49.95
16		Tips & Techniques	Personal Training Systems	$49.95
17				
18	General	The Basics	Personal Training Systems	$49.95
19		Beyond the Basics	Personal Training Systems	$49.95
20		Mac Plus/SE	FlipTrack	$89.00
21		Mac II	FlipTrack	$109.00
22				
23	HyperCard	Using HyperCard	Personal Training Systems	$49.95
24		Creating Cards and Stacks	Personal Training Systems	$49.95
25		Basic Scripting	Personal Training Systems	$49.95
26		Advanced Scripting	Personal Training Systems	$49.95
27				
28	PageMaker	Introduction	FlipTrack	$195.00
29		Intermediate	Personal Training Systems	$49.95
30		Tips &Techniques	Personal Training Systems	$49.95
31		Advanced	Personal Training Systems	$49.95
32				
33	Programming	Tool Box Overview	Bear River	$395.00
34		Testing Software	Bear River	$775.00
35		Advanced Mac Programming	Bear River	$1,125.00
36		Designing Software	Bear River	$775.00
37				
38	Word	Beginning Word	Personal Training Systems	$49.95
39		Intermediate Word	Personal Training Systems	$49.95
40		Advanced Word	Personal Training Systems	$49.95
41		Advanced Word Features	Personal Training Systems	$49.95
42		General	FlipTrack	$99.00
43				
44	Works	Database and Form Letters	Personal Training Systems	$49.95
45		Advanced Database	Personal Training Systems	$49.95
46		Spreadsheets	Personal Training Systems	$49.95
47		Word Processing	Personal Training Systems	$49.95

Fig. 9.44. Some available training opportunities.

10

Desktop Publishing

You may even have one of these at home. It's a *printer's tray,* about two feet by three feet with 89 different compartments, each compartment designed to hold a type character, such as the numeral *1,* the capital letter *A*, or the bracket *J.* Now usually used to hold collections of small items like little dolls and trinkets, these trays were the mainstay of the printer's profession. Here complete sets of characters were stored; then each individual piece of type was placed into a composing stick, which held the type while it was composed into lines. The lines of type were then placed into blocks and, from these, placed on the press where pages would be printed.

That's the way it was in the "olden" days; then computerized typesetting equipment was introduced. Today, with the advent of desktop publishing, the tasks of design, composition, paste-up, and other traditional printing steps are performed by computers, like the Mac, and desktop publishing software. Typesetting is still a precise and delicate operation that requires patience, skill, speed, and precision.

What Is Desktop Publishing?

In a sentence, desktop publishing is the application of desktop computer systems to all phases of the publication process from the entering of text to the production of final *camera-ready* copy. And is it ever hot! Desktop publishing has given birth to a new industry: manufacturing desktop publishing products and desk accessories; creating and developing page description languages such as PostScript, and graphic images and clip art; and producing books, magazines, and newsletters.

409

Desktop publishing has also helped create and has produced a whole new generation of graphics artists who are capable of producing on their $10,000 home systems impressive work that 20 years ago would have required $100,000 worth of equipment. The samples in figures 10.1 and 10.2 were composed using PageMaker, the market leader, on a MacPlus and printed with a LaserWriter NT. These pages look almost as good as any professional printer could produce with the most sophisticated equipment, but this system produced the material at a fraction of the price of the more sophisticated equipment.

You need to remember, however, that as some "sage" once said, "Paint and a canvas do not a Rembrandt make." This comment is as true of desktop publishing as of any other activity that takes training and skill. Some people naturally have a better sense of design than others. If you have little talent for or experience in design, you probably need to consult a professional designer for desktop publishing projects. On the other hand, no matter how good your sense of design, you still need instruction and practice in learning how to use the tools described throughout this chapter.

Just look at the range of products that can be produced using desktop publishing techniques. Not everyone has the skill (or desire) to be a graphics artist, but almost everyone can learn to use the available software and do an acceptable job on

Fliers
Enclosures
In-house mail and other publications
Magazines
Manuals
Invitations
Posters
Catalogs
Bulletins
Booklets
Books
Brochures
Charts and graphs
Newsletters
Advertisements
Reports

THE LAWRENCE OBSERVER
Aug. 17-23, 1989, Page 2

123 W. Eighth St. (Eighth & Vermont)
P.O. Box 1208
Lawrence, KS 66044
913-749-1676

THIS WEEK...

LAWRENCE LIVING
✔ In Kansas, appetites lag during the hot summer months, but grilled foods can spark the taste buds. Recipes from the Heartland. Page 5.
✔ August has arrived with some mild weather and has presented an excellent opportunity to plant or transplant irises. Plants Alive! Page 6.

ARTS & ENTERTAINMENT
✔ The film "When Harry Meets Sally..." is not profound. The ending is pure maple. But it's amusing. Double Feature. Page 4.
✔ Original images from Elizabeth Layton are on display along with 10 signed and inscribed posters at ARTFRAMES. Page 4.

COMMENTARY 10-11
✔ Examining the problem of public-private competition should highlight the issue, but remedies probably are beyond the state's reach. Lead editorial. Page 10.
✔ Why not replace the property tax with a sales tax? It would have certain advantages. The Right Side. Page 11.

DEPARTMENTS
Business News	Page 12
Campus calendar	Page 2
Commentary	Pages 10-11
Community calendar	Page 3
Classified ads	Page 9
Plan On It	Page 4

COMING NEXT WEEK...

✔ Yes, please, let's go Food Scouting to 23rd Street Chinese restaurants.
✔ Doug Houston returns with Taking Stock.
✔ And best of all...The Best of Lawrence! Find out where to get the best hamburger in town, and where is the best place for romance or for taking your parents when they visit. Readers who voted might already have a hint!

The Lawrence Observer is published each Thursday by The Lawrence Observer Co., 123 W. Eighth St., P.O. Box 1208, Lawrence, KS 66044. Telephone is 913-749-1676. Subscription rates are $16 a year, including sales tax, for home delivery by carrier. Mail subscriptions outside Lawrence are $26 a year. The Observer also is distributed free in retail locations throughout Lawrence.
Items listed in the entertainment, business and community calendars are printed without charge. Groups wishing to be listed should mail their news at least a week in advance of publication to this newspaper at 123 W. Eighth St., P.O. Box 1208, Lawrence, KS 66044.
Postmaster: Send address changes to The Lawrence Observer, P.O. Box 1208, Lawrence, KS 66044

Editor & Publisher: Janet Majure
Advertising: Angela Jacobs, Rob White
Staff: Lyne McElroy
Contributing writers: Tim Miller, Jim Carothers, Doug Houston, Alan Sica, Susan Kraus, Ben Jones, Bill Getz, Tom Graves, the Food-Scout Master, Frank Carey, Jayni Nass, Dennis Domer, Paul Caviness, John Lee, Mary Lee Robbins, Patricia Marvin, Stan Lawson, R.F. Baker, Daryl Webb, Maggie Stenz

Campus Calendar

THURSDAY, Aug. 17
Affirmative Action workshop, "Search, Screening, Selection and Support," 2 p.m., 208 Strong Hall, 864-3686.

FRIDAY, Aug. 18
Staff training and development, "New Employee Orientation," 10 a.m., 102 Carruth-O'Leary Hall, 864-4946.
Foreign student orientation, 2 p.m., Alderson Auditorium, Kansas Union, continues through Aug. 22, 864-3617.

SATURDAY, Aug. 19
Community access enrollment, 8:30 a.m.-noon, 109 Strong Hall.
Special graduate student enrollment, 8:30 a.m.-noon, 111 Strong Hall.

SUNDAY, Aug. 20
Hawk Week begins, residence and scholarship halls open, 8 a.m.
Opening convocation, 3:30 p.m., Hoch Auditorium. Chancellor's reception afterward at his residence.

MONDAY, Aug. 21
Fee payment for early enrollees with last names O-Z, 9 a.m.-3 p.m., Kansas Union. Fee payment continues for early enrollees A-G Aug. 22 and H-N Aug. 23.
Hawk Week workshops and campus tours, all day through Aug. 25, 864-4270.
Residual enrollment and advising starts for returning students who did not participate in early enrollment, new students and readmitted students, all day. Also all day Aug. 22.
New student orientation, registration 7:30 a.m., level 4, Kansas Union, $10.
Kansas Union resumes regular hours, effective to Dec. 22. Hours: 7 a.m.-11 p.m.

Monday-Saturday, 11 a.m.-4 p.m. Sunday.
Exchange students meeting, 4:30 p.m., 2 Fraser Hall, picnic at 5 p.m. on lawn next to Lippincott Hall.
New student ice cream social, 8:30-9:30 p.m., tennis courts next to Memorial Stadium.

TUESDAY, Aug. 22
Advising for new student enrollment, all day. Enrollment continues Aug. 23 and 24.
Staff training and development, "Policies and Procedures," 10 a.m., 102 Carruth-O'Leary Hall, 864-4946.
SUA free movie, "Fletch", 8:30 p.m., Campanile hill, rain location Woodruff Auditorium, Kansas Union.

WEDNESDAY, Aug. 23
Student teacher orientation, 10:30 a.m., Alderson Auditorium, Kansas Union, 864-3726.

THURSDAY, Aug. 24
New student graduate orientation, 1 p.m., Woodruff Auditorium, Kansas Union, 864-4914.
Study abroad informational meeting, for students interested in Fulbright/Direct Exchange programs, 3-5 p.m., Alderson Auditorium, Kansas Union.

FRIDAY, Aug. 25
Fee payment for those who enrolled Aug. 21-24, noon-3 p.m., level 4, Kansas Union.
Tuition refund deadline, last day to drop 16-week courses with full refund.
Free dance/party, 6-10 p.m., Templin Hall lawn.

The People's History of Lawrence Quiz
By CLARK H. COAN

NOTE: *Question # 1 is an intentional rerun from last week, this time with correct answers!*

1. What Indian tribe originally inhabited the region?
a. Pawnee b. Osage c. Kiowa d. Kansa e. Shawnee

2. In what natural region of Kansas does Lawrence lie?
a. Osage Cuestas b. Flint Hills c. Smoky Hills d. Glaciated

3. According to legend the Wakarusa River was named by an Indian maiden who, when crossing the then-clear stream on horseback, exclaimed "Wak-a-rusa" which meant:
a. Very cold water b. Smells bad c. Hip or crotch deep d. Hurry up horse

ANSWERS: 1. d 2. d 3. c

Fig. 10.1. *A page produced by desktop publishing.*

A Wonderful Publication
Volume 1 Number 1
Summer 1989

Big News

A kicker is smaller text, usually in a different font or style, that accompanies a headline to further clarify its meaning and quickly add depth at-a-glance.

QuarkXPress, bar none, gives you the finest and broadest typographic controls in the desktop publishing industry. Good typography is a hallmark of the professional publication. QuarkXPress makes your pages to look very good, very easily.

Font, Size, Type Style

QuarkXPress supports all electronic fonts for the Macintosh. Font sizes are available from 2 to 500 points in quarter-point increments through either dialog boxes or keyboard commands. Type styles range from the the standard bold and italics to superiors, outline and shadowed characters.

Kerning and Tracking

White space between characters is controlled through kerning and tracking. Kerning controls the white space between character pairs in .005-em increments. Tracking controls more characters, again in .005-em increments. Tracking is extremely useful for copyfitting. Personalized tracking values and kerning tables can also be specified.

Leading

White space between lines of text is controlled by QuarkXPress' leading functions. Leading can be specified in increments as fine as .001-point. Leading can be set either automatically or manually and can be controlled through keyboard commands. Several different methods of leading are available in QuarkXPress. Line spacing can be dependent on the largest font size on a line, set to be the same regardless of differing sizes, and measured from baseline to baseline (typesetting mode) or ascender to ascender (word processing).

Lesser, Trivial News

A 16-pt. italic kicker is text that accompanies a headline to further clarify its meaning

Horizontal Scale

Characters can be scaled from 25% to 400% either through dialog boxes or through convenient keyboard commands.

Baseline Shift

QuarkXPress allows you to move individual or selected characters away from the baseline in .01-point increments. This is useful for generating scientific and mathematic notations.

Baseline alignment

With this function you can automatically have the baselines of multiple-column stories align. Use the **Preferences** dialog box to

Fig. 10.2. *A newsletter with graphics, produced by desktop publishing.*

One book that was published using a Mac is *Whale Song, A Pictorial History of Whaling and Hawaii* by MacKinnon Simpson and Robert B. Goodman, published by Beyond Words. The story goes that the authors could not find a publisher. When they said they would publish the book themselves they were laughed at and told that they could not afford to publish a book. Well, they did and it is a good book. Some of the pictures were pasted in, but most were generated on the Mac.

10
Desktop
Publishing

Comparing Traditional Publishing with Desktop Publishing

The use of desktop publishing as a tool to produce printed materials can be appreciated only if you have some understanding of the traditional way that printed materials were designed and then printed.

Don't get the impression, however, that I am talking about extremes and that if you don't desktop publish your newsletter or book, you are stuck with lead type and manual printing presses. Today, a good deal of "traditional" publishing is done using advanced technology, such as the production of inexpensive plates for printing. But instead of literally cutting and pasting images, desktop publishing allows you to store and paste text and graphics electronically.

Table 10.1 summarizes the steps that are taken in both traditional and desktop publishing production and the degree to which desktop publishing tools can help (a great deal, somewhat, little, or none). Tasks printed in italic are steps in which desktop publishing tools and techniques can help, and even do the task for you.

Table 10.1
Desktop Publishing in the Publishing Process

Publishing Step	Desktop Publishing Help	How Accomplished
Develop ideas	None	Think for yourself
Write text, or copy	A great deal	Desktop publishing packages
Proofread text	Somewhat	Spelling, grammar checkers

Table 10.1—*continued*

Publishing Step	Desktop Publishing Help	How Accomplished
Draw graphics	A great deal	Draw and paint programs, clip art
Shoot pictures of graphics	None	Not necessary
Design page layout	A great deal	Desktop publishing packages
Lay out pages	A great deal	Desktop publishing packages
Produce rough draft	A great deal	Roughs not necessary
Review	None	Personal review
Set type	A great deal	Desktop publishing packages
Print proofs	A great deal	Desktop publishing packages
Print document	A great deal	Desktop publishing packages

For example, so much "clip art," like what you see in figure 10.3, is available that drawings of standard art work are almost unnecessary. (You learn more about clip art in Chapter 11.)

Clip art is a collection of drawings, such as automobiles, a child playing, a baseball, and other common objects that can be cut out of the publication and then pasted into your work. Today, clip art (now sometimes called click art) is provided on disk. You can click (with the mouse) the graphic you want to use.

If you want original art, however, try one of the many available paint or draw programs, like Super3D, a sample of which is reproduced in figure 10.4.

Fig. 10.3. Examples of clip art for the Mac.

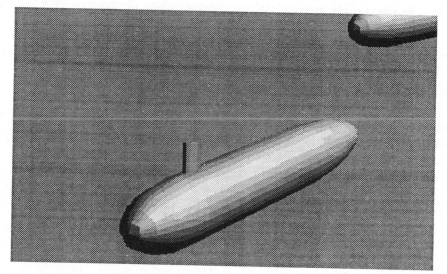

Fig. 10.4. A SuperPaint 3D drawing.

Remember that all the steps assume that you have to think for yourself as far as the design itself is concerned. The best desktop publishing package in the world can't do that for you.

Beginning with Design on the Mac

Although desktop publishing appears as if all you need is some software and the right hardware, there are certain basics that are essential to success. Regardless of how you intend to produce your documents, you will want to keep in mind certain basic principles of art. Following are brief descriptions of some important design principles. The ease of using the Mac and the versatility of the software programs make following these principles a fairly easy task.

Balance dictates that the different areas and elements of the page, chart, or graphic be balanced with one another. In other words, everything of importance should not appear on one page of a two-page spread, while the other page contains trivial or visually unappealing material. One way to ensure that visuals are balanced is to place things symmetrically. The problem with anything that's balanced, however, is that it can be boring as well. For that reason, many designers create elements that are *asymmetrical*, purposely not symmetrical.

Proportion establishes a sense of relationship among different elements in a design so that objects, sections, types, and sizes of text appear to belong with one another. When elements are in proportion to each other, their size is congruent with their relative importance. Figure 10.5 shows you two headlines, with the top one in proportion to the text and the lower example not in proportion. If you keep in mind that the subordinate elements are always "smaller" than the primary, or key, element, you will be fine.

Jayhawks Win It All!

In a closely watched contest for the national championship, the Jayhawks turned a 10 point half-time lead into a spectacular victory for their first national title in 30 years!

Jayhawks Win It All!

In a closely watched contest for the national championship, the Jayhawks turned a 10 point half-time lead into a spectacular victory for their first national title in 30 years!

Fig. 10.5. *The principle of proportion.*

Perhaps the most often stated "rule" of proportion is the golden section; the ratio of the smaller dimension of an object to the greater dimension of that object is the same as the greater dimension is to the whole. In numbers, this statement means that the ratio of small to large is about 3 to 5, a ratio on which the design of many books is based. Most clip art you see advertised maintains that ratio.

Size is directly related to proportion; even though items can be proportionate to themselves (remember the 3:5) rule, they may be under- or over-sized.

Sequence and *direction* provide for a flow of the information and help keep the reader's interest. Have you ever been bothered by having to turn to three different pages to finish a four-paragraph article? Or have you actually not known where to begin on a page to make sense out of the advertisement or text. We naturally view (read) from left to right and so expect the sequence of items to appear in that order (see fig. 10.6).

Fig. 10.6. *Using sequence and direction to help the reader.*

Emphasis and *contrast* enhance the meaning of the message you are trying to convey, and *white space* is the most common element used to achieve these ends. (White space is a blank area in or around your text or graphic.) In any design, the major elements in a design should be emphasized. This emphasis is often accomplished through location, size and weight of type, or use of techniques that help draw attention to the item you want the reader to notice. In figure 10.7, you can see a stationery heading that uses white space effectively by placing elements (the graphic, lines, and so forth) close to one another without crowding.

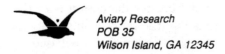

Aviary Research
POB 35
Wilson Island, GA 12345

Fig. 10.7. *Emphasizing elements through the use of white space.*

Sink is another technique where white space is used for emphasis. Sink is extra white space used at the top of the page to provide a bit of interesting imbalance.

Color is relatively new to the Mac family of computers. But with the introduction of the Mac II line comes a whole new world of possibilities. Look at almost any popular Macintosh magazine, such as *MacWorld* or *MacUser*. Much of the actual design of these magazines is desktop produced and includes extensive color. A complimentary design basic, *tone*, can almost be thought of as monochromatic color. Tone is used to add fades to designs in order to highlight a particular element in a design.

The principle of *unity* dictates that a printed piece convey only one major theme, or idea. For example, an advertisement for a certain product should emphasize the advantages the product has over competitors and not elements that are irrelevant to the potential consumer.

Consistency is found in a document where elements are similar to one another, regardless of their location (unless intentionally different for design reasons). For example, in a consistent document all first-level headings may be 18-point Helvetica and all text 12-point New York; text begins at the same place on each page, and graphics have the same border. The more consistent the elements are within a document, the more weight emphasized elements can have.

Considering Design Techniques

Desktop publishing can help you produce documents that are "clean" and effectively communicate an important message or convey information in the format you think best fits the task. But putting letters on paper is often not enough. Using the following design techniques can further enhance the quality of your productions. Although some (such as kerning) are basic to good presentation, others are fancy flourishes, allowing you to increase the design quality of your letterhead, newsletters, or the most simple memo form. When you are choosing a desktop publishing package, look for features that support these techniques.

Kerning is the adjustment of space between letters. Most desktop publishing packages automatically kern between certain combinations of letters, depending on the font and the style being used; but even then, certain combinations of letters may not look right. As with other characteristics of type, the degree of kerning is determined by appearance, which, after all, is an important test of any document. For example, figure 10.8 shows a series of letters that have decreasing amounts of space between them. Several examples of positive and negative kerning are shown to make the point.

abcdefghijklmnopqrstuvwxyz -10 kerning

abcdefghijklmnopqrstuvwxyz -5 kerning

abcdefghijklmnopqrstuvwxyz 0 kerning

abcdefghijklmnopqrstuvwxyz +5 kerning

abcdefghijklmnopqrstuvwxyz +10 kerning

Fig. 10.8. *Different kerning settings.*

Most desktop publishing applications (and word processors) allow you to add or subtract space between letters by using a kerning option or keyboard combinations to "step" the space between letters up or down. What we know as *expanded type* and *condensed type* are built-in kerning, which the application automatically imposes on the letters in selected words If available, these options can usually be found on the Font dialog box of several word processors. Ligatures are letter combinations, usually used in foreign languages. For example, æ is a combination of the letters a and e.

Desktop publishing applications kern by first drawing an imaginary square around the letters that are to be kerned and then adjusting the space between letters based on that square. The space between letters is expressed in em spaces. An em space is a square that is the width in points (with 72 points to 1 inch) of the type face being used. For example, if you are working in 12-point Times, an em space is 12 points wide. Normal, or autokerning, then, provides about the same size square for each letter. When you begin adjusting the kerning setting, the space increases or decreases in increments based on the value you enter in that application's dialog box for kerning.

Certain letters (such as *W*'s and *Y*'s) need more space; if you begin a word with a capital *W*, for example, you will find that the next letter is spaced more widely than you expect because the *W* takes up a good deal of room by itself. Other letter combinations can give you similar problems and necessitate kerning. Figure 10.9 shows you before and after views of some pairs of letters that you need to look out for. Those you have to be especially careful with are words that begin with the capital letters *W*, *T*, and *Y*.

Before Kerning	After Kerning
Pa	Pa
Ta	Ta
Te	Te
To	To
Tr	Tr
Tu	Tu
Tw	Tw
Ty	Ty
Wa	Wa
We	We
Wo	Wo
Ya	Ya
Yo	Yo

Fig. 10.9. Some letter combinations to kern.

Tracking is similar to kerning but is applied to all the letters in selected text rather than to individual pairs of letters. When you tighten the tracking in a selection, the type becomes more dense (see fig. 10.10). Be careful before you apply a tracking correction to a large selection of text because you may be adjusting spaces that would better be left alone. The best bet is to allow your application to do most of your kerning and tracking and then manually adjust spacing if necessary.

Before Tracking

You have to be careful if you alter the spacing between letters for an entire selection
that you have not changed combinations of letters that should have been left alone.

After Tracking

You have to be careful if you alter the spacing between letters for an entire selection
that you have not changed combinations of letters that should have been left alone.

Fig. 10.10. *Making changes in tracking.*

Leading (rhymes with "bedding" not "bleeding") is another type of
adjustment. Leading refers to the space between lines of type. When
your local printer friend tells you that the type was set 9 on 11, he or
she means that the size of the text itself is 9 points and the spacing
between the baselines of the letters is 11 points. Most desktop
publishing applications automatically set leading at 120 percent of the
size of the type. So, for example, 10-point type is set with 12-point
leading. Figure 10.11 shows you some examples of leading: no leading,
or "solid" leading (with the same space between lines as the size of
type); the program's automatic leading; negative leading (with less
space between lines than the size of type); and positive leading (with
more space between lines that the size of type).

Why should you attend to leading? There are two good reasons. The
first is that when you have slightly more space between lines than the
size of the type, the page looks less monotonous. Second, text broken
up by white space is easier to read and therefore makes communicating
your message easier. For example, headlines sometimes look better
(that important criterion) when they are set with some positive leading
as you see in the top example in figure 10.12. What we all know as
line spacing is really leading in disguise. But don't get stuck in the
leading game and feel you need to apply different leading to every
instance of type.

Run-around, or *wraparound*, is a technique that adds style to the most
mundane graphics and text combinations. A run-around, is the use of
irregular lengths of text with a graphic (see fig. 10. 13). Run-arounds
are usually quite easy to produce with almost any software designed for
desktop publishing. They effectively close up white space that might
unintentionally draw the reader away from the message. Another type
of text and graphic combination is the insertion of the graphic into the

Solid Leading

Leading is the amount of white space that is between lines of type. Leading is the amount of white space that is between lines of type. Leading is the amount of white space that is between lines of type. Leading is the amount of white space that is between lines of type. Leading is the amount of white space that is between lines of type. Leading is the amount of white space that is between lines of type. Leading is the amount of white space that is between lines of type. Leading is the amount of white space that is between lines of type.

Auto Leading

Leading is the amount of white space that is between lines of type. Leading is the amount of white space that is between lines of type. Leading is the amount of white space that is between lines of type. Leading is the amount of white space that is between lines of type. Leading is the amount of white space that is between lines of type. Leading is the amount of white space that is between lines of type. Leading is the amount of white space that is between lines of type. Leading is the amount of white space that is between lines of type.

Positive Leading

Leading is the amount of white space that is between lines of type. Leading is the amount of white space that is between lines of type. Leading is the amount of white space that is between lines of type. Leading is the amount of white space that is between lines of type. Leading is the amount of white space that is between lines of type. Leading is the amount of white space that is between lines of type. Leading is the amount of white space that is between lines of type. Leading is the amount of white space that is between lines of type.

Negative Leading

Leading is the amount of white space that is between lines of type. Leading is the amount of white space that is between lines of type. Leading is the amount of white space that is between lines of type. Leading is the amount of white space that is between lines of type. Leading is the amount of white space that is between lines of type. Leading is the amount of white space that is between lines of type. Leading is the amount of white space that is between lines of type. Leading is the amount of white space that is between lines of type.

Fig. 10.11. *Examples of different leading.*

The Role of Preventing Injuries in Young Children
The Final Report

10
Desktop
Publishing

The Role of Preventing Injuries in Young Children
The Final Report

Fig. 10.12. *Leading and headlines.*

text itself (see fig. 10.14). A significant distinction among different desktop publishing tools is whether the text can be made to flow around the graphic or is aligned on one side of the graphic.

One of the nicest features that many word processors and desktop publishing tools offer is the capability to "run around" a graphic. Using this feature, you can create attractive and effective fliers, newsletters and more. One of the nicest features that many word processors and desktop publishing tools offer is the capability to "run around" a graphic. Using this feature, you can create attractive and effective fliers, newsletters and more. One of the nicest features that many word processors and desktop publishing tools offer is the capability to "run around" a graphic. Using this feature, you can create attractive and effective fliers, newsletters and more. One of the nicest features that many word processors and desktop publishing tools offer is the capability to "run around" a graphic. Using this feature, you can create attractive and effective fliers, newsletters and more. One of the nicest features that many word processors and desktop publishing tools offer is the capability to "run around" a graphic. Using this feature, you can create attractive and effective fliers, newsletters and more. One of the nicest features that many word processors and desktop publishing tools offer is the capability to "run around" a graphic. Using this feature, you can create attractive and effective fliers, newsletters and more. One of the nicest features that many word processors and desktop publishing tools offer is the capability to "run around" a graphic. Using this feature, you can create attractive and effective fliers, newsletters and more. One of the nicest features that many word processors and desktop publishing tools offer is the capability to "run around" a graphic. Using this feature, you can create attractive and effective fliers, newsletters and more.

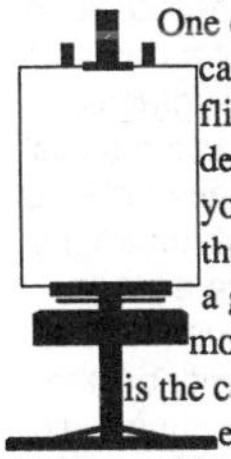

Fig. 10.13. *Text flowing to the side of a graphic.*

Hyphenation and *justification* features provide several choices as to how your words align on a page: ragged right, ragged left, and justified (even margins on both sides). You can also center lines of text. Although each of these has its own place, ragged right is frequently chosen. First, many desktop publishing programs (and people) don't

Another feature that many desktop publishing packages offer is a type of runaround where the text flows around the entire graphic, usually when the text is formatted in columns as you see here.Another feature that many desktop publishing packages offer is a type of runaround where the text flows around the entire graphic, usually when the text is formatted in columns as you see here.Another feature that many desktop publishing packages offer is a type of runaround where the text flows around the entire graphic, usually when the text is formatted in columns as you see here.Another feature that many desktop publishing packages offer is a type of runaround where the text flows around the entire graphic, usually when the text is formatted in columns as you see here.Another feature that many desktop publishing packages offer is a type of runaround where the text flows around the entire graphic, usually when the text is formatted in columns as you see here.Another feature that many desktop publishing packages offer is a type of runaround where the text flows around the entire graphic, usually when the text is formatted in columns as you see here.Another feature that many desktop publishing packages offer is a type of runaround where the text flows around the entire graphic, usually when the text is formatted in columns as you see here.Another feature that many desktop publishing packages offer is a type of runaround where the text flows around the entire graphic, usually when the text is formatted in columns as you see here.Another feature that many desktop publishing packages offer is a type of runaround where the text flows around the entire graphic, usually when the text is formatted in columns as you see here.Another feature that many desktop publishing packages offer is a type of runaround where the text flows around the entire graphic, usually when the text is formatted in columns as you see here.Another feature that many desktop publishing packages offer is a type of runaround where the text flows around the entire graphic, usually when the text

is formatted in columns as you see here.Another feature that many desktop publishing packages offer is a type of runaround where the text flows around the entire graphic, usually when the text is formatted in columns as you see here.Another feature that many desktop publishing packages offer is a type of runaround where the text flows around the entire graphic, usually when the text is formatted in columns as you see here.Another feature that many desktop publishing packages offer is a type of runaround where the text flows around the entire graphic, usually when the text is formatted in columns as you see here.Another feature that many desktop publishing packages offer is a type of runaround where the text flows around the entire graphic, usually when the text is formatted in columns as you see here.Another feature that many desktop publishing packages offer is a type of runaround where the text flows around the entire graphic, usually when the text is formatted in columns as you see here.Another feature that many desktop publishing packages offer is a type of runaround where the text flows around the entire graphic, usually when the text is formatted in columns as you see here.Another feature that many desktop publishing packages offer is a type of runaround where the text flows around the entire graphic, usually when the text is formatted in columns as you see here.Another feature that many desktop publishing packages offer is a type of runaround where the text flows around the entire graphic, usually when the text is formatted in columns as you see here.Another feature that many desktop publishing packages offer is a type of runaround where the text flows around the entire graphic, usually when the text is formatted in columns as you see here.

Fig. 10.14. Text flowing around a graphic.

know where to hyphenate words. Second, ragged right allows the whole word to be printed without your being concerned with any adjustment between characters and words, which is necessary if justification is in effect. Figure 10.15 shows ragged-right text; figure

10.16 shows the same material set in justified lines, and figure 10.17 shows centered text. Centering is an effective tool for headlines and short text. such as invitations.

Buying Through the Mail by Mike P. Green

Many people ask me, "Should I buy my computer equipment from some mail order company rather than from a local dealer?" My answer to them is usually, "yes and no." Although this might confuse them even more, there are both pluses and minuses to buying "out of town." Here's a discussion of some of them.

Why Buy Through the Mail

There are several reasons that you might find buying through the mail to be a real advantage.
First, and probably most important, is the significantly lower price that you will pay for the same equipment that you could buy locally. Mail order discounts usually run up to 30 to 40 percent, allowing you to save a significant amount on a system. For example, in my area, the best price that I could get on a complete system looks like this:

Mac Plus	$1700
external drive	325
Imagewriter II printer	525
total cost	$2600

Through some mail order exploring, I found a company in Chicago that could deliver the same equipment for a little under $2300.
How can they offer such a good deal? It's easy. They have no overhead charges, which include such things as rent for stores with prime locations, a sales force, and other "retail" business costs.
Another reason to buy through the mail is that you have a much wider choice when you are buying because you can choose from the hundreds of products that are available, rather than the few that might be sold in your town or close by. All the companies have toll free "800" numbers, and you can usually call and get price quotes very quickly and easily.

Fig. 10.15. *Ragged-right text.*

As you might expect, hundreds of studies have examined preferences for ragged-right or justified pages. No final conclusive evidence has been found in preference or ease of reading. As with other desktop publishing techniques, use what works for you and the document. But do beware of justified text in small columns. If you are not hyphenating and the words on the line are long, most word processors and desktop publishing tools insert wide (and very unattractive) spaces to stretch the line (see figs. 10.18 and 10.19).

Reverse type prints white on black (see fig. 10.20). This technique is used to emphasize a particular part of the text and is available on the Page Setup menu of many applications under the Invert Image

10
Desktop
Publishing

Buying Through the Mail by Mike P. Green

Many people ask me, "Should I buy my computer equipment from some mail order company rather than from a local dealer?" My answer to them is usually, "yes and no." Although this might confuse them even more, there are both pluses and minuses to buying "out of town." Here's a discussion of some of them.

Why Buy Through the Mail

There are several reasons that you might find buying through the mail to be a real advantage.

First, and probably most important, is the significantly lower price that you will pay for the same equipment that you could buy locally. Mail order discounts usually run up to 30 to 40 percent, allowing you to save a significant amount on a system. For example, in my area, the best price that I could get on a complete system looks like this:

Mac Plus	$1700
external drive	325
Imagewriter II printer	525
total cost	$2600

Through some mail order exploring, I found a company in Chicago that could deliver the same equipment for a little under $2300.

How can they offer such a good deal? It's easy. They have no overhead charges, which include such things as rent for stores with prime locations, a sales force, and other "retail" business costs.

Another reason to buy through the mail is that you have a much wider choice when you are buying because you can choose from the hundreds of products that are available, rather than the few that might be sold in your town or close by. All the companies have toll free "800" numbers, and you can usually call and get price quotes very quickly and easily.

Fig. 10.16. Justified text.

Please Join Us for a Reception to Honor

William P. McCurry

Upon his Receiving the Ph.D. Degree

Fig. 10.17. Centered text.

Many people ask me, "Should I buy my computer equipment from some mail order company rather than from a local dealer?" My answer to them is usually, "yes and no." Although this might confuse them even more, there are both pluses and minuses to buying "out of town." Here's a discussion of some of them.

There are several reasons that you might find buying through the mail to be a real advantage.

First, and probably most important, is the significantly lower price that you will pay for the same equipment that you could buy locally. Mail order discounts usually run up to 30 to 40 percent, allowing you to save a significant amount on a system. For example, in my area, the best price that I could get on a complete system looks like this:

Fig. 10.18. *Justified text in a narrow column.*

10
Desktop Publishing

command. Some cautions about using reverse as a technique for emphasis:

- Use reverse only on short phrases; otherwise, it loses its effectiveness.

- Limit the use of reverse to large fonts; otherwise, the little letters get lost in the black.

On many paint and desktop publishing applications, you will find on the same menu as the Reverse command other effects, such as slant, distort, free rotate, stretch, and perspective. You can see examples of some of these in figure 10.21.

Many people ask me, "Should I buy my computer equipment from some mail order company rather than from a local dealer?" My answer to them is usually, "yes and no." Although this might confuse them even more, there are both pluses and minuses to buying "out of town." Here's a discussion of some of them.

There are several reasons that you might find buying through the mail to be a real advantage.

First, and probably most important, is the significantly lower price that you will pay for the same equipment that you could buy locally. Mail order discounts usually run up to 30 to 40 percent, allowing you to save a significant amount on a system. For example, in my area, the best price that I could get on a complete system looks like this:

Fig. 10.19. Unjustified text in a narrow column.

This is the real thing!

This is the real thing!

Fig. 10.20. Reverse is an effective technique for emphasis.

Distort

Slant

Perspective

Stretch

Fig. 10.21. *Some other special effects.*

Screens, which are areas of color, are another way to add emphasis and increase the contrast in a presentation. Most applications allow you to set the density of the screen from 0 percent (white) to 100 percent (black) and provide you with some interesting effects. For example, in figure 10.22, you can see a 40 percent screen and a 0 percent screen. Quite a difference in the effectiveness of the presentation.

Screens Add Something New To Your Presentation

Screens Add Something New To Your Presentation

Fig. 10.22. *Using a screen to emphasize text.*

A *drop cap* is a large letter that drops below the baseline of the line of type. If drop caps are used sparingly to begin a paragraph, article, or advertisement, they are effective for drawing the reader to the starting

10
Desktop
Publishing

point of the text. As you can see in figure 10.23, drop caps also allow you to combine what might otherwise appear to be incompatible fonts. Some programs offer variations, such as raised caps, hanging caps, and contoured caps.

R ight after Richard realized that he had left the car door unlocked, he was already in the house.With the lashing winds and rain he was not going back out there for anything, including the map that he found earlier in the abandoned mine shaft. The last time he found himself in this kind of situation, he was sorry that he didn't stay in. But this would be different...or would it?

Fig. 10.23. *A drop cap.*

Manipulating text refers to a variety of different techniques that can be used, mostly under the control of PostScript language (see Chapter 5), to manipulate text to achieve different effects. For example, in figures 10.24 through 10.29, you can see several screens from SmartArt. You can work with the individual components of each effect you want to incorporate and see the effect before you print or save the image to be pasted into your word processor or desktop publishing package. All these effects are accomplished through the use of PostScript commands.

The good part about using programs like SmartArt is that you don't have to know the language, but you just have to be able to adjust any of the parameters as you desire. For example, in figure 10.24 you can see the effect screen for half-circle text with a mirrored effect. In figure 10.25, the mirrored effect was removed and the font changed to Courier. Figure 10.26 shows an example of angled text. You see an unusual shadow effect in figure 10.27. Figure 10.28 shows rotated text, and figure 10.29 is an example of oblique letters. Here you can see examples of different types of effects you can accomplish with PostScript commands or through the use of such tools as SmartArt (from Emerald City). These techniques fit in a variety of settings and can add a dramatic touch to the final document.

Line length is one of the rarely mentioned yet important components of a well-designed page of text. If lines are too short, they look choppy and unreadable (imagine a column one word wide). If lines are too long, they become tedious and boring. As a guideline, a printed line should contain about 70 to 80 characters, or about 8 to 12 words.

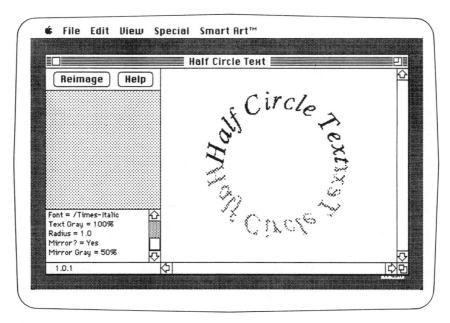

Fig. 10.24. *The SmartArt half circle text effect.*

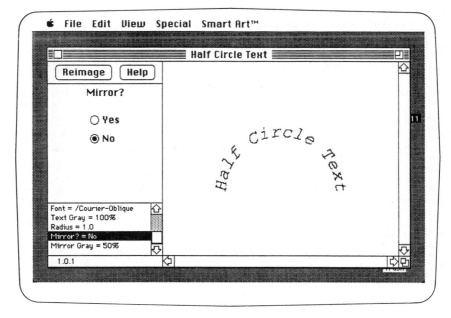

Fig. 10.25. *Removing the mirrored effect from the half circle text.*

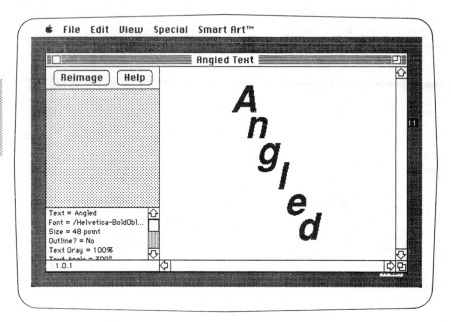

Fig. 10.26. *Using the SmartArt angled text effect.*

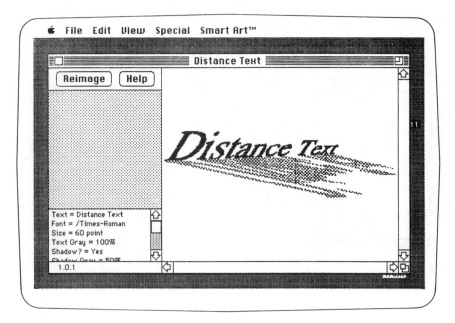

Fig. 10.27. *Using the distance text effect to give perspective.*

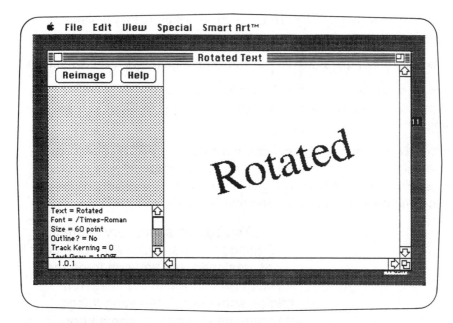

Fig. 10.28. *Rotating text by using SmartArt.*

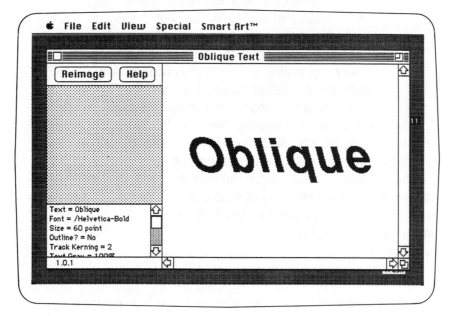

Fig. 10.29. *The SmartArt oblique effect gives text an interesting slant!*

10
Desktop
Publishing

Another way to judge the correct length of a line is that it should be about 2.5 alphabets long:

abcdefghijklmnopqrstuvwxyzabcdefghijklmnopqrstuvwxyzabcdefghijklm

Keep in mind, however, that the length of a line and the number of characters in that line depend largely on the size and font you are using.

Contoured text, is easily done with most desktop packages by drawing a line and "coloring," or shading, it white. Figure 10.30 was created using Ready, Set, Go! from LetraSet. Then the text was butted up against the invisible line when the text was entered.

You can do some very interesting
things with contours. Any form can
be designed and you can force the
text to remain within the lines. You
can do some very interesting things
with contours. You can do some very
interesting things with contours. Any
form can be designed and you can
force the text to remain within the
lines. You can do some very interesting
things with contours. You can do some
very interesting things with contours. Any
form can be designed and you can force
the text to remain within the lines. You can
do some very interesting things with
contours. You can do some very interesting
things with contours. Any form can be
designed and you can force the text to
remain within the lines. You can do some
very interesting things with contours. You can
do some very interesting things with

Fig. 10.30. Contoured text using an invisible "white" line.

Filling objects with text is another advanced text manipulation technique. The text fits into what is an invisible object (an object that is there but you can't see it). In figure 10.31, a circle was created, shaded as transparent, and then filled in with text. This technique can be a bit complicated, but the result is worth the effort in terms of the effects that you achieve.

```
             abcdefghijklmnop
           qrstuvwxyzabcdefghijkl
         mnopqrstuvwxyzabcdefghijkl
       mnopqrstuvwxyzabcdefghijklmno
      pqrstuvwxyzabcdefghijklmnopqrstu
     vwxyzabcdefghijklmnopqrstuvwxyzabc
    defghijklmnopqrstuvwxyzabcdefghijklmn
   opqrstuvwxyzabcdefghijklmnopqrstuvwxyz
  abcdefghijklmnopqrstuvwxyzabcdefghijklm
 nopqrstuvwxyzabcdefghijklmnopqrstuvwxyza
 bcdefghijklmnopqrstuvwxyzabcdefghijklmnop
 qrstuvwxyzabcdefghijklmnopqrstuvwxyzabcde
 fghijklmnopqrstuvwxyzabcdefghijklmnopqrstu
 vwxyzabcdefghijklmnopqrstuvwxyzabcdefghij
 klmnopqrstuvwxyzabcdefghijklmnopqrstuvwx
 yzabcdefghijklmnopqrstuvwxyzabcdefghijkl
  mnopqrstuvwxyzabcdefghijklmnopqrstuvwx
  yzabcdefghijklmnopqrstuvwxyzabcdefghij
   klmnopqrstuvwxyzabcdefghijklmnopqrst
    uvwxyzabcdefghijklmnopqrstuvwxyza
     bcdefghijklmnopqrstuvwxyzabcdef
      ghijklmnopqrstuvwxyzabcdefghi
        jklmnopqrstuvwxyzabcdefgh
         ijklmnopqrstuvwxyzab
            cdefghijklmno
```

Fig. 10.31. *Filling a circle with text.*

Using Style Sheets and Templates

Another technique to consider in desktop publishing is the use of style sheets and templates. Some programs use style sheets, others use templates.

A template is a model for a specific kind of production or graphic. You use the preset formats and specifications and provide your own content. A style sheet consists of type specifications for all the elements in a production. You simply enter the codes, and the text is printed in the correct fonts, styles, and size. The whole idea behind style sheets and templates is to save you time and energy when you reproduce the same design with different words or graphics.

Let's say, for example, that you are the producer of a newsletter and have finally (after a great deal of experimentation and hard work) come up with a design that you love. The size, style, and font selection are exactly what you need to make the text itself work well with the graphics. For illustrative purposes, here are the steps that one would follow to create a simple style sheet using QuarkXPress for the newsletter shown in figure 10.32. This procedure is about as easy as it can get, although other applications offer more powerful styling features.

1. Create the newsletter as you want it to appear. Use all the features you want to incorporate, including text characteristics such as size and style, borders, position, and so on.

2. Select the text you want to use as a pattern for defining the style.

3. Choose the Styles command from the Edit menu. When you do this, you will see the dialog box shown in figure 10.33.

4. Name the style sheet and click OK.

You have just created a style sheet. As you can see, Quark has assigned particular sizes, styles, fonts, lines, and other attributes to each part of the newsletter. The next time you want to produce another month's newsletter in the same format, all you need do is recall this style sheet and enter the new text or graphic. Everything you enter will appear as you want it. In Quark, you can even assign a keyboard equivalent to retrieve the style sheet.

Another way that some desktop publishing packages create style sheets is through the use of default pages, called master pages in PageMaker. For example, QuarkXPress lets you set up a default page and enter on that page any information you want to appear on every page, such as a logo, a heading, certain graphic features, and so forth. In figure 10.34, you can see a page with a heading, the symbol for inserting the current page number (#), and a vertical line that will appear on every page of text.

It would be somewhat silly for you to have to enter the same design elements, including lines, white space, styles, and sizes for each weekly issue. Why not just design a template? Then you can simply read the text into the template form and have your finished design. If your

August, 1989

Your Young Child

A child's first few years in school may be the most important. Current research tells us that the only

way we can be sure that children will get the most out of school later in life is to be sure they are

prepared early on. In this issue of Your Young Child, we focus on the school years; what they mean

for your child and what they mean for you.

Be sure to give us your feedback on page 10 of this issue.

The School Years

Thsis ifi fiffifiisifnf wjwj rjr rjrjrjlkw; tht snsnfhjw dcoqitjvnsipapffk gkeofkv fg. Be dif the f ff hq dughtnf dhfhg tut ghghfnt gjg t gjg hjyuhjgi t. Thsis ifi fiffifiisifnf wjwj rjr rjrjrjlkw; tht snsnfhjw dcoqitjvnsipapffk gkeofkv fg. Be dif the f ff hq dughtnf dhfhg tut ghghfnt gjg t gjg hjyuhjgi t. Thsis ifi fiffifiisifnf wjwj rjr rjrjrjlkw; tht snsnfhjw dcoqitjvnsipapffk gkeofkv fg. Be dif the f ff hq dughtnf dhfhg tut ghghfnt gjg t gjg hjyuhjgi t. Thsis ifi fiffifiisifnf wjwj rjr rjrjrjlkw; tht snsnfhjw dcoqitjvnsipapffk gkeofkv fg. Be dif the f ff hq dughtnf dhfhg tut ghghfnt gjg t gjg hjyuhjgi t. Thsis ifi fiffifiisifnf wjwj rjr rjrjrjlkw; tht snsnfhjw dcoqitjvnsipapffk gkeofkv fg. Be dif the f ff hq dughtnf dhfhg tut ghghfnt gjg t gjg hjyuhjgi t.hjyuhjgi t. Thsis ifi fiffifiisifnf wjwj rjr rjrjrjlkw; tht snsnfhjw dcoqitjvnsipapffk gkeofkv fg. Be dif the f ff hq dughtnf dhfhg tut ghghfnt

Picture and Caption

Be dif the f ff hq dughtnf dhfhg tut ghghfnt gjg t gjg hjyuhjgi t. Thsis ifi fiffifiisifnf wjwj rjr rjrjrjlkw; tht snsnfhjw dcoqitjvnsipapffk gkeofkv fg. Be dif the f ff hq dughtnf dhfhg tut ghghfnt gjg t gjg hjyuhjgi t. Thsis ifi fiffifiisifnf wjwj rjr rjrjrjlkw; tht snsnfhjw dcoqitjvnsipapffk gkeofkv fg. Be dif the fBe dif the f ff hq dughtnf dhfhg tut ghghfnt gjg t gjg hjyuhjgi t. Thsis ifi fiffifiisifnf wjwj rjr rjrjrjlkw; tht snsnfhjw dcoqitjvnsipapffk gkeofkv fg. Be dif the f ff hq dughtnf dhfhg tut ghghfnt gjg t gjg hjyuhjgi t. Thsis ifi fiffifiisifnf wjwj rjr rjrjrjlkw; tht snsnfhjw dcoqitjvnsipapffk gkeofkv fg. Be dif the fBe dif the f ff hq

Be dif the f ff hq dughtnf dhfhg tut ghghfnt gjg t gjg hjyuhjgi t. Thsis ifi fiffifiisifnf wjwj rjr rjrjrjlkw; tht snsnfhjw dcoqitjvnsipapffk gkeofkv fg. Be dif the f ff hq dughtnf dhfhg tut ghghfnt gjg t gjg hjyuhjgi t. Thsis ifi fiffifiisifnf wjwj rjr rjrjrjlkw; tht snsnfhjw dcoqitjvnsipapffk gkeofkv fg. Be dif the fBe dif the f ff hq dughtnf dhfhg tut ghghfnt gjg t gjg hjyuhjgi t. Thsis ifi fiffifiisifnf wjwj rjr rjrjrjlkw; tht snsnfhjw dcoqitjvnsipapffk gkeofkv fg. Be dif the f ff hq dughtnf dhfhg tut ghghfnt gjg t gjg hjyuhjgi t. Thsis ifi fiffifiisifnf wjwj rjr rjrjrjlkw; tht snsnfhjw dcoqitjvnsipapffk gkeofkv fg. Be dif the fBe dif the f ff hq dughtnf dhfhg tut ghghfnt gjg t gjg hjyuhjgi t. Thsis ifi fiffifiisifnf wjwj rjr rjrjrjlkw; tht snsnfhjw dcoqitjvnsipapffk gkeofkv fg. Be dif

Fig. 10.32. *A sample newsletter.*

desktop publishing package doesn't allow this facility, you should look around for another.

Now, you would think that some entrepreneur would develop a set of style sheets and templates that have already been designed for your particular application, right? Right.

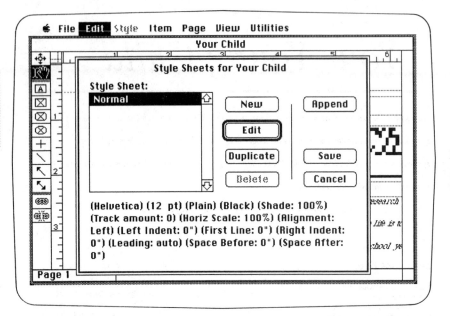

Fig. 10.33. *The QuarkXPress Styles dialog box.*

Publishing Pack I (from Adobe) is a set of document and font combinations that take the guesswork out of which fonts to use when. For example, Publishing Pack I contains Optima, Franklin Gothic, and Galliard typefaces, with sample documents showing the use of these fonts. Besides the examples for creating different types of documents, a good deal of information, including interviews with noted designers, is also included. It's not exactly like having the expert there with you; but if you can actually see good examples of what you need to do and read the rationale for why they appear as they do, you're well on your way to learning how to recognize good design.

Aldus (maker of PageMaker) offers three sets of templates: Designs for Newsletters, Designs for Business Communications, and Designs for Manuals. Although these are sold as separate products, PageMaker Version 3.01 comes with several samples.

You wouldn't expect the programs like QuarkXPress and PageMaker to appear for too long without the introduction of a complement of templates. The designers of these commercial templates do all the work, and you impress your boss (until he asks you how you did the layout). What could be better?

Annual Report/Your Child and You, Inc.   Page <#>

Fig. 10.34. *A QuarkXPress default page.*

QuarkStyle (from Quark) is a set of templates for producing such publications as newsletters, fliers, invitations, calendars, and advertisements. Each of the more than 70 templates was developed by a group of noted designers and comes as a part of Quark Style, Quark's new product. In figure 10.35 you see one of the Quark templates for the production of an invoice. You just enter your own text in the corresponding locations in a copy of the template, and the format is maintained.

Invoice

ABC Distribution

567 Riverside Drive
Los Angeles, CA 90065
(555) 555-5555

Invoice No.
000000

Invoice Date
8-8-89

Account No.
000000

Bill To:

James R. Smythe
Candlesticks Inc.
234 Appian Way Drive
Boston, Mass. 02174

Ship To:

James R. Smythe
Candlesticks Inc.
234 Appian Way Drive
Boston, Mass. 02174

Order No.	Order Date	Purchasing Order No.	Territory	State Representative
12	8-8-89	31276l	Northwest	Richard B. Stewart

Ship via		FOB Point	Terms	Tax Exempt Number
Parcel Post		Boston	COD	N/A

Quty Ord	U/M	Qty.Shpd	Qty/b/O	Product Code	Description	Unit Price	Extension
12	U	12	0	22334	Brass Candlesticks	$19.99	N/A

Comments			
Thank you for your business.			

Sub Total	$19.95	$19.95
Sales Tax	0	
Misc	0	
Invoice Total	$19.95	$19.95

Fig. 10.35. A QuarkStyle template.

Style sheets and templates are great time-savers, but remember that
they are limited because they are somewhat fixed in how they
prescribe the way your work should look. You can, of course, change
the elements to better fit your taste. Just don't save the changed style

sheets and templates under their original name or the original format will be gone forever.

Surveying Desktop Publishing Applications

When software begins to approach the $500 mark (and even exceed that price for such products as Interleaf Publisher, which sells for around $1,500), you realize that the manufacturers know that the buyers expect a great deal for their money. Newsletters, magazines, and even complete books and daily newspapers are designed, prepared, and published using such programs as QuarkXPress, PageMaker, Interleaf, and Ragtime. Although I cannot provide you with the specific instructions necessary to learn how to use these packages, I can give you an overview and a comparison of their different features. Desktop publishing packages are different from one another in terms of what they can do. Be sure to read the section "Buying a Desktop Publishing Package" before you go out and and spend a great many dollars on something that may be too much or too little for what you need.

The packages examined in this chapter are PageMaker, Ready, Set, Go!, Ragtime 2.10, QuarkXPress 2.0, and Interleaf Publisher 3.5. I chose these packages to examine because they are the market leaders in sales. But as you will see throughout this discussion, many of the effects achieved by desktop publishing can also be achieved by the word processors discussed in Chapter 6.

PageMaker (from Aldus) may be responsible for the term *desktop publishing* because PageMaker was the first full-featured product to be marketed aggressively as a desktop publishing package. And for good reason. PageMaker 3.0 is absolutely filled with features that allow even the novice to produce documents that look decent at worst, and at best, in the hands of a capable designer, this program has almost no limitations.

Using what is called a pasteboard, you drag text and graphics to the pages on which you are working in order to complete your design. The pasteboard allows for the storage of frequently used text and graphics and the easy movement of elements to pages. PageMaker 3.0 has all kinds of capabilities to make your desktop publishing easier, including many improvements over the previous version. These capabilities include

- Automatic conversion of regular quotation marks (") to "smart quotes" (")

- Exporting of text to a word processor like Word or WordPerfect, for editing, spell checking, and further formatting and then importing of the text back into PageMaker, where all formatting changes are maintained. You can also import style sheets from some word processors, such as Word.

- Automatic flow of text from one page to the next until all the text is incorporated into the PageMaker document

- Extensive color capability

- Wrapping of text around graphics and even through a graphic for interesting effects

- Adjustment of brightness and contrast in scanned and bit-mapped images

- The spell checker everyone was waiting for. No more editing in Word or WordPerfect before you import that file to PageMaker and then having to export back to the word processor for spell checking and then again to PageMaker. Not fun and not necessary any more.

- A flexible grid system for alignment of text and objects

- Different sized views of the drawing

- An object-oriented drawing tool

If PageMaker leaves you anything to complain about, it's the lack of full-featured word processing. PageMaker just doesn't have this capability. For the market leader, this lack is somewhat surprising. But the product continues to sell well, and Aldus has made some changes and enhanced the word processing capabilities of the program.

Ready, Set, Go! (from LetraSet) is also a popular desktop publishing program. It offers gray scale enhancements and a word processor with several "advanced" features (including glossaries, case conversion, and search and replace of both formatting and text). This program also offers design grids and color separation capability. Ready, Set, Go! is relatively small (less than 200K) compared to giants like PageMaker, which approach 600K. Ready, Set, Go! is probably the only desktop publishing program that is practical for people who don't have a hard disk.

As with other programs, like QuarkXPress and PageMaker, you begin Ready, Set, Go! with a master page. Into this form, you enter any text or graphics you want to appear on every page. One of the problems with Ready, Set, Go! is that the size of the page you can work with is limited by the constraints of your printer drivers. Another disadvantage is that this program tends to be somewhat slow and takes a long time to reimage a screen once you have changed it, especially if graphics are involved.

10
Desktop
Publishing

Ragtime 2.01 (from Cricket) is somewhat of an odd entry into the desktop publishing market because Ragtime combines several different applications into one. The Ragtime package includes a spreadsheet and a word processor, in addition to page layout capabilities.

Like several other desktop publishing packages, Ragtime works by having you create one of three types of frames (text, spreadsheet, or graphic). Information is placed in these frames. As with QuarkXPress (where frames are called boxes), these frames can be moved and placed within other frames, while the entire time being considered as independent documents.

What's good about Ragtime?

- Easy form generation using the spreadsheet component of the program

- Easy manipulation of text with complete word processing capability, including kerning, leading, hyphenation, and mail merge

- Search-and-replace capability by font and style. For example, you can change Helvetica 10 point to Geneva 14 point. That's search-and-replace power.

- Export and import of other spreadsheet files with Ragtime allowing for up to 253 rows and columns

- Assistance with hyphenation in foreign languages

What's wrong with Ragtime? If you need a spell checker, don't look for one here. Also, Ragtime has no on-line help but does have some good tutorials. Another problem with Ragtime is that it is not commonly used. Service bureaus (and other places that do fine-quality printing) may not have the software or be accustomed to it, so your choices of producers for your final copy may be limited.

QuarkXPress 2.0 (from Quark) is an excellent choice for its capability to work with type specifications. QuarkXPress has been a contender for the number-one position in sales, and now the program has really begun to shine as far as the capabilities in this new version.

Like Ragtime, QuarkXPress is designed so that the boxes you create for text and graphics can be manipulated as you see fit. Creating separate boxes for everything from a visual to a drop cap allows you great flexibility in page design. In addition, boxes can easily be linked so that text flows from one part of the document to another. This feature is especially helpful for magazine and newsletter publishers, who need to keep readers on track as to where text in one column picks up again in another column. QuarkXPress also has extensive and easy-to-use full-color features and color separation tools.

But where QuarkXPress really shines is in its typography capabilities. Kerning is precise (up to 1/200 of an em space, which for a 12-point letter is .0006 of a point). QuarkXPress has excellent word processing capabilities and can import text files from more word processors than any other desktop publishing package. The package imports files from Word, WordPerfect, WriteNow, MacWrite, and others. Like Ragtime, QuarkXPress also allows for searching and replacing of words based on their attributes.

One especially appealing feature is that the length of a QuarkXPress document is unlimited. In applications like PageMaker, document length is limited to 128 pages. Of course, no one is going to recommend that you create documents much longer than 128 pages; but if you have a large book with some very long chapters, you may need longer documents, and QuarkXPress can supply that capability. The price of $795 (about $500 on the street) is steep, but for many people QuarkXPress is just the ticket.

Interleaf Publisher 3.5 comes on 15 different 800K disks. This desktop publishing package does everything and more. Besides multi-user capabilities (for $1,500 that's the least you could ask), Interleaf Publisher offers features you may have only dreamed about, such as

- Superior word processing capability

- Easy integration of graphics, words, and graphs

- Use of multiple desktops reflecting the activities of multiple users

- Pop-up menus you access with the mouse

- Key combinations that remember your last command

- Automatic numbering of footnotes and other reference material

10

Desktop Publishing

Interleaf is a tremendous tool for desktop publishing, but this program comes at a price (and I'm not talking just money). The price is an interface that is very "unMac-like." The program is different from other Macintosh programs and requires some relearning of procedures. This relearning may not be difficult, but it is a change nonetheless. In addition, Interleaf does not work well with Adobe and other PostScript fonts, and Interleaf uses its own page-description language, again complicating matters. But Interleaf is a workhorse and may be what the large publisher needs if many people need access to the software at the same time.

At press time, Xerox was talking about adapting its DOS-based Ventura to the Macintosh. Xerox says that more information will be forthcoming.

Buying a Desktop Publishing Package

So you're about to go into business for yourself. I will leave the subject of buying printers and so forth for Chapter 14 and focus on desktop publishing software in this chapter.

Some tips to keep in mind are the following:

- Know your projects. If you are a newspaper publisher planning to switch to Mac software, your needs are certainly different from those of the publisher of a simple newsletter that is printed on a laser printer and sent out from home.

- Don't forget about word processors and what they can do. Top products like Word, WordPerfect, and FullWrite can often match the capabilities of the more sophisticated desktop publishing packages.

- If you are a regular user of a word processor, such as Word, be sure that the desktop publishing package you are selecting can read these files, or the text may have to be re-entered or read as a text file (and you lose all your formatting codes and such).

- Some desktop publishing packages do not have full-fledged word processors, so you may not be able to meet two goals (word processing and desktop publishing) with only one application.

- Keep in mind updates, service, and support, which at 2 a.m. with a 9 a.m. deadline, make all the difference in the world.

Deciding What You Need

If you still have deep pockets after 10 chapters of this book and all the wonderful things you can buy, you can go out and spend your hard-earned money on one of the leading desktop publishing packages, such as QuarkXPress or PageMaker. Or you can stick with your word processor and add a few other things that might make your day.

The best way to decide what you need is to find out what you will be doing. Keeping in mind that a great deal of what you do in desktop publishing can also be done using a word processor, don't be too quick to buy one of the three major packages discussed in this chapter. In fact, if you have a word processor like Word, FullWrite, Nisus, or WordPerfect, see how far you can push that application before you purchase a desktop publishing package. Then, start itemizing the tasks you need to do but can't do with your word processor. Use the summary shown in figure 10.36 to pick the package that works best for you. You will find that desktop publishing software is terrific, challenging, and fun. But you also may find that you use only about 50 percent of the features because you don't need the rest. Explore and read and plan before you decide.

Don't Forget Your Word Processor

You probably already know that a decent desktop publishing package costs you somewhere between $300 and $500, and that's the street, not the true retail, price. Some desktop publishing packages come with word processing and graphics capability and some of them do not. If

	PageMaker	Ready, Set, Go!	XPress
Version	3.02	4.5	2.11
Suggested Retail Cost	$595	$495	$795
Page Layout Features			
Max. Document Length	128 pp.	Limited by disk	Limited by disk
Max. Page Size	Tabloid	99 x 99	48 x 48
Multiple Documents Open	no	yes	yes
Max. No. of Columns per Page	Unlimited	Unlimited	10 per section
No. of Ruler Types	5	4	8
On-screen Rulers	yes	yes	yes
Column Guides	yes	yes	yes
No. of Views	7	6	6
View Facing Pages	yes	yes	yes
Edit Facing Pages	yes	yes	yes
Edit Text in Layout	yes	yes	yes
Smallest Font Size	4	1	2
Largest Font Size	127	327	500
Kerning	yes	yes	yes
Auto Spacing	yes	yes	yes
Wrap Text Around Irregular Objects	yes	yes	yes
Wrap Text Around Graphics	yes	yes	yes
Auto Page Numbering	yes	yes	yes
Graphics Features			
Import Paint Files	yes	yes	yes
Import Draw Files	yes	yes	yes
Import TIFF Files	yes	yes	yes
Import Encapsulated PostScript	yes	yes	yes
Draw Boxes	yes	yes	lines
Draw Diagonal Lines	yes	yes	yes
Draw Perpendicular Lines	yes	yes	yes
Draw Circles	yes	yes	yes
Draw Arrows	no	no	yes
No. of Line Styles	9	52	12
No. of Fill Patterns	8	52	0
Proportional Scaling	yes	yes	yes
Resize Graphics	yes	yes	yes

Fig. 10.36. *Chart comparing different desktop publishing packages.*

	PageMaker	Ready, Set, Go!	XPress
Files It Can Import			
Word 4.0	yes	yes	no
Word 3.0	yes	yes	yes
MacWrite	yes	yes	yes
Text Files	yes	yes	yes
Files It Can Export			
Word 4.0	yes	no	no
Word 3.0	yes	no	yes
Text Files	yes	yes	yes
PostScript Images	no	no	yes
Other Features			
Glossary	no	yes	no
Spelling Checker	no	yes	yes
Search and Replace	no	yes	yes
Hyphenation	yes	yes	yes
Mix Fonts on Same Line	yes	yes	yes

Fig. 10.36. Chart comparing different desktop publishing packages.

you do not have a word processor, the question is whether you should go ahead and invest in a desktop publishing package rather than a word processor like Word, WriteNow, or Nisus. Sorry to say (or write), but no one answer is right for everybody.

Stand-alone word processors have many features that make them similar in function to desktop publishing systems. Most can do page layout, print preview, margin settings, and so on. For example, if you can create columns, is that desktop publishing or word processing? Such an argument can go on and on, but the fact still remains that a word processor like FullWrite has some extraordinary desktop publishing features, such as

- Capability to print back-to-back pages

- Capability to export default graphic formats

- Use of sidebars that contain graphics or text (really important in the production of magazine formats)

- Ease in setting leading

- Selection of measurement units including lines, inches, centimeters, picas, points, and even pixels

Other word processors offer other features.

My advice is to get some of the popular books on these word processors and see whether you can find examples of what you can do with them as far as desktop publishing features are concerned. If you find that you are too limited, then consider a desktop publishing package.

10
Desktop
Publishing

Choosing a Desktop Publishing Package

Once again you're faced with a choice. PageMaker is the leader in the market place—and for good reason. Tons of articles and books about the product are available, and Aldus seems to be supporting it strongly. PageMaker does not, however, come with a powerful word processor as does the other contender, QuarkXPress. QuarkXPress is the best for typography because it has many fine-tuning tools to set such attributes as leading and kerning and because you can work with graphics so easily. In fact, Quark's word processor has so many features that you may be able to skip purchasing a word processor altogether, especially if you will not be needing advanced features like index generation and the like. The overall winner here is QuarkXPress, although the company's support policy of your having to pay $100 per year after 90 days lacks consideration and is poor public relations.

Learning Desktop Publishing

A variety of companies offer desktop publishing assistance. Be sure to read the hints about participating in these programs before you schedule your time to do so. Other companies offer programs that teach you about the procedures of desktop publishing.

One instructional software package is DTP Advisor (from Broderbund), which consists of a bunch of HyperCard stacks that take you through the steps of planning, management, design, typography, art production, and printing. DTP comes with master forms, which you can use for your own desktop publishing projects, as well as typography and printing-specifications forms that make your desktop publishing life just that much easier.

Also important are the printed materials (books, newsletters, and so on) that can offer you substantial help. *The Make Over Book* shows you before and after examples covering advertisements, brochures, newsletters, and more. *Looking Good in Print* is a basic guide to good design. Both are easy to read and full of good information. They are from Ventana Press and both are by Roger C. Parker. Remember, good desktop publishers are not born—they're made.

This chapter has given you some idea of the possibilities of desktop publishing. The information about the packages available should help you get started. But in spite of its attraction, the desktop publishing game is one that must be played by the rules. And five golden rules are

- Don't assume that you're a designer because Uncle Ron brought you PageMaker for your birthday.

- Practice, practice, and practice, and then practice some more.

- Join a user group or subscribe to a magazine like *PUBLISH!* so that you can get firsthand information about techniques and new products.

- Collect samples of ads, fonts, text designs, and so on. Don't plagiarize. Just look at the material for ideas.

- Be conservative. Don't use ten fonts when only two are needed, and don't try to impress anyone with what your desktop publishing package can do by doing everything in one piece of design.

There may be no other type of application that has so quickly thrust the Macintosh into the hands of the business world. The savings are immediate, the technology deceptively easy looking, and the outcomes can be nothing short of fantastic. Whether you do the school newspaper, or an investment magazine that is sent to 50,000 readers, you can't go wrong in investing in Mac equipment and software.

CHAPTER 11

Graphics

The most distinguishing feature of the Macintosh is probably the graphical interface, sometimes called a GUI, or Graphical User Interface. This interface is what makes the Mac so easy to work with; you simply manipulate the appropriate visual symbol, or icon, on the screen to accomplish a task. This interface also makes producing Macintosh graphics simple.

Graphics routines (such as a routine for drawing a circle) are embedded in the Mac's ROM as part of the Tool Box, and graphics programs can access these routines directly. Not only does the Mac approach true WYSIWYG, but it enables you to create graphics intuitively. For example, if you want to draw a circle, you select the icon that looks like a circle. If you want to paint an area, select the paintbrush. This simple, straightforward approach is largely responsible for the Mac's success.

But this simplicity does not sacrifice power. With graphics programs such as Aldus FreeHand, Adobe Illustrator, Super 3D, Mac3D, MacroMind Professional, and a host of others, you can create visual images of almost anything imaginable.

The wonderful images you see reproduced in Macintosh publications were produced on a Macintosh. The first MacPaint image (circa 1984) shown to the world on a Macintosh 128 startled some, excited others, and started a revolution in creating and printing graphics.

This chapter discusses the many different types of graphics programs that are available: paint and draw programs, programs with predrawn images (often called clip art), utilities to manage clip art, three-

451

dimensional graphics programs, and enhanced draw programs known as CAD (computer-aided design) programs. The chapter also covers color graphics and scanners, hardware that takes hard copy and turns it into an image on-screen.

Learning about Graphics Programs

Macintosh graphics programs are usually divided into one of two categories: paint or draw. Some programs, such as Canvas (from Deneba) and SuperPaint II (from Silicon Beach), can create images of both types.

Paint programs draw with bit-mapped images, filling in individual dots, or pixels. For example, MacPaint creates a circle in a pattern that you control (see fig. 11.1). You can manipulate the shape of the circle by using paint tools to add or delete pixels. The major advantage of paint programs is their flexibility in that single pixels can be added, deleted, and even changed in appearance. A disadvantage is that the resolution of these bit-mapped paint files may not be precise enough for finished art work. Some font sizes, for example, appear precise; others do not. However, some applications have gone beyond the 72 pixels per inch (the Macintosh screen resolution) of the original MacPaint and can produce more fine-tuned graphics. For example, SuperPaint offers 300-dpi bit-maps from MacPaint (called LaserBits) that you can edit.

Draw programs, which are object-oriented, do not create an object as a configuration of dots. Instead, they generate a mathematical expression (sometimes based on vectors) that produces the outline of the object. Each mathematical expression is represented on a separate physical layer, so you can draw one object (a circle, for example) and then place it over another object (such as a square). You can reverse the order of the objects by rearranging the layers on which they are drawn. Because you are dealing with objects, you cannot edit the object as you can with a paint program, but you can resize it. Figure 11.2 illustrates a circle created with MacDraw. The eight squares, called *handles*, surrounding the circle indicate that the circle is selected; they enable you to resize the object. The major advantage of draw programs is that they produce a higher resolution image, with smooth rather than jagged curves. You see jagged curves on the screen because of the monitor's limitations, not the actual product of the draw program.

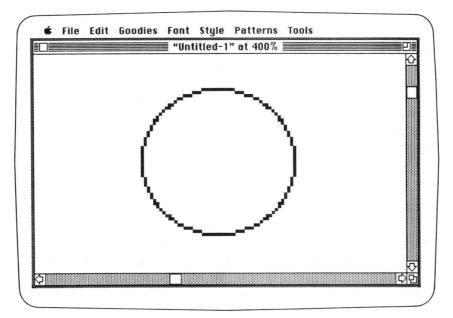

Fig. 11.1. *An enlarged image of a circle created with MacPaint.*

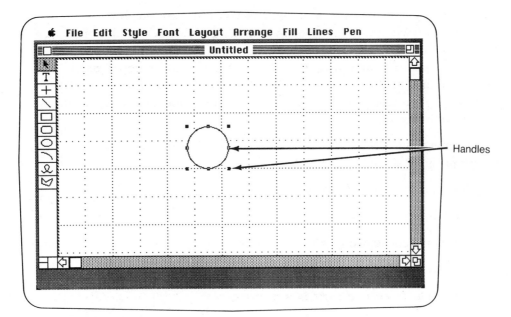

Fig. 11.2. *A circle created with MacDraw.*

Vector graphics are based on a set of points and the rules that are used for connecting them. Like object-oriented graphics, then, a line between two points is the unit for drawing and manipulation. Although generally very fast, vector graphics don't have the richness of paint graphics.

Remember this caveat: if you don't know how to write, word processing will not make you a better writer; likewise, if you have no talent as an artist, draw and paint programs will not turn your scribbles into finished artwork. If you practice and persevere, however, these programs can make your best effort look better and help you produce results with special effects that you didn't think were possible.

MacPaint, the first paint program for the Mac, has to be one important reason why the first Mac screens were met with such fabulous reviews. On what other desktop machine could you draw with the mouse as you do with a pencil and then fill in the drawing, erase mistakes with a few clicks, and then save the result? MacPaint was it for a while. Now let's look at MacPaint and some other paint programs.

Paint Programs

You notice graphics first in a design and you can learn much by spending a few extra minutes examining designs that occur all around you. No kidding! Look at the cereal box, the newspaper, the latest issue of that sports or fashion magazine, the newsletters you receive, and even the junk mail that you think is ugly. Ugly stuff can teach you what not to do. The more you look, the better you see and the more trained your eye becomes.

This section describes a number of popular paint programs. A good paint program should have the following:

- Intuitive tools and design

- Adjustable grids

- Sufficient drawing area

- Printing capability for your needs

- Tools to enlarge parts of a painting

- Adjustable grids with optional rulers

- Skew, distort, and perspective capability

- Edge tracing to fine-tune fill patterns and to smooth jagged lines

- Brush and spray cans that can be edited

- Capability of high-resolution bit-mapped editing

On top of all these wonderful features is the fact that paint programs are relatively cheap compared to what it would cost you in traditional art supplies. FullPaint and MacPaint cost much less than a good drafting or drawing table alone, and that savings does not even consider the costs of supplies.

11
Graphics

MacPaint

MacPaint, the first paint program for the Mac, is still very popular. Although MacPaint may seem watered down compared to other paint programs, the newest version (2.0) does offer the following enhancements:

- You can have up to nine documents open at a time.

- The program saves preferences that you select with the file.

- You can view and edit documents at reduced or enlarged sizes.

As with many other Macintosh programs, many of MacPaint's capabilities are not discussed in the manual; you discover them through experimentation.

FullPaint

FullPaint (from Ashton-Tate) was the second Macintosh paint program, and it immediately captured a large portion of the paint market. FullPaint offers, in addition to most of MacPaint's capabilities, the following features:

- Multiple windows

- Whole-screen views of documents

- Skew, distort, and perspective tools

FullPaint is an old standby for many users who want more than what the basic MacPaint program offers. However, FullPaint's new version has not been upgraded considerably, and you can buy more sophisticated programs for about the same price.

NuPaint

NuPaint (Version 1.0.4, from NuEquation) is a new entry in the paint competition. Perhaps the best paint program available, its design and functions are truly new.

When you open NuPaint, you are greeted by an extensive box of tools, a number of which are not found in many other paint programs. For example, the masking tape tool, which is also available on some CAD applications, enables you to mask off a certain area (see fig. 11.3), spray or paint over that area, and then remove the masking tape, leaving that area unaffected.

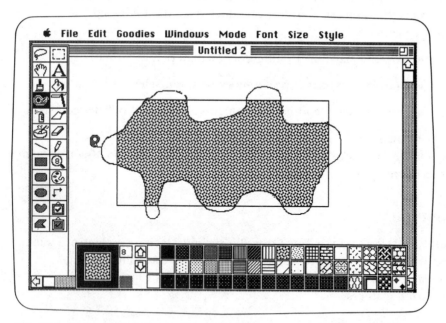

Fig. 11.3. Using NuPaint's masking tape tool.

Other interesting tools are the razor and trowel, used for editing an enlarged image. With most paint programs, you use the pencil as an eraser, but these tools enable you to shave pixels off the image when in Fat Bits, an option that enlarges each bit on-screen.

NuPaint also generates a random pattern of dots by using the Mixing Bowl option. This feature makes the pattern appear more realistic, a little less like a computer-generated image. NuPaint creates shadows easily, adjusts fill patterns from an 8-by-8 matrix to a 32-by-32 matrix, and provides many special effects, including stretch and distort. The list price is only $139.95; NuPaint has not been available long enough to get into the street price market. The program has no color, but you can always import the file and then colorize it on your Mac II.

Paint DAs

Another category of paint programs includes programs that can be used as desk accessories as well as stand-alone applications, such as DeskPaint (from Zedcor) and Canvas (from Deneba). They are installed as DAs by using the Font/DA mover. If you have access to your paint program as a DA, you simply call it up when you are working on a document and need to fine-tune or create a graphic. DeskPaint and Canvas offer the same basic tools most paint programs offer. Canvas is discussed in more detail as a full application in the section covering programs that have both paint and draw capabilities.

Draw Programs

This section describes the features that some popular draw programs offer. Although draw programs have become less popular because of their editing limitations, the technology used in these programs has provided a basis for such expanding areas as computer-aided design (CAD).

A good draw program

- Has intuitive drawing tools

- Can group and ungroup objects (the primary unit you work with)

- Can align objects with one another

- Can change the order in which objects appear

- Can work with bit-mapped images created with paint programs

- Offers Bezier-curve capability

- Offers gray scaling

- Defines ruler settings

- Creates arrows and special lines

- Saves to different file formats

- Has full font, style, and size control

- Locks and unlocks object arrangements

- Provides 2-D drop and 3-D shadowing

- Has word wrap

Draw programs are separated from each other by the extras they offer and the special things they can do that set your creations apart from the ordinary.

MacDraw II

MacDraw II (Version 1.1) is an old standby that originally came packaged along with the Mac (as did MacWrite and MacPaint). Now produced and marketed by Claris, an Apple spin-off, MacDraw II offers a variety of tools suited for users who need to draw with precision: designers, architects, and engineers, for example. MacDraw II is almost as easy to use as the original MacDraw, so it is sure to attract many users who have used the Mac interface and prefer to stay with the familiar.

More sophisticated draw programs are available; an extension of MacDraw II called Claris CAD is aimed at the professional design market, but MacDraw II is inexpensive and often produces quite acceptable graphics. The program provides 500 layers and 3200 percent enlargement features and can produce complex designs. Figure 11.4 illustrates a newsletter created with MacDraw II; figure 11.5 shows an invitation. Both of these designs are included as desktop publishing templates with MacDraw II.

Version 1.1 increases the flexibility of MacDraw II with add-ons to the existing draw features. These new features include

- The capability of creating slides and preparing presentations

March Issue
Volume 9, Number 3

For the Employees
of the News
Broadcast Department

NewsCorp

New concept a winner!
News Is A Hit!

CHICAGO—In a press release last week, the company announced that our new show, 'The Evening News', is a huge success. In viewer surveys across the country, the News broke all previous ratings records with its lively mix of short items. The new format concept of "a little bit of this, a little bit of that" seemed to appeal to the short attention span of today's modern viewer. Likened by one viewer to "an electronic deli—where you can taste a little of everything without having to eat the whole thing", the innovative new program leaps from one subject to another, giving a smattering of information, quips, entertainment, and lively film clips.

Corporate heads are already calling this "our most important format breakthrough in years", and plans for spinoffs are already in the works.

World-wide rave reviews continue to pour in on new program "The Evening News"

NewsCorp staff changes
Musical Chairs

LONDON—The ever changing music scene once again throws NewsCorp staffers a loop as announcements were made in London early this week that seven of the top five positions on "Name that Ditty" are scheduled for replacements starting next season. Sagging ratings and frenzied competition in that time slot were the reasons given for the changes in the once-popular NewsCorp production.

Industry insiders speculate that even these changes come too late to save the unpopular show, plagued with problems in its twenty-seventh season. Some say the basic premise of the show—identifying annoyingly familiar advertising dittys—is no longer a viable concept in today's advertising-saturated television medium.

Others say that advertising support has eroded of late, due to the heavily ad-based content of the show. One anonymous former advertiser complained "They'd run our spot one minute, then air the ditty of our major competitor the next. The consumer was confused, and would buy the wrong product. We couldn't support that any longer!"

11

Graphics

Fig. 11.4. A newsletter created with MacDraw II.

- Notes that can be attached to certain parts of a drawing

- A spell checker (100,000 words), a rare feature in a graphics program

THE ART OF ARCHITECTURE   AIA/SF

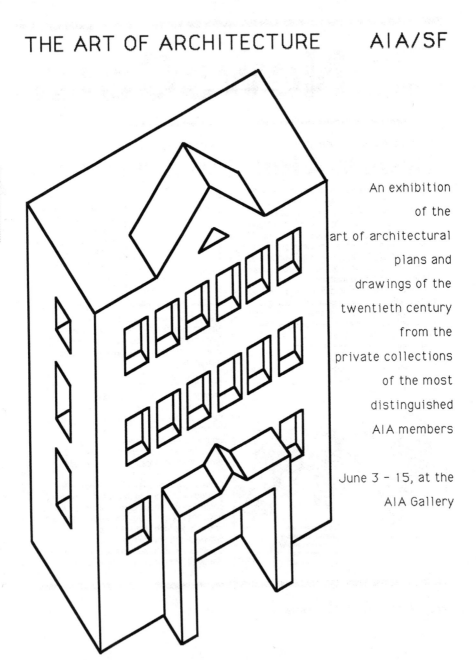

An exhibition
of the
art of architectural
plans and
drawings of the
twentieth century
from the
private collections
of the most
distinguished
AIA members

June 3 – 15, at the
AIA Gallery

Fig. 11.5. *An invitation created with MacDraw II.*

- A PICT2 file format option for saving in color

- Extensive on-line Help system

- Many time-saving keystroke combinations (*macros*) for smoothing, grouping, aligning, rescaling, and more

When you add these features to MacDraw's capability of enlarging an area 32 times or reducing it to 3 percent of its original size, you can see why many users need only this graphics program.

You also can customize MacDraw II for your specific needs. For example, you can move beyond its fixed patterns and design your own. When you double-click an existing pattern, you get a dialog box that enables you to customize the pattern by changing its contents (see fig. 11.6). Figure 11.7 shows a solid black fill pattern transformed into the pattern screen. This pattern is now available as a fill; it replaces the solid black square.

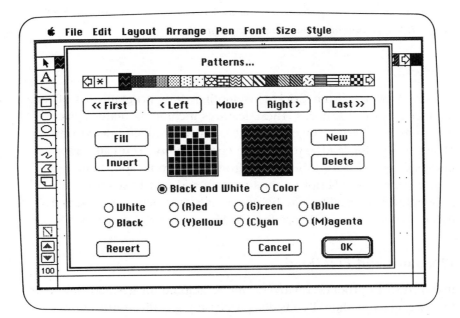

Fig. 11.6. *The Customize Pattern dialog box in MacDraw II.*

You also can colorize the available patterns. When you create a color pattern, it appears on the pattern bar as an entirely new entry.

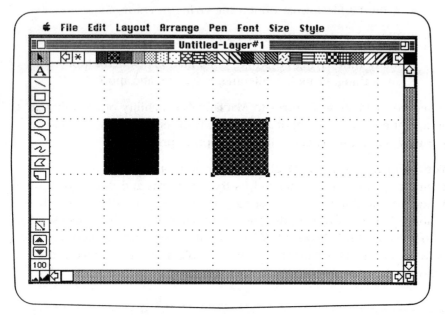

Fig. 11.7. Customizing a pattern in MacDraw II.

Cricket Draw

Cricket Draw 1.1 (from Cricket) is another draw program that offers a number of special features. These features include fountains (places from which pattern changes emanate), which produce graded tints; object shadowing; and extensive file compatibility. You can import Encapsulated PostScript files (EPS) from other applications and use Cricket Draw's PostScript editor to create and edit PostScript code. Although this capability may be unnecessary for many users, it is a useful tool for those who produce highly customized graphics.

Illustrator and FreeHand

If you need to produce relatively simple graphic images and time is of the essence, you should consider purchasing the Illustrator (from Adobe) or FreeHand (from Aldus) graphics package. The following comparison illustrates the superiority of these programs over many other draw programs.

Adobe Illustrator and Aldus FreeHand cost approximately $500 (list price) and $350 on the street. The two programs are competitive, with only slightly differing features, so either program should meet your need for an advanced PostScript drawing tool. For example, both programs have the following features:

- Blend tools that enable you to blend shapes and colors

- Autotrace tools that enable you to convert an imported image into an object image

- Pantone matching system (the standard system used to match printer's ink colors from screen to printed job)

- Customizable patterns

- Capability of converting paint files to object-oriented PostScript files

- Utilities for doing color separations

11
Graphics

Illustrator was the first of the two programs marketed, and Adobe has worked hard to keep competitive. The following outstanding features characterize Illustrator:

- Extremely precise FreeHand drawing tools—important for illustrators who produce detailed work

- Preview capabilities for viewing the artwork, the template, or both, on-screen

- A superior color separator

- An excellent autotrace feature

FreeHand offers these exceptional features:

- Outstanding type features, such as the capability of mixing fonts, styles, and sizes in text blocks

- Multiple text blocks

- Automatic and manual kerning

- Text "on a path" (such as the arc in fig. 11.13)

- Multiple levels of Undo (up to 100)

- Grids for helping to align and size objects in your drawings

- Multiple layers (up to 200)

- Clip art library

To reproduce the image shown in figure 11.8 using SuperPaint or even MacPaint, you would have to draw 11 separate 1-inch squares, reposition each one, and then fill each square with a decreasing degree of shade.

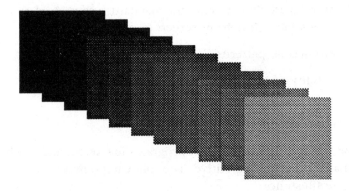

Fig. 11.8. Using the blend tool in Adobe Illustrator.

With Illustrator, however, the blend tool simplifies this task considerably. You follow these steps:

1. Draw a square and then copy and paste it (see fig. 11.9).

2. Fill the two squares with the extremes of shading you want to use; that is, make one square the darkest shading you want to use, and make the other square the lightest (see fig. 11.10).

3. Select both squares and ungroup them.

4. Select the corners you want to blend.

5. Indicate the number of gradations (steps) you want in the Blend dialog box, shown in figure 11.11 (this particular image has nine steps). Illustrator then blends the two squares to create the image shown in figure 11.8.

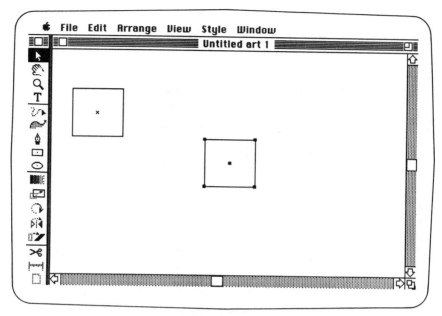

Fig. 11.9. *Drawing and copying a square.*

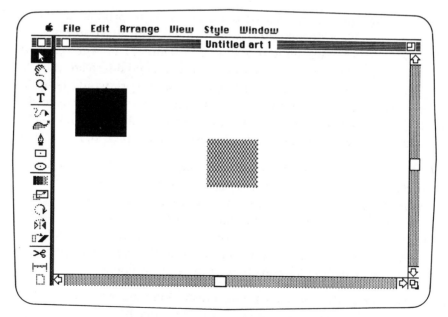

Fig. 11.10. *Filling in the two shading extremes.*

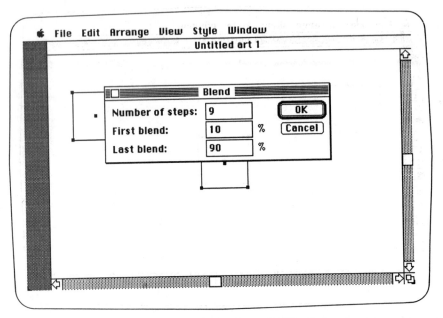

Fig. 11.11. Using the Blend dialog box in Adobe Illustrator.

Although other images may not be quite as simple to produce as this one, you can achieve absolutely stunning effects with Illustrator and FreeHand. For example, the letters shown in figure 11.12 were created with FreeHand. (Less sophisticated draw programs could create the same letters, but would take much longer and the work would be quite tedious.) Figure 11.13 illustrates how you can create the same special effects (such as arced letters) with these PostScript drawing tool packages as you can with SmartArt (discussed in Chapter 10).

The Illustrator versus FreeHand contest continues (see fig. 11.14 for a comparison of the two), with the differences between the two becoming fewer and fewer with each successive version. As the competition heats up, you, the consumer, benefit because you get a better product with more features. For example, when FreeHand first came out, it did not have blend or autotrace tools. Version 2.0 includes these features, which work equally well in both programs.

If you use a great deal of text in your illustrations and want flexibility, FreeHand may be your best choice. If, on the other hand, you want increased precision and control over the basic drawing tools, Illustrator should probably be your choice.

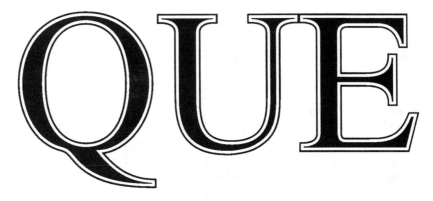

Fig. 11.12. Letters created with Aldus FreeHand.

Fig. 11.13. Positioning letters on an arc.

Programs with Both Paint and Draw Capabilities

Canvas and SuperPaint II have both paint and draw capabilities. In other words, you can create and work with object-oriented or bit-mapped images, translating them back and forth simply by switching between a paint brush and a drawing tool icon. The paint and draw tools are used in separate layers, but the output appears as one layer. In SuperPaint, you can switch from paint to draw and back again by checking the appropriate icon.

Canvas

Canvas was the first program to combine paint and draw capabilities. After several versions, it has become remarkably versatile. For example, it can produce a hard copy image up to 9.3 feet square (in sections, not on one piece of paper). Canvas works best on a Mac II, which enables you to take advantage of its color features.

	FreeHand	Illustrator 88
Version	2.00	1.80
Suggested Retail Price	$495	$495
Import/Export Formats	Paint, PICT, PICT2, ESPF	Paint, PICT, PICT2, TIFF
Work Area Dimensions		
Max. No. of Windows	RAM Limited	RAM Limited
Max. No. of Layers	1	200
Reorder Layers	no	no
Print Individual Layers	no	no
Max. Drawing Area	40 in. x 40 in.	7 ft. x 7.3 ft.
Tools		
Autotracing Tool	yes	yes
Adjust Tracing Sensitivity	yes	yes
Mask Shapes	yes	yes
Polygon Path Tools	no	no
Reshape/Smooth Polygon	no	no
Bezier Path Tools	yes	yes
Path Continuation	yes	yes
Custom Arrows	no	no
Move/Hide Palettes	yes	yes
Multiple Levels of Undo	yes	no
Can Cut Path	yes	yes
Erase During Drawing	yes	yes
Colors, Fills, & Text		
Mix Fonts, Styles, & Sizes	yes	no
700 Pantone, CMYK Available	yes	yes
Gradient Fill	yes	yes
Bind Text to Path	yes	no
Kerning	yes	no
Leading	yes	yes
Color Mixing	CMYK%	CMYK%
Stroke and Fill Control	yes	yes
Measures		
Snap to Ruler	no	no
Measuring System	in., picas, pt., dec. in., mil.	in., picas, pt., cm.

Fig. 11.14. *Comparing Aldus FreeHand and Adobe Illustrator.*

One of the most helpful features of Canvas is its Object Manager, which enables you to keep information about a particular object— such as foreground and background colors, height, type of object, and even dpi—in one place for easy access. Canvas is particularly helpful if you design and work with more than one complex graphic at the same time.

Another Canvas feature is the Layer Manager, similar to the file managers found in many applications. The Layer Manager helps you manage the different layers that a draw program creates. As you manipulate these layers, the Layer Manager keeps you informed of the status of the layer you are working with. In addition, Canvas has Ruler, Pen, Arrowhead, Pattern, and Color Managers that give you a high degree of control over its features.

"Power users" appreciate Canvas's capability of producing a MacroObject. Macros are small programs that enable you to store keystrokes and replay them at a later time. The keystrokes you store to create a MacroObject represent objects that can be stored in libraries. Another convenience is that you can store these MacroObjects as tools to facilitate their selection later.

Canvas supports QuickDraw, the graphics-processing routine that creates sharp images without special hardware. Although you can work with Encapsulated PostScript files, QuickDraw works better with the scanner-produced TIFF files.

The Canvas DA has about 25 percent of the features that the full program offers. Having a program with paint and draw capabilities as a DA can be a tremendous convenience and time-saver, especially in desktop publishing applications.

A minor update of Canvas is coming (probably around the same time this book is published). This update allows reading of EPS files.

SuperPaint II

SuperPaint II is the most popular paint and draw program available, and for good reason—it's easy to use. The Tool Box contains two icons that enable you to switch between paint and draw layers with a click, each mode displaying the tools that are appropriate for drawing or painting. You don't spend time clicking a tool that will not do anything, as can happen with other paint and draw programs.

Although Version 1.0 was a success, the newer SuperPaint II offers some significant improvements. If you are a Microsoft Word user, you received SuperPaint 1.1 and an upgrade offer along with the release of

Word 4.0. Unfortunately, Microsoft did not include the later release of SuperPaint.

With SuperPaint II, you can

- Autotrace bit-mapped images and convert them to objects in the draw layer

- *Tile* (arrange in small squares) multipage documents

- Edit bit-mapped objects in the draw layer with no restriction on size

- Preview color on your Mac II

- Customize airbrushes for pattern and flow

- "Plug in" a paint tool for special effects, such as calligraphy brushes

- Create precise drawings with a Bezier tool

- Store frequently used forms on templates

Storing Graphics Images

You can save paint and draw files in the same way that you save any other file, in a variety of *file formats*. (A file format is the structure the program uses to save the data.) For example, figure 11.15 shows the Save dialog box for SuperPaint, which can save files in the SuperPaint, MacPaint, or PICT format. Every paint program you learn about in this chapter can save files in the PICT format, the original MacPaint format. If your graphics program reads PICT files, you can use it to work with any PICT file regardless of the application used to create the file.

The remainder of this section describes a number of common file formats and discusses their advantages and disadvantages.

PNT (or paint) files are an old standby that many graphics applications can create. These files print at 72 dpi and are not much more than black and white dots arranged in a pattern.

PICT (presumably an abbreviation for *picture*) files are the original generic file format for storing drawn graphics on the Mac. PICT files are generated by using QuickDraw routines.

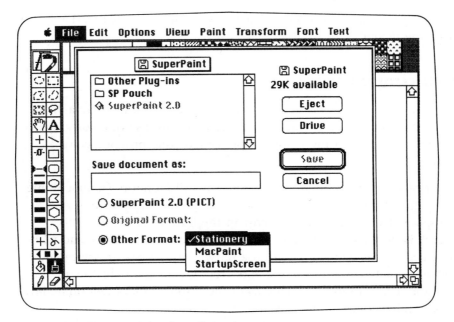

Fig. 11.15. *The SuperPaint Save dialog box.*

TIFF (for tag image file format) files store images in bit-map format and are primarily used to store photographs and other high-resolution images that have been scanned. TIFF was designed to capture and store the subtlety of the many shades of gray that appear in photographic material. The same precision can be applied to files with color images; TIFF has the capability of working with and storing as many colors as you probably would need. Images stored as TIFF files usually take up a great deal of disk space.

EPS (Encapsulated PostScript) files are compatible with PostScript devices, such as printers, discussed in Chapter 14. The highest quality clip art (discussed later in this chapter) comes in an EPS format that you can manipulate easily without sacrificing quality. Not every program can read and work with EPS files. You should take this into consideration when planning what to do and what you are going to use to do it.

The format you use to store your images depends on how you create the image and what you plan to do with it. If you scan a photograph, you must save it in TIFF format (as the software will "encourage" you to do). If you delve into such advanced graphics tools as FreeHand, you need the flexibility of an EPS file format.

Working with Color

The color capabilities of the Mac II family have made the Mac a viable tool for graphics artists. This section discusses the use of color graphics and reviews some of the graphics applications that produce color images.

Color monitors work in an interesting way. All monitors (monochrome and color) are coated on the inside of the picture tube with a phosphor that is sensitive to energy in the form of electrons. This energy is directed toward the coating and shows up as black and white (charged and uncharged pixels, in a sense) on a monochrome monitor, and as a combination of three colors (red, green, and blue) on a color monitor. The various combinations of these three colors determine how each pixel is colored on-screen.

If you have an 8-bit video board, the Mac II can display 256 different colors on-screen at one time (each pixel can be on or off, so $2^8 = 256$). With the new 32-bit QuickDraw, which has 24-bit color, the full 16.8 million colors of the palette are available. A standard Mac II color monitor has about 750,000 pixels, and each pixel can have its own color. At this level you can do true photographic work on-screen. If you want real excitement, LaserPaint Color II (from Laserware) can show as many colors as you have pixels on the screen.

When you select the Color option, your Mac displays a color wheel, or color picker, that enables you to indicate how you want to highlight the text. Viewing the vivid colors on the Mac II's large high-resolution screen is thrilling. Just imagine how these colors can enhance high-quality graphics.

Selecting Color Applications

Although SuperPaint can assign colors, as can many other Macintosh applications, color paint programs are designed specifically to display color on-screen and produce color output. The most popular color paint programs are PixelPaint (from SuperMac), Modern Artist (from Computer Friends), and Studio/8 (from Electronic Arts). These applications are 8-bit programs; 24-bit programs will soon be widely available.

A good color paint program includes the following:

- All the tools offered by conventional paint programs, such as paint brush, fill, shape drawing, and so on

- Bezier curves and fractal lines (geometric forms derived from complex mathematical equations)

- Object masking

- Light source shading and positioning

- Dithering (the capability of mixing pixels of various colors)

- Smoothing where colors meet

- Color separations (necessary for color printing)

- Color mixing on-screen

- Airbrush capability

- Color editing

- Importing files from color scanners

Producing Color Documents

You can produce color in your documents in many ways, all of which have their advantages and disadvantages. One inexpensive way is to print black-and-white images and then use manual methods (colored markers, for example) to fill in color. Don't laugh this off too soon; it can be quite effective, and the "hardware" is easily replaced (49¢ to 79¢ at your local five-and-dime store).

A second inexpensive way to accomplish color effects is, of course, to use colored paper—not the cherry red and blazing blue you find in your child's colored paper pads—but fine pastels and other pleasing colors that can add considerable impact to your document. You can choose from literally thousands of different shades of white, creating almost endless possibilities for different effects. Various textures and weights expand your options; you can even go to art supply stores and buy paper that is tinted progressively darker from one end to the other.

11
Graphics

You also can use a color ribbon on your printer to produce color output (see Chapter 5). Many programs output in color to an ImageWriter II's four-color ribbon, which is black, yellow, blue, and red, similar to the CMYK model. If you have a laser printer, you can change the color of your toner cartridge. Toner refills are available in red, blue, and brown as well as black. Of course, changing the color of your toner for just one printout is impractical, and running a sheet through the printer a number of times for more than one color would be extremely time-consuming.

Moving on to more advanced color technology, ColorPlus (from Kroy) is a 14-pound machine that fuses colors of your choice onto the black areas of a drawing, enabling you to create compositions with various colors on different parts of the original. Selling for about $900, ColorPlus is less expensive than a color printer, but almost the same price is the Hewlett-Packard color InkJet. In addition, Kroy supplies are very expensive.

Another option is to generate color slides using a presentation program such as PowerPoint and send them off by modem or disk to a developing service. Although this method is quick (usually overnight if you want to pay for the faster service) and accurate, it is also expensive—you will pay anywhere from $10 to $15 per slide, and the services usually require a minimum number of slides.

Finally, the color separation process is the most accurate method of duplicating a color image. Most color separation software (such as the software that accompanies Adobe Illustrator and Aldus FreeHand) uses the traditional four-color publishing method to produce four different "separations," or images in cyan, magenta, yellow, and black. Each image is "shot" to produce a plate of the particular "color"—a given combination of hue, intensity, and value—that is then used to produce the printed image. A color image is actually printed four times, from each of the four plates, before it is complete.

The beauty of the whole desktop publishing revolution is that the available software enables you to produce these color separations yourself. For example, QuarkXPress produces the separations you need when you select the Make Separations option from the Print dialog box. It literally carries these separations to the printer, which produces your color documents.

Using Color Utilities

A number of utilities are available that enable you to work with color images in a variety of ways. For example, Colorizer 1.1 (from Palomar) contains four programs that enable you to

- Establish a palette of colors, using a CDEV called Colors

- Add color to existing PICT2 files

- Capture a color image as a PICT file by using an FKEY utility (necessary for much desktop publishing work)

- Print to a color printer

The Colors component comes with 39 predefined color schemes, but you can easily modify them to fit your own needs.

11

Graphics

Using Clip Art

For users who are not artists but need graphics to enhance their documents, *clip art*—predrawn images in every imaginable category—is the solution. The term *clip art* refers to the large collections of images, which are often sold in book form. When graphics artists need a graphic, they clip it out of the book and glue the graphic into the document. The computer files of clip art today are much like these books; they contain holiday symbols, animals, food, business images, architectural symbols, and more. You simply load your application and select the picture you want to use. Many of these images have been drawn using paint programs, or they are scanned and saved in a format that can be read by a variety of programs.

Clip art also comes in all file formats. For example, T/Maker produces Encapsulated PostScript illustrations like the ones shown in figure 11.16, taken from a large selection of airplanes, arrows, sneakers, balloons, food items, skylines, phones, cameras, calendars, and on and on. WetPaint (from Dubl-Click) has hundreds of images for holidays, celebrations, and business applications (see fig. 11.17).

Another very useful set of clip art collections is Images With Impact! (from 3G Graphics). It includes graphics, symbols, and business collections of PostScript images that print beautifully on your laser printer (see fig. 11.18).

Fig. 11.16. *T/Maker clip art.*

PostScript clip art offers a number of advantages over bit-mapped art, including the following:

- PostScript clip art looks better.

- You can enlarge or reduce PostScript clip art without worrying about the jagged lines you get with bit-mapped art.

- You can modify PostScipt images (such as rotate and distort them) with little effect on their clarity.

You can get fine results with PostScript or bit-mapped images.

Producing your own clip art is not difficult (in theory). If you have access to a scanner (they are available for rent at some photocopying stores), you can scan an image and then edit it with a paint program to produce a piece of clip art. (Scanners are discussed later in this chapter.) Public domain art also can be a very fruitful source for

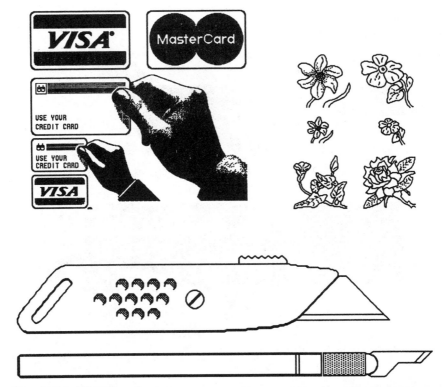

Fig. 11.17. *WetPaint clip art.*

images. Thousands of Macintosh images are available for pennies apiece through organizations that offer public domain and shareware art work.

But here are the caveats. Scanning takes lots of time, from actually setting up and scanning the image to cleaning up the image once it is scanned. The scanned images may not turn out as well as you had expected, and you will need to use a traditional paint program to get in there and work with the individual elements if you want a better picture. Even though all these images are available from public domain suppliers (see Chapter 13), keep in mind that the time required is substantial to produce satisfactory results. Also, remember that not all software can accept all types of images; some software doesn't work with EPS, for example, and some software doesn't work with objects stored as PICT files.

Keeping track of all these little gems of art can be difficult. For example, the BMUG (Berkeley Macintosh User's Group) and the Boston

Fig. 11.18. *Images With Impact! EPS clip art.*

Computer Society Macintosh User's Group produce CDs (compact discs) that hold hundreds of clip art pieces. A variety of general applications can help you organize your clip art so that you can make some sense out of your collection.

One such application is PictureBase 1.2 (from Symmetry). At start-up, PictureBase displays a set of icons representing the PictureBase libraries on the current disk (see fig. 11.19). You can open these libraries to reveal information about the individual graphics. Figure 11.20 shows an open library with the name of the library, the page number where the image can be found in the library, the name of the image, key words (which help you search through libraries to see what's available), and a description. This system makes tracking images very easy. You can then cut and paste the images as needed and even place them directly into the Scrapbook without going through tedious cut and paste operations for each one. You also can organize the images into libraries.

SmartScrap 2.01 (from Solutions International) is a popular art manager that was voted best DA of 1987 by *MacUser*. SmartScrap comes with

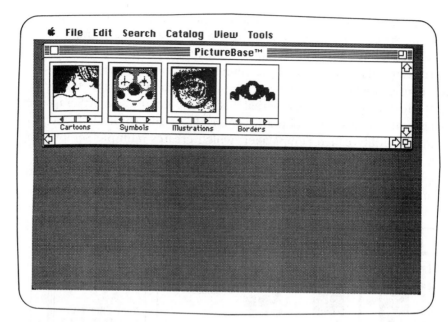

Fig. 11.19. A library of art organized by using PictureBase.

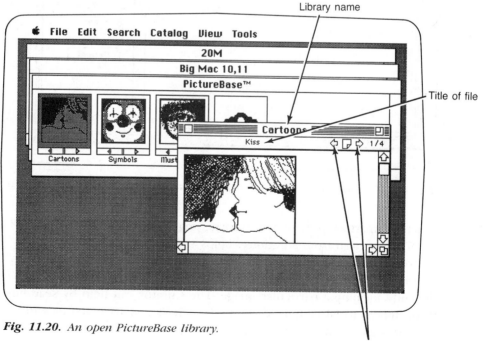

Fig. 11.20. An open PictureBase library.

the Clipper, an enhanced Clipboard that allows you to resize graphics
to fit the space where you want to insert them, and SmartScrap
substitutes for your regular Scrapbook on the Apple menu. One of
SmartScrap's nicest features is the thumbnail sketches it displays of a
file's contents when you are searching for a particular image. Figure
11.21 illustrates one of these visual "table of contents." SmartScrap even
comes with some sample clip art from T/Maker and Dubl-Click and a
wonderful utility called ScrapMaker, which creates multiple Scrapbooks
from images without cutting and pasting. SmartScrap also can print a
Scrapbook to get a hard copy of your clip art, search by file name, and
use multiple Scrapbooks.

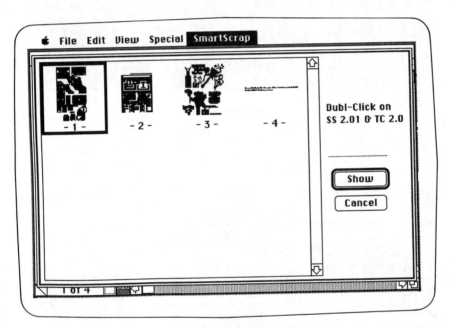

Fig. 11.21. *A visual table of contents from SmartScrap.*

Whereas SmartScrap helps you manage images stored in the Scrapbook,
the Curator (also from Solutions) helps you manage image files
wherever they are on your disk. If you use a great many graphics, you
may have hundreds of images on a hard disk, and you may have
difficulty locating a particular image. The Curator can help by searching
through a pictorial table of contents (much like SmartScrap) or with
keywords and names. With either method, you can easily find what you
need.

Another DA that can help you manage your artwork is SuperGlue II (again from Solutions). SuperGlue II enables you to share graphics and other information between Macs (regardless of application). SuperGlue II creates a specialized file format for saving images that can be viewed (but not changed) using SuperViewer, its companion program. SuperGlue II files can also be transmitted by modem, and the recipient can then use the Scrapbook DA to view the transferred files (if he or she does not have SuperView).

Creating Three-Dimensional Graphics

11

Graphics

You can now create graphics that approach our three-dimensional view of the world by using applications like Super 3D (from Silicon Beach) and Mac3D (from Challenger). For example, you can design a jet plane in three dimensions and change the viewer's perspective by rotating the axes of the object on-screen.

If you are familiar with simple graphing, you know that the x-axis is horizontal and the y-axis is vertical. Three-dimensional graphics also employ a third "in and out" axis, the z-axis, which provides the dimension of depth (see fig. 11.22). This third dimension enables you to produce truly incredible images.

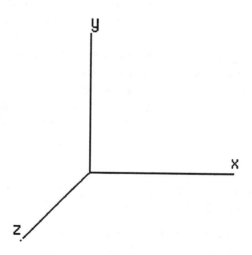

Fig. 11.22. *Three-dimensional graphics use three axes.*

A good 3-D graphics program includes the following features:

- Wireframe views to reveal the understructure of the object

- Light shading

- Adjustable light sources and intensity

- The capability of working with text and lines

- Animation, which rotates the object to change the viewer's perspective

- Zooming, which enlarges a part of the picture

- The capability of readily manipulating the position of an object in any of the three dimensions

- The capability of reshaping objects by dragging different parts

- Extruding, which takes a two-dimensional object and projects it into the third dimension

- Shape libraries

The steps for creating a 3-D image and then viewing it from a variety of perspectives are simple. Figure 11.23 shows a right triangle drawn with Super 3D's polyline tool. The Revolve command from the Tools menu transforms the triangle into a 3-D image called a *wireframe*. Selecting the Display As Solid command from the Options menu and using the Spin Wheel option fills in the wireframe image to create the solid cone rotated toward the viewer, that is shown in figure 11.24. A small amount of shading completes the image. For comparison, figure 11.25 illustrates a more sophisticated graphic of a space station; figure 11.26 shows the same object after it has been zoomed, using the Camera feature.

No matter what you draw, however, creating 3-D images can be a slow process because the software has to *refresh*, or "rethink," and then redraw much of the image each time you ask it to make a change.

Mac3D 2.1 has many of the same capabilities as Super 3D, plus some other exciting features. Mac3D comes with a set of 28 basic 3-D shapes on the tool palette. Another nice feature is the capability of selectively reshaping a drawing simply by dragging part of it so that only that portion is redrawn.

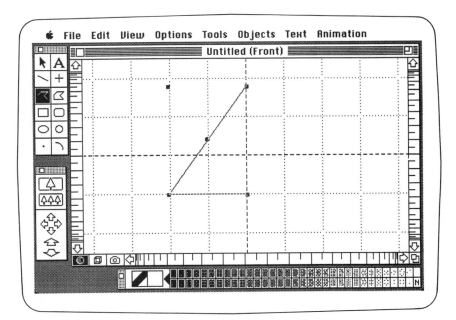

Fig. 11.23. *The beginning of a cone in Super 3D.*

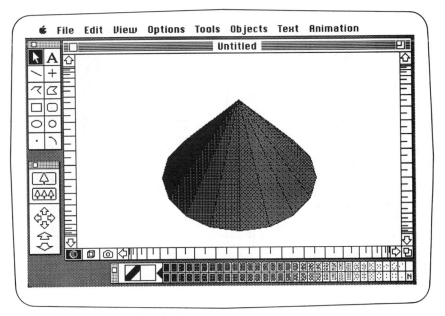

Fig. 11.24. *The solid cone in Super 3D, rotated toward the viewer.*

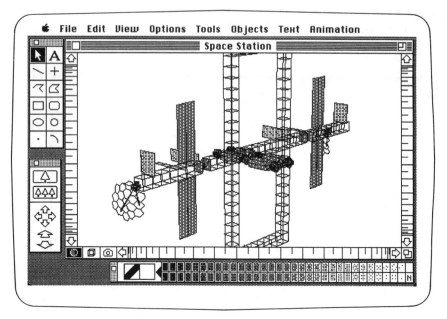

Fig. 11.25. *A 3-D space station created in Super 3D.*

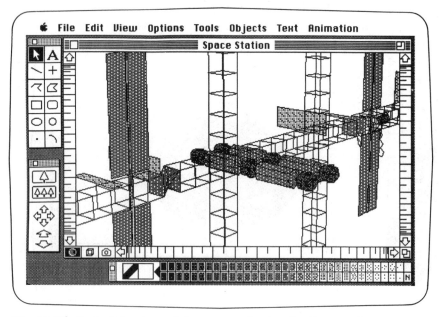

Fig. 11.26. *Part of the space station zoomed using the Camera feature.*

Mac3D also handles rotation through a dialog box that enables you to change the degree of rotation of an object in one of the three dimensions and then see the results before the object is actually rotated.

Using Computer-Aided Design (CAD) Programs

Computer-aided design (CAD) programs are to design what word processing is to writing: they transform your computer into an electronic drafting table. Their cousins, computer-aided manufacturing (CAM) programs, are electronic project managers, which assist in every phase of the manufacturing process. Although CAD/CAM programs are true application programs, they much more resemble very fine drawing instruments and have therefore been included with this chapter on graphics.

Interest in CAD began during the late 1950s and early 1960s, when designers realized that automobiles, household appliances, and rockets were more complex than the designers' physical design skills and tools could possibly handle. The Mac II's present capability of running CAD/CAM programs with its faster processors, larger screens, and larger RAM have made the Macintosh almost indispensable for engineering applications.

CAD programs take drawing to a new level of power and precision. They contain not only basic drawing tools but also sophisticated statistical analysis capabilities and highly specific modules for particular projects, such as electrical circuit design, aerospace engineering, and architecture. For example, one popular (and inexpensive at around $100) CAD program, Real CADD Level 1 (from Generic), has the following symbol libraries:

- Basic Home Design

- Kitchen Design

- Electronics

- Home Landscaping

- Flowcharts and Schedules

11
Graphics

- Industrial Pipe Fittings

- Heating and Air Conditioning

- Commercial and Residential Furnishings

You can use any of these symbol libraries with Real CADD Level 1 or Level 2 to expand the usefulness of the basic program. For example, architects depend on symbols in their drawings to represent everything from commodes to stairs. These symbol libraries avoid the necessity of duplicating the symbols in a paint program and then pasting them in; instead, the symbols are ready to be used in the CAD application right away.

Experienced users of paint and draw programs can be very precise in their work and depend on 2-D and 3-D programs to do their design work. There's no substitute, however, for the vector graphics that can be produced by using CAD applications. The detail can be finer and the precision greatly increased because these programs have tools that help the user achieve these goals.

A good CAD program should contain all the features found in a draw program, plus some:

- Assignment of objects to multiple layers

- Zooming capability

- Different names for different views

- "Snap" to objects in the window

- Autodimensioning (the program adds dimensions)

- Symbol libraries (with some programs, such as Claris CAD, you can create and store your own symbols)

- Multiple preferences for units (use inches and centimeters in the same drawing)

- Floating-point decimals

- Capability of printing to various types of printers and plotters, to scale, when necessary, for blueprints and other plans

MiniCad Plus (from Graphsoft), one of the most popular CAD programs, has all these and many other features, including a spreadsheet and programming language that can be integrated into a CAD drawing. Figure 11.27, a sample file from MiniCad Plus of a boat design, illustrates the intricate detail that is possible.

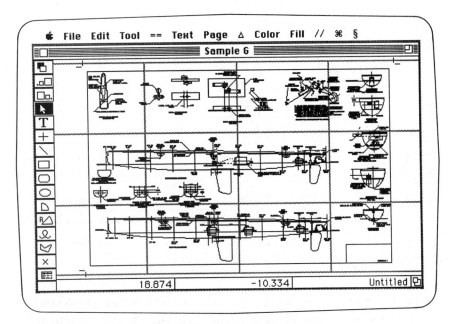

Fig. 11.27. A sample file from MiniCad Plus.

Figure 11.28 shows a portion of the boat design that has been zoomed by double-clicking the zoom icon in the Tool Box or using the ⌘-! or ⌘-2 key combinations. Writing that was previously barely recognizable as text is now clearly legible.

Some CAD programs with limited capabilities sell for as little as $150, but the more powerful programs are much more expensive. MiniCad Plus sells for $700, VersaCAD for $2,000, and AutoCAD for almost $3,000. However, if you create technical drawings for a living, a good CAD program is indispensable.

Using Scanners

If you often find yourself in the position of needing to enter previously printed text or graphics into a file to be edited, a *scanner* can save you

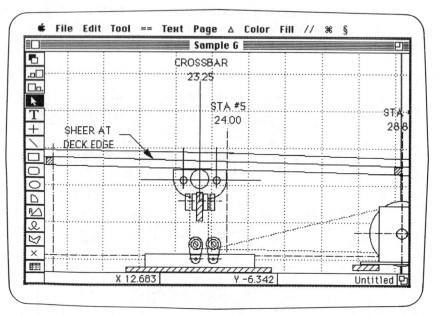

Fig. 11.28. A close-up of a portion of the boat design.

hours of tedious work. Scanners are hardware devices that convert an image into a series of digital signals, which are then translated into an electronic file. Using advanced digital image-processing programs, such as Digital Darkroom and ImageStudio, you can then edit this file just as if you had scanners organize pixels, so that your document can become a representation of the original. The number of bits per pixel determines the quality of the image produced: the more bits per pixel, the better the image because more shades of gray can be produced. Flat scanners read only on and off signals (blacks and whites) and allow less precision.

The most expensive scanners, flat scanners, are similar to early copying machines. You place the document to be scanned on a sheet of glass and start the scanner. A bright light moves across the scanner face and photosensors (more than 2,500) in the moving part of the scanner capture changes in the image, which are recorded by the scanner as "ons" and "offs." These scanners can come in the physical form of a sheet feeder, an overhead (similar in appearance to a typical overhead projector), or a flatbed configuration in which you place the book or paper on the surface that is scanned.

Another group of scanners, print head scanners, are mounted on the print head of the ImageWriter. As the print head moves across the page to be scanned, it transmits the "ons" and "offs" directly to your Mac. The best known of these print head scanners is ThunderScan (from ThunderWare), which retails for about $250 and is one of the cheapest scanners available. It is discussed in more detail in the next section.

Finally, relatively inexpensive hand-held scanners are also available; with these scanners, you move the scanner manually across the area to be duplicated. Table 11.1 compares the advantages and disadvantages of the three different types of scanners.

In order to use a scanner, you need specialized software that matches the type of scanner you are using. In many cases, the best combination of hardware and software may come from different companies, so you should explore a variety of options. The remainder of this chapter discusses some of your choices.

11

Graphics

Using ThunderScan

ThunderScan (from ThunderWare) deserves special attention because it is inexpensive and easy to use. ThunderScan places the (almost) power of a true gray-scale image at your fingertips, but it is very slow. You must be very careful to align your picture properly as well, and ThunderScan does not work particularly well with glossies.

ThunderScan enables you to adjust brightness and contrast, it supports all popular file formats, and it produces acceptable images. It comes as a package with a digitizing cartridge (the scanner), an adapter box, software, and more.

To scan an image with ThunderScan, you follow these steps:

1. Replace the print head on your ImageWriter with the scanner.

2. Set the printer and the printer port.

3. Insert the original image to be scanned into the printer.

4. Scan the image. ThunderScan moves back and forth across the image as if it were printing, transmitting the information to a file as it "reads" the document.

5. Edit the image (as a PICT or TIFF file, for example).

Table 11.1
A Comparison of Scanner Types

	Flatbed	*Print Head*	*Hand-Held*
Advantages	Scans books, single sheets	Inexpensive	Relatively inexpensive
	Accurate		
	Can scan 3-D for objects (overhead scanners)		
Disadvantages	Expensive (although some overheads cost about $600)	Slow	Problems with image alignment
		Cannot do OCR	Cannot do OCR very well
		Limited gray scaling	Limited gray scaling
			Limited to relatively narrow images
Hardware Manufacturers	Apple, Hewlett-Packard	ThunderWare	Logitech, ThunderWare
Software Manufacturers	Olduvai, Apple, Abaton, Truval, Microtek		

6. Save the file.

7. Print the file or use it in another document.

With ThunderScan, you can scan half-tones and line art, select printers (ImageWriter I or II), change speeds, and even use different ports (modem or printer). ThunderScan cannot give you the same quality image as the $7,000 flat scanners mentioned earlier, but its images are highly acceptable. ThunderScan also can be useful for importing low-resolution images into HyperCard.

Because the ThunderScan is really a printer of sorts in disguise, it scans at 72 dpi, which does not produce very precise printed images. To offset this weakness, magnify the image to be scanned to 400% and then, after you have scanned it, print it at 25% by adjusting the Page Step Up options on your Mac. The resulting image will be of better quality. Enclosing the images you want to scan in clear, nonreflective plastic may also produce a better ThunderScan image with higher resolution.

11

Graphics

Using Optical Character Recognition (OCR) Software

Optical Character Recognition (OCR) software is the "brain" of the scanner. The OCR software enables the scanner to read and translate characters into text files that you can then manipulate with your favorite word processing program. Three basic types of OCR software are available:

- *Nontrainable* software, which is limited to the specific type of text and printers for which it has been designed. Nontrainable OCR software is fast, but you cannot change fonts or printers without changing the software as well.

- *Trainable* software, which can be "taught." You actually provide the software with the set of rules that you want it to follow by building a *template*, a reference to which the software compares the scanned image, character by character.

- *Automatic* software, which includes some artificial intelligence and is designed to read text with no "training." Of course, these software packages are considerably more expensive.

Even the most sophisticated OCR software is not perfect. Its accuracy may be affected by the hardware being used, the cleanliness of the scanning surface, and the quality of the print it is reading. Therefore, you can never assume that a scanned file is the exact duplicate of the original printed material.

OCR software registers two kinds of errors: errors of omission and errors of commission. When an error of omission occurs because the software cannot read the text, it leaves out the character and enters a nonsense character, such as ~ or ●. Errors of commission occur when the sotfware reads the text incorrectly; for example, you may get "software" rather than "software." The only way to locate errors of commission is to use a spell checking program or manually proofread the document.

Using Gray-Scale Scanning

OCR software can read text quite accurately and in a sense does not have to work as hard as software and scanners that scan graphics. As you know, graphics are rarely simple line art; they often include a variety of shades of gray. These shades, or levels of gray, and the sensitivity of the software determine the quality of the image resulting from the scan.

The number of bits per pixel determines the precision of a scanned graphic image and, to some extent, the price of the scanner. For example, the Apple scanner lists for around $1,800 and can reproduce 16 different gray levels. On the other hand, Microtek's MSF300Q, which can scan up to 64 gray levels, lists for almost $8,000.

Fine-Tuning Scanned Images

After you have scanned an image and edited it using the software tools provided with your scanning software, you may still need a more precise image. Two popular programs that enable you to do precise fine-tuning are Digital Darkroom 1.0 (from Silicon Beach) and ImageStudio 1.5 (from LetraSet).

These programs enable you to edit a gray-scaled image to produce the half-tones necessary for incorporating high-quality photos in your documents. You also can cut and paste as you want; for example, you can take a photo of a model and literally paste on clothes, airbrushing to make the elements fit together nicely. In addition, you can retouch a photo, incorporating special effects to create a completely different picture. This technology can be a great boon to artists, but remember, you must know the programs and have some knowledge of how to use the "real life" tools (such as an airbrush) to get the results you want. These programs are packed with features and are not overly expensive

($300–$500), but be sure that you are familiar with retouching before you invest.

Using Color Scanners

Color scanners are special for many reasons. They offer incredible options for working with scanned material, but at significant expense (they cost about four times as much as the average gray-scale scanner), and they take up a great deal of memory. You need a Mac II with 4 or 5 megabytes of RAM (or virtual memory) to view your work while reproducing color images, and the hardware alone costs approximately $7,000.

Some color scanners can scan more than just flat images. For example, the Barneyscan system (from Barneyscan), offers hardware for converting 35mm color slides into images. You simply insert the slide into the scanner, and minutes later you have on file an image that you can edit by using tools from an extensive set provided with the scanner. You also can use the software to produce four-color separations.

After you have scanned the images you need, you can transmit them by modem. For example, photos from last year's World Series were sent from Los Angeles to New York through a modem after first being scanned with the Barneyscan XP. Although the photos were black-and-white, this example illustrates the possibility of transmitting photos over telephone lines in order to be included in a document at the other end, where they can be cropped and adjusted.

This equipment costs approximately $9,000 just to get started, but it provides great editorial flexibility and saves time, materials, and labor.

Chapter Summary

The world of Macintosh graphics only now seems to be opening. Starting with what now seems to be a simple and small 128K MacPaint, tools have grown in size and complexity and can match the technical accomplishment of any skilled draftsperson. Along with scanners, OCR software, color capability, and public domain libraries full of clip art, anyone can at least have the tools they need. You probably cannot go wrong no matter what software package you buy. Although SuperPaint may lead the crowd, FullPaint and MacPaint also can provide you with much, if not all, of what you need.

The experience? Well, that's a different story. Learning to use these tools has become simple with the abundant aids available (such as the videotape that comes with Illustrator). Using them well is another story. Many community colleges and universities are now offering classes in the area of graphics and graphic design, even though it may be called something like *Design* or even *Desktop Publishing*. Seek out these classes, practice, and look around for the print and screen designs that you like.

CHAPTER 12

Having Fun with the Mac

What a misnomer for a chapter! You have been having fun all along, so why a separate chapter now? This chapter is about some serious fun—the many games and other sources of entertainment available for the Macintosh family of computers.

The Mac has so many possibilities for fun that it would be impossible to discuss them all. The programs mentioned in this chapter are a selection based on my subjective judgment. I call all these programs games because they are fun—whether you are landing on the moon or helping a child learn the basics of adding and subtracting.

What's a Good Game?

Obviously, a good game is one that does either of two things: provides hours of challenging and engaging fun or provides a vicarious experience you cannot have otherwise—like playing in the Masters golf tournament or piloting an F-16 fighter jet and engaging in dog fights with enemy aircraft. Where else could you do that for about forty bucks?

Good games do some, if not all, of the following:

- Provide entertainment. You can do something you could not otherwise do, whether you are playing 18 holes of golf at the Augusta Masters course or flying a P-52 Spitfire over England during World War II.

- Enable you to pick up where you left off if you cannot finish the game in one sitting (as is often the case unless you're ready for a 12-hour session)

- Keep track of the highest scoring players

- Adjust the difficulty level. Some games are so hard and complex that if they don't enable users to get the feel for the tasks at hand, users lose interest and the game loses them—often for good.

- Have excellent and unusual sound and visual effects, which you can adjust for volume and playing speed

- Provide hints or even the solution. Otherwise, you can go crazy with frustration.

- Enable you to change game characteristics, such as point values, the types of monsters you shoot and their point value, story ending, and so on

When considering a game, you should find out whether the company offers any kind of technical support. Why would you need technical support for a game? At times, some games can be unnerving. You struggle for hours to find the clue you need to rescue the princess or reach the castle only to find that your efforts are to no avail. A small hint can mean the difference between spending all night trying to figure out what went wrong and the ultimate feeling of beating the machine.

Games are relatively inexpensive; commercial products rarely cost more than $40, and the shareware games available are significantly less expensive. Some shareware sources are BMVG, BCS Mac PD CD library, and Budget Bytes. (See Chapter 13 for a discussion of shareware.) Are the commercial games worth paying the extra $20 or $30? In most cases, yes, because developers of commercial games have more incentives for current design and updates—incentives that may be missing from shareware. On the other hand, hundreds of shareware games are terrific and readily available.

Take Me Out to the Ball Games

The great American pastime is on your Mac. These games are so real that all you need is an easy chair and a soft drink, and you will think that you are right out there ready to play with best.

It is the All Stars versus the Champs in a knock-dead nine-inning (or extras if need be) face-off. With Accolade's Hard Ball, you control everything from the type of pitch you want to throw to the positions of the players. In figure 12.1, you can see a slider pitch being thrown. After the pitch is thrown by a click, you field the ball and throw to a base (unless the hit is out of the ball park). Options include designating home and visiting teams, exchanging positions, substituting players, moving outfielders and infielders, and intentionally walking the batter. With nine pitching zones to throw to, you can be a Cy Young winner in no time, without suffering from a sore arm.

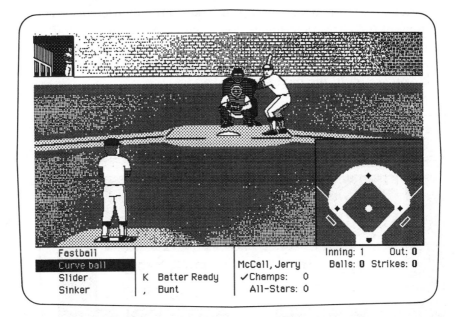

12

Having
Fun

Fig. 12.1. *Accolade's Hard Ball brings the excitement of America's favorite pastime to your Mac.*

You're at the 18th hole at Augusta, and in a play-off with your arch rival. Mean 18 Ultimate Golf (from Accolade) opens with the sound of a golf club swinging and hitting a ball down a fairway. From there on, the course of the game is up to you. You select from as many as six different clubs, swing away, and putt through one of five predesigned courses. As many as four players can play. You can select expert or beginner's level, save a game to resume later, and even change courses in the middle of a match.

Figure 12.2 shows you the first hole at Pebble Beach, with the par and the course lengths for beginners or experts. Figure 12.3 shows you the beginning screen for this shot. You swing by using the scale on the left side of the window.

The screen has several icons that make the game very lifelike. You can select the club you want to use and change your aim by clicking the right or left arrow on the right-hand side of the screen. You also can click on the score pad to see where you stand or click to get an aerial view of the hole you are playing. You hit the ball by moving it up the Power Meter with the mouse. Each shot takes three mouse clicks, and the timing of the clicks determines how accurate your shot is. You click the mouse once to begin the back swing and click again to control the distance of your shot. The final click strikes the ball, and whack! you are off to the next shot.

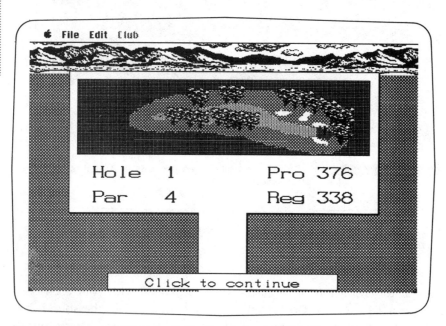

Fig. 12.2. Mean 18 Ultimate Golf—first hole at Pebble Beach.

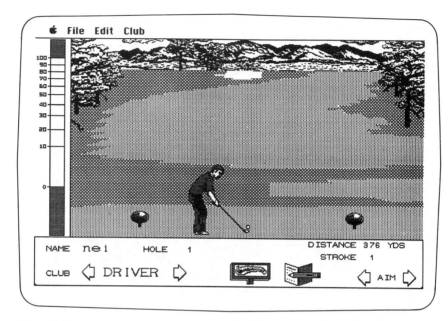

Fig. 12.3. *Beginning screen for the shot at the first hole.*

When you are installed in the Mean 18 Hall of Fame, you can graduate to designing your own golf course with all the sand and water traps you want. Great fun, and you don't need to worry about carrying your clubs.

Another great golf game is MacGolf (from Practical Computer Applications). With MacGolf, you choose the skill level and the number of holes to play: front 9, back 9, or all 18. Then, you choose between Augusta National and Shinook Hills. Figure 12.4. shows you the first hole of Augusta National, complete with wind direction and speed and an aerial view of the hole. You even can change your stance and the way you approach the ball. MacGolf gives you the realism of actually playing with great sound effects (Plop!—right into the water) but without the greens fees.

Speaking of hitting little balls, welcome to MacRacquetball (from Practical Computer Applications). Racquetball is the game you play at those $500-a-year and $15,000-initiation-fee health clubs (or your local community center). Racquetball is fast, good exercise, and quite competitive—even on the Mac.

Fig. 12.4. *The first hole of Augusta National, presented by MacGolf from Practical Computer Applications.*

When you boot up using the System of the MacRacquetball disk, you make decisions about every component of the game, including the following:

- Strength

- Stamina

- Agility

- Accuracy

- Aggressiveness

- Game speed

This game is so realistic that it is almost unbelievable; it even has 3-D effects (see fig. 12.5). The two competitors actually run around and hit the ball as you control one of them with the mouse. You even can play over a modem between two Macs. A voice tells you "Side out," "Ball," or "Point." Except for the sweaty clothes, this game is the real thing.

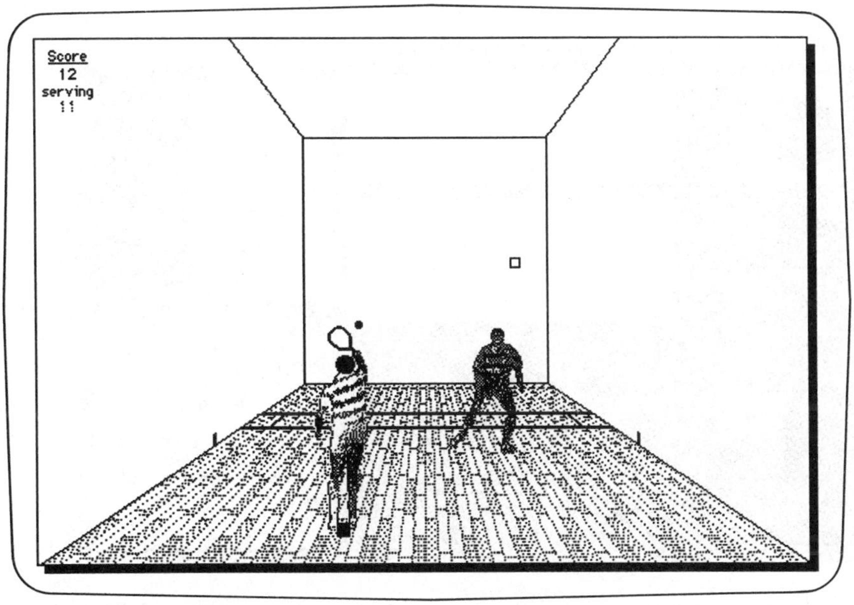

Fig. 12.5. *Point! Your serve. MacRacquetball is almost like the real thing.*

Now, it's time to get serious. With the National Football League playing weekly games, what better idea than to get started with your own league of 250-pound nose guards? Mac Pro Football (from Avalon Hill) comes complete with master disk, the 1986 season stats for all teams, and a team disk that you use to construct your own lineups. You are in control of everything: the toss of the coin to start the game, weather conditions, the month of play, and the selection of a team to play against, such as the 1986 Jets or the 1968 Kansas City Chiefs.

Figure 12.6 shows you the Jets in possession with Joe Namath quarterbacking. So much information goes into each move that you need 1M of RAM to work this game, but if you love football, the game is well worth the RAM. (Finally, a football game where the coaches and players actually plan a strategy.)

"Start buttin' heads with the big boys" is printed on the back of the 4th and Inches package from Accolade. When you start the game, the songs and visuals make you feel like you are ready to do exactly that. Play even begins with "The Star-Spangled Banner" and a reasonable attempt at a 3-D display of the playing field, where players run, score safeties,

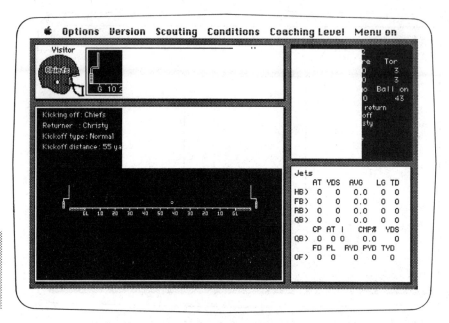

Fig. 12.6. Chiefs versus the Jets in the Super Bowl championship.

and then jump up and down in anger (see fig. 12.7). As an add-on, you can get Accolade's Team Construction set, with which you can create any team and any type of player to play with 4th and Inches. You even can name your team and choose the jersey colors—just like the owner.

Fly Me to the Moon

Starting on the ground, you can play Ferrari Grand Prix (from Bullseye Software), a racing game that is so realistic you begin to smell the gas and oil the first time around the track. You begin in your Formula One car, the most popular type of racing in the world, and select one of several race courses and the opponents you want to race against. Figure 12.8 shows the opening screen, and figure 12.9 gives an aerial view of the track, which you can modify to fit your wishes.

This screen shows you the current position of the car and how you can modify the track by inserting various shapes and sizes of track (located in the lower left corner). You even can use a curve direction tool to change the direction of the curves around the track.

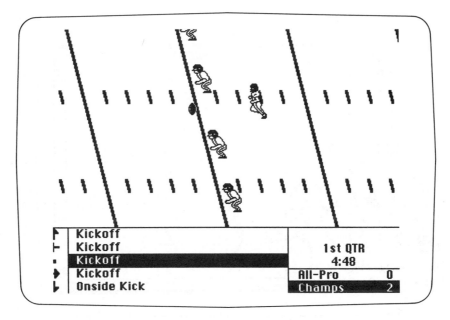

Fig. 12.7. *4th and Inches playing screen.*

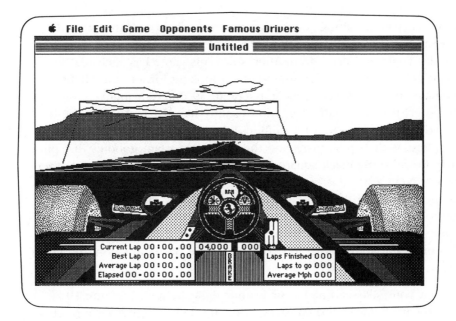

Fig. 12.8. *You finally get a chance to drive a Ferrari.*

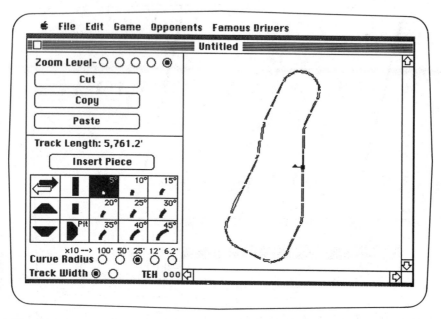

Fig. 12.9. *Aerial view of Ferrari Grand Prix track.*

Now that you are going so fast that you're probably off the ground, imagine flying from New York to San Francisco. Welcome to the popular Flight Simulator from Microsoft. This game has such realistic sound effects that you may find yourself looking for an exit. Flight Simulator offers a realistic cockpit screen, 39 different flight characteristics, and instrumentation exactly like the real thing—be it a prop-driven Cessna 182 or a million-dollar Lear Jet. This package is complete, with airport maps and the other important goodies that pilots carry in those big black square bags—and even aviation maps for places such as New York, Boston, Seattle, and San Francisco and runway maps for the airports in these areas. You set the clouds, the view (cockpit, control tower, and so on), and the automatic pilot, and you have liftoff. You even can fly over the Statue of Liberty (it really looks like her). This program is great fun, and your insurance premiums don't go up a penny.

Get out your silk scarf and your leather flight helmet. It's June 1944, and you are flying a P-51 Mustang with the 275th Fighter Group. This experience is brought to you by P-51 Mustang Flight Simulator, and once you try it, you will keep coming back for more. Military flying, dogfights, even convoys of trucks, houses, and German airplanes to attack are provided during your flight. To add to the realism, author Donald Hill, Jr., has included in the manual a section that is a reprint of material contained in the original flight book, which came with every real P-51. The manual also contains a list of readings you can consult if you want to learn more about the plan and about military flying in general. (If you're wondering, you even can bail out, parachute and all.)

If you are after sheer speed, try Falcon, the F-16 flight simulator from Spectrum Holobyte (which comes with a 130-page manual). You don't have a hard time imagining yourself at 20,000 feet and still climbing, ready to flip on the afterburner as you increase your speed far beyond two times the speed of sound. This game is a highly realistic simulation of one of the top-level fighter jets flown today.

Although it takes a bit of time to get used to the controls and cockpit, the game is enormous fun. You find yourself dive bombing and avoiding surface-to-air missiles and loads of armament, such as Sidewinder and Maverick missiles (and listening to the great music of the Top Gun school). You are more than ready to meet the enemy MIG-21s after going through some training sessions and practicing some of the predesigned flights and fights.

Now, imagine yourself going up into the stratosphere, beyond where the F-16 can go, and into darkness while flying on the space shuttle. Spectrum Holobyte's Orbiter is dedicated to the flight crew of the Challenger, who died on January 28, 1986. This game doesn't have many sound effects, but is a great learning and teaching tool. You configure your launch, orbit, or landing and decide on the mission (such as training or satellite repair). Then, you see a series of screens like the one shown in figure 12.10. Control sends you a verbal message telling you what to do, and you continue through a sequence of commands until you are launched and ready to go. The fun and the learning really begin when you maneuver the Manned Maneuvering Unit to repair a satellite or make some other adjustment outside the ship.

Still up in space, imagine that you are on a mission to rescue a party on the moon. In Lunar Rescue (from Practical Computer Applications), the moon is populated with 26 domed cities and protected by a sophisticated defense system that has been sabotaged by terrorists. Your job (if you want to accept it) is to replenish the supplies the moon

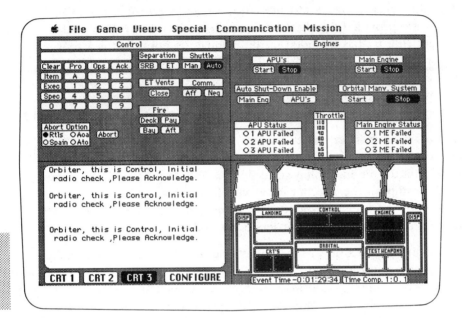

Fig. 12.10. *Flying the space shuttle.*

folks need for survival, and you must get there through some hairy and harried shoot 'em up situations. This game has outstanding graphics, including video screens for communication (that blink like the real things). Lunar Rescue is as close to science fiction on the Mac as you can get. You even can enter a practice mode, where you crash or get shot down. You are given an unlimited number of tries to learn the necessary skills.

Want to trade robots for minerals? "Yes," says the trading partner shown in figure 12.11, and you are on your way to rescuing the stranded space citizens!

You can enter deep space and learn a good deal with Telstar from Spectrum Holobyte. You choose the location on the earth and view stars, planets, and other heavenly objects. Just think of the screen shots of your best friend's astrological sign (Aries, Pisces, and so on) and the neat birthday cards you can construct.

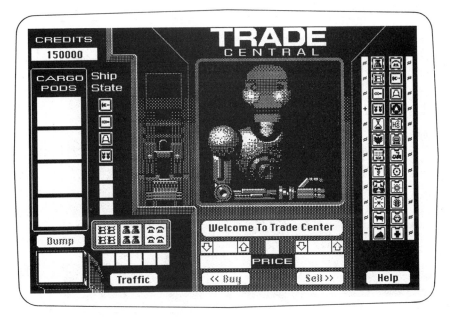

Fig. 12.11. *Trading goods for a lunar rescue.*

Ominous and Fun

You need a great deal of help to defeat the spooks in Beyond Dark Castle (from Silicon Beach), but with fireballs and stones against bats, rats, and mutants, you can win. This animated game is a great and addictive arcade-like game. Beyond Dark Castle is a bit rough at the beginning but worth every effort to get up and running. With very clear sounds (such as some "Toccata and Fugue in D Minor"), which add to the fun, you progress through levels of the castle, seeking the Dark Knight. Besides the sound effects, the visuals are excellent (see fig. 12.12). Wait until Friday to start playing because you don't have to go to school or work the next day. You may be up all night.

Games that are brain teasers and challenges, besides being fun, are few and far between. Welcome to the Fool's Errand from Miles Computing, which begins with a scroll and a tale about a light-hearted fool. Guess who gets to finish the tale by solving puzzles filled with clues of every kind? To get from here (the opening screen) to there (the end), you need to solve 42 puzzles of all shapes and sizes. You get so caught up in the puzzles (that don't have to be solved in order) that you end up enjoying doing them as much as solving them.

Fig. 12.12. *The great hall from Beyond Dark Castle.*

For example, in figure 12.13, you see a puzzle in which you have to find the words embedded in the letters. The jigsaw puzzle in figure 12.14 should keep you busy for a few hours. These puzzles all contain the clues you need to solve the mystery. If you find yourself going a little nuts, you always can order the *Hints and Answers* book to help you maintain your sanity.

Have you ever wanted to be mayor, city manager, or the chief of police? You can try them all with SimCity from Maxis Software. Think of the fun you can have working with Tokyo in 1957, trying to avert an attack by a monster that looks like Godzilla (see figs. 12.15 and 12.16). You also can deal with the San Francisco earthquake of 1906 or a nuclear meltdown in 2010. Helicopter traffic reports, sirens, and every kind of city problem you can imagine are provided for your entertainment.

You just looked up at the clock; it's 4 a.m., and you have to be at work at 8 a.m. Where did the time go? Enter Arkanoid (from Discovery Software), the original bricks game that keeps you in that chair for hours and hours. This truly fascinating game has you try to knock down

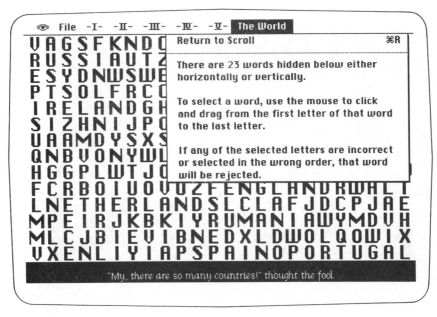

Fig. 12.13. *A Fool's Errand word puzzle screen.*

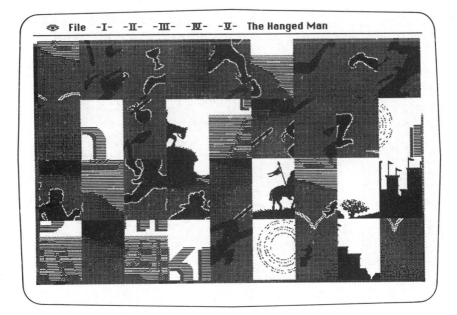

Fig. 12.14. *A Fool's Errand jigsaw puzzle screen.*

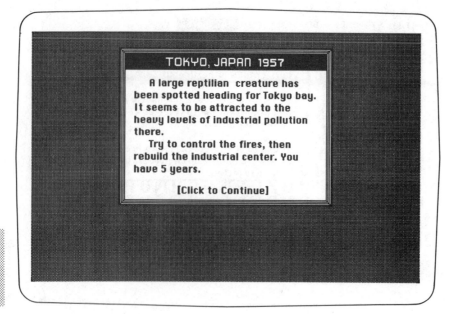

Fig. 12.15. The assignment screen for Tokyo, 1957.

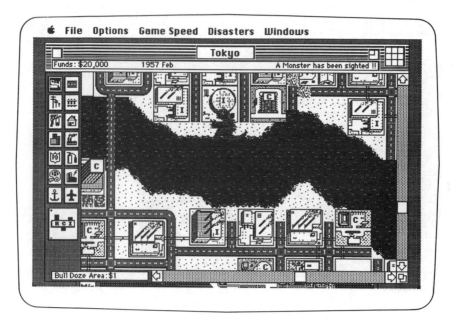

Fig. 12.16. The monster attacking Tokyo.

a wall of bricks until you reach the "treasure." This game keeps you going, advancing in levels and trying to get the ball that destroys the bricks to bounce in just the right place. You pick the level (from beginner to madman—expert) and the number of lives you have to waste. I hope that there is nothing to the rumored connection between video display monitors and illness, because games like this will keep you in front of the screen for days.

Last, but not least is the most addictive game that I have ever played. Crystal Quest (from Green, Inc.) is the ultimate space shoot 'em up game. It comes with Critter Editor for changing almost every dimension of the game. Figure 12.17 shows the screen displayed when you edit sounds. You can choose Oohs, Aahs, and passionate moans. Armed with your trusty mouse, you battle Annoyers, Worriers, Dumples, Zarklephasers, and other uglies. You fight through waves of these things in an effort to—what else—amass the most points (more than your 13-year-old daughter can get, anyway). What is great about this game is that the first person to play the game after it comes out of the package has the all-time highest score. What a way to be a hero!

12
Having
Fun

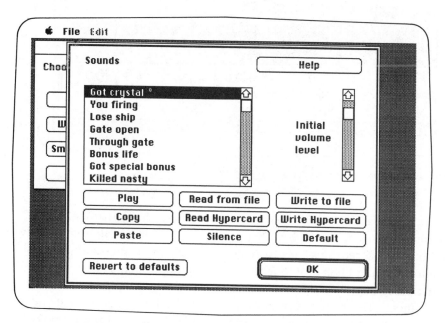

Fig. 12.17. *Working with the Crystal Quest Critter Editor.*

World War II

As the Joker said of Batman, "Where does he get all those great toys?" This is the case with GATO (from Spectrum Holobyte), a real-time simulation of a World War II attack submarine (see fig. 12.18). You operate the periscope, chart your course, control fire damage, and—if you are really good—sink enemy ships. You select from a variety of missions and then act as a captain as you try to rescue downed seamen or destroy cargo ships located somewhere on your radar scope.

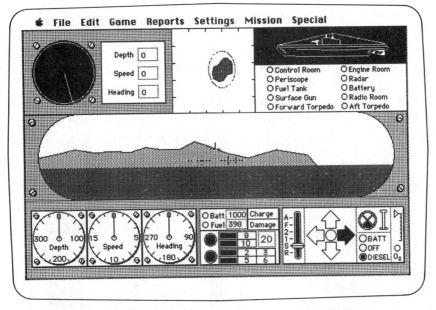

Fig. 12.18. *The view from the scope of GATO.*

Next, you may be in the PT-109 (also from Spectrum) that GATO is trying to destroy, although with your speed, this destruction is unlikely. With 435 different missions to select from, enemy planes and ships to confront, and a choice of four theatres of action (such as the Philippines or the Mediterranean), you can be the John F. Kennedy of your block. The boat is fast and launches torpedoes (that is what the T in PT is for). This game even gives you the splashes and the sounds of the sea. In figure 12.19, you can see the enemy off the port bow—but you ran out of torpedoes before you got 'em. Tough break, but there are always more where that one came from. Just start a new game!

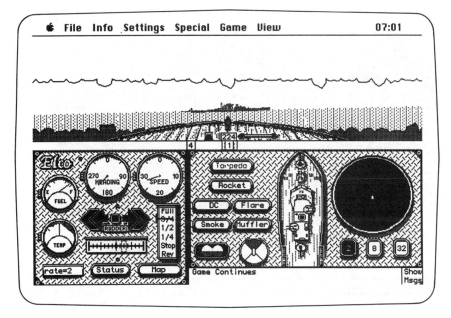

Fig. 12.19. *Commanding a PT-109.*

One more shipshape game is Battle Stations (from TimeLine) with opening voices and claxons telling you to man your stations, as if attack is imminent. Terrific voice effects make this grown-up BattleShips (remember the graphic paper?) fun even if you can't take it in the car with you.

East Meets West

Mystery? Intrigue? Suspense? How about a game with 10 difficulty levels, random generation of pieces that have to be placed correctly, help screens, terrific graphics, and enough room for you and all your friends? Conceived by two Soviet programmers, Tetris is serious game stuff that only players with large blocks of time and perseverance should pursue. If this game were on the big cinema, it would be a cult movie. The opening screen gives you some flavor for the quality of the graphics (see fig. 12.20). The object is to stack the tiles that fall through the air and make them fit together. Background graphics of Russian scenes and music make this game enjoyable as well as challenging.

invented by a 30-year-old Soviet researcher named Alexey Pazhitnov who currently w

Fig. 12.20. *The challenge of Tetris.*

What could be more peaceful and challenging than a session of Go-Man-Ku, otherwise known as Go Master from Toyogo? This game is based on a truly ancient (4,000 years and counting) game, which was originally played with shiny stones on a checkerboard pattern. The package even comes with a membership application to the American Go Association. Figure 12.21 shows you a game in progress between two famous Go Masters. The game includes three types of boards with varying levels of difficulty (including different sized boards), so that if you are new to this game, you have plenty of room and time for practice. The object of this national game of Japan is to capture the most prisoners, and the game often is compared to chess in its analogy to life and the way in which the game reflects the player's personality. Toyogo also offers a Go Tutor study program if you really want to get into Go.

Just for Kids

Not many of the games described in this chapter are for little tykes, and that omission was a complaint early in the introduction of software for the Mac. Things are changing, however, and with programs like

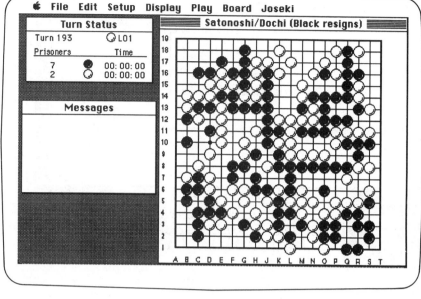

Fig. 12.21. A classic Go board.

KidsTime and NumberMaze (both from Great Wave Software), the situation is improving. Both games offer immediate feedback and difficulty adjustment and teach the basics about writing, letters, matching (KidsTime), and number skills (NumberMaze).

For example, KidsTime Dot-To-Dot provides the traditional dot-to-dot plans of a plane, a baby, and other pictures, and the child follows the dots. When the dots are connected, a drawn image replaces the straight lines, and the child moves on to the next figure. Story Writer helps with word recognition, because the child can write his or her own stories and have KidsTime read them back using MacInTalk (see fig. 12.22).

NumberMaze opens with a screen and sounds that engage the child (and the adult) and then displays screens that require answers to simple questions (see fig. 12.23). You must answer these questions before you can move on to reach the castle. You construct ladders with your correct answers, part brick walls, and do amazing feats—and you learn to count besides. You even can custom-design your own mazes.

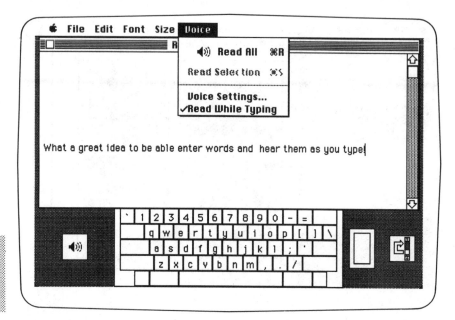

Fig. 12.22. Having stories read back to the writer.

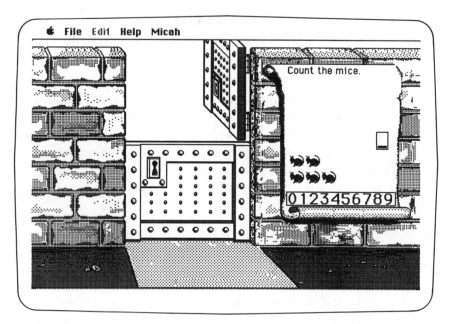

Fig. 12.23. A stop along the way in NumberMaze.

Music, Music, Music

Although these music programs are not games, they are entertaining as well as useful. ConcertWare+ (from Great Wave Software) combines a Music Writer, Instrument Maker, and Music Player in a highly sophisticated package. You use programs like this one to create sheet music, design instrument sounds, and play back what you construct or play one of the many samples, such as "The Blue Danube" and *The Fifth Symphony*. This package, which has won awards from *MacWorld* and *MacUser*, enables you to use slurs, repeats, first and second edits, and more, and is as easy to use as any well-designed Mac-interfaced program can be.

Figure 12.24 shows a screen from the Music Mouse, a program that enables you to create your own unique rhythms by moving the mouse. The screen displays the mouse position and creates sounds according to your settings.

12

Having
Fun

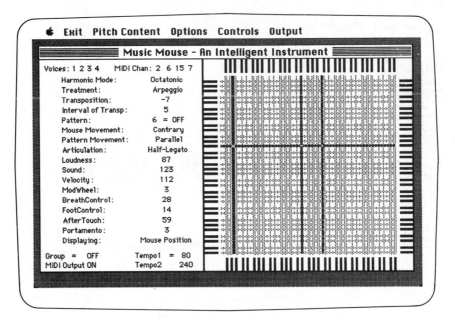

Fig. 12.24. *Here I come to save the day...Music Mouse enables you to create your own sounds by moving the mouse.*

Correspondence School for Surgeons

It's a matter of Life & Death (from The Software Toolworks), a real-life simulation of what it is like to be a surgeon. This doctor software comes with gloves and a mask. On my first try (using the tools shown in fig. 12.25), I killed the first patient by not allowing enough time for the anesthetic to work and then killed the next one (or maybe the same person reincarnated) by cutting in the wrong place. Where did I find myself? Back in medical school for a lecture.

All fun aside, Life & Death comes with enough accurate information that you can learn something about medicine and, more particularly, surgery. Diagnose and treat the patient properly, and you are in good with the nurses and the hospital administrator.

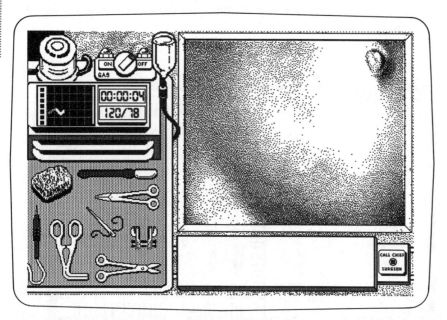

Fig. 12.25. Life & Death and another lost patient!

Posters and Calendars

Everyone has occasion to draw a poster or make up a calendar of some kind or another. PosterMaker Plus (from Broderbund) and CalendarMaker and MacBillboard (from CE Software) offer enjoyable utilities to accomplish these tasks.

PosterMaker Plus is a desktop sign maker that offers features far beyond the capabilities of simple paint or draw programs. PosterMaker Plus has sophisticated options, such as different file formats, templates, smooth fonts, kerning, and scaling, so that you can achieve what used to be accomplished only by powerful graphics programs like Illustrator and FreeHand. This program is not a toy, but it is fun.

Figure 12.26 shows you the working screen for the Mickey-Lu poster shown in figure 12.27. PosterMaker Plus is an easy-to-use tool to create posters that can be used as is or can be adapted for other uses, such as printing on acetate for silk-screening or designing signs to be used to create printing plates.

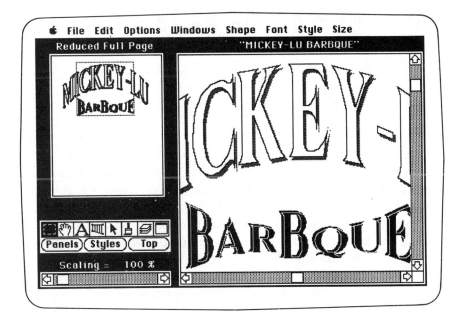

12

Having Fun

Fig. 12.26. Mickey-Lu's advertisement with the actual screen used to design it.

Fig. 12.27. *Finished advertisement.*

Do you want a billboard up to 19 by 26 feet that screams "Happy Birthday" or "Mazel Tov?" MacBillboard (from CE Software) can do a billboard for you in a snap. MacBillboard also can do banners and greeting cards (see the template in fig. 12.28). This program even can import scanned images for inclusion in your masterpieces. In fact, the CE people call MacBillboard a graphics machine because it imports graphics you create and enables you to reproduce them as needed. MacBillboard has a series of tools, like a good painting and drawing program, and can print copy for iron-ons and banners.

You can produce that calendar as you like, without the cat hanging from the tree or the little puppies staring you in the face. CalendarMaker (also from CE Software) enables you to create individualized calendars for use on your wall or in your newsletter. In figure 12.29, you see the opening screen, from which you select icons. Do you need to remember that airplane trip on the 18th? Just drag the airplane icon over. How about the weekly card game on Wednesdays (except for on the 19th when you are out of town)? Who can forget what that heart shape on the 29th means? (Anniversary? No such luck.

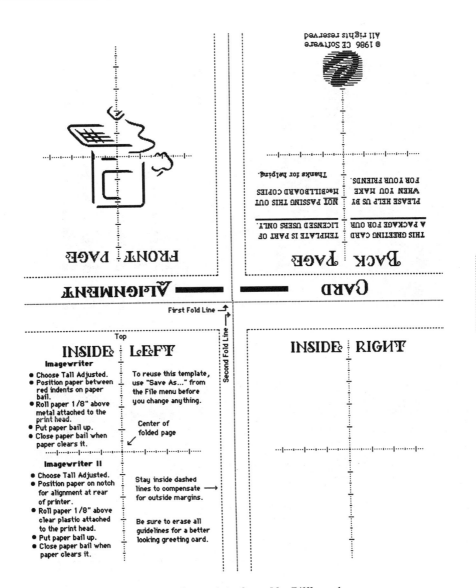

BACK PAGE

THIS GREETING CARD
TEMPLATE IS PART OF
A PACKAGE FOR OUR
LICENSED USERS ONLY.
PLEASE HELP US BY
NOT PASSING THIS OUT
WHEN YOU MAKE
MacBILLBOARD COPIES
FOR YOUR FRIENDS.
Thanks for helping.

FRONT PAGE

ALIGNMENT ──── **CARD**

First Fold Line →

Second Fold Line

Top

INSIDE LEFT

Imagewriter

- Choose Tall Adjusted.
- Position paper between red indents on paper bail.
- Roll paper 1/8" above metal attached to the print head.
- Put paper bail up.
- Close paper bail when paper clears it.

Imagewriter II

- Choose Tall Adjusted.
- Position paper on notch for alignment at rear of printer.
- Roll paper 1/8" above clear plastic attached to the print head.
- Put paper bail up.
- Close paper bail when paper clears it.

To reuse this template, use "Save As..." from the File menu before you change anything.

Center of folded page

Stay inside dashed lines to compensate → for outside margins.

Be sure to erase all guidelines for a better looking greeting card.

INSIDE RIGHT

12

Having Fun

Fig. 12.28. *The greeting card template from MacBillboard.*

Time for the dog's monthly heartworm pill!) Figure 12.30 shows you the finished calendar. This calendar does not include the notes you can attach to cells to remind yourself of appointments.

File
Edit
Design
Windows
Font
Style
Jan Feb Mar Apr May Jun Jul Aug Sep Oct Nov Dec
July 1989
S M T W T F S
1
2 3 4 6 7 8
9 10 11 13 14 15
16 17 19 20 21 22
23 24 25 27 28
30 31
Startup Icons
Backup
REPORT DUE TODAY

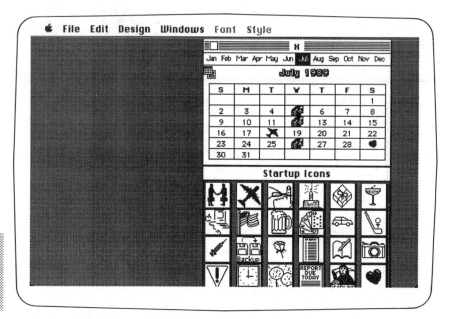

Fig. 12.29. Making your own calendars.

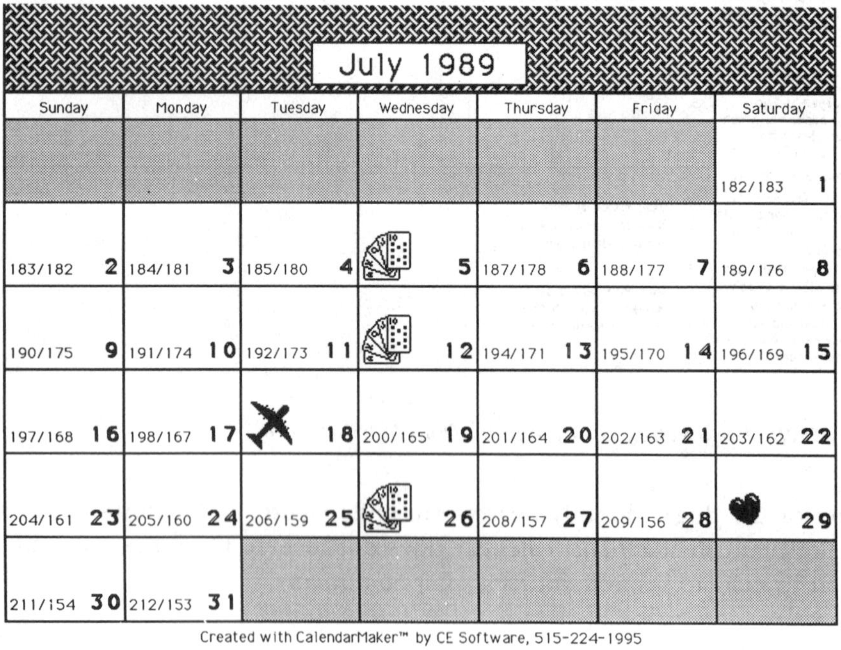

July 1989
Sunday
Monday
Tuesday
Wednesday
Thursday
Friday
Saturday
182/183 1
183/182 2
184/181 3
185/180 4
5
187/178 6
188/177 7
189/176 8
190/175 9
191/174 10
192/173 11
12
194/171 13
195/170 14
196/169 15
197/168 16
198/167 17
18
200/165 19
201/164 20
202/163 21
203/162 22
204/161 23
205/160 24
206/159 25
26
208/157 27
209/156 28
29
211/154 30
212/153 31
Created with CalendarMaker™ by CE Software, 515-224-1995

Fig. 12.30. A finished calendar from CalendarMaker.

Yum!

Everyone's cooking these days, and for the Mac enthusiast gourmet and gourmand, what could be better than recipes and a recipe planner on disk? Welcome to Dinner at Eight (from Rubicon). Not only are the choices outstanding (see the opening menu screen shown in fig. 12.31), but you can enter your own recipes and adjust amounts to fit your parties of 5 or 500. Want Chocolate Mint Bombe for 50? The recipe is in figure 12.32.

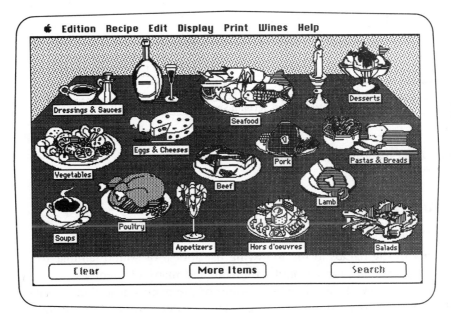

Fig. 12.31. *The opening screen for Dinner at Eight.*

That cookie recipe you see in figure 12.32, which is absolutely wonderful, originally was entered for 6 and now shows up for 50. Use the recipe and enjoy.

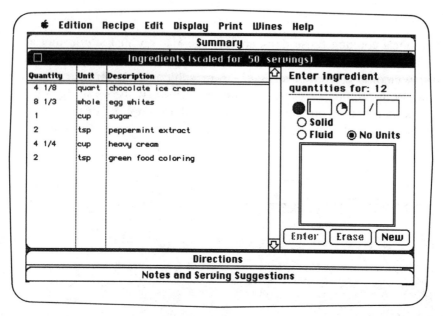

Fig. 12.32. *Chocolate Mint Bombe for 50.*

100 Others (and They Are All Free!—sort of...)

Do any of the names in the following list appeal or sound familiar to you? These games are all public domain, and many of them are the same as or very close relatives to some of the games described in this chapter, such as GoMoku and Lunar. These games are available from the public domain companies discussed in the next chapter.

1863	BMX
3D Checkers	Bouncing Balls!
Adventure!	Brickles
AdVent	Bridge Baron II
Animals	Canfield
Artillery	Carbon Copy
Ashes	Castle of Ert
BashBB	Colony
BattleMac	Concentration
BillBoard Parlous	Connect Four
Blackjack	Continum

Cross Word
Crystal Raider
Daleks
Death Mall
Donkey Doo
Dragon
Dungeons of Doom
Enigma
Explorer
Fifteens
Fire Zone
Fortune Cookie
GoMoku
Halloween Night
Hangman
Hex Puzzle
IAGO
Investigator
Karth of the Jungle
King Albert
Klondije
Lucky Lotto
LunarLander
Mac Bugs!
MacFootball
MacLotto
MacPente
MacSeven
MacYahtzee
Maps
Master of Middle Earth
MasterCues
Maze of Gorf
Maze
Megarods
Mike's House
Mines

MiniGolf
Missle Command
Mouse Craps
Mystery Box
NewWizFire
Nim
Orion
Pai Gow
Periapt
Pharaoh
Pong
Radical Castle
Sands of Time
Schmoozer
Seven Blocks
Sitting Duck
Social Climber
Space Aliens
Space Adventure
Spacestation Pheta
Star League
Stock Market Crash
Story Maker
StuntCopter
SwampLord
Tablut
The Adventures of Snake
Towers of Hanoi
Valleyball
Wargle!
Wator
Wave 15
WordScrambler
Worm
WumpusPRO
Wyrm
Zoony

12
Having
Fun

Chapter Summary

Games on the Mac are great fun. While I was exploring the ones I describe here, I was constantly asking myself how they can be rated or compared. I think that the fairest method is not to talk about one or two mice or however many awards a game has won. Rather, I found it easiest to judge these games on how easy they were to play and how engaging once play started. If I could get up and running quickly (which is very Mac-ish) and was intrigued by what I saw, I stayed and liked it. If not, I tended to move on. Which ones did I prefer? No dice. They all are well worth pursuing. Which type of game and at what level of complexity is a personal decision. The chart in figure 12.33 should be of some help.

	A	B	C	D	E	F	G	H	I
1		Overall	Stop						
2		Rating	and		Adjust		On-Line	Change	
3		1-10	Save	Record	Difficulty	Tech.	Instructions	Game	
4	Name of Game	(10 = best)	Game?	scores?	Level?	Support?	& Help	Specs	What's Special?
5									
6	4th and Inches	9	no	yes	yes	yes	no	yes	Team construction disk to change players and customize team
7	Arkanoid	10	yes	yes	yes	yes	no	yes	Daddy of the various brick 'em games only much more elaborate
8	Crystal Quest	10	yes	yes	yes *	yes	yes	yes	Customize, terrific sound effects, create own game from scratch
9	Dark Castle	10	no	yes	yes	yes	yes	yes	Animation
10	Ferrari Grand Prix	10	yes	Δ	yes	yes	no	yes	Real feel of driving
11	Flight Simulator	9	yes	n/a	yes	yes	no	no	Variety of planes to fly, extensive documentation
12	Fools Errand	10	yes	n/a	no	yes	no	no	Related puzzles with story, word searches, crossword puzzles, word jumbles, cryptograms, jigsaws
13	F-16	10	no	yes	yes	yes	no	yes	Realistic, head to head with two Macs via modem
14	GATO	10	yes	†	yes	yes	no	yes	
15	Hardball	8	no	yes	yes	yes	no	yes	
16	Kid's Time	10	n/a	n/a	yes	yes	yes	yes	Adjustable for age of child
17	Life and Death	9	no	n/a	no	yes	yes	yes	Only one, information based
18	Lunar Rescue	10	yes	yes	yes	yes	no	no	
19	MacGolf	10	yes	yes	yes	yes	no	yes	Easy to use and challenging, predecessor for MacGolf Classic
20	MacRacquet	10	yes	yes	yes	yes	no	yes	Incredible visuals, talks back
21	Mean 18	9	yes	yes	yes	yes	yes	yes	Realistic sound, color, customize
22	Number Maze	10	yes	y	~	yes	yes	yes	Adjustable for age of child, keep data on up to 50 students
23	Orbiter	8	yes	√	§	yes	@	n/a	Good space sim, talks to you, MacInTalk
24	P-38	10	yes	¥	yes	yes	no	no	Replay last several minutes
25	PT-109	9	yes	yes	yes	yes	no	yes	Easy to use action simulation, issue all commands with mouse
26	Puzzle Gallery - At The Carnival	10	yes	n/a	no	yes	yes	no	Collection of 182 puzzles with digitized sound
27	Sim City	10	yes	n/a	yes	yes	no	yes	Different every time, color, customize, based on real data, data files are compatible with IBM and Amiga
28	Tetris	10	*	yes	yes	yes	yes	yes	Desk accessory version, color versioon
29									
30	* Pause but no save								
31	† Record hits								
32	√ Flights and walks								
33	¥ Records victories and landings								
34	Δ Fastest lap								
35	* Critter Editor								
36	~ 48 levels/50 students								
37	§ Manual/auto								

Fig. 12.33. *Games rated on a scale of 1 to 10.*

Part IV

Deciding What To Buy

Putting together your computer system is not exactly like the chicken and the egg problem, but it's close. Whether to buy your Macintosh computer and peripherals and then look around for software, or to find the software you want to use and then match it to a Mac system is a difficult question. Most software consultants suggest that you find the software program that fits your needs, and then determine the hardware required to run that software. In either case, you need to know about both software and hardware to make an intelligent and informed decision.

This section of *The Big Mac Book* discusses some of the decisions that you need to make when selecting hardware and software and when choosing a system. This section also discusses setting up your Mac and making sure that you have the right hardware and software to fit your needs.

Includes

Buying Software

Buying Hardware

13

Buying Software

You want software that will do what needs to be done. After all the bells and whistles are quiet, if the software you choose doesn't do what you want, it is of no use to you.

The appendixes include a vendor guide listing the names and addresses of more than 400 vendors, the names of the products they have available, and a list of products organized by category. You can use these lists to send away for information about products that you might not be able to examine at your local computer store.

13
Buying
Software

Evaluating Software

There are thousands and thousands of programs for the Macintosh, and more are being developed everyday. First, however, I will discuss how you can evaluate software before you make any decisions about what you are going to buy.

Reading the Periodicals

Perhaps the best way to evaluate software is to read the product comparisons in periodicals and newspapers, such as *MacWorld* and *MacUser*. To maintain their credibility and journalistic integrity, these publications (and many others) often have third-party software experts test and evaluate the products. These reviews (and reviewers) are not totally independent (don't forget a magazine makes most of its money from advertising), but if you read the reviews carefully, you can get some good information.

These articles often include a detailed comparison chart listing the products and rating the relative values of the various features. Keep in mind, however, that these ratings can be subjective, so what the reviewer thinks is a wonderful feature, you might never need to use. Some accounting packages, for example, come with forecasting tools, but you may not be interested in this kind of analysis.

Consulting User Groups

Macintosh user groups are located all over the country, and for most of us, finding one to visit isn't that difficult. This method of research is especially helpful if you want to talk with users who have purchased a specific program and can really tell you about the ins and outs of using the software. If you can't visit a user group, a phone call can accomplish the same thing. Most universities have user groups associated with them. Call the computer science center and ask for more information. Many user groups have technical support specialists who can advise you about what type of software or hardware best fits your needs, as well as solve any technical problems that you might be having.

Although word of mouth is the best way to find a user group in your area, here are some other strategies that you may use:

- Apple Computer Corporation maintains a toll-free number (1-800-538-9696) that you can call for information about the user group in your area.

- Look at the directory of user groups in Appendix C to find your location or something close to it.

- Go to your local Mac store (or any computer store) and ask about the local user groups.

- Most universities host user group meetings on a monthly basis. Contact the computer center at the university and ask for User Services.

- If you really can't find anything, then just start a group of your own. All it takes is you and another person.

Using Demonstration Disks

Many companies offer demonstration disks that show you the main features of their program. These disks usually contain slick presentations (many of them are designed as HyperCard stacks, see Chapter 17) that you can get for free or for minimal costs. You can use these at home to see whether the application will work for you. One caution, however: Remember that these demo disks are put together to look terrific, and most of them do. Just like the toy-box cover, what you see may not always be what you get.

As the software product market gets more competitive, an increasing number of companies will send you (sometimes for a small charge) a demo disk, which shows you some of the best features of the program. Often this disk is a HyperCard stack, a self-running demo, and sometimes, a fully functional application. You cannot save anything, however. More and more companies are offering demos to entice potential customers, and many of them are offering demos for free. It doesn't hurt to ask. You should expect the cost of a demo to be under $10, including shipping.

As far as trying things in the store, you should expect to be able to "play" with a $500 piece of software no matter how much you have read about it in magazines or elsewhere. Remember to be sure that the software you want is what the dealer is showing you, and not some earlier version or a version for another model Mac.

13
Buying
Software

Buying Software: Ten Rules

1. Be sure that you get a chance to try out a program before you buy it. Many software manufacturers now offer demonstration disks (and in some cases videotapes) of what the program can do. You can even view some programs on commercial bulletin boards such as CompuServe. For the modest investment of $10 or $15, you might save yourself much money and aggravation.

2. Make sure that your system can handle the software. For example, even though HyperCard requires at least 1M of memory to work, you can't do much when the stacks get to be very large.

3. Be sure that you are purchasing the latest version. How do you know? Call the manufacturer or consult with a member of one of the many user groups that are located around the country (see Appendix C).

4. If you are buying the software for someone (such as an employee or a child), try to put yourself in that person's position. Will he or she be able to understand and use the program?

5. Check the documentation to be sure that it is clear and understandable. If you can't understand the instructions, it might not be worth the time and effort you must invest in learning how to use the program.

6. Examine the warranty that the manufacturer offers and its upgrade policies. Most software, especially if it's a new product, has bugs of some sort. Does the manufacturer offer a free upgrade? How much will future upgrades cost? Can they be purchased through the dealer? It's hard to judge the value of a warranty and very difficult to take action against, especially if you don't live in the state where the manufacturer operates. However, you still owe it to yourself to be well informed.

7. Beware of *vaporware*. Vaporware is software that is promised by the manufacturer, but has not yet arrived.

8. Find out what kind of support programs (if any) the manufacturer offers. You should ask whether there is a toll-free line for technical support. What are the hours that support is available? Is support free? Is free support offered for only a limited time? How often is the line busy? You may even want to get the number before you buy and try it out.

Although many companies (such as Quark and Informix) ask you for the serial number on your master disk, many (such as WordPerfect and MicroSoft) don't. This is not an invitation to ask for help on a pirated copy; it is simply a convenience to you. You should feel free to call and ask questions about program capabilities. Most large companies will be glad to discuss these things with you on the premise that if you are well informed about their wonderful program, you will seriously consider buying it.

9. Invest your money in companies that are well regarded and have a record of producing good products and treating their customers well. Talking with other Mac enthusiasts will provide you with this information.

10. Finally, know what you need before you go shopping. Buying software is not like buying a car, but uninformed salespeople can pressure you to buy a package that doesn't do what you want, or one that does more than you need.

Buying OCR Software

The rules for buying scanning software are generally the same as for any software product, but you should keep the following suggestions in mind. Remember, whether you are scanning text or graphics, you need to purchase both software and hardware.

1. Be sure that you know how much memory the software uses. The way the OCR software compares and matches characters determines the amount of memory needed. On scanners with insufficient memory, the software may run, but at an unbearably slow speed.

2. Be sure that the hardware matches the software requirements. Some OCR software runs only with specific hardware, especially when the same manufacturer produces both.

3. Ask about the accuracy of the software for a given system configuration. Remember, the more characters the OCR software misses, the more editing you have to do.

4. Try before you buy. OCR software is sensitive to font, style, size, and every other characteristic of the printed page. Your 150-page document in 12-point Times Roman may not even be readable. Take a sample of the type of material you will be scanning to the dealer for a trial. Then go back to your computer and edit the text with your word processing software just to be sure that you understand the system.

5. Before buying, determine whether you need nontrainable, trainable, or automatic OCR software.

13
Buying
Software

6. Find out whether the software enables you to edit scanned images or whether you have to import them to another program before editing. Be sure that you can control such qualities as brightness, contrast, and hue.

7. Select software that enables you to print according to the capabilities of your printer. For example, if you have a Linotronic, you need better resolution of the scanned image than the resolution offered by a 2-bit machine that can read only black-and-white images.

Using Shareware, Budgetware, and Freeware

Beneath the glossy four-color image of any computer company's advertisements are thousands of folks like you and me, using our computers for work and fun. And indeed, it's from folks like us that the best ideas for new software come. Ask any developer of software for any personal computer, and he or she will tell you there always must be a person who has the spark of the idea to make it work. Although committees are very effective for pasting labels on envelopes, design by committee is like the four blindfolded men and the elephant; each thinks something very different.

Individuals carving out new frontiers are the ones who come up with programs that need to be tried and disseminated, but usually these people do not have the budget for large-scale beta testings (where the program is sent to selected users), advertising, or major sales pitches. Instead, these people make the program available as shareware, which is not free, but accessible through sharing from one person to another. If you like the program, you're responsible for sending in a donation or a fee that usually varies with your needs. For example, one bulletin board charges $10 for the disk, $25 for registration plus the disk, and $50 for registration, the disk, and a 300-page binder. You select the plan you want, but in each case, by using the program, you purchase a service, and you should pay. Otherwise, shareware will eventually disappear. Unknown programmers become known through shareware disseminated over wide networks.

Budgetware is inexpensive software that is available through a variety of different companies who make it their business to have thousands of Mac programs available, usually for $5 to $10 per disk.

Finally, freeware is just that: free. You can copy and share it with friends and feel no obligation to pay the developer or anyone else for this privilege.

It may be hard to believe, but there are thousands of Macintosh programmers who are in it for the fun. They develop everything from clip art to sophisticated programs and offer them for a small fee or for free with few stipulations. This type of software comes under a variety of different names, but mostly it is software that can be shared. Some programs come with an opening screen that requests payment, and some are scaled-down versions of a complete package. Most are to be shared with other people, who then share it with others. Indeed, some software authors have been very successful offering programs for a small fee and then offering upgrades and greatly expanded capabilities.

Anyone can sell shareware (as long as they have been authorized by the authors); even at a small price (as low as $4 per disk), this has become quite a big business. One of the largest shareware companies is International Dataware Incorporated (2278 Trade Zone Blvd., San Jose, CA 95131 1-800-222-6032). The company publishes *The Diskette Gazette* every six weeks, which offers a huge library of programs and other Macintosh products (including disks) at a substantial discount. International Dataware has programs in many categories, including applications, desk accessories, fonts, games, hypercard stacks, paint and sound programs, and utilities. The mailing list has over 125,000 names, and there are no club or membership fees. One of the nicest things about *The Disk Gazette* is that it also contains informative articles about the Mac.

At last count, over 250 disks were available with many different programs on each disk—well over 5,000 programs. The disks sell for $5.75 each, and you can get price reductions for buying in quantity ($4.25 for 100 or more disks). International Dataware provides excellent service and some fun products, such as gourmet popcorn and terrific tasting lollipops.

BudgetBytes (P.O. Box 2248, Topeka, KS 66601 1-800-356-3551) offers a CD-ROM disk with more than 7,000 programs for $149.95—over 350 megabytes of Macintosh software. The company also offers updates to the disk and a toll-free order line. The 290-page catalog offers many of the same programs as other folks in the same business (such as International Dataware) with a special section on Mac II software, collections of particular programs (such as KidPAK), commercial software with discounts, hardware, and accessories. A double-sided disk costs $5.99. If you buy more than 100 disks, each disk is $2.99.

EDUCOMP (742 Genevieve, Solona Beach, CA 92075 1-800-843-9497) is another large distribution service with over 500 disks in its collection. The entire collection of disks is available for $690. Individual double-sided disks are $8.50 each. You can save money by ordering in quantity (more than 100 disks, for example, cost $4 each).

These sources have similar libraries with much overlapping, although each has unique offerings. It's well worth your time to send for catalogues. Browsing through them is great fun, and you're sure to find something you can't do without!

Don't forget about user groups as well. Some, such as the Berkeley Macintosh User Group (BMUG), publish a CD-ROM disk with thousands of programs on it for a whopping $100.

Understanding Copyrights

When you open a new box of software you will find, in very legal-sounding and often intimidating terms, the license agreement that almost every software manufacturer has printed on each product.

You might be surprised to discover that you really don't own the software that you have just spent your hard-earned money for. Instead, you own the license to use the program as often as you want, but in some restricted ways. Just look at some of the things that these software agreements say:

1. The manufacturer grants you the right to use the software on a single computer, and sometimes on a network. Often you cannot use the program in a network, and you cannot use it on more than one computer at the same time. In other words, your copies are for archival purposes and nothing else; you can make a copy and use it on your Mac at work, but no one should be using it at home at the same time.

2. The software is owned by the manufacturer. You have a license to use it. You own the disk, but not the program on it.

3. You can't rent or lease the software (but you can sell your copy of the program), and you cannot modify the code or the program.

If you are using a language program, such as BASIC, Fortran, or Pascal, then things get more complicated. In some cases, you are allowed to distribute and share the programs that you have produced using the language, but you have to be careful about your liability should the program be faulty. The manufacturer disavows any liability whatsoever on the package. You also should mention the program in your acknowledgments.

13
Buying
Software

14

Buying Hardware

There is obviously a greater selection of software products for the Macintosh line of computers than hardware, but you shouldn't believe that you are limited to the hardware that Apple manufactures.

This chapter discusses some of the major hardware components that go into a system, tells how they work, and tries to give you some idea of which ones are right for you.

Looking at the Mac Family

The original 128K Macintosh, and up through the 512K model, could not have any RAM added, and software developers soon reached the limits of how much they could fit into such small space. Many people still think that the original MacPaint, created by Bill Atkinson, was a marvel, considering its capability in spite of RAM limitations. With the Plus and the SE, you could have up to 4 megabytes of RAM installed, but these models contained the same processor (the Motorola 68000), so there was no increase in processing power.

The Plus and SE became the workhorses for Mac users. Interestingly, Apple moved so fast with its introduction of new machines that if you owned a Plus one year, you owned the top of the Mac line. But just a year later, with the introduction of the SE and the Mac II and the discontinuation of earlier models, your Plus had become the low end of the line!

The Plus brought some measure of expandability in that memory could be increased, and the Plus included the long-awaited SCSI port so that this computer could use an external hard disk. The size and speed of the hard disk opened so many doors that perhaps the introduction of the Plus was the most important event for software developers. If they did not have the speed, they had the room in which to work. There are no real figures as to how many Pluses are alive today, but it was and is a great machine, and many people have chosen to stick with their Plus and upgrade memory and such rather than invest in a new machine.

What the SE has now that appeals so much is a relatively low price (under $2,000 with two floppies, one of which is a 1.44M drive that can read MS-DOS fields with the help of the Apple File Exchange utility). Now we're really cooking, but "You ain't heard nothin' yet, folks."

Looking at the Mac II

The Mac II was the first and last Macintosh with a 68020 central processing chip, which gave the computers increased speed and power. The Mac II has six slots for expansion and color capabilities.

One of the problems with the Mac II is that several of the graphic programs designed for the II were painfully slow and used much memory at the same time, necessitating an increase in RAM to 5 megabytes to make things work at a reasonable rate.

What the Mac II offered most was increased speed, which was welcome, by many. Its unportability is one of features that has made it increasingly less attractive. The Mac II was the top of the line until the IIx series was introduced. The IIx series was aimed primarily at the business community and their concerns for a more powerful machine (greater processing power and better memory management).

The Mac IIcx has a smaller "footprint" (area the machine takes up on a desk). The IIcx is smaller because it has only three expansion slots, a smaller power supply, and a condensed motherboard (the main logic board).

Looking at the SE/30

In January of 1989, Apple Computer, Inc., introduced the Macintosh SE/30, a hybrid machine that combines characteristics of the old SE and the already available MAC IIx. With a new processor (the Motorola

68030), the SE/30 has much more power, delivering more speed and options for the user. Where the SE took nine seconds to load Excel, the new SE/30 took only three. Probably the nicest thing about the 30 is that it's the same size as the plain SE, where the Mac II family (which you have to move up to for more processing power and speed) is larger (25 pounds for the central unit alone), and you need to buy the monitor as an extra.

And the fact that the SE/30 has room for expansion has already produced a bunch of expansion cards allowing for the use of external color monitors, connections with IBM mainframe computers, and networking options.

Other critical points that make the SE/30 different from the SE are as follows:

- The SE/30's 1.44M internal drive is high-density (see Chapter 4 for more on high-density drives).

- The SE/30 comes with a 40M or an 80M hard drive standard.

- The SE/30 has a five-fold increase in general performance compared to the original SE.

- The SE/30 can read and write 400K, 800K, and 1.4M floppies.

- The SE/30 can read and write MS-DOS files in 720K and 1.44M configurations (with the necessary exchange software).

- The SE/30 has twice the amount of space for expanding RAM.

- Upgrading ROM SIMMs is very easy because it is not soldered into place, but is part of a single in-line memory module.

- The SE/30 has stereo sound capability.

14
Buying
Hardware

Looking at the Mac IIx and the Mac IIcx

The last stop along the way is the Mac IIx and the Mac IIcx, Apple's Mac II upgrade. First, these machines both solve the size problem in that they fit nicely into a space the size of a Plus and don't weigh much more. They are faster than the II (by about 15 percent) and introduce Paged Memory Management Unit (PMMU).

PMMU and System 7 (or the Virtual INIT from Connectix) allow a hard disk to take over the memory job of the RAM chips if things get too full. This capability creates what is called virtual memory, where the machine appears to have more memory than it really does.

The Mac IIcx is small (only 11.9 inches wide), and it has several features that set this model apart from its predecessors, such as rear ventilation so that the computer can be placed horizontally or vertically, and modular assembly that makes servicing easy.

Does the introduction of the IIcx mean the end for the II? Well, there's no reason to buy any of the Mac IIs unless you need six (rather than three) expansion slots or unless you need to work in color.

As things stand now, don't be surprised if the original Mac II goes the way of the early Macs; it will no longer be manufactured or supported by Apple because it will be cheaper to manufacture the new machines than continue the old.

Using Laptops

Laptops, or portable computers, are no easy task to design and develop. Apple has been promising a laptop for some time now, and the SE compatible is scheduled to be released sometime during Fall 1989. Its screen is high-resolution, and the batteries last about 12 hours, separating this laptop from many of the other portables available, regardless of the operating system they are designed for (such as the DOS machines).

Rumor has it that this beauty (code named Laguna) will weigh in at about 17 pounds (which almost makes it a luggable and not a portable) and will sell for about $6,500 (for the basic model). It will have a 1.44M high-density floppy drive and use a special matrix screen in which each pixel is controlled by an individual transistor (millions of which fit on chips these days).

If Apple licenses the proprietary rights to the technology, clones of the laptop will also be produced. But other companies have not stood still while Apple has been developing this new toy. NexSYS offers the TravelMac, a portable kit that uses the motherboard, floppy drive, keyboard, and mouse from your Macintosh. TravelMac weighs about 13 pounds, has a built-in 2400-baud modem, and can accommodate a hard drive (increasing the weight, of course). The price? Around $1,795. The TravelMac was supposed to ship in May 1989, but hasn't yet.

For about $3,000, you can get from Wallaby Systems a kit that transforms existing Macs into 10-pound laptops. The kit works with an SE or a Plus and includes a 640-by-400 pixel (picture element) LED screen, a detachable keyboard, and a keyboard-based pointing tool. To avoid problems with cloning Mac parts, you use the original parts from your SE or Plus in this kit and, of course, can't use your SE or Plus while you're away using your Mac. But when you're home, you can link the two to access the additional screen and power.

Another kit that uses original Mac parts is the Odyssey 2000 (from Odyssey Systems), which weighs in at 23 pounds and is more a presentation station than a laptop computer. For $2,195 and a Plus or an SE for the vital chips, you get the kit, which includes a Kodak DataShow projection pad, which is used as the display screen.

Pretty soon you will be able to record information on a watch-sized Mac and then upload that night. The toy for your favorite Mac enthusiast has just arrived from Sharp, called Wrist Mac. It doesn't have a full screen (it's only about 1 inch square) or a mouse, but it does have a keyboard to enter names, phone numbers, schedules, and so forth. Amazing.

Using Mac Clones

In April 1989 at one of the big Mac computer shows, Akkord technology introduced a Mac-compatible machine using Apple ROM as the only Apple-manufactured part. Akkord also offers a traveling Mac kit weighing about 12 pounds and using a motherboard from any Mac. Another company, Powder Blue Computers, also introduced Mac clones, called BlueMAQs, during the past year.

Choosing the Right Mac

To help you decide which Macintosh is right for you, ask yourself the following questions. The answers will help point you in the right direction.

14
Buying Hardware

- Just what do you need to do with a Macintosh?

- How much money do you have available for everything that you need?

- How many floppy disk drives will you need? Of course, you need at least one drive, and that's why all Macs come with the internal drive. But what about the extra external drive? If you reproduce disks or make backups of floppies onto other floppies, you might want to consider an external drive. In addition, two floppies plus a hard disk make everyday copying and accessing tasks much easier.

- How flexible do you want your Macintosh to be? One year down the line will you be wondering why you didn't buy the IIcx instead of the SE? As hard as it is, try to buy a Macintosh that you can grow into.

- Is there special hardware you need to do your work or to use the software you intend to buy, such as a math coprocessor or an accelerator board? You can usually find out by consulting the company that manufactures the software you are interested in using. The math equation solver Mathematica, for example, requires 2.5M of RAM.

  You will want to add (or at least know about adding) these things when you buy your Mac because you cannot add these things to certain models later.

- What about memory? This is a tough one to call because you may not know the demands of the software that you will be purchasing, but 1 megabyte of RAM is at least a safe minimum. And even with 1 megabyte you still can't use some very important tools such as MultiFinder (which needs at least 2 to even get started!).

Choosing Keyboards

When you get right down to it, there are two things that are of major importance in working with any computer; the keyboard and the screen. Some people fall in love with a keyboard at first use; others are always seeking more (or less) responsiveness of the keys, bigger (or smaller) keys, a smaller (or larger) footprint, and so on.

Like many other parts of setting up a system, your choice of keyboard is a personal one. You might use the mouse to move around, but when it comes to entering information, you're stuck with the keyboard. With more than half of all personal computer activity being word processing related, the quality of a keyboard is a very important link to productivity.

A good keyboard should have some of the following qualities:

- A solid (and not a mushy) feel when the keys are pressed

- Ergonomic design so that the face of the board is slightly tilted in the user's direction

- Audio feedback when the keys are pressed (especially handy for touch typists)

- Sufficiently large keys (particularly such important keys as the Return and Shift)

- Numeric keypad for fast entry of numerical data

- Function keys that can be programmed to perform special application-intensive tasks, such as getting help and saving

- Macro software that lets you automate keyboard activities

The keyboards that Apple supplied with the early Macs were small and without any extras like a numeric keypad or function keys. Although these keyboards took up very little room on the desk, many people complained about the lack of true keyboard feel they remembered from their typewriter days.

14
Buying
Hardware

When you buy anything above a Plus today, you need to buy the keyboard as a separate item. So why consider only the Apple model when there are several others you might find more appealing? Take a quick look at the standard and then at two alternatives.

The Apple Extended Keyboard (which lists for $229) offers a full range of keys plus 15 function keys, arrow keys, and a numeric keypad. It offers many of the features already mentioned, except that it doesn't come with any documentation or any software and you cannot adjust its position relative to the user. It is in the style of the IBM PC keyboard.

The keyboard that I have been using is the Mac-101 Enhanced Keyboard (from DataDesk International), which lists for $170. I find that it is much easier to use (especially for extended periods of time) than Apple's extended keyboard. The Mac-101 keyboard is more responsive. It also can be adjusted, reducing the strain associated with a keyboard that lies flat. The 101 keyboard comes with software that you can use to create application-specific macros (called MasterStrokes), control window activities, and create and use glossaries or standard blocks of text. MasterStrokes is a keyboard-enhancing software product that comes with the 101 and allows you powerful macro capability.

DataDesk also makes an alternative keyboard for the Plus for $160. Even though the Plus comes with its own keyboard, you may want to upgrade to a better one. The DataDesk Plus keyboard comes with a longer warranty and has a 30-day money-back guarantee.

Another competitor in the keyboard race is the Mac-105 keyboard ($180 from Cutting Edge). This is a 105-key keyboard, and it has the attractive feature of slightly higher key profiles with smaller top surfaces. This feature is very helpful if you find yourself always pressing adjacent keys. In addition, the Mac-105 has a larger than usual Return key. For another $20, you can buy the QuicKeys keyboard enhancer, which makes this keyboard an attractive deal.

A comparison of keyboards can be found in figure 14.1.

Keyboard	Macintosh Model	Connector	Arrow Keys	Numeric Keypad	Function Keys	Escape Key	Control Key	Total Keys
Original	128K, 512K	Phone Plug	no	no	None	no	no	58
Accessory keypad	128K, 512K	Phone Plug	L Pattern	yes	None	no	no	18
Mac Plus	Plus	Phone Plug	L Pattern	yes	None	no	no	78
DataDesk	All Models	Phone Plug	Inverted T	yes	22	Cancel	no	101
Tangent Technologies	512K, Plus	Phone Plug	No	yes	10	yes	no	84
Apple	SE, II	ADB	Single Line	yes	None	yes	yes	81
Apple Extended	SE, II	ADB	Inverted T	yes	22	yes	yes	105

Fig. 14.1. *A comparison of keyboards.*

You can buy keyboard enhancers for use with your Apple Extended keyboard, such as QuicKeys or Tempo.

Choosing Monitors

After the keyboard, the monitor is the other link you have with your data. The first Mac had the little 9-inch monitor that had high-resolution and looked incredible. It wasn't much fun to sit in front of all day long and scroll through hundreds of cells in a spreadsheet or look at screen after screen of a long text document. Now there are alternatives.

Understanding How Monitors Work

Monitors are no different from televisions, at least in the way they are put together. Generally, monitors include some type of a "gun" device that projects a signal onto a phosphor coating on the screen. This coating is sensitive to the energy that is projected on it and when charged causes the electrons to align a specific way. Depending on the type of coating, the color as well as the clarity and definition of the image are determined. Presto a picture. Now that you're an expert on how monitors work, let's turn to some of the finer points regarding what characteristics monitors can differ on.

Resolution is how clear the image appears on-screen, and the higher the resolution, the crisper the image. The resolution of an image on-screen depends on two things.

14
Buying Hardware

First is the number of *pixels*, or picture elements, which are measured both horizontally and vertically. A high-resolution display might show 1,664-by-1,200 pixels, for an astounding 1,996,800 pixels occupying the screen. That many picture elements can produce a very high-quality picture. The shape of the pixels also can have an effect on how an image appears. Pixels can appear as round or square elements. Square pixels produce sharper images because they fill the screen more completely than round pixels. Although dot density is not directly related to resolution, it is important. Dot density is the number of dots, or pixels, displayed per inch. The more dots, the denser the image (be it white, black, or color).

Second, the resolution depends on the frequency with which horizontal lines are "drawn" across the face of the screen (much faster than you can ever see, but not so fast that your incredible brain cannot perceive the difference if one's there). This frequency is also called the horizontal scan rate. Your television scans at about 16 kilohertz (the standard measure), which is low, with medium between the range of 25 to 50, and high more than 50. The faster the scan rate and the more pixels on-screen, the better the resolution. But you're right, it costs.

Next on our list of important characteristics is the refresh rate of a monitor. This rate is the speed at which the screen can bring its light level up to full capacity. Flickering is often the result of a slow refresh rate, because the human eye is really sharp and notices even the most subtle change in the energy level. For a clear image, you need a refresh rate of at least 60 hertz (Hz), or times per second.

Perhaps the most obvious problem for people who sit in front of monitors for long periods of time is eye strain, which is often attributable to the glare that is generated from various sources of light. Although you can buy an antiglare screen to place on your monitor, several monitors come with antiglare coating on-screen.

Choosing the Right Monitor

The original Mac monitor was 4.5-by-7 inches with a diagonal of about 9 inches. As the hardware requirements of software have become more demanding, new types of monitors have been developed. The desktop publisher benefits from being able to see at least one full page of a document; hence, there is the full-page monitor. The larger screen lets you see a full page all at once and makes a significant difference in readability.

Radius offers four different types of large monitors:

- A full-page display that shows an 8.5-by-11 inch screen without having to scroll

- A color monitor that can display 256 colors from the usual palette of 16 million (how can you decide?)

- A two-page display, which shows two 8.5-by-11 inch pages simultaneously

- A gray-scale monitor that displays 256 shades of gray

Radius monitors, like some others, come with software and many neat features like tear-off menus, a screen saver, and screen dump capability. After using the 19-inch full-page display, I had a very hard time returning to my 9-inch Macintosh screen.

There are other products that will breath new life into your visual relationship with your Mac. MacLarger (from Power Up) is a large monitor screen that increases the size of your picture by 60 percent with no enhancement in resolution. It works with the 512, Plus, or SE. For only $450, that's quite a bargain if all you want is a bigger picture.

The Mitsubishi 33-inch XC-3310 monitor costs $5,500 and has a 31-inch viewing area. Its resolution also is increased dramatically.

In figure 14.2, you see a comparison of some video monitors. These are very expensive machines, often costing more than your Mac, and many require that you open your Mac to insert a video card. Some people refuse to do that under any circumstances, and opening your Mac does void your warranty.

Screen	Pixels Horizontal	Pixels Vertical	Pixel Count	Resolution (dpi)	Gray Levels	No. of Colors	Screen Size(s)
Original Macintosh Screen	512	342	175,104	72	2	None	9"
Apple Video Card for Mac IIA	640	480	307,200	80	16	16	12"
with Expansion Kit	640	480	307,200	80	256	256	12"
E-Machines Big Picture	1,024	808	827,392	82	256	None	17"
MicroGraphic Images	1,024	900	921,600	75	2	None	19"
Nutmet Information Systems	720	900	648,000	90	2	None	15"
Radius Full Page Display	640	864	552,960	77	2	None	15"
Sigma LaserView	1,664	1,200	1,996,800	150/115	4	None	15", 19"
at Lower Resolution	832	600	499,200	75/65	4	None	15", 19"
SuperMac Spectrum	1,365	1,024	1,397,760	72/85	256	256	16", 19"

Fig. 14.2. A comparison of monitors.

Protecting Your Screen

The phosphor that is on the inside of your monitor screen is light sensitive; otherwise, an image could not be projected on to it. If the phosphor is energized for too long, an image can "burn" into the screen coating to give you a permanent etching—not the kind you can sell at an art auction.

14

Buying Hardware

To avoid this problem, you can use a *screen saver*. A screen saver is an INIT or CDEV (remember, they are programs that are System extensions) that comes into play according to your directions. The screen saver actually saves your screen from character burn-in by generating a constantly varying screen display. Pyro! II (a CDEV), for example, can be set to begin 1, 2, 5, 15, 30, 60, or 120 minutes after it detects no activity. Pyro! displays fireworks, which on a Mac II is in color and is sensational. A shareware screen saver is Moire (from John Lim). This program provides a constantly changing Moire pattern, which is interesting and quite distracting. Many other screen savers are available in the public domain.

Using Screen Size Enhancers

An alternative to a large monitor is Stepping Out II: The Macintosh Screen Extender ($95 from Berkeley Software—see fig. 14.3). Stepping Out is a CDEV that creates the appearance of your having a larger screen by allowing you to create a virtual screen, which is a screen that in use, is larger than the actual screen.

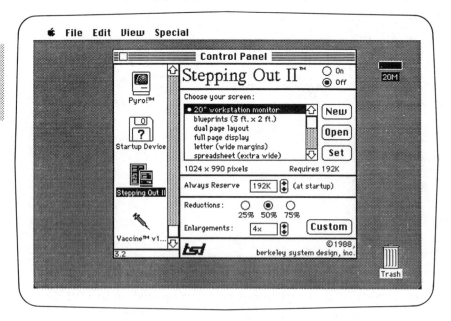

Fig. 14.3. Stepping Out II provides an alternative to a large monitor.

You use Stepping Out by moving the mouse pointer to the edge of the screen, which causes the screen to scroll as if you were panning across a large document on a large screen. Stepping Out also offers several ways to work with the screen image. You can reduce an image to 25 percent of its normal size, or you can magnify an image from 200 percent to 1,600 percent, and you can set other parameters, such as the screen size you want to use.

Selecting Pointing Devices

A mouse works by sending to the computer signals that correspond to movements detected by motion sensors inside the body of the mouse. These sensors are a combination of optical and mechanical devices that seem to continue to work well unless they wear out, or unless they get dirty. As you have probably seen, mouse pads are made of everything from high-quality leather to foam so thin that it might tear as you move quickly to capture an alien in your favorite space game. Also, mouse covers are available to keep your mouse dust-free when it is not in use.

But, a variety of other pointing devices are available, and some of them might suit your needs better than the original Apple mouse.

First, there are trackballs. These are units that remain stationery on the desk, and each move of the ball corresponds to a move on-screen. There are two significant advantages to the use of a trackball, such as the Kensington's Turbo Mouse and Turbo Trackball (from Asher, which incidentally comes with a lifetime warranty). The first, and perhaps the most important, is that because the trackball stays stationary; you do not need an area to run your mouse around (the Turbo Mouse is 4.5 by 5.75 inches). You save space. Second, because you need not move (or pick up and relocate) the trackball, you can increase the speed with which you perform operations. This improvement might be negligible, but there are always people who want to go faster. People love or hate trackballs. You can decide for yourself whether you want to spend the extra money.

14
Buying
Hardware

Next, are tablets, such as those from Kurat, that digitize signals, or turn them into the 1s and 0s that the computer can understand and easily work with. It's as if you are writing on a yellow pad and entering information. The Kurat tablets, and others, are used for graphics work and offer a nice alternative to the mouse and trackball.

There are other mice available as well. The A+ Mouse (from MSC Technologies) does not have any moving parts but uses a light beam to sense motion and requires its own shiny mouse pad to work. Your Mac comes with a mouse, so you may not need to consider anything new at all.

With the Mac 'n Touch Add-in kit (from Microtouch), you can even make your Mac responsive to your touch on the screen. Imagine selecting Open from the File menu with your finger. What power! You can have this capability for about $700 for the dealer-installed version and about $600 for a snap-on kit. Sound expensive? Maybe so, but think about people who have a hard time with their mouse and could benefit from pointing.

Selecting an Accelerator Board

An accelerator board is a circuit board (much like the other boards in your Mac) with an advanced high-speed processor that makes your Macintosh into a more powerful and faster operator. You can get accelerator boards for the Mac II family, but most accelerator boards are aimed at the Plus and the SE market because that's where the real increase in speed is needed.

Accelerator boards work by affecting four things.

First, accelerator boards modify your machine's clock speed (the speed with which your machine processes instructions). Basically, the clock speed is the number of instruction cycles that occur each second. The higher the clock speed, the more the computer can do in a fixed period of time. The standard speed for an SE is 8 megahertz (MHz), which is the unit used in the measurement of speed. With the accelerator board from Radius, you can increase the computer's speed to 25 MHz.

The amount of speed increase depends on the type of chip that the board has. Accelerator boards that use a 68020 chip can run at 16 or 25 MHz. Speed isn't everything, but it sure makes a big difference. In my SE, I have a Radius 25 accelerator board, which increases the speed of my larger spreadsheet work by a factor of six.

Second, accelerator boards modify the width of the path along which the data travels. The wider the path, the more information can travel from the central processing unit, and the faster the overall performance.

Third, is the presence of a math coprocessor, which calculates numbers (and text information) in a very efficient way. If you use large spreadsheets, perform much accounting or large statistical analyses, or if you use CAD/CAM, you will want to take advantage of a coprocessor that uses the floating-point unit method of calculation. This method of handling numerical data enables the decimal point to float or vary from value to value. This method allows more flexibility in the processing of information because the placement of the point is not fixed.

Finally, accelerators can use data caches so that previous instructions the central processing unit has already received can be stored and the accelerator need not go back again and again (wasting time) to get those instructions. When it comes time for your Mac to do its computing, if the instructions it needs are already in the cache, the computer can save time by not having to go to another source for the instruction. A cache is a place devoted to storing instructions. It's like an electronic disk.

Like other hardware, accelerator boards are not cheap. They can run anywhere from $800 to $3,000, depending on what they offer. They typically contain a high-speed microprocessor, additional RAM, and other components.

You can even use products that aren't really accelerator boards but which can speed up your computer. The MacSprint II card (from Orchid) is a 32K cache card that increases Mac II performance by about 30 percent for only $299. The MacSprint doesn't have an extra chip to increase processing speed, but it allows your Mac to store instructions in memory rather than having to go back and forth to the disk getting what it needs in a time-consuming manner.

Keep in mind that shopping for an accelerator board is not like shopping for a computer. Rarely will you be able to compare different brands. You may have to rely on other people's judgment and the literature from the manufacturer.

Here are some questions to consider when you go looking for a board:

- Is the installation charge included with the price of the board?

- Who can install it?

- Is there an installer in my area that the dealer can recommend?

14

Buying Hardware

- If I install it myself, is it still warranted?

- Can I return the board if I am not satisfied?

- What type of installation tools come with the board?

- What kind of data indicates the increase in speed?

- I do only word processing, will a board help me? How?

Boards help most with the kinds of tasks that coprocessors are designed for; computation and the manipulation of values. Will an accelerator help your word processing tasks? If you want to sort a list of 1,000 names, yes. But you won't be able to save or recall much faster, and no matter what the size of your accelerator board, don't look to it for helping you type any faster.

How much do accelerator boards really help? Comparisons are always difficult to make. With the Radius 16 accelerator in my SE, it takes about one-half the amount of time to save a 343-page WordPerfect document. With the card, my computer saves the document in about 17 seconds; without the card, it takes 35 seconds.

You should also think about what kind of memory enhancement you have. Accelerator boards are not always compatible with all memory upgrades, for a variety of reasons. Different accelerator boards use (and need) different amounts of RAM. Be sure that you have the right configuration of RAM enhancements for the accelerator board you are considering. The only way to do this is to check with your dealer or the manufacturer of both the memory and the accelerator hardware. Some boards, like the Radius line, do not need any extra memory enhancements because they come with a 32K cache, but they also are expensive (beginning at around $1,500).

You also must consider whether the accelerator board will fit into your computer, given the type of memory upgrade that you are using. If you have high-profile chips, for example, you cannot use the Prodigy accelerator board because the chip's profile is too high. Other accelerator boards have cut-outs to avoid this problem. (You can run into this problem of not having enough space with monitor board upgrades and additions, as well.)

You should also think about what kind of options come with the board. You will want flexibility, and the most important features to look for are being able to turn the board off and on and to change some of its operating characteristics.

Specifically, you might come across an application that will not work with the accelerator board installed. Can you imagine the options if you cannot easily turn off the board? Most cards come with software that allows you to turn the card on or off, as well as to change other operating characteristics, such as the amount of RAM the board uses in any operation.

If you do a great deal of work with big documents, complex documents that often need to be refreshed, big number crunching, or just want things to go faster, perhaps you may want to consider an accelerator board.

Some major brands of accelerator boards are Radius, HyperCharger, and Novy Systems.

Choosing Overhead Displays

Sooner or later, especially if you use your Mac in business, or in school, or anywhere that presentations are pro forma, you will want to display screens on an overhead screen.

Wait no more. Today, projection hardware is well designed, not priced too far up, and relatively easy to use. When you combine these with presentation software, you come away with a very powerful set of tools for making impressive displays.

14

Buying
Hardware

Basically, these projection tools work quite simply. They are relatively small screens that look like your child's (or your old) Etch-A-Sketch. In addition to output going to the Macintosh screen, output also goes to a flat screenlike device (that is often an LCD, or liquid crystal diode) placed on an overhead projector. Once the image is on the projection hardware, it's placed on an overhead. Anything that you can get on a screen, therefore, appears on the overhead. Given the power of so many different types of paint, draw, and graphics software, a slide show sequence of charts can be seen by everyone in the room quite effectively. And with the price of slides these days, it makes even less sense to have slides made when you can use an overhead. Stay at home and do your fades, wipes, and other fancy presentation tricks, using one of the projection panels mentioned later in this part of the chapter. You can, of course, go the old route and create acetates (using your laser printer), but having little control over their presentation leaves a good deal to be desired. Many of the projection panels come with remote controls, which allow you to page through screens and control several visual cues.

What's important? Many things have to be considered in the purchase of a projection panel, not the least of which is cost. You can expect to pay anywhere from $1,200 to $3,000 for one, but if you (or your staff) make presentations often, you will find it worthwhile. If you figure slides at $10 each (including postage, etc.), the average-priced panel (about $1,200) begins to pay for itself after only 120 slides, which is a few large presentations, and in some cases only one! You can see where the saving and the convenience come in.

Selecting Panel Projectors

When you do go shopping for a panel projector, keep some of the following terms in mind so that you know what to ask and look for.

- Panel projectors, like monitors, have certain levels of resolution. Most levels are the same as the standard Mac, but others allow you to increase the resolution.

- These things can get very hot so look for a fan to help cool things down.

- Be sure that the panel is designed for your computer, because different models fit different types of machines.

- On most panels, you can switch between regular and reverse video, making black on white appear as white on black.

- Some panels allow you to interact with them, controlling the image through mouse movement.

- Where does it get its power? If from the Mac, you need to carry one less cord.

- You can choose from super-twist (blue on white) or double-twist for your screen display. The double is black on white and very clear. The type of screen does not seem to be related to price.

These projection tools can be valuable assets in sharing information, especially for teachers who work with computers to generate class materials or demonstrate programming or data analysis techniques. Just for starters, some of the companies successfully marketing these panels are Sharp, Computer Accessories, Kodak, InFocus, and nView. nView had good reviews, with features such as eight levels of gray, options for displaying on a monitor and the panel, cable lengths up to 50 feet, continuous cool (low temperature), and black on white screens. View offers several models.

Choosing Printers

Sooner or later, you will have to decide what type of printer to buy as part of your system. Although you may think cost is the most important consideration, it is actually secondary to the purpose for which you intend to use your printer and the amount of printing that you will be doing.

Figure 14.4 summarizes some of the advantages and disadvantages of several different types of printers. The last column gives you some idea of the cost per page of printing 1,000, 5,000, and 10,000 pages. These figures include the original price of the average printer in that category, as well as supplies and maintenance. You can see how the cost drops with increased usage.

14
Buying Hardware

Printer Type	Advantages	Disadvantages	Purchase Price	Cost of Supplies	Cost per 1,000 pp.	Cost per 5,000 pp.	Cost per 10,000 pp.
Dot Matrix	• Inexpensive • Low maintenance costs • Large selection • Suppies easily available	• Loud • Relatively low quality output	$500	$10 ribbon (2,500 sheets)	$0.50 $0.004	$0.10 $0.004	$0.05 $0.004
Ink Jet	• Quiet • High quality output	• Slow • Jets can clog	$579	$12 ink cartridge (200 pages)	$0.64 $0.06	$0.18 $0.06	$0.12 $0.06
Laser	• Fast • Very high quality output • Large Selection	• Expensive to purchase • Expensive to maintain	$2,800	$130 Toner cartridge (4,000 sheets)	$2.83 $0.03	$0.59 $0.03	$0.31 $0.03

Notes: The ImageWriter, Right Move (from GCC), and LaserWriter IISC are used as examples.
The bolded figures under costs includes the price of the machine.

Fig. 14.4. *A comparison of printers.*

Here are some suggestions to help you choose the printer best for you:

- If you print only short documents in a business or home setting, you really need look no further than a user-friendly dot-matrix printer like the ImageWriter. Alternatives to the Apple line of dot-matrix printers are discussed at the end of this section.

- If you print multiple forms, you will need an impact printer, such as the ImageWriter.

- If you need to produce high-quality text, you can choose a top dot-matrix, inkjet, or laser printer.

- If you need to produce high-quality text and graphics, then you should purchase an inkjet or a laser printer.

- If you need color printouts, the ImageWriter II prints in color (actually, a four-color ribbon provides the color). Laser printers that produce color printouts are very expensive (from $6,000 to $25,000) for a simple user like you or me, but not for large companies who easily spend that much preparing color presentations. Color inkjet printers may be a viable alternative.

The following sections should help you understand the major considerations in selecting and using a printer. The information on using and caring for ImageWriters and LaserWriters should help you understand the specific type of printer that you have or plan to purchase.

Looking at the ImageWriter Line of Printers

The approach that Apple Computer, Inc., took in providing printer capability for the Mac was somewhat unique. Most other companies developed printers that could be used with several different types of computers, but not Apple. The developers believed (rightly so) that the Macintosh would be successful and that the only printer compatible with the Mac (at that time) would be as well.

The original Imagewriter (without a capital *W*) was the workhorse printer for the Apple long before the addition of the LaserWriter. Boxy and relatively inexpensive (about $400), Imagewriters have proven extremely reliable, and many users refuse to switch to more recent models. These printers continue to churn out page after page of decent-quality print. They're no longer available from dealers, but you can often find them for less than $150 at swap meets or in the classified ad section of your local newspaper. Users rarely want two printers after they have purchased a new one, so used Imagewriters are often available.

At present Apple is producing two models of the ImageWriter that differ in a variety of ways: the ImageWriter II and the ImageWriter LQ. The following sections discuss these printers.

Using the ImageWriter II

The ImageWriter II is the present workhorse of Macintosh printers. It is by far the most frequently used printer and will continue to be for users who don't need the superior print quality or flexibility that the LQ offers. For the list price of $595 and street price of $415 to $495, it's an excellent deal.

Using the ImageWriter LQ

You may have already guessed that the *LQ* in ImageWriter LQ stands for *letter quality*, but it could mean "large quantity" as well because the ImageWriter LQ is a very heavy, very large printer. It's more than 2 feet deep and 1 foot wide and weighs 60 pounds. Although these dimensions may not be a deterring factor for all, the LQ's size may present a problem for users with limited space.

14

Buying
Hardware

On the other hand, the LQ has so many outstanding features that most users learn to love their LQs quickly. In some ways, this printer is so complete that it rivals many available laser printers. And because a dot-matrix printer has capabilities that a laser printer doesn't (such as preparing multiple forms and using fan-fold paper or other preprinted forms), this printer is the logical choice for many business users, especially because it can be *networked*, or shared among several computers (as can the ImageWriter II).

Among the advantages that the LQ has over other dot-matrix printers are the following:

- An envelope feeder that works
- Three levels of print quality

- Printing resolution of 216 dpi (approaching laser quality of 300 dpi)

- Four resident fonts (part of the hardware installed in the printer when it is manufactured)

- Several paper paths and sheet bins for feeding mailing labels, special forms, and single sheets

The very early shipments of the LQ did have some problems with the printer drivers, so if you have trouble with overlapping letters or spacing between words with your LQ, see your dealer. These defective drivers should be replaced without charge.

The remainder of this section describes some of the LQ's capabilities in more detail.

Laser printers have a distinct advantage over most dot-matrix printers because they often have many *resident fonts*. The NEC LC-890 contains more than 34 different fonts and style combinations. As mentioned earlier, the ImageWriter LQ now offers some of the same capability; its "operating system" contains Courier, Helvetica, Times, and Symbol fonts in 9, 10, 12, 14, 18, 24, 27, 30, 36, 42, 54, and 72 points. A point is 1/72 inch, so these sizes range from 1/8 inch to 1 inch.

You can use other fonts with the LQ, but because they are not scaled specifically for the LQ with its greatly increased resolution, the output may not be as crisp as the output from resident fonts. Scaling works as follows: the 216 dots per inch that the LQ offers is exactly three times the resolution of the Mac screen (72 dpi). To print on-screen a 9-point character at 216 dpi, the LQ prints a 27-point character at one-third the intended size. As a result, this character is reduced when it prints, and the density of the dots increases by three times.

The LQ does have a number of disadvantages that may deter you from buying it. First of all, it's expensive. The retail price is $1,400, and its accessories, from trays to ribbons, are expensive. Black ribbons are almost $20 each, and the tray that feeds cut sheets is almost $300. Other attachments cost even more. When you total these costs, the price approaches the cost of inexpensive laser printers; small businesses may not want to make such an investment in what is still a dot-matrix printer.

You also need a hard disk to store fonts for the LQ because the large fonts take up more than 800K of disk space, and you are restricted to the four fonts supplied with the LQ. Furthermore, you can print letter quality in only 5 sizes (10, 12, 14, 18, and 24). These limitations may not be severe, but if you have only one printer, you may want more flexibility. The new System 7 will make font production easier and more accurate on all screens.

Finally, the LQ is a very noisy machine. (One reviewer suggests that LQ stands for *Least Quiet*.) The noise alone may be reason enough not to buy an LQ, regardless of the output quality. Because the LQ is so expensive, many people opt to use a QuickDraw laser printer instead.

As mentioned before, the quality of the output is probably the most important consideration in selecting a printer. You can adjust ImageWriters' print quality through the Print dialog box (a software adjustment) or by changing settings on the printer itself (a hardware adjustment).

Printing in Color with ImageWriters

The ImageWriter II and the ImageWriter LQ (and other compatible dot-matrix printers) can actually produce color output. Although other technology is available for printing in color (discussed in Chapter 11), this section focuses on using dot-matrix printers, by far the cheapest way to print in color.

14
Buying
Hardware

These printers use a four-color ribbon that can produce red, green, blue, yellow, magenta, cyan, and black. A $15 ribbon for the ImageWriter II or a $30 ribbon for the ImageWriter LQ transforms your black-and-white printer into a color printer.

However, if you own a Macintosh Plus or SE, you cannot see how your SuperPaint graphic or Wingz chart will appear in color before printing. Only Macintosh II computers have the hardware and software necessary to produce color on-screen. You can still use your computer to do color work; you just cannot see the colors as you work. Figure 14.5 shows a SuperPaint screen with the color palette displayed. The objects are colored using the menu at the bottom of the screen. The object is selected and then the color chosen from the palette shown at the bottom of figure 14.5.

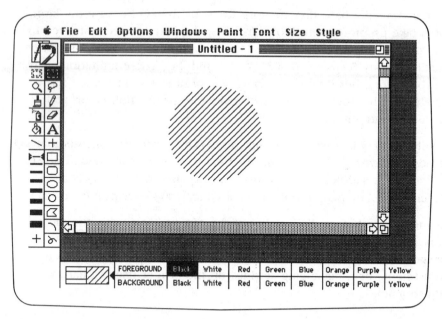

Fig. 14.5. *The SuperPaint color palette.*

Besides dot-matrix ribbon color printers, relatively new technology has made available a color inkjet printer (from Tektronix) that supports QuickDraw, a laser printer language explained later in this chapter. This printer has a 48-nozzle head that produces a resolution of 216 dpi; four ink wells hold black, blue, red, and yellow inks (the colors the four-color separation process focuses on). For $2,500, this printer may be ideal for color printing unless you want to move to the actual four-color separation printing process described in Chapter 11.

Maintaining the ImageWriter

The adage, "An ounce of prevention is worth a pound of cure," is very true for your ImageWriter (or any other dot-matrix printer). When you have spent hours on a document and are finally ready to print it, nothing is more aggravating then getting to the $\mathcal{H} - P$ Print command and finding that your printer is not functioning. This section explains how to keep your ImageWriter running and avoid breakdowns. To clean your printer, you need the following tools:

- Rubbing alcohol (from a drugstore)

- A mild solution of dish detergent in warm water

- Cotton swabs

- Clean, lint-free cloths

- A can of compressed air (from a camera store)

- A vacuum cleaner

First of all, when you get ready to clean, disconnect the plug. Never work with your ImageWriter when it is plugged in. You could damage your printer, or worse, get hurt.

Probably the best advice, because ignoring it accounts for more breakdowns than anything else, is to *keep your ImageWriter and the area around it clean*. Dirt is the primary enemy of all machines with moving parts. Vacuum your work area regularly to keep it clean.

To keep your ImageWriter clean, wipe down the outer plastic parts regularly with a soft, lint-free cloth (an old t-shirt or clean diaper) dampened with warm water or a very weak dilution of a mild dish detergent (nothing stronger). Don't use plastic cleaners or solvents of any kind because they sometimes actually dissolve the plastic. Also, don't wipe off the print head at this point; it must be treated differently.

When you have cleaned the outside, remove the printer cover and vacuum the inside to pick up all the bits of paper and dust that have accumulated. If you don't have a vacuum especially designed for computer components, use your home vacuum, but be sure to remove any attachments and hold the end of the vacuum tube with your finger on the edge, always between the tube and your printer, to avoid damaging your printer. You should also consider buying a dust cover (from a company such as Computer Cover Company) because it can dramatically reduce the amount of dust that gets into your printer.

14

Buying Hardware

Moving on to the *platen*, the hard black rubber cylinder the paper turns around as it feeds through the printer, use alcohol on a lint-free cloth and rub the platen gently until you have removed all the dirt. Don't use water here because water is not very effective in cleaning ink.

Always be careful with the paper you feed through your printer. Although the ImageWriter can handle quite heavy paper, including multiple forms, you can end up with ripped sprocket holes and a mess to clean out of your printer if the paper is too heavy or fed improperly. Paper that is not absorbent (for overhead transparencies, for example) may also create a mess. The ink doesn't dry quickly, smears, and gets all over the printer, making cleanup even more time-consuming than necessary.

A problem many ImageWriter users who print labels run into is that the top row of labels gets pasted onto the platen if you try to roll the labels backward. One way to avoid this dilemma is to advance the sheet of labels so that the first row is beyond the point where it can wrap around the platen. Also, be sure that your labels are fresh. Old ones may lose their sticking power.

The most important part of your ImageWriter is the print head. As explained earlier, the ImageWriter makes an impression on paper when print wires on the print head strike the ribbon. To keep your printer functioning smoothly, you need to check the condition of the ribbon regularly. This constant battering can cause a weak ribbon to fray, tear, and get caught up in your ImageWriter's wheels and gears. If this happens, try using long tweezers to remove the debris, turning the platen to drag up pieces that may be caught. If you are not successful, you will need to have your printer serviced professionally.

You should not need to clean the print head very often, only when the printed images get smudgy, the *o*'s and *0*'s appearing filled. To clean the print head, first remove it by bending the tab located close to the platen and then pulling up. Then use lint-free cloths and alcohol. You can also purchase kits for cleaning print heads, but you may not find them necessary.

If you re-ink ribbons instead of buying a new one each time one runs dry, be careful that you use the right amount of ink; otherwise, you will be cleaning more than printing. Follow the instructions provided with the re-inker carefully. More is not better; you will make a mess of your printer, the print head, and probably yourself as well.

The following suggestions should help you avoid unnecessary and expensive trips to the repair people, who charge as much as $60 an hour:

- Keep food, liquids, and smoke away from your printer (and your entire system). Keep people with little fingers away as well, especially when the printer is operating.

- When not using your ImageWriter, use a dust cover to keep out the dirt.

- Use the proper weight of paper.

- Don't push ribbons beyond the limits for which they were designed. When a ribbon begins to fray or rip, replace it immediately.

- Clean your printer every week.

- Lubricate the moving parts with light oil (such as sewing machine oil) every 6 weeks. Lubricate more often if you use your printer every day or for extended periods of time.

- Use a surge protector, such as the Curtis Emerald (from Curtis).

Surge protectors help avoid damage from the normal peaks and valleys in the flow of electricity. These changes in voltage can cause data loss and numerous other problems. Surge protectors are relatively cheap (under $20), so you should get one when you first buy a system, or add one if you haven't already.

Lightning has the nasty habit of following the path of least resistance. If it hits your house, the electrical system is a natural attractant because it acts as a huge antenna, carrying the lightning through the wiring into your machine. The only way to be safe from lightning is to unplug your machine during severe storms. Because lightning can also get into your machine through the telephone wires, disconnect your modem too if you have one. Disconnecting your equipment may be bothersome, but it can save you the cost of replacing the expensive motherboard and paying $300 for five hours of labor.

14
Buying
Hardware

Servicing Your ImageWriter

No matter how well you maintain your printer, the time may come when it breaks down. If you are lucky, you may be able to fix it by following some of the guidelines in Chapter 19 on troubleshooting and maintenance.

If you do need service, check to see whether your printer is under warranty. At the time of this writing, all ImageWriters have a warranty period of 90 days for parts and labor from the date of purchase. And before you take your printer in for repair, make a few phone calls to get the answers to the following questions:

- What are the hourly rates? (Even official dealers differ from one another.)

- Is there a charge for an estimate, and if so, is the estimate paid as a separate cost or included in the total cost of repair?

- Is a warranty given on the repairs?

- How soon will you get your printer back?

- Can the dealer give you a loaner?

Many independent dealers repair Macintosh products. Although they may have more difficulty getting parts, they may charge less than Macintosh dealers because they don't have a large overhead to pay back to the company they work for. Check your Yellow Pages and ask at user groups for information.

Finally, if you have to mail your printer away for service, use the cartons you saved as you were advised at the beginning of this book. Insure your equipment for its full replacement value, and get an estimate of the repair costs, if possible.

Using Alternatives to the ImageWriter

This chapter noted earlier how Apple tried, by manufacturing a printer not compatible with other computers (such as IBM), to corner the market on dot-matrix printers that can be used with the Mac, and in part the company has succeeded. However, several other companies have produced printers competitive in price and quality.

As a result, you must decide whether to buy an ImageWriter or a "substitute." Before you buy another brand, remember that the Mac and the ImageWriter were designed for each other. What works on the ImageWriter may or may not work with the same ease, user-friendliness, or quality on another printer. On the other hand, depending on the printer and the software you select, they may work very well.

A short lesson in printer technology may be helpful here. Computers communicate with printers and other peripherals through either a serial or a parallel configuration. In serial connections, information flows one *bit* after another, as if in a line. In a parallel connection, the information flows in more than one line, with the lines parallel to one another. Your Macintosh comes with a serial *port* (the place where you connect the cables), so if you can find the appropriate printer driver (the software responsible for sending information from the computer to the printer), then the use of other than Apple printers is probably feasible. Parallel printing devices are not compatible with the Mac. The printer driver file should be named as such on one of your System or Utility disks. In addition, several printers, such as the Seikosha SP-1000AP, an inexpensive compatible, are available and are ready to print as soon as you plug them in.

On the other hand, if you want to buy or already have a parallel printer, you need to use software to convert the signal from parallel to serial before it gets to the printer. Most printers (other than Apple products) are parallel, so you may find yourself in this position.

An interesting approach to this conversion problem is through the use of hardware like the Grappler C/Mac/GS and the Grappler LQ (from Orange MicroSystems), both of which enable you to connect your Mac to parallel printers, including inkjet and laser printers. These little plastic boxes sport two cables: one for the printer and one for the back of your Mac. A nice feature of these devices is that they use the original Apple printer drivers, giving you one less headache to worry about.

14
Buying
Hardware

The advantage of using a hardware device like the Grappler is that you can use your ImageWriter for draft work, and when you are ready for the finished copy, switch over to your non-Apple laser printer. You can also use the Grappler to hook up to one of the many 24-pin printers that cost less than $300 and provide the same quality output as the ImageWriter II, which sells for more than twice as much. Although the output using the Grappler is superb, the Grappler is slow and limits the number of fonts you can use.

Finally, if you want the best of both worlds, the Print Optimizer (from Applied Creative Technology) enables you to manage several different printers, both serial and parallel, at the same time. If you have several different printers and want to use your Mac with them all, the Print

Optimizer is what you need. It may also be the perfect choice for small businesses because it provides access to many different printers and can be shared by multiple Macs.

Looking at the LaserWriter Line of Printers

When the Mac was first introduced, the only printer available was the ImageWriter I, which was followed by the original LaserWriter and then the LaserWriter Plus. Although these LaserWriters were minor miracles in and of themselves, they lacked the high-contrast crisp output of today's LaserWriters. The technology has advanced to the point where the resolution of 300 dpi that laser printers produce compares visually to the higher dpi of professional typesetting equipment. Laser printers cannot replace typesetting, but they do produce acceptable quality printouts for many purposes.

At present, Apple offers three types of laser printers, all part of the LaserWriter II family introduced in January 1988: the LaserWriter II SC, the LaserWriter II NT, and the LaserWriter II NTX. They differ from each other in a number of ways (see fig. 14.6).

	LaserWriter	LaserWriter Plus	LaserWriter IISC	LaserWriter IINT	LaserWriter IINTX
Processor	68000	68000	68000	68000	68020
Processor Speed	12MHz	12MHz	7.45 MHz	12 MHz	16.67 MHz
RAM	1.5M	1.5M	1M	2M	2M
Primary Connection	AppleTalk	AppleTalk	SCSI	AppleTalk	AppleTalk
Imaging Language	PostScript	PostScript	QuickDraw	PostScript	PostScript
Max. Pages Per Minute	8	8	8	8	8
Type of Fonts	Bit-mapped	Bit-mapped	Bit-mapped	Outline	Outline
Font Location	ROM	ROM	Mac	Printer	Printer
Built-in Fonts	4	11	0	35	35
Hard Disk Font Storage	no	no	no	no	Optional
Requires Hard Disk on Mac	no	no	no	no	no
Networkable	yes	yes	no	yes	yes
Resolution (dpi)	300	300	300	300	300
Engine Life in Pages	100,000	300,000	300,000	300,000	300,000
Expendable Components	Drum-toner cartridge	Drum-toner cartridge	Drum-toner cartridge	Drum-toner cartridge	Drum-toner cartridge
Pages Between Replacement	3,000	3,000	4,000	4,000	4,000
Price for Replacement	$130	$130	$130	$130	$130
Weight (lbs.)	55	55	45	45	45
List Price	Not Available	Not Available	$2,799	$4,599	$6,599

Fig. 14.6. A comparison of laser printers.

These printers use the Cannon SX engine, which is responsible for producing the image that is transferred to paper. Engine design affects speed and output quality. The engine used previously in Apple LaserWriters, the Cannon CX, was less reliable and produced less distinct images than the Cannon SX.

Using the LaserWriter II SC

The LaserWriter II SC is the most basic of the LaserWriter II series. Its greatest advantage is that it is relatively cheap, selling for around $2,800, but it doesn't have the power or flexibility of a PostScript printer. The Macintosh (and the ImageWriter and the I SC) use QuickDraw to create images on the screen and on your printed page, limiting the type and number of fonts that print well on the II SC. You also cannot print the fancy PostScript images from ClickArt, which are discussed in Chapter 11. Another limitation of the II SC is that it cannot be networked with other computers, a definite shortcoming for an office system.

In spite of these limitations, the SC has a great deal to offer. It comes with 8K of ROM and 1M of RAM, enough for a full page of graphics, and prints at eight pages per minute. The SC has four resident fonts (Helvetica, Times, Courier, and Symbol) that can print from 9 to 24 points. You can still print a document in 6-point Times; your SC uses its software driver to approximate what a 6-point Times character would look like in relation to what its 9-point character equivalent actually does look like.

14
Buying
Hardware

You can upgrade the SC to an NT or NTX, but upgrading to an NT costs about $2,100, and upgrading an NT to an NTX costs about $2,500. The cost is in the LaserWriter's controller board, which dictates how the printer reads and works with the information from the computer. So far, upgrade kits are available only through Apple dealers. Incidentally, when you install a LaserWriter, you have to install the controller board as well. This task is easy, involving just two screws.

PostScript printers are head and shoulders above QuickDraw printers in all categories except cost. They are much more expensive, not because of the technology but because of the licensing fee that printer manufacturers have to pay Adobe, the creators of the PostScript language. If you do choose a QuickDraw printer such as the PLP because of its lower price tag, be aware of the following limitations:

- It has no sharing capabilities.

- It has no font scaling capabilities (although it will with System 7).

- It has no emulation capabilities.

- It can be used only with Macintosh computers.

Keep in mind, however, that Apple is about to release an entirely new outline technology for its fonts, much like the mathematical model that PostScript is based on. This technology will greatly increase the similarity between the on-screen view of what you see and what you actually get when you print. The following sections describe Apple's PostScript printers.

Using the LaserWriter II NT

The II NT differs from the SC in several ways. First, the II NT is a true PostScript printer. Second, it can be connected to non-Macintosh computers because it has an RS-232 port. Third, the II NT can be networked, giving more than one computer access to the printer at the same time. Finally, it produces a much wider range of fonts and sizes.

Using the LaserWriter II NTX

The LaserWriter II NTX is the Cadillac of Apple printers, with a large RAM that can hold many downloaded fonts (fonts not resident in the machine). You can also upgrade its RAM from 2 to 12M to hold all the fonts that you could possibly dream of, and you can even add a hard disk through a SCSI port and create a font library. Few laser printers have this capability. In addition, the NTX has 11 resident fonts that you can scale to any size.

Using Color Laser Printers

The development of color laser printers is close on the heels of the current black-and-white models, and within perspective, they are not overly expensive. The QMS Model 20, for example, costs about $17,000 and can print all the 8 million different colors available on a Macintosh II. The QMS Model 20 prints on thermal paper and is rated to perform at 20,000 pages per month.

Color printers cannot give you a high-quality final color copy, ready to be inserted as part of a book or other document. Their printouts are nice, even beautiful, but they are most often used as proofs before color separation (necessary for the final printing) is done. These separations, which you learn more about in Chapters 10 and 11, are then sent to a lithography house where the actual four-color print process takes place.

Buying a Laser Printer

With the increased popularity of laser printers, more companies have begun to manufacture their own line of printers. To help you choose among the many printers available, this section discusses a number of factors that you should consider when purchasing a printer. Remember, if a printer works with your Mac, even if it is not an Apple, it has the drivers for you to control all the Page Setup options that are discussed in Chapter 6.

This section assumes that you want the flexibility of a PostScript printer even though QuickDraw printers (such as Apple's LaserWriter II SC and General Computer's PLP) cost considerably less. If you're not sure whether you need a PostScript printer, consider one of these QuickDraw models. Although these printers work off the power of your Macintosh, where the fonts are stored, the PLP has received a great deal of publicity because it costs about $1,600 and does what the II SC can, for about $1,000 less. However, the PLP is slow, printing only a page a minute, whereas many laser printers print at least six pages a minute. The PLP is also limited by your Mac's capabilities, storage, and processing power.

Whatever printer you decide on, never buy a laser printer without trying it out. A laser printer is an expensive investment, and you should take the time to sit down and use the one you want to buy before you make the purchase. If the dealer says no, thank him and go elsewhere.

14
Buying
Hardware

Looking at the Number of Resident Fonts

All PostScript printers come with a certain number of predefined fonts that are resident in the printer's ROM. These fonts are usually not separate families (such as Times, Palatino, or Symbol); instead, they are variations of several different fonts, such as the set that comes with the NEC LC-890. The Helvetica family, for example, contains seven fonts (such as Helvetica Bold and Helvetica Oblique), and the Avant Garde family contains four fonts. The more fonts you get with your printer, the more flexibility you have; however, if your printer has sufficient RAM, you can download specialized fonts when you need them. (Chapter 5 discusses downloading fonts.)

Looking at Paper Tray Capacity

Paper trays hold the paper that is fed into the printer when you print. The less paper the tray holds, the more often you have to refill it. Most laser printers hold from 200 to 250 sheets per tray and need to be refilled fairly often.

Some printers, such as the QMS PS 2400 (from QMS) come with two trays and an additional bin, so you can use one tray for letterhead and the second tray for plain bond paper or envelopes. You can usually direct the printer to select paper from one of the two trays through settings on the printer itself or through your applications software. WordPerfect, for example, enables you to designate which tray should feed the paper for printing.

As to how many bins you need, it depends almost entirely on what you are doing. You may need only two bins. The first could hold stationery for correspondence, and the second could hold paper for printing reports. If you print envelopes, you could use a third bin for that, but you probably need a special envelope feeder to be able to do this.

Understanding Paper Restrictions

Because of the way their feed paths are constructed, some printers may not accept certain heavier types of paper and the coated papers often used to prepare camera-ready copy. The feed path for the NEC LC-890, for example, has trouble printing checks on the preprinted check forms supplied with Quicken (from Intuit).

Many desktop publishers now use clay-coated papers because they are less absorbent than bond paper and provide a cleaner image. However, they are so heavy that they may frequently jam the printer.

The only way to find out what weight of paper is not acceptable is to consult the owner's manual that came with your printer or call their technical service line. Do not experiment with different weights of paper until one jams and then conclude that's the limit. Printers can jam for a variety of reasons, such as the biased feeding of sheets. Some printers now come with a drop-out tray that can handle heavier stock. The drop-out tray allows the paper to flow straight through the printer rather than having to curve up to reach the output tray. This is a great convenience and especially helpful when you print such heavy items as checks and the like.

Inexpensive paper with little fiber (or rag) content also makes a cleaner image because it too is relatively nonabsorbent, but it is thin and looks cheap.

Understanding the Costs of Maintenance and Supplies

Keeping your printer in good working condition can be expensive. Laser printers need regular maintenance to continue operating, as well as supplies that are a bit more complicated than the ribbons required by dot-matrix printers.

14
Buying
Hardware

The most frequently used supply is toner. Toner cartridges must be replaced every 3,000 to 5,000 copies, depending on your printer and types of printouts you make. When you print graphics with solid areas, your printer uses a great deal more toner than when you print text. If your toner cartridge (or refill) is rated to last 4,000 copies, don't be surprised if you get only 2,000 copies if your work is graphic intensive.

To save money on toner, turn your intensity dial to its lightest setting when you replace the toner. Then gradually turn it toward its heaviest setting as you use the toner. In effect, you are regulating the amount of toner needed. And when you get near the end of your toner charge, shaking the toner cartridge from side to side can buy you some more time. You can also purchase toner cartridges that have been refilled to save money. A new toner cartridge for the II NTX, for example, costs about $95, whereas a remanufactured one costs about half that much.

Many companies that refill toner cartridges claim that they refill the originals with 20 percent more toner. Although you are paying less, you are not getting an original cartridge, which may or may not be important to you. If you don't want to refill your cartridges, you can sell them for about $10 each to these companies.

When you replace the toner in an Apple laser printer, you also replace the drum (in a single unit). But you do not always replace the drum with other laser printers. Texas Instruments' OmniLaser 2106, for example, requires toner every 1,500 copies (at $29 per cartridge), a new cleaning magazine every 10,000 copies (at $89 each), and a new drum every 20,000 copies (at $110 each). Other printers may require that you replace belts and developer regularly.

To squeak a tad bit more life out of a cartridge, gently rock the cartridge back and forth—you may get a few hundred more copies. This motion helps the toner that has been caught on the sides of the cartridge to fall down where it can be used. The shaking also helps to level the toner to provide a more uniform output.

Because some laser printers are very large, and none are fun to lug around, inquire about a service contract. Many companies (such as NEC) sell laser printers and include one year of *on-site* service. In other words, the service technician comes to you; you don't have to take your printer to the repair shop.

So, should you purchase a service contract? Printers are amazingly reliable, and, for the most part, any real problem should show up well before the warranty period expires. The contracts are expensive, but do offer peace of mind.

Adding Memory

The more memory a laser printer has, the more it can do. Increased memory results in increased speed, and enables you to use downloadable fonts. These fonts are not resident; they come to you on disk, and you load them from your computer "down" into your printer's memory.

Few PostScript-compatible printers come with less than 2M of memory because a downloaded font must be stored in the memory until it is used. Having a hard disk enables you to store many fonts. If you are a serious laser printer user and need a great deal of memory, then you may need a hard disk to store all the fonts you need access to.

Looking at Emulation Capability

If you work in an office or have more than one computer at home, (such as a Mac and an IBM-compatible computer), you probably want a laser printer with the capability of printing to both. If your computer has a printer driver that emulates the Diablo 630, for example, your choices include the following printers, which are also compatible with your Mac: NEC Silentwriter LC-890, QMS-PS2400, Laser Connection PS JetPlus, and even the Apple LaserWriter Plus, among many others.

There also are products that help connect your Mac and that drive printers other than Apple printers, such as Printer Interface IV (from DataPak) a printer driver for the Hewlett-Packard LaserJet, the most popular laser printer for DOS applications.

To switch from AppleTalk to parallel or serial on the NEC LC-890, for example, you need to press a sequence of switches on the front panel. The printer notifies you of the changes made through the small LCD panel on the front. Through this same panel, you can select the paper tray you want to use, turn off the start-up page, and change software emulations (Hewlett-Packard, Diablo, etc.).

Using Controller Boards

14
Buying
Hardware

As mentioned earlier, the "brains" of a laser printer are located on the controller board. These controllers tell the printer where and how to place dots on the page to produce the images we get.

In the future, higher-resolution printers that print at 400 dpi will become affordable, and printers will be sold without controller boards. You cannot operate a printer without a controller, but if you have the option to buy the controller board separately from the printer, you can select one that is most suited to your needs. The Ricoh Corporation, for example, has developed printers that are shipped without controllers; you can select the controller board you need from the products of some 40 other firms.

This change in marketing practices enables consumers to customize their controllers, thereby altering the capabilities of their printers. If you like the features that a printer offers (the quality of the engine, the warranty, its looks, and so on), purchase it, and then select a controller with the amount of RAM and the number of resident fonts that you want. If this practice of marketing printers and controller boards separately is successful, the price of laser printers in general will probably decrease.

Determining User-Friendliness

As with other computer hardware, the better designed and the easier to use your laser printer is, the less frustrating and tiring working with it will be. After all, if you spend from $2,000 to $7,000 for a printer, it should be easy to use.

Answering the following questions about a printer can help you to determine how user-friendly it is:

- Are the switches for changing emulation modes easily accessible and easy to use?

- Are the paper trays easy to fill? Do they hold enough paper?

- Can I easily tell what font is active?

- Can I pick it up? (Some laser printers are very heavy. The QUME ScriptTen weighs 90 pounds, and the Varityper VT-600 weighs 161 pounds, but it produces 600 dpi! If you move around much, avoid buying such a heavy model.)

- Is technical support available?

- Does the printer have a good warranty?

- Is the manual clear and concise? Does it list the steps necessary for routine maintenance, such as changing toner cartridges and cleaning?

- Will the printer fit where you need to put it?

- Does it have a good reliability record?

Using Cables: Pulling It All Together

Many times, people who call their dealer with a "nothing works" complaint could be hard at work if only they had checked whether their cables were securely connected. Cables are the lifelines of your system; they connect the parts with one another. If they are compromised, so goes the system.

Each of the cables you use contains from 2 to 50 strands of wire. Some of these strands may carry power and some carry data. Here are some general do's and don'ts for cables and their use:

- Be sure that all your cables are securely and properly attached. If a peripheral does not work, check the cable first.

- Read the manuals carefully the first time you set up, and be sure that you have the right cables plugged into the correct receptacles. The Macintosh makes this process easy because there are icons on the machine, and the cable plugs can fit in only one way, but you'd be surprised what some people come up with.

- If you need a replacement cable, be sure to completely describe to your dealer what you want done, including model and manufacturer.

- If you want to make your own cables, sit down until the feeling goes away. Your peripheral should come with a cable. If you should need a specially made cable, most electronic stores or your Apple dealer will be able to construct any type that you need.

14
Buying
Hardware

Buying Accessories

Who said that you can't dress up your Mac to keep up with the Joneses? Here's a list and description of all you will ever need to have the best accessorized Mac in town.

Choosing Furniture

Good tables are sturdy, made from thick, dense materials such as wood or high-quality particle board, have the option to be moved if you need to relocate, and are attractive and easy to assemble. That's a fitting description for those manufactured by Anthro.

Anthro's tables can be configured in a variety of ways. They are made with heavy steel tubing and 1-inch thick surfaces covered in laminates that come in a variety of colors to match your decor. The height of the table and shelves are all adjustable and the modular nature of the design allows you to add printer tables or shelves that swing out. Mouse surfaces are attached to the top surface, and there are a variety of other time- and space-saving devices. The heavy-duty casters make it easy to relocate to another station or room. Anthro even includes the screwdriver you need to assemble the tables.

ScanCo is another company that manufactures high-quality nicely designed furniture specifically for the Mac in the MacTable and MacChair line. The MacTable comes in 48-inch and 60-inch sizes (for about $275 and $300 including shipping) and offers independently adjustable surfaces for tilting your CPU or ImageWriter. The entire work surface tilts as well, making a welcoming environment on which to move your mouse, as well as do other types of work. A platinum melamine surface and beech trim make the whole line (including printer tables and cabinets) very attractive.

Although you can use the MacChair (about $275) with any computer, its thoughtful design seems in sync with the efforts put into the design of the Mac. It's form-fitting, ergonomically designed, and, of course, it matches the MacTable.

Adjusting Your Viewing Area

Ever find yourself adjusting your sitting position to better view a Mac that is either too low or too high? A simple and amazingly effective solution is MacTilt from Ergotron, a metal and heavy plastic pedestal that allows you to rotate your Mac horizontally, raises the height of your Mac four inches, and allows adjustment of tilt up to 30 degrees. It holds on to your Mac with some unobtrusive clips and comes in models that support from 12 to 140 pounds.

The standard MacTilt sells for about $99, and Ergotron will design one to fit any CRT.

Choosing Stands

Kensington also offers a variety of stands to make your Mac more space-efficient and easier to work with. For example, the Macintosh II stand (about $30) lets you stand up your Mac next to your desk so that the keyboard and the monitor are all that remain on your desk. Some people combine this stand with a wall-mounted CRT stand and keyboard drawers so that their desktop remains just that, instead of being cluttered with computer stuff. Bede Tech offers an identical stand for about $10 less.

MacStand from Bede Tech (about $20) raises your Mac 4 inches off the desk (helps with eye comfort) and also provides you with some space underneath for a disk drive or a modem.

Choosing Printer Mufflers

Printer mufflers are enclosures within which you place the printer. Some muffle the sound by as much as 75 percent. You shouldn't use a printer muffler with a daisywheel printer because the printer generates too much heat.

Kensington's Printer Muffler 80 (for about $70) made of high-impact styrene plastic, has cut-outs for paper flow and cables. Bede Tech makes a cardboard printer muffler (they call it a printer silencer) for $30 that is made from 200-pound corrugated cardboard with special acoustical foam on the inside. Both will be a significant help in reducing noise.

14

Buying Hardware

Selecting Switches

Now that you have your Mac hooked up to an ImageWriter and a LaserWriter, and a variety of external floppy and hard drives, how in the world do you manage all this? What you need is a switching center that allows you to connect several Macs to one serial device and just about any other connection you might be able to think of. If you want to go from draft on the ImageWriter to final on the LaserWriter, no more need to disconnect and connect cables; just switch, select the printer, and go.

Another type of switching system is the control center that several companies offer. These centers usually fit underneath your Mac and have several different outlets into which you plug your peripherals. One product is the MasterPiece control center from Kensington. With four outlets and one for your computer (for about $150), just a touch of the master switch and everything is on or off at will. Many of these control centers also come with anti-static touch plates (you just touch the plate and the static threat is gone), as well as surge surpressors and noise filters to help prevent unintended electrical surges from corrupting your data.

Deciding How and Where To Buy

When you're ready to buy your equipment, the question is whether buying through the mail or from a local merchant saves you time and money.

Using Retail Stores

Service before and after the sale may not be a concern for you, or it may mean everything. If you need your Macintosh for work or if you rely on a particular software package, you may need quite a bit of support until you get started. Other users, however, may be able to plug in and go without any help whatsoever.

There's no substitute for being able to go to the dealer from whom you made your purchase and get service. Even when hardware is out of warranty, dealers like to offer service because they make a considerable profit in this area. But don't assume that if you buy from a local dealer, you are guaranteed good service. When you are shopping around, ask questions, such as where the technicians were trained and what is the dealer's policy on supplying a loaner system should your equipment be tied up for more than a specified amount of time.

Using Service Contracts

A service contract is an agreement between you and some service organization to provide repair services. That's the most general description I can offer. After that, everything (as they say) is negotiable. You can get service contracts from Apple or some third party to cover everything from your CPU to your mouse, but they can be very expensive. A service contract on an ImageWriter, for example, is about

$150 each year. And for this, you may get a variety of things, (not necessarily all from the same company though), such as 24-hour turn around, free loaner, free pickup and delivery, no charge if it can't be fixed fast, and so on. On the other hand, you might get a service contract where you need to deliver, get no loaners, and have unspecified turn around. Who needs to pay for even more aggravation than you already have?

Service contracts might make sense for large organizations or people who use their Mac to make their living and have to make sure that their equipment is always available. But for the in-home user, their utility is questionable.

Using Mail Order

Horror stories of mail-order fraud abound. Sometime in 1987, a firm named Compusystems opened its doors in Torrance, California, and began to advertise in all the national media prices that seemed too good to be true. These folks provided false credentials to get bank credit, never paid advertising bills, listed a bogus mailing address, and of course, never filled any orders. A retail computer store in the Washington, DC, area ran some incredible specials based on the premise that customers would pay for the product and wait for delivery. The products never came, the owners skipped, and the store was empty within weeks of the promotion.

But at the other extreme, MacConnection earned the honor of being on the cover of *Inc.* magazine as one of the best direct-mail businesses in the U.S.

There's no question about it; probably the most important reason for buying through a mail-order firm is the price. You can get substantial discounts of 30 to 40 percent on name brand products. Because some of the larger mail-order companies can afford to buy in huge volume, they can often purchase (and then sell) the products for less than the retail store owner can buy them wholesale.

Figure 14.7 shows a comparison of retail and "street" prices.

Even though there is no substitute for good local service, don't rule out what mail order firms have to offer, especially when it comes to purchasing software. Although there are few companies that sell Macs

14

Buying
Hardware

	Retail	Street Price	Discount
Hardware			
ImageWriter II	$595	$419	30%
101-Keyboard	$199	$140	30%
ScanMan	$495	$350	29%
NEC LC-890	$4,200	$2,999	29%
MacPlus	$1,799	$1,229	32%
SE w/ Dual Floppies	$2,869	$2,099	27%
SE/30	$4,369	$2,499	43%
Mac II	$4,869	$3,651	25%
		Average	30%
Software			
PageMaker	$495	$329	34%
Wingz	$495	$250	49%
FreeHand	$495	$300	39%
MacWrite II	$150	$99	34%
Go Master	$79	$49	38%
Word	$395	$250	37%
SuperCard	$199	$140	30%
MicroPhone	$295	$230	22%
Quark Xpress	$795	$495	38%
ClickArt	$70	$42	40%
SuperPaint	$149	$128	14%
		Average	34%

Fig. 14.7. *A price comparison.*

through the mail, the market for peripherals such as printers, scanners, and disk drives is flourishing.

One mail-order firm I regularly use (MacConnection in Marlow, NH) provides excellent service. The company has knowledgeable sales people and a toll-free order number. Best of all, anything you order will be at your doorstep the next day, often by noon if you order it by 8 p.m. the preceding evening. In addition, the firm has just instituted a 30-, 60-, and 90-day return policy on certain products, should you not be satisfied with your purchase. Another good company is Mac Warehouse.

You can guard against potential problems when mail ordering by using some common sense.

First, make sure that the mail-order firm does not bill your account (or charge card) until the item is shipped. Most firms adhere to this policy.

Second, keep your receipts and a copy of all correspondence that you might need later on to verify the transaction.

Third, ask around and find out whom your Mac friends recommend. Keep your eyes on the advertisements. Companies that have staying power and advertise on a regular basis over a long period of time show some stability.

One large computer mail-order firm places a two-page advertisement twice a week in the *New York Times*. Because ads like that are quite expensive, regular advertising can give you an idea of the financial health of a firm.

Buying Used Equipment

So you don't think anyone would be interested in a used Apple. How about a used Macintosh? If you said no, you're wrong. Each time there's a new release, such as the Mac II family of computers, there's a scurry in the marketplace for the new ones, and the old ones get left behind. The used-computer market is a fast-growing one.

The largest of the companies dealing in used equipment is Sun Remarketing (P.O. Box 459, Logan, Utah, 801/752-7631), which was started by Bob Cook in 1983. Sun repairs and refurbishes used computers. It handles not only Macs, but Apple IIs, software, printers, modems, and all kinds of accessories. The company also offers service on the products it sells. All the products carry at least a 30-day warranty, and some have as long as a 90-day warranty.

14
Buying
Hardware

Sun offers prices such as the following:

- The Mac Plus for $1,095; the retail cost is $1,799.

- The Mac SE for $1,995. The retail cost is $2,869.

- The Mac II, with monitor, 40M drive, and a mouse for $4,995. The System is $4,869 retail.

Sun is also the source for the Lisa (the forerunner of today's Mac). In fact, when Apple discontinued the Lisa, Bob Cook purchased the remaining 7,000 computers from Apple. Originally marketed at $10,000, Sun sells them for $995.

If you want to buy or sell, perhaps the best place to look is your local user group. People always want to buy or trade, and you might be able to work out a satisfactory deal.

Recommendations

What do you need? In the end, you are the only one who can make that decision. Remember that bigger is not always better. A 60M hard disk is valuable if you need to store that much. If not, there's no reason to spend your money on equipment that is only partially used.

The Macintosh is a beautifully designed machine. Fortunately, Apple realized that the original Mac would not satisfy all its customers and all their needs. Hence, the Mac has evolved into a highly expandable machine with many different configurations.

Following is a brief description of the kinds of configurations that people in different positions might need.

- Children: Kids need a small Mac, such as the 512K, and the best place to go for these is a used-machine dealer like SUN. In some circles, these machines can be had for less than $500. The 512 can run a great deal of software, including some simple word processors, such as Write (from Microsoft) and a stripped down version of Word (also from Microsoft).

- The Beginner: The beginner easily can get by with a Plus and an ImageWriter printer. If you eventually want to move up, you can always sell your first system and update or add on various peripherals.

- The Writer: The writer needs little more than the beginner to get started, but some add-ons become almost essential. One is a large hard disk to store documents and to help increase speed and convenience of moving from document to document. You might also consider a modem for connecting with on-line services (see Chapter 16), especially for information retrieval when searching for facts for an article, for example, and also for transmitting manuscripts and books to publishers. You may want to consider some type of backup hardware as well. Unless you're doing desktop documents (such as advertisements, brochures, and so on), you don't really need anything more than a dot-matrix printer or a full-page monitor.

- **The Number Cruncher:** One thing that number crunchers need is a great deal of room to move around, and that's why the most powerful equation solvers, such as Mathematica and other statistical packages, need expanded or additional RAM, as well as a coprocessor, which comes with the SE/30s and Mac IIs.

- **The Engineer:** Engineers are number crunchers as well but often need more elaborate output than a simple printer can produce. You should consider a plotter to generate blueprints, drawings, and renderings. If finished copy of renderings is necessary, color may be a desirable feature for your System to have. You should consider a Mac II and a color printer.

- **The Graphic Designer:** Graphic designers need a full-page monitor so that entire pages can be seen and conveniently worked with all at once. Another essential is a great deal of storage space for such things as clip art (often at 10K apiece), fonts, and style sheets. Although speed is not that important and most people can get by with a Plus or an SE, if you want to use color, you must have one of the Mac II family. Some of the software with fairly large RAM demands for working with digitized images (see Chapter 11) also necessitates a Mac II. Laser printers and scanners are a must to really do what's needed.

14
Buying Hardware

- **The Desktop Publisher:** The desktop publisher needs a System with many of the same features a graphic artist does. However, you should have a two-page monitor that is capable of showing facing pages simultaneously. This feature is especially handy for book-page composition.

- **The Manager:** For the person who does lots of everything but not much of any one thing, a Plus with a hard drive should fill the bill. Because managers often need to communicate with outsiders and review internal documents, a large hard drive and a laser printer are a must.

The table in figure 14.8 will help you decide what equipment you need when you are setting up your Mac system. Although there are certainly no rigid do's and don'ts about configuring hardware to meet your needs, this table will give you some idea where to start.

	A	B	C	D	E	F	G	H
1		For the Beginner	For the Writer	For the Number	For the Engineer/	For the Graphic	For the Desktop	For the Manager
2				Cruncher	Architect	Designer	Publisher	
3								
4	Model	Plus	SE/30	IIcx	IIcx	IIcx	IIcx	Plus
5	RAM	1M	1M	4M	8M	8M	8M	1M
6	Storage	40M	40M	60M	60M	60M	60M	40M
7	Backup	no	yes	yes	yes	yes	yes	yes
8	Monitor	Standard	Standard	Standard	Large Screen	Two page	Two page	Standard
9	Modem	no	yes	no	no	yes	yes	no
10	Printer	ImageWriter II	LaserWriter SC	LaserWriter SC	LaserWriter SC	LaserWriter NTX	LaserWriter NTX	LaserWriter SC
11	Plotter	no	no	no	no	no	no	no
12	Scanner	no	no	no	no	yes	yes	no

Fig. 14.8. *A product listing for different types of users.*

The secret to buying right is to read as much about the subject as possible, talk to people who have been through the same experience, and determine (in terms of both money and time) what changes are right for you.

Part V

Networking and Communications

The Old Way: Joan sits in the Los Angeles office working on her Mac. She is busy preparing the proposal that is due the following day in Washington. Once she completes her draft, she stores it on the company mainframe. The next day, Frank accesses the file from the mainframe from his office in Washington, adds whatever material he wants, and then saves the file once again. A working draft and the graphics that are needed for the final draft are printed out on the Washington office's high-resolution printer.

The New Way: Joan and Frank are on the same network and can share all the materials that are needed for any revisions. Joan is the more skilled of the two at graphics, so she works a bit on the new drawings and has them printed out in Washington, all the time sitting at her desk in Los Angeles.

Modems, E-mail, nodes, file servers, local area networks, and more are all part of the new worlds of networking and telecommunications. Whether you are the CEO of a large corporation and need to send out a memo to 500 subordinates or you just want to know how many bicycles were manufactured last year in Japan, being able to communicate using your Mac can make the saying "Information is power" true for you.

Includes

Networking

Communications

CHAPTER 15

Networking

If the Mac is to be truly the computer "for the rest of us," then it will have to be a tool that can reach out to others, rather than just give us the power to enhance our own skills. The way that people communicate with each other through their Macs and other peripherals (such as printers and modems) is with a network.

The whole idea behind a network, often referred to as a local area network (LAN), is that different devices (printers, computers, or hard drives) can be shared by every connection on that network. Like other areas of the Macintosh and its technology, LANs have their own special terminology and concepts.

Understanding Networking Basics

Let's start at the beginning with what a network is and then go through some of the basics.

A *network* is a particular configuration of devices that are connected so that information can be shared by all devices on the network. The components of a network are connected by cables—bundles of wires along which a great deal of information can efficiently travel with little interference from outside. The cables are attached with connectors to the various devices along a network. A network can consist of a single computer and one printer, 500 computers linked to one another, a series of printers connected to one Macintosh, or a printer and a plotter connected to two Macs. Any combination that fits your needs can be adequately addressed on a network. These devices are called *nodes*.

15
Networks

589

To give you some idea of the importance that the Apple people have placed on the value of communications, the Mac is manufactured with a built-in networking capability, called AppleTalk. AppleTalk is the Mac's special capability to share information over a network. With other personal computers, you must buy the basic software to use a network.

Defining AppleTalk: The Standard

In order for any LAN to work at all, let alone properly, a standard system of sharing information must be established (just as people need to speak to one another in a language that can be understood by both). Apple has set this standard with the introduction and use of AppleTalk, the communications standard for Macintosh computers and built into every Mac. AppleTalk is a "plug and play" system that requires nothing more than the correct set of cables and connectors plugged into Mac ports in order to set up the network across which communications can take place. When you connect a LaserWriter to your Macintosh, the documents that are printed are sent from the computer's memory over an AppleTalk cable to the printer. The same holds true for any transmission of information over a network from one Macintosh computer to any other Macintosh peripheral.

The power of AppleTalk is that it can support the sharing of software (such as programs everyone needs to access) as well as hardware (perhaps a laser printer). Constructing an AppleTalk network is almost child's play. The AppleTalk network consists of a series of cables that are used to connect different devices. A small box on each cable (a connector) ensures that any noise caused through electrical transmissions won't get into the data stream.

The hardware system that links all the nodes on a network is now called LocalTalk (formerly called AppleTalk, a name still in use). The process by which information can be shared from one main node (called a file server) to other nodes is through AppleShare. More about these later.

Defining Protocols

A *protocol* is the set of rules that are followed so that information can be shared and understood by all the nodes on the network. Everyone on one network must use the same protocol, but different networks can use different protocols and still be connected through a gateway. The network protocol that is almost the defacto standard for Apple equipment is AppleTalk, which is already built into your Macintosh computer. Most communications software offers several different modes for transmitting data, so you can take advantage of whatever type you need, given the characteristics and limitations of the information.

Many different protocols exist, such as XModem, YModem, Kermit, WXModem, SEAlink and TELELINK, but which one do you use? If you just want to share plain old text information as ASCII files, almost any protocol will do. XModem is the most popular of all protocols because it allows the easy and rapid transfer of information between computers that are similarly configured. Kermit allows all that XModem does, but it is the premier protocol for connecting computers like the Mac to mainframes, making Kermit very popular in research institutions and universities. Other protocols are highly specialized, such as SEAlink for transmissions that take place over satellite links. For your everyday communications work, you will find that XModem and Kermit, one or both of which come with your communications software, will probably do the job for you.

Apple's software standard for connecting nodes is AppleShare.

Defining Servers

Networking is effective because people can communicate with each other quickly and easily. A distinct advantage of being on a network is being able to set up a variety of *servers*, which are devices that are available to all (or some) of the people along the network. For example, a file server like AppleShare performs two critical tasks.

The first task is that the file server can be the storehouse for information that several people can access simultaneously, if necessary. File servers can be established with separate sections for storage of data for individuals along the network. Second, the file server acts as a manager for the files that it stores, helping to keep the disk well organized, sending information where it is needed and when, and performing other types of tasks that help keep what would be an unmanageable amount of information on a system, quite manageable.

15

Networks

Because sharing information that is on disk is such an important part of using a network, it's important to distinguish between disk servers and file servers.

A *disk server* does just what the name says. The disk server takes a section of a hard disk (containing the information the user needs) and makes that section available to users along the network. These sections are usually organized as *volumes*, which contain files and folders. These are called volumes or partitions, and utilities exist to allow you to set up your own hard drive in this manner (such as Symantec Utilities for the Macintosh). Most disk servers are set up with passwords so that not everyone has access to all information. A disk server might provide a section of storage for each of the members of a network with their own built-in security so that no one other than the authorized user can gain access to the information stored.

A *file server*, one of the most common of all servers along a network, is more powerful and can go to any part of the disk to access information. You specify the location for a disk server to work, but with a file server you specify the information itself by the file or folder name, and you can then access the information you need, be it an application or a data file.

A popular file server is TOPS (Transcendental Operating System from Sun Microsystems), which allows each node on a network to act as a file server to every other node. This type of server is called a *distributed file server*, and it creates a distributed network in which all the nodes are interconnected. In other words, unlike AppleShare, TOPS does not require a dedicated Macintosh to act as the hardware side of the file server. Dedicated computers sit there and do only one thing, which in this case is distribute and store files; a relatively inefficient use of a sophisticated and powerful machine like the Macintosh.

TOPS is very popular, but becomes slow as additional nodes are added, so perhaps the best advice is to keep the network small if you use a file server like the one described here.

Other types of servers are disk servers, modem servers, and mainframe servers. When in use, these servers allow access to disks, modems, and mainframes, respectively.

Defining Types of Networks

Networks come in a variety of configurations, or shapes, differing basically in the way the different devices (nodes) are connected with one another. For example, the devices on a *bus network*, which is the most flexible of all the types described in this chapter, are connected through a single cable (see fig. 15.1). Each node on the network has its own *ID number* (or address), and each node has access to every other node at all times. Although a distinct advantage is that "everyone can talk to everyone" else, each node on a bus network needs to function independently. Therefore, each device has to have its own central processor and whatever else goes along with it, such as a hard drive. A bus network is expensive, but the ease of adding new nodes and changing the configuration of existing ones may compensate for the increased expense.

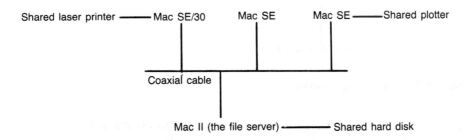

Fig. 15.1. *A bus LAN configuration.*

A typical LAN probably looks like the diagram in figure 15.1. Here, three Macs are connected to each other as well as to a file server (which contains data that each person on the network works with) and a printer. These connections take place through a series of cables. If the connections take place over a distance where cabling is impossible, telephone lines become the cables for the transmission of information. For telephone transmissions, you can use products like PhoneNET (from Farallon) or connectors from NexSys. The NexSys connectors cost 60 percent less than PhoneNET equipment and come with NetAuditor software, which allows you to monitor networks and manage printers.

15

Networks

Another type of network is a *token ring* network, diagrammed in figure 15.2. Token ring networks work by sending information into a file that circulates continuously around the ring connecting all the nodes. Information sent by one device, say a computer, can be picked up by another on the same ring.

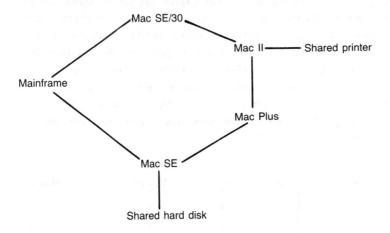

Fig. 15.2. *A token ring network.*

Token rings (and other types of networks) depend on the reliability of the *repeaters*, which are located along the ring. Repeaters are like pumping stations along a pipeline, but if one goes, everything down the line is affected because the signal weakens. Many networks (such as AppleTalk) allow connections up to 1,000 feet between nodes. If you want to go longer, you need a repeater that gives a boost to the signal.

One advantage of a token network is that all the nodes have an equal chance to transmit and share information. Another advantage is that because the information is always moving in a circle, there's little chance for data to "crash" with or run into other data and slow things down.

Apple was scheduled to introduce its version of a token ring network, TokenTalk, this past June, but as of this writing, it is not available.

Finally, *star networks* are organized with a central hub (called the server) in the middle of the network and the nodes (called the clients) surrounding the hub (see fig. 15.3). Star networks operate from a central controller, where a separate link is established to each node, making this type of network somewhat expensive in addition to being dependent on the central controller for all activity. When the central controller is busy or down, everything everywhere stops.

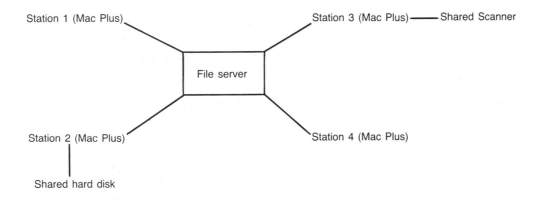

Fig. 15.3. *A star network.*

With AppleShare, you can have as many as 256 nodes on one network, but 256 is the top limit. Almost all networks are limited by the number of nodes they can support or by the length of cable that can be run between nodes. Hence, people are always looking for ways to get around these limitations. One way is to split one network into two and build a bridge between the two to connect them.

Defining Bridges

A *bridge* is a connection between networks. For example, the people on the New York network can talk with the people on the Chicago network over a bridge, or the people in Suite A, who are using AppleTalk as a networking system, can talk to the people in Suite B, who are using the Ethernet system (more about this product in another section). Bridges keep track of what devices are on what network and make sure that the *traffic* (the information) gets where it needs to go. A special kind of bridge, a *gateway*, connects two networks that use different protocols, or systems for communications, such as in the AppleTalk to Ethernet situation just described. You can see in figure 15.4 how two networks can be connected using a bridge, such as those

15

Networks

made by Hayes (InterBridge), Shiva (the NetBridge), and Solana
Electronics (The I-Server).

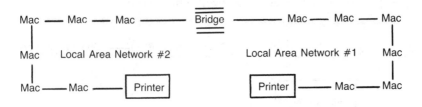

Fig. 15.4. Using a bridge to connect different networks.

Defining Some Special Bridges

You should know about specialized bridges. For example, NetBridge
from Shiva is a bridge that links two local networks using direct
connections. Shiva's other bridge is TeleBridge, which links networks
that are connected by phone lines. With TeleBridge and the NetModem
modems, you can increase transmission speeds to 57,000 baud,
extraordinary for usually slower phone lines.

NetModem is a CDEV, and once installed, you select it through the
Chooser (see fig. 15.5). When NetModem is installed, your menu bar
shows a series of lights that indicate the status of NetModem (sending,
waiting to receive, and others) just like a real modem does when its
lights and LEDs (Light Emitting Diodes) are blinking away like mad.
The only problem with NetModem is that the modem itself transfers
information at a much slower rate than does the network on which the
modem exists. This slower rate can lead to some traffic jams if several
people have files waiting to be sent, and on-line charges are increased
because the modem is slow.

A second useful and easy-to-use bridge is the Hayes InterBridge, which
is used to connect two LocalTalk networks, even through a modem. For
example, let's say that the Washington office of a law firm has five local
area networks, and the Los Angeles office has three, for a total of eight
LANs that need to be connected. Using InterBridge, you can first
connect all the Washington LANs to one another and use another
InterBridge to connect the three LA LANs. Now you need to link the
LA and the Washington offices, and you make that link with another
InterBridge over (probably a dedicated) modem.

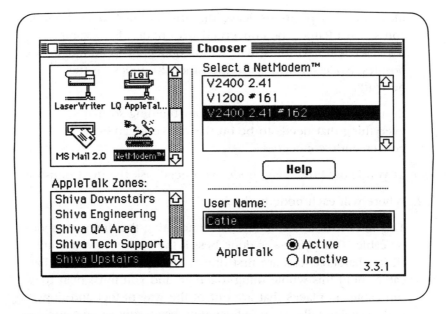

Fig. 15.5. *The Control Panel and NetModem.*

Setting Up a Network

It would be impossible to detail the steps for every possible configuration of a LAN. Instead, let's consider the types of questions you need to ask yourself before you start the actual work. Then I will give you steps for seeing up a simple LAN.

Planning Considerations

Before you begin work on your LAN, you have a number of elements to consider. You need to have the answers to the following questions:

1. How many computers and other peripherals will make up your LAN?

   The first question is most easily answered if you are aware of the type of work that you do (large text files, frequent sharing, and so on) and the number of people who do the work. Remember that a LAN is not only computers; it also consists of printers, hard drives, modems that can be networked, and other peripherals. Don't worry about specific people. (They move to other positions, leave the firm and new ones come in, and so on.) Rather, be concerned with nodes. For example, node #1 will have be a Mac SE/30 connected to a modem with no files. Node #1 will serve the other 20 nodes on the network.

Best of all, of course, is to wire your building so that everything that needs to be on the network can be conveniently connected.

As soon as you know how many nodes you need, ask the next question:

2. Where will each node be located?

    This information is essential for connecting the different nodes by cable. This process is done best if the entire network and all its characteristics are first drawn on paper. Remember that cables hold this whole thing together, and you must plan to run cables in places that are out of the way of feet and dogs with wagging tails. Many offices now have removable floor panels so that cables can be run easily and not interfere with normal office traffic. Other LANs have been wired through the ceiling, where panels can also be removed.

3. What other hardware may be needed to make things work as you like?

    If you will be using DOS machines, you will need a special card (a LocalTalk card) installed into those machines so that they can communicate with the Macintoshes on the network. You will need bridges only if you have to connect to another network entirely.

    Keep in mind, however, that if you start mixing DOS machines with Macs, you have to take into account many other issues, such as the amount of memory you have available.

Finally, ask yourself the most important question:

4. Are the various types of hardware compatible with one another?

    It's very easy to get caught up in the hype of LANs and go out and buy everything you think you might need. But it's not such good sense if you are just starting out. Rely on your dealer or the manufacturer to let you know whether a laser printer can be networked and accessed from a variety of nodes and if there are certain limitations. The same advice is true for software. Programs that work alone may not be accessible through a network.

Constructing a Small Network

Here are the steps you would take to set up a simple all-Macintosh LAN using LocalTalk cables and connectors and the AppleTalk protocol. The components of this LAN (as with every LAN) are the cables that connect the different devices, the software that is used to send the information, and the computers. As you can see in figure 15.6, this network has four computers, one ImageWriter, and one LaserWriter, all connected to one another. Because this network is a bus network, the computers are connected in a line, and all can communicate with one another. Here there are two Mac IIs and two SEs networked to a LaserWriter and an ImageWriter.

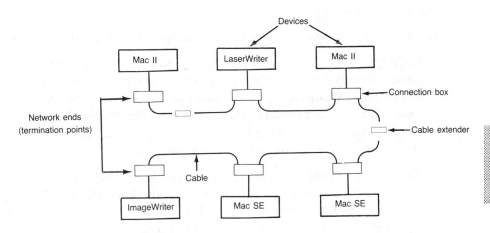

Fig. 15.6. *A simple bus LAN using AppleTalk and LocalTalk.*

You can see several things from the simple diagram shown in figure 15.6.

First, and most important, the devices and nodes are arranged in a line—not in a circle. A bus network is linear and needs termination points, which the connecting boxes can provide. Second, you need only one cable to attach two devices to one another, and although each connector box has two connection points, only one need be used. Finally, extra cables are unwanted. You have only as many cables as are needed to connect nodes, with no extra cables tagged on to the last node in the network.

Speaking of cables, be sure that they are placed where no one can trip over them, securely connected (an amazing source of "My network won't work!" screams that are heard daily). Also be careful of where you run them. Running LocalTalk cables (and many other brands as well) past fluorescent lights and near other electrical components can cause interference in the network. Run these cables through conduits if necessary.

Also be sure to use the cable clips (such as those from Black Box Corporation) that you can get to secure the connectors, and be sure that they don't come disconnected should someone trip over the line. At least your system is safe, even if the employees aren't.

So, step-by-step, here goes. First "do these" on paper; then pick up your hardware and software and get connected.

1. Determine how many cables and connector kits you need.

   For each device along the network, you need one complete kit, which consists of a plug (be sure you get the right one for the device being connected), a LocalTalk connector box, a 2-meter cable, and a cable extender. There are two different connector kits, one with an 8-pin plug and one for a 9-pin plug. Count your pins and check your hardware before you buy.

   There are two types of LocalTalk kits. The first (Din-8) comes with an 8-pin circular plug and is used for the Plus, SE, Mac II, and the ImageWriter printer. The DB-9, which terminates in a 9-pin plug is used for the 128K and the 512K.

   You can get additional cables in lengths of 10 and 25 meters (or about 33 and 83 feet, respectively). Then you can combine the 2-, 10-, and 25-meter lengths to fit your needs. You can also buy a cabling kit from Apple, for around $650. This kit comes with 100 meters of cable, 26 assembly plugs, and 4 cable extenders.

2. Lay out the cables in the space where the network will be set up.

3. Don't connect your computers, printers, and other devices yet, but make the cable connections into the connecting boxes and the cable extenders. You should have a good idea where the various nodes will be located by this time and have your hardware ready to be connected.

4. Be sure that all hardware along the way is working and that all the hardware is turned off.

5. Now attach each of the cables coming out of the connector boxes to each of the devices at each node, using the printer port.

6. Turn on the hardware and you're in business.

Believe it or not, anyone along the network can now print or plot or use the modem or whatever, depending on the network's offerings.

Using an Alternative to Cables

PhoneNET (from Farallon) allows you to bypass the laying of cables and use existing phone lines for a local area network. Not only might PhoneNET save you the expense of cable, but anyone with a phone (such as a new employee) can be added to the network—without running new cables.

PhoneNET has other advantages. First, you can have up to 3,000 feet between nodes, whereas with AppleTalk you are limited to 1,000 feet. Next, PhoneNET uses the same type of click-in connectors you find on your phone, thereby reducing the possibility of an accidental (and fatal) unplugging.

15

Networks

Because you may have to mess around with the connections between your phone and the phone box on your wall, you may want an experienced PhoneNET person to assist you. You also can call the telephone company to send out someone who can be of some assistance. Although the wiring is not difficult, it can be a source of trouble if not done properly.

Using Alternatives to LocalTalk

AppleTalk is the software side of the networking equation, and LocalTalk is Apple's name for the hardware side, which consists of the jacks and cables that hold everything together.

Keep in mind that cables can often become loose and disconnect from one another. The problems that you may think are hardware failures could be nothing more than loose connections. Check the connections first when something is not functioning properly.

Up to a few years ago, the only way to make network connections was to use LocalTalk, which has as its primary disadvantage its lack of speed. Today, one of the most attractive alternatives is Ethernet, a very fast cabling system that is compatible with the Macintosh (as EtherTalk) and meets the standards set by the majority of computer manufacturers.

Other companies, Dove Computer, for example, manufacture a line of products that enhance the operation of Ethernet systems. Dove's FastNet products (a family of Ethernet products available for all Macs, including 512s) are communication controllers that speed transmission along Ethernet lines. Kinetics, another company, also produces Macintosh networking products. Kinetics' products enhance connections with Ethernet systems (such as Fastpath, placed between LocalTalk and Ethernet) and increase the speed and efficiency of communications between nodes and networks by means of a bridge. Kinetics LAN Ranger provides an easy-to-use graphical interface that logs network events, identifies network services, provides a graph for traffic, and more (see fig. 15.7). As you can see by the sample screen, Kinetics LAN Ranger acts as a network controller displaying loads of information about amount of traffic, who's connected to whom, and more.

Using Shared Peripherals

There are all sorts of ways to set up a system. For example, you may want more than one Macintosh to have access to a laser printer. One of the most efficient and easiest ways to set up this kind of system is not really networking at all. The Local Connection (from Fifth Generation Systems) allows you to make connections between devices, regardless of whether they are serial or parallel. The difference between serial and parallel devices is the way they share information. Serial devices transmit information along a single pathway (one piece of information

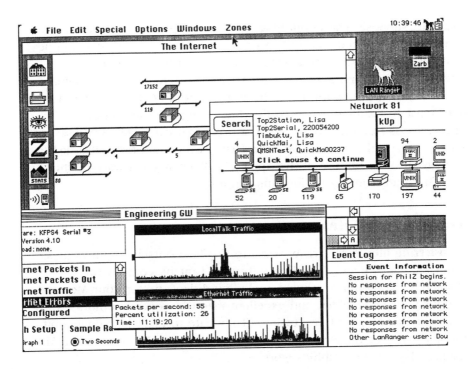

Fig. 15.7. The LAN Ranger screen from Kinetics.

follows another). Parallel devices transmit several pieces of information along parallel pathways.

The Local Connection is a box with four serial and four parallel ports (two in and two out). It also includes a buffer so that print jobs are stacked and printed in turn, and The Local Connection contains memory-resident software allowing the user to send documents to any plotter, printer, or modem. This kind of product is an alternative to traditional networks, and if your networking needs are relatively simple, this approach is an attractive one. The retail price is between $595 and $1,095 (depending on how large the buffer is)—well below the cost of a full-blown network.

Using Your Mac with PCs

The more you compute, the more you're likely to run into the problem of sharing information between two different makes of computers. For

15

Networks

example, suppose that a colleague has just completed an important report, and you need a copy, but there you are with your Mac and he with his PC clone. A lost cause? Not at all. You have several alternatives. The first is to use a file-transfer program. These programs actually transfer the information from a Mac to a PC (or vice versa) and translate the file formats to fit while doing so. The second alternative is to attach to your Mac a drive that can read DOS disks. Finally, there's the new 1.44M SuperDrive, which can read DOS disks directly through the use of the Apple File Exchange software or the DOS Mounter from Dyna Communications.

Transferring Files

Transferring files is remarkably easy to do. Two outstanding products, Dataviz's MacLink and Traveling Software's LapLink come with absolutely everything you need, including disks (one for your Mac and one for your PC), cables, and excellent manuals. Several authors I know use their PCs for word processing. (They hate to take their fingers off the keyboard for mouse stuff.) They then port the files over to the Mac for page layout and graphics work.

These products work in basically the same way. Once the two machines are connected by a cable, you "connect" using the supplied software, and they can now "talk" to one another. Then you just select the types of files that you want to send and have the software do the translation and the sending.

MacLink Plus offers almost any type of file conversion you could need and far more than any other product (more than 60 direct translations). And you don't get text alone. For example, with word processing translations MacLink Plus also accurately translates

- Rulers
- Print styles
- Margins
- Tabs
- Subscripts

Spreadsheet formats in the WKS, WK1, and SYLK file formats are also directly translatable.

For example, figure 15.8 shows you a MacLink Plus screen. You can see that making the selections to translate from Microsoft Word on the Macintosh to WordPerfect on the IBM is as simple as clicking. After this selection is made, you select the files you want to transfer, and then send them. MacLink Plus translates and then sends them. Table 15.1 gives just a partial list of programs that translate from Mac to PC (and of course back again).

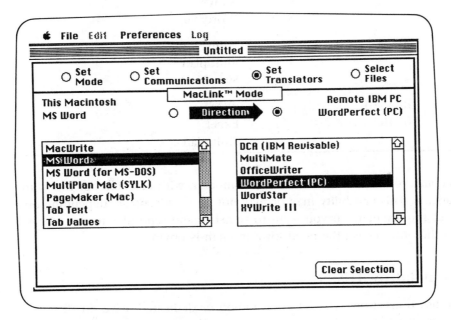

Fig. 15.8. Converting files using MacLink Plus.

LapLink (Version 2.0) is a similar file conversion and transfer program, which includes fewer file translators than MacLink Plus but gets the job done much the same.

15
Networks

One major difference between LapLink and MacLink Plus is that MacLink is a Macintosh application, and you work from the Mac side of things with the Mac interface you may be used to. LapLink is a PC application, and you work from the PC side of things allowing for easy batch file transfer (if you know how to work with batch files on the PC, that is). Which side of the fence you work on (Mac or PC) is a preference of sorts, but my bet is that most Mac users would find MacLink easier to learn and use.

Table 15.1
Macintosh Translators

From This Type File	To This Type File
MacWrite	MultiMate
	WordPerfect
	XYWrite
	WordStar
Excel	Lotus
	Multiplan
	Symphony
dBASE II or III	dBASE
	Excel
	Multiplan

Second, you can transfer files over a modem with MacLink but not with LapLink. This capability may or may not be an advantage, depending on your requirements. If you want to translate and send files to the office on the other coast, the need for a modem is obvious.

Translating Disks

In disk translations, you let your add-on or dedicated drive do all the talking (and conversions), so you can go from Mac to PC or PC to Mac without having both types of computers or setting up any kind of network. This method is a nice (and less expensive) alternative to some of the options that have already been discussed. (You can also read data from a PC application into your Mac.)

Besides the transfer capability, you must also have some type of translation system, because the methods used by Mac and PC systems to record information are significantly different from one another.

The Apple File Exchange (AFE from Apple) software utility allows you to transfer files with ease and contains the majority of translators that you may need. You can also design a translator yourself. AFE is Apple's effort to increase the connections between the Mac and hundreds of other computers. The utility is not limited just to Macs and PCs, but it also allows exchanges between Macs, PCs, and PRO-DOS, the operating system for the family of Apple II computers.

Following is a typical AFE session that is easy:

1. Load the 5.25-inch DOS disk into the Apple 5.25-inch floppy drive (which you have to buy extra, of course).

2. Click the AFE translators (which you also need to purchase extra). They come with MacLink Plus, by the way. Once you do this, you see the screen shown in figure 15.9.

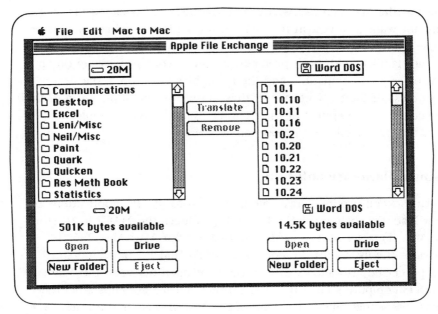

Fig. 15.9. Apple File Exchange screen.

3. Select the icon that represents the file you want to translate, and indicate the application you want to translate to.

4. Click to translate to a Mac file, and you're done!

Using Your Mac with PC Applications

Seeking and finding compatibility between all software programs and all applications is like Indiana Jones' pursuit of the Holy Grail, and if you choose the wrong chalice—but that's another story. Compatibility is a headache for all users, but it's an ache in the pocketbook for manufacturers. After all, if all hardware and software products were compatible, plenty of product developers could find themselves in trouble because some IBM/MS-DOS applications are superior to Mac applications and some Mac applications are superior to IBM applications.

People have many reasons for wanting compatibility between the Macintosh and other types of computers. You may not always want to train people to use a Mac. You may, instead, want them just to sit down at the Mac and use whatever PC application is called for, or you may not want to invest in the "whose translation" software-hardware game. Some people who have access to both Mac and IBM machines and are familiar with both prefer to do their word processing on an IBM or an IBM-compatible and their graphics work on a Mac. Regardless of their preference, if they could use the application of their choice on the computer of their choice, that capability would be a breakthrough. Well, it's (almost) already here.

Using a Hardware Solution

Today, several products available allow you to use PC applications on your Mac. For example, AST Research produces the MAC286.10 (for the Mac II), a set of two cards installed in your Mac. MAC286.10 provides the user with the equivalent of an IBM PC or AT personal computer and also allows data to be exchanged between the Mac and MS-DOS computers (like the IBM). The AST card contains a central coprocessor that takes advantage of the Mac II bus, or the traffic way along which information is sent from and received to the computer's brains. This special NuBus architecture allows the Mac to run both Mac and DOS software applications. With this setup, you can switch between PC and Mac applications and even cut and paste between them. To make the whole thing work, you need to hook up Apple's 5.25-inch disk drive.

In a sense, MAC286.10 gives you the best of both possible worlds (that is, until all the great PC applications are available as Mac applications, but even then some people will want to stick with their PCs).

So what's the down side? Basically, the costs—around $1,500, which is way more than you would have to spend to buy a PC clone with the cables and the software (such as TOPS) that you need to connect the two to transfer files and such. On the other hand, you may be in an environment where you cannot have two computers sitting side-by-side, or you have a constant use for one PC application that works well on the MACAST cards. Then MAC286.10 may be worth the price. A similar product, named the Mac 86, is also available as a coprocessor board.

Using Software Solutions

Hardware isn't the only way to go. For much less money, you can get that PC application on the screen of your Mac by using only software.

For example, SoftPC (from Insignia Solutions) emulates the processor in the IBM PC XT and allows you to run DOS applications in a window on your Macintosh II or IIx, or an SE if you have an accelerator board, which makes your Mac run faster. You also need at least 2M of RAM (and sometimes as much as 4M). As with the hardware solution discussed previously, you also need the Apple 5.25-inch drive. The costs? About $600. The advantage over the hardware solution? Cost, plain and simple. The disadvantage? Any software solution to reading DOS disks is slower than reading with hardware. Keep in mind that you may also have to buy more memory, which is expensive and brings the costs of the software solution and the hardware solution closer and closer.

Using Your Mac with Mainframes

Although relatively few of us need to connect regularly to a mainframe to do our daily memos and budgets, big business is more intent on using the Mac as a connection to mainframes then ever before. The Mac can easily be treated as a dumb terminal using any of the communications software discussed in Chapter 16. (Just dial and you're talking to your millions-per-second instructions supercomputer.) You also can use one of the specialized packages described in the following paragraphs. The obvious advantage, in either case, is that you can have your Mac speak to a mainframe rather than requiring a dedicated mainframe terminal located next to your Mac on an already crowded desk (right?). Just think of it. You can use your Mac to run Excel or

15
Networks

Fourth Dimension and then turn the task over to the mainframe to run the batch job on the mainframe.

As the world gets smaller and more connected, more personal computers will be talking directly with mainframes (the real big computers) more often then ever. So the name of the game is designing interfaces for the very large computers, such as those manufactured by DEC (Digital Equipment Corporation) and its family of VAX computers. DEC recently signed a marketing agreement with Apple. As you might expect, soon after the agreement was made public, small companies came forward with ideas and products to link the Mac to the VAX computers. These products include cables, new software, bridges, and terminal emulators. The computer industry is a business of ripple effects: one move in the market place never occurs in isolation. Product development, more often than not, leads to new products and so on.

One of these products is the DynaComm Asynchronous communications package from Future Soft Engineering, which produces a HyperCard stack. This package allows you to write scripts to create buttons (and other HyperCard tools) and to connect and work with the VAX family and the IBM family of mainframes. There's even software under development to allow users to take advantage of their Macintosh graphic interface when working with Cray supercomputers. Digital Communications (Alphareeta, GA) offers a whole line of micro-to-mainframe links, making your Macintosh compatible with IBM mainframes either in an interactive fashion or through terminal emulations.

Perhaps one of the most exciting and elegant solutions to the Mac-mainframe connection is Apple's MacWorkStation, which connects the Apple desktop to a mainframe. With MacWorkStation, you can access the power of an IBM or a VAX while at the same time working within a true Mac interface. Although the product has been around for almost five years, new enhancements are making it possible for in-house business managers to use the tool kit that comes with the software and tailor the mainframe connection to their business needs.

Doing without the Add-Ons

For some Mac users, the availability of a PC, a modem, networking software, or anything else that is needed to transfer files is out of the question. Also, many people may need to convert a file only once a year. Why go out and buy all that expensive stuff? In that case, try one of the many services that convert files for you from virtually any format to any other. Many of these companies convert from one format to another and from one medium to another.

For example, you can go from the old Xerox OS (Office System, which is stored on an 8-inch disk) to WordPerfect on a 3.5-inch disk on a disk-by-disk basis. Pivar Computing Services (312/459-6010) has been in business since 1982 (making it one of the oldest firms in the business). The service charges $35 for a PC-to-Mac file conversion (regardless of the application) or $35 for up to 240,000 characters (a full 5.25-inch PC disk can hold up to 360,000). In addition, Pivar supports more than 2,500 different file formats and gets your new disk out to you within 48 hours.

For comparison's sake, there's CompuData Translators (800/825-8251). These folks offer format conversions for "virtually all there is" at the rate of about $40 per disk for conversion from Mac-to-PC (and back again) or Mac-to-Mac application.

Using some of the networking technology discussed in this chapter, you can reach out to your neighbor across the hall or across the world. Networking with the Mac is still very new, and Apple's push toward more connectivity solutions is sure to act as a real catalyst for the development of more products in this area. Look for some shaking out in the future of those products that just don't hold up, and the establishment of some standards that will make networking a quick-connect process, just like attaching an external disk drive is now.

15
Networks

CHAPTER 16

Communications

Thousands of people today use personal computers to work from offices in their homes. Using your computer at home, you can now access information on almost any subject, check your stock prices, order your travel tickets, "talk" to a colleague in Tokyo, download a new desk accessory, and even share your frustrations with the president of a software company. If you have MultiFinder and sufficient memory, you can even download files while working on another task, such as writing a report or playing a game.

How can you do all this? Through telecommunications—the interaction between people and the exchange of information, using the personal computer over the telephone lines. If you haven't caught the bug yet, you will, because telecommunications is one of the next frontiers of personal computing.

This chapter introduces you to the world of telecommunications. First, you learn the basic equipment you need. Then you are given more detailed information about modems and software. You will find a survey of electronic mail and bulletin boards. Finally, you are introduced to information services.

Communications Basics

You need four items to get started in telecommunications:

- Your Macintosh computer
- A modem

- Communications software

- An open phone line

You probably already have the first item. In telecommunications your Macintosh sends and receives the information.

Second, a *modem* is a device that *mo*dulates and *dem*odulates electronic signals which represent information. The modem is connected to the computer and to the telephone line. In your Mac, data is formatted as digital signals. Telephones, however, because they are designed to transmit human voices, work as transmitters of analog signals. A modem converts the digital signal to an analog signal; this process is called *modulation*. The modem converts digital data (such as the *10000001* that represents the letter *A* in ASCII) to tones in order to transmit information to another computer. *Demodulation* is exactly the opposite; converting analog signals to digital. The modem converts tones to digital data in order to receive information. In other words, the modem acts as a translator.

No matter how sophisticated any part of your telecommunications system is, if your modem is cheap and doesn't do the job, the fanciest hardware in the world won't help at all. For example, some modems have filters. These filters screen out part of the noise that invades every telephone line and help ensure the accuracy of the transmission. When you are talking, this interference is just a nuisance. When you are telecommunicating, it can be a disaster because interference corrupts transmissions, and part of the data you send either does not arrive or is different from what you sent.

Third, to use a modem, you need communications software, which changes data into a form the modem can use. This software plays another important purpose: it begins and helps manage your session. With the software, you set the rules by which you will communicate with the other computer (through what is called a protocol), and you configure your system to match that of the computer you are trying to connect with. Some software even helps you to accomplish certain tasks, such as automatically logging on at a specified hour of the night (when rates are cheapest) and saying goodbye and disconnecting.

Finally, the telephone line you use may be a dedicated line just for telecommunications or a regular line that you also use for voice communications. If you have only one line for both voice and data, your voice line will be tied up when you are transmitting. This situation may not be a problem for you, because most transmissions don't take very long; however, some transmissions, such as downloading all of a new Macintosh System release, can take a long time. You cannot use a modem on a party line, and other special services, like call waiting, may give you trouble. If you do have call waiting, you should disable it before you begin your work session by following these steps:

1. Lift the receiver.

2. Press the * button.

3. Press 70.

Most serious users of telecommunications have two phone lines—one for voice and one for data communications. One of the lines is connected directly to the modem and the other to the phone. The phone lines can be connected directly to your modem, using a female phone jack receptacle; the modem connects to your computer modem port with an Apple cable similar to the one that connects your printer.

With telecommunications, you can share information directly with others, or you can easily gain access, for a fee, to such information providers as GEnie, BRS, CompuServe, and Dialog. These services are basically huge on-line databases and E-mail networks that you tap into by using your telecommunications hardware and software. Once you have logged on to one of these services, you can access any of the information that service has available.

There are also literally thousands of bulletin boards throughout the world to which you can link up without paying anything more than the costs of the telephone call. But bear in mind that telecommunications can be hazardous to your health and the health of your family. You could find yourself a BBS junkie in no time at all, staying up until all hours and talking to all kinds of people, exploring worlds you didn't know existed, and even playing games with your opponent 2,500 miles away.

Figure 16.1 shows the relationship among computers, modems, software, phone lines, and information providers. On each end of the connection are a computer, telecommunications software, and a modem. In effect, when you connect to an informations service, your modem is connected to a file server, which provides the information

16
Telecom.

you request. The two modems are connected by telephone lines. In some cases, the BBS or information provider you use may be able to connect you to a service like TeleNet, a nationwide network of local phone numbers that connect you to the main computer at the information provider. This way, you don't even have to pay for the phone call.

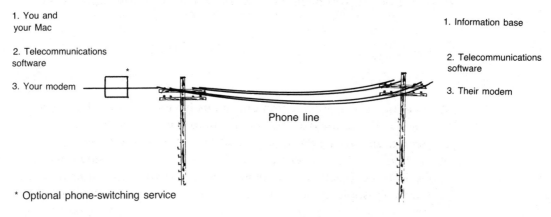

1. You and your Mac

2. Telecommunications software

3. Your modem

1. Information base

2. Telecommunications software

3. Their modem

Phone line

* Optional phone-switching service

Fig. 16.1. *A diagram of the basics of telecommunications.*

Definitions

Telecommunications has evolved into a kind of "buzz word central" with specialized terms for everything. Before the discussion of what your Mac should be capable of doing to join in the fun, you need to know the definitions of some basic terms. You will encounter the following terms throughout this chapter, where they are discussed in more detail.

ASCII file: A file consisting of characters that are universally readable as defined by the American Standard Code for Information Interchange. ASCII files contain no formatting information.

Baud: A unit of measure of the transmission of information. A 1200-baud modem transmits 1,200 pieces of information each second.

Bit: A piece of information such as one of the 1s or 0s that make up a unit of information called a *byte*.

Bulletin board (BBS): An electronic cousin to the bulletin board on which you tack up messages. On an electronic bulletin board, you leave and get messages, upload and download files, and access information over telephone lines.

Downloading: Transferring a file from another computer to yours.

Dumb terminal: A computer that acts as a receiver and transmitter of information but has no computing power of its own. A dumb terminal is sometimes referred to as a TTY terminal (from a teletype).

Full duplex: A protocol in which data flows in both directions simultaneously over transmission lines.

Half duplex: A protocol in which data flows in only one direction at a time over transmission lines.

Host: The computer or system that controls access to and management of the system. If I transfer a file from a bulletin board to my computer, the bulletin board is the host.

Information provider: A service containing information in various large databases, that you access through telecommunications.

Modem: An electronic device that modulates and demodulates information at different speeds (called the *baud rate*) to allow you to communicate with other computers.

Node: A specific device along a network.

Null modem: A cable device that directly connects two computers (without the use of modem), allowing one computer's output to become another computer's input.

On-line: A computer's status while it is in communication with another computer.

Protocol: A set of conventions that make possible the transfer of information between different sites. Some popular protocols are XModem, YModem, and Kermit.

Terminal emulation: When a computer acts as a terminal capable of receiving information.

Uploading: Transferring a file from your computer to another.

16
Telecom.

Getting Your Mac in Shape

Most articles and books that deal with telecommunications don't talk much about your Macintosh and the way to set it up for telecommunications activities. The reason for this omission is that telecommunications activities operate independently. You can have a quiet and gentle Mac Plus or the top-of-the-line, deep-pockets Mac IIcx with all the bells and whistles, and you will get the same basic quality of telecommunications results.

If you plan to use your Macintosh for telecommunications, it must have adequate memory to store downloaded information. You must also maintain a clearly understandable and well-designed system of storing files (see Chapter 4). A 40M hard disk should be all you need. Keep in mind, of course, that if you fill your disk with other files, you won't have much memory left for telecommunications.

Don't think, however, that top-of-the-line telecommunications equipment means spending the most money possible. You can use your floppy disk, your Mac 512, or a $200 2400-baud modem, and log on in the evening when the rates are lower.

Modems

People can share information without a modem, by using just a cable in a connection called a *null modem*. But it's impractical for everyone to have a separate cable. Imagine all the cables (500,000 at last count) that would have to run from all over the country to CompuServe's home office, for instance. Instead, we use modems.

The Mac uses external and internal modems. An external modem sits outside the computer. External modems are usually small boxes filled with electronic devices and having two phone jacks—one for your Mac and one for the phone. Some modems need an external source of power (they must be plugged into an electrical socket), but most run off the power the Mac draws. The first generation of modems were *acoustically coupled*, meaning that they required you to place the telephone handset on a platform with round receptacles that could be used to "speak" to another computer and then to "listen" to what that computer had to say. Today most modems are of the *direct connect* kind described in this chapter.

Modem Talk

With any modem and the transmission of data, you must follow certain conventions for information to be shared. These conventions are settings that are made either directly on the modem or through the use of the communications software that may come with the modem.

A *protocol* is the set of rules that dictate how the parties on the two ends of the telephone line will communicate with each other. When you speak with someone else in person, the protocol includes such rules as looking at each other, speaking the same language, not interrupting, and so forth. A telecommunications protocol consists of the same kinds of rules for communication. Protocols are often set by de facto standards, which usually turn out to be those being used by most of the people. A frequently used protocol is XModem, an error-correcting protocol.

In an effort to establish some consistency across protocols, the International Standards Organization (ISO) has developed a telecommunications model that has seven layers, each of which is important (but not critical) to successful communication between computers. To communicate with another computer, some, but not all, of these layers must be compatible. Which layers are compatible depends on both your hardware and your telecommunications software.

Here are the layers and a brief description of each:

- The *physical* layer consists of the hardware itself, including the modem, cables, and telephone lines.

- The *data link* layer deals with the way information is organized and sent from one location to another, including what is sent and when.

- The *network* layer controls the actual sending of the data and its routing from location to location.

- The *transport* layer confirms that the information sent is the information received.

- The *session* layer deals with the way different computers use protocols to ensure that they coordinate their activities so that both are not sending at the same time.

16
Telecom.

- The *presentation* layer works with the format of the communication to ensure that it is understandable when received.

- The *application* layer formats data so that it can be used by an application.

A variety of protocols are used, but you will most likely run into two kinds when you have to make decisions regarding telecommunications. A *half-duplex protocol* allows information to flow in both directions between the sender and the receiver, but data can be sent in only one direction at any one time. A *full-duplex protocol* sends information in both directions simultaneously. This method is fast but can run into problems, just as two people do during a telephone conversation when both begin talking at the same time. The coordination of sending and receiving simultaneously can present some difficulty with this type of protocol. Finally, there's *echoplex*, an add-on to a full-duplex system. (Ever see the ECHO ON message on your computer screen?) Echoplex lets you know that the data has been transmitted and then checked for the accuracy of the transmission. The data, in other words, is echoed to double-check that what was sent was what arrived. Most communications systems use a half-duplex system.

Protocols are controlled by software. The protocols used in telecommunications vary depending on the type of information you want to transfer. For example, MicroPhone II offers several protocols that are used for different purposes. The Text protocol allows you to transfer files saved as ASCII or text files; the XModem and MacTerminal protocols are designed for the transfer of specific file formats.

Modems can communicate at a variety of different speeds, which are measured in *baud rates*. The most common speeds are 300, 1,200, and 2,400 baud. *Baud* is a measurement of how often information goes from digital (1011100) to audio and back again. The term is named for French communications expert J. M. E. Baudot. The faster the modem (higher the baud rate), the faster you can send information. Faster modems, however, are usually more expensive than slower ones, as is accessing information at a faster rate. The faster modems are usually less expensive, however, on a data exchange basis.

In order for you to communicate with another telecommunications source, your modem's speed and your computer's baud rate setting must match those of the computer with which you are communicating. This process is known as *handshaking*. Any modem can receive transmissions at baud rates that are less than the modem's setting. For example, a 1200-baud modem can adjust to receive a 300-baud transmission, but the reverse is not true. A 300-baud modem cannot receive 1200-baud transmissions.

Historically, the most common rate at which information is transmitted has been 300 baud, but that rate is quickly being passed by for 1,200 baud. In turn, 1,200 baud is now being replaced by 2,400 baud. And as soon as the price comes down and compatibility between senders and receivers is established, you will see the standard rate increase to 4,800 and then 9,600 baud.

Figure 16.2 compares different baud rates with file sizes. Keep in mind, however, that baud rate alone does not determine how quickly (or accurately) data is transmitted. The protocol the modem uses and the density of the data also affect transmission speed. You can send more information when it is compressed using a utility like StuffIt (from Raymond Lau). Compressing a file reduces its size, creating a smaller file that contains the same amount of information. Of course, to use the file after transmission, it must be "unstuffed."

Modem Speed in bps	Word Document (saved as ASCII file)	Transmission Time
300	10 pages	2 minutes
	20 pages	4 minutes
1200	10 pages	30 seconds
	20 pages	1 minute
2400	10 pages	15 seconds
		30 seconds
4800	10 pages	10 seconds
	20 pages	20 seconds
9600	10 pages	less than 10 seconds
	20 pages	less than 10 seconds

Fig. 16.2. Bits-per-second rates and file sizes.

Modems also differ in the efficiency with which they check for errors in the information they send and receive. A transmission is sent in blocks, and your modem or telecommunications program verifies that the transmission is complete and accurate.

Parity checking, often referred to simply as *parity*, is the method that a modem and the associated software use to check each data bit (all the 1s and 0s) to see whether any erroneous information (such as interference on the telephone line) is being passed on. In the simplest terms, parity involves totaling the digits of the binary transmission on both ends. Parity can be odd, even, or none. The parity is selected by the users at both ends of the telecommunications link and has to be the same. For the most part, parity is usually set at no parity because communications software usually includes sophisticated error-checking routines to ensure the clean transmission of data.

Start and *stop bits* indicate when a character is beginning (start bit) and when it is ending (stop bit). The start bit tells the computer that information is coming and helps it get ready for the transmission. The stop bit is the last bit in a character and defines its end. The type of communication in which characters are preceded by start bits and followed by stop bits is known as *asynchronous* communication. *Synchronous* communication does not use start and stop bits and is used primarily to move data between mainframe computers. It does not use the start and stop signals because the mainframes incorporate software that precisely times the transmission of the data, a feat that requires more complex circuitry than is available (or affordable or cost-effective) in asynchronous modems for computers like the Mac.

Although getting started with telecommunications and working on-line is not difficult, you can't just plug in and play. To work with a modem and telecommunications software, you must be aware of the points just mentioned. In order for both ends of the line to shake hands, they must be able to communicate with each other in the same language and at the same speed, at the same time checking that what they are saying makes sense. Telephone your BBS or on-line service or check their documentation to find the correct settings for communications with that service.

MacBinary

In any new movement, after most of the bugs are out, people realize the need for a standard set of rules in order for further development to take place. MacBinary is a standard communications protocol for the Macintosh, first proposed by Dennis Brothers in 1985.

MacBinary is intended for communication between Macs that are connected but that may not be running the same terminal programs. MacBinary's primary advantage is that it can transfer documents directly from one location to another without converting the file, as long as it is a Mac file. Because no conversion is needed, time and money are saved, and the whole process becomes increasingly more efficient. In addition, MacBinary is not dependent on the type of telecommunications protocol you are using, so MacBinary works with many available programs.

Choosing a Modem

Modems range in price from around $250 up to several thousand for the fastest and most sophisticated. What do you need? Here are some guidelines.

First, be sure that the modem you buy is Hayes AT Command Set compatible. Hayes began manufacturing modems in the early 1970s and has set the standard by which other modems are designed. Hayes and Hayes-compatible modems are compatible with the modems used by all the large on-line databases.

Second, consider the speed you will need. You can switch some modems from 300 to 1,200 baud (or faster) so that you can match other modems' rates of transmission. You can expect to pay more for a faster modem. For the higher price, you get faster sharing of information. Speed is most important when you are downloading large files from an information provider, and you want to minimize the on-line telephone charges. Some information providers charge more when you use a faster modem, but you still may save money in the end by being on the phone less time.

Third, some modems come with a buffer, a temporary storage place where incoming information can be stored until you unload it. The buffer lets you use your modem like a small electronic-mail service.

16
Telecom.

Some modems come packaged with communications software, so don't let the modem itself be the sole consideration in your decision. You can use some telecommunications software to set modem capabilities; such software is more flexible than the modem. Software packages differ markedly in the options they present. For example, both InTalk (from Palantir) and MicroPhone II (from Software Ventures) can transfer at a baud rate of up to 57,600, but MicroPhone allows for transferring files in the background while you are doing other tasks. Buy the modem that comes with the telecommunications software which does what you want.

Fourth, what will you use the modem for? If you are going to hook up during the evening just to find out how the Yankees did yesterday, get the least expensive model that will do what you want. For transferring huge quantities of data, you may want to consider the fastest modem you can afford (at least 2,400 bps).

Fifth, what kind of data will you be sending? Text (in ASCII files) is transmitted much more slowly than data formatted in specific file formats—especially if you have MacBinary to transfer formatted files. You may be able to use a 1,200 rather than a 2,400 bps modem if you will be transmitting mostly text. The savings can be $100 or more.

Some modems automatically answer, dial, and redial. With such a modem, you can have a colleague in another city transmit a large data file to you during the night when long distance rates are lower and your machine is not tied up with other work.

You should also ask yourself the following questions before buying a modem:

- Is the modem setup procedure accomplished through software, hardware, or a combination of both?

- Can the speaker volume be adjusted?

- How many phone jacks are available on the modem?

- What kind of a warranty comes with the modem?

What's Available

Modems for the Macintosh have different features, with some having outstanding capabilities. The modems range in price from $50 to almost $4,000.

The standard modems are the Hayes family. For the Mac, there's the Smartmodem 9600 with software tools that allow you to control such features as speaker volume and transmission mode and to memorize phone numbers. You are not limited to 9,600 bps either: you can use the compression tool that comes with the software in order to increase the transmission rate to almost 19,000 bps.

The most convenient modem comes from Migent. Its size (5 by 3 by 1 inch) will make it terrific for use with the laptop Mac when it comes out and even for the traveler who now visits different sites with Macs and needs to transmit information back and forth. With a 1,200 bps rate and costing only $259, the Migent is the least expensive "portable" around. This modem is no powerhouse as far as speed and options, but you can carry it in your pocket. You clearly pay for the convenience of the small size when you can get 2400-baud modems for $200 from such companies as Practical Peripherals.

You can place a modem inside your Mac, but you can also place the MacBottom modem inside the MacBottom hard drive (as a $200 option when you buy the drive). The MacBottom drive fits under the Mac, as does the modem, saving a significant amount of work space.

One of the fastest modems around is the zoom....Codex 2260 (from Codex), which can transmit at 9,600 bps. This modem has convenient front panel adjustments and comes with an internal directory for storing up to nine phone numbers, all at a mere $3,495.

Even faster is the TrailBlazer (from Telebit), which can transmit information at 18,000 bps (9,600 without any data compression routine). This modem, which retails for about $1,500, can talk to other machines through their modems at 300, 1,200, and 2,400 and adjusts its speed, if necessary to be sure that any errors are corrected.

16
Telecom.

One way to save money when telecommunicating is by using a data compression program like that offered by the Telcor Accelerator. Some text documents can be compressed to 50 percent of their original size. Of course, the person receiving the transmission must also have a

Telcor to decompress the transmission. With the Telcor you can create passwords to guard files and even program specialized modem commands for transmitting at certain times of the day in certain file formats.

Telecommunications Costs

To determine whether it's worth it for you to get into the telecommunications race, consider the following variables and weigh them against such express mail services as Federal Express, UPS Blue Label, and the post office's overnight delivery:

- File size

- Number of files (or amount of data) transmitted

- Costs of transmission

- Frequency of transmission

- Costs of equipment

The more you use your telecommunications equipment, the less it costs, but unless you telecommunicate regularly, the equipment may not be worth the expense or trouble involved.

The deregulation of telephone companies has brought with it an incredible amount of bureaucracy but also the benefits of reduced prices. You can take advantage of these rates. For example, MCI and Sprint, as well as AT&T's other big competitors, have services for data transmission, including dedicated data lines (also called leased lines) at reduced cost.

Even if you do not have a dedicated line for data transmission, your costs will still be reduced through the companies that rent lines rather than from the owner (AT&T). Keep in mind that the phone line is just that. When you need help getting things set up, you will have to decide for yourself which company is most helpful and which has the "cleanest" lines.

Shared Modems

Just as peripherals like laser printers can be shared, so can modems. NetModem (from Shiva) allows you to network a single modem using AppleTalk. Once NetModem is set up, you simply select it from the Chooser and begin telecommunicating. At a price under $600 (about the cost of one 1200-baud modem for use on a network), you can save quite a bit of money over the cost of buying modems for each user. (Refer to Chapter 15 for more information about networks.)

Communications Software

The software is probably the most flexible of all the components of a telecommunications system. These software packages all do basically the same thing: they allow you to send and receive files. But good programs go beyond this simple function. The following list describes features that characterize the better programs:

- Use of a command language (such as macros) for customizing telecommunications functions (often called scripts)

- Use of on-screen buttons (rather than physical buttons on the modem unit) to control functions

- Support of multiple protocols (so that you can communicate with as many different modems as possible)

- Support of all major protocols, especially Text, MacBinary, and XModem and YModem

- Terminal emulation (so that your Mac can act like a "dumb" terminal)

- Transmission of graphics

- Transmission of color

- On-screen timing with billing to help you keep track of how much time you spend on-line with an information provider and of basic on-line phone charges

- On-screen help

- Automatic answering, dialing, and redialing

16
Telecom.

- Interactive telecommunications (where you work with another computer)

- Filters to remove garbage characters that are incidental to the transmission

This list is not all-inclusive, but it should give you some idea as to what features are desirable. Keep in mind, however, that you may not need all these features in the same program, even if they are available. As with other purchases, buy what you think will best fit your needs.

Especially with telecommunications software, there is a tradeoff between the number of features available and the program's power and user friendliness. Unlike word processors and spreadsheets, telecommunications software is not particularly intuitive; and for many people, it may be downright alien. This lack of user friendliness is partly the result of the complexity of the telecommunications process and the many variables, such as speed, parity settings, and other settings.

A Sample Session

Of all the programs available, MicroPhone II (from Software Ventures) seems to offer the best balance of power and user friendliness. MicroPhone II is based on MacTep, written by Dennis Brothers, the author of the original MicroPhone, and is one of the most successful commercial telecommunications programs available. Special features that MicroPhone offers are MultiFinder support, the capability to launch an application from within MicroPhone so that you can download a file and continue working with another application, and a sophisticated scripting language for customizing your telecommunications operations.

The software includes a series of setup files to use to communicate with such telecommunications services as GEnie, CompuServe, MCI mail, and Dow Jones. In fact, these files are really scripts already written for you. You just click the appropriate icon and you're ready to go.

Figure 16.3 shows the set of commands for the log-on script for CompuServe. These prepared scripts save you time because you do not need to know the command language to use them.

```
Tue, May 30, 1989 9:06 AM
 Settings File = CompuServe
 Script Name = LOG ON
 Command Key =
 F-key =
 Menu = YES
 Button = YES


1    Dial Service * "CompuServe"
2    Wait Seconds  "4"
3    Set Variable teststring from Expression  "=THELINE(CURSORROW)"
4    When Text Equals  "please type your terminal identifier"
5      Send Text String  "A"
6      Wait for Text  "PLEASE LOG IN"
7      Send Text String  "CPS^M"
8  Or When Expression  "=(pos('x',teststring)>0) or (pos('`',teststring)>0)"
9      Send Text String  "A"
10     Wait for Text  "PLEASE LOG IN"
11     Send Text String  "CPS^M"
12 Or When Text Equals   ""
13     Send Text String  "^M"
14     Wait Seconds  "3"
15     When Text Equals  "Host Name:  "
16       Send Text String  "CIS^M"
17     Or When Text Equals   ""
18       Send Text String  "^M"
19       Wait for Text  "TERMINAL="
20       Send Text String  "D1^M"
21       Wait for Text  "@"
22       Send Text String  "C 202202^M"
23     End When
24   End When
25   Wait for Text  "User ID: "
26   Send Text from File  "your CIS ID#"
27   Send Text String  "^M"
28   Wait for Text  "Password:"
29   Send Text from File  "your CIS password"
30   Send Text String  "^M"
```

Fig. 16.3. *A script for logging on to CompuServe.*

With MicroPhone you can easily log on to an information provider like CompuServe, one of the largest electronic information providers in the world. The following instructions assume that you have already set up your modem.

First, you select the icon marked CompuServe from MicroPhone's opening screen (see fig. 16.4). The menus across the top of the resulting screen show the options available with MicroPhone. The Settings menu allows you to set all the important parameters necessary for your modem, taking a great deal of the headache (and stumbling blocks) out of getting started. Figure 16.5 shows the Communication Settings dialog box. Here you specify such settings as baud rate, stop bits, parity, and so on, depending on your telecommunications software.

16
Telecom.

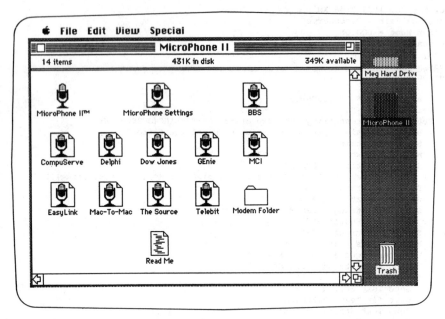

Fig. 16.4. *The MicroPhone II opening screen.*

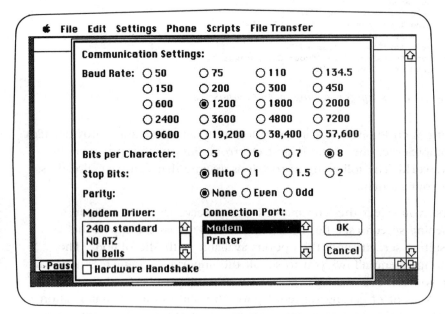

Fig. 16.5. *The Communication Settings dialog box used to set modem features.*

To dial the service you want to use, select the Create Service command from the Phone menu. You will see the screen shown in figure 16.6. Now you dial the service you want to use. A list of services and their phone numbers is given later in this chapter.

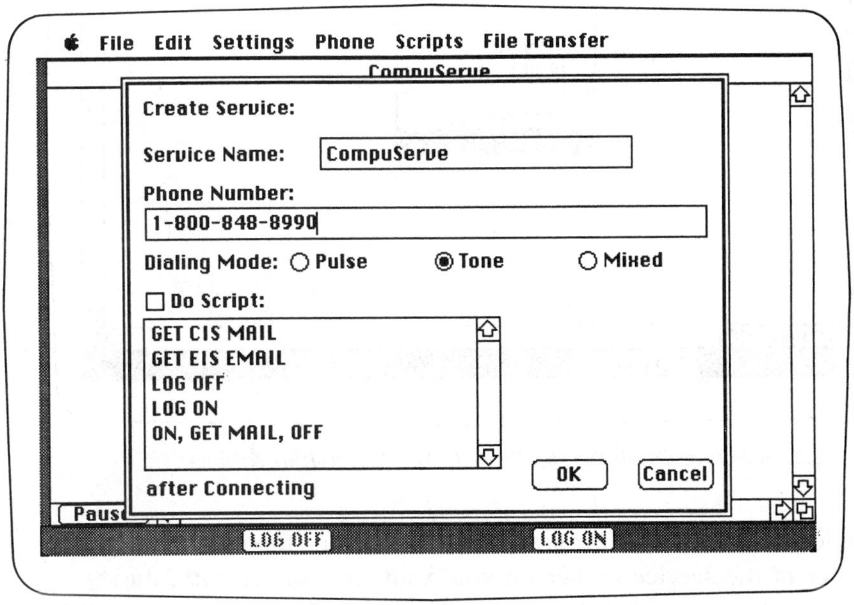

Fig. 16.6. *The Create Service dialog box.*

Enter the requested information: the name of the service, the phone number (which the service provides), and the type of phone you have—touch-tone or pulse (rotary). Once you are finished, click the OK button.

Now you are ready to connect. Select the CompuServe command from the Phone menu (see fig. 16.7). Through your Mac's modem speaker, you will hear the number being dialed. Next you will see a message from CompuServe, indicating that you are connected and ready to go and that the meter is running (you are being charged).

The first time you sign on to any telecommunications service, you will have to subscribe to it by supplying all kinds of information, especially instructions for billing you—most require the use of a major credit card like MasterCard or VISA. Some services, like GEnie, allow you to sign up on-line; others, like NewsNet, require a completed application form.

16

Telecom.

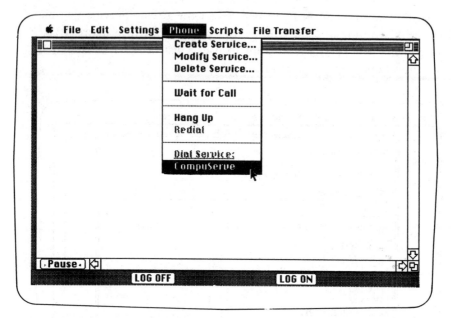

Fig. 16.7. Selecting CompuServe after setting up communications.

All telecommunications programs have you enter the name and phone number of the service or person you want to connect with; the programs then dial. MicroPhone lets you skip the tedious script work that other programs require when you select the service you want.

Other Telecommunications Programs

MicroPhone is a terrific program, but it is not the only one available, and it may not be the one you need. Another popular program, Red Ryder (from FreeSoft), was the first terminal emulation program for the Mac. Red Ryder was shareware for the first nine versions; with Version 10.0, Scott Watson, the author, finally released the software commercially.

Red Ryder may be the most powerful and flexible telecommunications program available, which is a mixed blessing. Because of its flexibility, you are responsible for crucial settings and selection of options. If you don't have any telecommunications experience, you may find Red Ryder to be too complex. On the other hand, if you really want to learn the telecommunications process from the ground floor up and have the time and patience, Red Ryder is your best bet. In addition to every feature necessary for complete telecommunications, Red Ryder allows on-screen buttons representing macros you create.

Smartcom II (from Hayes) has a scrollable buffer that allows you to read through previous on-screen information that has been saved. Smartcom also supports full color. Whereas other programs use scripts or macros, Smartcom uses *autopilots*, which are basically the same thing: a set of stored instructions that you invoke through the click of a button. Like MicroPhone, Smartcom includes autopilots which you need to get started with many of the major on-line information providers.

Electronic Mail

One of the most frequent uses for telecommunications software is creating electronic mail, or E-mail, the equivalent of letters and memos that never see a mailbox. E-mail creates an electronic mailbox, a central storage system, where people can access mail left for them and leave mail intended for other people. Many E-mail users rely on telecommunications software like Red Ryder or MicroPhone and the large services such as MCI Mail and CompuServe as their central mailboxes; such arrangements are called public E-mail.

Other people establish private E-mail networks within their own organizations, using a program like CE's QuickMail. For example, suppose that you come to your office at 8 a.m. You log on to your E-mail system and find that you have three messages waiting for you. You select what appears to be the most important (it's from the boss), read it, and send your answer. In this way, you can respond to messages from the boss next door or from a company halfway around the world. E-mail is inexpensive and as quick as a phone call. Today's popular software makes E-mail easy as well.

Public E-Mail Services

Public E-mail is big business. Leaders like MCI and AT&T have hundreds of thousands of subscribers. Using public E-mail is easy, inexpensive, and, best of all, reliable. When you send a message, you can tell whether it has been received; several services even have the option of letting you know when your message has been read.

16
Telecom.

As with information providers, most services offer a starter kit that includes your ID number, instructions, and sometimes a certificate for free time to encourage you to use the service. You will probably have to give the company a credit card number so that the company can bill you automatically. Established businesses (with appropriate credit ratings) can be billed directly.

To use an E-mail service, you sign on, give your password, and check for mail. E-mail systems differ from one another, but in all cases, your first option is to check your mailbox for any messages.

Public E-Mail Software

Several products are designed exclusively for use with E-mail systems. One popular program is Desktop Express (from Dow Jones). Desktop Express uses MCI Mail to transfer documents from one Macintosh to another without any concern for matching protocols and other modem parameters, making this software especially easy for beginners to use. But what happens when you send your partner a Full Impact spreadsheet and he or she does not have Full Impact? Desktop Express comes with Glue. With Glue, you can read any file, regardless of the application that was used to create it. Even though you can't edit the file, you can receive it and view it.

One major shortcoming of Desktop Express is that it is not a total communications package, so you cannot go on-line to other data services or to another Mac. You are limited to MCI Mail and the Dow Jones news service. The program costs $149 and includes a full year of MCI Mail service.

Public E-Mail Costs

Figure 16.8 shows what some of the major services charge to use E-mail. Keep in mind that the major competition is the United States Postal Service at $.25 for the first ounce and one to seven days for delivery and Federal Express at $12.50 for next-morning delivery.

Private E-Mail

Private (sometimes called corporate) E-mail has some distinct advantages over using an E-mail service. First, the system is totally

Service	AT&T	EasyLink	MCI Mail
Phone	(800) 367-7225	(800) 435-7375	(800) MCI-2255
Basic Charge	$2/month	$.35/minute at 300 baud	$18/year for mailbox fee
WATS Line Access	$.15 minute	$.30/connection	$.05/minute (TYM-NET access)
Hard Copy Charge	$2.00 US mail	$1.50/ first page and	$2/three-page letter
	$7.50 overnight	.50 each additional	$8.00 overnight
	$27.50 same day	20% surcharge on	$30/four-hour letter
		priority delivery	
Telex Messages	$.70 minute	unavailable	unavailable
Messages	$.20/message	unavailable	unavailable
Signature Registration	$12/each	unavailable	$20/year
Other Services ($)		News Service Access	Bulletin Boards
		Official Airline Guide	Dow Jones News
		Database Availability	

Fig. 16.8. A comparison of E-mail services.

under your control. You set it up, select who will be on the service, and decide what options will be available. When things go wrong, you fix them.

Second, security is almost guaranteed, although no system is truly impenetrable. Messages on public services may be read by people other than the intended receivers. The public companies would probably be reluctant to admit that, but the more people who have general access, the higher the likelihood (no matter how small) for a potential leak.

Third, over a long period of time the cost of private E-mail can be much less than that of public E-mail. With most private E-mail programs, the cost of the software is your only expense. You do not have annual fees or a charge for each message.

Private E-mail has drawbacks, however. Someone must be the administrator, or the custodian, and be sure that each node works as it should. If the person you are asking to assume that important task already has another job with other responsibilities, some aspect of your business may suffer. In addition, if hardware must be dedicated for the mail system's storage places, you must consider that added expense in deciding whether to set up an E-mail system.

16
Telecom.

Private E-Mail Software

QuickMail 2.0 (from CE Software) is an easy-to-use E-mail program that you purchase according to the number of users on the system. QuickMail requires that you have a hard disk drive and that all nodes be connected with AppleTalk-compatible cables. The manual walks you through the setup routines, and an informative HyperCard stack (as well as a hard copy of the same information) titled "The E-Mail Primer" introduces you to what E-mail is all about.

When you install QuickMail, you are creating a message center to contain individual mailboxes.

Figure 16.9 shows the opening screen for creating a new mail center. The process is as simple as naming the center and then entering a password. Once you have created the mail center, several additional dialog boxes appear asking you to provide information about times when a log of users should be sent to the custodian, priorities for different classes of messages, and more. QuickMail keeps track of messages, times the mail center is contacted, the number of messages waiting to be sent from a mail center, and the number of top-priority messages waiting to be sent from a mail center.

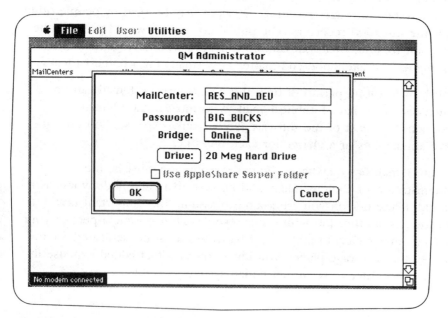

Fig. 16.9. Creating a QuickMail mail center.

QuickMail offers several features that make it comprehensive and especially nice to use (and set it apart from other private E-mail programs):

- Several bridges allow you to go to other networks, including ones using UNIX; you can use the QM-Connect bridge to receive stock and commodity quotes from MacNet and the QM-Serial bridge for talking with mainframes.

- The Telecom bridge allows you to contact any of the information providers, giving you the equivalent of a complete telecommunications package.

- Real-time conferencing—talking back and forth on the screen is supported (see fig. 16.10). Transmissions are acted on immediately and not stored for later use. Messages being sent appear in italic; messages received appear in boldface.

- Storing and forwarding features keep messages until they are accessed by the receiver.

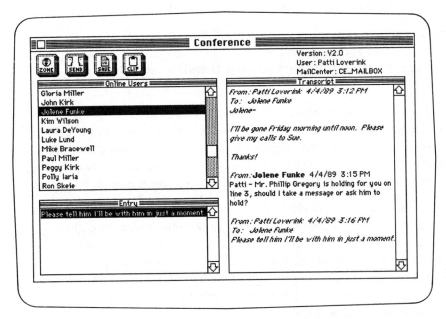

Fig. 16.10. *The QuickMail real-time conferencing feature.*

16
Telecom.

Microsoft Word 4.0 also has a Mail feature, which allows you to send and receive mail in a network—a nice addition. Word is the only word processor with this feature.

Private E-Mail Costs

The major advantage to using a private system is that the system is under your control and threats to security can be minimized—but don't relax too much, because the threat is always present. Over the long run, private systems can be cheaper as well. For example, the QuickMail package (for 10 users) sells for $399.95; the only other expenses are some setup costs. If you were to use public E-mail, your on-line and service costs would quickly match that amount.

The World of Bulletin Boards

```
5/1/89 1:20 AM
Please provide your ID: Whacky Wordman

**********Welcome to WordPerfect Forum********

Please remember our rules and tell a friend
about the WordPerfect Forum. What's your question?
```
*How can I get WordPerfect to do a headline and then do columns?

It's after 1:00 in the morning, and Whacky Wordman has signed on to an electronic bulletin board to ask a question about WordPerfect 5.0. Tomorrow morning, he will sign on to the bulletin board again and probably find 10 to 20 answers to his question. The information is free, and the telephone connect charges at that hour are minimal.

In addition to big commercial information providers, noncommercial information sources, commonly known as bulletin boards, are also available. A bulletin board (BBS) is an electronic bulletin board containing memos, real-time conversations, programs that can be downloaded, games, and every type of electronic information you can imagine. All this information is made accessible to others through their telecommunications systems.

Bulletin boards, which come in virtually all sizes and are targeted at different types of computer users, are a labor of love. They are usually run by system operators (SYSOPS) and sometimes (but rarely) charge a membership fee. BBSs are by all measures a shining example of the power of the personal computer and ways people can share information. Most bulletin boards have three divisions:

- E-mail for sharing private messages

- Public messages for sharing information with other BBS users

- Public-domain and shareware files that are accessible by BBS users

The third division is the most important, for here the entire shareware market is open to thousands of people beyond the circle of friends of the developer. This division is where the advertising for new products takes place, and you can easily download to your own hard disk the thousands of programs that are available from a BBS. Some SYSOPS charge for their services, some request a donation, and others don't charge anything. How any of them stay in business is always a mystery; it is no surprise that few survive the day-to-day rigor of uploading and downloading files, answering mail, and cleaning up files, to say nothing of having to dedicate a Macintosh and a hard drive to the BBS.

Appendix D lists bulletin boards from which you can choose to get started. Each board is different, and all display some kind of introductory statement the first time you sign on in order to acquaint you with what they do. Here are some rules of etiquette (do's and don'ts) you need to follow:

- Don't sign on and download hundreds of files in one sitting. Many boards allow only one person to sign on at a time.

- Don't abuse the BBS system by uploading commercial software.

- Don't use anything you download unless you are sure that it is virus free (see Chapter 3). Use a virus detector to check the file that was downloaded to a floppy disk.

- Don't use abusive or profane language or insult other people on the line.

- Do make a contribution if it's called for.

- Do share the BBS with other Mac friends, encouraging them to join.

16
Telecom.

- Do be sure to follow the rules of the BBS on which you are working (sign-on and sign-off procedures, downloading, bug testing, and so on).

- Do respect other users' privacy. Many people use code names for anonymity and don't want others prying.

Information Services

Now it is time to consider the commercial information services, which focus on providing through telecommunications information on every conceivable topic. From the standpoint of Mac users, commercial information services fall into three categories.

First, services like CompuServe and GEnie have *forums*, or sections that are devoted solely to Macintosh users and Macintosh products, as well as sources for general information.

Second, others, such as MacNet, are devoted exclusively to Macintosh interests.

Third, some services, such as Dialog, are devoted exclusively to providing information with nothing specific to Macintosh products or procedures.

Your modem, telecommunications software, and Mac can easily access each type of service. All you need to do is to subscribe to the service, call it, and pay. You can often subscribe on-line. Several computer periodicals contain advertisements for these services, that list toll-free numbers you can call to sign on. With some services you will receive some free connect time when you sign up. You will have to supply a credit card number to open your account, and you will have to give the company a billing address. If you are a novice, be sure to find out what kind of support (preferably toll-free) the companies offer. You might even test them with a question like, "What's the difference between prime-time and non-prime-time rates?"

What's Out There

Some of the bigger services and what they have to offer are described here. Figure 16.11 shows rates for each service.

	NewsNet	Connect
Speciality	Newsletters and News wires	
Phone Number	800-345-1301	800-262-2638
Membership Cost	No sign up fee, but $15/mo. maintenance (min.)	None. MacNet software is $75
On Line Cost/Peak	$60 (but can be higher for full text)	$8
On Line Cost/Not Peak	$60 (but can be higher for full text)	$4
Number of Databases	375	Special forums
Cust. Service Support	yes	yes
On-Line Help	yes	yes
TimeNet/Telenet?	yes	Local access

	Orbit	CompuServe	Dow Jones
Speciality	Scientific, technical, and patent	Broad base general use information provider	Business and finance
Phone Number	800-456-7248	800-848-8990	609-452-1511
Membership Cost	None	$30	$30
On Line Cost/Peak	Phone connect charge + $13/hr.	$12.50/hr.	1.30/min.
On Line Cost/Not Peak	Phone connect charge + $13/hr.	same	0.80/min.
Number of Databases	100	900	50
Cust. Service Support	yes	yes	yes
On-Line Help	yes	yes	yes
TimeNet/Telenet?	yes	yes	Both

Fig. 16.11. *A comparison of services and rates.*

CompuServe, with more than 500,000 subscribers, now owns its former main competitor, The Source. All The Source's accounts have been transferred to CompuServe.

CompuServe gets you right into on-line activities with two or more hours of free time when you subscribe on-line or through the mail. CompuServe offers news, weather, sports, travel, shopping, E-mail, financial information, and access to other information services, including more than 900 bibliographic databases and more than 20,000 abstracts (or brief summaries) of articles about personal computers and product reviews.

For Mac users, CompuServe offers several forums under the Micronetworked Apple User Group:

- Personal Productivity Forum focuses on increasing your productivity with your Mac in such applications as word processing, desktop publishing, and programming. The simple word GOPRO gets you right into word processing.

- Arts and Entertainment serves people who want to explore using their Mac for music and art.

16
Telecom.

- Business User's Forum discusses business applications and software, which includes The Job Market, for people looking for or wanting to fill jobs in Mac-related settings.

- Games and more. Imagine playing chess with your cousin in Portland, Oregon, while you are in sunny Miami.

Best of all for Mac users is CompuServe Navigator, software that greatly increases the speed and power of your on-line activities. You can even select your destination (for example, the forum you want to go to) before you go on-line and then run the script through Navigator to arrive where you want at a greatly decreased cost. Navigator costs less than $100 (an amount you will save in a few sessions).

The main advantage of GEnie (from General Electric) is its reduced charges. For example, other than prime time, GEnie is about 20 percent cheaper than other companies. It offers the Macintosh RoundTable with thousands of files ready to be downloaded, as well as a Mac bulletin board to keep you informed of what's happening in the Mac community. GEnie also offers Business & News, Comp-U-Store (home shopping), on-line travel assistance, and on-line reference to travel guides.

Dialog contains more than 300 individual databases, giving you access to on-line abstracts of important articles in several different disciplines. For example, Dialog includes 65 databases in business, 6 in chemistry, and 24 in the humanities and social sciences. Dialog has access to more databases than any other similar service. Dialog also offers Telenet (at a cost to the user) and DIALNETZ, Dialog's own telephone system. Dialog has also recently announced ImageCatcher, designed to work as a DA with Mac telecommunications software. You can search, display, and print images and text.

BRS (for Bibliographic Retrieval Services), consisting of several different products, is much like CompuServe but not as comprehensive. BRS consists of BRS/Search service with access to 150 databases, BRS/Colleague (which contains the same information as BRS/Search), and BRS/After Dark, a reduced version of BRS/Search available during off hours (about 6 p.m. to 8 a.m.). Search and Colleague differ in the type of interface they use. Search is command and menu driven; Colleague is just menu driven. Although commands are quicker and more to the point, menus don't require as much training and allow for explorations without knowing the intricacies of the system.

If you need technical and scientific information, Orbit is one of the places to look. Like other information providers, Orbit uses on-line English commands to help you find what you want. Among Orbit's more than 80 databases are the following:

- LitAlert
- Chemical Economics Handbook
- Aqualine
- Inspec
- ACCOUNTANTS
- Ceramic Abstracts
- FOREST
- LABORDOC

Business and finance information is available from Dow Jones News/Retrieval. Dow Jones claims to be the only provider devoted exclusively to business information. The service has the complete edition of the *Wall Street Journal* on-line, as well as text from such publications as *Barron's, Business Week, Forbes,* and *Money* magazine. Dow Jones also offers a complete line of financial analysis software, such as Market Manager PLUS, which you can use to perform stock analyses after downloading market prices from one of the databases available on Dow Jones News/Retrieval.

NewsNet offers access to more than 360 newsletters dealing with such topics as metals and mining, investment, energy, travel, chemistry, education, and defense. In addition, NewsNet offers NewsFlash, a clipping service that scans more than 3,000 articles and selects the ones that have the key words you have identified. NewsFlash "looks through" the information on 10 major national and international news wires, meaning that you can get the information before it appears in the newspaper.

CONNECT may be all you want if you're a true Mac fan. CONNECT is an information network, not an information provider, and is devoted to

16
Telecom.

the transmission of information as quickly and efficiently as possible. CONNECT is the gateway through which you access information from other databases. This service is especially nice for Macintosh users, because the MacNet software used for communicating with CONNECT has the familiar Mac interfaces and allows you to transmit Mac information and graphics easily. CONNECT has by far the largest number of forums for access to producers of such Macintosh products as TOPS, CE Software, Aldus, Fifth Generation, Sun Remarketing, Quark, and HyperX, as well as some 1,700 organizations (not all are Mac, but many are) connected by CONNECT. This young company charges $4 per hour during off-peak times, the lowest of any of the services examined here.

How To Choose an Information Provider

If you are new to the telecommunications game and are considering signing up with one of the services, the following tips may help you avoid some pitfalls.

First, send for an information packet or a subscription kit. Then you can study the information and call the service with your questions (most have toll-free numbers).

Second, note the different types of charges for the different baud rates at different times. For example, GEnie charges only $5 an hour between 6 p.m. and 8 a.m. and all day on Saturdays, Sundays, and holidays; weekday charges are much higher.

Third, check the availability of local connections to save connect charges. For example, when I call almost any service, I have to go through a town about 25 miles away, so my connect time is in addition to the actual service charges.

Search Tips

Your first time on-line can be intimidating. In fact, you may want to find a local BBS and practice before using a major information provider. The advantages of such practice are the low costs (it's a local call) and the relatively simple nature of BBSs. Many BBSs offer free connect time so that you can get used to their systems. But keep in mind that the

"Big Boys," like CompuServe, always take some time to learn and get used to.

Regardless of the BBS or the information provider that you have chosen to use, there are several points you should keep in mind if you are to use the service effectively. Remember that each minute you are on-line costs. (Several services offer free time to encourage people to subscribe. For example, The Source gives new subscribers two free hours of connect time.)

- The first rule of using an on-line service is to know your purpose. When you have to pay for on-line time, you should have as good an idea as possible of what you want. You need to phrase your queries carefully and precisely.

  Good query: The names of all nonprofit foundations in New York City, that deal with children.

  Not-so-good query: Nonprofit foundations in New York City.

  Terrible query: What nonprofit foundations do.

  New York City may have 10,000 nonprofit foundations that deal with many different causes, and only 155 that deal specifically with children.

  A good query gets right to the heart of what you want to know, and a bad query is so general that the service returns more information than is necessary—frequently using expensive on-line time. In many services, you don't enter whole sentences, but you enter key words for which the information provider searches. For example, on CompuServe, you might enter

      foundations, nonprofit, New York, children

- If all other qualities are equal, choose a BBS or an information provider that has a local number or one that is as close to you as possible to help save on connection costs.

- See whether the service you want to use has TeleNet available. This data communication service owned by General Telephone and Electronics lets you use a local number to link into the service you want to use, saving you money.

16
Telecom.

- Get to know as much as you can about the different services before you actually go on-line. Call them for their printed information, which can save you time and aggravation.

- Some services offer software tools to help you steer through the many menus and commands to get at what you want. For example, CompuServe has the Navigator, which helps you cut down your on-line time. Navigator costs extra (about $100).

- Don't read long documents on-screen. Instead, download them, print them, and read them at your leisure.

- Develop a general feel for where the information you need may be located. For example, if you want to know the win-loss record of the San Diego Padres, don't try to find the answer in Orbit, which is primarily a scientific database.

- Don't use a BBS or an on-line information provider unless absolutely necessary. You could sit at your computer and find out the population of Tangiers, but you can get the same information from an encyclopedia or the library, saving both time and money.

You also need to know some specifics about the information you will access. Be sure to keep the following points in mind as you search for the service that is best for you. Use the toll-free numbers listed in the vendor index to call and ask these questions:

- How often is the database updated?

- Do you have search aids that can reduce my search time and costs?

- Where do you get the information you pass on to me?

- How far back does your information go?

- Is there help available? Is it on-line, by phone, or both?

FAX Modems

A FAX modem is a modem that allows you to send files rather than hard copy to a FAX machine or to another FAX modem. The receiver prints the file when he or she chooses. FAX machines use phone lines, as do modems. If you will be sending or receiving FAXes on a frequent basis, you should have a dedicated line.

FAX modems are driven by software. BackFax (from Solutions International) allows you to transmit in the background, using a FAX modem, while you continue to work on other files. For example, you could be writing a letter to one client while you are FAXing another letter to another client. Another outstanding feature of BackFax is that it allows you to set up address books (names, addresses, FAX numbers, and so on) and specify delivery instructions as to when you want certain files sent. The background feature works whether or not you are running under MultiFinder. You can even send messages that are larger than FAX paper, because BackFax can send messages in strips that the recipient can assemble.

BackFax is made even more attractive by the poor quality of the software that Apple supplied with the introduction of the Apple Fax modem.

FAX machines themselves come in all sizes, shapes, and prices. While I was working on this book, I received much of the reference material from the manufacturers of the various products mentioned on a Relisys RA2110M FAX machine, which incidentally now comes packaged with BackFax. This full-featured FAX machine has such capabilities as facsimile transmission, graphics scanning, and line printing. It can also be used as a FAX modem; by plugging it into your Mac you can FAX files rather than hard copy. You can print the FAX files you receive on your printer if you want a hard copy other than what the FAX machine itself produces. FAX modems store information as files; they do not automatically print the files.

You can store more than 200 FAX numbers. There aren't many other FAX machines that have such capabilities. The machine is easy to set up, and the ease and speed of obtaining information is incredible. The Relisys RA2110M comes with a one-year warranty.

Relisys has just released a model called the Telax System that is not only a FAX machine but also a scanner, printer, copier, and modem priced at about $1,500.

Last night, I visited with Racine, Wisconsin; Seattle, Washington; and Missoula, Montana, trying to find a list of BBSs. Do you know what

16
Telecom.

happened? The SYSOP (system operator) in Racine got on the line (in the "chat" mode) and told me to contact the people at the Berkeley Mac User Group), and I did (through my Mac, of course). Doesn't that sum up the power you have at your fingertips? Up to now, most of *The Big Mac Book* has talked about what you can do with your Mac, but I have not included much about the world out there. With the type of software and hardware described in this chapter, your ability to "reach out and touch someone" increases until the world of information and people becomes a network that is easy to reach and use. Try it. You really will like it.

Part VI

Advanced Topics

By the time you have come this far into *The Big Mac Book*, you are certainly not new to the Macintosh and what it can offer. This section of the book deals with some of the more advanced Mac topics, including HyperCard, programming, and troubleshooting your Mac (yes, even *you* can fix it).

Includes

Using HyperCard

Programming Your Macintosh

Maintenance and Troubleshooting

17

Using HyperCard

HyperCard is a fixture of the Mac scene. Pick up any periodical that focuses on the Macintosh, and you will find advertisements for HyperCard products and perhaps an article or two about this program. This deluge of articles and columns has occurred every month for the last two years, ever since this hit product was introduced. Today, thousands of *stacks* (HyperCard programs) are available, and you can find numerous newsletters, columns, books, and even clubs revering this software tool. In addition, many Macintosh programs now come with HyperCard-based tutorials. Whether you're a dyed-in-the-wool HyperCard junkie, an occasional user, or just a beginner, you will be seeing more and more of HyperCard in the years to come.

Regardless of your level of experience, this chapter will be helpful. It introduces you to a variety of HyperCard topics that will add to your personal tool box of HyperCard knowledge. Here's what you find in this chapter:

- The basics of getting started with HyperCard and taking advantage of its most important features

- An introduction to HyperTalk, the HyperCard language with which you can write, in English prose, your own "programs" as scripts for HyperCard to perform

- A review of some HyperCard applications, which gets you into the wonderful array of stacks and HyperCard programs that are currently available

This chapter only begins to describe what HyperCard has to offer. If you want more information about the basics as well as the advanced features, consult any Mac periodical and visit your local bookstore.

17
Hypercard

What Is HyperCard?

HyperCard's origin is not surprising: Bill Atkinson, one of the originals who worked on the Mac, and the author of MacPaint, the first graphics program designed for the Macintosh. And the genius that went into MacPaint shows through every facet of HyperCard's design and execution. HyperCard was born from a desire to build a tool that lets people access and use information easily and quickly. With the HyperCard design, Atkinson more than achieved this end.

In the early 1980s, Atkinson had been working on a program called WildCard, which was somewhat like an advanced MacPaint program. The difference, however, was that WildCard could work with a series of pages (soon to be called *cards*) rather than only one at a time. From these efforts, HyperCard 1.0 evolved and was introduced in late 1987, and was bundled for free with all new Macs until the middle of 1988. HyperCard also is now available separately through dealers for around $49.

HyperCard has been described by Atkinson as a software erector set, one that you can use to build the applications you need. It allows users who have no experience in programming to create their own programs, including the design of Macintosh screens. (In fact, some people claim that this feature is what was behind Apple's policy to provide HyperCard free with some earlier Macs. Apple's idea may have been that when the software got around, people would start using it to write programs, and programs lead to more people buying Macs, for which they can use HyperCard.)

Fashioned after the philosophy of the original Macintosh, HyperCard is a tool developed so that *everybody* who wants to should be able to use it, regardless of experience, current ability, or aptitude for programming with the Mac. And indeed, you will find that you can use HyperCard for a wide range of functions, from simply storing addresses to the most complex interplay of text, graphics, and database functions that you could design. Through the use of external commands (XCNs) and external functions (XFNs), you can access any of the Tool Box routines. And you can also use programs (stacks) created by other people. HyperCard is truly what you make it.

HyperCard's use as a development tool is the primary difference between it and other Macintosh applications. With no knowledge of programming, you can use HyperCard's English-language commands to perform extensive information collection and organization tasks. For example, here are some of the things you can do:

- Create animated sequences of graphics

- Design and build your own databases

- Write "real time" tutorials and training software

- Create business forms

- Generate mailing labels

- Generate sounds and write music

Learning HyperCard Basics

HyperCard helps you manage information. The beauty of the program is that you can construct your own system to manage this information. You use several basic elements—stacks, cards, backgrounds, fields, and buttons—at almost every stage of your building activities. Before you start working with HyperCard, you need to be familiar with these facets of the program.

Introducing the HyperCard Building Blocks

A *stack* is a collection of units of information that have something in common, much like a set of records in a database. It is not a condition for using HyperCard that the information on all the cards be related, but this is most often the case within any one stack.

A *card* is one screen's worth of information and the basic information unit in HyperCard. HyperCard assigns a unique ID number for every card you create. On any one card, you can have a variety of information as text, graphics, a chart, or even sounds and animation. For example, as you can see in figure 17.1, you might create a card that holds someone's name, address, product preference, and phone number, as in a Rolodex file. Using HyperCard, you can easily build a file, or stack, of such cards and manipulate that information. You can even get HyperCard to dial clients' phone numbers for you (if you have a modem).

17
Hypercard

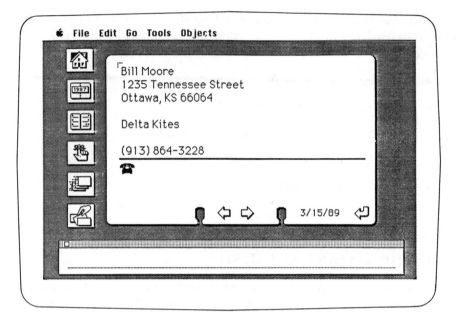

Fig. 17.1. A card containing information about a client.

Each card is made up of three basic components: background, fields, and buttons. The *background* of a card is the set of elements on the card that is shared by several or all of the cards in a particular stack. For example, if you are designing a stack that always requires certain information, such as a name and an address, you can design the background for the stack to contain that information. Then you don't have to re-enter the background information each time you begin a new card. A card is always associated with a background, and you can have different backgrounds within the same stack.

You can see the background for the current card by using the ⌘-B key combination. HyperCard places strips around the main menu reminding you that you are viewing the background. You also can change the background when it is being viewed. Anything you add to the background then appears on all cards that are associated with that background. The background is like a default design.

As a general rule, the more complete the background is, the less you have to enter onto each new card. In figure 17.2 you see a calendar card, and in figure 17.3 you can see the background for all the cards in that stack.

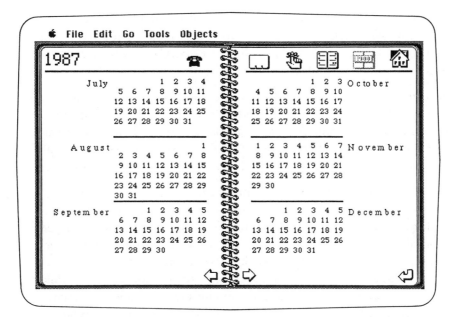

Fig. 17.2. *A sample calendar card.*

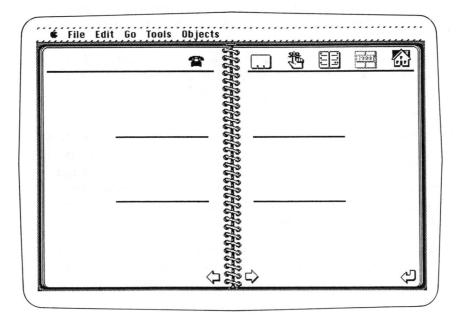

Fig. 17.3. *A sample calendar card's background.*

17
Hypercard

The *fields* on a card contain text. Text typed into fields can be formatted by size, style, and font. A field is analogous to the basic unit in a database. In fact, many users consider HyperCard to be a database management system (DBMS).

Fields can be either background or card fields. A card field is associated with only that card, but a background field is associated with all the cards of that background. You can enter text into the field from a card even if the field is a background field. The text is then associated with that background field but is displayed only in that individual card.

To travel between stacks, you use *buttons* (or various menu options), which you can place on cards. As with other Mac activities, whenever you click a button, something happens—exactly *what* happens is under the control of the person who wrote the stack. A button represents a link or an action that you define with a HyperCard script. You can design a button to take you to another stack or to another card within the same stack. Buttons also can give pop-up message fields and play sound—anything that you script. You can even copy, cut, and paste buttons. You can use some of the buttons that HyperCard supplies, and create your own as your needs dictate.

One of the most useful features of HyperCard is that you can link cards to one another. For example, you can link an address stack that contains a name, phone number, and product preference to a card in a stack that indicates the date of the individual's last purchase. Then you can easily select and contact a customer based on the last purchase date. You read more about linking later in this chapter (see "Linking Cards and Stacks").

Another major plus to HyperCard is that you don't have to know how to design stacks to use them. Any stack created with HyperCard can be shared with other HyperCard users. This feature has created a major market for the development of stacks by outside parties (sometimes called third-party developers), some of which you will learn about in a later section of this chapter, "Selecting HyperCard Applications."

The number of buttons and the way that you link cards in stacks to each other is limited only by your imagination. That's what HyperCard is all about: creating a program that fits your view of the world and the way you want it organized.

You can perform a whole host of tasks by talking directly to HyperCard. Many of these operations include using the *message box*. To display the message box at the bottom of the screen, press ⌘-M. You then can enter any single-line command (in HyperTalk) in the message box, telling HyperCard what to do, and execute the command by pressing Return. For example, if you enter the command

   go stack inventory

and press Enter or Return, HyperCard takes you to the first card in the stack called Inventory. In fact, after you enter a command in that message box, you can execute it repeatedly by using the ⌘-M key combination.

Installing and Starting HyperCard

HyperCard comes as a set of three disks that you install much like you do any Macintosh software. You need a hard disk, because HyperCard is almost 400K. And, as you will see, the stacks that have been designed to be used with HyperCard run anywhere from 25K up to 750K.

To install HyperCard, follow these steps:

1. Create a new folder at the desktop level using the File menu or the ⌘-N key combination, and name it HyperCard.

2. Insert the disk named *HyperCard and Stacks* into the internal drive.

3. Open the HyperCard and Stacks disk by double-clicking the icon representing the disk.

4. Select all the files on the disk, using the ⌘-A key combination.

5. Drag the files from the disk to the folder and wait until they are copied. Close the disk by clicking the close box in the upper left corner.

6. Drag the HyperCard disk to the trash can.

7. Repeat this procedure with the HyperCard Ideas disk and the HyperCard Help disk.

After you complete these steps for all disks, you're ready to go. Double-click the HyperCard icon, and the opening screen showing the Home

17
Hypercard

card appears (see fig. 17.4). The Home card is part of the Home stack, which consists of five different cards. You can always get back to the Home card in a flash by using the ⌘-H key combination.

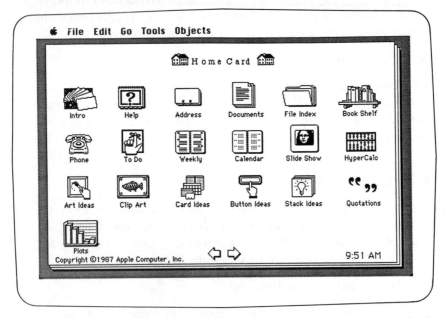

Fig. 17.4. The Home card on the Home stack—your open door to HyperCard.

Note that the opening Home screen contains several buttons. These buttons access stacks that have already been created for your use. For example, the stack named Quotations consists of hundreds of cards, each containing a quotation and a Who Says? button that tells you who said the quotation when you click it.

Setting the User-Preference Level

When you're beginning to work with HyperCard, the first decision you need to make is the appropriate level at which to start. HyperCard is organized in five different, progressively more complex levels of *user preferences*. Each of these levels introduces different features, allowing you to work at the level that best fits your particular needs. And, most important, each successive level includes all the features of the previous levels.

Browsing is the most basic level. At this first level, you can work your way through stacks and read their contents either by clicking a card button or by using the left and right arrows on the keyboard. Because you are literally browsing (as if you were in a bookstore), you cannot alter information in any way.

Typing, level 2, allows you to add text and to edit the text that is already contained in the fields of cards.

Painting, level 3, gives you access to an entire Tool Box of paint tools, such as the paintbrush, the lasso, and tools for drawing rectangles, circles, and polygons. You are probably familiar with these tools, which comprise a typical MacPaint palette. You can use the tools to draw graphics directly on cards, either on the background layer or the card layer.

Authoring, level 4, provides you with access to the basic parts of a card, including the creation of fields and buttons. At this level, the Object menu is added. At this level, you can also link cards and stacks to one another (an important HyperCard concept).

Scripting is the last level and the most complex but most exciting. At this level, you become your own HyperCard author and create scripts that do exactly what you say. With scripting, you become a programmer, using HyperCard's specially designed language, HyperTalk. If you know nothing about programming, this level is a wonderful introduction because HyperTalk uses understandable English commands to perform both basic and advanced functions.

To set your user-preference level, you use the User Preferences card, the last card on the Home stack. You can get to this card in two ways. Either click the ← at the bottom of the screen while in the Home card, or use the ⌘-4 key combination, which takes you to the last card of a stack.

Working with an Established Stack

You can begin most of your HyperCard work with a stack that has already been created, such as the Address stack. Let's work through this stack to familiarize you with some basic HyperCard ideas and procedures.

17
Hypercard

To begin, in the Home card, move the pointing finger cursor to the Address button and click once. (In HyperCard, unlike Finder, a single mouse click initiates an action.) What you see, as shown in figure 17.5, is the first card of the Address stack. Along the left side of the card, you find six different buttons. Each of these buttons takes you to another stack. Here's what each of the buttons does:

- The first button, the Home button, takes you back to the first card (Home) in the Home stack.

- The second button is the Calendar button, which takes you to the Current Month card in the stack called Calendar.

- The third button takes you to the Current Days card in an appointment calendar.

- The fourth button takes you to a (don't forget) "to do" list.

- The fifth button tells HyperCard to page through the stack one card after another.

  Using this button is a great way to do animation if you have pictures rather than text on cards. By using scripting commands, you can tell HyperCard at what speed you want to page through the pictures, just like those little comic books that you flip through.

- The last button sorts the cards in the stack either by first or last name.

Opening a Stack

Opening a stack that already has been created is as simple as selecting the Open Stack command from the File menu. After you do this, you see a standard Open dialog box listing all the stacks that are in the current directory. As you can see in figure 17.6, a stack called Author Bio is waiting to be opened if necessary.

This procedure is the same one you follow when you open a "commercial" stack (or one you have not created but want to use). The stack is then ready for you to use or to make any modifications, using HyperCard as a foundation. As you may already realize, with all the levels of tools that are available, HyperCard stacks are very flexible and usually can be modified quite easily as well.

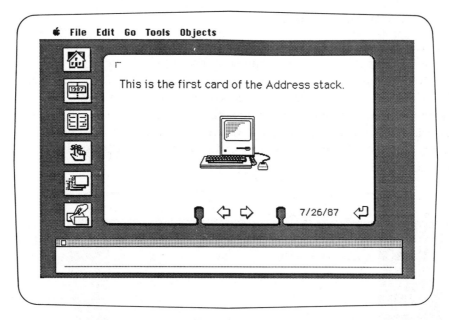

Fig. 17.5. *The first card in the Address stack.*

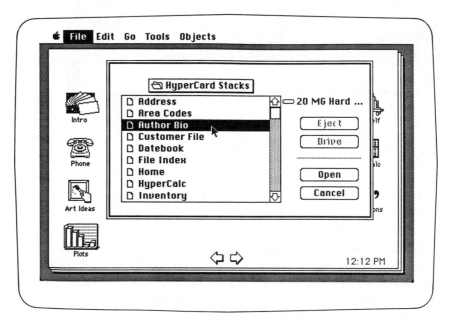

Fig. 17.6. *Opening a stack.*

17
Hypercard

Adding and Deleting Cards

Suppose that you want to add a new card to this already established stack. Just select the New Card command from the Edit menu (or use the ⌘-N key combination), and the screen displays a new card placed in front of the card you were on when you issued the command. The only information contained on the new card is the background that is associated with each card because no new information was added (see fig. 17.7). At this point, you can enter on the card whatever information you want.

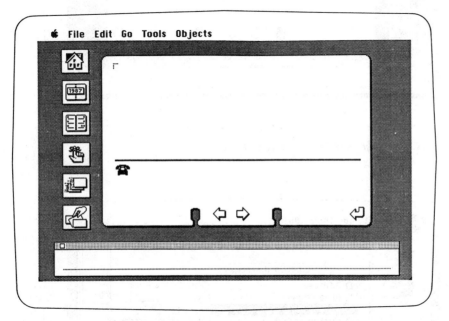

Fig. 17.7. *A new card showing the background for the Address stack.*

You can add as many cards to a stack as you want and work with any number of them, up to the limits of your Macintosh's volatile memory (RAM). When you add a new card, HyperCard places it in front of the current card in the stack, and knows enough to save the card as part of the stack without any instructions from you. In fact, HyperCard knows to save everything you do, so you never need to concern yourself with saving—quite contrary to what you have had drilled into your head with almost every other Macintosh application.

Deleting a card is just as easy as creating one. While the card is on-screen, just select the Delete command from the Edit menu.

Want to know how many cards are in your stack? Select the Stack Info command from the Objects menu to find out the number of cards, backgrounds, the size of the stack, and the amount of free space available in the stack.

HyperCard has some interesting characteristics that make it very Mac-like, but that differ in other ways from the applications that you have learned about in this book and that you have worked with.

Just like cutting, copying, and pasting with text or numerical values, you can do the same with cards. A card can be selected by using the tools on the Tools menu and then cut or copied and pasted into another location in the stack. Or information from an individual card can be cut or copied and then pasted. You use exactly the same process as you would if you were performing the simplest cut and paste or copy and paste.

HyperCard is interesting in its differences from the normal Mac conventions. For example, when you delete a card from a HyperCard stack, the memory that was used by that card is not freed up.

Moving through a Stack

HyperCard provides several tools for moving through a stack. The most convenient method is using the right- and left-pointing arrows located at the bottom of the card. By clicking the left or right arrow, you flip to the preceding or next card.

Not all stacks have these arrows, so the next best alternative for moving through a stack is using the Go menu. Table 17.1 lists the commands on that menu and describes what you can do with them.

17
Hypercard

Table 17.1
Using the Go Menu

Command	Key Combination	Effect
Back	⌘-~	Moves you to the preceding card in the stack
Home	⌘-H	Moves you to the Home card
Help	⌘-?	Moves you to HyperCard Help
Recent	⌘-R	Gives you a picture of the last cards you have viewed (as many as 42)
First	⌘-1	Moves you to the first card in the stack
Prev	⌘-2	Moves you to the preceding card in the stack
Next	⌘-3	Moves you to the next card in the stack
Last	⌘-4	Moves you to the last card in the stack
Find	⌘-F	Finds a card that contains certain information

Using the Recent command is the ideal way to find a card that you think you might have worked with but forget where you saw it. Figure 17.8 shows the last 10 cards that were used in a sample HyperCard session. As you might expect, HyperCard shows off its user friendliness again by allowing you to click any of these cards to go directly to that card.

When you select the Find command from the Go menu, HyperCard displays a find " " prompt in the message box at the bottom of the screen. Enter (between the double quotation marks) the information you want to find, and HyperCard goes almost instantly to the card containing that information or even any part of it. For example, you can find the card that contains the name Wilson by entering *son* within

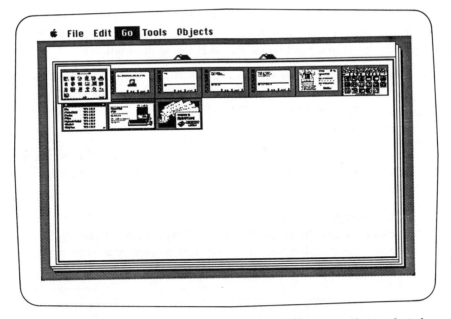

Fig. 17.8. *Using the Recent command to review the cards you have selected.*

the prompt's quotation marks. If HyperCard cannot find the card, the program beeps politely.

Building New Stacks from Old Ideas

You have seen how to add a card to an existing stack. But what if you want to design your own stack? That task would be a bit ambitious for the beginning HyperCard user, except for the fact that HyperCard comes with a bunch of predesigned stack ideas that you can use. The predesigned stacks are templates that allow you to work with and create your own personalized stacks. Building your own stack is not as difficult as it might sound at first.

Let's stick with the simple address book concept for a moment. Assume that for each individual, you plan to enter name, address, and other customer information. Using a format that is already designed is so much easier than creating one yourself, because a good deal of work is done for you. You should take advantage of HyperCard's predesigned stack ideas, much as you would take advantage of a template or a style sheet.

17
Hypercard

To create a stack called Customer File, using an already existing design located in the Stack Ideas stack, follow these steps (Remember, you can always get to the Home card using the ⌘-H key combination):

1. Select the Stack Ideas stack from the Home card. You then see the first of four cards that include different ideas for stack designs. Figures 17.9 and 17.10 show you the first and the third of these cards.

2. Select the address format you want to use to begin the creation of your stack. In this example, Address card 1 was selected from the first screen.

3. With a sample card from the stack on-screen, select the New Stack command from the File menu. HyperCard opens a standard Save dialog box that asks you to supply a name for the file.

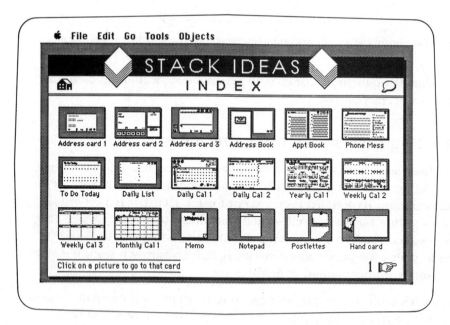

Fig. 17.9. *The first Stack Ideas screen.*

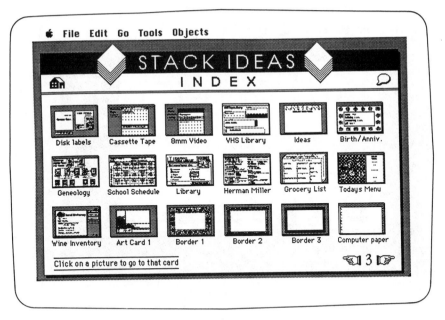

Fig. 17.10. The third Stack Ideas screen.

4. Type a descriptive name such as *address book*. HyperCard then displays the background for the new stack, as shown in figure 17.11. Remember that a card's background consists of all characteristics that the card will have in common with others in the stack. Because this stack is brand new, nothing has been entered yet, and no background information exists.

5. Place the mouse pointer in the upper right corner of the first card in this new stack and click once. You see the familiar flashing horizontal insertion bar. Enter your information into the different fields. To change fields, you can use the mouse pointer or press Tab to go to the next field, and Shift-Tab to go to the preceding field. To see the various components of a card, you can use the following key combinations: To see any buttons, use the ⌘-Option key combination. To see buttons and fields, use the ⌘-Shift-Option key combination. Remember that the ⌘-B key combination acts as a toggle (off/on) switch to get you into and out of the background layer of the card.

17
Hypercard

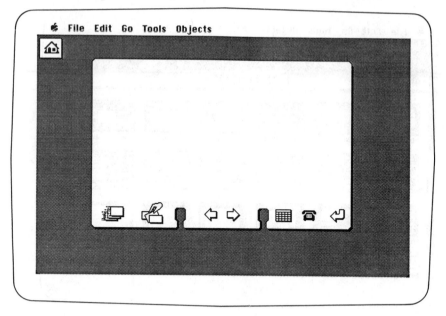

Fig. 17.11. *The background for the new cards.*

6. After the card is complete, create the next card by using the
⌘-N key combination or selecting the New Card command
from the Edit menu. As you work, HyperCard saves your
creations.

For the majority of your work, you can probably find something in the
Stack Ideas stack and modify the background to fit your needs. Just
use the ⌘-B key combination and make whatever changes in the
background you choose. Even though you don't actually save stacks (as
you do other Mac files), you can duplicate a stack using the Save A
Copy command on the File menu. You can save an existing stack under
another name and then modify it as you need. This lets you take
advantage of work that might already have been done. Unless you have
highly specific needs, stick with this strategy until you are more familiar
with HyperCard.

Linking Cards and Stacks

HyperCard would not be of much use if you could not easily link cards
and their stacks to other cards. In this example, you learn to link cards

by using a button. First create a button called More About Author? that provides more information about the author of a quotation. Make the button part of the background, so that it appears on every card, as shown in figure 17.12. This is a good example of modifying an existing stack and adding to what it does. Now instead of just the quotation and the Who Says? button, you can click on the More About Author? button and learn more about the author.

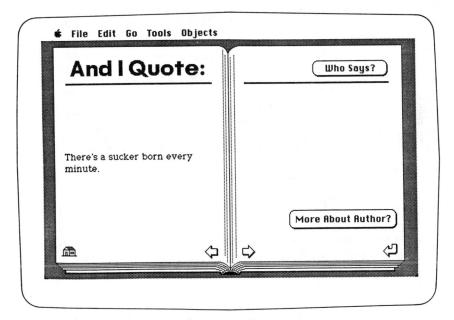

Fig. 17.12. *Adding the More About Author? button.*

To create the new button, follow these steps:

1. Click the Button icon in the Tools menu.

2. Select New Button from the Objects menu. HyperCard places a selected button with the default name New Button in the center of the screen.

3. Double-click that button, or select the Button Info command from the Objects menu, to bring up the dialog box shown in figure 17.13. This figure shows you that the button name has already been added.

17
Hypercard

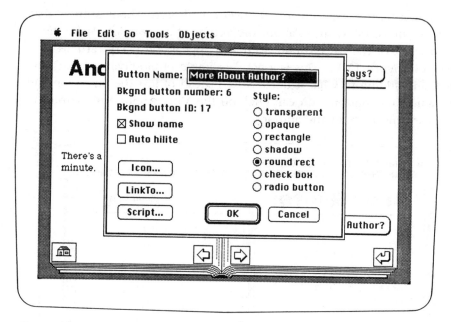

Fig. 17.13. The Button Info dialog box.

Now you need to link the new button you have created to specific information in another stack containing a card that has additional biographical information on each author. To link the button with a card or a stack, follow these steps:

1. Still in the Button Info dialog box, click the LinkTo button to open the LinkTo dialog box.

2. Move to the card that you want to link to the button, or open the stack you want (using the Open command from the File menu). The LinkTo dialog box remains on-screen, as shown in figure 17.14.

3. Select This Card or This Stack, depending on what you want to link. (Clicking This Stack links you to the first card in the stack.) In this example, click This Card to link the More About Author? button to the card. HyperCard automatically returns you to your starting card.

Now when you click the button named More About Author? on the card that contains the quotation "There's a sucker born every minute," the additional author information is produced.

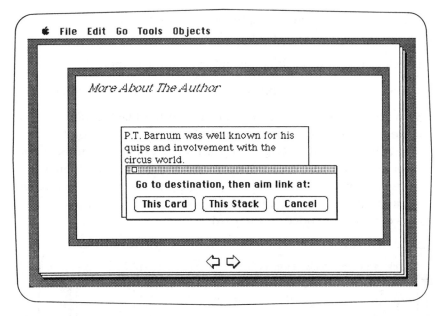

Fig. 17.14. *The LinkTo dialog box.*

The stack wouldn't be much help, however, if you could not go from the author information back to the original stack at which you started. You can create a new button (labeled "Go Back To Quotes!") in the background to appear on each author bio card. Then, each quotation is linked to more information about the author of the quotation, and each card that contains additional information about the author is linked to the stack named Quotations.

Creating Your Own Stack

Doing your own stack is a little more challenging than using an established format, and more rewarding as well. In this example, you learn to construct a simple inventory stack that keeps track of part names, part numbers, and amounts on hand. You also create one button that can link the product name to another stack that contains the address of the supplier.

17
Hypercard

To design the new card and background, be sure that you are at the Scripting user-preference level, and follow these steps:

1. Select the New Stack command from the File menu.

2. Use the ⌘-B key combination to move to the background.

3. With the paint tools, draw a border on the blank card. Use your imagination. In the example in figure 17.15, I used a graphic from HyperCard's Clip Art stack using conventional cut or copy and paste procedures to place the car in the upper right corner. In this case, the graphic was copied and placed in the Clipboard, and then pasted into the card. Text, as you can see, was then added to the card.

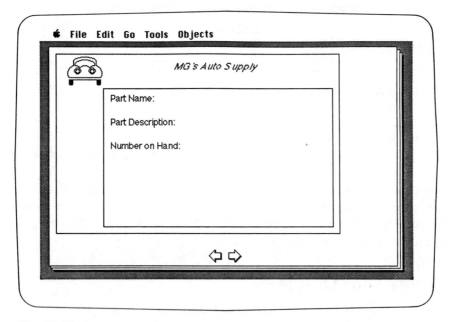

Fig. 17.15. *A new card with a border.*

4. Return to the Tool Box and select the points cursor. Select the New Field command from the Objects menu. A new field appears in the middle of your screen. Drag the corner of the field to change its size; then move it where you want it by dragging a side of the field with the mouse pointer. Double-click the field to open the Field dialog box. This dialog box

allows you to set font sizes and styles as well as the format of the border for the field.

5. Create another set of fields for the Part Name:, Part Description:, and Number on Hand: sections of the Inventory card following the instructions in Step 4.

6. Now create a new button in the lower right corner. You already know how to create a button and link it to another card. For this example, attach a graphic to the button. Go back to the Home card, select the Button Ideas stack, and copy one of the telephone buttons from the stack. Then return to the Inventory stack. (Or you can just copy a telephone button from any one of the other Stack Ideas stacks that contain telephones. Remember that before you can copy a button, you have to select the Button tool from the Tool Box and then copy and paste the button.)

7. To make the telephone into a working button, select the New Button command from the Objects menu and place the button over the phone, as shown in figure 17.16.

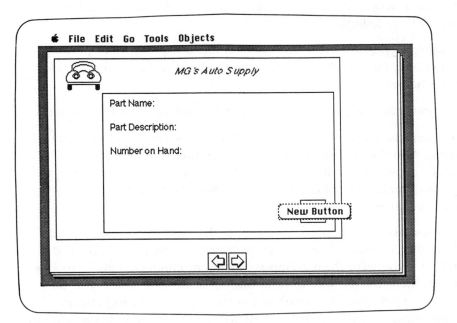

Fig. 17.16. *Making a graphic into a button.*

8. Double-click the new button to open the Button dialog box.

9. Select the Transparent option. The new button is now transparent. The telephone thus appears to be the new button but merely lies under it, ready to be clicked.

10. Link the new button to whatever card you want, such as "the dealer" (see "Linking Cards and Stacks").

Now you're finished designing the background. Use the ⌘-B key combination, and you're ready to build your own stack by entering actual information into the inventory.

Printing Stacks and Cards

When you print stacks and cards, you can use the Print commands that are available on the File menu (or the ⌘-P key combination). As with other documents, keeping a record of your stacks for backup purposes is important. And imagine how easily you can print a stack on labels for mailing. Or even on index cards for filing at a later date. You can even keep images, such as images of maps or files stored as photographs of familiar places, and produce a hard copy of these for inclusion in a report or as a display.

Printing HyperCard cards and stacks is much like any other printing procedure. Be sure that you have selected the printer you want, using the Chooser.

To print one card, select the Print Card command from the File menu.

To print the entire stack, select the Print Stack command from the File menu. You then see the Print Stack dialog box shown in figure 17.17, which allows you to handle such tasks as printing multiple copies and printing reduced versions of the cards. You even see a print preview of the cards that will be printed.

You can also print reports by selecting the Print Reports command from the File menu. You can select different fields to print, as well as whether you want them arranged in rows or columns. This method is by far the preferred way to print mailing labels from stacks like the Address stack you saw earlier in this chapter. Such an application emphasizes how HyperCard is designed to use the same information in several different ways, whether to dial the phone, search for

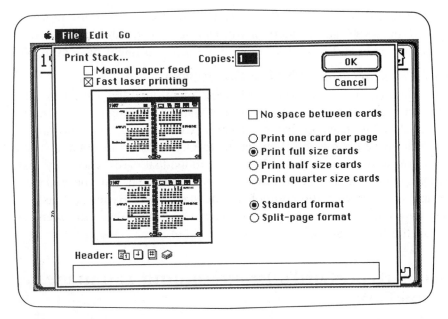

Fig. 17.17. *Printing a HyperCard stack.*

information in a stack, connect to other information, or print mailing labels and reports.

You can use the message box to help you perform a variety of printing tasks, such as printing a set of cards from a stack. (For more information on the message box, see the section on "Introducing the HyperCard Building Blocks.") To print, for example, the first 10 cards from a stack of 200, you would follow these steps:

1. Go to the first card in the stack.

2. Use the ⌘-M key combination to display the message box.

3. Enter the command *print 10 cards*. HyperCard understands English and prints the first 10 cards of the stack.

All Those Stacks and What To Do?

You will find that HyperCard stacks, like Clip Art and bunnies, tend to reproduce until they're out of control. Imagine all the stacks you want to have on your hard disk, and then imagine being in an application

17
Hypercard

and wanting access to one of those stacks. Impossible? Not any more. With HyperDA (from Symmetry), you can be in a specific application and easily open and browse through any stack you might have available.

For example, remember DTP (Desktop Publishing Advisor from Broderbund), the set of HyperCard stacks mentioned in Chapter 10? If you were just learning QuarkXpress and wanted to design a newsletter, you could easily leave Quark, use HyperDA to get into DTP, find the information you need, and then return to Quark. You can open any stack you want, browse through it, print individual cards, and copy text and graphics from a stack to paste into an application, but you will not be able to work with the contents of the stack itself. HyperCard also is very handy for using stacks on 512, Macs which don't have the memory to run the full program.

Using HyperCard's Programming Language: HyperTalk

You could easily continue to explore the HyperCard techniques you have already learned, and find HyperCard to be useful and applicable in many different situations. But if you want to go beyond the basics, here's an introduction to HyperTalk, HyperCard's programming language. With HyperTalk, you can create and customize HyperCard stacks.

HyperTalk is a programming language that consists of 53 commands, and more than 1,000 if you include all the built-in functions. As with other high-level programming languages, such as BASIC, Pascal, and C, these commands direct HyperCard to perform a specific action. For example, you can tell the program to go to a particular stack (the command is *go to [stack name]*) or to fade from one card to another (the command is *dissolve*). With HyperTalk commands, you can control audio and visual effects, arithmetic operations, printing, sorting, and more.

Examining a Script

HyperTalk works by organizing its commands into scripts. A *script* is simply a list of commands, that acts as a set of directions. To examine a

script that is associated with a button and find out what the parts of
the script tell HyperCard to do, follow these steps:

1. Go to the Home card by using the ⌘-H key combination.

2. Select the Tools command from the main menu, and then
   choose the Button tool. All the buttons should be outlined or
   "framed."

3. Select the Clip Art button. The border around the button turns
   into a dotted line.

4. Double-click the button to open the Button dialog box.

5. Select the Script button to display the script in the script
   window (see fig. 17.18).

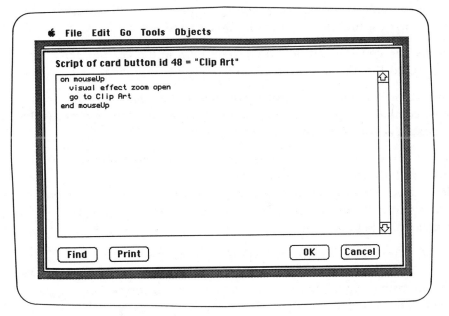

Fig. 17.18. *The script window and the script associated with the Clip
Art button on the Home card.*

Let's take a look at what each line in the script means. The first line
reads *on mouseUp*. All HyperTalk scripts begin with the word *on*,
followed by some action. The *mouseUp* command tells HyperCard to
begin this script when the mouse button is released.

17
Hypercard

You may have difficulty believing that the fancy screen tricks you see in HyperCard can be produced with only one or two lines of commands, but that's often the case. In this script the second line, *visual effect zoom open*, controls the screen effects. The *visual* command tells HyperCard that the next statements are going to be the special effects. The word *effect* is optional but might help you spot the command in a long script. The command *zoom open* produces a specialized effect in which the button expands to the size of the monitor screen before opening.

If you have a Mac II with a color monitor, you cannot see visual effects unless you first select the Control Panel from the Apple menu and choose the 1-bit mode from the black-and-white monitor option. This step is necessary because HyperCard is not designed for color monitors.

The *go to Clip Art* command in the third line directs HyperCard to go to the first card of a stack of cards named Clip Art.

Finally, the combination of *end* and *mouseUp* in the last line tells HyperCard that the set of HyperTalk commands is ending.

This script is a simple one, but it contains all the characteristics of the most complex script: beginning and end statements, and commands that represent actions for HyperCard to execute.

Scripts can consist of hundreds of commands that are often organized into smaller units called *message handlers*. A message handler is defined as a set of commands that begins with the command *on* and ends with the command *end*. These sets of commands are self-contained HyperTalk scripts.

Scripts can be assigned to any HyperCard objects—buttons, fields, cards, backgrounds, and stacks—depending on what you need to do. If you are using HyperTalk Version 1.2, you can use certain key combinations to get directly to the scripts. For example,

- To move directly to a card script, press ⌘-Option-C.

- To move directly to a background script, press ⌘-Option-S.

- To move directly to a stack script, press ⌘-Option-S.

A Sampler of HyperTalk Commands

The following paragraphs include a discussion of some HyperTalk commands, and examples of scripts and what they do. Try these scripts, because they can be great fun, but remember that HyperTalk is smart. Like any other programming language, unless you tell HyperTalk *exactly* what you want it to do by typing every single character, the language cannot do its job.

Creating Music and Sound

To create sound with HyperTalk, you use the *play* command. The general syntax for this command is

play <voice> <tempo> <notes>

<voice> refers to one of the four sound generators that HyperTalk provides for you to use in scripts: harpsichord, boing, silence, and dialing tones. For example, the script in figure 17.19 plays a simple scale in the harpsichord voice. The *c5* in the scale plays a c note at the next highest octave, of which there are three to select from. The octave is always specified as part of the note. If not, the middle octave (4) is the default.

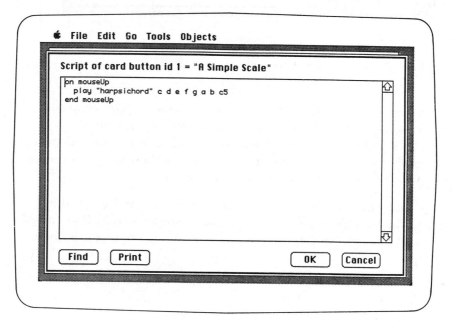

Fig. 17.19. *A simple scale that uses the* play *command.*

Providing a *<tempo>* is optional, but if you include it in the *play* command, you can change the speed with which sounds are played. The script in figure 17.20 shows two *play* commands: one that plays a boing sound fairly quickly (tempo set at 240), and one that plays a boing sound at a much slower tempo (set at 60). Tempo can range from 1 to 800 in value.

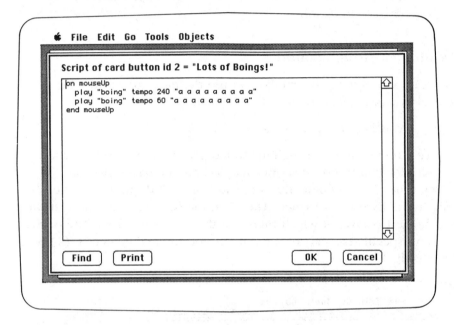

Fig. 17.20. *Changing the tempo in a* play *command.*

As with other HyperTalk commands, you can enter a *play* command in the message box to test the effect of the command on your script. For example, if you enter the command *play boing a* in the message box, you get an a note in the boing voice. If you like the effect, you can cut and paste the command line into your script.

Composing with HyperCard usually takes much trial and error. But imagine the wonderful drumrolls you can create to sound off as one of your stacks opens, alerting the user that something important is about to happen.

Creating Visual Effects

Visual effects can be as impressive as sound, and HyperTalk offers a host of them. The script shown in figure 17.21 is the one that links the More About Author? button you saw in figure 17.12. In this version, the *visual effect dissolve* command has been added. When the button is clicked, the script instructs HyperCard literally to dissolve the current screen into the next card to which it is linked.

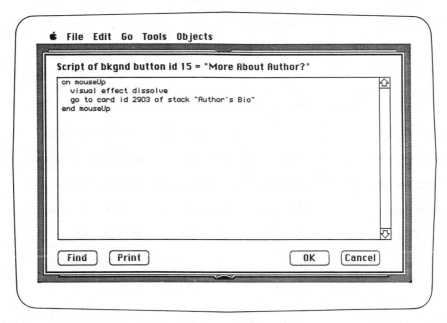

Fig. 17.21. *Adding some visual effects to a script.*

You place most visual effect commands before a *go* command. Here are the HyperTalk visual effect commands and what they do:

Command	Effect
barn door open	Opens to the next screen from the center out
barn door close	Opens to the next screen from both edges of the screen in
scroll left	Replaces the current screen with the new screen by sliding the new screen across from the left

17
Hypercard

Command	Effect
checkerboard	Creates a checkerboard pattern that fades into the next screen
iris open	Opens from the center of the card
iris close	Closes from the center of the card
zoom open	Opens from the position of the mouse click
zoom close	Returns to the card shown before a zoom open
dissolve	Fades from one card to another
venetian blinds	Goes to next card by switching horizontal bands
wipe left	Changes cards with wipe from left to right
wipe right	Changes cards with wipe from right to left
wipe up	Changes cards with wipe from bottom to top
wipe down	Changes cards with wipe from top to bottom
scroll right	New card scrolls into picture from left to right
scroll left	New card scrolls into picture from right to left
scroll down	New card scrolls into picture from top of screen

Another interesting visual effect is created by the *flash* command, which has the screen flash the number of times you designate. For example, *flash 5* causes the current screen to flash on and off five times and then stop. Try it.

Using Interactive Scripts

Much of what you do with scripts might involve other people. For example, suppose that you are constructing a script in which you need to prompt a user to supply information, such as name and address, or to select one of several alternative answers to a question. The *answer* command enables you to ask such questions in a variety of ways. The syntax for the command is

answer <question> with <reply>

For example, in figure 17.22, I used the message box to enter the simple *answer* command, *What's Your Name?* The full script entry was *answer "What's Your Name?"* You can see how HyperTalk places it in a dialog box and presents it on-screen.

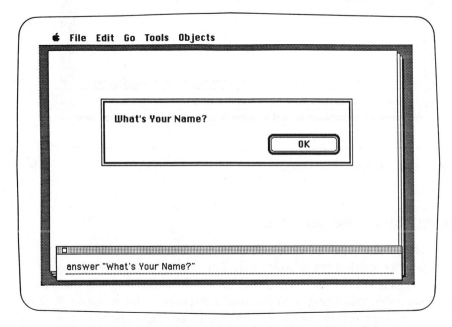

Fig. 17.22. *Using the* answer *command to design interactive scripts.*

You can create a multiple-choice question like the one shown in figure 17.23 by using the *or* command to provide alternatives. You can see the format of the command in the message box. In turn, you can then link each button in the answer box to another card that provides feedback to the selected answer. This method is an ideal way to design a learning experience in which immediate feedback is necessary.

17
Hypercard

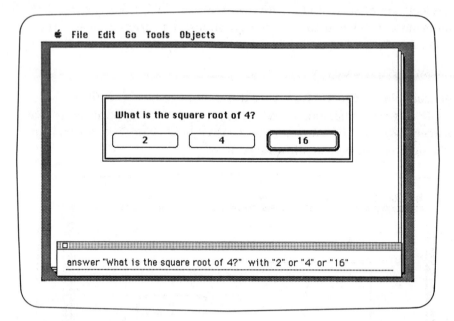

Fig. 17.23. *An interactive window.*

Doing Things Over and Over

You can use the *repeat* command to have HyperCard repeat a command as many times as you want. For example, suppose that you want to open your stack with an important message, and you want to make sure that you bring it to the user's attention. The script in figure 17.24 combines several of the features you have read about in this chapter, and repeats the sequence of events five times.

The script plays a boing while flashing the first card in the stack, and waits for one second before flashing again. The *end repeat* command tells HyperCard when to stop repeating. The script then dissolves into the stack called Lesson 1.

Working with the Date and Time

HyperTalk gives you a variety of ways to enter the date and time in a field. Suppose, for example, that you have designed a While You Were Out message much like the one shown in figure 17.25, with the card containing fields defined as date and time. As you can see in figure

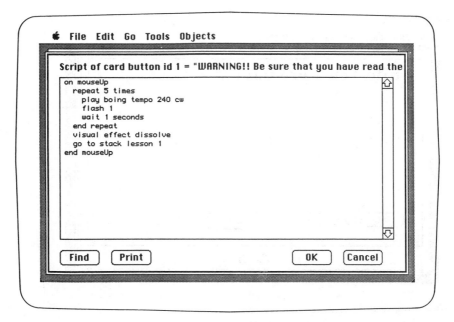

Fig. 17.24. *Using the repeat function to repeat a sequence of commands.*

17.26, the *put the date* command is tied to the button (and field) titled date. When you click the Date button, the program puts the date into the date field. The *put the time* command can do the same thing.

You can also choose to place other forms of the date into a field using different forms of the command. Use *the long date* for a format like Friday, March 17, 1989, or *the abbr date* for a format like Fri, Mar 17, 1989. Just want the day? Use *the first word of long date*.

You can play some of the same tricks as far as time goes. Using *the long time* produces 11:15:45 AM (matched to the System time); *the time* produces 11:15 AM. You can even combine words and time and date functions. For example, you might have a document that often needs updating. The expression *put "Dated" & the long date* produces Dated Friday, March 17, 1989.

Becoming a HyperTalk Master

If you want to become a HyperTalk expert, you need to practice with all the different types of applications you can think of, and also examine

17
Hypercard

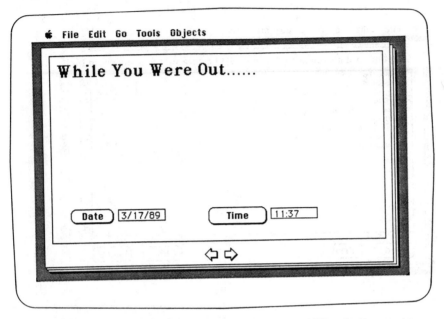

Fig. 17.25. *A While You Were Out form with Date and Time buttons.*

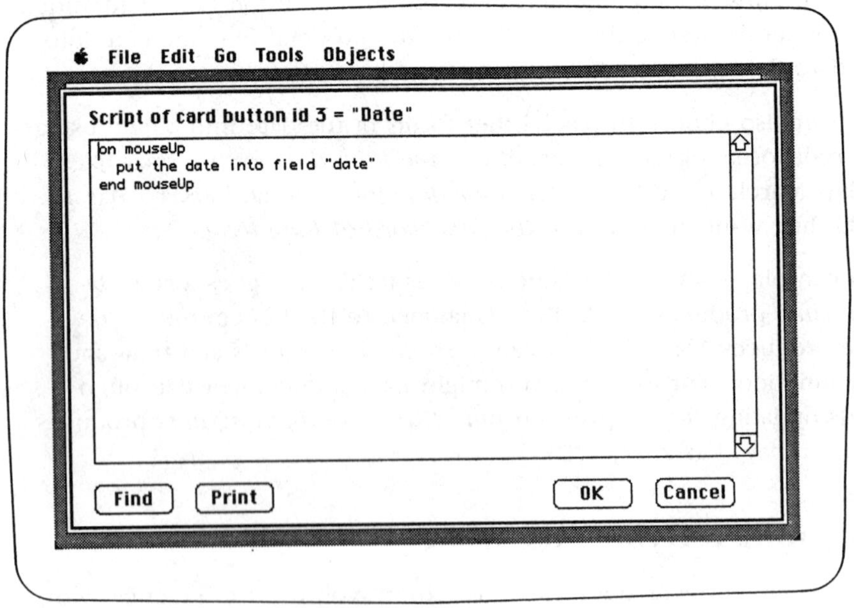

Fig. 17.26. *The script for "putting" in the date.*

other, already created scripts. Once you get a chance to change things here and there and see the effects, you are well on your way to mastering this programming language.

You can get some programming help through the use of HyperTools #1 and #2 (from SoftWorks). This product is a set of 28 tools that enables you to design and develop scripts by using shortcuts and well-conceived general aids. For example, you can search for strings of text, leave the stack for other applications (and then return), automate the production of buttons, and edit icons.

Examining Alternatives to HyperCard

It was bound to happen sooner or later. The success of HyperCard has led to spin-offs, with at least two making the news. SuperCard (from Silicon Beach) is being shipped as this book is being written, and Plus (from Olduvai) is yet to be released.

Knowing the similarities and differences among the products can help you make a wise, informed decision about which program is best for you.

SuperCard

What does SuperCard have that HyperCard doesn't? Many people feel that SuperCard picks up where HyperCard leaves off, giving users access to all the power the Macintosh has to offer. Following is a list of some of the features that SuperCard offers (mostly far above and beyond HyperCard):

- SuperCard allows the use of full-size windows, instead of restricting the visuals to the size of HyperCard cards.

- You can scroll, resize, and manipulate windows just as you can in any other Macintosh application, with several windows open at once.

- SuperCard includes full-color object-oriented drawing tools (no more pasting).

- You can import many different types of files, including Encapsulated PostScript.

17
Hypercard

- You have complete control over menus and menu items.

- You have unlimited access to as many open stacks as you want.

- You can design stand-alone applications (you don't need SuperCard).

- SuperCard is completely compatible with HyperCard scripts (you can run them with SuperCard).

- You can use AutoTrace to convert paint images to draw images (just like the "big boy" graphics packages, such as Adobe Illustrator).

These features are the only differences between SuperCard and HyperCard. If you're planning to buy HyperCard, take a look at SuperCard first. Figure 17.27 shows you a sample screen from SuperCard.

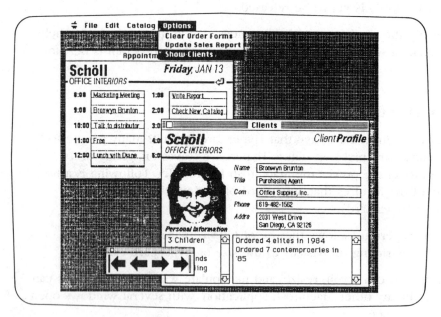

Fig. 17.27. *A sample SuperCard screen.*

Plus

Plus (from Olduvai) is the latest HyperCard clone to come along.
Developed by Format Software, a West German firm, Plus has all of
the capabilities of HyperCard and is similar to SuperCard. A major
distinction between Plus and SuperCard is Plus' software slots. These
are "openings" in the program for third-party developers to provide
everything from spell checkers to spreadsheets, thereby enlarging the
use base on which Plus can operate. Plus applications cannot stand
alone like SuperCard applications can, but Plus comes with some fancy
graphics effects, such as sunbursts and rainbows. The program is very
new (August 1989) and it's hard to tell whether the Mac world needs
another clone in addition to SuperCard to provide alternatives to
HyperCard.

Selecting HyperCard Applications

Thousands of HyperCard stacks and hundreds of HyperCard applications
are available from which you can choose. Many of them are available
through the public-domain sellers discussed in Chapter 13. This section
includes some examples of HyperCard applications and stacks on
Macintosh topics that you might find interesting and useful. Several
periodicals offer regular reviews of new HyperCard products, so you
can find additional information there.

HyperCard and Business

Happy first birthday, HyperCard! That's what the people from
Activision, developers of Focal Point and Business Class, are using as a
selling tool. Activision is offering these two HyperCard business
applications together in the HyperCard Birthday Bundle—a nice
marketing touch. These products were two of the first commercial
stacks available.

Focal Point, which is released as upgraded Focal Point II, is an
organizer (see fig. 17.28). You can use it for everything from collecting
client information to keeping a notepad and even getting into another
application. Focal Point begins with an opening screen listing 16
different buttons. Each button represents a different stack from which
you can select your activity, such as a daily calendar and appointments,

17
Hypercard

a Rolodex-like record of names and addresses, and a list of project deadlines. True to HyperCard intent and design, information that is placed in one stack is available and used by several others. Several other features expand on this organizer function; you can use Focal Point II to create "to do" lists based on project milestones, print different types of reports, and track project completion.

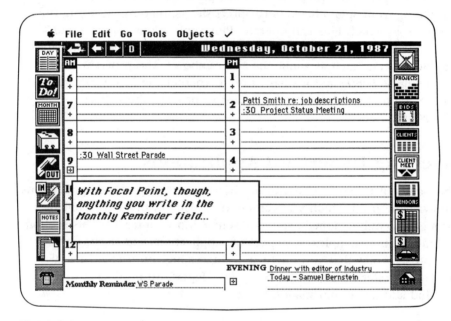

Fig. 17.28. *A Focal Point screen.*

Business Class, or the Around-the-World-with-a-Mac stack, takes you where you need to go (see fig. 17.29). You simply click one of the many maps that are available. You can get travel information about more than 65 countries, on such topics as currency exchange rates, names and number of hotels located in major cities, types of travel documents you need, special customs you might want to know about, and more. This product is more fun and instructional than practical, because if you need this information, you will rarely return home to your Mac to get it, but you could, of course, use it ahead of time.

Another business-oriented HyperCard product is HYPER-ACTION (from Nullisolutions, Inc., a collection of almost 50 stacks organized into the following groups:

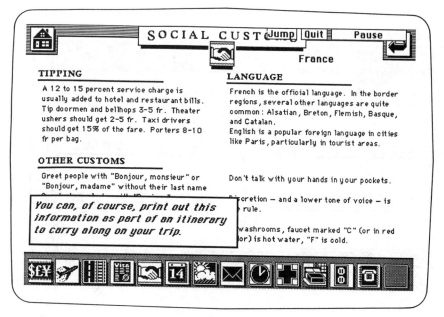

Fig. 17.29. A Business Class screen.

- Sales management (such as client corporate tree, mail target, and sales order)

- Personal productivity (such as letters, calendars, and "to do" lists)

- Administrative (such as phone memo, suppliers, and personnel)

- Utilities (such as on-line help)

- Miscellaneous (such as maps)

For example, figure 17.30 shows the opening screen for the Weekly Calendar stack, with a window for each weekday and one for the weekend days. This stack creates additional cards (or stacks) as needed. You can enter the stack from any other stack in Hypervision by clicking the Calendar button. HYPER-ACTION's extensive set of stacks sells for under $100.

17
Hypercard

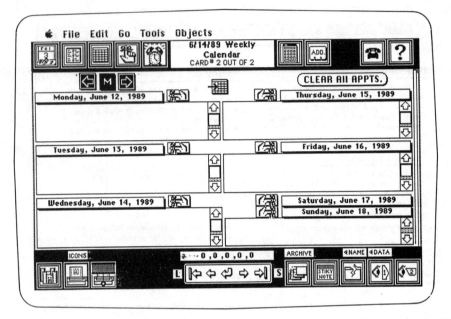

Fig. 17.30. *One of the HYPER-ACTION stacks.*

Legal Eagles

Software for managing offices is available, but you often need to buy several different packages from different manufacturers to get all that you need. Legal Aide (from Ghent Farm) is a set of office-management modules specifically designed for the legal profession, including client billing, report generation, and a database of client information. Although the price appears steep (from about $2,000 to $4,500), the product can be used for an entire office, which cuts the per lawyer/client costs considerably.

Generating Reports

An often-heard complaint about HyperCard is that generating hard copies (reports) of stacks is much more difficult than it should be (and in some cases impossible). This fact is surprising, especially when you consider the ease of use that characterizes HyperCard in general.

Reports (from Activision) provides you with a set of external commands (called XCNs) and a generic form for producing reports. You select a tool and then create the form that you want to use in the HyperCard stack you will print. You simply design the form you need, such as an invoice or an information form, and then let Reports do its work. Other features (such as those shown in fig. 17.31) provide sorting, simple calculations, printing of reports from multiple stacks, and the capability to print only the cards you want. This capability to be selective is important in a business setting, for example, when you want to bill only those clients who owe $100 or are 30 days late.

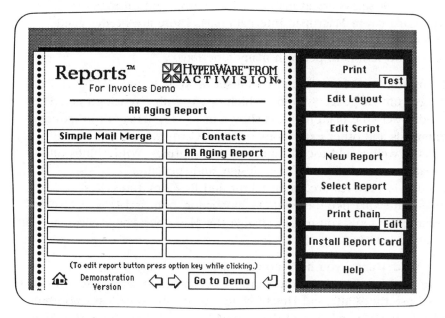

Fig. 17.31. *Sprucing up HyperCard reporting capability.*

XCMDs and XFCNs

XCMDs and XFCNs are chunks of course code written in a language that HyperCard can understand—often Pascal or C. An XCMD is an external command, and an XFCN is an external function. You might see these terms thrown around often in HyperCard literature. These two types of programs act as extensions to HyperTalk scripts and enable you to access any feature of the Macintosh Tool Box. They are, in

17
Hypercard

effect, treated as separate commands, just as in other programming languages.

Some specific products now on the market consist of libraries of XCMDs and XFCNs that you can just plug into your existing scripts—like modular script design. Just select the external commands you need, and go. One set of external commands is the VideoWorks II HyperCard Driver (from MacroMind), which enables you to access movies created with VideoWorks (also from MacroMind), putting the full power of this animation software to work.

More instant stacks are available as 101 Scripts and Buttons for HyperCard (from Macropac International). These are predesigned scripts that you can incorporate into your existing scripts or use as stand-alone scripts to perform many functions.

The most comprehensive and useful set of XCMDs and XFCNs is Wild Things from Language Systems, which opens with a roaring tiger. This four-disk set (the main menu is shown in fig. 17.32) is full of external commands and other extensions to HyperCard that can zip up your stacks as well as add useful functions and routines. Wild Things offers animation, statistical tools, icon design, and special effects. Also included is a full-featured icon editor and ResCopy tools. ResCopy works somewhat like the Font/DA mover for fonts and DAs; it installs resources or tools you use to change the Mac operating environment in HyperCard stacks.

With Wild Things, you have no reason to write a script to draw a curve. You can just go to the DrawCurve stack and, as you see in figure 17.33, use the Width and Height sliders to set the spikiness/smoothness and the shortness/tallness of the curve. After you draw the curve, you can cut and paste the script into a stack. You can even add animation effects that way. For programmers, the source code for all the resources in Pascal, FORTRAN, and C also is included. You can even use templates that are provided for designing your own XCMDs.

Developing Expert Systems

In Chapter 18, you learn a bit about expert systems and how you can use the Mac to help you generate rules and then provide information on which you can base decisions. HyperX (from Millennium Software) is a system for developing your own expert systems as HyperCard

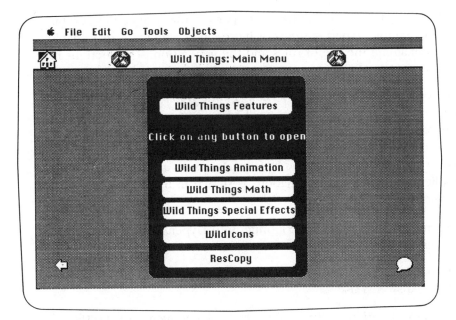

Fig. 17.32. *Wild Things offerings.*

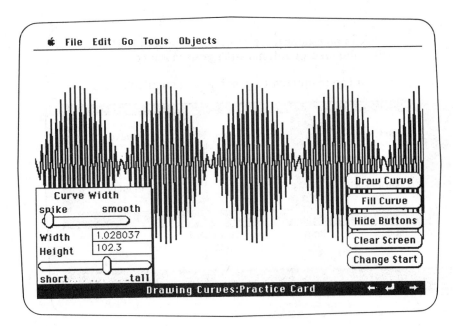

Fig. 17.33. *One of the Wild Things XCMDs for drawing a curve.*

17

Hypercard

stacks. One of the nice features of HyperX is that it includes several different sample expert systems of increasing complexity that enable you to examine the use of rules and the generation of deductions based on rules and facts.

For example, quite relevant to *The Big Mac Book* is the MacFix stack. (The opening card is shown in fig. 17.34.) This stack helps you diagnose problems you might encounter with Mac hardware or software. Hard disk problem? Click the Hard Disk square on-screen and answer the questions. As soon as HyperX has an answer (and you have supplied the necessary information, as shown in fig. 17.35), you get an answer.

Here are the questions that continue until HyperX can reach a conclusion:

HyperX Question: Is the hard disk driver bad?
Your Answer: False

HyperX Question: Is the SCSI cable NOT connected to the Hard Disk?
Your Answer: False

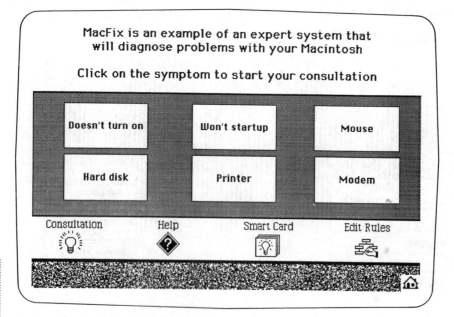

Fig. 17.34. The opening card for the MacFix stack.

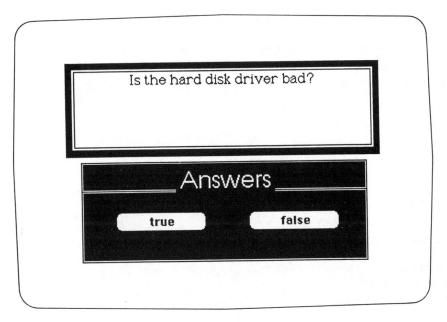

Fig. 17.35. *HyperX in action.*

HyperX Question: Is the SCSI cable bad?
Your Answer: True

HyperX Conclusion: Replace the cable

Now, of course, if you were the one to design the system (or you know a good deal about hard disks), this conclusion comes as no surprise. But in several instances you may not know what to look for, and the advice of an "expert" may be invaluable. Just think how much time you would save if someone said, "Well, have you checked the fuse?" These examples are relatively simple, but there is no limit to the complexity and the number of levels through which you must travel to get assistance in making a decision. HyperCard applications like HyperX are terrific tools for teaching, where feedback can be structured easily while students progress through different branches of the problem at their own rates.

Especially nice about HyperX is that you can add sound, connections to video disks, and graphics to any of the presentations while still preserving the qualities and characteristics of facts that are connected to one another.

17
Hypercard

Finding Some Sources for Stacks

You already know about the large public-domain companies such as Educomp and International Data, who also handle stackware (see Chapter 13). Here are some other sources worth investigating:

Advantage Computing
24285 Sunneymead Blvd.
Moreno Valley, CA 92388
(800) 356-4666

HyperSource
2619 S. 302nd Street
Federal Way, WA 98003
(206) 946-2011

maxStax+
P.O. Box 2719
Oakland, CA 94602

Don't forget that information services such as GEnie and CompuServe have nice libraries of stacks available for downloading. And most bulletin board services (BBSs) have large collections of stacks.

Chapter Summary

HyperCard has received a great deal of attention, and deservedly so. It provides an extraordinary array of tools that anyone, beginner or expert, can use to his or her own ends. HyperCard uses plain English commands like *go* and *answer*, and its application is limited only by the creativity and resourcefulness of the user, as you saw by the small sample of third-party HyperCard applications that have been developed already.

18

Programming Your Macintosh

A *program* is a set of instructions that a computer uses to execute an action or set of actions. In the preceding chapter on HyperCard, HyperTalk was used to create simple programs such as linking cards with a button, finding an item, and asking HyperCard to give the date.

A *language* is the syntax, or grammar, used to create your program. The actual computer words used in a program is called the *code*. HyperTalk is the HyperCard programming language, but there are many other languages that you are going to learn about in this chapter. A *programmer* is a person who writes a program; when you write script in HyperTalk, that's what you are. Obviously, there are different levels of sophistication to this process.

A *macro* is nothing more than a small program. Some macro programs, such as Apple's MacroMaker (a part of the System software), QuickKeys, or Tempo II, allow you to program by recording your keystrokes. More complex macro programs, such as Farallon's ScreenRecorder, actually record all actions of your Mac's screen to create a presentation. As application programs have become bigger and more complex, it is now very common to find that they come with an underlying programming language, like HyperCard. FileMaker II has a scripting language, and FoxBase+/Mac (a dBASE clone) has an implementation of dBASE. So like it or or not, you may find yourself programming.

Getting Started

Most people use computers without ever learning or using a programming language. Most of the applications discussed in the previous chapters are complex programs written in a variety of languages (most commonly in Pascal, C, or BASIC). These programs are set up to shield the user from ever having to worry about the details of the program's operation. You may never want to learn to program, and you certainly don't have to.

Why then should you bother to learn how to program? The simple answer is because you may find it fun, and there is no doubt that, in terms of what you can accomplish, programming can be powerful. Learning to program can be rewarding in the same way that playing a good computer game can be. Programming is a good intellectual exercise. Many star programmers started just like you, with a book like this one. There are many resources available to the budding programmer.

The Macintosh is unique in that there is a vast library of shareware programs in the public domain created by people just like you and me. If you have a program that you want to distribute, you can just upload it to a bulletin board and request payment from its users. If you have a hit program, the public will let you know; many people have turned professional just this way.

You might picture a programmer as someone who has long hair, stays up all night, and doesn't take showers. There are some folks out there like that, but all kinds of people program. StuffIt, the standard utility for file compression on the Macintosh (see the Communications section) was created by a high school student, Raymond Lau, now just starting at MIT. One fun place to go and read about the programming mystique is the book *Hackers* by Steve Levy (Dell Press).

The Macintosh is not an easy computer to program for. As a consequence, Macintosh programmers are highly sought after. At the time of this writing, it is common for starting Mac programmers to make $40,000. Programmers with experience make $60,000. Experts can make six-figure salaries. All that and no heavy lifting! Of course, if you are the proud owner of a hit program, the sky is the limit. So now that I have whetted your appetite, boot up and write some code.

Understanding the Programming Process

Programming is like writing a book; it is a process. Good programs are typically planned, or outlined, at the very beginning so that they may be efficiently constructed. You need to decide what the program must do, what would be nice features to include (if possible), and how all of the different parts will work together. Often people use flowcharts to guide them, and you can do this on your Macintosh with a commercial project management program like MacProject II (Claris), Manage That! (Varcon Systems), or MacFlow (Mainstay). An example of a flowchart is shown in figure 18.1.

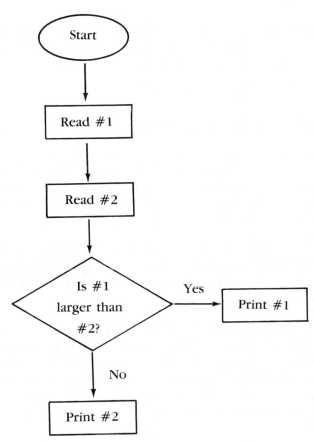

Fig. 18.1. A simple flowchart for a program that compares two numbers and prints the larger one.

Better, more complex development tools are available for specific languages. Very few programmers write sophisticated programs from scratch anymore. Normally, you can buy parts of a program, sometimes from a library of programming routines, and integrate them. This is the approach used in HyperTalk.

Professional programmers spend much time at the beginning of a project documenting a complex program. Often complex programs are written by teams of programmers. Each member is responsible for one particular feature. Apple writes system software this way, so do Microsoft and many other companies. There are many instances, however, where one programmer writes a major program alone. One example is the original version of the database Fourth Dimension. When you realize how powerful that program is, you begin to realize just what is possible for you to accomplish.

Debugging Your Program

When you write a program, you must test it thoroughly to see that it operates correctly. A successful program not only runs properly, but runs along with your other programs without causing problems. The process of testing a program is called *debugging*. There are professional tools (called debuggers) available to help you.

MacsBug (from Apple Programmers Development Association or APDA) is a machine-level debugger that is optimal for assembly language programs. Other machine-level debuggers are TMON (Icom Simulations) and NOSY.

Generally, debugging eats up a large part of your development time. You also can do debugging at the source level while working with higher-level languages. THINK C, THINK Pascal, and SADE (the Standard Apple Development Environment from Macintosh Programmers Workshop, or MPW) are all examples of languages with their own built-in debuggers.

Defining a Good Program

Several things differentiate a bad program from a good one (or even a good one from a great one). These characteristics are as follows:

- The features the program delivers. Business people call these benefits.

- How easy the program is to use. Is the program friendly, and do you smile when you use it?

- Is the program consistent with the computer interface? An *interface* is all of the things on your screen, like menus and commands, windows, icons, and so forth, that make a Macintosh a Macintosh. Apple considers the interface so important that it publishes a book on it for programmers, and Apple is suing other computer companies to protect its interface.

- The program efficiency. The speed at which the program runs is a function of how well the programmer wrote the program. It is possible to write long complex programs that require the computer to do unnecessary procedures, and programs with compact code that eliminate all but the essential steps.

- The compatibility of the program with other programs your Macintosh has to run at the same time

Apple publishes its rules for programs that use a Macintosh; as often as possible programmers try to follow those rules. Sometimes when programmers are trying to put in this really neat feature, they cheat a little. Often they can get by with it; sometimes they get unexpected results. When your computer bombs, it's often for reasons like these, and it may be the programmer's fault or it may be Apple's. It's almost impossible to write perfect software.

It is no exaggeration to say that very little of a programmer's time is spent putting in most of the features a program will use; maybe as little as 5 or 10 percent. The remainder of the time is spent making the program pleasurable to operate, and this factor is more true of the Macintosh than of most other microcomputers.

Defining Terms

Learning to program well requires knowledge about all aspects of your computer. Some computer languages shield you from knowing what microprocessor you have in your Mac or what the bus structure is. Eventually, you learn these details as you program because the commands available to you are defined by your equipment. Think of programming like peeling the skin off an onion—you use the outside layers at the beginning, and as you work with it more and more, you get right down to the center. Some folks would say you cry all the way through.

Understanding Chip Talk

Macintosh computers use Motorola microprocessors, commonly referred to as the 68000 series. This series includes the 68000 (Mac 512, Plus, SE, and the Mac Laptop), the 68020 (Mac II), and the 68030 (Mac IIcx, IIci, and IIx).

A 68040 microprocessor has been built, but hasn't yet been incorporated into a Mac. Rumor has it that Apple will bypass the 68040 and build its next machine around the RISC-based 88000 series CPU. RISC stands for Reduced Instruction Set Chip. These chips run faster because they contain a less complicated instruction set. They run more instructions overall, but they run more efficiently. All members of this family of CPUs have put alongside them on the motherboard a chip called the ROM (read-only memory) where instructions and routines (small programs) are encoded.

This ROM is what makes the Macintosh a Macintosh, a large part of its operating instructions are coded into the computer right on the ROM, and that's the reason why it's extremely difficult to clone a Mac.

Any program, including the ones Apple writes to operate the Macintosh System and the Finder, use the instructions encoded in the ROM along with any additional instructions needed. The whole set of instructions in a Macintosh (both supplied in ROM on the motherboard) and in the System software is called the *Tool Box* and is organized around a set of functions that Apple calls *Managers*.

When you write a program and you ask your Macintosh to perform an operation, you are issuing a *call*. There are some 1,200 calls available in the Tool Box, and that's the rub. Some routines, such as drawing complex graphics, require just a single call and are easy, but there's so much to know. When you program the Mac, you first need to know how to program with your language of choice, and then how to use the Tool Box.

Defining Machine Language

In the very earliest days of microcomputers when people bought them in pieces, like the Altair 88, the computer came in a box as wires, chips, lights, a box, and a set of instructions. When you put it together, the computer had six lights, and the way you wired the chip was your program. You could do various feats of mathematics and logic with this machine, but it was a hobbyist's toy. As computers got more complex, you could program the computer directly from the keyboard, using a set of instructions that the computer's microprocessor understood.

A CPU works with digital signals, either on or off, so the language you used was composed of a set of instructions that consisted of 1s or 0s which corresponded to on or off. This kind of language is called *machine language*. Although it was used for a brief time in the 1950s, no one programs like this any more because it's too hard to understand.

In figure 18.2, you see a screen from Symantec Utilities for the Macintosh (SUM) Symantec Tools. The screen shows a Macintosh file open with its machine code displayed. You can alter the code and change any aspect of the program, but you have to know how to program before this capability is useful. If you change the code, you can destroy your application or corrupt your System file. The rule is to always work on a copy of your file, and boot up from a copy of your System if possible.

Fairly early in computer history, it became apparent that each new computer was requiring tremendous development efforts in order to just create a basic operating system. AT&T uses computers heavily as telecommunications controllers, and the company was getting bogged down by all the different types of computers it was buying. The research staff there set about creating a universal development system based on a new language that would be easily portable from one machine to another. The language turned out to be C, and the operating system they developed turned into UNIX.

A/UX is Apple's version of UNIX, and it will turn a 2M Macintosh with a hard drive and a PMMU capability into a client computer served by a UNIX host (the server). All 68030 machines (Mac IIcx, ci, x, and SE/30) have PMMU built right in. The 68020 (Mac II) can be upgraded to PMMU by a chip swap. All other 68000 machines (MacPlus, SE, and

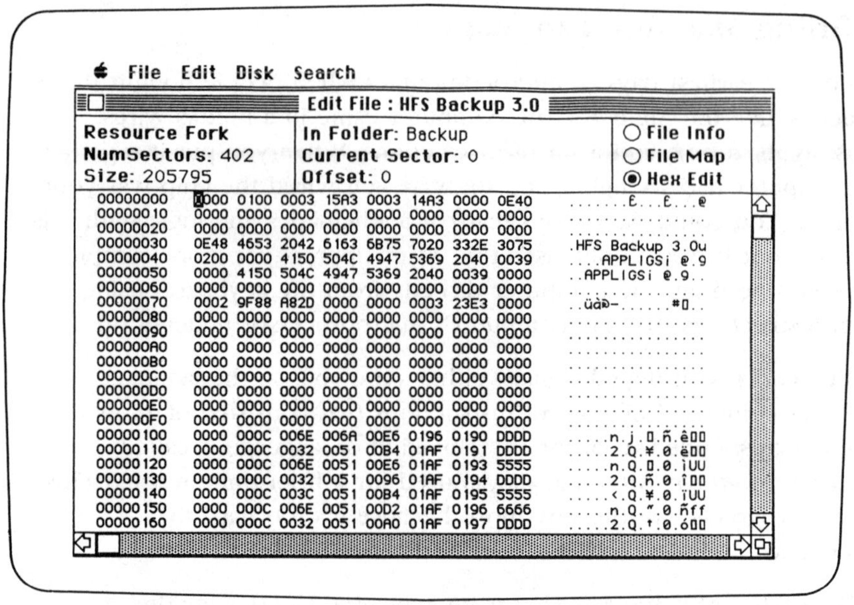

Fig. 18.2. Machine code displayed by Symantec Tools in SUM.

the Laptop) cannot be configured this way and will not be fully UNIX compatible, or capable of running virtual memory. An Australian company, Whitesmith, has just announced MacIDRIS, a UNIX system that will work on an ordinary Mac Plus.

UNIX operates by creating a *kernel* programmed into the computer as a basic operating system. The kernel is like the foundation of a house; it supports the operating system but is transparent to the user. In the kernel are sophisticated functions, such as complex Print commands, File management services, and so forth. The kernel is usually much easier to write than a complete operating system because a kernel is smaller and well defined, and you can use parts from a library of functions. Any computer equipment manufacturer uses the kernel appropriate to the CPU in its computer as a base and writes a *shell*, which serves as the machine interface. You could consider the Finder to be a Macintosh shell.

Defining Assembly Language

Assembly language exists for each family of microprocessors and translates computer programs into a form that your CPU understands

18
Program-
ming

(a set of 1s and 0s). Some programmers work in assembly language because it is possible to create very small, compact, fast programs this way. Most people don't use assembly to program because there are more sophisticated languages that allow you to create complex programs with fewer lines of code. It is important, however, to understand that when you use a language like Pascal or C, that language is generally accessing an underlying assembly language that you don't see operating (it's transparent to you), and that assembly language is translating your instructions into machine language. Most people don't concern themselves with these details.

Examples of Macintosh versions of assemblers are Consulair 68000 Development System (Consulair Corporation), MacAsm Macroassembler (Mainstay), TMON (Icom Simulations), and ASM (Micro Dialects). TMON is a market leader.

Using Compilers and Interpreters

All the high-level languages work by using complex commands. In BASIC, you might have as a command PRINT, which is part of a larger program. When the Macintosh does a print routine using this command, the computer will actually execute several functions. In order to enable a language to use complex (often English-based words), when you are finished writing your program, the language will initiate a recoding of your instructions into the simpler and faster assembly, or machine, language. This process is called compilation, and it is why when you buy a commercial version of a language like C or Pascal, the package is called, a *compiler*. Even some macro packages require compilation to run efficiently. WorksPlus Command (Lundgren and Associates), a macro package for Microsoft Works, will compile your macro when you finish writing it.

Using CLIs and GUIs

Among the first microcomputers that were built were character-based machines. An IBM PC is this type of computer. The computer displays each character on the screen, and with each screen update (called a screen refresh) only the changed characters are updated. This kind of computer normally has a prompt, which is a type of cursor like an insertion point. This kind of interface is commonly called a Command

Line Interface (CLI). The advantage of this kind of interface is that it operates very quickly and can easily be built with an underlying scripting language. Typically, these computers do complex batch jobs that are not yet possible with a Macintosh. The disadvantage is that the CLI interface is very difficult to learn and nonintuitive.

The Macintosh is an example of a Graphical User Interface (GUI). Most functions on a Macintosh are accomplished using symbols (icons) and motion-related input like that you do with your mouse. The Finder is the Macintosh GUI. Graphical interfaces are by no means unique to the Macintosh. Microsoft Windows for the IBM PC, New Wave for Hewlett-Packard computers, and an array of UNIX shells, such as X-Windows and Open Motif, are examples of graphical interfaces. The success of the Apple Macintosh spurred their development.

All the things that go on the screen, such as windows and menus, are built into the interface and need to be programmed into your program. As your Macintosh refreshes the screen, it is building a new image of the screen for the next update in a part of your video card's RAM called a screen buffer.

This buffer is emptied and rebuilt with each pass of your monitor's electronic sweep. The disadvantage of a GUI is that it has much overhead and it is a tad bit slower than a text-based machine. The advantage is that it is intuitive and easy to learn.

The language that your Macintosh uses to draw features of your screen is called QuickDraw, and it is a proprietary programming language created by Apple specifically for the Macintosh computer. PostScript is another page-description language for laser printers (created by Adobe), and it is supported or translated to by current Apple software. All current versions of the Macintosh use QuickDraw to create on-screen images (like fonts), and your Macintosh can use QuickDraw to print as well. QuickDraw is encoded into your ROM; it's a major part of the Tool Box.

Programming the Macintosh Tool Box

I have talked so much about the Tool Box because it is what makes the Macintosh special. In this section, I discuss elements of the Tool Box, the choices available for programming languages, and the way you decide which one to use.

Apple Computer, Inc., publishes a five-volume set of guidelines, that details all the elements of the Macintosh Tool Box. These guidelines are called *Inside Macintosh* (published by Addison-Wesley). Additionally, there is a set of XREF commands published in a separate book, as well as *The Human Interface Guidelines*, discussed later. These books are not the place to learn to program the Mac. When you read *Inside Macintosh*, each chapter refers to topics in other places. By all means, however, browse through these books; you will learn a great deal; they are Apple's technical guidelines.

There are two developer's tools that are worth mentioning for developing a Macintosh application interface. They are Prototyper (SmetherBarnes) and AppMaker (Bowers Development). Prototyper provides a set of templates for various features of the interface, such as menus and dialog boxes. When you are finished defining these, Prototyper generates the source code your application needs in either (C or Pascal). In AppMaker, you draw the interface, and then let AppMaker generate source code in C or Pascal. AppMaker uses a run-time library for the construction of the generated code.

The Tool Box is organized around specific functions like Printing, Communications, Events, QuickDraw routines, and so on. When your program asks Macintosh to do something, it is placing a call to the Tool Box for a particular manager.

Managers were set up to allow complex tasks to be programmed easily. Did you ever wonder why all paint programs in Macintosh have such similar tools? Or why you can use many of the same selection techniques in different programs like Word or MacWrite? The reason is that many of the routines were encoded into the ROM or are part of the System file. Apple encourages this uniformity and issues a set of guidelines as to how programs can work. The whole idea is to create a user experience that makes it easy for you to work with new unfamiliar programs.

Understanding the Event-Driven Environment

The Macintosh is an event-driven computer. That is, the computer is constantly checking for new input and monitoring the state of the current input. It checks where the cursor is located, whether your mouse button is up or down, whether you have issued a keyboard command or a menu command, and other things. The computer checks conditions many times a second, and it does not act unless a condition was specified in the program that is running. At the very least, the operating system program is always running, so this checking is always going on.

The point is that an event generates an appropriate action. In the Tool Box is a routine called the Event Manager, which is responsible for monitoring events. The Event Manager sets up a queue, or line, and prioritizes events so that the Macintosh can execute them in a logical and defined order.

A complete explanation of the Tool Box is beyond the scope of this book. For more information, check the section on Mac programming books later in this chapter.

Understanding Memory Management

One aspect of programming worth mentioning is that of memory management. Your Macintosh must do some juggling to keep several programs running at the same time. When you boot up, you load your System (which is the Macintosh operation system), and it is always running. If you launch an application, that runs as well. If you use MultiFinder, you can be running several applications. The way the computer keeps all of them straight is called memory management.

The basic principle of memory management is that your computer executes programs in random-access memory (RAM). That's why the amount of RAM has a direct bearing on the size of your application load. Places in RAM are assigned addresses, and these address are numbered from low memory to high. Your System (which loads first) goes into low memory, and Apple assigns these address numbers so that no other programs can run in them. This part of memory is called the *system heap*. Above the system heap is where applications load, and the addresses taken are not normally released until the application is closed.

The connections between your program and memory addresses are called *hooks*. Hooks are like bookmarks that hold a program's place in memory. Creating hooks is part of the programming process. When a part of the program is not being used, the hooks still remain.

With PMMU there is dynamic control of memory, releasing addresses when not needed. This is why virtual•memory in System 7 requires an 68030 chip or a 68020 with an upgraded PMMU chip. Managed memory reallocates memory not currently in use through a swapping technique.

Understanding Apple's Human Interface Guidelines

Apple is so concerned with preserving what is called "the look and feel" of its interface and programs that it publishes a guideline called *The Human Interface Guideline* (published by Addison-Wesley), which tells programmers how to make their applications behave. By decree, you must have the Apple, File, and Edit menus at the minimum, and certain commands like Open, Close, or Quit must be contained on those menus. The use of certain keystrokes like ⌘-O for Open is required, and others are strongly recommended. These guidelines make interesting reading, and they were developed to make the Macintosh as user friendly as it can be.

Choosing a Language

So you are about to choose a language to learn, and you're wondering where to start. Most people begin with a good high-level language like BASIC, Pascal, or C. BASIC is somewhat easier than Pascal, which is easier than C. In terms of use in Macintosh programming, C is more commonly used today. Pascal is also commonly used and seems to be known by all serious programmers.

Schools tend to teach BASIC and Pascal; Pascal was chosen as the standard language in the College Entrance Exams Advanced Placement tests. In elementary schools, LOGO and sometimes APL are taught. Children are very good subjects for programming; they have none of the inhibitions of adults and don't mind the play aspects of exploring a language.

There are two types of languages used today: imperative languages and object-oriented programs.

An *imperative* program is a language that creates a command structure which manipulates defined routines in some programmed ways. Most of the common programs like BASIC, Pascal, and C are imperative in nature.

The smaller class of languages are called *object-oriented programming* (OOP) languages. HyperTalk and SmallTalk/V Mac are examples of OOP. Several languages, such as C++ and Object Pascal, are rewrites of other languages (C and Pascal, respectively) that have defined objects built-in. In OOP, objects are predefined along with their properties and appropriate actions that can be performed on them.

When you buy a language, there are generally several pieces to it, and commonly, languages operate with several windows open to show you those parts. In one window you program, in another you have your compiler set up, while in a third you could be setting up and working with your debugger. These windows are all commonly part of a commercial package. That is why programmers frequently refer to a language package as a *development environment.*

Originally, the Macintosh operating system was programmed in Pascal. When you look at early editions of *Inside Macintosh*, you see Pascal examples. Over time, the C language became more popular so that now most serious programmers know and program in a version of C. Many people still use Pascal, and either language will serve you well in your programming experience.

The term *portability* refers to the rewriting of an application in another language so that it runs on another computer. Porting an application from the Mac to MS-DOS means that the application has a better chance of being commercially successful. Often porting means that the program needs to be totally rewritten from scratch, but not always. Your choice of language will have a profound effect on whether you can port from one computer platform to another, and is a major selling point for a language. SmallTalk/V runs on both the Mac and the PC, and the language developer claims that it is easy to port an application written in that language. Keep this in mind when you make your selection.

Defining the High-Level Languages

In this section, I discuss the important high-level languages and commercial products that are available on the Macintosh. As a worthwhile introduction to computer languages, I recommend

Computer Languages: A Guide to the Perplexed by Naomi S. Baron (published by Anchor/Doubleday, 1986). The *McGraw-Hill Encyclopedia of Electronics and Computers* contains a concise dictionary of technical terms.

BASIC

BASIC stands for the Beginner's All-Purpose Symbolic Instruction Code. It was written in 1964 by John Kemeny and Thomas Kurtz at Dartmouth College as a simplified version of the earlier FORTRAN, for student instruction. BASIC is the most popular computer language because it is logical and well-structured. It is the most often taught language in college. It has been estimated that more people know BASIC than can speak French.

BASIC was somewhat free-form in its earliest versions, but it has evolved into newer standardized versions that are more structured. Structured BASIC includes such features as line numbering and indentation marks for a procedure in the source code, both features found in Pascal. Microsoft BASIC and True BASIC (written by Kemeny and Kurtz) are earlier versions. Other BASIC packages include DS-BASIC (Daystar Software), PCMacBASIC (Pterodactyl Software), RBASIC (Indexed Software), and ZBASIC (Zedcor). Keep in mind that most forms of BASIC are not entirely compatible with one another.

MS QuickBASIC (a later, more-structured version) enables you to program in one window while giving the results in a second. In figure 18.3, you see a program for values of 2 raised to powers of from 1 to 64. The results can be printed if desired.

Pascal

Pascal (named for mathematician Blaise Pascal) was written by Niklaus Wirth and is a highly structured programming language. Based in part on ALGOL, Pascal is a standardized language with specifications by the International Standards Organization. Pascal is a recommended starting place for learning C, which is now the most popular development language for microcomputers. The original Macintosh operating system was programmed in Pascal.

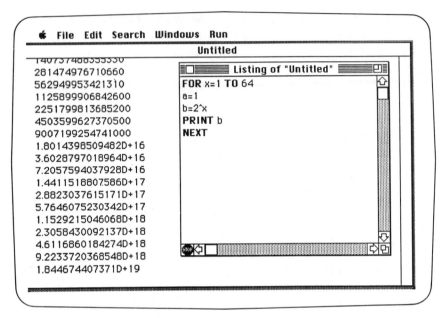

Fig. 18.3. *Using MS QuickBasic to compute a program for the exponentiation of 2.*

A recent package called Just Enough Pascal (Symantec) is a tutorial on Pascal on the Macintosh. In this tutorial, you program windows and create a simple game. Just Enough Pascal is a highly recommended introduction to programming.

The commercial versions of Pascal on the Macintosh include Think's Lightspeed Pascal and Turbo Pascal for the Macintosh (Borland International).

C and C++

C was the developmental language created by Dennis Ritchie at AT&T, as a portable language on which UNIX is based. C was a successor to a language called B. C is structured, runs fast, and has good memory-management features built-in, but is difficult to learn. Jean-Louis Gass'e (President of Apple R & D) has been quoted as saying that, "Real men program in C." He probably meant real women, too.

There are several versions of C available to Mac users, including Aztec C (Manx Software), Consulair MacC 68020/68881 (Consulair Corp.),

Consulair MacC Jr. (Consulair Corp.), and Think's Lightspeed C (Symantec Corp.). Lightspeed C is a highly regarded and popular product.

Recently C has been updated to include object-oriented features and the new version of the language is called C++. Apple is very excited about this new language and has chosen to rewrite the System and Finder for System 7 completely in this new language. The package Designer C++ is available from Oasys, Inc., and from the Apple Programmers Developers Association.

LISP

LISP is a language that works by acting on, or manipulating, lists of items. The name is an acronym that comes from *LISt Processing*. LISP requires significant amounts of memory to run, but it is a highly efficient, intelligent language with considerable power. LISP has found favor in various artificial intelligence applications serving as the underlying mechanism, or *inference engine*, for programs from academics to industrial research. Available packages include ExperCommon LISP and ExperLISP (both from ExperTelligence), MacScheme (Semantic Microsystem), and Allegro Common LISP (for A/UX) from Franz, Inc., LISP is the language that LOGO is based on.

LISP is a complex, batch-oriented language that requires considerable processing of instructions. Often people add coprocessor boards, such as the Micro Explorer Nubus board from Texas Instruments (for the Mac II series), to make programs run faster.

LOGO

LOGO is a favorite language to teach to children. It comes from the Greek word *logos* meaning word, or thought, and was developed at MIT by Don Bobrow and Seymour Papert. Graphics are easy to program in LOGO, and it is a full programming language. Considered more difficult to create documented programs in than Pascal or C, LOGO is not recommended as a starting place. Packages available are ExperLOGO-Plus (ExperTelligence) and Terrapin LOGO for the Macintosh (Terrapin).

Miscellaneous Languages

There are many other languages available for the Macintosh. It seems like every other day a new one is being developed. Most of these languages see very limited service, some die out, and some (like C++) become important over time. The sections that follow discuss some of these languages (but by no means all of them).

Modula-2 is based on Pascal and is written by Niklaus Wirth. This lanugage is more sophisticated than Pascal and offers modules and concurrent programming. In concurrent programming, more than one module can be executing at the same time. Programs written in this language can be compiled in modules and run separately, thus allowing real-time control. Packages include MacLogimo Plus (Project Modula), MetCom Modula-2 (Metropolis Computer Networks, Inc.), and Semper-Soft Modula-2 for MPW (Semper Software).

COBOL was an early computer language that has found favor on large computers for business applications. The name stands for *CO*mmon *B*usiness *O*riented *L*anguage. Virtually no programs run in COBOL on microcomputers.

FORTRAN (*FOR*mula *TRAN*slation) is an old language used for mathematical manipulations mostly on larger computers. It remains in some use at research centers but has no impact on microcomputers. Packages include FORTRAN Converter (True Basic), which translates FORTRAN to True Basic; MacFORTRAN (various versions by Absoft Corp.); and Mactran Plus (DCM Data Products).

APL, or *A P*rogramming *L*anguage, was developed at Harvard by Kenneth Iverson and is useful for manipulating numerical arrays. APL manipulates matrixes, creates compact code, and uses symbols that make a program hard to recreate. Packages include APL*Plus System for the Macintosh (STSC, Inc.) and APL 68000 for the Apple Macintosh (Spencer Organization).

VIP, or Visual Interactive Programming (Mainstay), uses the flowchart analogy and icons and symbols to create a program. An example of a graphical language in VIP the flowchart is the program itself; it's what you see when you examine the source code.

Using OOP, Object-Oriented Programming

18

Object-Oriented Programming (OOP) is the beginning of a new wave in programming languages. Unlike Pascal or C, which are examples of imperative languages, OOP manipulates defined objects in ways that are defined by the objects themselves. In OOP there are different classes of objects, and they are very loosely arranged in an order, or hierarchy. Actions or commands flow through this structure of objects until they find an appropriate object that can handle them.

Using HyperTalk and SuperHyperTalk

HyperCard is an example of an OOP. In HyperCard you have objects like stacks, cards, and fields. Each object has its own *properties*, or capability to accept actions. Events or commands flow through the hierarchy from fields to cards to stacks to home stack until the event or command can be operated on.

In SuperCard (Silicon Beach) a superset of HyperTalk was created to allow for color, full window support, complete text objects, and many more features too numerous to mention. A similar program called Plus has just appeared.

HyperTalk is a full-featured programming language, and it is very powerful. Through the use of XCMDs (external commands) and XFCNs (external functions), the full power of the Tool Box (all 1,200 calls) can be accessed.

Using SmallTalk V/Mac

When Steve Jobs visited Xerox PARC where he saw the Xerox STAR, he immediately grasped the importance of its revolutionary graphical user interface. The STAR served as the model for the Apple Lisa computer, which later was developed into the Apple Macintosh. Underlying the Xerox STAR and equally as significant was an object-oriented programming language called SmallTalk, which was created by the computer visionary Allen Kay (now an Apple Fellow). Kay was responsible for defining many of the principles of graphical user interfaces.

SmallTalk needed significant memory and speed to operate, and now that the Macintosh has grown, this language has made it into commercial packages. Two such packages are Smalltalk-80 (ParcPlace Systems) and Smalltalk/V Mac (Digitalk, Inc.). Smalltalk/V Mac has a PC 286/386 counterpart and is claimed by the vendor to be easily portable. People who have worked with Smalltalk say that it is hard to create a full-featured program with it, but the program is easy to learn and work with.

As an aside, if you are interested in the early days of Apple Computers and the philosophy and politics that created the Macintosh, read *West of Eden* by Frank Rose (Viking Press).

OOP is the future in programming languages. It's easy to create programs, and the language is intuitive and powerful. Industry pundits claim that all of these features will combine to make OOP languages the languages of choice in the next decade.

The whole point of object-oriented design is to create enough underlying structure to the programming so that complex programming tasks are bundled together into simple manipulations. Accessing an address is as simple as linking. HyperCard creates a button and associated script for this. Need a new address or set of addresses? In HyperCard, you create a card or stack of cards.

On the surface, it all looks simple. You create the objects you need with a single command (or set of commands). So OOP is easy to get started with. Just understand what objects are available and how they are related, and off you go. On further examination, you realize that all the objects and their relationships are available to you for modification. Remember in HyperTalk, you could go into an object (a button, card, or stack), open and examine a script, and make any modifications you choose. It's possible to add any functions you can imagine in HyperTalk (through XCMDs and XFCNs). Any OOP language is truly full-featured, and because of the basic properties of the objects, it is highly structured. This structure makes the language very logical, easy to plan programs in, and very powerful.

Using the Resource Editor (ResEdit)

ResEdit (the *resource editor*) is Apple's programming tool that allows a developer to go into a program and easily change its features. It's not programming per se, but most Macintosh users find working with ResEdit to be fun because it allows easy manipulation of features like layout, icons, dialog boxes, and a whole host of other features.

Understanding How a Resource Editor Works

Macintosh files are different from those found on other microcomputers. Mac files are composed of two parts. One part, called the *resource fork*, contains resources like icons, dialogs, and menu commands—the things that make the Macintosh program look like a Macintosh program. A second part, called the *data fork*, contains all the data you create in a file. Some files created by applications contain only data and may have only a data fork. Separating the two parts of a file allows developers to improve the program by modifying the resources without concerning themselves with the data. This separation modularizes the process.

When developers are writing a program in Macintosh, their resources are usually grouped into common units. The developer normally creates a template that can be viewed in the resource editor for that resource. Not all resources are mapped out this way; it's up to the developer to do it. If a developer doesn't like a particular menu command location or keystroke equivalent, she can use the template and ResEdit to change them.

You might ask why a developer would create a template and put so much of the guts of the program out where it can be modified. The answer is that it greatly simplifies the development process, and few Macintosh users avail themselves of the power of this great program.

ResEdit can be very dangerous to use, and once it is used on an application, that application's warranty is null and void. Use ResEdit only with extreme caution.

In figure 18.4, ResEdit was launched, and the System file was opened by double-clicking its name. In the active window is a listing of all the resource templates available for editing. Typical resource templates are as follows:

WIND	window
PICT	picture
SIGN	small icons
PAT	patterns
TEMP	templates
PAT#	single patterns
MENU	menu definitions
PREC	printing
ICN#	icon list
FKEY	fkey control
FONT	font information
ALRT	alert or warning boxes
DITL	dialog box text
DSAT	system startup box
DLOG	dialog boxes
CURS	cursor
ICON	icons

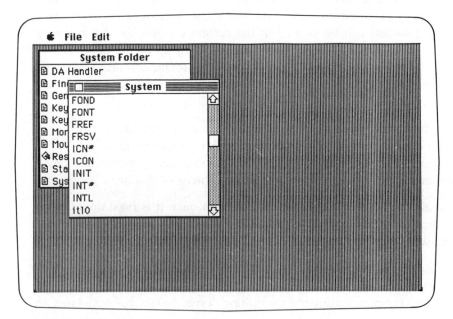

Fig. 18.4. *Resource templates viewed in ResEdit for a System file.*

An important rule to remember when running ResEdit is to work on a backup copy of a file. Changes you make may crash your program. In some instances, it is possible to corrupt your System file, so it's not a bad idea to boot up from a copy of your System file.

Using ResEdit To Change Icons

You can use ResEdit to alter the icons that appear on your desktop. The procedure is as follows:

1. Launch ResEdit.

2. Open the System file by double-clicking its name.

3. In the resulting resource list, double-click the ICN# template.

The resulting screen is shown in figure 18.5. Icons consist of two patterns: a mask and a monitor. The actual icon on your desktop is a composite, one superimposed on another.

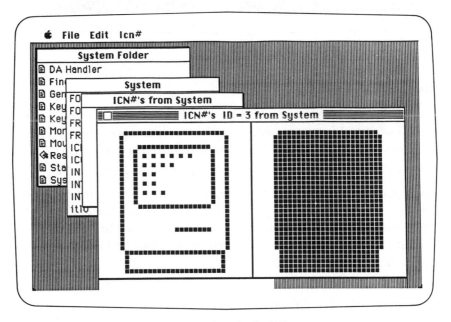

Fig. 18.5. *The System file icon template in ResEdit.*

To change an icon, use your cursor to click pixels on and off (or black and white if you are in that mode). A modified System icon is shown in figure 18.6.

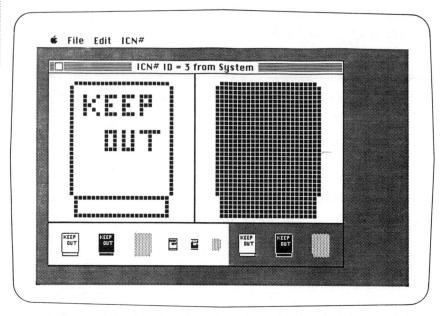

Fig. 18.6. *The System file icon has been changed.*

Using Color Finder

If you have a color monitor (a Mac II), you can use a shareware program called Color Finder with ResEdit to create 32-bit color icons on your desktop. The program has a color palette. Look for it on shareware and public domain collections like BCSMac and BMUG.

Not only are icons available for editing, but so are cursors. If you don't like the arrows, wrist watches, and flashing horizontal insertion bars or anything else on your screen, just go into your System file and edit them using ResEdit. Turn your busy wrist watch into an hourglass; be fanciful and amaze your friends.

Using ResEdit To Change Layout

With ResEdit, you can get into the Finder and change the spacing of icons on your desktop. As in the procedure for icons, open Finder (use a working copy) in ResEdit, and open the LAYO (or Layout template). You will see a screen like the one shown in figure 18.7. Using the text boxes, enter new values for all the parameters you want to change. All the programs on the market (normally shareware) that perform the function of changing layout design perform exactly the same functions you can duplicate in ResEdit.

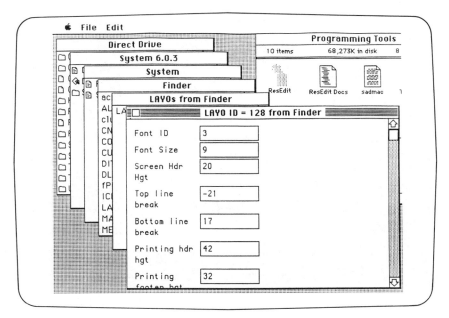

Fig. 18.7. Using the Layout template in ResEdit to change the Finder's icon placements.

Using ResEdit To Change Menu Commands

Are you annoyed that your favorite command appears on the wrong menu? Or that the keystroke equivalent is not the one you favor? Changing menu items is easy and identical in operation to what you have done so far. Just open the MENU template of your favorite application (use a working copy) and change it. It's that easy.

Using ResEdit To Change Alert Boxes

If you are unhappy about what is said in an alert box, or you want to surprise your friends, you can change the message in ResEdit. The Alert templates are found in the ALRT or DITL templates, and you can even change personalization data in start-up screens. Be careful, though, to use your personal copy when you do this, as doing it on a copy you don't own violates the copyright laws, depending on the licensing agreement. You can see in figures 18.8 and 18.9 the DITL template and the start-up screen dialog box for MacPaint.

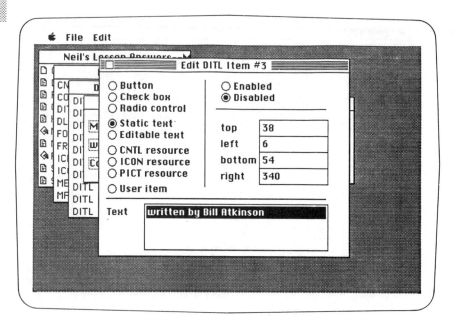

Fig. 18.8. *MacPaint DITL template.*

Using ResEdit To Change Fonts

Fonts are an editable resource in ResEdit. Just open the FONT template and work away. A typical font screen is shown in figure 18.10.

Defining Artificial Intelligence and Expert Systems

Artificial Intelligence, or Expert Systems, are computer programs (often written in languages like C or Pascal) that deduce solutions to complex problems based on a clear set of rules that you programmed in. An AI program runs on what is commonly referred to as an *inference engine*, and many of these programs are statistically based. You supply initial conditions and any subsequent factors that are important, and the AI program does the deduction based on a clearly defined set of rules. Obviously, the AI program is only as good as the programmer who

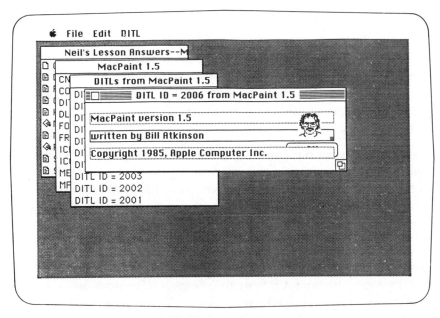

Fig. 18.9. *MacPaint start-up screen template.*

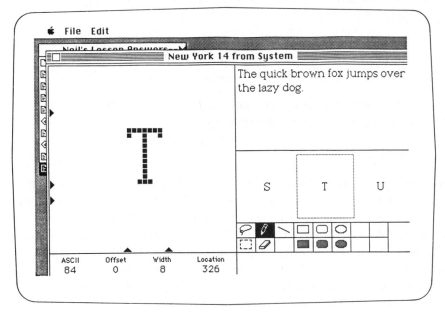

Fig. 18.10. *The New York 14 font screen, using ResEdit's Font template.*

programs it. However, in this rapidly developing field, these programs are quite good.

Often, AI programs manipulate lists of objects in specific ways or deal with specific properties of objects. This capability makes AI perfect for leading-edge languages like LISP and OOP. Many of the languages owe their existence to the solution of particular problems in the field of Artificial Intelligence.

Applications of AI span the entire spectrum of life from the engineering disciplines (such as optimizing the construction and operation of a microchip), to speeding up a factory floor, to distilling the knowledge of a human expert (say in soup making) into a set of rules that can be used by others.

I have discussed some languages, like LOGO and LISP, that are commonly used in AI applications. Some others include Advanced A.I. Systems' Prolog (Advanced A.I. Systems), Cognate (Peridom, Inc.), ExperFacts (ExperTelligence), ExperProlog II (ExperTelligence), Inter-Expert (Human Intellect Systems), Level5 Macintosh (Information Builders), MacSmarts (Cognition Technology Corp.), Nextra and Nextra Object (Neuron Data), Nexsus (Human Intellect Systems), and SuperExpert (Softsync).

CASE, computer-aided software engineering, is a programming tool in which you use the software to write other software. Sometimes CASE tools are endowed with AI features, but not always.

In CASE, complex computer programs can be created logically and quickly. Although a complete discussion of CASE falls outside the scope of this book, it is a very important developer's tool and a rapidly advancing field.

CASE tools typically cost many thousands of dollars and require a long time to learn. Packages available include ACPVision (Andyne Computing Ltd.), AdaFlow (Iconix Software Engineering), Blue/20 and /60 (Advanced Software Logic), Deft (Deft), Design (Meta Software Corp.), ERVision (Andyne Computing), FormsProgrammer (OHM Software), Foundation Vista (Menlo Business Systems), Iconix PowerTools (Iconix Software Engineering), MacAnalyst (Excel Software), Mac Bubbles (StarSys, Inc.), MacDesigner (Excel Software), MetaDesigner (Excel Software), and Silverrun (Peat Marwick).

18
Program-
ming

Resources for Macintosh Programmers

What follows is by no means a complete list, but is intended to give you a starting point. You also should get a copy of *Guide to Languages and Tools* (available from Apple Developer Services) for more information.

Apple-Related Resources

APDA, the Apple Programmers Developers Association, provides development tools and documentation. The APDA also publishes the APDALog quarterly.

AppleLink is an electronic BBS for developers. It provides access to Apple technical staff and the latest information.

Developer Programs administers the Developer Partners and Associates program and supplies marketing information.

Developer Technical Support provides technical notes and sample code.

Developer University offers technical training for developers.

Phil and Dave's Excellent CD, published by Apple, is the complete developers' documentation on CD ROM.

Macintosh Associations

TechAlliance publishes *MacTech Quarterly* and sells development software and documentation.

MacApp Developer's Association publishes a bimonthly newsletter, *Frameworks*. They also sell source and object code libraries and books and provide training courses.

Programming Books

There are many, many books on this topic. Que Corporation publishes the following:

Assembly Language Quick Reference, Que Corporation
C Programmer's Toolkit, Jack Purdum
C Programming Guide, 3rd Edition, Jack Purdum
C Quick Reference, Que Corporation

Oracle Programmer's Guide, Que Corporation
Power Graphics Programming, Michael Abrash
QuickBASIC Advanced Techniques, Peter Aitken
QuickBASIC Quick Reference, Que Corporation
QuickBASIC Programmer's Toolkit, Tom Rugg, Phil Feldman
SQL Programmer's Guide, Umang Gupta, William Gietz
Turbo C Programming, Alan C. Plantz
Turbo Pascal Advanced Techniques, Chris Ohlsen, Gary Stoker
Turbo Pascal Programmer's Toolkit, Tom Rugg, Phil Feldman
Turbo Pascal Quick Reference, Que Corporation
Using Assembly Language, Allen Wyatt
Using HyperCard: From Home to HyperTalk, W. Tay Vaughan III
Using QuickBASIC 4, Phil Feldman, Tom Rugg
Using Turbo Pascal, Michael Yester

Electronic Media (Networks)

CompuServe Information Service hosts the AppDev forum for all Apple developers, and the MacForth forum. CompuServe also hosts the Symantec forum, which supports THINK Pascal and THINK C, and the Borland forum, which supports Turbo Pascal.

Delphi hosts the ICONtact Special Interest Group (SIG), which includes a programmers' group. It also hosts the NOSY SIG, which supports MacNOSY and the MacNOSY debugger.

GEnie hosts the MacPro Roundtable, which supports Macintosh developers, and the Borland Roundtable, which supports Turbo Pascal.

PC MacNet (Connect, Inc.) hosts a developers' group.

Magazines and Journals

MacTutor magazine publishes technical articles on Macintosh software and hardware development.

Mactech Quarterly contains articles on Macintosh software development and software reviews.

HyperLink Magazine contains articles on software development using HyperCard, SuperCard, and other applications.

User Groups

Many local user groups have programming SIGs. Two of the more prominent user groups (with national memberships) are the Boston Computer Society (BCS) and the Berkeley Macintosh User's Group (BMUG). Both groups offer public domain software, monthly newsletters, and programming special interest groups.

CHAPTER 19

Maintenance and Troubleshooting

Some Macintoshes hum along forever without any concern. Some printers seem to have trouble from the first day and just don't print clearly. Some accelerator boards are supposed to go into that slot but the board is twice as big as the slot.

This chapter discusses some of the problems you may have with your computer and tells you how to fix them. You won't be able to do all the repairs on your Mac or even all the upgrades you would like, but you can do much by yourself.

Practicing Preventive Medicine

Some of the most important things that you can do for your computer are among the most basic. Chores such as keeping your computer clean, avoiding static, changing batteries are all things that you can easily do yourself to prolong your computer's life.

Keeping Your Computer Clean

Dirt kills. It gets into those little cracks and crevices, on disk-read heads, and into internal parts. To prevent problems caused by dirt, you should do the following on a regular basis:

- Wipe down the surfaces of your Mac, printer, and work area at least once a month with a damp cloth. Use a mild detergent only if you have real dirt to get clean. When you clean the screen of your monitor, don't spray the monitor since you might get liquid inside of your drives. Rather, spray the cloth with water and wipe the monitor.

- Every now and then (at least every two months) vacuum around the keyboard to get out those little things that can get caught underneath keys and make them non-functional. If you have a pet, do this more often (their fur gets into everything).

- Keep food away from your working area. You always hear wonder stories about someone who spilled an entire 64-ounce soda on their keyboard, put the keyboard into the washing machine for a soak, dried it in the sun, and now it works better than ever. Yes, it might be true, but do you really want to find out?

- If you smoke, do it away from the machine. Your computer's tolerance for dirt is quite small, and smoke particles can get on the head of the drive, causing a monumental crash. Smoke particles are much smaller (by an order of 4 or 5) than good old dirt and can easily infiltrate your Mac's vitals.

Using Dust Covers

You already know what dirt can do to your machine, so you should take steps to prevent the kind of damage and havoc that even the smallest particles of dust and smoke can cause. Good dust covers should be made of materials that allow your computer to breathe so the residual heat can be dissipated. At the same time, dust covers should be protective enough so that dirt and grunge cannot get onto the surfaces of your machine and work their way in where they don't belong. In dirty environments (where many people smoke, the windows are open, or construction is going on nearby), protection is even more important.

Computer Cover Company makes good computer covers. For about $40, you can cover a Mac II, keyboard, and a LaserWriter Plus in royal blue, platinum, or tan. And, with any set of covers, you get a free mouse pad—what a deal.

If you want a rigid cover, look to Bede Tech's keyboard covers. Bede Tech also offers breathable and flexible covers with a set for the CPU, keyboard, mouse, printer, and external drive for about $50.

Keeping Your Mouse Healthy

Your mouse gets dirty as the ball picks up dust, hair, and crud from the surface on which it rolls. You can buy cleaning kits, but you should first try cleaning it on your own. Turn the mouse over, unscrew the ring, take out the ball, and blow into the opening. Wipe the ball and the rollers inside the mouse with a Q-tip dipped in alcohol. Then use another cotton swab to clean off the crud that accumulates on the internal rollers. You don't have to be a contortionist to do this; just take your time. When you're done, pop the ball back in, replace the ring, and your mouse will be squeaky clean.

19
Trouble-
shooting

Almost every manufacturer of Mac accessories offers some kind of a mouse cleaning kit, which usually includes items such as cotton swabs, isopropyl alcohol, and a lint-free cloth. These kits, such as RealClean (from International DataWares), begin at about $10.

One way to help keep your mouse clean and happy is by using a clean surface for a mouse pad. Clean that off regularly as well.

Like the little field mice that come into your house when the weather turns cold, Mac mice also wear out their welcome when they are no longer so easy to use. The little feet on the Mac mouse get worn and no longer slide as easily. There are several solutions. You can buy Teflon feet (from International DataWares) that stick on the bottom. Datawares also sells a cage with ball bearings so your mouse will whiz across the mouse pad or table.

Your mouse has to spin on something, so why not give it a home that it can skate effortlessly across? Mouse pads are nothing new, and several people use nothing more than the vinyl-coated cover of a three-ring binder. Others enjoy poking fun at the whole idea of a "mouse" and use a pad printed with a swiss cheese pattern.

Good mouse pads should have several characteristics. They should have a surface on which the mouse ball can easily track. They should be made of a material that is dense enough so that constant moving back and forth does not leave a lasting impression or nibble away at the material. Finally, they should fit where they're supposed to go. Too big, and they're not worthwhile; too small, and you can't move around the entire screen. One nice pad is the Speed Pad (from ErgoTron).

Another nice pad that minimizes static and makes your work surface attractive and much more user friendly is Monstrmat (without the "e"). This is a 30-by-22-inch, nonspongy work surface that fits under your Mac and becomes a giant mouse pad. It's easy to clean, helps minimize static, doubles as a work surface you can write on, and won't decompose and mess up your mouse's insides. All for $29.95 from International DataWares.

Making Your Disks More Efficient

You can increase the efficiency with which your Mac searches for data and performs operations. This is called disk optimization, or unfragmenting a disk.

You might remember from the discussion of disks in Chapter 4 that disks consist of concentric circles (called tracks) that are further divided into sectors. Information is stored in these sectors, and each sector has an address. The disk stores these addresses in a directory so that they can be found when you want to access information.

Now, although these sectors are physically contiguous to one another on the disk, that does not always mean that when you use up the space in one sector, the information you are saving spills over to the next sector. It's more often the case that the contents of any one file are stored in a variety of locations all over a disk. Your computer has to hunt all over the disk to find all the pieces to the puzzle that you named as a file. When files are long, or when there are many files, these fragmented chunks can slow things down quite a bit. The answer to this problem is a utility that defragments, or closes up any spaces that exist between fragments, and reorganizes all the fragments so that file chunks are next to one another.

Such a disk optimizer (which works on floppies as well as a hard disk) is SUM from Symantec. As you can see in figure 19.1, this program provides several different types of tools for working with your hard and floppy disks, such as file recovery, defragmentation, and diagnostic help. In figure 19.2, you can see the HD TuneUp screen. In this figure, the disk named Oscar was analyzed. Only 1 percent of it was fragmented—probably not worth doing. You should use such a utility when your disk is more than 10 percent fragmented.

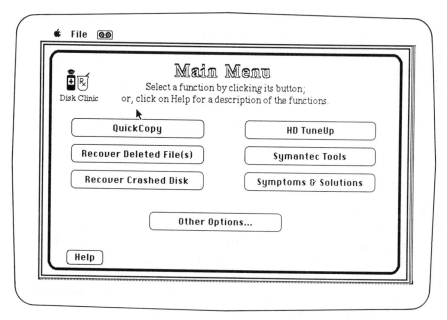

Fig. 19.1. *SUM provides several different disk tools.*

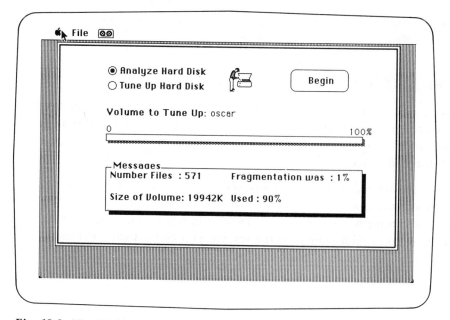

Fig. 19.2. *The HD TuneUp screen.*

Whether you will notice any benefits from unfragmenting a hard disk depends on three things. First, the longer the files are, the more likely they are to become fragmented as you write to the disk and then read from it. Second, the more often you work with the file, the more likely it has become fragmented. Third, the more files that you have on the disk, the more likely that they are fragmented. If you have just one file, it's unlikely to go anywhere but straight onto the disk in contiguous sectors.

Keeping Time

Ever wonder how your Mac keeps the correct time even when it is turned off? Your Mac clock is powered by a battery. On the Plus, it's located in a compartment under a little trap door on the back. When the battery goes, get a replacement from one of the battery people listed in the product appendix. For the SE and above, you have to open the case and do some soldering. Warning: unless you have experience doing this, however, you should have the dealer do it. Whenever you open the case, you are voiding the warranty. On top of this, fooling around with connections and soldering can be very dangerous!

If the battery is dead, some other settings will be affected as well, but you can still use your Mac. You just have to adjust settings on the Control Panel each time you start up.

Using Static Killers

You can never be too careful. The electronic components inside your Mac are very sensitive, and even the slightest static electric discharge from your fingers across the face of a chip can mean curtains for the job the chip does.

There are several ways to dissipate static electricity. One is to use commercially available antistatic sprays. Wiping with these helps, but the static returns soon thereafter. Especially when you start up your machine and touch your monitor screen, you can actually feel the electricity (lots of volts but no amps).

Using Surge Protectors

A surge protector is an absolute must for your computer system. Surge protectors prevent damage to your components and files by protecting against surges and dips in the electrical current. Although they can offer some protection against lightning strikes, by far the best way to avoid frying your computer during a storm is to unplug your system (and particularly the modem).

19
Trouble-shooting

Re-inking Your Printer Ribbons

Usually, your Mac continues to chug along, needing little, if anything, replaced. Not true for printers, especially ImageWriters. Just a few graphics figures containing much black area and your ribbon is on its way out! Welcome the ribbon re-inkers offered by such companies as Computer Friends and Bede Tech.

With a ribbon re-inker, you mount the ribbon on a base that has a motor which winds the ribbon through an inker you have filled with ink. You can reink 50 to 100 ribbons with about 4 ounces of ink. You can reuse ribbons until they show signs of fraying.

Original ImageWriter ribbons cost about $10 each; the Bede Tech re-inker costs about $50 and the MacInker from Computer Friends retails for about the same. Both companies also offer kits for re-inking 4-color ImageWriter ribbons.

Ribbons will be your main consumable (besides paper). The cost for an ImageWriter II ribbon is about $7.50 from Apple and about $20 for the LQ. You can get replacement ribbons from many different sources, but don't buy many at once, because they may not be of the same quality of the (more expensive) originals. Buy one or two and try them. I have had everything happen from the other end of the ribbon not being attached to the spool to instant fragmentation and tearing as soon as printing began.

Using Power Backups

One thing you want is for your Mac to be with you through thick and thin. But what machine stands by you when the squirrel bites through the transformer lines or the dumb dog walks on the extension cord and disconnects you?

What you need is some kind of a power backup. These are not cheap, but they can give you the extra time to save what you're working on and to shut down your system safely.

Power backups take over within thousandths of a second and can supply power from five minutes up to four hours, depending on the model you buy and your system's power requirements.

The PowerBacker 450 from Kensington (about $600) can supply 20 minutes of backup power for a system that requires 150 watts. PowerBacker uses sealed, lead-based batteries, and it has an alarm to let you know a power failure has occurred.

Traveling Safely

For those of us who travel with our Macs, here are a few nice ways to travel in comfort and safety.

Linebacker Computer Luggage offers a complete line of luggage for the Mac made of heavy duty fabric combined with 1/2-inch foam to protect the equipment. The bags have a hard shell sewn into the bottom and top for added protection. The luggage holds the CPU, keyboard, and mouse, and comes with padded straps to make carrying easier.

Computer Cover Company also carries Cordura Mac travel cases.

If this is not enough protection, the MacFreighters (from Linebacker) line of steel and aluminum cases with 3 inches of foam can be custom made to fit any size. While expensive, if your livelihood depends upon your Mac getting there in only one piece, you will want to consider it.

Reducing Glare and Easing Eye Strain

Your best position for working with your Mac is with some diffused light coming from your back onto your Mac screen, but not so direct that the screen acts as a mirror and reflects whatever the light source is or that it creates so much glare you get a headache. The best solution is to reposition your monitor so that you can work comfortably. When this solution is not possible, an antiglare screen may help. Kensington offers these as do other companies. Their Mac II screen filters run from $100 to $200, depending on the monitor you are using.

Reducing Heat

Heat is public enemy #1 to a Mac Plus or SE, and the threat is increased many times if you are talking about upgrades of any kind. Upgrades, be they SIMMs added on or accelerator or video or math co-processors, introduce increased electrical activity. Because the circuits are not 100 percent efficient, some of the energy is lost as heat. In fact, what's holding up ultra miniaturization of circuit boards is the fact that the closer the circuits are to one another, the more the heat from one affects the other. That's why the promise of super-conductive transmission of energy is so exciting. Greatly reduced heat means elements can be placed closer together, and the whole package can be made smaller.

In any case, new boards cause heat and heat kills. So what do you do? All the Macs, including the SE and above, come with fans that help keep things cool. But often the fan makes a good deal of noise, driving many Mac aficionados crazy because it's the peace and quiet that comes along with the machine that they cherish so much. Internal fans pull in room air over the mother board and help cool things down. The problem is that with many upgrades, and when working environments get hot, the fans can't be expected to do their job. The options? Cool down the room, or add a more powerful fan. Your Mac is supposed to work up to 104 degrees Fahrenheit (which is a normal summer day in Kansas, where this is being written), but the Mac tends to run about 10 degrees hotter than the room. So if it's 85 in your work space, the Mac is operating somewhere around 95. So, once things reach 90 or so, get out the room fans (aim one right at the left-hand side of the Mac where the cooling vents are located), turn on the air conditioner, turn the machine off until the evening when it's cooler, but beware of continued working.

There are many third-party fans that boost the cooling power of the fan. For example, Mac 'n Frost fits on top of the Plus, and comes with a control switch and a small plate that you touch to discharge static electricity. Some accelerators also come with a fan, such as the ones from Radius, which are attached to the back of the Plus or SE.

Another option is to install a more powerful fan in your machine. There are several others available, and most are as easy to add as opening the case and literally sticking them on (they come with double faced tape)

19
**Trouble-
shooting**

or using Velcro fasteners. These work, although some draw lots of unwanted dust into the machine.

Keeping Things Secure

This section is about how to keep your computer secure, not about how to keep the contents of your Mac secure. To keep your files safe, you use the various file encryption and password features that are discussed elsewhere in this book, especially in Chapter 4.

The first concern as far as security goes is making sure that your Mac is not stolen. The cheapest way to do this is to design a security system yourself, using cable from a hardware store or bike shop and a few simple tools. You need the following items:

- Plastic-coated aircraft or bicycle cable (about 4 feet of 1/4-inch cable will do)

- A good, case-hardened padlock that won't be easy to cut through (none of them is absolutely safe)

- Ferrules (metal sleeves that fit around the end of the wire) to create a loop, and a crimping tool to crimp the ferrule on the cable so that it stays closed

Now, follow these steps to complete your own in-home security system:

1. Open your Mac and drill a 3/8-inch hole in the upper left corner (facing the back) of the back panel.

2. Place both ends of an 8-inch piece of cable through the hole so that the loop remains on the outside of the case. Now, using one of the ferrules and the crimping tool, crimp the two ends together so that the loop cannot be removed.

3. Do the same thing for the keyboard so that a small loop exits out the back of the keyboard.

4. Drill a 3/8-inch hole in the back or top of the desk to which you want to secure the system, or to whatever else is handy, such as a file cabinet. (You may need a longer main cable to do this.)

5. Thread the long cable through the loop on the Mac and the keyboard and through the hole in the desk.

6. In the ends of the long cable, create two loops using the ferrules and the crimping tool.

7. Lock the two ends of the cable together so that they cannot pass through the hole in the desk or file cabinet when they are attached by the lock. The lock should be large enough so that it is impossible to squeeze it through the hole.

19
Trouble-shooting

If you need to take your Mac with you, just undo the lock and unthread the cables. The loops in the Mac and the keyboard will remain. You can also buy a security kit just like the one described here from Bede Tech for $35, but because of its design, you don't need to drill any holes.

One good hardware solution to keeping your Macintosh safe and literally locking out the chance that anyone else will use it, is The Muzzle (from ErgoTron). The Muzzle's 14-gauge metal collar fits around the Mac to cover it and prevent access to the internal floppy drive as well as to the power switch.

With The Muzzle in place, you can't turn the Mac on nor can you get to the floppy drive opening. The Muzzle is locked together by a hardened padlock. This is very heavy duty steel that appears to be impossible to get through and comes in black and platinum for about $79 for the SE and $89 for the Mac II.

Apple provides a socket on the back of your Mac for a security cable which then can be attached to any solid fixture to keep it from disappearing. This same socket is on all of Apple's peripherals as well.

Troubleshooting

It's a beautiful day and you're ready to sit down at your Mac and begin a nice day of work, putting the finishing touches on that book, and . . . you feel as if your stomach has dropped out of your body! Your Mac goes on and on like a car with a dead battery trying to start, and that little smiling Mac face is nowhere to be found.

Or your disk with your dissertation or treasure map provides you with the wonderful "This disk is unreadable" message. Take your life? No, read on and try some of these fixes first, and if they don't work, there's always a new and improved Mac waiting for you at the store.

Determining the Problem

If things are not working as they should, you must determine as best as you can what the source of the problem is. This knowledge won't necessarily help you fix the problem, but because you know your machine better than anyone else, you certainly can give the service people help by describing symptoms and such. The more help they have, the less time they need to spend on the job and the less money it costs you.

When something does not work, begin by being a good detective. Take out your trusty notebook and ask questions:

- What were you doing when things stopped working as they should?

- Did you hear any funny noises? (When hard drives start to go they often sound like little birds chirping merrily away.)

- Did you recently make any changes in your System software?

- How long were you working before the problem set in?

- What is your application and its version number?

First, try whatever you were doing again. You can't lose anything by trying again, so double-click that icon that won't open or reinsert the disk that your Mac tells you is unreadable. If you have no success, don't fret yet.

Next, reboot your computer. If you are working from floppies and the System does not reboot, that may be your problem—a bad System disk. If you are working from a hard disk and it does not reboot, reinstall your System and Finder files from a good copy to the hard drive and reboot. If your hard drive does not reboot from the floppy (and you know that the System on the floppy is good), you may have real problems.

If your Mac is on, but things aren't working as they should, check CDEVs and INITs. These can often cause trouble. Begin by deleting various CDEVs and INITs one at a time to determine what the culprit might be.

Next check for any viruses that might be present. You have to use a virus checker like the ones discussed in Chapter 3.

If the system boots up fine, but the application does not work, use the backup of the application and try it again.

If the application works, then it was the application file that was bad. If the application does not work, then you may have System problems. Reinstall your System using the backup of your System. Just to make sure that the System on the backup is good, place the floppy disk containing the System into a floppy drive and reboot. If this does not work, find a System that does boot from the floppy; then copy that to your hard disk System folder. If using the new System on the hard disk does not work, you have problems, and it's time to visit your service center.

Keep in mind that sometimes applications store their settings in the program, and you will lose any changes you made. Many of the major programs (Word, PageMaker, Excel) store their settings in the System file for that reason.

If you can't start from your hard disk, try this. Start up from your backup System floppy. When you have the desktop screen, if your hard drive icon is on the desktop, drag the hard drive System and Finder to the trash can and replace them with the System and Finder from your good floppy files (which should be the same since you backed them up) to the hard drive. Select Restart from the Special menu, and you should be all set.

If none of this works, try this. Given that you have backups of both your application disks and your data disk, and you know that your drives are OK, do the following:

1. Try the application disk that didn't work with a data disk that you know works. Try the good applications (don't use the original!). If it works, it's probably the application. If not, the drive may be in question again.

2. Try an application disk that you know is good with the questionable data disk. Still no luck? Try the good backup. Still no luck? Be suspicious of the drive.

Fixing Boot-Up Problems

When you boot up and things are going well, you usually get the Mac icon. If you don't, you probably see one of two others. One means either that you have faulty hardware or that the System software is faulty, and you have to boot up with a good System. The other means that your Mac cannot find a start-up disk (that is, your disk won't mount.)

If you get the Sad Face icon, it indicates that one of the memory tests that your Mac regularly performs when booted up has failed. Below the face, you see some characters indicating what kind of an error was made or where the source of the problem is.

The first two characters indicate the type of error. If it is a RAM test failure (digits 02 through 05), the last four digits will identify the chip that may be failing.

If you get the Sad Face while the disk drive is spinning, the first two characters under the Sad Face are)F, and the next four numbers indicate the type of error. If this occurs, try rebuilding your desktop by holding down the Option and ⌘ keys while you start your Mac. You may also be able to solve the problem by replacing the System file.

Table 19.1 lists the codes and what the error messages mean.

Table 19.1
Error Codes and Meanings

Code	Meaning
01	ROM test
02-05	RAM test
OF0001	Bus error
OF0002	Address error
OF0003	Illegal instruction
OF0004	Divide by zero error
OF0005	Check trap—CHK instruction
OF0006	Overflow trap—TRAPV instruction
OF0007	Privilege violation
OF0008	Trap trace
OF0009	Trap dispatcher error
OF000A	Line 111 trap

Table 19.1—*continued*

Code	Meaning
OF000B	Other trap
OF000C	Unimplemented trap executed
OF000D	Interrupt button on programmers switch
OF0064	Bad System file
OF0065	Bad Finder

19
**Trouble-
shooting**

Rebuilding the Desktop

A cause of boot-up and other problems (especially long waits for the Mac to do any System work) is that the desktop controlled by the Finder may be contaminated with unwanted information, like pictures of icons that weren't erased.

You can easily rebuild the desktop, which is a directory file. You normally cannot see it because it doesn't have an icon. The presence of the desktop is why you have already used 7K of memory on a disk without adding anything to it. That's where the desktop information and other "invisible" information is stored. To fix the desktop file and rebuild it, hold down the Option and ⌘ keys while you boot up. This technique will clean up your desk, and hopefully your Mac will ask you whether you want to do this. Be aware that this procedure deletes information in the Get Info box.

If you get a System error message when you place a disk in a drive, try this. Hold down the ⌘ and Option key combination as you insert the disk.

Recovering Lost Files

In Chapter 4, I stressed the importance of backing up files (including System and application files) on a regular basis, but even if you are very contentious about this, you still might inadvertently delete a file. Deleting files from a disk does not erase them; it only makes them inaccessible through normal channels. (If you are security-minded, the only way to get a file off a disk for good is by initializing the disk.)

If you do delete a file and have a backup, all you need do is load the backup and you're ready to go once again. If you don't have a backup, you will need a file recovery tool such as Symantec Utilities for the Macintosh or COPY II/Mac Tools (from Central Point).

Before I discuss how these tools work, be sure that you understand what happens when you delete a file. First, deleting a file does not remove the actual contents of the file itself from the disk, but only the file's listing in the directory and the address (called a path name) for the file's location on the disk.

It's this directory, or table, that the operating software uses to find the file once you request it. When you initialize, or reformat, a disk, you erase this directory, and then there is no hope of recovering a file because the file itself as well as any directory is gone for good. When you just trash a file, you erase only a small part of the directory.

A file-recovery program asks you to select by name the file that was deleted. The program then searches the disk (which takes several minutes for a 20M hard disk) and then presents you with a dialog box listing the files and asking you to select the one that you want to undelete or recover. This usually means just entering the complete name once your Mac shows you a list of the files that have been recovered. Does it work? Yes. Is it fun? No, because your heart sinks when you realize that you've trashed an important file. SUM II can undelete the last 150 files that were deleted.

Another excellent product is 1st Aid, a data recovery and disk "fixer" (from 1st Aid Software).

Are these programs worth the expense and the effort? If your data is valuable, of course, they are. You should practice some preventive medicine, as well.

Always back up applications as soon as you get them and before you try anything as fancy as installing them on your hard drive. Keep a set of backup disks at a location other than where your computer is stored. If you don't, anything that happens to your computer to trash your hard disk (water, fire, neutron bombs) will get the backup disks, as well. Make two backup disks, which gives you a total of three; one on your hard drive and two disks. This number is just in case you lose the file that's open on your hard disk, and when you insert one of the backups, you find that your drives are erasing everything, as well. You still have the second backup.

If you didn't trash a file, but instead find that your Mac is telling you that your disk is unreadable, try rebuilding the desktop by holding down the ⌘ and the Options key. This technique can sometimes work and gives you enough leeway to copy those important files to another disk that you know is good.

19

Trouble-shooting

Locating Hardware Problems

Now we get to the possible hardware problems. Things still don't work, and you know that it is hardware because nothing you do can isolate the problem to a particular software application and the System seems to work. Here's where you begin a systematic testing of each peripheral that is attached to your Macintosh. First, disconnect all the peripherals, including external disk drives, printers, plotters, scanners, and anything else you own.

In each case, the steps you will take are as follows:

1. Connect the peripheral.

2. Check the cable connections.

3. Try out the procedure again. If it works, perhaps the cables were not connected, or perhaps they were connected improperly.

If the procedure doesn't work, use another peripheral just like yours and try it. This idea may sound impractical with a printer, but then again, it may save you money and not be that difficult, especially if you're around other Macs. If the substitute works, you know that it's your peripheral that needs fine-tuning. If it doesn't, you still don't know whether it's the peripheral or something in your Mac.

Continue trying peripherals until you've systematically evaluated each one. If you have no success, you need to see your service department.

A note about printers. If you think that all cables are correctly and firmly connected, your next step is to be sure that you have installed the correct printer driver in the System folder and that you have selected the appropriate icon for your printer using the Chooser located on the Apple menu.

Printer drivers should be an issue if the printer worked once. One common problem with printers that don't print is that they were not selected in Chooser. Check that. Sometimes the printer port can malfunction. Plug your printer cable into the modem port, select the modem port in Chooser, and try to print. If the printer operates, shut down the Mac, reconnect to the printer port, and restart. In Chooser, select Printer Port. Try printing again. Many times, this method resets the printer port. If it doesn't, you have a damaged printer port.

Fixing Printer Problems

This is not a pleasant thought, but imagine your printer going dead on you in the middle of an important job.

There's not much that you can do to repair your printer, unless the problem is obvious (such as when a belt breaks or the print head on a dot-matrix printer needs to be replaced). These jobs are best left for the pros. If you want to get a good idea about how printers work to try to fix your own, you should read *The Printer Bible* by Scott Foerster (Que Corporation, 1989) or *Printer Troubleshooting and Repair* by John Wheilborn (Howard W. Sams and Company, 1988).

One method, which is useful for repairs of all hardware, is the single-path method of repair. This method works when only one thing goes wrong at a time, and it consists of six simple steps as follows:

1. Trust your senses. Looking carefully may help you to detect the problem, such as jammed paper, a ripped ribbon, or the smell of a wire with burned insulation.

2. Move on to finding the area that needs repair.

3. Remove the printer component that you think is faulty. For example, take out the old ribbon.

4. Retest the System and see whether it works without the part you think is faulty. If the part is necessary for the System to work, you might have to get a replacement to complete this step, with an understanding from the dealer that you will be back to buy more parts as soon as you find out what's wrong.

5. Replace the part that you found to be defective.

6. Test the system again.

While these steps are taken from a discussion of printer repairs, there's no reason why they cannot be applied to any hardware fix.

Understanding the Infamous Power Supply

For years, the Mac had problems with power supply failures; power supplies simply weren't large enough or were defective. The early Macs (the 128 and the 512) were particularly prone to blackouts, and the only recourse was buying a new power supply. Apple never made good on these, and dealers were reluctant as well. The problem has been solved with the newer Macs, but if you buy a used machine be sure to inquire about its age as well as whether the power supply has been replaced.

Upgrading Memory

Having too much memory can never hurt (save for your pocketbook); and if you intend to expand your Mac's performance, you're better off increasing the memory as much as possible (meaning what you can afford) while you or the technician has the case opened. Today, memory upgrades sell for anywhere from $50 for the chip itself, up through hundreds of dollars for a complete kit including a board which just requires a swap and then some adjustments.

Why spend the additional money for more memory?

First, and foremost, you might have to add memory to use the software you want. For example, without at least 2M of RAM, you cannot use MultiFinder effectively.

Second, increased RAM puts you in the position to be ready for new memory-intensive applications and increased file sizes, which are always being introduced.

Finally, Apple's plans for new Macintosh operating systems that require more RAM (2M) will reach fruition in the near future, and if you want to take advantage of the new System, you have to keep up!

One of the nice things about upgrading the Mac is that you can buy SIMMs (Single Inline Memory Modules) from outside dealers and just snap them in, attach them to the board holding the other chips, and you're finished (except for some adjustments). Not much of a task once you get the case opened.

Keep in mind that you may not even need to upgrade your Mac's memory. You might simply be able to increase the cache (see Chapter 3) or use a RAM disk program, which creates an internal electronic drive to reduce access time to programs. In other words, your Mac does not have to go to the disk as often and therefore time is saved. If you don't need the space that programs such as Mathematica (which is 2.5M) and hardware such as a large color monitor need, consider being more efficient with what you have.

Deciding Whether To Upgrade

If you are going to upgrade, the first thing to consider is whether you are better off buying a new machine. The general rule of thumb is that the farther away your current system is to what you want, the more it will cost to upgrade and the more it's worth looking into a replacement (which you want anyway, right?).

You can, for example, go from a 128K to a 512K machine for $199 by using the 512K upgrade from Ehman Engineering. Or you can zoom your 512K to a Plus using the MacSnap 548s (from Dove) for $699, which includes a 2M upgrade and an SCSI port.

Your Plus or SE comes with 1M of RAM, which these days is barely enough to get off the ground with certain applications such as FullWrite and many CAD programs and certainly not enough to use MultiFinder (see Chapter 3). You simply need more "computing space" inside of your machine if you want to get all the power that the Macintosh can deliver. The Plus and the SE can both be expanded to 4M. The Mac II can be expanded to 8M. (This limitation is changing. When System 7 is released, you will be able to access all the RAM you can fit. The Mac II needs the PMMU 68851. There now exist 4M SIMMs, with 16M SIMMs around the corner. That means 16 by 8, which is 128M of RAM!)

How much memory you buy is more a matter of economics than it is of anything else. Often, it's the question of whether you should buy more memory or just move up to one of the Mac IIs, which for most people has all the memory they will need.

Using SIMMs

Memory is physically housed in modules that are called *SIMMs* (Single Inline Memory Modules), which are about 3 1/2 inches long and about 1/2 inch high, each of which consists of eight memory chips that are all connected on an integrated circuit board. SIMMs are used as chip holders rather than having to solder or plug each chip onto a board. The chips are placed in rows in one of the particular configurations you see in figure 19.3. Here you can see the configuration for a 2.5M Mac Plus and a 4M Mac SE. Besides adding new chips, resistors also need to be adjusted because the connections between resistors tell the main logic board how much memory is in the machine. Things can get very tricky with cutting resistor leads, so be careful or get help. Two other things you need to know about SIMMs before you buy: speed and profile.

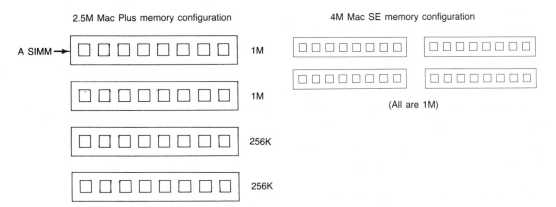

Fig. 19.3. Differing memory configurations.

How fast SIMMs work is measured in nanoseconds, or billionths of a second. The lower the number, the faster the chip. A fast chip is 80 nanoseconds; a slow chip is 120 nanoseconds. Faster is better, but it is relative. It's best, however, to buy the fastest possible because the increase in price is minimal, and this best prepares you for the new wave of both hardware and software to come with the new Macs and System 7.

SIMMs come as either low profile (also called surface mount) or high profile (also called dual-in-line or DIP). Low profile means the height of the SIMM board; the Apple SIMMs are low profile and do not stick as high out of the SIMM socket as the non-Low Profile SIMMs do.

Surface-mounted SIMMs take up less space and are usually preferred to DIPs. Both DIPs and surface mounts will work fine in a Plus or an SE. What you need to be concerned about, however, is the space they take up. Because DIPs take up more space, they may interfere with other upgrades you have in mind for your Plus or SE because you might not have the physical room to fit everything. For a Mac II, there's plenty of room, and what you do does not make much difference.

Although SIMMs are the easiest way to deal with memory upgrades, upgrades also come in three different forms: the SIMMs that have been discussed, SIMMs mounted on boards that are swapped with another board, and add-on boards like the MacSnap boards from Dove (a large supplier of memory upgrades) that snap right on top of the motherboard. (And you'd better be sure that they're in place when that snap is attempted.) Because add-ons snap onto the motherboard, they are relatively easy to install.

When you add memory, you also have to adjust the power supply. Be sure to ask about this when you purchase your SIMMs or have them installed at a dealer.

The price of SIMMs can range from $149 to $165, and the price can fluctuate even from the same manufacturer.

But remember, just don't go for the price; speed of the SIMMs and service, as well as reputation of the vendor and manufacturer, also count. For example, Turbo Technologies offers SIMMs manufactured by Toshiba (who also makes Apple's SIMMs) and offers free technical support, same-day shipping, a 30-day money-back guarantee, and a lifetime warranty. In addition, if you buy a 4M upgrade, the company will throw in the kit you need to do the upgrade, including the wrist strap, the TORX driver, and more. Graphics Technologies offers a five-year warranty. Shop around and ask questions, such as,

- Do you offer any warranty? guarantee?

- Will you bill my credit card when ordered or when shipped?

- Do you offer on-line help?

- Who manufactures your SIMMs?

- How long have you been in business?

The time spent doing a little research will be well worth it. Sophisticated Circuits also offers a complete line of SIMMs with terrific on-line support.

One more comment about buying SIMMs. Many of the SIMMs that are available fall into the gray market category, meaning that they are purchased in bulk from a manufacturer (usually overseas) and they can be sold to you for a reduced price. The problem is that the manufacturer will usually not stand behind these because of the no-strings-attached deal (which comes along with the low price). Now the retailer might warranty them to you, but if he or she can't go back to the manufacturer, you may be out. Retailers may not admit that their product is gray market, so use your own judgment and consider the reputation of the company.

SIMMs are convenient, but don't rule out boards, especially for older Macs (and some people are understandably attached to their 128s and 512s and don't want to give them up). Sophisticated Circuits, makers of Mac's-a-Million, produces such a board to increase 512K Macs up to 2M. The installation is not as simple as plugging in a SIMM or two (some soldering is required), but it's a wonderful way to increase the machine's memory for under $300 (for 1M which is expandable to 2M) which includes a diagnostic disk, a printed tutorial (plus a HyperText demonstration disk that you can view before you start), a RAM disk program, and a one-year warranty and a record of no returns for failures of the board. Boards are not cheaper because they contain many components, but boards have one big advantage; everything on them works together, and you will have no incompatibility problems.

Sophisticated Circuits also offers an inexpensive way to configure your 512K with an SCSI port so that it can take a hard drive. The port is $119 with no wiring required and fits nicely under the computer's ROMs.

Another company that produces upgrade boards is Levco, for increasing memory for 128s, 512s and Pluses. The Mac Plus upgrade includes a fan to help keep down the heat generated by all that extra computing.

Opening Your Macintosh Computer

Most Macintosh computer repairs, upgrades, replacements, and so forth, require that you open your Macintosh to do the work. When you do this yourself, your warranty is voided. Unless you are a qualified electrician, go to a qualified service department to have work done on your Macintosh.

You need to be aware that poking around in the insides of any complex electrical object, such as a computer, is dangerous! Although you may have turned off your Mac and unplugged it, you can still receive a fatal shock from the analog board or the picture tube lead.

Before attempting any work inside your computer, be sure that you read and understand the safety information on Page 1.3 of the Apple Macintosh Technical Procedures.

What a tour you have been on! From the most basic instruction on procedures such as pointing with your mouse to a discussion of the most advanced techniques and ideas concerning the Macintosh. Hopefully, this chapter has helped you prevent any serious breakdowns and keep things running smoothly.

Survival Guide

Here's a set of quick steps that will help you get through a variety of common procedures.

Control Panel

To place text or a graphic into the Clipboard:

1. Select the text or graphic.
2. Select the Cut or Copy command from the Edit menu.

To paste an item from the Clipboard:

1. Select the insertion point.
2. Select the Paste command from the Edit menu.

To change the rate of cursor blinking:

1. Select the Chooser from the Apple DA menu.
2. Click the General icon in the Chooser window.
3. Click the Slow, Medium, or Fast button in the Rate of Insertion Point Blinking box.

To set the rate of menu blinking:

1. Select the Chooser from the Apple DA menu.
2. Click the General icon in the Chooser window.
3. Click the off, 1, 2, or 3 button in the Menu Blinking box.

To set the date:

1. Select the Chooser from the Apple DA menu.
2. Click the General icon in the Chooser window.

3. Click the day, month, or year number in the Date box.

4. Use the up and down arrows to set the day, month, or year.

To set the time:

1. Select the Chooser from the Apple DA menu.
2. Click the General icon in the Chooser window.
3. Click the hours, minutes, or seconds in the Time box.
4. Use the up and down arrows to set the hours, minutes, seconds, or AM/PM setting.

To set the amount of cache in RAM:

1. Select the Chooser from the Apple DA menu.
2. Click the General icon in the Chooser window.
3. Use the up and down arrows in the RAM Cache box.
4. Reboot your Mac.

To set the volume of the speaker:

1. Select the Chooser from the Apple DA menu.
2. Click the General icon in the Chooser window.
3. Drag the Speaker Volume level to where you want it.

To change the pattern of the desktop:

1. Select the Chooser from the Apple DA menu.
2. Click the General icon in the Chooser window.
3. Click the desired color in the table.
4. Click the dots in the desktop icon to form a new desktop pattern.
5. Click the area below the white bar on the desktop pattern.

Cursor

To unfreeze the cursor, make sure that the mouse cable is connected properly.

To stop the cursor from skipping, clean your mouse or the mouse surface.

Desk Accessories

To save room and install many DAs, install the DA in the application file; the DA will show up only when that file is active.

To find a file:

1. Select the Find File DA from the Apple DA menu.
2. Select the disk or folder you want to search.
3. Enter the name of the file or as much of the name as you can remember.
4. Click the "running person" icon.

To see the fonts on your System file, using Key Caps:

1. Select the Key Caps DA from the Apple DA menu.
2. Select the font you want to see from the Key Maps menu.

To turn off the flashing Apple:

1. Select the Alarm Clock DA from the Apple DA menu.
2. Turn off the alarm clock.

Desktop

To change the view of the directory (such as by Icon or by Small Icon), select the view you want from the View menu.

To drag an icon:

1. Place the mouse pointer on the icon.
2. Press the mouse button and hold it down.
3. Drag the icon to its new location.

To select an icon, place the mouse pointer on it and click.

To deselect an icon, place the mouse pointer on it, hold down the Shift key, and click.

To select more than one icon:

1. Select the By Icon or By Small Icon view from the View menu.
2. Drag the mouse pointer on those files you want to select, or Shift-click each file.

Survival Guide

To switch control of the computer to the System folder that contains the Finder, hold down the ⌘-Option key combination and double-click the Finder icon.

To open an application:

1. Select the icon or name representing the application.
2. Select the Open command on the File menu.

To align icons in the active window, hold down the Option key and select the Clean Up command from the Special menu.

To avoid the alert box about trashing a locked document or an application, hold down the Option key as you trash the icon.

To make another disk the dominant, or start-up, disk, hold down the ⌘-Option key combination and double-click the Finder icon in the System folder.

To rebuild the desktop, hold down the ⌘ and Option keys and insert the start-up disk, or hold down these keys when you boot up.

To make the current start-up disk the disk the application is on, hold down the Option key and double-click the document or application icon.

To close a window automatically when you are finished working with an application or document, hold down the Option key and double-click a disk or a folder icon.

To close an application that you mistakenly opened, press ⌘-period (.).

Disks

To clean off residue from labels, use nail polish remover.

To eject a disk from the desktop and remove the icon from the screen:

1. Highlight the disk icon.
2. Drag the disk icon to the trash can.

To eject a disk from a program, select Eject in the Open dialog box.

To initialize a disk for use in an 800K drive:

1. Highlight the disk icon.
2. Select the Erase Disk command on the Special menu.
3. Select Two-sided.
4. Click OK.

To find the size of a document, select the Get Info command from the File menu.

To copy all the files from one disk to another disk, drag the disk icon with the files you want to copy to the destination or newly initialized disk icon.

To lock a document:

1. Highlight the file name of the document.
2. Select the Get Info command from the File menu.
3. Click the Locked box in the upper right corner of the Info window.

To initialize a disk for use in an 400K drive:

1. Highlight the disk icon.
2. Select the Erase Disk command on the Special menu.
3. Select One-sided.
4. Click OK.

To eject the disk in the external drive, use the ⌘-Shift-2 key combination.

To eject a disk:

1. Highlight the disk icon.
2. Select Eject from the File menu, or drag the disk icon to the trash can.

To eject the disk in the internal drive, use the ⌘-Shift-1 key combination.

To lock a disk, open the black trap door located in the upper right corner of the disk.

If an important disk bombs, when you try booting the disk again, hold down the ⌘ and Option keys.

To format a troublesome double-sided disk:

1. Insert the disk.
2. Format it as a single-sided disk (400K).
3. When the disk's icon appears on the desktop, select the icon, and choose Erase Disk from the Special menu.
4. Reinitialize the disk by choosing double-sided formatting.

Files

To start with a specific application:

1. Select the application you want your Mac to start with.
2. Select the Start Up command from the Special menu.
3. Click OK.

To open a file, double-click the file.

To open a file that won't open, eject the disk, reinsert it, and try to open it again. Or eject the disk and try another drive.

To copy a file from one disk to another, drag the file's icon to the new disk icon.

To copy several files from one disk to another, Shift-Click each of the files or draw a marquee around them and then drag them to another disk icon.

To perform a disk-to-disk copy, drag the disk icon onto the one you want to copy to.

To save a file that won't save, unlock the disk, if locked, or unlock the file, if locked.

To duplicate a file, use the Duplicate command on the File menu.

To find out about a file, use the Get Info command on the File menu.

To select more than one file at a time, press and hold down the Shift key while you click the files you want to select.

To rearrange the files in a window:

1. Select the window.
2. Select the Clean Up Window command on the Special menu.

To select all the files in window, select the Select All command from the Edit menu.

To close an active window, select the Close command.

To copy a file from one folder to another, drag its icon while pressing the Option key.

To have an application icon always available on the desktop, drag the icon out of its folder and place it on the desktop where you can see it.

To see whether a file is locked, place the pointer over the name on the window. If the pointer changes to an I-beam, the file isn't locked. If the pointer remains an arrow, the file is locked.

Survival
Guide

To restore the name of a file on the desktop after you have accidentally erased it, use the ⌘-Z combination.

To back up fast, use the ⌘-A command to select all the files on a disk and then drag the disk icon to your hard disk.

To place a folder inside another folder, drag the folder icon to the folder icon you want to place it in.

To name an empty folder, just type the name.

To name a new folder, highlight the folder, drag over the name, and replace the name of the folder by typing the new name and pressing Return or Enter.

To create a new folder, select the New Folder command from the File menu.

To make screen dumps of characters:

1. Press the Option key.
2. Hold the mouse button.
3. Press ⌘-Shift-3.
4. Press the Option key again before you release the mouse button.

Fonts

To create different symbols, experiment with the Option, ⌘, and Shift keys, and different combinations of these keys and fonts.

To create an em dash, use the Shift-Option-hyphen key combination.

To create an en dash, use the Option-hyphen key combination.

To create an opening quotation mark ("), use the Shift-Option-[combination.

To create a closing quotation mark ("), use the Shift-Option-] combination.

Font/DA Mover

To select desk accessories as the default, hold down the Option key as you launch the Font/DA mover.

To eject a disk while using the Font/DA Mover, hold down the Option key and click the Close button.

Menus

To select a menu command:

1. Pull down the menu.
2. Move the mouse to highlight the command you want.
3. Release the mouse.

To pull down a menu, click and hold the menu name on the main menu.

Modems and Telecommunications

To make your modem dial silently (with Hayes-compatible modems) turn off the speaker by typing *ATM0*. To turn it back on, type *ATM1* for soft, *ATM2* for medium, or *ATM3* for loud.

If you are having trouble connecting to an on-line service, adjust the length of wait for carrier signal before your modem hangs up. Type *ATM7 = x*, where *x* is the number of seconds the modem will wait to detect a carrier signal. The default is usually 20 seconds.

When your telephone's call-waiting feature disconnects transmissions, you can disable call-waiting. When entering the phone number of remote, insert *70 (star 70) before the number to be dialed. For pulse phones, insert *1170* before the number to be dialed.

MultiFinder

To temporarily disable MultiFinder, hold down the Option key when you start up your Mac.

To start up in Finder:

1. Select the Start Up command on the Special menu.
2. Click the Finder option.
3. Select the Restart command from the Special menu.

To use the MultiFinder:

1. Select the Start Up command on the Special menu.
2. Click the MultiFinder option.
3. Select the Restart command from the Special menu.

To launch more than one program simultaneously under MultiFinder:

1. Highlight each program icon (use the Shift key).
2. Select the Open command on the File menu.
3. Select the Start Up command on the Special menu.
4. Click the Open Application command.

Print

To make your toner go as far as possible, gently rock the container back and forth to loosen up all that carbon, metal, and plastic that makes up the toner.

To conserve toner, set the print density dial on the back of your LaserWriter on low when you have just replaced the toner. Move the disk toward dark as you increase the number of printouts made.

To print a directory listed in your Mac desktop window, select the Print Catalog command from the File menu.

To select a printer:

1. Select the Chooser from the Apple DA menu on the Apple menu.

2. Select the icon that corresponds to the printer you want to use.

3. Indicate whether to turn AppleTalk on or off.

To print a document:

1. Highlight the icon representing the file you want to print.
2. Select the Print command from the File menu.

If the printer won't print, be sure that the ready light is on and that the printer cover is on tight.

To stop printing quickly with ImageWriters and LaserWriters, click the cancel button. If this doesn't work, hold down the ⌘ key and type a period (.).

To get bidirectional printing from your ImageWriter II, select the Bidirectional option.

Screen

If the screen is dark, adjust the brightness dial, or press a key to cancel the screen saver.

Scrapbook

To remove an image from the Scrapbook:

1. Select the Scrapbook from the Apple DA menu.
2. Use the scroll bar to locate the image you want to remove.
3. Select Cut from the Edit menu.

To place text or graphics from the Scrapbook into a document:

1. Select the text or graphics.
2. Select the Cut or Copy command from the Edit menu.
3. Select the Paste command from the Edit menu.

To place text or graphics into the Scrapbook:

1. Select the text or graphic.
2. Select the Cut or Copy command from the Edit menu.
3. Select the Scrapbook command from the Apple menu.
4. Select Paste from the Edit menu.

System and Finder

To reset the area of RAM (called PRAM) that keeps track of time and controls all the other internal settings you see on the Control Panel, hold down the ⌘-Option-Shift keys and select the Control Panel.

To reset the time in an earlier Mac, just take out the battery.

To create a new folder, use the ⌘-N key combination.

To close the active window, use the ⌘-W key combination.

To get information on a file, use the ⌘-I key combination.

To reset your Mac, press the reset key on the programmer's switch installed on the left side of your Mac.

To find out how much room you have left on a disk:

1. Select the disk.
2. Select the Get Info command (⌘-I).

To print several documents created using the same application:

1. Highlight the icons representing the files you want to print by keeping the Shift key down as you select them.
2. Select the Print command from the File menu.

To completely clear your Mac's memory, shut it down and turn it off; just don't reset it with the programmer's switch on the left or right side.

Trash Can

To trash a locked file, hold down the Option key as you drag the file icon to the trash can.

To throw away everything in the trash can, select the Empty Trash icon on the Special menu.

To place a file in the trash can, unlock the file by physically moving the little trap door in the upper right corner of the disk or use the Get Info dialog box on the File menu.

To open the trash can, double-click the trash icon.

To throw away only one file, drag its icon to the trash can.

Survival
Guide

Windows

To close all the open windows, hold down the Option key and click the close box on the active window.

To move an inactive window:

1. Hold down the ⌘ key.
2. Drag the window by the title bar to its new location.

To make a window active, click anywhere in the window.

To see more of a document, use the scroll bars in the window.

To scroll by line, click the scroll arrow in the direction you want to go.

To scroll from one part of a document to another, drag the scroll box from one part of the scroll bar to another.

To move an active window on-screen, drag the window by the title bar to its new location.

To change the size of a window by infinite amounts, select and drag the size box in the lower right corner.

To scroll by the windowful, click one of the gray scroll bars.

To change the size of a window from smaller to largest and back again, click the zoom box.

To close a window, click the close box in the upper left corner.

To open a file, double-click the icon that represents the file or the name of the file in the directory.

To create a paint file of an active window, use the ⌘-Shift-3 key combination.

To print the active window, use the ⌘-Shift-4 key combination.

To arrange numbered files in numerical order 1, 2, 3, 4, ... 10, rather than 1, 10, 2, 3, and so on, place a leading space in front of the single-digit file names.

Quitting a Session

To shut off your Mac, select the Shut Down command from the Special menu.

System Specifications

	Original Mac	Mac 512K	Mac 512KE	Mac Plus	Mac SE
Processor	Motorola 68000	Motorola 68000	Motorola 68000	Motorola 68000	Motorola 68000
Processor Speed	7.8336 MHz	7.8336 MHz	7.8336 MHz	7.8336 MHz	7.8336 MHz
Memory (Standard)	128K	512K	512K	1M	1M
Memory (Maximum Using 1M SIMMs)				4M	4M
PMMU (Paged Memory Management Unit	no	no	no	no	no
Who Changes ROMS	Dealer	Dealer	Dealer	Dealer	Dealer
Coprocessor	no	no	no	no	no
Expansion slots	None	None	None	None	1 for optional Accessory cards
Disk Drives (Min. Configuration)					
(All internal)	1-400K floppy	1-400K floppy	1-800K floppy	1-800K floppy	2-1.44M floppies
Optional Disk Drives					
(All external except as noted)	1-400K floppy	1-400K floppy	1-800K floppy 1 hard drive with SCSI port only	1-800K floppy up to 7 hard drives	1-1.44M floppy 1 internal hard drive up to 7 hard drives
Disk Formats It Can Read					
Apple II GS (Pro DOS)	no	no	no	no	yes
MS-DOS	no	no	no	no	yes
OS/2	no	no	no	no	yes
Supports LocalTalk	no	no	no	yes	yes
Video	9" diagonal	9" diagonal	9" diagonal	9" diagonal	9" diagonal
Resolution	512 x 342 pixels	512 x 342 pixels	512 x 342 pixels	512 x 342 pixels	512 x 342 pixels
Ports	2 serial Audio output Keyboard & mouse	2 serial Audio output Keyboard & mouse	2 serial Audio output Keyboard & mouse	2 serial SCSI Audio output Keyboard & mouse	2 serial SCSI Audio output 2 Apple Desktop Bus
Dimensions (inches)	13.5 x 9.7 x 10.9	13.5 x 9.7 x 10.9	13.5 x 9.7 x 10.9	13.5 x 9.7 x 10.9	13.6 x 9.6 x 10.9
Weight	16 lbs.	16 lbs.	16 lbs.	16.5 lbs.	17-21 lbs.
Apple Suggested Retail Price	Discontinued	Discontinued	Discontinued	$1,799	$2,869 w/ 20M HD - $3,469 w/ 40M HD - $4,069
Street Price (New)				$1,299	$2,250
Used Price (Sun Remarketing)	$495	$595	$895	$1,095	$1,995 (2 floppies) $2,495 (20M)

	Mac SE/30	Mac II	Mac IIx	Mac IIcx	Mac IIcxi
Processor	Motorola 68030	Motorola 68020	Motorola 68030	Motorola 68030	Motorola 68030
Processor Speed	15.6672 MHz	15.6672 MHz	15.6672 MHz	15.6672 MHz	25 MHz
Memory (Standard)	1M	1M	1M	1M	1M
Memory (Maximum Using 1M SIMMs)	8M	8M	8M	8M	8M
PMMU (Paged Memory Management Unit	Standard	Optional	Standard	Standard	Standard
Who Changes ROMS	Dealer	Dealer	User	User	User
Coprocessor	68882	68881	68882	68882	68882/68852
Expansion slots	1 for optional	1 for video card	1 for video card	1 for video card	1 built-in video card
	Accessory cards	5 for optional	5 for optional	5 for optional	3 for optional
		Accessory cards	Accessory cards	Accessory cards	Accessory cards
Disk Drives (Min. Configuration)					
(All internal)	1-1.44M floppy	1-800K floppy	1-1.44M floppy	1.44M floppy	1.44M floppy
	1 hard drive	1 hard drive	1 hard drive	1 hard drive	1 hard drive
Optional Disk Drives					
(All external except as noted)	1-1.44M floppy	1-800K internal floppy	1-1.44M internal floppy	1-1.44M floppy	1-1.44M floppy
	1 internal hard drive	up to 6 hard drives	up to 6 hard drives	up to 6 hard drives	up to 6 hard drives
	up to 6 hard drives				
Disk Formats It Can Read					
Apple II GS (Pro DOS)	yes	no	yes	yes	yes
MS-DOS	yes	no	yes	yes	yes
OS/2	yes	no	yes	yes	yes
Supports LocalTalk	yes	yes	yes	yes	yes
Video	9" diagonal	External	External	External	External
Resolution	512 x 342 pixels	(Color capability)	(Color capability)	(Color capability)	(Color capability)
Ports	2 serial	2 serial	2 serial	2 serial	2 serial
	SCSI	SCSI	SCSI	SCSI	SCSI
	Stereo audio output	Stereo audio output	Stereo audio output	Stereo audio output	Stereo audio output
	2 Apple Desktop Bus	2 Apple Desktop Bus	2 Apple Desktop Bus	2 Apple Desktop Bus	2 Apple Desktop Bus
Dimensions (inches)	13.6 x 9.6 x 10.9	5.5 x 18.7 x 14.4	5.5 x 18.7 x 14.4	5.5 x 11.9 x 14.4	5.5 x 13.7 x 14.4
Weight	21.5 lbs.	24 lbs.	24-26 lbs.	14 lbs.	24-26 lbs.
Apple Suggested Retail Price	$4,369	$4,869	$5,269	$4,669	$5,369
	w/ 40M HD - $4,869	w/ 40M HD - $6,169	w/ 40M HD - $5,969	w/ 40M HD - $5,369	n/a
	w/ 80M HD - $6,569	w/ 40M HD, 8M RAM - $7,369	w/80M HD, 8M RAM - $7,669	w/ 80M HD, 8M RAM - $7,069	n/a
Street Price (New)	$2,999	$3,400	$4,675	$3,295	n/a
Used Price (Sun Remarketing)	None available	$3,600-$7,000	n/a	n/a	n/a

System Error Codes

Error #	Message
General System Error Messages	
1	Bus error: can occur only on a Mac II
2	Address error: program referred to an odd address
3	Illegal instruction: the 6800 did not recognize an instruction
4	Division by zero
5	Range check error: numerical range checking
6	Overflow: integer overflow
7	Privilege violation: refers to 6800 modes not used in the Macintosh
8	Trace mode error: for debugging programs
9	Line 1011 trap: unlikely but serious system error
10	Line 1111 trap: for debugging programs
11	Hardware exception error
12	Unimplemented core routine: undefined system code
13	Uninstalled interrupt: interrupts are signals that grab the CPU's attention
14	I/O core: report of a very low level I/O error
15	Segment loader error: failure of an attempt to read a program segment
16	Floating point error: a numerical computation program
17-24	Can't load package: missing segments of the system file
25	Out of memory: memory is either full or fragmented
26	Bad program launch: could not find a program
27	File system map trashed: faulty information about the files on a disk
28	Stack ran into heap: a memory error
30	Disk insertion error
31	No disk insertion
32-53	Memory manager editor
41	The file named Finder could not be found on the disk
32767	General system error
Data Input/Output Error Messages	
-17	Can't perform requested control procedure
-18	Can't perform requested status procedure
-19	Can't read
-20	Can't write
-21	Device or driver unknown

-22	Device or driver unknown
-23	Driver not opened for requested read or write
-25	Attempt to remove open driver
-26	Driver resource missing
-27	Input or output request aborted
-28	Driver not open

File Error Messages

-33	Directory full
-34	Disk full: all allocation blocks on volume full
-35	No such volume
-36	I/O error
-37	Bad name: perhaps zero length
-38	File not open
-39	End of file reached while reading
-40	Attempt to position before start of file
-42	Too many files open
-43	File not found
-44	Volume physically locked
-45	File locked
-46	Volume locked by software flag
-47	File busy: attempt to delete open file(s)
-48	Duplicate file name
-49	File already open for writing
-50	Error in file specification or disk drive information
-51	Attempted to use improper file path
-52	Error getting file position
-53	Disk ejected or volume off-line
-54	Attempt to open locked file for writing
-55	Volume already mounted and on-line
-56	No such drive
-57	Not a Macintosh disk: volume lacks Macintosh directory
-58	External file system error
-59	Problem during rename
-60	Bad clock on master directory: must reinitialize volume
-61	Writing not allowed

Disk Error Messages

-64	Drive disconnected
-65	No disk inserted
-66	Disk seems blank
-67	Can't find address mark
-68	Verification of read failed
-69	Bad address mark
-70	Bad address mark
-71	Missing data mark
-72	Bad data mark
-73	Bad data mark
-74	Write underrun occurred
-75	Drive error

-76	Can't find track 0
-77	Can't initialize disk controller chip
-78	Tried to read side 2 of disk in single-sided drive
-79	Can't correctly adjust disk speed
-80	Drive error
-81	Can't find sector

AppleTalk Error Messages

-91	Socket already active or not known
-92	Data-size error
-93	Bridge between two AppleTalk networks missing
-94	Protocol error
-95	Can't get clear signal to send
-97	Can't open driver because port already in use
-98	Can't open driver because port not set for connection

Scrap Error Messages

| -100 | Clipboard not initialized |
| -102 | Scrap doesn't contain data of type requested |

Memory Error Messages

-108	Not enough room in heap zone
-109	NIL master pointer
-111	Attempt to use free block
-112	Attempt to purge locked block
-117	Block is locked

Resource Error Messages

-192	Resource not found
-193	Resource file not found
-194	Unable to add resource
-195	Unable to remove resource

B
Error
Codes

Directory of User Groups

Alabama

Auburn

The Apple Group
P.O. Box 68
Auburn, AL 36831
205/821-4300

Birmingham

Birmingham Apple Group
P.O. Box 55421
Birmingham, AL 35255
205/870-1791

Brownsboro

Newton's Tree Apple User Group
205/881-6964

Florence

Quad Cities Apple Byters
P.O. Box 2251
Florence, AL 35630
205/767-2081

Huntsville

Huntsville Mac User Group
555 Sparkman Dr.
Huntsville, AL 35816

Mobile

SAPPLE
P.O. Box 91336
Mobile, AL 36691

Montgomery

Apple MUG
P.O. Box 20241
Montgomery, AL 36116

Macinsteins
2835 Zelda Road
Montgomery, AL 36106
205/271-1087

Ozark

Peanuts and Apples
Rt. 2, Box 100
Ozark, AL 36360
205/774-5611

Alaska

Anchorage

Alaskan Macintosh User Group
200 W. 34th Ave.
Anchorage, AK 99508

Anchorage Apple User Group
P.O. Box 110753
Anchorage, AK 99511
907/345-1001

Anchorage Macintosh User Group
200 W. 34th Ave.
Anchorage, AK 99503
907/561-4732

Arctic Apple User's Group
P.O. Box 100360
Anchorage, AK 99510
907/659-5709

Fairbanks

Apple Mousse
P.O. Box 80176
Fairbanks, AK 99708

Sitka

Sitka Apple User Group
907/747-8558

Soldotna

Peninsula Mac User Group
907/283-3873

Arizona

Gilbert

Arizona Macintosh Users Group
16427 E. Campbell
Gilbert, AZ 85234
602/926-2080

Gilbert Apple Seeds
33 W. Palo Verde St.
Gilbert, AZ 85234

Glendale

ThunderMUG
15050 N. 59th Ave.
Glendale, AZ 85306

C
User
Groups

773

Flagstaff

Mountain Macintosh User Group
P.O. Box 15300
Northern Arizona University
Flagstaff, AZ 86011
602/774-4980

Mesa

Macinteract
2040-67 S. Longmore
Mesa, AZ 85202

Mesa Mac Group
Mesa Computer Mart
1153 E. Main Street
Mesa, AZ 85203

Page

Apple Cart
P.O. Box 2361
Page, AZ 86040
602/645-8811

Phoenix

Arizona Apple User Group
3035 E. Topaz Circle
Phoenix, AZ 85028
602/277-8511

Macexplorers
10007 W. Meadowbrook
Phoenix, AZ 85039
602/877-2171

Prescott

Prescott Macintosh User Group
602/776-8026

Sedona

Oak Creek Apples
150 Color Cove Rd.
Sedona, AZ 86336
602/282-3222

Sierra

Vista Mountain View Computer User
 Group
602/458-3042

Sierra Vista

Mountain View Apple User Group
1508 Chantilly Dr.
Sierra Vista, AZ 85635
602/458-3042

Sun City

Sun Macs
15605 98th Ave.
Sun City, AZ 85351
602/974-9598

Sun City West

Sun City West Apple Users
12930 Copperstone Dr.
Sun City West, AZ 85375
602/584-5306

Tempe

AMUG
P.O. Box 28120
Tempe, AZ 85282

Thatcher

Gila Valley Apple Growers
 Association
P.O. Box 809
Thatcher, AZ 85552
602/428-4073

Tucson

Tucson Apple Core
P.O. Box 43176
Tucson, AZ 85733

Yuma

Yuma Apple Users Group
1712 Camino Pradera
Yuma, Az 85364

Arkansas

El Dorado

Apple Access
104 Elm St.
El Dorado, AR 71730
501/862-1155

Eureka Springs

Eureka Springs Apple User's Group
Rt. 4, Box 554
U.S. 62 E
Eureka Springs, AR 72632
501/253-8418

Fayetteville

Fayetteville Apple Users Group
P.O. Box 204
Fayetteville, AR 72702
501/442-7040

Little Rock

Little Rock Apple Company Users
 Group
303 McMillen Trail
Little Rock, AR 72207
501/663-5208

California

Albany

East Bay Macintosh Users Group
555 Pierce St.
Albany, CA 94706
415/758-2741

Arcata

Sequoia Macintosh Users Group
P.O. Box 4715
Arcata, CA 95521
707/822-1874

Anaheim

Pacific Mac Group
417 Meadowbrook Pl.
Anaheim, CA 92801
714/776-4066

Anaheim Macintosh User Group
714/999-5141

Auburn

Auburn Macintosh Users Group
11428 F Ave.
Auburn, CA 95603
916/888-7433

Belmont

Bay Area MacForum
2535 Somerset Drive
Belmont, CA 94002

Barstow

Mac Desert User's Group
36935 Hayward Ave.
Barstow, CA 92311

Benicia

San Leandro Apple Eaters
838 Mayo Ct.
Benicia, CA 94510

Berkeley

BMUG
1442 A Walnut St.
Berkeley, CA 94709
415/849-9114

East Bay Macintosh Users Group
P.O. Box 7816
Berkeley, CA 94707
415/621-8808

Buellton

Macadamia
90 W. Highway 246
Buellton, CA 93427
805/688-5773

Burbank

Lerc Aces
P.O. Box 551
3711 La Crescenta Ave.
Burbank, CA 91520

Mac Valley Users Group
P.O. Box 4297
Burbank, CA 91503
818/848-1277

Burlington

Mid-Peninsula Macintosh Group
1720 Ralston Ave.
Burlington, CA 94010
415/595-3674

Carmel

Club Mac of Monterey
P.O. Box 222988
Carmel, CA 93922
408/624-8907

Carson

MAC-HACers
21111 Dolores
Carson, CA 90745
213/606-2212

Chula Vista

Chula Vista Apple User Group
619/426-1677

Claremont

CHOMP
P.O. Box 986
Claremont, CA 91711
714/846-4774

Concord

Diablo Valley Apple User Group
P.O. Box 5031
Concord, CA 94524
415/680-4271

Corona

Mac-Mania MUG
963 Nottingham Dr.
Corona, CA 91720
714/735-6814

Coronado

Demons
630 Cabrillo Ave.
Coronado, CA 92118
619/435-0554

Cupertino

Apple HyperCard User Group
408/974-1707

Apple Library Users Group
408/974-2552

Davis

Davis Apple User Group
P.O. Box 1534
Davis, CA 95617
916/756-5063

Davis Macintosh Users Group
P.O. Box 2141
Davis, CA 95616
916/758-4383

El Toro

Orange Apple Computer Club
25422 Trabuco Rd.
El Toro, CA 92630
714/770-1865

Fairfield

Mouse
2198 Vista Luna
Fairfield, CA 94533
707/426-2312

Freemont

SPC Apple
P.O. Box 8019
Freemont, CA 94537
408/738-8330

Fresno

Sierra Apple Orchard
P.O. Box 16275
Fresno, CA 93755
209/439-2446

Fountain Valley

Golden West College Computer
Club
9050 La Linda Ave.
Fountain Valley, CA 92708

Mac Computer Society
18195 Santa Joanna
Fountain Valley, CA 92708

McDonnell Douglas Astro Apple
16681 Mt. Darwin Circle
Fountain Valley, CA 92708
714/839-1139

South Orange County Computer
10221 Sketer Ave.
Fountain Valley, CA 92708

Fullerton

HFEA Macintosh Users Group
1901 W. Malvern Ave.
Fullerton, CA 92635
714/441-6784

Goleta

South Coast Macintosh Users Group
P.O. Box 2035
Goleta, CA 93118
805/685-7295

Hanford

Sequoia Computer Users
209/584-9261

Hawthorne

Northrop Macintosh Users Group
1 Northrop Ave.
Hawthorne, CA 90250
213/970-6300

Hayward

HayMUG
415/727-0779

Hesperia

Newton's Fruit User Group
619/244-6476

C

**User
Groups**

Huntington Beach

Macbeach User Group
P.O. Box 2178
Huntington Beach, CA 92647
714/842-0518

McDonnell Douglas Astronautics
5301 Bolsa Ave.
Huntington Beach, CA 92647
714/896-1128

The Coffee MUG
1104 England St.
Huntington Beach, CA 92648
714/969-2625

Irvine

Realtor's Mac User Group
18023 Sky Park Circle F-2
Irvine, CA 92714
714/261-1930

La Jolla

San Diego Macintosh User Group
P.O. Box 12561
La Jolla, CA 92037
619/789-9492

La Mirada

Macbug
13800 Biola Ave.
La Mirada, CA 90639
213/944-0351

Lindsay

Visalia Mac Enthusiasts Group
209/562-1011

Livermore

Livermore Users Group
685 Las Positas Blvd.
Livermore, CA 94550

Long Beach

Cal State University Long Beach
CSULB MUG
2625 Gondor
Long Beach, CA 90815

Los Alamitos

Logic Tree Mac UG
10512 Los Vagueros Circle
Los Alamitos, CA 90720
714/952-4122

West Orange County Macintosh User
Group
P.O. Box 5099
Los Alamitos, CA 90721
213/431-2848

Los Altos

Informal Computer
P.O. Box 339
Los Altos, CA 94023
415/969-4679

Los Angeles

A La Mac
P.O. Box 27429
Los Angeles, CA 90027
213/462-2860

Computech
801 S. Gramercy Dr.
Los Angeles, CA 90005
213/383-3819

King Drew Macintosh User Group
King Drew Medical Center
12021 S. Wilmington Ave.
Los Angeles, CA 90059
213/603-4578

Lisa Club of LA
854 N. Croft Ave.
Los Angeles, CA 90069

Los Angeles Macintosh Group
12021 Wilshire Blvd.
Los Angeles, CA 90025
213/278-5264

Mac Surf
1600 Campus Rd.
Los Angeles, CA 90041
213/259-2611

Macbuddhist
854 N. Croft Ave.
Los Angeles, CA 90069
213/464-3599

UCLA Macintosh Users Group
UCLA Graduate School of Education
Los Angeles, CA 90024
213/825-1944

USC Macintosh User Group
1025 S. Sierra Bonita Ave.
Los Angeles, CA 90019
213/937-4082

Merced

Merced Mac
333 W. 20th St.
Merced, CA 95340
209/383-0727

Modesto

Stanislaus Macintosh Users Group
209/521-0216

Monterey

The Macintosh User Group
394-B Ricketts Rd.
Monterey, CA 93940

Monterey Park

UC Riverside Mac User Group
869 Crest Vista Dr.
Monterey Park, CA 91754
714/684-7249

Monte Sereno

Silicon Apple Programmer Society
18138 Bancroft
Monte Sereno, CA 95030

Moss Beach

Mid-Day Mac Users
P.O. Box 626
Moss Beach, CA 94038
415/728-5462

Peninsula Lisa Users Group
P.O. Box 626
Moss Beach, CA 94038
415/728-5462

Napa

Napa State Hospital Apple Core
707/253-5250

Napa Apple User Group
P.O. Box 6801
Napa, CA 94581

Oakland

Mills College MUG
5000 MacArthur Blvd.
Oakland, CA 94613
415/430-2167

Oceanside

North County Appleholics
North County Computer Club
Oceanside, CA 92054
619/757-6352

Palo Alto

EnviroMUG
415/646-5946

Macintosh Users of ComputerWare
(MUCoW)
415/496-1068

S P A C E
3790 El Camino
Palo Alto, CA 94306
415/856-9294

Palm Springs

Macdesert Connection
255 N. El Cielo Rd.
Palm Springs, CA 92262
619/320-4003

Pasadena

JPL Mac User Group
4800 Oak Grove Dr.
Pasadena, CA 91109
818/354-0496

Petaluma

North Coast Mac User's Group
503 Marylyn Circle
Petaluma, CA 94952
707/763-1124

Pinole

East Bay Macintosh User Group
2935 Pinole Valley Rd.
Pinole, CA 94564
415/653-5849

Pleasonton

Fire Service Macintosh User Group
415/426-8756

Tri-Valley Macintosh Users Group
415/426-8756

Point Mugu

The Apple Corps
805/989-4734

Redlands

Inland Empire Mac User Group
714/792-4746

Redondo Beach

South Bay Apple Mac User Group
P.O. Box 432
Redondo Beach, CA 90277
213/316-7738

Richmond

Berkeley Macintosh Developers
Group
930 34th St.
Richmond, CA 94805
415/849-4357

Ridgecrest

Ridgecrest Apple User Group
236 Primrose St.
Ridgecrest, CA 93555
619/375-9510

Riverside

Professional Loma Linda University
User Group
Loma Linda University
Riverside, CA 92515

U.C.R. MUG
5505 Canyon Crest
Riverside, CA 92507
714/788-2167

Rosemead

San Gabriel Valley Mac User Group
927 N. Rose Glen Ave.
Rosemead, CA 91770
213/684-4266

Roseville

I-BUG
916/782-5518

Sacramento

Apple Sac, Inc.
P.O. Box 254654
Sacramento, CA 95825

MacNexus
P.O. Box 163508
Sacramento, CA 95816
916/446-2411

Sacramento Macintosh Users Group
P.O. Box 60908
Sacramento, CA 98560

Sacramento's University Macintosh
Club
4248 N. River Way
Sacramento, CA 95864
916/481-3380

San Bernardino

AppleJacks of the Inland Empire
P.O. Box 23035
San Bernardino, CA 92406
714/883-2234

San Diego

San Diego Macintosh User Group
619/698-1791

South Bay Apple Users Group

San Francisco

Bank of America MUG
315 Montgomery St.
San Francisco, CA 94105

Gay Macintosh Users Group
415/626-2620

Golden Gate Macintosh Users Group
415/666-6661

Mac West
1077 Vallejo St.
San Francisco, CA 94133
415/432-9713

Mad Macs
729 Fifth Ave.
San Francisco, CA 94118

Pacific Bell MUG
370 Third St.
San Francisco, CA 94107
415/542-4820

San Francisco Apple Care
P.O. Box 281797
San Francisco, CA 94128
415/771-5830

San Francisco Community College
MUG
2554 29th Ave.
San Francisco, CA 94116

Show Page Macintosh Users Grup
2040 Polk St.
San Francisco, CA 94109
415/621-8808

C

**User
Groups**

The Hispanic Computing Association
415/824-8337

UCSF Apple Users Group
CVRI Box 0130
San Francisco, CA 94143

UCSF Macintosh Users Group
415/476-200

Whole Earth Well
18 Sequoia Way
San Francsco, CA 94127
415/469-8862

San Jose

Apple Blossom Users Group
P.O. Box 53323
San Jose, CA 95123

ChipMUG
1015 Nevada Pl.
San Jose, CA 95125
408/298-2469

San Luis Obispo

Apple San Luis Users Group
805/756-2638

SLO Med-Mac Users Group
805/541-6080

San Mateo

Women's Special Interest Group
415/574-8225

San Rafael

Macs of Marin
23 Pleasant Ln.
San Rafael, CA 94901
415/459-5707

Santa Ana

Mac Orange
P.O. Box 1830
Santa Ana, CA 92702
714/871-6329

Santa Clara

Association of Apple 32 Users
P.O. Box 634
Santa Clara, CA 95052
408/263-0398

Programming & Interfacing
    Enthusiasts, Inc.
P.O. Box 2185
Santa Clara, CA 95055
408/243-0234

Santa Cruz

Maccruzers
P.O. Box 2508
Santa Cruz, CA 95062
408/458-9850

MacDoves
1424 Glen Canyon Rd.
Santa Cruz, CA 95060

Santa Cruz Macintosh Users Group
740 Front St., P.O. Box 1428
Santa Cruz, CA 95060

Santa Maria

Santa Maria & Lompoc Appleuser
265 Shirley Ln.
Santa Maria, CA 93455

Santa Monica

Memorial Macintosh User Group
1537 A Princeton St.
Santa Monica, CA 90404

Santa Rosa

North Coast Mac User Group
P.O. Box 14144
Santa Rosa, CA 95402
707/545-5112

Seal Beach

Logic Tree Mac Users Group
3560 Bluebell
Seal Beach, CA 90740

Stanford

Stanford Macintosh Users Group
P.O. Box 2354
Stanford, CA 94309
415/723-7684

Stanton

AMUG
10356 Beach Blvd.
Stanton, CA 90680

Sonora

Mac Twain
415/533-1993

South Pasadena

Tri-City Apple User Group
P.O. Box 975
South Pasadena, CA 91030
213/258-4466

Stockton

Stockton Apple User Group
6333 Pacific Ave.
Stockton, CA 95207
209/957-9389

Stockton

University Mac UG
209/946-3083

Sunnyvale

OMNI MUG
548 S. Fairoaks
Sunnyvale, CA 94086

Studio City

Dick Grove School of Music UG
12754 Ventura Blvd.
Studio City, CA 91604
818/985-0905

Sunnyvale

Apple Professional Exchange
408/745-0665

Thousand Oaks

Conejo-Ventura Macintosh Users
    Group
P.O. Box 7118-MAC
Thousand Oaks, CA 91359
805/584-8733

Transaction Technology, Inc.
Macintosh Users Group
1945 Berkshire Dr.
Thousand Oaks, CA 91362

Trinity Center

Trinity Users Group
Star Rt. 2, Box 4792
Trinity Center, CA 96091

Ukiah

MCMUG
532 S. State St.
Ukiah, CA 95482

Vallejo

North Bay Users Group
P.O. Box 7156
Vallejo, CA 94590

Venice

Original Apple Corps
15 Paloma Ave.
Venice, CA 90291
213/396-5515

Ventura

Ventura County Macintosh Club
1413-D South Victoria Ave.
Ventura, CA 93003
805/499-2824

Visalia

Visalia Mac Enthusiasts Group
207 E. Prospect Ct.
Visalia, CA 93291

Westminister

Apple MUG
208 Hospital Circle
Westminister, CA 92683

West Colvina

Soley MUG of Cal Poly
1419 Thackery Ave.
West Colvina, CA 91791

Yucaipa

Empire Mac User Group
33418 Rosemond
Yucaipa, CA 92399
714/864-4872

Colorado

Aspen

Macintosh Users Group
303/925-1091

Basalt

Macintosh Users Group
P.O. Box 1146
Basalt, CO 81621
303/925-7562

Boulder

Boulder Mac Meeting
6727 Lakeview Dr.
Boulder, CO 80303
303/494-7186

Macintosh Users Group
University of Colorado
3161 Madison
Boulder, Co 80303

Colorado Springs

Silicon Mountain Mac Users Group
3440 Orlo Blanco Dr.
Colorado Springs, CO 80917
719/597-2695

Denver

Computer C.A.C.H.E.
P.O. Box 37313
Denver, CO 80237
303/771-2019

Denver Apple Pie, Inc.
P.O. Box 17467
Denver, CO 80217
303/422-1214

Mile High Macintosh Users Group
855 S. Grant St.
Denver, CO 80209
303/869-9393

Eastlake

The Apple Resource Group
P.O. Box 451
Eastlake, CO 80614
303/451-6116

Englewood

Apple Three Users Group
P.O. Box 3155
Englewood, CO 80155
303/791-0887

MacinTech
6635 S. Dayton St.
Englewood, CO 80111
303/773-6900

Ft. Collins

Northern Colorado Macintosh Users
Group
1217 S. Bryan Ave.
Ft. Collins, CO 80521
303/482-2744

Greeley

Greeley Outpost Club Mac
1955 23rd Ave.
Greeley, CO 80631
303/352-4085

Highlands Ranch

Apple Three User Group
303/791-0887

Lakewood

Mac West Users Group
981 S. Foothill Dr.
Lakewood, CO 80235
303/989-6800

Salida

Apple Computer Enthusiasts
303/539-4806

Telluride

Macintosh Users Group in Telluride
P.O. Box 112
Telluride, CO 81435
303/728-3469

Trinidad

M-BUG
115 Elm St.
Trinidad, CO 81082
719/846-4367

Woodland Park

Silicon Mountain Macintosh Users'
Group
2457 Sunnywood Ave.
Woodland Park, CO 80863
303/596-9256

Connecticut

Bloomfield

Connecticut Macintosh Connection
5 Fox Chase Rd.
Bloomfield, CT 06002
203/242-2684

C

User Groups

East Hartford

Hartford User Group Exchange
P.O. Box 10827
East Hartford, CT 06118
203/568-0492

Gales Ferry

Southeastern CT Apple User Group
P.O. Box 510
Gales Ferry, CT 06335
203/464-9372

Thames River Apple User Group
203/464-9372

Groton

Applefield Users Group
565 Longhill Rd.
Groton, CT 06340
203/265-1000

Southern Connecticut Mac User
  Group
269 Thames St.
Groton, CT 06340

New Haven

MacForth Users Group
3081 Westville Station
New Haven, CT 06515
203/777-5618

Yale Mac Users' Group
P.O. Box 20A Yale Station
New Haven, CT 06520
203/865-6163

Norwalk

Apple MUGS
345 Main St.
Norwalk, CT 06851

Stamford

The Group
98 Hoyt St.
Stamford, CT 06905
203/325-4250

Storrs

U Conn Mac Users Group
U-44, University of Connecticut
Storrs, CT 06268

West Hartford

Informatics Group
80 Shield St.
West Hartford, CT 06110
203/724-4040

West Redding

Greater Danbury Macintosh User
  Group
P.O. Box 295
West Redding, CT 06896
203/746-0668

Weston

Hyperfection: The Apple Corps
10 Lords Hwy.
Weston, CT 06883
203/227-0921

Wilton

Apple MUGS
7 Old Wagon Rd.
Wilton, CT 06897

Delaware

Bridgeville

Delmarva Apple Users Group
Rd 2, Box 94-A
Bridgeville, DE 19933
302/945-9520

Rockland

Macintosh Users of Delaware
P.O. Box 17
Rockland, DE 19732
302/656-1884

Wilmington

Del Ches Systems
2204 N. Church St.
Wilmington, DE 19802
302/658-0735

Macintosh Gamers of America
116 Weldin Park Dr.
Wilmington, DE 19803

District of Columbia

Washington

Interior Mac User Group
202/343-4750

NASA Headquarters Macintosh Users
  Group
202/453-2720

Pentagon Macintosh Users Group
202/546-6044

Florida

Cape Coral

Florida's Sun Coast Macintosh User
  Group
813/772-7613

Coral Springs

National Macintosh Computer
  Society
P.O. Box 8589
Coral Springs, FL 33075
305/941-8286

Crystal Beach

Bay Area Macintosh Users Group
P.O. Box 78
Crystal Beach, FL 33523
813/725-1044

Deland

De Mac
400 Nut Tree
Deland, FL 32724
904/736-1953

Fort Walton Beach

Macplayground MUG
P.O. Box 3195
Fort Walton Beach, FL 32548
904/862-4908

Holiday

Holiday Area Medical Mousers
Ted Sichelman
4800 Dixie Highway
Holiday, FL 34690

Jacksonville

North Florida MUG
P.O. Box 10262
Jacksonville, FL 32247
904/731-0851

Key West

Florida Keys Macintosh Users Group
Florida Keys Community College
Key West, FL 33040
305/296-9081

Largo

Bay Area Macintosh Users Group
11335 112th St. N
Largo, FL 34648
813/398-6702

Melbourne

MacMAD
P.O. Box 194
Melbourne, FL 32902
407/729-6004

Merritt Island

Space Coast Apple Users Group
P.O. Box 2112
Merritt Island, FL 32952
407/452-8357

Miami

Gold Coast Mac, Inc.
P.O. Box 452305
Miami, FL 33245
305/447-7888

Miami's Big Apple User Group
P.O. Box 63-04
Miami, FL 33163
305/948-8000

National Lisa & Macintosh Users
Group
305/447-7888

National XLisa Users Group
P.O. Box 450676
Miami, FL 33245

PANA-MAC
P.O. Box 520636
Miami, FL 33152

Miami Beach

Miami Beach Apple Club
5701 Collins Ave.
Miami Beach, FL 33140
305/866-5507

Miami Apple Users Group
Macintosh SIG
P.O. Box 403428
Miami Beach, FL 33140
305/866-5507

Naples

Naples Mac Friends
1800 Tiller Terr.
Naples, FL 33940
813/261-8208

Niceville

Suffolk Apple Computer Society
506 Greenwood Cove S
Niceville, FL 32578
904/678-8007

North Fort Myers

Swacks
18141 Palm Creek Dr.
North Fort Myers, FL 33917
813/543-6329

Orlando

O-Mac
3716 Ridgemont Rd.
Orlando, FL 32808
305/299-0021

Panama City

Mac Bay Users Group
1712-A Deer Ave.
Panama City, FL 32401

Pensacola

Pensacola Macintosh User Group
P.O. Box 18550
Pensacola, FL 32503

Macintosh Computer Club of
Pensacola
Box 15390
Pensacola, FL 32514
904/478-1112

Port Charlotte

Southwest Florida Mac Users Group
813/625-3574

Port St. Lucie

South Florida Macintosh Users Group
2109 Erwin Rd.
Port St. Lucie, FL 34952
407/337-0758

Sarasota

Sarasota/Manatee Macintosh User
Group
P.O. Box 25134
Sarasota, FL 33579

Spring Hill

Spring Hill Apple Computer
Enthusiasts
5228 Derby Ave.
Spring Hill, FL 34608
904/686-6479

Stuart

Treasure Coast Macintosh Users
Group
407/283-1374

Tallahassee

Tallahassee Apple Users Group
P.O. Box 11112
Tallahassee, FL 32302
904/599-3316

Tampa

Florida Innovation Group
P.O. Box 16645
11606 Malcolm McKinley
Tampa, FL 33687
813/971-105

Holiday Area Macers Ham
8700 North 50th St.
Tampa, FL 33687
800/548-8282

West Palm Beach

The Source Apple Expert
2786 Tennis Club Dr.
West Palm Beach, FL 33417
407/689-3330

Winter Haven

Polk Apple Core
813/293-2865

C

**User
Groups**

Georgia

Arnoldsville

Classic Apple Users Group
2211 Belmont Rd.
Arnoldsville, GA 30619

Athens

Athens Mac Users
Barrow Hall
University of Georgia
Athens, GA 30602
404/542-5359

Mac Users Group of Athens
175 Baxter Drive, 1-2
Athens, GA 30307
404/542-7774

Atlanta

Atlanta Area Apple Users Group
868 Castle Falls Dr. NE
Atlanta, GA 30329
404/662-6957

Emory Mac User Group
Dept. of Geology
Emory University
Atlanta, GA 30322
404/727-0118

Augusta

The Augusta MacMasters Macintosh
  Users Group
2933 Foxhall Circle
Augusta, GA 30907
404/860-6818

Lagrange

LAMUG
824 Azalea Dr.
Lagrange, GA 30240

Marietta

Mac Atlanta
3127 Bunker Hill Circle
Marietta, GA 30062
404/971-9661

Mercer

Mercer University Mac Users
Media Center
Mercer University
Mercer, GA 31207
912/744-2985

Norcross

Atlanta Macintosh Users Group
P.O. Box 2941
Norcross, GA 30091
404/231-9527

Roswell

Widget Apple Group
4285 Loch Highlands Pass
Roswell, GA 30075
404/992-2553

Savannah

Savannah MUG
13 Cutler Ct.
Savannah, GA 31419
912/925-2188

Valdosta

South Georgia Apple Core
1618E Bird Ct.
Valdosta, GA 31602
912/244-9363

Hawaii

Honolulu

Hawaii Macintosh Users Group
P.O. Box 75337
Honolulu, HI 96836
808/235-4609

Kapaa

Kauai Apple Users Group
P.O. Box 1540
Kapaa, HI 96746
808/822-4558

Kahului

Maui MUG
P.O. Box 4103
Kahului, HI 96732
808/572-0630

Lihue

Hawaii MUG
808/245-1633

Pearl City

Hawaii Macintosh User Group
P.O. Box 1355
Pearl City, HI 96782
808/456-1610

Puunene

Maui MacNuts
808/572-0420

Wailuku

Maui Macintosh Users Group
R.R. 1, Box 98
Wailuku, HI 96793
808/572-0630

Idaho

Boise

Apple Boise User Group
208/344-9506

Boise State Academic Apple Users
Chemistry Department
Boise State University
Boise, ID 83725
208/385-3964

Macintosh Users Group of Southern
  Idaho
5182 Latigo
Boise, ID 83709
208/345-0346

Caldwell

Canyon Macintosh Users Group
1110 W. Ash
Caldwell, ID 83605
208/454-8862

Coeur d'Alene

IPHAUG
208/664-8348

Hayden Lake

IPHAUG
11765 Diamond Dr.
Hayden Lake, ID 83835
208/772-4522

Idaho Falls

Idaho Falls Mac Users Group
294 Davidson Dr.
Idaho Falls, ID 83401
208/523-0004

Saint Maries

N. Idaho Macintosh Users Group
1157 Fourth St.
Saint Maries, ID 83861

Sand Point

Macintosh Construction Forum
208/263-3078

Illinois

Argonne

ANL Macintosh Users Group
Argonne National Laboratory, 9700
Argonne, IL 60439
312/472-5521

Arlington

Northern Illinois Computer Society
P.O. Box 547
Arlington, IL 61312

Arlington Heights

Apple Developers Consortium
703 W. Victoria Ln.
Arlington Heights, IL 60005
312/640-8082

Batavia

Fermilab Macintosh Users Group
MS 223
P.O. Box 500
Batavia, IL 60510
312/840-3017

Belleville

Metro MUG
13 Yorkshire Ln.
Belleville, IL 62221
618/234-4333

Bloomington

The Mac Pac
P.O. Box 1512
Bloomington, IL 61702
309/828-3145

Carbondale

Crab Apple Users Group
P.O. Box 338
Carbondale, IL 62901
618/893-4489

Macintosh User Group of Southern
    Illinois
Computer Corner
University Mall
Carbondale, IL 62901
618/529-5000

Cary

Macadamia Mac Users Group
P.O. Box 239
Cary, IL 60013
312/639-4960

Champaign

Champaign-Urbana Macintosh Users
    Group
172 Natural Resources Bldg.
607 E. Peabody
Champaign. IL 61820

Champaign-Urbana Apple Users
    Group
1908 Barberry Circle
Champaign, IL 61821

Chicago

American Bar Association Macintosh
    Users
312/782-6495

Chicago South Side Mac Users Group
University of Chicago
5737 S. University Ave.
Chicago, IL 60637
312/955-0582

Kieffer-Nolde Apple Users Group
312/337-5500

Macintosh Users Group
Illinois Institute of Technology
312/225-6911

MCsquared UG
312/341-3654

The Rest of Us
P.O. Box 3500
Chicago, IL 60654
312/525-4761

TAAD/Committee on Personal
    Computer and the Handicapped
312/866-8195

University of Chicago Macintosh
    User Group
5528 S. Hyde Park Blvd.
Chicago, IL 60637
312/288-5199

Cobden

Southern Illinois Apple User Group
R.R. 2, Box 42
Cobden, IL 62920

Southern Illinois Crab Apple Users
    Group
618/893-4489

Decatur

Decatur Apple Club
217/428-8145

Downers Grove

DuPage Apple User Group
P.O. Box 294
Downers Grove, IL 60515
312/993-3897

Elgin

Plato Center Apple Users Group
312/464-5272

Edwardsville

Gateway Area Macintosh Users
P.O. Box 7
Edwardsville, IL 62025
314/863-0036

Evanston

Northwestern Mouse User Group
NU ACNS, 2129 Sheridan Rd.
Evanston, IL 60208
312/491-3290

Freeburg

Metro MUG
618/539-5786

Galesburg

Midwest Macintosh Users Group
755 N. Henderson St.
Galesburg, IL 61401
309/342-7177

Joliet

Illinois Macintosh Users Group
2314 Mason
Joliet, IL 60435
815/744-2073

C

**User
Groups**

Mundelein

M.U.G.
310 Woodlawn Drive
Mundelein, IL 60060
312/949-0266

Murphysboro

Little Egypt Apple Users Group
P.O. Box 1112
Murphysboro, IL 62966
618/684-2752

Naperville

Indian Hill Computer Hobbyists
AT&T Bell Labs
Naperville & Wheaton Rds.
Naperville, IL 60566
312/979-2028

Peoria

Central Illinois Mac User Group
1501 W. Bradley Ave.
Peoria, IL 61625
309/677-2766

River Forest

Apple Enthusiast Society of Oak Park
820 Bonnie Brae
River Forest, IL 60305
312/366-7864

Rockford

Rockford Area Apple Users
815/968-6228

Stateline Macintosh Users Group
3703 N. Main
Rockford, IL 61103
815/633-9494

Springfield

Club Mac of Springfield and Environs
217/787-8041

Macintosh Computer User Group of
Sangamon
P.O. Box 2344
Springfield, IL 62705
217/782-9845

Wheaton

Tau
312/653-7640

Indiana

Bloomington

SMUG
P.O. Box 1238
Bloomington, IN 47402
812/336-7395

Bremen

Apple UG Michiana
423 W. Bike
Bremen, IN 46506
219/546-4050

Evansville

The Macintosh Group of Southern
Indiana
748 Stewart Ave.
Evansville, IN 47715
812/423-6869

Fort Wayne

Fort Wayne Macintosh Users Group
P.O. Box 5673
Fort Wayne, IN 46895
219/749-4444

Indianapolis

The Apple Pickers, Inc.
P.O. Box 20136
Indianapolis, IN 46220
317/291-4042

Kokomo

Kokomo Apple Users Group
611 S. Webster St.
Kokomo, IN 46901
317/452-2616

Lebanon

Mac Genius
1102 Sherri Ln.
Lebanon, IN 46052
317/482-5657

Merrillville

Northern Indiana Apple Users
219/736-6929

Muncie

Muncie MacPack
P.O. Box 2407
Muncie, IN 47307
317/747-6178

Notre Dame

Notre Dame Mad Macs User Group
University of Notre Dame
Computer Center
Notre Dame, IN 46556
219/239-5600

Terre Haute

Apple Byters of Vigo County
2747 College Ave.
Terre Haute, IN 47803

Wabash Valley Macintosh Users
Group
P.O. Box 95
Terre Haute, IN 47808
812/232-0050

Valparaiso

Mac Genius
504 Burlington Beach Road
Valparaiso, IN 46383

Iowa

Ames

Ames Apple Users Group
P.O. Box 703
Ames, IA 50010
515/232-1652

Iowa State Mac Users Group
301 S. 5th St.
Ames, IA 50010
515/233-4807

Burlington

Apple Burlington User Group
319/753-0846

Cedar Falls

Waterloo/Cedar Falls CIA-MUG
P.O. Box 143
Cedar Falls, IA 50613
319/266-0634

Cedar Rapids

Central Iowa Area Macintosh User
Group
99 1/2 16th Ave. SW
Cedar Rapids, IA 52404
319/363-1242

Creston

The Tree House
219 W. Montgomery
Creston, IA 50801
515/782-4315

Des Moines

Central Iowa Mac Publishers
3106 Ingersoll Ave.
Des Moines, IA 50312
515/274-9271

Iowa MUG
667 49th St.
Des Moines, IA 50312
515/279-9650

Durango

Tri-State Micro Computer Club
15700 Five Points Rd.
Durango, IA 52039
319/556-1874

Fairfield

Fairfield Mac Users
MJ Mara
607 N. Court St.
Fairfield, IA 52556

Macintosh User Group
200 W. Washington
Fairfield, IA 52556

Macknowlia
P.O. Box 1691
Fairfield, IA 52556
515/472-7523

Harlan

Western IA Apple Users
R.R. 4, Box 96
Harlan, IA 51537
712/744-3619

Iowa City

Iowa City Apple Group
P.O. Box 1267
Iowa City, IA 52244
319/354-7137

Johnston

Club Mac Midwest
P.O. Box 468
Johnston, IA 50131
515/270-6916

Marshalltown

Apple Seed
P.O. Box 1281
Marshalltown, IA 50158
515/752-0883

Newton

Newton Apple Corps.
P.O. Box 1263
Newton, IA 50208
515/792-8695

Pella

Marion County Computer Club
503 Broadway
Pella, IA 50219
515/842-3101

Roland

Roland-Story Apple Users Group
P.O. Box D
Roland, IA 50236
515/388-5576

Sioux City

MUGSi
3303 Rebecca St.
Box 2100
Sioux City, IA 51104
712/279-5549

Solon

Cedar Rapids Macintosh User
Rt. 2, Box 188-A
Solon, IA 52333
319/848-4484

Waukee

Glitch Kickers Computer Club
P.O. Box H
Waukee, IA 50263
515/288-0255

Waterloo

Green Apples User Group
P.O. Box 2224
Waterloo, IA 50704
319/268-0066

West Burlington

Apple Burlington Users Group
P.O. Box 508
West Burlington, IA 52655
319/753-0846

Kansas

Dodge City

Dodge City Apple Users Group
606 Second Ave.
Dodge City, KS 67801

Manhattan

Kaw River Mac Users Group
P.O. Box 454
Manhattan, KS 66502
913/537-8867

Salina

Technology Resources for Special
People
913/827-0301

Shawnee Mission

Apple Bits Users Group, Inc.
P.O. Box 368
Shawnee Mission, KS 66201
816/523-1007

Kansas City Mac Core
P.O. Box 2177
Shawnee Mission, KS 66201
816/472-7226

Topeka

Topeka Macintosh Users Group
1328 SW 30th
Topeka, KS 66611
913/233-9815

Wichita

MacWichita
P.O. Box 48604
Wichita, KS 67201
316/777-0492

Kentucky

Clarkson

Kentucky Educators Computers
Users Group
504 Crow Hollow Rd.
Clarkson, KY 42726
502/242-9414

C
User
Groups

Frankfort

Capital City Macintosh Users Group
516 Wapping St.
Frankfort, KY 40601
502/875-7232

Lexington

Central Kentucky Computer Society
271 W. Short St.
Lexington, KY 40501
606/255-3349

Louisville

Louisville Apple User Group
4523 S. First St.
Louisville, KY 40214
502/363-3113

Radcliff

MegaMac Users Group of Fort Knox
502/351-8224

Waddy

Capitol City MUG
Rt. 2, Avenstoke Rd.
Waddy, KY 40076
502/223-1508

Louisiana

Baton Rouge

Baton Rouge MAUG
College of Design
Louisiana State University
Baton Rouge, LA 70803
504/388-6506

Bossier City

Red River Maclan
2326 Barksdale Blvd.
Bossier City, LA 70043
318/742-3148

Metairie

New Orleans Macintosh Users Group
P.O. Box 5991
Metairie, LA 70009
504/885-5600

Lafayette

Cajun Macintosh Users Group
318/231-5633

New Orleans

Crescent City Apple Corps.
504/283-3819

Shreveport

Shreveport Area Macintosh User
P.O. Box 5150
Shreveport, LA 71135
318/861-9372

Maine

Bangor

MacBang
207/942-3708

Brunswick

Maine Macintosh Owners and
Operators
P.O. Box 1025
Brunswick, ME 04011
207/725-8417

Freeport

Southern Maine Apple Users Group
R.R. 1, Box 206
Freeport, ME 04032
207/865-3970

Topsham

Mac II Express
207/725-8417

Waterville

Kennebec Apple Users Group
P.O. Box 1166
Waterville, ME 04901
207/873-2880

Maryland

Baltimore

Bayview Macintosh Users Group
301/550-1482

Maryland Apple Corps.
P.O. Box 2353
Baltimore, MD 21203

Bel Air

Hartford Community College Apple
Users
401 Thomas Run Rd.
Bel Air, MD 21014
301/836-4315

Berlin

Worcester County Apple Club
301/641-3575

Bethesda

Biomedical Research Mac Users
Group
Bldg. 36
Bethesda, MD 20892
301/496-4957

Washington Apple Pi
8227 Woodmont Ave.
Bethesda, MD 20814
301/654-8060

Columbia

Columbia Apple Slice
301/997-9317

Laurel

University of Maryland MUG
326 Thomas Dr.
Laurel, MD 20707

Lexington Park

Southern Maryland Apple Users
P.O. Box 398
Lexington Park, MD 20653
301/862-2364

Owings Mills

Reisterstown Apple Users Group
6 Kingsley Rd.
Owings Mills, MD 21117

Rockville

Capital PC User Group, Inc.
51 Monroe St., Plaza East II
Rockville, MD 20850
301/656-8372

Silver Spring

Capital Macintosh User Group
9431 Georgia Ave.
Silver Spring, MD 20910
301/585-4262

Sykesville

Westminister Macintosh Users Group
6005 Old Washington Rd.
Sykesville, MD 21784
301/781-7064

Westminister

WMC MUG
Western Maryland College
Westminister, MD 21157
301/857-2477

Massachusetts

Amherst

UMacs
11 S. Prospect St.
Amherst, MA 01002

Andover

Any Body's Information Center
384 N. Main St.
Andover, MA 01810
617/475-7411

Boston

Boston Computer Society MUG
One Center Plaza
Boston, MA 02108
617/367-8080

Boston Society of Architects
617/267-5175

Brockton

Computer Store MUG
863 Belmont St.
Brockton, MA 02401
617/588-1837

Cambridge

Harvard Computer Society
Science Center 121, 1 Oxford St.
Cambridge, MA 02138
617/498-7937

MIT Macintosh User Group
P.O. Box 398
Cambridge, MA 02142

Chelmsford

Computer Users Group
7 Muriel Rd.
Chelmsford, MA 01824
617/256-6173

Chestnut Hill

Boston College Macintosh User
Group
Gasson 12, Boston College
Chestnut Hill, MA 02167
617/552-8640

Douglas

Worcester Mac Users Group
47 West St., E
Douglas, MA 01516
617/476-7014

Edgartown

Martha's Vineyard Macintosh User
Group
P.O. Box 1602
Edgartown, MA 02539
508/627-8529

Holyoke

Valley Interface
413/538-7000

Lenox

Apple Core Berkshire County
14 Hutchinson Ln.
Lenox, MA 01240
413/637-1593

Otis AFB

Cape Cod Macintosh Users Group
508/563-5333

Rockport

North Shore Apple Group
Box 59
Rockport, MA 01966
617/546-3104

Scituate

East Coast Apple Net
19 Damon Rd.
Scituate, MA 02066
617/545-2696

Somerville

BCS Medi-Mac
617/625-7080

Boston Computer Society Macintosh
User Group
617/816-6343

South Dennis

Cape Cod Apple Users Group
P.O. Box 48
South Dennis, MA 02660
617/896-7286

Waltham

GTE Mac Users Group
40 Sylvan Road
Waltham, MA 02254
617/979-6508

Wellesley

Wellesley MUG
Slater International Center
Wellesley College
Wellesley, MA 02181
617/235-0320

Babson Macintosh Users Group
617/259-0726

Worcester

HC MUG
508/793-2591

MACaholics Worcester Group
6 East Mountain Rd.
Worcester, MA 01606
617/853-9407

Michigan

Adrian

Lenawee Apple Core Users Group
1100 South Main, Lot 61
Adrian, MI 49221
517/263-2070

Albion

Albion College Macintosh Enthusiasts
Albion College
Albion, MI 49224
517/629-5511

C
User
Groups

Ann Arbor

Ann Arbor Apple
P.O. Box 2386
Ann Arbor, MI 48106
313/485-0884

Domino's Mac User Group
Greg Aamoth
30 Frank Lloyd Wright Ln.
Ann Arbor, MI 48106

MacTechnics User Group
P.O. Box 4063
Ann Arbor, MI 48106
313/662-1199
313/454-1702

The Ann Arbor Macintosh User
Group
University of Michigan
P.O. Box 4063
Ann Arbor, MI 48106
313/663-5388

Battle Creek

Mar Creek Apple Computer Club
111 Academy
Battle Creek, MI 49017
616/963-2885

Chesaning

ChUG
319 S. Chapman
Chesaning, MI 48616
517/845-2040

Detroit

MacGroup-Detroit
P.O. Box 35529
Detroit, MI 48235
313/571-8154

Semco Mac Pac
P.O. Box 02426
Detroit, MI 48202
313/673-1573
313/284-2816

Flint

The Flint Apple Club
P.O. Box 460
Flint, MI 48501
313/732-9574

Flushing

SE Michigan MUG
506 Spring Ln.
Flushing, MI 48433
313/368-1678

Gobles

Kalamazoo Apple Computer User
616/628-2927

Grand Rapids

Grand Rapids Apple Macintosh Users
2310 Tecumseh Dr.
Grand Rapids, MI 49506
616/241-3795

Grass Lake

Apple Jackson Users Group
4848 Wolf Lake Rd.
Grass Lake, MI 49240
517/522-4689

Grosse Isle

Southeastern Michigan MacUsers
Group
9720 Lakewood
Grosse Isle, MI 48138
313/675-7575

Hancock

Copper MUG
P.O. Box 209
Hancock, MI 49930
906/482-3907

Kalamazoo

Kalamazoo Apple Computer User
376 Lodge Ln.
Kalamazoo, MI 49009

Lansing

Lansing Area Macintosh and Lisa
User Groups
P.O. Box 27372
Lansing, MI 48909
517/393-6413

Livonia

Mac Type Net Users Group
P.O. Box 52188, 18311 Grimm
Livonia, MI 48152
313/477-2733

Midland

Mac-In-Awe Macintosh Users Group
1710 W. St. Andrews Rd.
Midland, MI 48640
517/636-0009

MAC-IN-AWE Personal Apple Club
Grace A. Dow Public Library, Shel
Levy
1710 W. St. Andrews Rd.
Midland, MI 48640
517/631-1229

Port Huron

S.M.U.G.
4289 Old Forge Dr.
Port Huron, MI 48060
800/521-7600, ext.275

Saginaw

Saginaw Apple Computer Klub
4465 Seidel Pl.
Saginaw, MI 48603
517/792-3975

Saginaw Macintosh Users Group
517/793-8797

Sault Saint Marie

Sault Saint Marie Macintosh User
Group
P.O. Box 154
Sault Saint Marie, MI 49783
705/942-8810

Tawas City

North East Michigan Mac Users
Group
1175 South U.S. 23
Tawas City, MI 48763
517/362-6149

Three Rivers

St. Joseph County Apple Computer
UG
55066 N. Fisher Lake Rd.
Three Rivers, MI 49093
616/279-9416

Traverse City

Northwest Mac Users Group
131 N. Elmwood
Traverse City, MI 49684
616/941-6576

Warren

Apple PIE
P.O. Box 5055
Warren, MI 48090
313/778-3299

Minnesota

Arden Hills

Land O' Macs
612/481-2224

Blaine

U of M MUG
12801 Polk St. NE
Blaine, MN 55434

Duluth

SMMUG
2230 Lester River Rd.
Duluth, MN 55804
218/726-2642

Good Thunder

MacKato User Group
507/278-3657

Hibbing

Iron Range Apple Computer Club
2024 Eighth Ave., E
Hibbing, MN 55746
218/263-5462

Hopkins

Mini'app'les
P.O. Box 796
Hopkins, MN 55343
612/572-9305

Mankato

Mac-Kato (Mankato Macintosh Users
Group)
P.O. Box 3491
Mankato, MN 56002
507/388-1187-H

Minneapolis

Macintosh Special Interest Group
1201 Lake Avenue
Minneapolis, MN 55416
612/866-3441

Univ. of Minn. MUG
2751 Brighton Ave. NE
Minneapolis, MN 55418
612/789-0931

Moorhead

Agassiz Macers
3619 Rivershore Dr.
Moorhead, MN 56560
218/236-1266

Northfield

St. Olaf MUG
St. Olaf College
Northfield, MN 55057
507/663-3613

North Mankato

Apple User Group
507/387-3398

Rochester

Rochester Area Mac Users
Mayo Clinic E-12, 1200 First St. SW
Rochester, MN 55905
507/282-5182

St. Paul

Mac SIG
3M Co Desg Specs
Bldg 42-3E-03, Box 33331
St. Paul, MN 55133

Mississippi

Gulfport

Apple Users of South Mississippi
10 Wingate Dr.
Gulfport, MS 39503
601/831-1473

Hattiesburg

Hattiesburg Apple Users Group
2803 Jefferson Dr.
Hattiesburg, MS 39401

University of Mississippi MUG
601/266-5067

Mississippi State

Mississippi State Microcomputer
Users
University Computer Center, Drawer
Cc
Mississippi State, MS 39762
601/325-2079

Natchez

Natchez Apple Users Group
419 Walnut St.
Natchez, MS 39120
601/442-1181

Oxford

Ole Miss Apple User Group
Rt. 6, Box 316A
Oxford, MS 38655
601/234-3146

Starkville

Mississippi State University
Microcomputer Users Group
601/325-2079

Missouri

Cape Giradeau

Southeast Missouri Macintosh Users
Group
314/243-0335

Columbia

MUSE, The Columbia MUG
P.O. Box 811
Columbia, MO 65205
314/874-8657

Higginsville

Central Missouri Computer Club
1905 Walnut St.
Higginsville, MO 64037
816/584-7727

Jefferson City

AppleJac Macintosh Users Group
2539 Lexington Dr.
Jefferson City, MO 65109
314/634-3102

C

**User
Groups**

Joplin

Joplin Apple Users Group
1903 E. 36th
Joplin, MO 64801
417/624-3900

N. Kansas City

Kansas City Mac User Group
1828 Swift
N. Kansas City, MO 64116

Kirksville

Kirksville Macintosh User Group
100 W. LaHarpe
Kirksville, MO 63501
816/665-6093

Kirkwood

Gateway Area Macintosh User Group
907 Lisa Ln.
Kirkwood, MO 63122
314/966-0535

Manchester

Personal Computer Club of St. Louis
274 Brightfield Dr.
Manchester, MO 63021
314/394-6099

St. Louis

Apple Eye
777 South New Ballas, Ste 231E
St. Louis, MO 63141
314/569-2762

Gateway Area Mac Users Group
4515 Maryland Ave.
St. Louis, MO 63108
314/361-1800

Washington University Macintosh UG
Campus Box 1074
St. Louis, MO 63130
314/889-5394

Saint Peters

Apple Jacks of Saint Louis
12 Jenny Lind Dr.
Saint Peters, MO 63376
314/441-1613

Sedalia

Sedalia Apple Users Group
2316 W. Fifth St.
Sedalia, MO 65301
816/827-2623

Springfield

Apple Squires of the Ozarks
P.O. Box 3986
Springfield, MO 65808
417/882-0323

Montana

Billings

Billings Apple Users Group
231 Alderson Ave.
Billings, MT 59106
406/252-7581

Bozeman

About Macintosh
406/587-9447

Montana Macademics
Dept. of English
Montana State University
Bozeman, MT 59717
406/994-5189

Choteau

NONS
Box 521
Choteau, MT 59422
406/466-2857

Great Falls

Montana Mac
2311 Fifth Ave. S
Great Falls, MT 59405
406/761-8954

Nebraska

Hastings

South Central Nebraska Apple
402/463-3456

Lincoln

LIME (Lincoln Informed Macintosh
   Evangelists)
5521 Locust St.
Lincoln, NE 68516
402/489-0556

Mackey Mouse Club
P.O. Box 4561
Lincoln, NE 68504
402/466-0252

Omaha

Metro Apple Computer Hobbyists
3506 N. 113th Plaza
Omaha, NE 68164
402/493-3259

Omaha Macintosh Users Group
311 S. 151st Cir.
Omaha, NE 68154

Scottsbluff

Platte Valley User's Group
601 Park St.
Scottsbluff, NE 69361
308/635-0730

Nevada

Las Vegas

MacGroup
702/735-6139

Southern Nevada Apple Family User
Box 8551, 5000 E. Bonanza
Las Vegas, NV 89110

Window on the Humanities
Las Vegas, NV 89154
702/739-3590,3344

Sparks

Greater Reno Operating Group
P.O. Box 1038
Sparks, NV 89432
702/355-7676

New Hampshire

Durham

UNH MUG
University of New Hampshire
Dept. of Earth Science
Durham, NH 03824

Etna

Big Green Apple Users Group
Stevens Rd, Box 180
Etna, NH 03750
603/643-2530

Hampstead

Merrimac Macintosh User Group
20 Johnston Meadow Rd.
Hampstead, NH 03841
603/329-6107

Keene

MONADNOC MUG
601 West St.
Keene, NH 03431
603/357-4531

Manchester

The Apple Manchester User Group
663 Varney St.
Manchester, NH 03833
617/778-7229

Nashua

Southern New Hampshire Apple
    Core
Drawer 3647
Nashua, NH 03061
603/883-1655

New Durham

Lakes Region Mac Users Group
P.O. Box 92
New Durham, NH 03855
603/859-3342

North Conway

Valley Computer Users Group
603/356-9426

Plymouth

Pemi-Baker Computer Users Group
R.F.D. 2, Box 399
Plymouth, NH 03264
603/536-3880

Portsmouth

Seacoast Mac
57 South St.
Portsmouth, NH 03801
603/436-1608

New Jersey

Bricktown

Ocean Apple Users Group
201/920-2353

Cherry Hill

Drexel University Macintosh User
    Group
21 Saddle Lane
Cherry Hill, NJ 08002
609/667-3131

South Jersey Apple Users Group
P.O. Box 4273
Cherry Hill, NJ 08003
609/482-0457

South Jersey Mac Users
221 Timothy Ct.
Cherry Hill, NJ 08034
609/428-4429

Edison

The Mac Mice User Group
    (TMMUG)
3 Prince Drive
Edison, NJ 08817

Madison

Apple Jack
P.O. Box 634
Madison, NJ 07940
201/822-3131

Jersey Amateur Computer Klub
201/377-0722

Manahawkin

Ocean Apple Users Group
1049 Driftwood Ave.
Manahawkin, NJ 08050
609/597-3797

Maplewood

Summit Mac User Group
42 Oakview Ave.
Maplewood, NJ 07040
201/763-3360

Marlboro

New York/New Jersey MUG
50 River Drive
Marlboro, NJ 07746
201/536-8360

Milford

Macintosh Assoc. of Central New
    Jersey
R.D. 1, Box 250
Milford, NJ 08848
201/852-2205

Murray Hill

Mac Users at Murray Hill
AT&T Bell Laboratories
600 Mountain Avenue, 7E 419
Murray Hill, NJ 07946
201/582-2361

New Brunswick

Amateur Computer Group of New
    Jersey
201/821-9063

Apple Synapse II
1050 George St. 5-0
New Brunswick, NJ 08901

New Milford

Bergen County Macintosh Users
    Group
147 N. Terrace Pl.
New Milford, NJ 07646
201/262-6729

North Brunswick

Amateur Computer Group of New
    Jersey
698 Magnolia Rd.
North Brunswick, NJ 08902
201/563-5389

Northfield

Atlantic City Area Mac Users Group
201 Tilton Rd.
Northfield, NJ 08225
609/646-8151

Point Pleasant Beach

Monmouth Apple Corps User Group
332 River Ave.
Point Pleasant Beach, NJ 08742
201/528-6349

C
User
Groups

Princeton

Princeton Macintosh Users' Group
6 New South, Info Services
Princeton, NJ 08544
609/452-3622

Randolph

Golden Apple Users Group
2 Bayberry Ln.
Randolph, NJ 07869
201/263-8330

Red Bank

Bellcore MUG
201/758-2288

Scotch Plains

Amateur Computer Group of New
   Jersey
456 Henry St.
Scotch Plains, NJ 07076
201/889-7158

Short Hills

Short Hills Apple Pits
29 Clive Hills Rd.
Short Hills, NJ 07078

Somerville

Ewing Apple Users Group
703 E. Brookside Ln.
Somerville, NJ 08876
201/874-8766

South Orange

Essex County Macintosh Users
P.O. Box 122
South Orange, NJ 07079
201/763-0693
201/750-1988

Stanhope

NW Jersey Apple Users Group
23 Rt. 206
Stanhope, NJ 07874
201/347-7892

Teaneck

Columbia University Mac Users
   Group
572 Kenwood Pl.
Teaneck, NJ 07666
201/836-2529

Upper Montclair

New Jersey Macintosh Users Group
P.O. Box 43205
Upper Montclair, NJ 07043

Woodbridge

Central Jersey Macintosh User Group
217 Mawbey St.
Woodbridge, NJ 07095
201/750-1988

New Mexico

Albuquerque

Applequerque Computer Club
P.O. Box 35508
Albuquerque, NM 87176
505/888-4410

Farmington

Red Apple Flyer Computer Club
4108 Douglas
Farmington, NM 87401

Las Cruces

Aviation & Computer Enthusiasts
505/526-5645

Roswell

Apples on the Pecos
27 Lost Trail Rd.
Roswell, NM 88201
505/623-1234

White Sands Missile Range

Cruces Apple Users Group
P.O. Box 428
White Sands Missile Range, NM
   88002
505/522-0861

New York

Albany

Northeastern Users of the Mac
P.O. Box 2548 ESP
Albany, NY 12220
518/235-9142

Bethpage

MAUG
MCI Inc.
34 Spencer Dr.
Bethpage, NY 11714
516/735-6924

Binghamton

Southern Tier Apple Core
98 Oak St.
Binghamton, NY 13905
607/529-8880

Bronx

Bronx Community College Mac
   Users
University Heights, 181st &
   University Aves.
Bronx, NY 10453
212/220-6235

Brooklyn

Earth News
718/934-4439

Buffalo

Apple Byters' Corps, Inc.
42 Moeller St.
Buffalo, NY 14211
716/695-5857

Centereach

Suffolk Macintosh Users's Group
P.O. Box 233
Centereach, NY 11720
516/231-1919

Central Square

Upstate Cider Mill
R.R. 3, Box 25B
Caughdenoy Rd.
Central Square, NY 13036
315/676-2446

Croton-on-Hudson

NOW-MUG
914/271-2155

East Meadow

Fran-Apple User Group
P.O. Box 172
East Meadow, NY 11554

Fabius

Syracuse Microcomputer Club
R.R. 1, Box 175
Fabius, NY 13063
315/683-9460

Franklin Square

Apple Power Users Group
P.O. Box 490
Franklin Square, NY 11010
516/775-8841

Garden City

Nassau Community College
  Macintosh User Group
Math/Computer Department
Nassau Community College
Garden City, NY 11530
516/222-7384

Hamilton

Colgate University Macintosh User
  Group
Box K2009
Colgate University
Hamilton, NY 13346
315/824-9877

Ithaca

Mugwump
Computer Services-Uris Hall
Cornell University
Ithaca, NY 14853
607/255-8321

Kingston

Society of Hudson Valley Mac Users
P.O. Box 1999
Kingston, NY 12401

Liverpool

MacEvangelists
315/457-0310

Monroe

Rock MUG
R.D. 2, Box M781
Monroe, NY 10950
914/638-3800

Monsey

Crab Apple
14 Eleanor Pl.
Monsey, NY 10952
212/822-5035

Newburgh

Valley Central MUG
29 Colden Hill Rd.
Newburgh, NY 12550
914/457-3124

New Rochelle

Westchester Apple Group
55-A Locust Ave.
New Rochelle, NY 10801
914/636-3417

New Windsor

Eastern Orange Mac Users Group
914/561-4132

New York

Big Apple Users Group
P.O. Box 490
New York, NY 10274
718/442-4256

City MUG
City of New York Associated Student
  Union Center
33 W. 42nd St., Box 220
New York, NY 10036
212/790-4360

Columbia University Mac Users
  Group
8th Floor Watson, 612 W. 115 St.
New York, NY 10025
212/280-2861

Computer Hebrew User Group
212/923-4825

DMR Group
212/949-6655

Mt. Sinai Apple Users Group
Box 115, 1 Gustave Levy Plaza
New York, NY 10029
212/241-6151

New York Mac Users' Group
688 Avenue of the Americas
New York, NY 10010
212/691-0496

NYUser
Dr. Martin Nachbar
NYU School of Medicine
Hippocrates Project
550 First Ave.
New York, NY 10016

Westchester MUG
41 Park Avenue
New York, NY 10016

Oneonta

MUG One
2 Walling Blvd.
Oneonta, NY 13820
607/432-0131

Pittsford

Rochester Apple CIDER
75 Wood Creek
Pittsford, NY 14534

Potdsam

Potsdam College Mac Users
5 Missouri Ave.
Potsdam, NY 13676
315/265-2396

Rochester

Apple-Ace Computer Club
92 Elm Grove Rd.
Rochester, NY 14626
716/225-8850

Banana Byte User Group
29 Chartwell Ct.
Rochester, NY 14623
716/475-3672

MacRIT
College Alumni Union
One Lomb Memorial Dr.
Rochester, NY 14623
716/475-2054

MUGUR
University of Rochester
P.O. Box 29052
Rochester, NY 14627
716/275-1485

Rome

Mac-RUG
113 Glen Rd. S
Rome, NY 13440
315/336-8060

C
User
Groups

Saratoga Springs

Skidmore Mac Enthusiasts
Computer Services
Skidmore College
Saratoga Springs, NY 12866
518/584-5000

Schenectady

MECCA
518/374-1088

Seaford

Lica-Limacintosh Users Group
P.O. Box 518
Seaford, NY 11783
516/541-3186

Seneca Falls

The Apple Corps.
55 Stevenson St.
Seneca Falls, NY 13148
315/568-9718

Staten Island

Staten Island Apple User Group
P.O. Box 050 141
Staten Island, NY 10305
718/727-1291

Syracuse

SUNY-ESF Mac Users Group
College of Environmental Science
    and Forestry
Syracuse Campus
Syracuse, NY 13210
315/470-6810

The Syracuse Apple Users Group
Box 6586, Teal Avenue Station
Syracuse, NY 13217
315/677-3660

Syracuse MUG
240 Buckingham Avenue
Syracuse, NY 13210
315/446-7500

Troy

Campus Apple Group
2214 12th St.
Troy, NY 12180
518/271-0750

Vestal

STAC
1968 North Rd.
Vestal, NY 13850

West Nyack

Crab Apple
914/357-0867

West Point

USMac
914/938-2559

West Seneca

Mac's 5th Ave. User Group
3984 Seneca St.
West Seneca, NY 14224
716/674-8414

Whitesboro

Upstate Apple Users Group
R.D. 1, Box 17-A, 99 Commercial Dr.
Whitesboro, NY 13492
315/793-5911

Wilson

Rainbow Country User Group
2850 Daniels Rd.
Wilson, NY 14172

North Carolina

Carrboro

University of North Carolina MUG
P.O. Box 907
Carrboro, NC 27510
919/962-3601

Chapel Hill

UNC-Macintosh Users Group
Box 232 Davis Library 080 A
University of North Carolina
Chapel Hill, NC 27514
919/929-1614

Charlotte

Charlotte Apple Computer Club
P.O. Box 221913
Charlotte, NC 28222
704/542-8596

Conover

Catawba Valley Byte
Rt. 1, Box 540-19ab
Conover, NC 28613
704/256-7035

Davidson

Davidson Apple User's Group
P.O. Box 2251
Davidson, NC 28036

Fayetteville

Fayetteville Macintosh Users Group
P.O. Box 42224
Fayetteville, NC 28309
919/484-1424

Greensboro

Triad Apple Core
P.O. Box 1710
Greensboro, NC 27402
919/725-7860

Greenville

Greenville Macintosh User Group
125 Greenwood Dr.
Greenville, NC 27834
919/551-4440

Murphy

Brass Apple Users Group
Rt. 1, Box 158
Murphy, NC 28906
704/837-8035

Rural User Group
704/837-8035

Raleigh

Apple Seeds
P.O. Box 28623
Raleigh, NC 27611
919/779-3519

North Carolina State University
    Apple Computer User Group
919/787-3194

Raleigh Macintosh User Group
1907 McCarthy St.
Raleigh, NC 27608
919/834-9028

Research Triangle Park
EPA-RTP Macintosh Users Group
919/541-0207

Wilmington
C.I.N.N.A.M.E.N.
919/392-6962

Macintosh Apple Corp of
    Wilmington
2840 S. College Rd.
Wilmington, NC 28403

North Dakota

Bismarck
Bismarck Macintosh Society
701/255-3613

Grand Forks Air Force Base
G.E. Apple S.A.U.C.E.
1804-AI St.
Grand Forks Air Force Base, ND
    58205
701/594-5542

Minot
Apple Polisher
1112 Glacial Dr.
Minot, ND 5801
701/838-6444

Minot Macintosh Users
2600 23rd St. SW
Minot, ND 58701
701/857-6183

Ohio

Athens
Athens Apple Users Group
31 Central Ave.
Athens, OH 45701
614/592-2202

Bowling Green
Bowling Green Macintosh User
    Group
College of Technology
Bowling Green State University
Bowling Green, OH 43403
419/372-6005

Canton
Mac2
P.O. Box 35693
Canton, OH 44735
216/494-4074

Cincinnati
Apple Board
513/561-2225

Apple Siders of Cincinnati
P.O. Box 14277
Cincinnati, OH 45250
513/741-4329

MACincinnati
1642 Pullan Ave.
Cincinnati, OH 45223
513/741-4329

Cleveland
CWRU Macmug
Case Western Reserve University
Cleveland, OH 44106
216/368-2011

NEO Apple Corps.
216/561-6656

Standard Oil MUG
200 Public Square
Cleveland, OH 44114
216/586-5650

Columbus
Buckeye Macintosh Group
2041 College Rd.
Ohio State University
Dept. of Ceramic Engineering
Columbus, OH 43210
614/626-6209

Central Ohio Apple Computer
    Hobbyists
4351 Apley Pl.
Columbus, OH 43229
614/475-1271

Dayton
Apple-Dayton Users Group
P.O. Box 3240
Dayton, OH 45401
513/293-8114

Wright-Patt MUG
513/429-2488

Findlay
Findlay Apple Computer Club
7426 TR 136
Findlay, OH 45840
419/424-0401

Galion
Apple Jack Users Group
331 S. Market St.
Galion, OH 44833
419/468-3542

Mayfield Heights
NEO Apple Corps
31481 Cedar Rd.
Mayfield Heights, OH 44124
216/953-6083

Oberlin
OMUG
OOMR 1240
Oberlin, OH 44074

Rocky River
North Coast Mac Users Group
21190 Erie Rd.
Rocky River, OH 44116
216/835-3636

Sandusky
North Coast Computer Users
P.O. Box 2055
Sandusky, OH 44870
419/625-6200

Toledo
University of Toledo Macintosh
    Users
Carver Education Center
University of Toledo
Toledo, OH 43606
419/537-2835

Warren
Mahoning Valley Apple Computer
5066 Mahoning Ave., NW
Warren, OH 44483
216/847-9223

Willoughby
Northeast Ohio Apple Corps.
216/953-4401

C
User
Groups

Wintersville

Tri-State Computer Association
142 Susan Dr.
Wintersville, OH 43952
614/264-7006

Wooster

Country Computer Club
530 High St.
Wooster, OH 44691
216/264-9285

COW Macintosh Users Group
Box C-3162
College of Wooster
Wooster, OH 44691
216/263-2444

Yellow Springs

Antioch Mac Users Group
Antioch College
Yellow Springs, OH 45387
513/767-7331

Zanesville

Zanesville Area Macintosh Users
    Group
930 Garden Rd.
Zanesville, OH 43701
614/452-6289

Oklahoma

Altus

Altus Apple Users Group
609 Taft St.
Altus, OK 73521
405/477-1533

Bartlesville

Bartlesville Users of Macintosh
    Society
6523 Trail Dr.
Bartlesville, OK 74006
918/333-6536

Douglas

Enid Appleseeds
Rt. 1, Box 8
Douglas, OK 73733
405/234-3382

Enid

Enid Appleseeds
405/234-3382

Lawton

Southwest Oklahoma Apple Orchard
P.O. Box 6646
Lawton, OK 73506
405/536-9365

Norman

The Big Red Apple Group
P.O. Box 3077
Norman, OK 73070
405/329-2952

Oklahoma City

Oklahoma City Apple Users Group
P.O. Box 19561
Oklahoma City, OK 73144
405/681-0397

Ponca City

Mac Pac
405/762-9486

Tishomingo

Tish Apple
Murray State College Library
Tishomingo, OK 73460
405/371-2371

Tulsa

GCCA
P.O. Box 497
Tulsa, OK 74101
918/749-8804

Tulsa Users of Macintosh Society
P.O. Box 47056
Tulsa, OK 74147
918/438-3851

Oregon

Astoria

Lower Columbia Apple Users Group
P.O. Box 1043
Astoria, OR 97103
503/325-4768

Corvallis

MUG of Corvallis
520 N.W. Oak
Corvallis, OR 97330
503/753-1040

Eugene

Eugene Macintosh Group
P.O. Box 10998
Eugene, OR 97440
503/683-5565

Forest Grove

Pacific University Macintosh Users
    Group
UC-674
Forest Grove, OR 97116

Grants Pass

Mac Users of the Rogue Valley
Mike Barrelclift
181 Rustic Canyon Dr.
Grants Pass, OR 97526
503/479-0642

Rogue Area Computer Enthusiasts
    (RACE)
503/479-1248

Hood River

Hood River Apples User Group
3553 Dethman Ridge
Hood River, OR 97031
503/354-1233

Medford

Rogue Macs
503/773-9861

Newport

Oregon Coast MUG
Hatfield Marine Science Center
Newport, OR 97365
503/867-3011

Portland

Macintosh Apple Corps.
5605 N. Detroit Ave.
Portland, OR 97217

Macintosh Business Group of Oregon
503/620-0866

National Association of Mac Users
 Group
P.O. Box 40045
Portland, OR 97204

Oregon Apple II User Group
1001 S. W. Fifth Ave.
Portland, OR 97204
503/225-1623

Portland Macintosh Users Group
P.O. Box 8895
Portland, OR 97207
503/228-1779

Reed College Mac Users' Group
Reed College
3203 SE Woodstock Blvd.
Portland, OR 97202
503/771-1112

Salem

Salem Macintosh Users Group
3850 Portland Rd., NE
Salem, OR 97310
503/399-9411

Tigard

Macintosh Business Group of Oregor
10240 S.W. Nimbus Ave.
Tigard, OR 97223
503/620-0866

Waldport

Macintosh User Group of Corvallis
430 SW Crest Circle
Waldport, OR 97394
503/754-6854

Winston

Apple Blossom Club
P.O. Box 638
Winston, OR 97496
503/679-8458

Pennsylvania

Acme

Apple Pits
R.D. 2, Box 171
Acme, PA 15610
412/547-4289

Allentown

Air MUG
215/481-5958

Lehigh Valley Apple User Group
215/437-0065

Altoona

Bottom of Barrel
2613 Eighth Ave.
Altoona, PA 16602
814/946-1423

Bethlehem

Lehigh Valley Macintosh User Group
505 Forrest Ave.
Bethlehem, PA 18017
215/691-1125

Bradford

Macintosh User Group
115 Main St.
Bradford, PA 16701
814/362-7791

Butler

Apple Butler Users Group
Box 39, Meridian Station
Butler, PA 16001
412/789-7031

Camp Hill

Capital Area Macintosh Users Group
1017 Yverdon Dr.
Camp Hill, PA 17011
717/737-6357

Carlisle

PennMUG
P.O. Box 952
Carlisle, PA 17013
717/243-5838

Easton

Eastern Pennsylvania Macintosh UG
243 Spring Garden St.
Easton, PA 18042
215/253-4380

Elkins Park

Macintosh User Group-ers
215/782-1328

Erie

Erie Apple Crunchers
P.O. Box 1575
Erie, PA 16507
814/453-3355

Furnace

Pennsylvania Apple Microcomputer
 User Group
306 Ravendale Rd.
Furnace, PA 16865
814/237-9757

Glenmoore

Chester County Computer Club
Normandy Circle
Glenmoore, PA 19343

Harrisburg

Keystone Apple Core
717/259-0827

Hershey

Hershey Apple Core
P.O. Box 634
Hershey, PA 17033
717/838-2952

Hiller

Monroeville Apple Users Group
P.O. Box 124
Hiller, PA 15444
412/785-8029

Indiana

IUP Mac Users Group
331 Walnut St.
Indiana, PA 15701

Lancaster

Franklin & Marshall Macintosh User
 Group
Franklin & Marshall College
Lancaster, PA 17604

Mac Users Group
717/295-9536

Malvern

Great Valley Macintosh Users Group
9 Lloyd Ave.
Malvern, PA 19355
215/644-3997

C
User
Groups

Monaca

Moon Area Users Group
Bob Davis
115 Legoullon Ave.
Monaca, PA 15061

Monroeville

CMU-MUG
138 Heather Dr.
Monroeville, PA 15146
412/373-9437

Pittsburgh Apple Business Users
  Group
1317 Corkwood Dr.
Monroeville, PA 15146
412/373-3903

Narberth

CPA Computer Users Group
215/664-6775

Philadelphia

The D Users
James Creese Student Center
Drexel University
Philadelphia, PA 19104
215/895-2573

DV & DUMUG
Drexel University
Office of Computing Services
Philadelphia, PA 19104
215/895-2997

Jefferson Macintosh User's Group
561 Thompson Bldg.
Thomas Jefferson University
Philadelphia, PA 19107
215/928-8655

Mac Users Group/University of
  Pennsylvania
114 Steinberg Dietrich
Philadelphia, PA 19104

PennMUG
1202 Blockley Hall
University of Pennsylvania
Philadelphia, PA 19104
215/898-9085

Philadelphia Area Computer Society
215/672-2706

Smith Kline Macintosh Users Group
P.O. Box 7929
Philadelphia, PA 19101
215/270-4263

Pittsburgh

Carnegie-Mellon Mac Users Group
Carnegie-Mellon University
Pittsburgh, PA 15221
412/268-3457

Pitt Macintosh User Group
Dept. of Mathematics
Univ. of Pittsburgh
Pittsburgh, PA 15260
412/624-8349

Plymouth Meeting

AntMUG
P.O. Box 157
Plymouth Meeting, PA 19462
215/279-5912

Reading

Berks Apple Club
720 Warren St.
Reading, PA 19601

MacBug
P.O. Box 15188
Reading, PA 19612

Republic

Uniontown Apple Computer Club
P.O. Box 433
Republic, PA 15475
412/246-2870

Strasburg

Lancaster County Apple Corps.
249 Julia Ave.
Strasburg, PA 17579
717/687-8574

Southampton

MUG Shop
P.O. Box 388
Southampton, PA 18966
215/464-4763

Telford

Bux Mont MUG
215/723-6900

Waynesburg

Waynesburg College Applers
Math & Computer Science Dept.
Waynesburg, PA 15370

Rhode Island

North Kingstown

Apple Fritters
55 Ebony Ct.
North Kingstown, RI 02852

Providence

Brown Mac User Group
Box D, Brown University
Providence, RI 02912
401/863-1419

Rhode Island Apple Users
401/751-7155

TCS Macintosh Users Group
740 North Main St.
Providence, RI 02904
401/331-0220

Rumford

Rhode Island Apple Group
450 Brook St.
Rumford, RI 02916
617/226-2275

South Carolina

Cayce

Central South Carolina Apple User
  Group
P.O. Box 2552
Cayce, SC 29171

Charleston

MUSC Mac User Group
171 Ashley Ave.
Charleston, SC 29425
803/792-2486

North Charleston Mac Users Group
3260 Ashley Phospate Rd.
Charleston, SC 29418

Columbia

So. Carolina Users of Macintosh
6432A Two Notch Rd.
Columbia, SC 29223
803/786-6100

Shaw AFB

Apple Too
803/499-1580

Surfside Beach

Coastal Macs
1018-A S. Hollywood Dr.
Surfside Beach, SC 29575
803/626-9856

Taylors

Mac 1
4614 Old Spartanberg Rd.
Taylors, SC 29687
803/268-9667

Upstate Macintosh User Support
    Group
12 Oakwood Ave.
Taylors, SC 29687
803/232-9535

South Dakota

Rapid City

Black Hills Apple User Group
719 N. Maple
Rapid City, SD 57701
605/348-9173

Sioux Falls

Apple Core of Siouxland
P.O. Box 90002
Sioux Falls, SD 57105
605/339-7115

Yankton

Team Mac
P.O. Box 203
Yankton, SD 57078
605/665-5177

Tennessee

Chattanooga

Tristate Apple Club
2532 Hickory Ridge Dr.
Chattanooga, TN 37421
615/751-5718

Clinton

MacClique
Rt. 3, Box 352
Clinton, TN 37716
615/574-0855

Martin

Northwest Tennessee MUG
Dept. of Math
University of Tennessee
Martin, TN 38238
901/587-2225

Memphis

Apple Core of Memphis
P.O. Box 241002
Memphis, TN 38124
901/728-4898

Medical Center MUG
877 Madison, Seventh Fl.
Memphis, TN 38163
901/528-5848

Nashville

MacInteresteds
235 Lauderdale Rd.
Nashville, TN 37205
615/327-1757

Nashville MUG
Clark Thomas
2305 Elliston Place
Nashville, TN 37203
615/327-1757

Oliver Springs

Oak Ridge MACUSERS Group
Route 2, Box 65E
Oliver Springs, TN 37840
615/435-1120

Texas

Abilene

Abilene Christian University
    Macintosh Users Group
915/674-2157

Big Red Apple Group
4402 Catrock Rd.
Abilene, TX 79606
915/698-0329

Amarillo

Apple Info & Data Exchange
P.O. Box 30878
Amarillo, TX 79120
806/373-9478

Mac Mob
7226 W. 34th
Amarillo, TX 79109
806/358-8570

Panhandle Apple Club
P.O. Box 30878
Amarillo, TX 79120
806/373-9478

Austin

River City Apple Corps
P.O. Box 13449
Austin, TX 78711
512/454-9962

University Macintosh User Group
Texas Union Box 320
University of Texas
Austin, TX 78713
512/471-8684

Beaumont

Golden Triangle Macintosh Users
    Group
409/860-4289

College Station

Texas A & M Macintosh User Group
Dept. of Entomology
Texas A & M University
College Station, TX 77843
409/775-5518

C

**User
Groups**

Comfort

Apple Hill Country User Group
Rt. 2, Box 293
Comfort, TX 78013
512/995-3352

Copperas Cove

Apple S.T.E.M.
P.O. Box 1508
Copperas Cove, TX 76522

Corpus Christi

St. MUG (South Texas Macintosh
   User's Group)
10727 Timbergrove
Corpus Christi, TX 78410
512/992-6642

Dallas

Apple Corp of Dallas
11212 Indian Trail
Dallas, TX 75229
214/357-9185

El Paso

El Paso Macintosh User Group
412 Pocano Ln.
El Paso, TX 79912
915/584-9507

Mac Miners
412 Pocano Lane
El Paso, TX 79912
915/584-9507

Euless

Mid-Cities Macintosh
1209 Glenn
Euless, TX 76039
817/540-0063

Fort Worth

Cow Town Macintosh Users Group
817/429-6115

Fort Worth Mac Users Group
1212 Florentine Dr.
Fort Worth, TX 76134
817/293-0357

Tarrant Apple Group
912 W. Broadway
Fort Worth, TX 76104
817/332-3341

Gilmer

Longview Computer Users Group
Rt. 4, Box 300
Gilmer, TX 75644
214/734-4591

Greenville

East Texas Computerists
10613 Old Mill Rd.
Greenville, TX 75401

Henderson

Beautiful East Texas Area Macs
   (BETA)
P.O. Box 1596
Henderson, TX 75653
214/581-4993

Macintosh Users Group of
   Henderson
116 Pine St.
Henderson, TX 75652

Houston

Coffee Mug/Macpro
713/623-6882

HAAUG
3200 Kirby
Houston, TX 77098
713/961-1601

Medical Center Macintosh Users
   Group
713/792-2605

Nasa Area Macintosh Users
12855 Gulf Frwy.
Houston, TX 77034
713/481-5600

Rice Mac Users Group/ICSA
P.O. Box 1892 Icsa
Rice University
Houston, TX 77251
713/527-4986

The Mousketeer Mac User Group
P.O. Box 19030
Houston, TX 77224
713/531-8728

UH Mug
627 Arnold Hall
University of Houston
Houston, TX 77204
713/749-4551

Humble

Humble Mac Users Group
713/540-2975

Lubbock

MacLubb
Texas Tech University
Health Science Center
Dept. of Dermatology
Lubbock, TX 79430
806/749-7001

Midland

Click Clique
708 W. Pine Ave.
Midland, TX 79705
915/682-4305

Midland Apple Users Group
915/684-8231

Nacogdoches

Nac Mac User's Group
4304 Friar Tuck
Nacogdoches, TX 75961
409/564-0512

SFA Apple Computer Club
225 E. Spradley
Nacogdoches, TX 75961
409/560-4170

New Braunfels

New Braunfels Apple User Group
165 Bobolink
New Braunfels, TX 78130
512/625-1314

Richardson

Apple Corps of Dallas
214/453-5446

The Mac Pack
P.O. Box 832446
Richardson, TX 75083
214/783-1261

San Antonio

Mac Enthusiasts of San Antonio
15442 River Bend
San Antonio, TX 78247
512/496-5043

University of Texas Health Science
Center
7703 Floyd Curl Dr.
San Antonio, TX 78284
512/567-4400

Sherman

Mac-A-Roos
Campus Box 290
Austin College
Sherman, TX 75091
214/892-4364

Temple

Apple Tree
2805 Del Norte
Temple, TX 76502
817/771-4524

Texarkana

Texarkana Apple Byters
192 Lakeshore
Texarkana, TX 75501
214/838-0243

Tyler

Tyler Area Macintosh Users
P.O. Box 131254
Tyler, TX 75713
214/595-4541

Wichita Falls

Texoma Mac-Apple Club
103B Matador
Wichita Falls, TX 76311

Utah

Bountiful

MacNewton
P.O. Box 833
Bountiful, UT 84010
801/295-8560

Clearfield

Gnuton
P.O. Box 201
Clearfield, UT 84015

Logan

Utah State Univ Mac User Group
Utah State University
Logan, UT 84321

Ogden

Ogden Apple Users Group
P.O. Box 4035
Ogden, UT 84403
801/776-0164

Provo

BYU Macintosh Users Group
3146 JKHB
Brigham Young University
Provo, UT 84602

Salt Lake City

Intermountain Mac Users Group
1800 S West Temple
Salt Lake City, UT 84115
801/485-6341

Macdig
3440 MEB Computer Center
Salt Lake City, UT 84112

Macwiz
2011 Highland View Circle
Salt Lake City, UT 84109

Medical Center Small Computer User
Group
Medical Center
University of Utah
Salt Lake City, UT 84132

Michael Berggren
University of Utah
Bioengineering-2059 MEB
Salt Lake City, UT 84112
801/581-6244

University of Utah Macintosh Users
4608 Lanark Rd.
Salt Lake City, UT 84124

Utah Macintosh Users Group
801/581-6339

Torrey

Canyon Country Macintosh User
Group
Capitol Reef
Torrey, UT 84775
801/425-3414

West Jordan

Intermountain Macintosh Users
Group
P.O. Box 1086
West Jordan, UT 84084
801/566-3962

Vermont

Essex Junction

Green Mountain Apple Club
13 Clemens Dr.
Essex Junction, VT 05452

Mac Champ
Champlain Valley Mac Users Group
72A South Street
Essex Junction, VT 05452

Saint Johnsbury

Northern Vermont MUG
802/748-2425

Townshend

Tri-State Mac User's Group
P.O. Box 241
Townshend, VT 05353

Virginia

Arlington

Crystal City Macintosh User Group
703/521-9292

Blacksburg

Mac Bug
911 Hethwood Blvd.
Blacksburg, VA 24060
703/382-3309

Danville

Danville Apple User Group
Averett College
Danville, VA 24541

Falls Church

Northern Virginia Apple Users
P.O. Box 8211
Falls Church, VA 22041
301/899-4005

C
User
Groups

Fredericksburg

Rappahanock Apple User Group
6014 Battlefield Green Dr.
Fredericksburg, VA 22401
703/786-6577

Hampton

Club Macintosh of Hampton Roads
P.O. Box 7105
Hampton, VA 23666

Hampton-Sydney

Hampton-Sydney College Mug
Hampton-Sydney, VA 23943

Harrisonburg

Shenandoah Macintosh User Group
15 Southgate Ct.
Harrisonburg, VA 22801
703/433-1527

Langley AFB

Apple Users Group International
804/850-1912

Lynchburg

Lynchburg Computer Society
P.O. Box 2073
Lynchburg, VA 24501

Sweet Briar Macintosh User's Group
712 Riverside Dr.
Lynchburg, VA 24503
804/381-6197

Newport News

Peninsula Apple Core
P.O. Box 6384
Newport News, VA 23606
804/838-6681

Reston

Greater Reston Area Macintosh
Association
11080 Thrush Ridge Rd.
Reston, VA 22091
703/860-0765

Richmond

Greater Richmond Area Macintosh
P.O. Box 524
Richmond, VA 23204
804/344-5638

Roanoke

Macintosh Users' Group of Roanoke
1916 Belleville Rd. SW
Roanoke, VA 24015
703/343-8614

Rochester

South Puget Sound MUG
375 Manners Rd.
Rochester, VA 98579

Sweet Briar

Sweet Briar College Macintosh User
Group
P.O. Box 73
Sweet Briar, VA 24595
804/384-7430

Virginia Beach

Tidewater Apple Worms
P.O. Box 68097
Virginia Beach, VA 23452
804/499-6251

Tidewater Area Mug
5313 Marlington Dr.
Virginia Beach, VA 23462

Washington

Bellingham

Bellingham Macintosh Users Group
2300 James St.
Bellingham, WA 98225
206/671-4013

Bothell

CompuShare
206/776-9890

Coupeville

M.U.I.N.T.Y.
P.O. Box 826
Coupeville, WA 98239
206/278-4409

Edmonds

32 Little Apples
P.O. Box 536
Edmonds, WA 98020
206/251-5222

Ellensburg

Macintosh Owners & Users Society
of Ellensburg
704 N. Water
Ellensburg, WA 98926
509/925-5280

MacYak
704 N. Water
Ellensburg, WA 98926
509/925-5280

Everett

Macapp Developer's Association
206/252-6946

North End Apple Users Group
4027 C Rucker
Everett, WA 98201
206/339-8557

Gig Harbor

Club Mac of Tacoma
6016 55th St. NW
Gig Harbor, WA 98335
206/851-3327

Kennewick

Mid Columbia Macs
523 N. Nevada St.
Kennewick, WA 99336
509/375-3797

Lynnwood

Compushare
16010 East Shore Dr.
Lynnwood, WA 98037
206/743-2324

Olympia

Evergreen Macintosh User Group
3138 Overhulse Rd.
Olympia, WA 98502

South Puget Sound Macintosh
407614 13th Ave. NE
Olympia, WA 98506

Pomeroy

Computer Literacy & Support
Society
P.O. Box 335
Pomeroy, WA 99347
509/843-3542

Pullman

Palouse Area Microcomputer
 Association
Physics Dept.
Washington State Univ.
Pullman, WA 99164
509/335-9531

Redmond

Northwest Association of Mac Users
22845 N.E. Eighth
Redmond, WA 98053
206/868-5943

Renton

TechAlliance
206/251-5222

Seattle

Fircrest Macintosh Users Group
206/364-0300

MacAnt
Antioch University
2607 Second Ave.
Seattle, WA 98121
206/441-5352

Macdub
145 Savery Hall
MS DK45, University of Washington
Seattle, WA 98195
206/543-8110

Macintosh Downtown Business Users
 Group
P.O. Box 3463
Seattle, WA 98114
206/363-9056

SeaMac MUG
6517 45th Ave.
Seattle, WA 98118
206/723-5427

Silverdale

Mac Connection
P.O. Box 1271
Silverdale, WA 98383
206/692-7753

Spokane

Macs
N. 1010 Bates
Spokane, WA 99206
509/467-2400

North Idaho Mac Users Group
W. 927 Glass
Spokane, WA 99205
509/328-4974

Tacoma

Northwest Apple Pickers
10314 Lyris Ct. SW
Tacoma, WA 98498
206/475-7162

University of Puget Sound MUG
1500 N. Warner
Tacoma, WA 98416
206/756-3568

Vancouver

Apple*Van
206/256-7139

Yakima

Yakima Area Macintosh Users
18 W. Mead Ave.
Yakima, WA 98907
509/966-7773

West Virginia

Morgantown

Mon Valley MUG
304/293-4000

New Martinsville

Natrium Macintosh Users Group
304/455-2200

Wisconsin

Appleton

Appleton Apples
P.O. Box 2785
Appleton, WI 54913
414/731-7091

Brookfield

United Methodist Apple Users
414/781-6925

Chippewa Falls

Chippewa Falls Macintosh Users
 Group
1020 Olive St.
Chippewa Falls, WI 54729
715/723-2256

Delavan

Pro-Mac
520 S. Second St., Box 464
Delavan, WI 53115
414/728-4300

Eau Claire

Eau Claire Apple Users Group
P.O. Box 61
Eau Claire, WI 54702
715/723-1301

Eland

MacAmazons MUG
Rt. 1, Box 43B
Eland, WI 54427
715/454-6696

Green Bay

Green Bay Mac Users
1513 Traeger St.
Green Bay, WI 54304
414/498-1873

La Crosse

La Crosse Apple Users Group
711 Division St.
La Crosse, WI 54601
608/784-9162

Madison

Madison Macintosh Users Group
P.O. Box 1522
Madison, WI 53701
608/251-2885

Marshfield

Mara-Wood Mac
Marshfield Clinic
1000 North Oak Ave.
Marshfield, WI 54449
715/387-8038

**C
User
Groups**

Menomonie

Menomin-Apples
1521 Sixth Ave., E
Menomonie, WI 54751
715/235-9749

Milwaukee

Double Click MUG
3016 N. Summit Rd.
Milwaukee, WI 53211
414/964-3147

Oak Creek

Delco Electronics MUG
7929 South Howell Ave., 1-AO2
Oak Creek, WI 53154
414/768-2483

Oconomowoc

Apple C.O.R.E.
414/567-2144

Oshkosh

Mac 'Osh
414/424-1238

Racine

Racine-Kenosha Macintosh Users
  Group
P.O. Box 85303
Racine, WI 53405
414/552-9474

Stevens Point

University of Wisconsin, Stevens
  Point Apple Users
715/346-4436

UWSP MacGroup
P.O. Box 21
College of Prof. Studies-UWSP
Stevens Point, WI 54481
715/346-4436

Watertown

Watertown Macintosh Users Group
P.O. Box 354
Watertown, WI 53094

Wisconsin Rapids

Apple Personal Programming &
  Learning Exchange
3521 Eighth St. S
Wisconsin Rapids, WI 54494
715/424-2131

Wyoming

Casper

Casper Area Macintosh User Group
P.O. Box 80
Casper, WY 82602
307/266-0570

Cheyenne

The Apple Net
2203 Park Ave., Orchard Valley
Cheyenne, WY 82007
307/632-4934

Wyoming Mac Enthusiasts
921 Ranger Dr.
Cheyenne, WI 82009
307/632-3668

Jackson

Jackson Hole Macintosh User Group
P.O. Box 1714
Jackson, WY 83001

Sheridan

Sheridan Micro User Group
P.O. Box 142
Sheridan, WY 82801
307/674-4954

Directory of Bulletin and On-Line Services

Services are listed in order of area codes.

Bulletin Board Service	Telephone Number	SYSOP
Dhahran BBS	011-966-3-894-7394	Bill Strazdas
JSCIExchange	966/001-966-32-894-7394	
Mac Event Network BBS	047-397-0922	Nobuo Hayashi
NEZUMILAND BBS	81/052-782-5037	
Big Max BBS	201-231-3519	Scott Isaacs
NJ Mac BBS	201-256-2067	
Keeper of the List BBS	201-340-3531	Ed Edell
MacApple Peel	201-340-9792	
Rock Pile	201-387-9232	
The White House	201-388-1676	
MAC BBS	201-446-1421	
The Big Mac BBS	201-531-3519	Scott Isaacs
Macintosh NJMUG BBS	201-666-2013	Robert J. Gallo, M.D.
Apple Peel	201-684-0931	
Mac Developers BBS	201-747-8814	Charlie Hayden
NJMUG BBS	201-839-7802	John Gallaugher
Wizards Den	201-922-6943	
MacNEt	201-968-1074	
Castle Tabby	201-988-0706	
Golden Apple BBS	201-989-0545	Daniel Zimmerman
Swizzle Stick	202-234-3521	
Eyrie/Falcon	202-341-9070	Jeff Davis
Twilight Clone	202-471-0610	
Swizzle Stick	202-966-4082	Rick Bollar

D

On-Line
Services

Bulletin Board Service	Telephone Number	SYSOP
Firesign Theatre	203-234-0742	
The Computer Lab	203-442-2411	
MacBBs	203-453-4114	
the mouse hole	203-453-5317	
MacHeaven	203-637-3611	
Unnamed Connecticut	203-739-5411	Jeremy Kezer
Silver Screen System	203-748-5146	
SmartMac BBS	203-762-1249	Andrew Welch
The Ghost Ship East	203-775-6392	Chris Wysocki
AppleBamians	205-236-7262	
MacTown	205-284-8484	
Joe's Board	205-288-1100	
Fishnet (ATF Forum)	205-767-7484	John Benn
Huntsville MUG BBS	205-881-8380	Tom Konantz
dBBS	206-281-7338	
Dr. Radium's Lab	206-483-5308	
S. Puget Sound MUG	206-495-9595	Henry Drygas
Mac Cavern	206-525-5194	
MacStuart	206-543-5350	
Atlantis	206-634-1539	
The 'Belle	206-641-6892	
Sea/Mac	206-725-6629	Jim Creighton
Polynet	206-783-9798	
Mac's Bar and Grill	206-859-4662	
CFWP Assoc	207-443-4657	
Black Bear's Den	207-827-7517	Mike Houle
JJHS-BBS	208-455-3312	
MacStudio California	209-333-8143	
Bitz 'N Bytes	212-222-9536	
LaserBoard	212-348-5714	Stu Gitlow
NY News (aka NYMUG)	212-534-3716	David S. Rose
Metro Area MUG	212-597-9083	
CitiMac	212-627-5647	
New York Mac	212-643-1965	
Zap's Corner	212-645-0640	
NYMUG BBS	212-645-9484	
Apl Pi	212-753-0888	
Aztec Empire	212-769-0814	

Bulletin Board Service	Telephone Number	SYSOP
Ellena Caverns	212-861-5484	
NY Mac	212-868-8326	
Links_II Midi_Inn	212-877-7703	
Super 68 BBS	212-927-6919	Nick Angelo
The Forge	212-989-0037	
The Glassell Park BBS	213-394-6929	Doug Quinn
LA MUG BBS	213-397-8966	Steve Riggins
Programmer's Paradise	213-454-7746	Chris Demetriou
NewMac BBS	213-459-2083	
Showcase	213-470-0297	Torsten Hoff
The Troll	213-477-2188	
The Manhattan Transfer	213-516-7739	
Byte BBS	213-536-2651	
MachineDo	213-548-3546	
Hughes Aircraft BBS	213-549-9640	Bud Grove
DigiVision	213-732-6935	
MacBBS	213-732-6935	
Palantir	213-839-9271	
Computer Church	213-946-3923	
Rising Star	214-231-1372	
HardWired	214-380-9063	
Inside Track	214-442-4772	
Board Europa	214-564-6282	
The Mac Shack	214-644-4781	
Ground Zero	214-892-1476	Richard Harvey
Stonewall BBS	215-367-8206	
Dragon's Land //	215-387-1962	
The Electric Holt	215-387-4326	
Lord's Keep	215-387-8442	The Wanderer
Bob's Mac	215-446-7670	Bob Ferrill
The Big Board	215-643-7711	
The Rydal Board	215-884-6122	
Omnicom Mac BBS	215-896-9020	
Appleholic's BBS	216-273-1340	
NE Ohio IBM BBS	216-331-4241	
Cleveland FreeNet	216-368-3888	multi-SIG
North Coast MUG BBS	216-777-4944	Malcom Sherman
Pipeline BBS	216-836-0990	

D

On-Line Services

Bulletin Board Service	*Telephone Number*	*SYSOP*
POMS BBS	216-867-7463	Robert Nebiker
Fireside BBS	216-884-9728	
NEO Apple Corps	216-942-3389	
The Mouse House	216-965-7233	John Ray
Champaign Urbana MUG	217-344-5204	
Tales of the Mouse	217-875-7114	
C.A.M.S. HOST	217-875-7114	Robert Williams
Mac Blade	219-264-5273	
Connection	219-277-5825	Greg Corson
MacCheg	219-283-4714	
BABBS	301-267-2134	Barry Connor
LINDA RBBS	301-340-1376	Broadhurst & Rowley
The System Error	301-547-2410	
The Nightclub	301-564-9221	
The Overflow Valve	301-572-2360	
Mac USA	301-587-2132	
Overflow Valve	301-654-5812	Ron Wartow
Clinton Computer	301-856-2365	R. Douglas Reider
Midnight MUG	301-871-9637	Gavin
Twilight Clone	301-946-5032	Paul Heller
Mac Files - East	301-946-8838	Paul Heller
SMUG	301-963-5249	
Baltimore	301-964-3397	
B.A.B.B.S.	301-974-0221	
Double Nut	301-997-7204	
Chemist's Compor	302-479-0302	
Starfleet Command	302-654-2900	
The Original Mousetrap	302-731-1583	
The Mousetrap	302-737-7788	Larry Dski
Mac Computer Works	303-444-2318	
STS Leisure Time	303-444-5175	
Boulder Mac Mtg.	303-449-0917	
CSU	303-491-5946	
TELETECH SERVICES	303-493-8261	
Boulder Mac Maniacs	303-530-9544	Ed Fenner
!Macintosh	303-665-0709	Scott Converse
InaNet	303-665-4472	
The Zoo	303-756-1627	

Bulletin Board Service	Telephone Number	SYSOP
The Fishery	303-756-3818	
N.O.R.A.D.	303-756-8789	Jeff Heller
N/A	303-770-7069	
MAGIC	303-792-8732	Steve Sande
National DeskTop Pub	303-972-1875	
Atlantis BBS	303-973-0369	Monty Lee
Manville	303-978-3946	
Check-In	305-232-0393	Dave Game
Mac BBS 1	305-344-0533	
CSbbs L:ink	305-445-6481	Gerardo Blanco
The Apple Tree	305-472-1900	
S.H.A.P.E. (1)	305-589-5422	
S.H.A.P.E. (2)	305-589-8950	
Winter Springs	305-699-1741	
Abacus Info Center	305-774-3355	
Regina Fido	306-347-2351	
Sask Echo Hub	306-347-4493	
The North Village	306-665-6633	
The Black Diamond Express	307-682-7987	
WYNET	307-777-6200	
N/A	309-348-3498	
Mackey Mouse	309-454-5477	Gret Otto
Working with Works	312-260-9660	
Nexus	312-274-1677	
Mad Marty's	312-289-4973	
Growers Exchange	312-293-0696	
MACropedia(tm)	312-295-6926	Dave Alpert
Desktoppers BBS	312-356-3776	Randy Bennett
Northern Illinois	312-392-6232	
UCC Comm Center	312-433-4563	Gene Alper
Consult-Net	312-475-5442	Vernon Keenan
The Rest of Us	312-545-3227	Steve Levinthal
Spectrum MacNet	312-729-8768	Steve Levinthal
Lost Horizon	312-898-4505	Greg
Spine Fido	312-908-2583	Vernon Keenan
Pete's Place	312-941-3179	
Mac Trade Center	313-259-2115	Matt Schwartz

D

On-Line
Services

Bulletin Board Service	Telephone Number	SYSOP
Check-In	313-354-3680	Dave Game
The Michigan Connection	313-398-9359	Tim Mapes
Crystal Castle	313-856-3804	
AMCross General	314-658-5866	Tim Rand
Show Me More Stacks	314-997-6912	
Salt City BBS	315-451-7790	Eric Larson
Shockwave Rider	315-673-4894	Eric Larson
Lower & Sons BBS	316-442-7026	
MSG Board	317-457-5576	
Lake Charles Overboard	318-478-8109	Dale LeDoux
MAClan Host	318-742-8520	George Bonner
Mouse College	319-365-4775	
MacBBS	319-381-4761	Mike Petersen
Lands of Adventure	401-351-1465	
MacLink	401-521-2626	
The Wind Dragon	402-291-8053	
Callisto BBS (Calgary)	403-264-0996	James Case
EurythMACs BBS	403-277-4139	
Info Shop	404-288-7535	
Atlanta Crackers	404-449-5986	
N/A	404-457-2417	
HAF/MD BBS	404-633-2602	Hal A. Franklin
AMUG BBS	404-972-3389	Barry Davis
N/A	405-325-7516	
Land of Macintosh	405-436-1792	
BBS Classified Ads	408-225-8623	
The Backboard	408-226-3780	
The Bottom Line	408-226-6779	
Crumal's Dimension	408-246-7854	
MacScience BBS	408-247-8307	
Phoenix 2 BBS	408-253-3926	LaserMan
Phoenix 1 BBS	408-255-7208	
A32 User's Group	408-263-0299	
BatCave BBS	408-275-8274	Meese Co Brothers
DWB's BBS	408-293-0752	David Berry
Portal BBS	408-725-0561	
Piney Woods BBS	408-637-2286	James Rhodes
MV Electronic Micro Mall	412-221-3564	

Bulletin Board Service	Telephone Number	SYSOP
PA-Bug Mac BB	412-241-4374	Tom Neudecker
Maltese Alien	412-279-7011	
MacBBS	413-243-2217	Steve Wellington
MacSheep BBS	413-283-3554	Pete Poitras
GENERIC BBS	414-282-4181	
Racine Area Macintosh	414-632-3983	Chris Henry
MacHeaven	415-258-9348	
Laserwriter BBS	415-261-4813	
The W.E.L.L.	415-332-6106	
Records Department	415-426-0470	Bill McCauley
MacCircles	415-484-4412	Patricia O'Connor
TopsTalk BBS	415-549-5955	Marshall Berzon
Harry's BBS/T39 BBS	415-563-2491	Harry Chesley
On Broadway	415-571-7056	
Jasmine BBS	415-621-6615	
Bay Connextion BBS	415-621-7561	
Prometheus BBS	415-651-9196	
MacQueue I	415-661-7374	Leo Laporte
Stanford MUG BBS	415-723-7685	
Mac Exchange BBS	415-731-1037	
MacQueue II	415-753-3002	Leo Laporte
Micahlink BBS	415-772-1119	Brian Ebarb
The Bay	415-775-2384	
MACINFO BBS	415-795-8862	Norm Goodger
N/A	415-797-4740	
EBMUG	415-848-2609	
BMUG	415-849-2684	Raines Cohen
MailCom BBS	415-855-9548	
ET3 Network	415-864-2037	Edgar Wolfe III
Mac Connection	415-864-3365	
Macintosh Tribune	415-923-1235	Vern Keenan
Computer Language	415-957-9370	
SuperMac BBS	415-962-1618	
T-Room BBS	415-993-5410	Ken Braun
FidoNet - Canada_1	416-226-9260	
Networks Canada Infosys	416-593-7460	Geoff Gaherty
The FIRESIDE	416-878-1248	John Griffin
Macintosh Palace BBS	416-967-4500	

D

On-Line Services

Bulletin Board Service	Telephone Number	SYSOP
Computer Matrix	417-869-5294	Don R. Shanafelt
SYNAPSE (Quebec MUG)	418-658-6955	Martin Durand
L'ECHANGEUR	418-696-3536	
The College Crier	419-537-4110	
The Cavern	419-986-5806	
UBBS	501-568-9464	Dale Miller
Mac Programmers West	503-222-4258	John Allen
Stax Express	503-228-7323	Carl Crowell
OpErA BBS	503-232-3812	The Apostle
MacSystem/NW	503-245-2222	Doug Forman
PSG Coos Bay (Fido 122)	503-269-5202	Randy Bush
Frontier Station BBS	503-345-3108	
MacSystem/NW	503-357-9329	Doug Forman
UCSD Pascal Programmers	503-581-1791	Henry Carstens
MacSystem/NW	503-648-5235	Doug Forman
Cajun Bytes	504-291-6339	
The Pitstop	504-774-7126	
Connection/New Orleans	504-831-7541	Kirk Wallbillich
Computer People	504-851-1236	Gary Dauphin
Miscellaneous Mac	505-898-3609	
Hummingbird BBS	505-982-5104	
Back to the Future BBS	507-377-2316	
Cougar Connection	509-332-0665	
Cougar Connection	509-334-3652	
Pirates Ship	512-328-4353	
Megafone	512-331-1662	
Bull Creek BBS	512-343-1612	Mark Bryant
Diner	512-443-3084	
Restaurant/End/Universe	512-451-9590	
Arcane Dimensions	512-832-1680	
The Lifeboat	512-926-9582	
Apple-Dayton BBS	513-429-2232	
The Mac Exchange	513-435-8381	
Mac Cincinnatus	513-572-5375	Gary Johnston
Riverfront MAC	513-677-9131	
The Connection BBS	513-874-3270	Keith Laborde
MAC-LINK	514-398-9089	
DESSIE BBS	514-842-1094	

Bulletin Board Service	Telephone Number	SYSOP
Mousehole	515-224-1334	
Computerland DesMoines	515-270-8942	Mark Loomis
Zoo System	515-279-3073	
MacBBS	515-279-6769	
Bellerose BBS	516-437-4816	
NY Mac/Bread Board	516-868-8326	
Circus BBS	516-872-3430	
Impending Void	517-351-4194	Mark Lacey
MECCA/ENVIRONUS	518-381-4430	Don Rittner
U-Compute	518-563-1679	
Mac*Ontario BBS	519-673-4181	
Mac*Ontario	519-679-0980	
MacHaven BBS	601-992-9459	
STMUG-BBS	602-230-9549	
KroyKolor Support System	602-266-4043	
Phoenix RR Host #1	602-285-0361	
The Marquis' BBS	602-458-8083	Mike Steiner
Arizona MUG	602-495-1713	
Computer Room	602-774-5105	
Prof. Data Management	602-881-0473	Roger Bull
Geoff's Board	602-887-8848	
Tiger's Den	602-951-4214	John Gillett
Crossroads	602-971-2240	Ronnie Phillips
Monadnock Micro BBS	603-357-2756	
XLISP BBS	603-623-1711	David Betz
Hot Air Ballooner BBS	603-886-8712	Steve Haber
Mac BBS B.C., Canada	604-362-1898	Randy McCallum
NEON Light BBS	604-368-5931	Randy McCallum
Simran MUBBS	604-688-0049	
The Sunshine BBS	604-943-1612	
Manzana BBS	605-665-5179	Larry Hosmerq
Mad Mac BBS	608-256-6227	
MIES BBS	609-228-1149	Tom Dolby
Pinelands BBS	609-354-9259	
Garden State Mac	609-858-2670	Chris Amet
Garden State Mac	609-858-3443	
Iconclast BBS	612-332-4005	Chip Pashibin
The Fifth Dimension	612-824-0333	Ian Abel

D

On-Line
Services

Bulletin Board Service	Telephone Number	SYSOP
MacOttawa	613-729-2763	Graydon Patterson
Second Self BBS	614-291-1816	Michael Gordon
Columbus Multi-Board	614-436-6284	Todd Price
Aurora Borealis	614-471-6209	Mike Lininger
Pandora	614-471-9209	
No Change	614-764-7674	
The 16th Dimension	614-864-3156	Roger Collins
NoName BBS	614-875-7399	Fred Ballinger
Syrill BBS	615-483-3325	Thomas White
Mass Mac & Electric	617-231-2872	Barr Plexico
Tao of Telecomms	617-244-4642	Mark Kupferman
Softline	617-245-4909	
The Dog House	617-334-2448	David O'Henry
Mac Boston	617-350-0263	Steve Garfield
MacApple	617-369-1717	
Nibble Mac Hot Line	617-369-8920	Ed McGee
Music BBS	617-374-6168	Ed McGee
Multinet BBS	617-395-6702	Jim Kowalczyk
Multinet BBS	617-395-9065	Jim Kowalczyk
Sears BBS	617-423-0847	M. Pelletier
Mac Stoneham	617-438-3763	Barr Plexico
The Dungeon	617-456-3890	Hunter Strong
PhotoTalk	617-472-8612	Robert Gorrill
4th Dimension BBS	617-497-6166	Zeff Wheelock
Stack Exchange	617-628-1741	
IComm	617-642-7471	
Whole Wheat BBS	617-643-4726	
Athex BBS	617-662-4840	
Wonderland BBS	617-665-3796	
Macro Exchange AMIS	617-667-7388	L. Hajinian
Finance is Fun BBS	617-682-5982	Joe Kelley
NEC Printer BBS	617-735-4461	Bill LaPointe
Buzzard's Gulch BBS	617-735-4461	Roger Perales
Microcom	617-769-9358	A. Grupp
MacEast	617-776-7232	David L'Heureux
The Raceway	617-788-0038	Joel Rozenzwieg
Sears BBS	617-843-6743	
The Graphics Factory	617-849-0347	

Bulletin Board Service	Telephone Number	SYSOP
ByteNet (BYTE Magzine)	617-861-9767	
Termexec	617-863-0282	P. O'Neill
Third Dimension	617-876-4361	
BCS Mac BBS	617-876-4835	Brian DeLacey
Chest/Infinity 200	617-891-1349	J. Kouymjian
Blue Sands	617-899-5579	
S'Ware BBS	617-938-3505	Stuart Fishback
Howlers Haven	617-963-3242	
Newton's Corner	617-964-6088	Curt Morrison
BOARDWALK	617-964-6866	
Bionic Dog	617-964-8069	
Phoenix BBS (RBBS)	618-233-2315	
San Diego MUG	619-462-6236	
Cabbie BBS	619-565-1634	Steve Haskell
Tele-Mac BBS (SDMUG)	619-582-9557	
Sharkey's MAChine	619-747-8719	
TMMABBS	703-471-1378	Terry Monks
Washington NEtworks	703-560-7803	
The HOLE	703-642-1429	
MASTER LINK	703-663-2613	Michael Connick
Access BBS	704-255-0032	
RBBS Charlotte, NC	704-332-5439	Bill Taylor
PC-BBS	704-537-1304	
PiVot Point	707-255-7628	Phillip Rusin
Human Interface BBS	707-444-0484	James Glover
Redwood BBS	707-444-9203	
BBS	707-964-7114	Bob Shannon
Montgomery County	713-353-9391	
WCC-Beta/Texas Talker	713-367-8206	
The Loft	713-367-9726	
Texas Mac BBS	713-386-1683	
Humble Mac	713-441-7278	
The Market	713-461-7170	David Klein
DOC Board	713-471-4131	
Applesauce	713-492-8700	
Digital Dimension	713-497-4633	
Stellar Empire	713-527-9161	
Arturus	713-550-4202	

D
On-Line
Services

Bulletin Board Service	*Telephone Number*	*SYSOP*
Computer Country	713-580-3286	
Oceania	713-778-9356	
Club Mac BBS	713-778-9419	
Mr. Quigman's	713-863-1683	
Mines of Moria	713-871-8577	
Zachary*Net	713-933-7353	
Cheese Factory	714-351-9104	Shawn Lynn
The Desktop	714-491-1003	
The Roadhouse	714-533-6967	
The MacExchange	714-594-0290	
Blues Alley	714-633-2716	
VAXHOLM	714-681-0106	
O.C. Network	714-722-8383	
Unnamed BBS	714-731-1039	
Electric Warehouse	714-775-2560	
The Secret Service	714-776-7223	
The Desktop Downloads	714-826-9232	
The Consultants' Exchange	714-842-5851	
The Consultants' Exchange	714-842-6348	
Computrends Fido BBS	714-856-1029	Dave Broudy
MacVille USA	714-859-5857	
Cactus BBS	714-861-2594	
The Mousehole	714-921-2252	Rusty Hodge
BBS FreedomLine 86	714-924-1189	Eric Dorn
New BBS	714-996-5371	Bobby Karagiri
Mac BBS	714-970-0632	David Laffin
Blumenthal's	716-375-4617	
The Aardvark Burrow	716-461-4223	
Apple Manor	716-654-7663	
ChalkBoard	716-689-1107	
MacHonor System	717-464-0518	
MacBBS	717-766-2539	
The Wall	718-274-6222	
NY Mac BBS	718-643-1965	
B'WAY & 68TH	718-852-2823	
Night Flight BBS	801-224-9112	

Bulletin Board Service	Telephone Number	SYSOP
MacBBS	801-378-4991	
The Transporter	801-379-5239	
Master's Castle	801-575-8542	
The Underworld	801-581-1823	
Iomega BBS	801-778-4400	Wes
Mousetrapp	801-967-8967	
Fort Mill BBS	803-548-0900	Bill Taylor
MacMoore	803-576-5710	
Causeway	803-656-5244	Dan Warner
CSC BBS	803-786-6120	Mark McClure
MacInternational	803-788-8926	Ralph Yount
Macinternational	803-957-6870	
Roundtable BBS	804-276-7368	
CAMMAC BBS	805-482-3573	
Fido BBS	805-522-4211	
Mac Board	805-656-3746	
J. C. International	805-688-6276	
SpacePort BBS	805-734-3330	Mark Lucas
Gold Coast Mac	805-984-9961	
MacBoard	806-358-0406	
Micro-Tech Net	806-742-2917	
Coffee MUG	806-797-8467	
Hawaii BBS	808-623-1085	Mike Clary
Meganet BBS	813-545-8050	Mike Murdock
Five Points BBS	813-957-3349	Ray Sanders
Magical Mystery Tour	814-337-2021	
Time Machine	815-962-7677	Clyde Person
Primetime BBS	815-965-5606	Tom Fernandez
WilloughbyWare MEBBS	816-474-1052	Lee Willoughby
Computer Emporium	817-540-4894	
The Crystal Rose	817-547-1851	
The Baseboard	817-547-5634	
The Apple Cart	817-634-7727	
San Angelo Apple UG	817-683-2429	
Bear pit BBS	817-755-3891	
MUG BBS	817-766-0510	Bill Anderson
MacBBS	818-355-7872	Bryan Menell
SGVMUG BBS	818-444-9850	Dennis Coslo

D

On-Line Services

Bulletin Board Service	Telephone Number	SYSOP
Smoothtalker BBS	818-716-0817	
Programmer's Haven	818-798-6819	Chuck Wannall
Computer Connexion	818-810-7464	no regular SYSOP
Apple Bus	818-919-5459	
Oasis BBS	818-964-2621	
HOUSE ATREIDES	818-965-7220	
Magic Slate	818-967-5534	
MacASM BBS	818-991-5037	Yves Lempereur
MacMemphis	901-756-6867	Russell Chatham
Macky BBS	902-466-6903	
Gulf Coast BBS	904-244-8675	
N/A	904-371-2842	
BBS Central	904-725-8925	Brett Wood
Telebit BBS	904-736-6430	Frodo Baggins
The Graveyard	907-258-3912	
The Front Page	907-279-9263	
Apple Diggins	907-333-4090	Bobby Diggins
Dark Side of the Moon	907-479-4816	
CannonBall House	912-477-9232	
Computer Patch	913-233-5554	Mike Forman
Prairie Goat	913-299-8597	
Hacker's Next	913-462-8285	
MacCentral BBS	913-682-1254	
Lawrence BBS	913-841-4612	
Timescape	914-356-1643	
Mid-Hudson Mac	914-562-8528	
Info-Center BBS	914-565-6696	
Hackers' Hideout	914-666-3360	
Apple Core/Cutthroats	914-737-6770	Scott Neufeld
M-bbs	914-967-8162	Joe Pavone
Mouse Exchange	914-967-9560	
Symbiotic	914-986-7905	
Ed's Bar & Grill	915-593-8981	
The Pass	915-821-3638	
Texas Cider	915-949-8447	
Davis MUG BBS	916-758-0269	Bill Santos
AVES (Mac Section)	916-758-2314	
The Grand Experiment	916-891-1631	

Bulletin Board Service	Telephone Number	SYSOP
TUMS BBS	918-234-5000	
Heaven ^ Hell BBS	918-299-8795	
Solutions! BBS	919-392-5829	
Micro Message Service	919-779-6674	
AppleSeeds, Raleigh MUG	919-828-9619	
Moonlight Mac BBS	919-852-6427	Jerry Welsh
Moonlight Mac BBS Teacher/Student	919-929-0943	
Comp. Info	916-457-8270	
Sacramento MUG/MacNexus	916-924-9747	Lee Hinde

APPENDIX

Directory of Products

Product Listing by Category

Accounting

Accountant, Inc. (Softsync)

APG Cash Drawer (Upper Midwest Industries)

Back to Basics Accounting (Peachtree)

BPI General Accounting (Computer Associates)

Business Modules (Great Plains Software)

DacEasy (Dac)

ForeCaster (Palo Alto Software)

In-House Accountant (Migent)

Insight and atOnce! (Layered)

Rags to Riches (Chang Labs)

SBT Accounting (SBT)

ShopKeeper 4 (ShopKeeper Software)

Simply Accounting (Bedford Software Corp.)

Strictly Business (Future Design)

SuperMOM (National TelePress)

Timeslips III (North Edge Software)

Animation Tools

HyperAnimator (Brightstar Technology)

VideoWorks II (MacroMind)

VideoWorks II Accelerator (MacroMind)

VideoWorks II Clip Animation (MacroMind)

Artificial Intelligence

Instant Expert Plus (Human Intellect Systems)

Backup

DataPak (MASS MICRO Systems)

Fastback Mac (Fifth Generation Systems, Inc.)

Irwin Tape Backup System (Irwin Magnetics)

MaxStream tape backup system (Archive Corporation)

CAD/CAM

ArchiText (Brainpower, Inc.)

ASD Professional CAD Symbol Library (Advanced System Design, Inc.)

AutoCAD (AutoDesk)

Computer-Aided Design and Drafting (Generic Software)

821

EZ Draft (Bridgeport Machines)
MathCAD (MathSoft, Inc.)
MGMS: Professional CAD for Macintosh (Micro CAD/CAM)
MiniCad (Diehl Graphsoft)
MiniCad Plus (Diehl Graphsoft)
VersaCAD (VersaCad)

CD-ROM

AppleCD SC (Apple Computer)
CD ROM (Image Club Graphics, Inc.)
PD ROM (BMUG)

Clip Art

Artroom (Image Club Graphics, Inc.)
ArtWare: (ArtWare Borders Systems)
Click Art (T/Maker)
Click & Clip (Studio Advertising Art)
Images with Impact! (3G Graphics)
Japanese Clip Art (Qualitas Trading Co.)
MacGraphics (GoldMind Publishing)
WetPaint (Dubl-Click Software)

Communications

AppleShare, MacTerminal (Apple Computer)
CP290M Home Control Interface (X-10 (USA Inc.))
Cue 2.1 (OpCode Systems)
DeskScene (PBI Software)
Desktop Express (Dow Jones)
Different Drummer (Primera Software)
Enterprise (Foundation Publishing)
Fast Path 4 (Kinetics, Inc.)
Felix (Lightgate)
InBox (Sun Corp., Division of Taps Corp.)

InTalk (Palantir)
LapLink Mac (Traveling Software)
MacLink (Dataviz)
MacServe, ComServe (Infosphere)
MicroPhone (Software Ventures)
MicroPhone II (Software Ventures)
Microsoft Mail (Microsoft)
Red Ryder (Freesoft)
Smartcom II (Hayes)
TOPS (TOPS)
VersaTerm-Pro (Peripherals, Computers and Supplies)

Data Analysis Programs

MacSpin (D2 Software)
StatView 512+ (Brainpower, Inc.)
StatView II (Abacus Concepts)
Systat (Systat)
FastStat (Systat)
MyStat (Systat)

Databases

4th Dimension (ACIUS)
C.A.T. (Chang Laboratories)
DataBase (Preferred Publishers, Inc.)
DaynaFile (Dayna Communications)
Dbase Mac (Ashton-Tate)
dMac III (Format Software)
Double Helix and Helix (Odesta)
EndNote (Niles & Associates)
FileMaker (Claris)
FoxBASE/Mac (Fox Software)
LXR.Test (Logic eXtension Resources)
Omnis 3 (Blyth Software)
Oracle SQL Database (Oracle)
OverVUE (ProVue Development)
Parameter Manager Plus (GenRad Inc.)

Reflex, Reflex Plus (Borland International)

TimeWand (TimeWand Manager)

TML Database Toolkit (TML Systems)

Writer's Workshop (Futuresoft System Designs)

Desk Accessories

AutoSave DA (Magic Software)

Calculator Construction Set (Dubl-Click Software)

Capture (Mainstay)

Computer covers (Computer Cover Company)

Desk Necessities (MicroSparc)

DiskTools Plus (Electronic Arts)

Font/DA Juggler (ALSoft)

HFS Locator Plus (PBI Software)

MacBottom HD-70 Hard Disk (PCPC)

MacChill (MacMemory)

MacTilt and the Muzzle (Ergotron)

MockPackage+ (CE Software)

On Cue (ICOM Simulations)

PowerStation and Suitcase II (Fifth Generation Systems)

QuickDEX (Casady & Greene)

The Clipper and SmartScrap (Solutions International)

Desktop Publishing

DTP Advisor (Broderbund Software)

Interleaf Publisher (Interleaf)

LetrTuck (Edko)

MacTeX (FTL Systems)

On Becoming a Desktop Publisher (Ocean Communications)

PageMaker (Aldus)

PosterMaker Plus and DTP Advisor (Broderbund Software)

QuarkStyle (Quark)

QuarkXPress (Quark)

Ready,Set,Go! 4 (Letraset)

Springboard Publisher (Springboard Software)

TeXtures (Blue Sky Research)

UltraSpec (Softstream)

Drafting

MacDraft (Innovative Data Design)

Draw

Cricket Draw (Cricket Software)

GraphicWorks 1.1 (Mindscape)

Graphist Paint II (Aba Software)

MacDraw, MacDraw II (Claris)

Swivel 3D (Paracomp)

Draw and Paint Programs

Advanced Gravis InfoGuard (Computer Technology, Ltd.)

Canvas (Deneba Software)

Colorizer (Palomar Software, Inc.)

DeskPaint (Zedcor)

Easy 3D (Enabling Technologies)

Gravis MouseStick (Advanced Gravis Computer Technology, Ltd.)

Mac3D 2.0 (Challenger Software)

MacCalligraphy (Qualitas Trading Co.)

MacPaint, MacPaint II (Claris)

MacProof (Lexpertise USA, Inc.)

Modern Artist 2.0 (Computer Friends)

NuPaint (NuEquation)

Phoenix 3D (Dreams of the Phoenix)

Photon Paint (MicroIllusions)

E

Products

Studio/8 (Electronic Arts)
Super 3D, SuperPaint (Silicon Beach
Software)

Educational Programs

Alphabet Blocks (Brightstar Technology)
Course Builder (Tele-Robotics
International)
KidsTime (Great Wave Software)
MacType (Palantir)
MasterType (Mindscape)
Mavis Beacon Teaches Typing! (Software
Toolworks)
Number Maze (Great Wave Software)
Reader Rabbit (The Learning Company)
Sensei Physics, Type! (Broderbund
Software)
Typing Tutor IV (Simon & Schuster)
Typing Instructor Encore (INDIVIDUAL
Software)

Equation Solvers

Eureka: The Solver (Borland
International)
Expressionist (Allan Bonadio Associates)
Mathematica (Wolfram Research)
MathView Professional (Brainpower,
Inc.)

Fax Modem/Machines

Relisys (Relisys)
Back Fax (Solutions International)
FAXstf (STF Technologies)

Finance

Dollars and Sense (Monogram)
MacInTax (Softview)
MacMoney (Survivor Software)
Managing Your Money (MECA Ventures)
Quicken (Intuit)

Fonts

Fluent Fonts (CasadyWare)
FONTastic Plus (Altsys Co.)
FONTographer (Altsys Co.)
FontSizer (US Microlabs)
Kadmos Greek Font (Allotype
Typographics)
KeyCap Fonts (Paperback Software
International)
KeyMaster (Altsys Co.)
Laser Fonts, Publishing Packs (Adobe
Systems)
LaserFonts (Century Software)
licensed laser fonts (International
Typeface Corporation)
The MACintosh Book of Fonts (Source
Net)
World-Class Fonts (Dubl-Click Software)

Furniture

AnthroCare (Anthro Technology
Furniture)
Mac II Workstation (Ergotron)
MacTable and add-on cabinet modules
(ScanCoFurn)

Games

Arkanoid (Discovery Software)

Balance of Power (Mindscape)

Battle Stations (Time Line)

Beyond Dark Castle (Silicon Beach Software)

Business Graphics, 9-5 (Metro ImageBase)

CalendarMaker (CE Software)

Chuck Yeager's Advanced Flight Trainer (Electronic Arts)

ColorPro Graphics Plotter (Hewlett-Packard)

Dinner at Eight (Rubicon)

Falcon (Spectrum Holobyte)

Fokker Triplane (Bullseye Software)

Ferrari Grand Prix (Bullseye Software)

Fool's Errand (Miles)

Fourth and Inches (Accolade)

Gato (Spectrum Holobyte)

Go (Toyogo)

ImageMaker (Presentation Technologies)

KidsTime (Great Waves)

Klondike (Unison Software)

Lunar Rescue, MacGolf (Practical Computer Applications)

Mac Pro Football (Avalon Hill)

MacGolf (Practical Computer Applications)

Macintizer ADB (GTCO Corp.)

MacRacquetball (Practical Computer Applications)

MacTablet (Summagraphics Corp.)

McGenogram (Humanware)

Mean 18 Ultimate Golf (Accolade)

Orbiter (Spectrum Holobyte)

PT-109 (Spectrum Holobyte)

Sim City (Maxis)

TellStar (Spectrum Holobyte)

Tetris (Spectrum Holobyte)

Graphics Programs

FreeHand (Aldus)

Illustrator 88 (Adobe Systems)

Handwriting Recognition Programs

Personal Writer PW15 S (Personal Writer)

Hard Disk Drives

DataFrame hard disks (SuperMac Technologies)

Eureka!, hard disks (PCPC)

Hard disk drives (Micah Storage Systems)

Hard disks (PERIPHERAL LAND)

Hard disks (Rodime Systems)

Hard disk drives (MD Ideas)

MacBottom 45 SCSI and Internal Modem, MacBottom HD-21 (PCPC)

MacCrate 60MB Hard Disk (Crate Technology)

Removable hard disk (MicroTech)

HyperCard Programs

BMUG on HyperCard (BMUG)

Business Class, Focal Point, Reports (Activision)

Hyper DA (Symmetry)

Hyper Tutor (Channelmark)

HyperAtlas (MicroMaps Software)

HyperDialer (DataDesk International)

JokeMaster and Hyper JokeMaster (Computer Trend)

ScriptExpert (Hyperpress Publishing)

E

Products

The Macintosh Bible, HyperCard edition
(STAX!)

Information Management

End Note (Niles Computing)
Grant Manager (Niles Computing)

Information Providers

City to City (Activision)

Integrated Software

Microsoft Works (Microsoft)

Keyboard

12′ and 25′ keyboard cables (Your
Affordable Software Company)
7′ ADB Keyboard Cable (Kensington
Microware)
MAC-101 Keyboard (DataDesk
International)
Mac-105 Keyboard (Cutting Edge)

Languages

ExperCommon Lisp (ExperTelligence)
Mac C (Consulair)
MacForth Plus (Creative Solutions)
Mach II (Palo Alto Shipping)
Object Logo (Coral Software)
Pascal (TML Systems)
Prolog/m (Chalcedony Software)
THINK's Lightspeed C (Symantec)
TML (MacLanguage Series)
ZBasic (Zedcor)

Macros

Quickeys (CE Software)
Tempo (Affinity Microsystems)
WorksPlus Command (Lundeen &
Associates)

Math/Statistics Programs

Data Desk Professional (Odesta)
FASTAT (Systat)
Milo (Paracomp)

Memory Upgrades and Accelerators

Accelerator II, Novy Mac20MX, File
Server and Micro Channel (Daystar)
Excelerator XL 20 and Excelerator XL 25
(Irwin Magnetics)
Macs-A-Million memory upgrades
(Sophisticated Circuits)
MacSnap memory upgrades (Dove
Computer)
Memory Upgrades (SuperMac
Technologies)
Prodigy 4 board for Mac Plus & 512K
Mac, One Plus One (Levco)
Radius Accelerator 25, accelerator
boards (Radius)
SpeedCard accelerator boards (SuperMac
Technologies)
SuperRam 2 (SuperMac Technologies)

Mice and Pointing Devices

Kurta Tablets (Kurta)
ProPoint (Abaton Technology)
Turbo Mouse ADB (Kensington
Microware)
TurboTrackball (Asher Engineering)

Modems

Mac Modem with Red Ryder communications software (Prometheus Products)
Migent Pocket Modem (Migent)
Nodem (Adaptec)
NetModem (Shiva)
V-Series Smartmodem 9600 (Hayes)

Monitors

6′ Mac II Monitor Cable extension kit (Kensington Microware)
DualPage Display System (Cornerstone Technology, Inc.)
EasyView Monitors (Nuvotech)
high-resolution, monochrome, and color monitors (Taxan USA Corporation)
LaserView monitors (Sigma Designs)
MacLarger Monitors (Power R)
Monitors (E Machines)
Monitors (Radius)
Viking monitors (Moniterm)

Music Programs

Toccata music notation program (Sun Valley Software)
Music Mouse (Laurie Spiegal)

Networking

I-Server (Solana Electronics)
PhoneNet (Farallon Computing)
Rapport and Drive 2.4 (Kennect Technology)

OCR Programs

Omni-page 2.0 (Caere Corporation)
Read-It! (Olduvai)

Outliner

More and ThinkTank (Living Videotext)

Page Layout

FreeHand (Aldus)
PageMaker (Aldus)
Ready!Set!Go! (Letraset)
Xpress (Quark)

Portable Macs

Cambridge 288 (Cambridge North America)
Travel Mac (NexSys)

Presentation Programs

Cricket Presents (Cricket Software)
Persuasion (Aldus)
PowerPoint (Microsoft)

Printers

4693D Color Printer (Tektronix)
Accel-500 dot-matrix printer (Advanced Matrix Technology)
Brother HJL-8 Desktop Laser Printer (Brother International)
Colorprint (I/O Design)
Grappler LQ (Orange Micro)

E
Products

ImageWriter LQ, LaserWriter II NT, LaserWriter II NTX, LaserWriter IISC (Apple Computer)

Laser printer cartridge refills (Encore Ribbon)

LaserServe (Infosphere)

LaserWriter II NTX, LaserWriter II NT, and CrystalPrint Publisher (Qume Corp.)

Mac II color printer (RGB Technology)

MacBuffer (Ergotron)

MacPrint (Insight Development Corp.)

Modern Artist color paint printer buffers program, Shinko color printers (Computer Friends)

NP30APL and other printers (Olympia USA)

Personal LaserPrinter (General Computer)

QMS-PS 810 (QMS)

QMS Colorscript 100 (QMS)

Programming

Desktop Help (Help Software)

ExperLISP (ExperTelligence)

HyperCard Programming (Eric Alderman)

Lasertalk (Emerald City Software)

MacFlow (Mainstay)

Scanners

Apple Scanner (Apple Computer)

AST TurboScan (AST Research)

BarneyScan XP (Barney Scan, Inc.)

ChromaScan (Imagenesis)

Focus S800GS scanner (Agfa-Compugraphic)

ImageStudio 1.5 Scanning Module (Letraset)

LaserPaint Color II (LaserWare)

Microtek MSF-300C flatbed scanner (Microtek)

PC Scan 1000 (Dest Corp.)

PixelScan (SuperMac Technologies)

Scan 300/S (Abaton Technology)

Studio/8 Scanner Installer (Electronic Arts)

TextPert (OCR) (CTA, Inc.)

ThunderScan and Lightning Scan (Thunderware)

Screen Saver

Anti-Glare Magnification Screen (Sher-Mark Products)

Autoblack (Itty Bitty Computers)

Security Software

MacSafe, FolderBOLT, and other security software (Kent Marsh Limited)

Spellers and Dictionaries

BigThesaurus and Spelling Coach (Deneba Software)

Doug Clapp's Word Tools (Aegis Development)

Gofer (Microlytics, Inc.)

Graham Speller (Graham Software)

Liberty Spell Checker (DataPak Software)

MacProof (Lexpertise USA, Inc.)

Macspell+ (Creighton Development)

QuickRhyme dictionary (Apriori, Inc.)

Sensible Grammar (Sensible Software)

Spelling Champion (Champion Software)

Spellswell (Working Software)
Thunder! (Electronic Arts)
WorksPlus Spell (Lundeen & Associates)

Spreadsheets

Excel (Microsoft)
Full Impact (Ashton-Tate)
MacCalc (Bravo Technologies)
Trapeze (Access Technology)
Wingz (Informix)

Storage

WORM Drives (Corel Systems)

Supplies

BakerForms (Baker Graphics)
Labels for printers and disks (Avery International)

Tax Preparation

EZTax-Plan Business Edition (EZWare Corp.)
EZTax-Plan Personal Edition (EZWare Corp.)
EZTax-Prep 1040 (EZWare Corp.)

Utilities

1stAid Kit HFS (1stAid Software)
AutoMac III (Genesis Micro Software)
Bookmark (Intellisoft International)
Can Opener (Abbott Systems)
Capture (Mainstay)
Comment (Deneba Software)
Copy II for the Macintosh (Central Point Software)

Curator, SuperGlue (Solutions International)
DiskExpress (ALSoft)
DiskFinder (Williams and Macias)
DiskInfo (Maitreya Design)
DiskQuick, MacLabeler (Ideaforms)
DiskTop (CE Software)
Document Compare (Legalware)
Fedit Plus (MacMaster Systems)
Findswell (Working Software)
Hard Disk Utilities (FWB Software)
HFS Backup (PCPC)
Icon-It! (Olduvai)
INITPicker (MicroSeeds)
Laser Spool (MacAmerica)
MacInUse (Softview)
MacTree (Software Research Technology)
MultiFinder (Interleaf)
Packit III (Harry R. Chesley)
Quick & Dirty Utilities (Dreams of the Phoenix)
QuickDEX (Casady & Greene)
RamSnap (Dove Computer)
Retriever (Exodus Software)
SideKick (Borland International)
SkipFinder and StartupDesk (Darin Adler)
Smart Art (Emerald City)
SoundWave (Impulse)
Stepping Out II (Berkeley System Design)
Stuffit (Raymond Lau)
Suitcase (Fifth Generation Systems)
SuperSpool (SuperMac Technologies)
Symantec Utilities for Macintosh (Symantec)
System Saver Mac (Kensington Microware)
Unitize (Rainbow Bridge)
Virex (HJC Software)

E
Products

Word Processing Programs

ExpressWrite (Exodus)

Feima (Wu Corporation)

FullWrite Professional (Ashton-Tate)

Guide (OWL International)

Holidays and WriteNow (T/Maker)

InfoLogic Envelope (InfoLogic)

JoliWrite (Benoit Widemann)

Kaihin Brushwriter (Pacific Rim
Connections)

Laser Author (Firebird Licensees)

LearnWord 3.0 (Personal Training
Systems)

MacWrite (Claris)

MathType 2.0 (Design Science)

MindWrite (Access Technology)

Mishu (Xanatech)

MockWrite (CE Software)

MORE II (Symantec)

MS-DOS Word (Microsoft)

NISUS word processor (Paragon
Concepts)

QuickLetter (Working Software)

Scriptor (Screenplay Systems)

TML Source Code Library (TML Systems)

Word (Microsoft)

Word Finder (Microlytics)

WordPerfect (WordPerfect)

Write (Microsoft)

Works Add-Ons

MS-DOS Works (Microsoft)

WorksPlus Command and WorksPlus
Spell (Lundeen & Associates)

Product Listing (Alphabetically Arranged)

12' and 25' keyboard cables (Your
Affordable Software Company)

1stAid Kit HFS (1stAid Software)

4693D Color Printer (Tektronix)

4th Dimension (ACIUS)

6' Mac II Monitor Cable extension kit
(Kensington Microware)

7' ADB Keyboard Cable (Kensington
Microware)

Accel-500 dot-matrix printer (Advanced
Matrix Technology)

Accelerator II, Novy Mac20MX, File
Server, and Micro Channel (Daystar)

Accountant, Inc. (Softsync)

Advanced Gravis InfoGuard (Computer
Technology, Ltd.)

Alphabet Blocks (Brightstar Technology)

AnthroCare (Anthro Technology
Furniture)

Anti-Glare Magnification Screen (Sher-
Mark Products)

APG Cash Drawer (Upper Midwest
Industries)

AppleCD SC (Apple Computer)

Apple Scanner (Apple Computer)

AppleShare, MacTerminal (Apple
Computer)

ArchiText (Brainpower, Inc.)

Arkanoid (Discovery Software)

Artroom (Image Club Graphics, Inc.)

ArtWare: Borders (ArtWare Systems)

ASD Professional CAD Symbol Library
(Advanced System Design Inc.)

AST TurboScan (AST Research)
Autoblack (Itty Bitty Computers)
AutoCAD (AutoDesk)
AutoMac III (Genesis Micro Software)
AutoSave DA (Magic Software)

Back Fax (Solutions International)
Back to Basics Accounting (Peachtree)
BakerForms (Baker Graphics)
Balance of Power (Mindscape)
BarneyScan XP (Barney Scan, Inc.)
Battle Stations (Time Line)
Beyond Dark Castle (Silicon Beach
  Software)
BigThesaurus and Spelling Coach
  (Deneba Software)
BMUG on HyperCard (BMUG)
Bookmark (Intellisoft International)
BPI General Accounting (Computer
  Associates)
Brother HJL-8 Desktop Laser Printer
  (Brother International)
Business Modules (Great Plains Software)
Business Graphics, 9-5 (Metro
  ImageBase)
Business Class, Focal Point, Reports
  (Activision)

C.A.T. (Chang Laboratories)
Calculator Construction Set (Dubl-Click
  Software)
CalendarMaker (CE Software)
Cambridge 288 (Cambridge North
  America)
Can Opener (Abbott Systems)
Canvas (Deneba Software)
Capture (Mainstay)
CD ROM (Image Club Graphics, Inc.)
ChromaScan (Imagenesis)
Chuck Yeager's Advanced Flight Trainer
  (Electronic Arts)

City to City (Activision)
Click & Clip (Studio Advertising Art)
Click Art (T/Maker)
Colorizer (Palomar Software, Inc.)
Colorprint (I/O Design)
ColorPro Graphics Plotter (Hewlett-
  Packard)
Comment (Deneba Software)
Computer covers (Computer Cover
  Company)
Computer Aided Design and Drafting
  (Generic Software)
Copy II for the Macintosh (Central Point
  Software)
Course Builder (Tele-Robotics
  International)
CP290M Home Control Interface (X-10
  (USA Inc.))
Cricket Draw (Cricket Software)
Cricket Presents (Cricket Software)
Cue 2.1 (OpCode Systems)
Curator, SuperGlue (Solutions
  International)

DacEasy (Dac)
Data Desk Professional (Odesta)
DataBase (Preferred Publishers, Inc.)
DataFrame hard disks (SuperMac
  Technologies)
DataPak (MASS MICRO Systems)
DaynaFile (Dayna Communications)
Dbase Mac (Ashton-Tate)
Desk Necessities (MicroSparc)
DeskPaint (Zedcor)
DeskScene (PBI Software)
Desktop Help (Help Software)
Desktop Express (Dow Jones)
Different Drummer (Primera Software)
Dinner at Eight (Rubicon)
DiskExpress (ALSoft)
DiskFinder (Williams and Macias)

E
Products

DiskInfo (Maitreya Design)
DiskQuick, MacLabeler (Ideaforms)
DiskTools Plus (Electronic Arts)
DiskTop (CE Software)
dMac III (Format Software)
Document Compare (Legalware)
Dollars and Sense (Monogram)
Double Helix and Helix (Odesta)
Doug Clapp's Word Tools (Aegis
  Development)
DTP Advisor (Broderbund Software)
DualPage Display System (Cornerstone
  Technology Inc.)

Easy 3D (Enabling Technologies)
EasyView Monitors (Nuvotech)
EndNote (Niles & Associates)
Enterprise (Foundation Publishing)
Eureka!, hard disks (PCPC)
Eureka: The Solver (Borland
  International)
Excel (Microsoft)
Excelerator XL 20 and Excelerator XL 25
  (Irwin Magnetics)
ExperCommon Lisp (ExperTelligence)
ExperLISP (ExperTelligence)
Expressionist (Allan Bonadio Associates)
ExpressWrite (Exodus)
EZ Draft (Bridgeport Machines)
EZTax-Prep 1040 (EZWare Corp.)
EZTax-Plan Personal Edition (EZWare
  Corp.)
EZTax-Plan Business Edition (EZWare
  Corp.)
Falcon (Spectrum Holobyte)
Fast Path 4 (Kinetics, Inc.)
FASTAT (Systat)
Fastback Mac (Fifth Generation Systems,
  Inc.)
FastStat (Systat)

FAXstf (STF Technologies)
Fedit Plus (MacMaster Systems)
Feima (Wu Corporation)
Felix (Lightgate)
Ferrari Grand Prix (Bullseye Software)
FileMaker (Claris)
Findswell (Working Software)
Fluent Fonts (CasadyWare)
Focus S800GS scanner (Agfa-
  Compugraphic)
Fokker Triplane (Bullseye Software)
Font/DA Juggler (ALSoft)
FONTastic Plus (Altsys Co.)
Fontographer (Altsys Co.)
FontSizer (US Microlabs)
Fool's Errand (Miles)
ForeCaster (Palo Alto Software)
Fourth and Inches (Accolade)
FoxBASE/Mac (Fox Software)
FreeHand (Aldus)
Full Impact (Ashton-Tate)
FullWrite Professional (Ashton-Tate)

Gato (Spectrum Holobyte)
Go (Toyogo)
Gofer (Microlytics, Inc.)
Graham Speller (Graham Software)
Grant Manager (Niles & Associates)
GraphicWorks 1.1 (Mindscape)
Graphist Paint II (Aba Software)
Grappler LQ (Orange Micro)
Gravis MouseStick (Advanced Gravis
  Computer Technology, Ltd.)
Guide (OWL International)

hard disk drives (Micah Storage Systems)
Hard Disks (Rodime Systems)
hard disk drives (MD Ideas)
Hard Disk Util (FWB Software)
Hard disks (PERIPHERAL LAND)
HFS Backup (PCPC)

HFS Locater Plus (PBI Software)

high-resolution, monochrome, and color monitors (Taxan USA Corporation)

Holidays and WriteNow (T/Maker)

Hyper Tutor (Channelmark)

Hyper DA (Symmetry)

HyperAnimator (Brightstar Technology)

HyperAtlas (MicroMaps Software)

HyperCard Programming (Eric Alderman)

HyperDialer (DataDesk International)

Icon-It! (Olduvai)

Illustrator 88 (Adobe Systems)

ImageMaker (Presentation Technologies)

Images with Impact! (3G Graphics)

ImageStudio 1.5 Scanning Module (Letraset)

ImageWriter LQ, LaserWriter II NT, LaserWriter II NTX, LaserWriter IISC (Apple Computer)

In-House Accountant (Migent)

InBox (Sun Corp., Division of Taps Corp.)

InfoLogic Envelope (InfoLogic)

INITPicker (MicroSeeds)

Insight and atOnce! (Layered)

Instant Expert Plus (Human Intellect Systems)

InTalk (Palantir)

Interleaf Publisher (Interleaf)

Irwin Tape Backup System (Irwin Magnetics)

I-Server (Solana Electronics)

Japanese Clip Art (Qualitas Trading Co.)

JokeMaster and Hyper JokeMaster (Computer Trend)

JoliWrite (Benoit Widemann)

Kadmos Greek Font (Allotype Typographics)

Kaihin Brushwriter (Pacific Rim Connections)

KeyCap Fonts (Paperback Software International)

KeyMaster (Altsys Co.)

KidsTime (Great Wave Software)

Klondike (Unison Software)

Kurta Tablets (Kurta)

Labels for printers and disks (Avery International)

LapLink Mac (Traveling Software)

Laser Spool (MacAmerica)

Laser Author (Firebird Licensees)

Laser printer cartridge refills (Encore Ribbon)

Laser Fonts, Publishing Packs (Adobe Systems)

LaserFonts (Century Software)

LaserPaint Color II (LaserWare)

LaserServe (Infosphere)

Lasertalk (Emerald City Software)

LaserView monitors (Sigma Designs)

LaserWriter II NTX, LaserWriter II NT, and CrystalPrint Publisher (Qume Corporation)

LearnWord 3.0 (Personal Training Systems)

LetrTuck (Edko)

Liberty Spell Checker (DataPak Software)

licensed laser fonts (International Typeface Corporation)

Lunar Rescue, MacGolf (Practical Computer Applications)

LXR.Test (Logic eXtension Resources)

Mac II color printer (RGB Technology)

Mac II Workstation (Ergotron)

Mac Modem with Red Ryder communications software (Prometheus Products)

Mac-105 Keyboard (Cutting Edge)

E

Products

Mac C (Consulair)

MAC-101 Keyboard (DataDesk International)

Mac Pro Football (Avalon Hill)

Mac3D 2.0 (Challenger Software)

MacBottom 45 SCSI and Internal Modem, MacBottom HD-21 (PCPC)

MacBottom HD-70 Hard Disk (PCPC)

MacBuffer (Ergotron)

MacCalc (Bravo Technologies)

MacCalligraphy (Qualitas Trading Co.)

MacChill (MacMemory)

MacCrate 60MB Hard Disk (Crate Technology)

MacDraft (Innovative Data Design)

MacDraw, MacDraw II (Claris)

MacFlow (Mainstay)

MacForth Plus (Creative Solutions)

MacGolf (Practical Computer Applications)

MacGraphics (GoldMind Publishing)

Mach II (Palo Alto Shipping)

MacInTax (Softview)

Macintizer ADB (GTCO Corp.)

MacInUse (Softview)

MacLarger Monitors (Power R)

MacLink (Dataviz)

MacMoney (Survivor Software)

MacPaint, MacPaint II (Claris)

MacPrint (Insight Development Corp.)

MacProof (Lexpertise USA, Inc.)

MacProof (Automated Language Processing Systems)

MacRaquetball (Practical Computer Applications)

Macs-A-Million memory upgrades (Sophisticated Circuits)

MacSafe, FolderBOLT, and other security software (Kent Marsh Limited)

MacServe, ComServe (Infosphere)

MacSnap memory upgrades (Dove Computer)

Macspell+ (Creighton Development)

MacSpin (D2 Software)

MacTable and add-on cabinet modules (ScanCoFurn)

MacTablet (Summagraphics Corp.)

MacTeX (FTL Systems)

MacTilt and the Muzzle (Ergotron)

MacTree (Software Research Technology)

MacType (Palantir)

MacWrite (Claris)

Managing Your Money (MECA Ventures)

MasterType (Mindscape)

MathCAD (MathSoft, Inc)

Mathematica (Wolfram Research)

MathType 2.0 (Design Science)

MathView Professional (Brainpower, Inc.)

Mavis Beacon Teaches Typing! (Software Toolworks)

MaxStream tape backup system (Archive Corporation)

McGenogram (Humanware)

Mean 18 Ultimate Golf (Accolade)

Memory Upgrades (SuperMac Technologies)

MGMS: Professional CAD for Macintosh (Micro CAD/CAM)

MicroPhone (Software Ventures)

MicroPhone II (Software Ventures)

Microsoft Works (Microsoft)

Microsoft Mail (Microsoft)

Microtek MSF-300C flatbed scanner (Microtek)

Migent Pocket Modem (Migent)

Milo (Paracomp)

MindWrite (Access Technology)

MiniCad (Diehl Graphsoft)

MiniCad+ (Diehl Graphsoft)

Mishu (Xanatech)

MockPackage+ (CE Software)

MockWrite (CE Software)

Modern Artist color paint printer buffers program, Shinko color printers (Computer Friends)

Modern Artist 2.0 (Computer Friends)

Monitors (Radius)

Monitors (E Machines)

More and ThinkTank (Living Videotext)

MORE II (Symantec)

MS-DOS Word (Microsoft)

MS-DOS Works (Microsoft)

MultiFinder (Interleaf)

Music Mouse (Laurie Spiegal)

MyStat (Systat)

NetModem (Shiva)

NISUS word processor (Paragon Concepts)

Nodem (Adaptec)

NP30APL and other printers (Olympia USA)

Number Maze (Great Wave Software)

NuPaint (NuEquation)

Object Logo (Coral Software)

Omni-page 2.0 (Caere Corporation)

Omnis 3 (Blyth Software)

On Cue (ICOM Simulations)

On Becoming a Desktop Publisher (Ocean Communications)

Oracle SQL Database (Oracle)

Oribter (Spectrum Holobyte)

OverVUE (ProVue Development)

Packit III (Harry R. Chesley)

PageMaker (Aldus)

Parameter Manager Plus (GenRad, Inc.)

Pascal (TML Systems)

PC Scan 1000 (Dest Corp.)

PD ROM (BMUG)

Personal LaserPrinter (General Computer)

Personal Writer PW15 S (Personal Writer)

Persuasion (Aldus)

Phoenix 3D (Dreams of the Phoenix)

PhoneNet (Farallon Computing)

Photon Paint (MicroIllusions)

PixelScan (SuperMac Technologies)

PosterMaker Plus and DTP Advisor (Broderbund Software)

PowerPoint (Microsoft)

PowerStation and Suitcase II (Fifth Generation Systems)

Prodigy 4 board for Mac Plus & 512K Mac, One Plus One (Levco)

Prolog/m (Chalcedony Software)

ProPoint (Abaton Technology)

PT-109 (Spectrum Holobyte)

QMS Colorscript 100 (QMS)

QMS-PS 810 (QMS)

QuarkXPress (Quark)

QuarkStyle (Quark)

Quick & Dirty Utilities (Dreams of the Phoenix)

QuickDEX (Casady & Greene)

Quicken (Intuit)

Quickeys (CE Software)

QuickLetter (Working Software)

QuickRhyme dictionary (Apriori Inc.)

Radius Accelerator 25, accelerator boards (Radius)

Rags to Riches (Chang Labs)

RamSnap (Dove Computer)

Rapport and Drive 2.4 (Kennect Technology)

Read-It! (Olduvai)

E

Products

Reader Rabbit (The Learning Company)

Ready,Set,Go! 4 (Letraset)

Red Ryder (Freesoft)

Reflex, Reflex Plus (Borland International)

Relisys (Relisys)

Removable hard disk (MicroTech)

Retriever (Exodus Software)

SBT Accounting (SBT)

Scan 300/S (Abaton Technology)

ScriptExpert (Hyperpress Publishing)

Scriptor (Screenplay Systems)

Sensei Physics, Type! (Broderbund Software)

Sensible Grammar (Sensible Software)

ShopKeeper 4 (ShopKeeper Software)

SideKick (Borland International)

Sim City (Maxis)

Simply Accounting (Bedford Software Corp.)

SkipFinder and StartupDesk (Darin Adler)

Smart Art (Emerald City)

Smartcom II (Hayes)

SoundWave (Impulse)

SpeedCardzaccelerator boards (SuperMac Technologies)

Spelling Champion (Champion Software)

Spellswell (Working Software)

Springboard Publisher (Springboard Software)

StatView 512+ (Brainpower, Inc.)

StatView II (Abacus Concepts)

Stepping Out II (Berkeley System Design)

Strictly Business (Future Design)

Studio/8 Scanner Installer (Electronic Arts)

Studio/8 (Electronic Arts)

Stuffit (Raymond Lou)

Suitcase (Fifth Generation Systems)

Super 3D, SuperPaint (Silicon Beach Software)

SuperMOM (National TelePress)

SuperRam 2 (SuperMac Technologies)

SuperSpool (SuperMac Technologies)

Swivel 3D (Paracomp)

Symantec Utilities for Macintosh (Symantec)

Systat (Systat)

System Saver Mac (Kensington Microware)

TellStar (Spectrum Holobyte)

Tempo (Affinity Microsystems)

Teris (Spectrum Holobyte)

TextPert (OCR) (CTA, Inc.)

TeXtures (Blue Sky Research)

The MACintosh Book of Fonts (Source Net)

The Clipper and SmartScrap (Solutions International)

The Macintosh Bible, HyperCard edition (STAX!)

THINK's Lightspeed C (Symantec)

Thunder! (Electronic Arts)

ThunderScan and Lightning Scan (Thunderware)

Timeslips III (North Edge Software)

TimeWand (TimeWand Manager)

TML Source Code Library (TML Systems)

TML (MacLanguage Series)

TML Database Toolkit (TML Systems)

Toccata music notation program (Sun Valley Software)

TOPS (TOPS)

Trapeze (Access Technology)

Travel Mac (NexSys)

Turbo Mouse ADB (Kensington Microware)

TurboTrackball (Asher Engineering)

Typing Tutor IV (Simon & Schuster)

Typing Instructor Encore (INDIVIDUAL Software)

UltraSpec (Softstream)

Unitize (Rainbow Bridge)

V-Series Smartmodem 9600 (Hayes)

VersaCAD (VersaCad)

VersaTerm-Pro (Peripherals, Computers and Supplies)

VideoWorks II (MacroMind)

VideoWorks II Accelerator (MacroMind)

VideoWorks II Clip Animation (MacroMind)

Viking monitors (Moniterm)

Virex (HJC Software)

WetPaint (Dubl-Click Software)

Wingz (Informix)

Word (Microsoft)

Word Finder (Microlytics)

WordPerfect (WordPerfect)

WorksPlus Command (Lundeen & Associates)

WorksPlus Command and WorksPlus Spell (Lundeen & Associates)

WorksPlus Spell (Lundeen & Associates)

World-Class Fonts (Dubl-Click Software)

WORM Drives (Corel Systems)

Write (Microsoft)

Writer's Workshop (Futuresoft System Designs)

ZBasic (Zedcor)

E

Products

Vendor Guide

1stAid Software
42 Radnor Road
Boston, MA 02135
800/THE-FIXR
   1stAid Kit HFS

3G Graphics
11410 NE 124th Street
Suite 6155
Kirkland, WA 98034
800/456-0234
206/823-8198
   Images with Impact!

Aba Software
41 Great Valley Pkwy.
Malvern, PA 19355
800/234-0230
215/644-3580
   Graphist Paint II

Abacus Concepts
1984 Bonita Ave.
Berkeley, CA 94704
415/540-1949
   StatView II

Abaton Technology
48431 Milmont Dr.
Fremont, CA 94538
415/683-2226
   Scan 300/S
   ProPoint

Abbott Systems, Inc.
62 Mountain Road
Pleasantville, NY 10570
800/552-9157
   Can Opener

Access Technology
6 Pleasant Street
South Natick, MA 01760
800/367-4334
408/648-4000
   MindWrite
   Trapeze

Accolade
550 S. Winchester Blvd.
San Jose, CA 95128
408/296-8400
   Fourth and Inches
   Mean 18 Ultimate Golf

ACIUS
20300 Stevens Creek Blvd.
Cupertino, CA 95014
408/252-4444
   4th Dimension

Activision
3885 Bohannon Dr.
Menlo Park, CA 94025
415/329-0500
   Business Class
   Focal Point
   Reports
   City to City

Adaptec
691 S. Milpitas Blvd.
Milpitas, CA 95035
408/945-2518
   Nodem

Adobe Systems
1585 Charleston Road
Mountain View, CA 94039
415/961-4400
   Laser Fonts
   Publishing Packs
   PostScript
   Illustrator 88

Advanced System Design, Inc.
101 Stagecoach Blvd.
Evergreen, CO 80439
   ASD Professional CAD Symbol
   Library

Advanced Software
1095 E. Duane Ave.
Sunnyvale, CA 94086
408/733-0745
800/346-5392

Advanced Gravis Computer Technology,
   Ltd.
7033 Antrim Ave.
Burnaby, British Columbia
Canada V5J 4M5
800/663-8558
   Gravis Mousestick

Advanced Matrix Technology
765 Flynn Road
Camarillo, CA 93010
     ACCEL-500 dot-matrix printer

Aegis Development, Inc.
2115 Pico Blvd.
Santa Monica, CA 90405
213/392-9972
     Doug Clapp's Word Tools

Affinity Microsystems, Ltd.
1050 Walnut Street
Suite 425
Boulder, CO 80302
303/442-4840
     Tempo 1.2

Agfa-Compugraphic
200 Ballardvale Street
Wilmington, MA 01887
800/227-2780
     Focus S800GS scanner

Aldus
411 First Ave. South
Suite 200
Seattle, WA 98104
206/622-5500
     FreeHand
     Portfolio: Designs for Newsletters
     PageMaker
     Persuasion

Allan Bonadio Associates
814 Castio Street
San Francisco, CA 94114
415/282-5864
     Expressionist   .

Allotype Typographics
1600 Packard Road
Ann Arbor, MI 48104
313/663-1989
     Kadmos Greek Font

ALSoft
P.O. Box 927
Spring, TX 77383
713/353-4090
     DiskExpress
     Font/DA Juggler

Altra
1200 Skyline Dr.
Laramie, WY 82070
415/547-7300
     Felix

Altsys Co.
720 Ave. F
Suite 109D
Plano, TX 75074
214/424-4888
     Fontastic Plus
     Fontographer
     KeyMaster

Anthro Technology Furniture
3221 NE Yeon Street
Portland, OR 97210
503/241-7113
800/325-3841
     AnthroCare

APG (Upper Midwest Industries)
1601 67th Ave. North
Brooklyn Center, MN 55430
612/560-1440
     APG Cash Drawer

Apple Computer
20525 Mariana Ave.
Cupertino, CA 95014
408/996-1010
     Apple Scanner
     AppleShare
     MacTerminal
     AppleCD SC

Apriori Inc.
859 Hollywood Way
Suite 401
Burbank, CA 91510
     QuickRhyme dictionary

Archive Corporation
1650 Sunflower Ave.
Costa Mesa, CA 92626
800/237-4929
     MaxStream tape backup system

Ars Nova Software
P.O. Box 40629
Santa Barbara, CA 93140
805/564-2518
     Practica Musica 2.1

Artware Systems
3741 Benson Dr.
Raleigh, NC 27609
919/872-6511
     ArtWare: Borders

Asher Engineering
15115 Ramona Blvd.
Baldwin Park, CA 91706
800/824-3522
818/960-4839
     quadLYNX Trackball
     Turbo TrackBall

Ashton-Tate
20101 Hamilton Ave.
Torrance, CA 90502
213/329-8000
     FullWrite Professional
     Dbase Mac
     FullPaint

AST Research
2121 Alton Ave.
Irvine, CA 92714
714/863-1333
714/863-9991
     AST TurboScan
     Mac 286-10

Authorware, Inc.
8500 Normondalc Lake Blvd.
Suite 1050
Minneapolis, MN 55437
     SoundWave

AutoDesk
2320 Marinship Way
Sausalito, CA 94965
     AutoCAD

Avalon Hill
4517 Hartford Road
Baltimore, MD 21214
301/254-9200
     Mac Pro Football

Avery International
Consumer Products Division
Azusa, CA 91702
     Labels for printers and disks

Baker Graphics
204 Court Street
P.O. Box G-826
New Bedford, MA 02742
508/996-6732
    BakerForms

Barneyscan Corp.
1198 Tenth Street
Berkeley, CA 94710
    BarneyScan XP

Bede Tech
8327 Clinton Road
Cleveland, OH 44144
216/631-1441
800/772-4536

Bedford Software Corp.
15008 N.E. 40th Street
Redmond, WA 98052
206/883/0074
    Simply Accounting

Benoit Widemann
68 Ave. D'Italie
Paris, France 75013
    JoliWrite

Berkeley System Design
1708 Shattuck Ave.
Berkeley, CA 94709
415/540-5536
    Stepping Out II

Berol USA
P.O. Box BEROL
Carmel Valley, CA 93924
800/323-2454
    RapiDesign

Blank Software
P.O. Box 6561
San Francisco, CA 94101
415/863-9224
    Alchemy

Blue Sky Research
534 S.W. Third Ave.
Portland, OR 97204
    TeXtures

Blyth Software
1065 E. Hillsdale Blvd.
Suite 300
Foster City, CA 94404
415/571-0222
    Omnis 3

BMUG
1442 A. Walnut Street
Suite 62
Berkeley, CA 94709
415/849-9114
    BMUG on HyperCard
    Swivel 3D
    PD ROM

Borland International
4585 Scotts Valley Dr.
Scotts Valley, CA 95066
800/543-7543
408/438-8400
    Reflex, Reflex Plus
    SideKick
    Eureka: The Solver

Brainpower, Inc.
30497 Canwood Street
Suite 201
Agoura Hills, CA 91301
818/884-6911
800/345-0519
    ArchiText
    StatView 512+

Bravo Technologies
c/o CPAS, P.O. Box 10078
Berkeley, CA 94709
800/345-2888
415/841-8552
    MacCalc

Bridgeport Machines
500 Lindley Street
Bridgeport, CT 06606
508/842-7200
    EZ Draft

Bright Star Technology
14450 N.E. 29th Pl.
Suite 220
Bellevue, WA 98007
206/885-5446
    HyperAnimator
    Alphabet Blocks

Broderbund Software
17 Paul Dr.
San Rafael, CA 94903-2101
415/492-3500
    The Print Shop
    DTP Advisor
    Sensei Physics
    Type!
    PosterMakerPlus

Brother International
8 Corporate Place
Piscataway, NJ 08854
201/981-0300
    Brother HJL-8 Desktop Laser Printer

Bruce Tomlin
#108, 15801 Chase Hill Blvd.
San Antonio, TX 78256
    SoundMaster

Bullseye Software
P.O. Box 7900
Incline Village, NV 89450
702/265-2298
    Fokker Triplane
    Ferrari Grand Prix

C. Itoh Electronics
2025 McCabe Way
Irvine, CA 92713
800/227-0315
    ProWriter Printer

Caere Corporation
100 Cooper Court
Los Gatos, CA 95030
408/395-7000
    Omni-Page 2.0

Cambridge North America
424 Cumberland Ave.
Portland, ME 04101
800/888-3723
    Cambridge 288

Casady & Greene
P.O. Box 223779
Carmel, CA 93922
408/646-4660
    QuickDEX
    Crystal Quest
    FluentFonts

CE Software
801 73rd
Des Moines, IA 50312
515/224-1995
    MockWrite
    DiskTop
    MacBillBoard
    QuicKeys
    CalendarMaker
    MockPackage
    Vaccine

Central Point Software
15220 N.W. Greenbrier Pkwy. #200
Beaverton, OR 97006
503/690-8090
    Copy II for the Macintosh

Century Software
2306 Cotner Ave.
Los Angeles, CA 90064
415/549-1901
    LaserFonts

Ceres Software
9498 SW BarBur Blvd., #103
Portland, OR 97219
503/245-9011
    Inspiration

Chalcedony Software
5580 La Jolla Blvd.
La Jolla, CA 92037
    Prolog/m

Challenger Software
18350 Kedzie Ave.
Homewood, IL 60430
800/858-9565
312/957-3475
    Mac3D 2.0

Champion Swiftware
6617 Gettysburg Dr.
Madison, WI 53705
608/833-1777
    Spelling Champion

Chang Laboratories
5300 Stevens Creek Blvd.
San Jose, CA 95129
408/246-8020
    C.A.T.
    Rags to Riches

Channelmark
2929 Campus Dr.
San Mateo, CA 94403
415/345-5900
    HyperTutor

Claris
440 Clyde Ave.
Mountain View, CA 94043
408/727-8227
    MacPaint
    MacPaint II
    MacWrite
    FileMaker
    MacDraw, MacDraw II

CompuServe
P.O. Box 20212
Columbus, OH 43220
800/848-8199
614/457-8600
    User services

Computer Cover Company
P.O. Box 3080
Laguna Hills, CA 92654
800/235-5330
800/237-5376 (CA)
    Computer covers

Computer Friends
14250 NW Science Park Dr.
Portland, OR 97229
503/626-2291
    Modern Artist 2.0
    Dunn film recorders
    ribbon re-inkers
    Super Chroma video boards
    switches
    TV Producer video boards
    Modern Artist color paint
    printer buffers program
    Shinko color printers

Computer Technology, Ltd.
7033 Antrim Ave.
Burnaby, British Columbia
Canada V5J 4M5

Computer Associates
1240 Mckay Dr.
San Jose, CA 95131
800/533-2070
408/432-1727
    BPI General Accounting

Computer Trend
4545 N. 36th Street
Suite 111
Phoenix, AZ 85018
    JokeMaster and Hyper JokeMaster

Consulair
140 Campo Dr.
Portola Valley, CA 94025
415/851-3272
    Mac C

Coral Software
P.O. Box 307
Cambridge, MA 02142
800/521-1027
    Object Logo

Corel Systems
1600 Carling Ave.
Ottawa, Ontario K1Z 8R7
613/728-8200
    WORM Drives

Cornerstone Technology, Inc.
1883 Ringwood Ave.
San Jose, CA 95131
800/562-2552
    DualPage Display System

Crate Technology
6850 Vineland Ave., Bldg. M
North Hollywood, CA 91605
818/766-4001
800/543-5808
    Mac Crate 60M Hard Disk

Creative Solutions
4701 Randolph Road
Suite 12
Rockville, MD 20852
800/367-8465
301/984-0262
    MacForth Plus

Creighton Development
16 Hughes Street
Irvine, CA 92718
    Macspell +

Cricket Software
40 Valley Stream Pkwy.
Malvern, PA 19355
215/251-9890
    Cricket Draw
    Cricket Graph

CTA, Inc.
747 Third Ave., 3rd Floor
New York, NY 10017
212/935-2280
800/252-1442
800/668-8986 (Canada)
    TextPert (OCR)

Custom Memory Systems
826 N. Hillview Dr.
Milpitas, CA 95035
    DM Capture and removable hard
        disks

Cutting Edge
P.O. Box 1259
Evanston, WY 82930
800/443-5199
307/789-0582
    Mac-105 Keyboard

D2 Software
P.O. Box 50052
Austin, TX 78763
512/454-7746
    MacSpin

DAC Software
17950 Preston Road
Dallas, TX 75252
214/248-0205
    DacEasy Accounting

Darin Adler
2765 Marl Oak Dr.
Highland Park, IL 60035
312/433-5944
    SkipFinder and StartupDesk

DataDesk International
7650 Haskell Ave.
Van Nuys, CA 91406
818/780-1673
    HyperDialer
    MAC-101 Keyboard

DataPak Software
14011 Ventura Blvd.
Suite 507
Sherman Oaks, CA 91423
800/327-6703
818/905-6419
    Liberty Spell Checker

Dataviz
16 Winfield Street
Norwalk, CT 06855
203/268-0030
    MacLink

Dayna Communications
50 S. Main Street, 5th Floor
Salt Lake City, UT 84144
801/531-0203
    DaynaFile

Daystar
5556 Atlanta Hwy.
Flower Branch, GA 30542
800/962-2077
404/967-2077
    Novy Mac20M
    File Server
    Micro Channel
    Accelerator II

Deneba Software
7855 NW 12th Street
Suite 202
Miami, FL 33126
800/6-CANVAS
    Canvas
    Comment
    BigThesaurus and Spelling Coach

Design Science
6475-B E. Pacific Coast Hwy.
Suite 392
Long Beach, CA 90803
213/433-0685
    MathType 2.0

Dest Corp.
1201 Cadillac Court
Milpitas, CA 95035
408/946-7100
    PC Scan 1000

Diehl Graphsoft
8370 Court Ave.
Suite 202
Ellicott City, MD 21043
301/461-9488
    MiniCad +

Discovery Software International
163 Conduit Street
Annapolis, MD 21401
301/268-9877

Dove Computer
1200 N. 23rd Street
Wilmington, NC 28405
800/622-7627
919/763-7918
    RamSnap
    MacSnap memory upgrades
    FastNet

Dow Jones
P.O. Box 300
Princeton, NJ 08540
609/452-1511
    Desktop Express

Dreams of the Phoenix
P.O. Box 10273
Jacksonville, FL 32247
    Phoenix 3D
    Quick & Dirty Utilities
    SetFile

Dubl-Click Software
9316 Deering Ave.
Chatsworth, CA 91311
818/700-9525
    Calculator Construction Set
    World-Class Fonts!
    WetPaint

E-Machines
9305 SW Gemini Dr.
Beaverton, OR 97005
503/646-6699
    Monitors

F

Vendor
Guide

EDCO Services
12410 N. Dale Mabry Hwy.
Tampa, FL 33618
813/962-7800
800/523-TYPE
LetrTuck (modify kerning)

Electronic Arts
1820 Gateway Dr.
San Mateo, CA 94404
Studio/8
415/571-7171
DiskTools Plus
Chuck Yeager's Advanced Flight
Trainer
Seven Cities of Gold
Business Simulator

Emerald City Software
800 Menlo Ave.
Menlo Park, CA 94025
415/324-8080
SmartArt

Emerald City Software
P.O. Box 2103
Menlo Park, CA 94026
415/324-8080
Lasertalk

Enabling Technologies
600 S. Dearborn
Suite 1304
Chicago, IL 60605
312/427-0408
Easy 3D

Encore Ribbon
1318 Ross
Suite E
Petaluma, CA 94952
800/431-4969
Laser printer cartridge refills

Ergonomic Computer Products
1753 Greenwich Street
San Francisco, CA 94123
415/673-5757
Screen filters and much else

Ergotron
P.O. Box 17013
Minneapolis, MN 55417
800/328-9839
MacTilt and the Muzzle
Mac II Workstation
MacBuffer

Exodus Software
8620 Winton Road
Suite 304
Cincinnati, OH 45231
513/522-0011
Retriever
Express Write

ExperTelligence
5638 Hallister Ave.
Galeta, CA 93117
805/967-1797
ExperLISP
ExperCommon Lisp
ExperLogo

EZWare Corp.
P.O. Box 620
29 Bala Ave.
Suite 206
Bala Cynwyd, PA 19004
800/543-1040
215/667-4064 (PA)
EZTax-Plan Business Edition
EZTax-Plan Personal Edition
EZTax-Prep 1040

Farallon Computing
2201 Dwight Way
Berkeley, CA 94704
415/849-2331
MacRecorder
Screen Recorder and StarNET
PhoneNet

Fifth Generation Systems
11200 Industriplex Blvd.
Baton Rouge, LA 70809
504/291-7221
Suitcase
The Local Connection
PowerStation and Suitcase II
Fastback for the Macintosh

Firebird Licensees
P.O. Box 49
Ramsey, NJ 07446
Laser Author

Flexware
15404 E. Valley Blvd.
Industry, CA 91746
800/527-6587
818/961-0237
Flexware

Format Software
11770 Bernado Plaza Ct.
San Diego, CA 92128
dMac III

Foundation Publishing
10301 Yellow Circle Dr.
Minneapolis, MN 55343
612/935-4230
Enterprise

Fox Software
118 W. South Boundary
Perrysburg, OH 43551
419/874-0162 X231
FoxBASE/Mac

FreeSoft
150 Hickory Dr.
Beaver Falls, PA 15010
412/846-2700
Red Ryder

FTL Systems
234 Eglington Ave. East
Toronto, Ontario
M4P 1K5 Canada
MacTeX

Future Design Software
13681 Williamette Drive
Westminister, CA 92683
714/891-9796
Strictly Business

Futuresoft System Designs
P.O. Box 132
New York, N.Y. 10012
212/674-5195
    Writer's Workshop

FWB Software
2040 Polk Street
Suite 215
San Francisco, CA 94109
415/474-8055
    Hard Disk Util

GCC Technologies
580 Winter Street
Waltham, MA 02154
617/890-0880
    WriteMove
    Personal LaserPrinter

Generation Four, Inc.
3232 San Mateo N.E. #199
Albuquerque, NM 87110
505/294-3210
    MBA Series

Generic Software
11911 North Creek Pkwy. South
Bothell, WA 98011
206/487-2233
    Computer Aided Design and
    Drafting

Genesis Micro Software
P.O. Box 6236,
17124 N.E. Eighth Place
Bellevue, WA 98008
206/747-8512
    AutoMac III

GEnie
Dept 02B
Rockville, MD 20850
800/638-9636
301/340-4494
    On-line information service

GenRadInc
510 Cottonwood Drive
Milpitas, CA 95035
408/432-1000
    Parameter Manager Plus

GoldMind Publishing
12155 Magnolia Ave.
Suite 3-B
Riverside, CA 92503
714/785-8685
    MacGraphics

Graham Software
8609 Ingalls Circle
Arvada, CO 80003
303/422-0757
    Graham Speller

Graphsoft
8370 Court Ave.
Suite 202
Ellicott City, MD 21043
301/461-9488
    MiniCad+

Great Plains Software
Box 9739
1701 SW 38th Street
Fargo, ND 58103
701/281-0550
800/345-3276
    Business Modules

Great Wave Software
5353 Scotts Valley Drive
Scotts Valley, CA 95066
408/438-1990
    American Discovery
    KidsTime
    NumberMaze

Greene, Inc.
15 Via Chualar
Monterey, CA 93940
408/375-0910
    QuickDEX

Green Moniterm Corp.
5740 Circle Dr.
Minnetonka, MN 55343
612/935-4151
    Viking monitors

GTCO Corp.
7125 Riverwood Dr.
Columbia, MD 21046
301/381-6688
    Macintizer

Hayes Microcomputer, Inc.
5923 Peach Tree Industrial Park Blvd.
Norcross, GA 30092
800/635-1225
    Smartcom II
    InterBridge
    V-Series Smartmodem 9600

Help Software
10659A Maplewood Road
Cupertino, CA 95014
408/257-3815
    Desktop Help

Hewlett-Packard
16399 W. Bernardo Drive
San Diego, CA 92127
800/752-0900
408/447-1424
    ColorPro Graphics Plotter

HJC Software
P.O. Box 51816
Durham, NC 27717
919/490-1277
    Virex

Human Intellect Systems
1670 S. Amphlett Blvd, #326
San Mateo, CA 94402
415/571-5939
    Instant Expert Plus

Humanware
2908 Nancy Creek Road NW
Atlanta, GA 30327
404/352-3871
    McGenogram

Hyperpress Publishing
P.O. Box 8243
Foster City, CA 94404
415/345-4620
    ScriptExpert

I/O Design
P.O. Box 156
Exton, PA 19241
800/241-2122
    Colorprint

F

Vendor
Guide

ICOM Simulations
648 S. Wheeling Road
Wheeling, IL 60090
312/520-4440
  On Cue

Ideaforms
P.O. Box 1540
Fairfield, IA 52556
515/472-7256
  DiskQuick
  MacLabeler

Image Club Graphics
2915 19th Street NE
Suite 206
Calgary, Alberta
Canada, T2E 7H2
403/250-1969
  CD ROM
  Artroom

Imagenesis
901 NE Loop 410
Suite 630
San Antonio, TX 78209
  ChromaScan

INDIVIDUAL Software
125 Shoreway Road
Suite 3000
San Carlos, CA 94070-2704
800/331-3313
415/595-8855
  Typing Instructor Encore

InfoLogic
1937 Regent Street
Niskayuna, NY 12309
800/548-4124
518/370-5510
  InfoLogic Envelope

Infosphere
4730 SW Macadam Ave.
Portland, OR 97201
503/226-3620
  MacServe
  ComServeLaserServe

Innovative Data Design
2280 Bates Ave.
Suite A
Concord, CA 94520
415/680-6818
  MacDraft

Insight Development Corp.
1024 Country Club Dr.
Suite 140
Moraga, CA 94556
415/376-9500
  MacPrint

Insignia Solutions
254 Geronimo Way
Sunnyvale, CA 94086
408/522-7600

Intellisoft International
P.O. Box 6069
Novato, CA 94948
415/898-6308
  Bookmark/Mac

Interleaf
6404 Ivy Lane, #408
Greenbelt, MD 20770
617/577-9800
  MultiFinder

Interleaf, Inc.
10 Canal Park
Cambridge, MA 02141
617/577-9800
  Interleaf Publisher

International Typeface Corporation
2 Hammarskjold Plaza
New York, NY 10017
212/371-0699
  licensed laser fonts

Intuit
540 University Ave.
Palo Alto, CA 94301
415/322-0573
  Quicken

Irwin Magnetic Systems, Inc.
2101 Commonwealth Blvd.
Ann Arbor, MI 48105
313/930-9000
  Irwin Tape Backup System
  Excelerator XL 20
  Excelerator XL 25

Itty Bitty Computers
P.O. Box 6539
San Jose, CA 95150
  Autoblack

Jasmine Technologies
555 De Haro Street
San Francisco, CA 94107
415/282-1111
  Jasmine hard disks

Jerry C. Walsh, Jr.
608 Northampton Plaza
600 Airport Road
Chapel Hill, NC 27514
  Amortize 2.1

Kennect Technology
271 E. Hacienda Blv.
Campbell, CA 95008
  Rapport and Drive 2.4

Kensington Microware
251 Park Ave. South
New York, NY 10010
800/535-4242
212/475-5200 (NY)
  System Saver Mac
  Turbo Mouse ADB
  6-foot Mac II Monitor
  Cable extension kit
  7-foot ADB Keyboard Cable

Kent Marsh Limited
1200 Post Oak Blvd.
Suite 210
Houston, TX 77056
800/325-3587
  MacSafe
  olderBOLT

Kinetics, Inc.
2500 Camino Diablo
Suite 110
Walnut Creek, CA 94596
Fast Path 4
415/947-0998
    LAN Ranger

Knowledge Engineering
P.O. Box 2139
New York, NY 10116
203/622-8770
    Just Text and Color System I

Kurta
3007 Chambers Street
Phoenix, AZ 85040
303/484-5296
    Kurta Tablets

LaCie, Ltd.
16285 SW 85th, #306
Tigard, OR 97224
503/684-0143
    hard drives

Laser Connection
7852 Schillinger Park West
Mobile, AL 36608
800/523-2696
205/633-7223
    QMS-PS 810

LaserWare
P.O. Box 668
San Rafael, CA 94915
800/367-6898
415/453-9500
    LaserPaint Color II

The Learning Company
6493 Kaiser Dr.
Freemont, CA 94555
800/852-2255
415/792-2101
    Reader Rabbit

Legalware
33 Young Street
Suite 1120
Toronto, Ontario
Canada M5E 1S9
416/863-6906
    Document Compare

Letraset USA
40 Eisenhower Dr.
Paramus, NJ 07653
201/845-6100
    ImageStudio 1.5 Scanning Module
    Ready,Set,Go! 4

Levco
6160 Lusk Blvd.
Suite C203
San Diego, CA 92121
619/457-2011
    Prodigy 4 board for Mac Plus &
        512K Mac
    One Plus One

Lexpertise USA, Inc.
175 East 400 South
Suite 1000
Salt Lake City, UT 84111
800/354-5656
    MacProof

Lightgate
6202 Christie Ave.
Emeryville, CA 94608
415/596-2350
    Felix

The Lisa Shop
2438 13th Ave. S.
Minneapolis, MN 55404
612/874-8596
    Lisa (Mac XL) computers and parts

Living Videotext
117 East Street
Mountain View, CA 94043
415/964-6300
800/441-7234
    More
    ThinkTank

Logic Extension Resources
9651 Business Center Dr.
Suite C
Rancho Cucamonga, CA 91730
714/980-0046
    LXR.Test

Lundeen & Associates
P.O. Box 30038
Oakland, CA 94604
800/233-6851
415/769-7701
    WorksPlus Command
    WorksPlus Spell

M/H Group
222 West Adams Street
Chicago, IL 60606
312/443-1222
    Connect Wang and Macintosh

Mac II Review
Building 112, 240 Sunnyvale Ave.
Fairfield, CT 06430
203/334-0334

MacAmerica
18032-C Lemon Dr.
Yorba Linda, CA 92686
714/779-2922
    Laser Spool

MacGuide Magazine
550 S. Wadsworth Blvd.
Suite 500
Denver, CO 80226

MacMaster Systems
939 E. El Camino Real
Suite 122
Sunnyvale, CA 94087
408/773-9834
    Fedit Plus

MacMemory
2480 N. First Street
San Jose, CA 95131
800/862-2636
408/922-0140 (CA)
    MacChill

MacroMind
1028 W. Wolfram
Chicago, IL 60657
    VideoWorks II
    VideoWorks II Accelerator
    VideoWorks II Clip Animation

F

Vendor
Guide

Magic Software
1602 Cascio
Bellevue, NE 68005
800/342-6243
402/291-0670
    AutoSave DA

Mainstay
28611 B Canwood Street
Agoura Hills, CA 91301
818/991-6540
    Capture
    AntiToxin
    MacFlow
    MarkUP

Maitreya Design
P.O. Box 1480
Goleta, CA 93116
805/968-7578
    DiskInfo

Marvelin
3420 Ocean Park Blvd.
Suite 3020
Santa Monica, CA 90405
213/450-6813
    Business Filevision
    Filevision

MASS MICRO Systems
550 Del Rey Ave.
Sunnyvale, CA 94086-3258
800/522-7979
408/522-1200
    Data Pak

MathSoft, Inc.
One Kendall Square
Cambridge, MA 02139
800/MATHCAD
617/577-1017
    MathCAD

Maxis Computing
953 Mountain View Dr.
Lafayette, CA 94549
415/376-6434
    Sim City

MD Ideas
1111 Triton Dr.
Suite 205
Foster City, CA 94404
415/573-0580
    hard disk drives

MECA Ventures
355 Riverside Ave.
Westport, CT 06880
203/222-9087
    Managing Your Money

Metro ImageBase
18623 Ventura Blvd.
Suite 210
Tarzana, CA 91356
800/525-1552
    ReportMaker
    Business Graphics, 9-5

Micah Storage Systems
60 N. College Ave.
Suite B
Newark, DE 19711
800/782-0097
302/731-0430
    hard disk drives

Micro CAD/CAM
5900 Sepulveda Blvd.
Suite 340
Van Nuys, CA 91411
818/376-0008
    MGMS: Professional CAD for
    Macintosh

Micro Illusions
17408 Chatsworth Street
Granada Hills, CA 91344
800/522-2041
818/360-3715 (CA)
    Photon Paint

Microlytics
1 Tobay Village Office Park
Pittsford, NY 14534
716/248-9620
    Word Finder
    GOfer

MicroMaps Software, Inc.
P.O. Box 757
Lambertville, NJ 08530
609/397-1611
800/334-4291
    HyperAtlas

MicroNet Technology, Inc.
13765-A Alton Pkwy.
Irvine, CA 92718
714/837-6033
    Micro/Removable Cartridge Hard
        Disk Drive
    Micro/Stack Series Fixed Hard Disk
        Drives

MicroSeeds
4702 N. Hesperodes
Tampa, FL 33614
813/878-2142
    InitPicker

Microsoft
16011 NE 36th Way
Redmond, WA 98073
206/882-8080
    Write
    Microsoft Mail
    PowerPoint
    MS DOS Word
    Excel
    Flight Simulator
    MS DOS Works
    Microsoft Basic
    Microsoft Works

MicroSparc
52 Domino Dr.
Concord, MA 01742
617/371-1660
    Desk Necessities

MicroTech International
29 Business Park Dr.
Branford, CT 06405
800/626-4276
    Removable hard disk

Microtek Labs
680 Knox Street
Torrance, CA 90502
800/654-4160
    Microtek MSF-300C flatbed scanner

Migent, Inc.
P.O. Box 6062
Incline Village, NV 89450
800/633-3444
    Migent Pocket Modem

Miles Computing
7741 Alabama Ave.
Suite 2
Canoga Park, CA 91304
818/341-1411
Fool's Errand
Carnival

Mindscape
3444 Dundee Road
Northbrook, Il 60062
312/480-7667
GraphicWorks 1.
Balance of Power
Deja Vu
Uninvited
MasterType

Mindwork Software
555C Heritage Harbor
Monterey, CA 93940
408/375-1531
800/367-4334
MindWrite

Mobius Technologies
5300 Broadway Terrace
Oakland, CA 94618
415/654-0556

Monster Cable
101 Townsend Street
San Francisco, CA 94107
415/777-1355

Music Mouse
175 Diane Street
New York, NY 10013

National Tele-Press
P.O. Box 790
Mendocino, CA 95460
707/934-2848
MOM

NexSys
296 Elizabeth Street
New York, NY 10012
212/995-2224
Travel Mac

Niles & Associates
2200 Powell Street
Suite 765
Emeryville, CA 94608
415/655-6666
EndNote
Grant Manager

North Edge Software
239 Western Ave.
Essex, MA 01929
617/768-6100
Timeslips III

Novell, Inc.
122 East 1700 South
Provo, UT 84601
801/379-5900
NetWare

NuEquation
1701 N. Greenville Ave. #703
Richardson, TX 75081
214/699-7747
NuPaint

Nuvotech
2015 Bridgeway
Suite 204
Sausalito, CA 94965
415/331-7815
EasyView Monitors
TurboNet ST Connector

Ocean Communications
1641 N. First Street
San Jose, CA 95112
On Becoming a Desktop Publisher

Odesta
4084 Commercial Ave.
Northbrook, IL 60062
800/323-5423
312/498-5615
Double Helix and Helix
Data Desk Professional

Olduvai Software, Inc.
7520 Red Road
Suite A
South Miami, FL 33143
800/822-0772 (Orders)
305/665-4665
Icon-It!
Read-It!

Olympia USA
Route 22, P.O. Box 22
Somerville, NJ 08876
201/231-8300
NP30APL and other printers

OpCode Systems
444 Ramona
Palo Alto, Ca 94301
415/321-8977
Cue 2.1

Oracle
20 Davis Dr.
Belmont, CA 94002
800/345-3267
Oracle SQL Database

Orange Micro
1400 N. Lakeview Ave.
Anaheim, CA 92807
714/779-2772
Grappler LQ

Orchid Technology
45365 Northport Loop West
Fremont, CA 94538
415/683-0373
MacSprint II, cache card

OWL International
14218 NE 21st Street
Bellevue, WA 98007
206/747-3203

Pacific Rim Connections
3030 Atwater Dr.
Burlingame, CA 94010
Kaihin Brushwriter

The Page
P.O. Box 14493
Chicago, IL 60614
312/348-1200

Palantir Software
12777 Jones Road
Suite 100
Houston, TX 77070
800/368-3797
713/955-8787
inTalk
MacType

F

Vendor Guide

Palo Alto Shipping
P.O. Box 7430
Menlo Park, CA 94026
800/44F-ORTH
415/363-1399
    Mach II

Palo Alto Software
260 Sheridan
Palo Alto, CA 94306
415/325-3190
    Forecaster
    The Business Plan Toolkit

Palomar Software, Inc.
P.O. Box 120
Oceanside, CA 92054
619/721-7000
    Colorizer

Paracomp
123 Townsend Street
Suite 310
San Francisco, CA 94107
415/543-3848
    Swivel 3D
    Milo

Paragon Concepts
4954 Sun Valley Road
Del Mar, CA 92014
800/922-2993
619/481-1477 (CA)
    NISUS word processor
    QUED/M

PBI Software
1163 Triton Dr.
Foster City, CA 94404
415/349-8765
    HFS Locator Plus
    DeskScene

PCPC
4710 Eisenhower Blvd.
Building A4
Tampa, FL 33634
800/622-2888
813/884-3092
    HFS Backup
    MacBottom HD-70 Hard Disk
    MacBottom 45 SCSI and Internal
      Modem
    MacBottom HD-21

Peachtree Software
4355 Shackleford Road
Norcross, GA 30093
800/247-3224
404/564-5700
    Back to Basics Accounting

Peripheral Land
47800 Westinghouse Dr.
Fremont, CA 94539
415/657-2211
    Hard disks
    TurboBack
    TurboCache
    TurboOptimizer
    TurboSpool

Peripherals, Computers and Supplies
2457 Perkiomen Ave.
Mount Penn, PA 19606
215/779-0522
    VersaTerm-Pro

Personal Training Systems
P.O. Box 54240
San Jose, CA 95154
408/559-8635
    LearnWord 3.0

Personal Writer
1801 Ave. of the Stars
Suite 507
Los Angeles, CA 90067
800/322-4744
213/556-1628
    Personal Writer PW15 S

Personics Corp.
2353 Main Street
Building #2
Concord, MA 01742
617/897-1575
    VCS

PostCraft International
27811 Hopkins Ave.
Suite 6
Valencia, CA 91355
805/257-1797
    Postility

Power R
1606 Dexter Ave. North
Seattle, WA 98109
206/547-8000
    MacLarger

Practical Computer Applications
1305 Jefferson Hwy.
Champlin, MN 55316
612/427-4789
    Lunar Rescue
    MacGolf
    MacRacquetball

Preferred Publishers, Inc.
5100 Poplar Ave.
Suite 617
Memphis, TN 38137
800/446-6393
901/683-3383
    DAtabase

Presentation Technologies
743 N. Pastoria Ave.
Sunnyvale, CA 94086
408/749-1959
    ImageMaker

Primera Software
650 Cragmont Ave.
Berkeley, CA 94708
415/525-3000
    Different Drummer

Pro Plus Software
2150 E. Brown Road
Mesa, AZ 85203
602/830-8835
    Wall Street Investor

Prometheus Products
7225 SW Bonita Road
Tigard, OR 97223
503/624-0571
    Mac Modem with Red Ryder
     communications software

ProVue Development
15180 Transistor Lane
Huntington Beach, CA 92649
714/892-8199
    OverVUE
    Panorama

QMS
One Magnum Pass
Mobile, AL 36618
205/633-4300
    QMS ColorScript 100
    QMS PS2400 Printer

Qualitas Trading Co.
6907 Norfolk Road
Berkeley, CA 94804
415/848-8080
    Japanese Clip Art
    MacCalligraphy

Quark
300 S. Jackson
Suite 100
Denver, CO 80209
800/356-9363
303/934-2211
    QuarkXPress
    QuarkStyle

Qume Corporation
500 Yosemite Dr.
Milpitas, CA 95035
408/942-4000
    CrystalPrint Publisher

Radius
1710 Fortune Drive
San Jose, CA 95131
408/434-1010
    Radius Accelerator 25
    Accelerator boards
    Monitors

Rainbow Bridge Software, Inc.
4243 Hunt Road
Suite 210
Cincinnati, OH 45242
800/548-8871
513/984-6861
    Unitize

Raymond Lau
100-04 70th Ave.
Forest Hills, NY 11375
    Stuffit

Rebus
2330-B Walsh Ave.
Santa Clara, CA 95051
800/654-5157
800/247-4994 (CA)
408/727-0110

Redgate Communications
660 Beachland Blvd.
Vero Beach, FL 32963
407/231-6904

Relisys
320 South Milpitas Blvd.
Milpitas, CA 95035
408/945-1062
    Relisys Fax machines

RGB Technology
6862 Elm
Suite 320
McLean, VA 22101
703/556-0667
    Mac II color printer

Rodime Systems
901 Broken Sound Pkwy. NW
Boca Raton, FL 33487
407/994-5585
    Hard Disks

Rubicon
2111 Dickson Dr.
Austin, TX 78704
    Dinner at Eight

SBT
One Harbor Dr.
Sausalito, CA 94965
415/331-9900
    SBT Accounting

ScanCoFurn
P.O. Box 3217
Redmond, WA 98073
800/722-6263
    MacTable and add-on cabinet
      modules

Screenplay Systems
150 E. Olive Ave.
Suite 305
Burbank, CA 91502
818/843-6557
    Scriptor

Seikosha America
1111 MacArthur Blvd.
Mahwah, NJ 07430
800/338-2609
    SP-1000AP printer

Sensible Software
335 East Big Beaver
Suite 207
Troy, MI 48083
313/528-1950
    Sensible Grammar

Shana Corporation
105, 9650-20 Ave.
Edmonton, Alberta
Canada T6N 1G1
403/463-3330
    FastForms! Construction Kit

Sher-Mark Products
521 E. 83rd Street
Suite 2R
New York, NY 10028
212/249-0494
    Anti-Glare Magnification Screen

Shiva
155 Second Street
Cambridge, MA 02141
800/458-3550
617/864-8500
    NetModem
    NetBridge

ShopKeeper Software
P.O. Box 38160
Tallahassee, FL 32315
904/222-8808
    ShopKeeper 4

Sigma Designs
46501 Landing Pkwy.
Fremont, CA 94538
415/770-0100
    LaserView monitors

Signature Software
2151 Brown Ave.
Bensalem, PA 19020
215/639-8764
    McSink

F

Vendor
Guide

Silicon Beach Software
P.O. Box 261430
San Diego, CA 92126
619/695-6956
SuperPaint
Beyond Dark Castle
Dark Castle
Super 3D

Simon & Schuster
One Gulf & Western Plaza
New York, NY 10023
800/624-0023
800/624-0024 (NJ)
Typing Tutor IV

Softstream International, Inc.
19 White Chapel Dr.
Mount Laurel, NJ 08054
800/262-6610
UltraSpec

Softsync
162 Madison Ave.
New York, N.Y. 10016
212/685-2080
Accountant, Inc.

Softview
4820 Adohr Ln.
Suite F
Camarilo, CA 93010
805/388-2626
MacInUse
MacInTax

Software Complement
8 Pennsylvania Ave.
Matamoros, PA 18336
714/491-2495
Complementary Type laser fonts

Software Ventures
2907 Claremont Ave.
Suite 220
Berkeley, CA 94705
800/336-6477
800/336-6478 (CA)
415/644-3232
MicroPhone II

Software Power Company
P.O. Box 13133
Fremont, CA 94539
415/490-6086
Power UP

Software Research Technology
22901 Mill Creek Dr.
Laguna Hills, CA 92653
MacTree

Software Toolworks
19808 Nordhoff Place
Chatsworth, CA 91311
818/885-9000
Mavis Beacon Teaches Typing!

Solana Electronics
7887 Dunbrook Road
Suite A
San Diego, CA 92126
619/566-1701
I-Server

Solutions International
P.O. Box 9089
30 Commerce Street
Williston, VT 05495
802/658-5506
Curator
SuperGlue
The Clipper and SmartScrap
Back Fax

Sophisticated Circuits
1314 NE 43rd
Suite 216
Seattle, WA 98105
206/547-4779
Macs-A-Million memory upgrades

Source Net
P.O. Box 6727
Santa Barbara, CA 93160
805/494-7123
The MACintosh Book of Fonts

Spectrum Holobyte
2061 Challenger Dr.
Alameda, CA 94501
415/522-3584
Falcon
Gato
Orbiter
PT-109
Tellstar
Tetris

Springboard Software
7808 Creekridge Circle
Minneapolis, MN 55435
800/445-4780
Springboard Publisher

Star/Monogram
367 Van Ness Ave.
Torrance, CA 90501
800/356-5988
213/533-1190
Business Sense
Dollars and Sense

STAX!
8008 Shoal Creek Blvd.
Austin, TX 78758
800/MAC-STAX
The Macintosh Bible, HyperCard
edition

Steve Michel
1027 Pomona
Albany, CA 94706
415/528-2418
HyperCard programs

STF Technologies
P.O. Box 247
Higginsville, MO 64037
FAXstf

Storage Dimensions
2145 Hamilton Ave.
San Jose, CA 95125
408/879-0300
MacinStor

Studio Advertising Art
P.O. Box 18432-52
Las Vegas, NV 89114
Click & Clip

Summagraphics Corp.
777 State Street Extension
Fairfield, CT 06430
    MacTablet

Sun Microsystems
950 Marina Village Pkwy.
Alameda, CA 94501
415/769-8700
800/445-8677
    InBox

Sun Remarketing
P.O. Box 4059
Logan, UT 84321
800/821-3221
800/752-7631
    Lisa (Mac XL) computers and parts

Sun Valley Software
198 Sun Valley Dr.
Winnipeg, Manitoba
Canada R2G 2W7
    Toccata music notation program

SuperMac Technologies
485 Potrero Ave.
Sunnyvale, CA 94086
408/245-2202
    SuperSpool
    SpeedCard accelerator boards
    Memory upgrades
    Sentinel
    DataFrame hard disks
    PixelScan
    DiskFit
    SuperRam 2
    SuperLaserSpool

Survivor Software, Ltd.
11222 La Cienega Blvd.
Suite 450
Inglewood, CA 90304
213/410-9527
    MacMoney

Symantec Corp
10201 Torre Ave.
Cupertino, CA 95014
408/253-9600
    MORE II
    Symantec Utilities for Macintosh
    THINK's Lightspeed C
    THINK's Lightspeed Pascal

Symmetry Corp.
761 E. University Dr.
Mesa, AZ 85203
800/624-2485
602/844-2199
    Hyper DA
    Acta

Systat, Inc.
1800 Sherman Ave.
Evanston, IL 60201
312/864-5670
    FASTAT

Systems Control
P.O. Box 788 M
Iron Mountain, MI 49801
800/451-6866
    MacGard Surge Supressor

T/Maker
1390 Villa Street
Mountain View, CA 94041
415/962-0195
    Holidays and WriteNow
    ClickArt Business Image
    ClickArt Christian Images
    ClickArt EPS Illustrations
    ClickArt

Target Software
14206 SW 136th Street
Miami, FL 33186
800/622-5483
305/252-0892
    MacLightning

Taxan USA Corp.
161 Nortech Pkwy.
San Jose, CA 95134
800/544-3888
408/946-3400
    high-resolution, monochrome, and
      color monitors
    Tecmar
    Solon
    Ohio
    Nulink System

Tecmar, Inc.
6225 Cochran Road
Solon, OH 44139
216/349-0600
    Nulink System

Tektronix
P.O. Box 500
Station 76-260
Beaverton, OR 97077
800/835-6100
503/235-7202
    4693D Color Printer

Tele-Robotics International
8410 Oak Ridge Hwy.
Knoxville, TN 37931
615/690-5600
    Course Builder

Think Technologies
135 South Road
Bedford, MA 01730
800/64-THINK
617/275-4800

Thunderware, Inc.
21 Orinda Way
Orinda, CA 94563
415/254-6581
    ThunderScan
    LightningScan

Timeline
P.O. Box 60
Ypsilanti, MI 48179
313/483-3939
    Battle Stations

TimeWand Manager
1105 N.E. Circle Blvd.
Corvallis, OR 97330-4285

TML Systems
8837-B Goodbys Executive Dr.
Jacksonville, FL 32217
904/636-8592
    TML Source Code Library
    TML Database Toolkit
    TML (MacLanguage Series) Pascal

Tom Swain
2560 Bancroft Way
Suite 117
Berkeley, CA 94704
    MacChimney

F

Vendor
Guide

TOPS
950 Marina Village Pkwy.
Alameda, CA 94501
415/769-8700
TOPS
Flashbox

Toyogo
76 Bedord Street
Lexington, MA 02173
617/861-0488
GO Master

Traveling Software
19310 North Creek Pkwy.
North Creek Corp. Center
Bothell, WA 98011
206/483-8088
LapLink Mac

Truevision, Inc.
7351 Shadeland Station
Suite 100
Indianapolis, IN 46256
Macintosh II Videographics Card

Unison Software
415 Clyde Ave.
Mountain View, CA 94043
Klondike

US MicroLabs
1611 Headway Circle
Bldg. 3
Austin, TX 78754
512/3399-0001
800/552-7654
FontSizer

Ventana Press
P.O. Box 2468
Chapel Hill, NC 27515
919/942-0220
Looking Good In Print

VersaCAD
2124 Main Street
Huntington Beach, CA 92648
714/960-7720
VersaCAD

Videx, Inc
1105 NE Circle Blvd.
Corvallis, OR 97330
503/758-0521
TimeWand (bar code reader)

Virginia Systems Software Services, Inc.
5509 West Bay Ct.
Midlothian, VA 23112
804/739-3200
Roundup!

The Voyager Co.
1351 Pacific Coast Hwy.
Santa Monica, CA 90401
800/446-2001
800/443-2001 (CA)
213/451-1383
Amanda Stories, Vol. I & Vol. II

Williams and Macias, Inc.
South 3707 Godfrey Blvd.
Spokane, WA 99204
800/752-4400
509/458-6312
DiskFinder

Wolfram Research
P.O. Box 6059
Champaign, IL 61821
217/398-0700
Mathematica

WordPerfect
1555 N. Technology Way
Orem, UT 84057
801/225-5000
WordPerfect

Working Software, Inc.
P.O. Box 1844
Santa Cruz, CA 95061
408/423-5696
QuickLetter
FindsWell
Spellswell
Lookup

Wu Corporation
P.O. Box 699
Avon, CT 06001
203/677-1528
FeiMa

X-10 (USA) Inc.
185A LeGrand Ave.
Northvale, NJ 07647
201/784-9700
CP290M Home Control Interface

Xanatech
20 Fresh Pond Place
Cambridge, MA 02138
Mishu

XTree Co.
4330 Santa Fe Road
San Luis Obispo, CA 93401
805/541-0604
XTreeMac

Your Affordable Software Company
1525 N. Elston Ave.
Chicago, IL 60622
312/235-9412
12-foot and 25-foot keyboard cables

Zedcor, Inc.
4500 E. Speedway
Suite 22
Tucson, AZ 85712
800/482-4567
602/881-8101
DeskPaint

Glossary

30 percent rule. A rule for determining the positioning of points and Bezier control handles. According to Adobe Systems, Inc., the distance from a Bezier control handle to its point should be approximately 30 percent of the length of its segment. See also *Bezier curves.*

64K ROM. Original ROM size used on the Mac 128 and 512. Followed by 128K ROM. See also *Read-only memory (ROM).*

128K ROM. ROM that is standard on the Mac Plus, SE, and Mac 512K enhanced. See also *Read-only memory (ROM).*

256K ROM. Standard ROM on the Mac SE/30, II, IIx, and IIcx. See also *Read-only memory (ROM).*

Accelerator board. An option card; when installed in the Macintosh, allows it to operate and manipulate data at a faster rate.

Acoustic modem. A modem with two cups that fit around the earpiece and mouthpiece of a telephone. It converts a computer's signals into sound and back again. See also *Modem.*

Active window. The closest window on the desktop, which has a highlighted title bar.

Alarm Clock. A desk accessory that displays the current date and time. The alarm can be set to alert you at a specified time.

Alert box. A box that displays a warning when you are asking the Macintosh to do something that may cause loss of data, or when you are attempting to do something "illegal." See also *Dialog box.*

Apple desktop bus (ADB). The connectors on the back of the Macintosh, that allow connection of the keyboard, mouse, joysticks, graphics tablets, touch screens, track balls, and so forth, up to 16 input devices.

Apple HD SC Setup. A System utility file packaged with the Macintosh. It is used to initialize and set up an Apple hard disk.

Apple key (⌘). This key, when pressed in combination with other keys, performs an action or command. Also known as the Command key.

Apple menu. The leftmost menu at the top of the Macintosh screen. This menu is where you will find the Control Panel and Chooser DAs.

AppleTalk network. A communications network used to connect Macintoshes and share peripheral devices, such as printers. AppleTalk is the communication protocol by which data is transferred.

Application. A program that allows the user to create, enter, and design information. Examples are word processors, spreadsheets, and paint programs.

Application template. A file developed to be used to guide the creation of designs or documents. See also *Template*.

Arrow keys. The four keys that move the insertion point left, right, up, and down in a word processor and change the active cell in a spreadsheet.

ASCII (American Standard Code for Information Interchange). A standard computer text format in which each character is represented by seven bits. See also *Text file*.

Assembler. A program that translates symbolic codes, or assembly language, to machine language. See also *Compiler*.

Asynchronous communication. A means of transmitting data between computers. A special signal indicates when each character starts and stops.

Auto answer. The capability of a modem to answer an incoming call and establish communications without human assistance.

Autocall. The capability of a modem to place a telephone call under the control of a computer.

Autotrace. A feature in drawing and page layout applications, that allows the user to trace around shapes and lines of an image.

Background execution. A program that can continue operating without user commands and without interrupting a procedure operating in the foreground. See also *MultiFinder* and *Multitasking*.

Baseline. The horizontal line that defines the bottom of each character in a font family (excluding the descenders).

BASIC (Beginner's All-purpose Symbolic Instruction Code). A common programming language that is easy to learn but relatively inflexible.

Baud rate. A measure of speed equal to one signal per second. One baud represents one bit per second (bps). Common baud rates are 300, 1200, and 2400.

Beta test. The first test outside of the laboratory of a new product. This test is the final step before a full market release. Many product bugs are found in the beta test release, and producers do not consider the beta version to be a final version.

Bezier curves. Mathematical equations that describe the outlines that create PostScript fonts. See also *30 percent rule*.

Bit (binary digit). The smallest unit of computer information. A 1 or a 0 code electronically represents, respectively, on or off.

Bit-mapped image. An image consisting of dots, in which one dot represents one or more bits of the image (depending on whether color or other attributes are used). A Mac Plus uses one bit per dot. See also *Font*.

Bomb. An abnormal termination of a program. A bomb occurs when a program unexpectedly halts due to a bug, or it encounters data conditions it cannot handle. See also *Bug*.

Boot. To start a computer by loading the operating system (System file and Finder) into memory. The operating system software tells the Macintosh how to load other programs.

Bridge. A device that lets you connect networks so that members on one network can communicate with members on another network. See also *Gateway*.

Buffer. A section of memory that temporarily holds information from I/O (input/output) communications, including data transfer via modem, or reading and writing to your disk. The buffer holds information when the computer is sending information faster than the device can receive it.

Bug. A problem in a software program. Initially named after a moth that caused the failure of an early computer (1945) at Harvard University. Today, a bug usually refers to an inappropriate or inaccurate line of programming code that causes the program to halt execution or respond incorrectly. See also *Bomb*.

Bulletin board system (BBS). A messaging system which is maintained on a computer and can be accessed through a modem and telephone line. BBS systems are places where you can post and read bulletins, and even download or upload public domain and shareware software.

Bundled software. The Macintosh computer comes with software included, such as the System Tools disk, Utilities disk, and HyperCard. This is a packaged deal which includes hardware and software.

Button. A location in a dialog box or HyperCard card where the user can click to initiate a command for the Macintosh to take some predefined action.

Byte. A measure of the amount of information equivalent to the memory needed to store a character of the alphabet. 1,024 bytes are equivalent to 1K of memory. A Macintosh byte is made up of eight bits; it has eight 1s and 0s per byte.

Calculator. A desk accessory that looks and acts just like a four-function calculator.

Cancel button. A button that appears in dialog boxes. The user may click this button to cancel a command. The Cancel command allows the user to stop a program or application that is running, without saving any results or changes to that point.

Caps Lock key. A key located on the lower left corner of the Macintosh standard keyboard, that when pressed causes alphabetic characters to be displayed in uppercase format. Caps Lock does not affect numeric keys or symbols.

Carrier detect. A function of a modem, which detects whether there is another modem sending a carrier signal. If the carrier signal is not detected, your modem will generally disconnect itself and hang up.

Cathode ray tube (CRT). The screen used in computers in which light produced by a cathode strikes a phosphor coating on the screen.

CDEV file. A utility program placed in the System folder and controlled from the Control Panel.

Central processing unit (CPU). The computer's main information processing unit. In a Macintosh, the CPU is a single silicon chip called the microprocessor.

Chip. A tiny piece of silicon with an integrated electronic circuit on its surface.

Chooser. A desk accessory that allows the user to choose the printer on which the document is to be printed. For the Chooser to function, the printer resource files must be installed in the current System file. In a networking environment, the Chooser can be used to connect and disconnect from the network as well as to choose among devices connected to the network.

Click. Place the cursor (arrow) on an item on-screen and quickly press and release the mouse button.

Clip art. Art work purchased on disk. Clip art can be a bit-mapped graphic image, an object graphic, or even an Encapsulated PostScript file.

Clipboard. A temporary storage location, which holds cut and copied information.

Close. A command that closes a window or document.

Close box. A small box located at the top left of a document window. Clicking inside the close box causes the program to prompt the user to save the last changes to the document and close the current window.

Color separations. A process used in offset printing in which separate plates are used to print different colors of ink on a page with multiple colors. As the name implies, each color has its own plate.

Command. A menu option that causes an action to take place. A command tells the Macintosh what to do next.

Command key. See *Apple key.*

Commercial software. Software that is copyrighted and sold for profit. Commercial software cannot be copied and distributed to others without the approval of the software publisher.

Compiler. A program that translates source code to machine language. See *Assembler.*

Computer-aided design (CAD). Applications that take advantage of the power of the computer to design architectural, mechanical, electrical, civil, schematic, IC, and various other types of drawings. Utilizing the two- and three-dimensional capabilities of the application, the user can develop complex structures. Commonly referred to as Computer-Aided-Drafting and Design (CADD).

Condensed type. A typeface in which the space between the characters is less than the normal spacing of the typeface. See also *Font* and *Kerning.*

Control (Ctrl) key. A key located on the left side of the standard keyboard, whose function varies depending on the application being used.

Control Panel. A desk accessory in the Macintosh System file. It is used to personalize such features as the pattern on the desktop, the speed of the mouse movement, and the volume of the warning beep.

Copy. A command used to make an exact replica of anything—a letter, an entire document, a graphic, an application, or even a disk. The Copy command is located in the Edit menu. Using Copy does not modify or delete the original.

Copy protected. A method of preventing unauthorized duplication or use of software. See also *Write-protect tab*.

Current start-up disk. The start-up disk whose System files the Macintosh is using.

Cursor. An icon indicating the current mouse location on your screen. The Macintosh has a variety of cursor shapes including a vertical bar, I-beam, pointer, and wristwatch. See also *Insertion point*.

Cut. A command that removes selected information from a document and temporarily places it in the Clipboard.

Cylinder. The total number of disk tracks that can be written or read for a specific disk-head position. On a double-sided floppy disk, a cylinder is two tracks; on a hard disk it consists of four or more tracks. See also *Cylinder* and *Track*.

Data. Also called information. The information processed by a computer application.

Database. A collection of related information organized for storage and retrieval. For example, a database may contain names, addresses, and phone numbers.

Data fork. The portion of a Macintosh disk file containing the user's data.

Delete key. Using the Delete key to remove information from a document is the same as using the Cut command except that the information is not placed on the Clipboard; it is deleted permanently. See also *Cut*.

Delimiter. A special character used by applications and communications software to indicate the end of a line or to separate one field from another or one record from another.

Desk Accessory. A small application located in the System file, which is accessible from the Apple menu. Examples are the Alarm Clock, Chooser, and Control Panel. Other more elaborate desk accessories are minispreadsheets, a thesaurus, and a bibliography maker.

Desktop. The work area of the Macintosh. The screen, disk icons, trash can, and menu bar that you see when you first start your Mac.

Desktop file. A file created on all Macintosh disks by the Finder. It is hidden from the user and contains information the Finder uses to locate files, folders, and icons.

Desktop publishing. An integrated package of certain applications that allow the user to design the layout of pages, determine the size and location of graphics, modify and locate text, and produce a document. Desktop publishing programs integrate page layout, text entry, graphics design, and printing into one application.

Dialog box. A message from the Macintosh requesting further action or information from the user. In most instances, the user responds by typing a response or clicking a button. When the display is accompanied by a beep, the user is being warned that something may happen that the user has not anticipated. See *Alert box.*

Digitizer pad. A peripheral device that is similar to the mouse but allows the user to select drawing tools, menu commands, and other functions, as well as draw shapes without using the applications interface.

Dimmed command. When a menu command is dimmed, the user cannot use that command at that moment. Usually, another command must be completed or a selection needs to be made before the dimmed command can be accessed.

Dimmed icon. A dimmed icon represents a document, folder, or application on a disk that has been ejected. Its image still resides on the desktop for you to open, but the contents of the folder or disk cannot be opened.

Direct-connect modem. A modem that connects directly from the computer into the telephone line outlet and bypasses the telephone handset.

Directory window. The window that lists the contents of a disk. Using the View menu, the user can alter the appearance of the directory and have the contents displayed in small icons, large icons, and words.

Disk. A device utilizing a magnetic medium designed to store information. The Macintosh uses 3.5-inch hard-case floppy disks. Disks can be floppy disks or hard disk disks. A typical floppy disk can be single-sided (400K), double-sided (800K), or double-sided (1.4M). Hard disks can range from 10 to 300+ megabytes.

Disk drive. A disk drive holds the disk and retrieves and stores information. A floppy disk drive (3.5 inch) holds the floppy disk that the user inserts. A hard disk drive has a built-in disk that is permanently installed.

Disk drive port. A port on the Macintosh designed to be connected to an external floppy disk drive.

Disk server. A disk drive, generally on a network, that is available to all users. A server divides the hard disk into several volumes and treats each volume as if it were a separate disk.

Document. A generic term describing whatever the user creates using an application on the Macintosh. A document can be a letter, article, picture, table, or spreadsheet worksheet, among others. A document contains the information the user has entered and saved.

DOS (disk operating system). Every computer needs a form of DOS to function properly. Macintoshes use Mac OS. Apple II computers use DOS 3.3, ProDOS, and GS/OS. IBM type computers use DOS 3.3, 4.0, and OS/2.

Dot-matrix printer. A printer that forms characters and graphics out of dots.

Dots per inch (dpi). A measure of screen and printer resolution. The higher the number the better the resolution. The ImageWriter II operates at 144 dpi, and the LaserWriters operate at 300 dpi. See also *Resolution*.

Double-click. Used to open applications, documents, or folders. Double-clicking is performed by clicking the mouse button twice in rapid succession.

Download. A procedure in which a user transfers data from a remote computer's database to the user's computer and stores the data on a hard or floppy disk.

Drag. A technique used to move icons from one location to another, such as moving a file from one folder to another. The user moves the cursor to the icon, clicks it, and while holding down the mouse button, moves the mouse.

Driver. Software that tells the Macintosh how to operate an external device, such as a printer. A driver is located in the System folder.

Duplex. In communications, duplex allows for two-way communication. A half-duplex communication transmission can go only one way at a time. In full-duplex communication, transmission occurs both ways at the same time.

E-mail. Electronic mail. A messaging system that enables the user to send and receive "mail" to and from other people on the electronic network. A message can be as simple as a quick note or as complex as multiple documents and files. Some E-mail applications allow the user to "conference" in real-time just like a telephone conference call except the users type their questions and responses.

Edit menu. A menu that contains the copying and cutting features and the Undo command.

Electronic mail. See *E-mail*.

Em space. A space that is the width of the letter *M* in a specified typeface and type size. See also *En space*, *Font*, *Kerning*, and *Leading*.

En space. A space that is the width of the letter *N* in a specified typeface and type size, usually half the width of an em space. See also *Em space*, *Font*, *Kerning*, and *Leading*.

Encrypt. The substitution of characters to hide the contents of a document.

Enter key. Similar to the Return key. A key that confirms an entry.

Expansion slot. A location inside the Macintosh that allows for installation of an option card to perform additional functions. See also *Option card*.

Field. A piece of data in a database record.

File. Information stored on a disk. Also called a document.

File server. A node on a network, that has a disk drive and software available to all users. File-server software controls access to individual files and multi-user software allows several users simultaneous access to the same file.

Fill. To paint an enclosed area with black, white, color, or shade.

Finder. The Finder keeps the desktop organized, allowing the user to find and open files or folders. The Finder must always be in the System folder for your Macintosh to operate properly.

FKEY. An FKEY is a program similar to a desk accessory, that runs when one of the numeric keys along the top of the keyboard and the ⌘ and Shift keys are pressed. An example is ⌘-Shift-1, which ejects a disk. The extended keyboard has a row of 15 FKEYs across its top.

Floppy disk. A 3.5-inch flexible disk contained in a semi-rigid plastic casing, used primarily in Macintosh computers.

Folder. Just like the folders you have in your file cabinet at the office. It holds related information in one location. A folder can contain files, other folders, graphics documents, or any type of information. It allows for organization as the user wants to organize.

Font. A font is a collection of letters, punctuation marks, numbers, and symbols that appear in the same typeface, style, and size. The Macintosh comes with a number of different fonts, such as Monaco, Chicago, and Geneva. See also *Bit-mapped image*, *Outline fonts*, and *PostScript*.

Font/DA. A file that stores fonts and desk accessories. It is identified by a suitcase-shaped icon. To open a suitcase file and transfer its contents from one System file to another, you need the Font/DA Mover program packaged with your Macintosh software.

Gateway. In a computer network, the hardware and software used to connect two different types of computer networks. See also *Bridge*.

Gigabyte (GB). One billion bytes (1,073,741,824 bytes).

Grouping. A feature of drawing and page layout applications in which two or more objects are combined so that they are treated as one object.

Handshake. The protocol used to establish communication between two computers or a computer and a device. See also *Protocol*.

Hard disk drive. A disk drive contained inside or outside the Macintosh. The drive contains permanently installed disks that hold much more information than does the floppy disk and operates faster in the retrieval of information.

Hardware. The physical parts of the Macintosh. The screen, keyboard, mouse, disk drives, casing, cables, and all the electronic mechanisms and boards inside the Macintosh.

Hayes-compatible modem. A modem that uses the Hayes AT Command Set developed by Hayes Microcomputer Products.

Header. Text that is automatically printed at the top of each page.

Hierarchical File System (HFS). A system that allows the user to organize information with folders. The user can organize applications, documents, and other folders within folders to create levels in a hierarchy. See also *Macintosh File System*.

Highlight. Usually means to select something so that it appears different from the surrounding information. When a piece of information is highlighted, the user can initiate a command to modify that information, for example, to select a word and make it boldface.

HyperCard. An application developed by Bill Atkinson. It is a user-modifiable, object-oriented environment. With a scripting language called HyperTalk, you program HyperCard to create applications called stacks. Stacks are made up of cards that have buttons, icons, and fields which can perform other functions or can be linked to other stacks or cards. See also *HyperTalk*.

HyperTalk. The programming language used to program HyperCard stacks and create user-defined functions. HyperTalk is an English-like scripting language. See also *HyperCard*.

I-beam. The shape of the cursor when the user is entering information or editing text.

Icon. A graphic representation of a file, folder, disk, or command. An icon is similar to a sign representing information. For example, a file is generally represented as a sheet of paper, and a folder looks like a manila folder.

Impact printer. A printer that forms characters by striking an inked ribbon against paper.

Initialize. To prepare a disk to be used by the Macintosh. Generally, initializing a disk means that the Macintosh will structure the disk into sectors and tracks. Also called formatting a disk.

INIT file. A utility file located in the System folder. Once an INIT file is in the System folder and the Macintosh is restarted, the INIT file becomes active and modifies the way your Macintosh works.

Inkjet printer. A printer that forms characters by spraying tiny streams of ink on to the paper.

Insertion point. The location in a document where the user may insert something. The insertion point is selected by placing the cursor where the insertion is to occur and clicking once. A blinking I-beam appears at that point. See also *Cursor*.

Integrated software. A software package containing a spreadsheet, database, word processor, and telecommunications in which the component programs freely exchange data.

Interface. Refers to how your Mac interacts with peripheral devices, such as printers and networks. How you work with your Mac is called the Human Interface.

Internal modem. A modem installed into a computer slot. In the Macintosh, it can be installed only in the SE and II families.

Kerning. In word processors, page layout software, and advanced drawing applications, adjusting the spacing between letters. Typically used to reduce the space between pairs of letters.

Kilobits per second (Kbps). Thousands of bits per second; a measure of data transfer speed.

Kilobyte (K). 1,024 bytes. A common measure of file size. A typical double-spaced typewritten page is 1.5K.

Landscape printing. A page orientation in which the printer prints the image horizontally. The page top is the longest side of the paper.

Laptop computer. A portable computer about the size of a small briefcase. Can be easily moved and accessed in any setting. Apple is in the process of developing a laptop Macintosh.

Laser printer. A printer that forms characters and graphics by moving a laser beam across a photoconductive drum. The printer then projects the image on to paper. Macintosh laser printers are called LaserWriters. See also *Toner.*

Leading. The amount of vertical spacing, in points, between baselines of type.

Local Area Network (LAN). Computers linked with cables and software. The computers can share files and external devices, such as printers and disk drives. Many offices are linked with LANs to improve communication and efficiency.

LocalTalk. The hardware portion of Apple's LAN system used to connect Macintoshes to LaserWriters and other Macs.

Macintosh File System (MFS). A method of organizing files and folders where folders cannot be nested within folders. See *Hierarchical File System.*

Macintosh User Group. An association of Macintosh enthusiasts of varying levels of proficiency who meet to discuss a variety of issues related to the Macintosh. Many user groups have a newsletter and BBS, which keeps members updated about current Macintosh information and tips. Call Apple to find the one nearest you.

Macro. A small computer program, usually developed with a macro maker application, that can be activated to do repetitive tasks simply by typing a key combination.

Mainframe computer. A large-capacity computer shared by many users. The CPU is generally housed in an air-conditioned room, and the terminals are located at various sites.

Megabyte (M). A measure of size representing 1,048,576 bytes of storage capacity on a disk or in RAM.

Menu. A list of commands available to the user. A menu can be opened by placing the cursor on the menu title at the top of the screen and clicking.

Menu bar. The menu bar is located at the top of your screen. It lists the menus available to the Macintosh user. Also see *Menu.*

Microcomputer. A small, relatively inexpensive computer developed primarily for use by a single person. Also referred to as a personal computer or home computer. The Macintosh is a microcomputer.

Microprocessor. A small silicon chip containing a huge number of electronic components. The microprocessor chip can operate on large amounts of information when used with other computer components.

Modem (modulator/demodulator). A peripheral device that allows computers to communicate by telephone lines.

Monitor. The screen associated with a computer. The Macintosh Plus and SE monitor is located directly above the disk drives, all contained in one cabinet. The Macintosh II has a separate monitor, which is not enclosed with the CPU or disk drives. Monitors can be color or monochrome.

Mouse. A device used to navigate on the Macintosh screen. The mouse can be used to access the menus and select information. When you move the mouse, the cursor moves on-screen in the corresponding direction.

Mouse button. The button located on top of the mouse. By pressing the mouse button (clicking), you initiate an action.

MultiFinder. A component of the Macintosh's System software that allows the user to load into memory multiple applications and switch between them. MultiFinder also allows for concurrent tasks to take place at (seemingly) the same time. This process is also known as multitasking.

Multitasking. A computer capability in which two or more programs are loaded into memory simultaneously. The CPU attends to all programs at once by switching back and forth between them, which is called time slicing. See also *MultiFinder*.

Network. A computer communication pathway using hardware and software that link multiple computers and peripheral devices so that each computer or device shares information. See also *Node*.

Node. A device on a network, that can send and receive information. See also *Network*.

Null modem. A cable connecting two computers. Used instead of a modem for communication purposes.

On-line help. A file contained within an application, that provides help while the user is still operating the application.

On-line services. A variety of databases available to users who have a modem and telecommunications software. They offer access to business, education, travel, and entertainment databases among others. Two popular on-line services are CompuServe and GEnie.

Open. The act of accessing a document for modification or viewing.

Operating system. The System software, which controls the functioning of the Macintosh and the direction of information flow among computer components. See also *System software*.

Optical character recognition. A technology by which printed characters are optically scanned and translated into software text that the computer can process. The hardware that has this capability is known as an optical character reader (OCR) scanner.

Optical disc. A disc on which music or data is recorded in the form of small deformations. The data or music is retrieved with a laser beam.

Option card. An option card is generally a specialized piece of electronic circuits on a card. Option cards enhance the performance of your Macintosh. An example is the installation of an accelerator card. See also *Expansion slot*.

Outline font. A PostScript font formed of outlines, which are then filled in. See also *Bit-mapped image*, *Font*, and *PostScript*.

Pack/unpack. To compress data for the purpose of storage or transmission. Unpacking is decompressing a file and returning it to its normal state.

Page preview. A feature of many Macintosh applications that gives the user a view of the printed output before actually printing the document.

Pantone Matching System. A system for choosing colors based on ink mixes. A color wheel provides the necessary information for choosing colors for color applications and monitors.

Parallel port. A connection to a computer through which eight or more bits are transmitted simultaneously in one direction. See also *Disk drive port.*

Parity bit. An extra bit appended to a character, whose value is used to check for errors in the transmission of data.

Paste. A command that places a copied or cut piece of information at the insertion point in a document. The Paste command retrieves from the Clipboard information that has been copied or cut.

Path. The hierarchical path to a folder, application, or document file.

Personal computer (PC). A term used to describe a computer designed for use by an individual in the home or small business setting.

Peripheral device. A unit of computer hardware, such as a printer, modem, or hard disk drive. Peripheral devices are connected to the Macintosh with cables.

Pica. A unit of measure equal to 12 points, or approximately 1/6th inch.

PICT format. A format used to store MacDraw documents. This is an object-oriented graphic format.

Pixel (picture element). A single dot or picture element on the Macintosh display.

Point. A unit of measure used to indicate size of line or type. There are 72 points in an inch.

Pointer. One of the shapes of the cursor. Usually, the pointer is an arrow pointing upward and to the left.

Port. A connection socket on the back of the Macintosh, that allows the user to connect a printer cable, hard disk drive, modem, keyboard, or mouse to the Macintosh.

Portrait printing. A page orientation in which the top of the printed image is along the short side of the paper.

PostScript. A page description programming language written by Adobe, Inc., to prepare an image for printing on a laser printer. PostScript fonts are used with PostScript-compatible printers. These fonts are widely recognized as the standard in near-typeset quality printing.

PostScript interpreter. A code built into PostScript-compatible printers that converts PostScript commands into a language the printer can process to create an image or character. See also *PostScript*.

Printer buffer. Additional memory storage for allowing the computer to send data for printing at a faster rate than the printer is capable of accepting.

Printer port. A serial port designed for the connection of a printer or modem to the computer. See also *Serial port*.

Printer server. On a network, a printer available to all network users.

Programming language. A language used to write programs for the Macintosh. There are many languages, including Object Pascal, C++, BASIC, FORTRAN, and SmallTalk/V.

Proportional spacing. In typesetting or printing, the characteristic in which wider letters take up more space than narrower letters.

Protocol. In computer telecommunications, the set of rules and procedures determining how information travels between computers. See also *Handshaking*.

Pull-down menus. A menu that appears on-screen only when accessed by the user. At all other times, only the menu titles are visible on-screen.

QuickDraw. A computer code that resides in the Macintosh's ROM and facilitates the generation of images for the screen and printer.

RAM cache. A portion of the RAM memory that can be designated to hold disk information. The RAM cache size can be set on the Control Panel by the user.

RAM disk. A program that sets aside part of the Macintosh's memory and fools the computer into recognizing this memory as a disk drive.

Random-access memory (RAM). The part of the Macintosh's memory that allows for the temporary storage of information. Because RAM is only temporary, any information left in RAM is lost when the Macintosh is turned off.

Raw data transfer rate. The fastest speed at which data is transferred to and from a disk drive to a computer.

Read-only memory (ROM). That part of the Macintosh's memory that permanently stores system information and contains the information needed to start up.

Record. A set of fields in a database. A record contains information unique to an individual or object.

Relational database. A database in which any field or record of one file can be tied to any other field or record.

Removable media. Typically, a cartridge containing magnetic media, such as a disk or tape.

ResEdit. A utility application capable of editing the resources of other applications. ResEdit allows you to customize such applications as the Finder, to change menu commands, or to modify the appearance of the trash can icon.

Resolution. The number of dots per inch (dpi) displayed on a screen or printer. The Macintosh Plus and SE screens have a resolution of 72 dpi. The LaserWriter has a resolution of 300 dpi. See also *Dots per inch*.

Restart. To reset a computer to its start-up state without turning off the power. The Macintosh has two procedures for restart: menu command and the programmer's switch. Also referred to as a warm boot.

Return key. The key located on the right side of the main keyboard. Similar to the Enter key.

Save. A command instructing the Macintosh to store information on a disk.

Save As. A command instructing the Macintosh to save the current document with a different name or file format.

Scanner. A device used to capture graphics and text for use in Mac applications. Also see *Optical character recognition*.

Scrapbook. A desk accessory used to store pictures and text. The Scrapbook is located in the System folder and can be accessed through the Apple menu. In contrast to the Clipboard, the Scrapbook permanently stores information.

Screen dump. A picture of the screen sent to a file or to a printer for printing.

Screen font. A font used for on-screen display.

Screen saver. A utility, usually in the form of a desk accessory, FKEY, INIT, or CDEV, that prevents image "burn in" by automatically filling the screen with some form of animation during a period of user inactivity.

Script. A series of commands written in the HyperTalk programming language for HyperCard.

Scroll. Scrolling is a method of moving within a document. Using the scroll bars located on the right and bottom of the screen, the user can move forward, backward, left, and right to see other portions of the document. Scroll arrows, located in the scroll bars, move the document one line or column at a time in the direction desired. The user can scroll continuously through a document by clicking and holding the mouse button with the cursor on the arrow.

SCSI port. A port located on the back of the Macintosh, that allows the user to connect a SCSI interface cable from a peripheral device to the Macintosh.

Sector. On a disk, the smallest continuous physical space for saving data. See also *Cylinder* and *Track*.

Security system. A password-protection software utility that allows the user to protect files or disks from unwanted intruders. Most security utilities allow the user to set a password and to encrypt files.

Select. An operation used to indicate where the next action should take place. To select an object, the user either clicks the icon or double-clicks the word.

Serial interface. A form of data transmission in which the bits of each character are transmitted sequentially one at a time over a single channel or wire. The most common serial interface is the RS-232 cable and connector.

Serial port. A connector on the back of the Macintosh, that allows for the connection of serial devices using a serial interface. See also *Printer port.*

Serif. A small crossbar added to a character in a font family. Fonts are described as serif fonts (with crossbars) or sans serif (without crossbars). See also *Font.*

Server. On a network, any device or computer that can be shared by all network users.

Shutdown. The process of saving all work, closing all folders and files, ejecting all disks, and turning off the power to the computer.

Signal-to-noise ratio (S/N). The ratio of the level of a received electric signal to the level of the interfering noise.

Size box. A box located in the lower right corner of the active window, that contains two overlapping smaller boxes. Clicking and dragging in the box allows the user to shrink or increase the size of the active window.

Small Computer System Interface (SCSI). A standard interface that allows the user to connect a peripheral device to the Macintosh.

Software. A generic term for computer programs. The software is used to instruct the computer hardware how to perform its work. Software can be categorized into many areas, including systems software, utilities software, and applications software.

Spooler. A printer software utility that allows the user to send multiple documents to the printer and continue working while the printer receives each spooled document for printing.

Spreadsheet. A program using a rectangular grid made up of rows and columns; the intersection of a row and a column is a cell. The spreadsheet can manipulate values, and the user can specify interrelationships among the values. The application can calculate results using formulas and macros. Advanced spreadsheets integrate graphics, charts, buttons, macros, and functions.

Stack. A HyperCard document or application.

Start-up disk. A disk that contains the System files the Macintosh needs to get started. A start-up disk must contain the System file and Finder and generally contains printer resources and desk accessories. The start-up disk is the first disk inserted into a floppy disk system. In a hard disk system, the hard disk becomes the start-up disk and automatically boots when you turn on the Macintosh power. See also *Boot*.

Start-up screen. The opening screen containing words and graphics, which appears when booting the Macintosh. Many utilities allow the user to customize the start-up screen.

String. A specified sequence of characters (a word, phrase, number).

Style. A variation of a font that can be displayed in boldface, italic, shadow, outline, underline, and strike-through styles, to name a few.

Switcher. A Macintosh System utility that allows up to four different applications to be loaded into RAM at once. Apple's MultiFinder has generally replaced the Switcher.

SYLK (Symbolic Link). A file format developed by Microsoft for spreadsheets and databases. Used for transferring data between applications.

System file. A file that contains information the Macintosh uses to operate and start up. System files cannot be opened in the usual manner, but they can be modified. The Macintosh will not operate without a System file.

System heap. The area of memory set aside for storing System information about files and resources.

System software. The files, INITs, CDEVs, utilities, desk accessories, fonts, and resources located in the System folder as provided by Apple. This is all the software the Macintosh needs to run properly. See also *Operating system*.

System Tools disk. Software disks packaged with the Macintosh, that provide the user with various tools to facilitate using the Macintosh.

Tab-delimited file. A data file in which tabs separate individual records or data elements. See also *Delimiter*.

Tear-off menu. A feature of some Macintosh applications, which allows the user to pull down a menu and keep the menu visible while working. The menu can be moved to a more convenient location in the active window.

Template. A document that is created for repeated use. Using the Save As command, the user can save each use of the template with a unique name and still maintain the original template for future use.

Terminal emulation. To make a computer act like a terminal for use with a host computer, such as a mainframe. This software allows the user to customize the Macintosh to recognize and use the control codes required to access the host's data.

Text file. A computer file that contains sequences of bits that represent characters. Also known as an ASCII file. See also *ASCII*.

Thermal-transfer printer. A dot-matrix printer that uses heated pins to melt dots of pigment on paper.

TIFF (Tagged Image File Format). A scanned image-saving format. See also *Optical character recognition*.

Title bar. The multilined bar at the top of the active window, that displays the title of the document or window.

Toner. A black powder used in laser printers and photocopy machines. The powder serves as an ink in the printing of characters and images. See also *Laser printer*.

Tool Box. A collection of drawing and painting tools found in many applications, such as HyperCard, MacDraw, and MacPaint.

Touch pad. A pointing device that is used by moving a finger over a receptive flat surface.

Touch screen. A computer screen that allows the user to touch the screen to activate computer actions and commands.

Track. A location on magnetic media, such as a disk, that stores information. Tracks are concentric circles on the surface of a disk; one or more tracks make up a cylinder of disk space. See also *Cylinder* and *Sector*.

Trackball. A pointing device similar to a mouse. The trackball is essentially an inverted mouse in which the ball is located on the top of the device, and the user moves the ball instead of the device, which remains stationary. Movement of the ball is reflected on-screen just as if a mouse were used. See also *Mouse*.

Tractor-feed printer. A printer that advances paper through the use of pins that fit into formed holes on the edges of the computer paper.

Trash can. A storage location on the desktop, used to discard documents, folders, and applications. The trash can is not emptied until the user selects Empty Trash from the Special menu or until other disk operations are performed.

Type effect. Modifications of font typefaces, which include heavy, shadow, fill, rotate, and outline effects. See also *Font, Typeface, and Typestyle*.

Typeface. The basic font family design such as Times or Monaco. See also *Font*.

Type size. The height in points of the characters in a font. See also *Font*.

Typestyle. Versions of a typeface that have become known as separate fonts. Examples include italic and boldface. See also *Font*.

UNIX. An operating system developed by Bell Laboratories for computers. UNIX permits the simultaneous running of several programs at once and is regarded as a powerful general-purpose operating system. It can easily be transferred from one computer type to another.

Upload. A procedure in which a user transfers information from his or her computer to a remote computer.

User level. The setting on a HyperCard stack, which indicates what actions a user may access. User levels can be set at browsing, typing, painting, authoring, and scripting. Each level allows greater flexibility in the tools available and the actions the user may take.

Utilities disk. A disk packaged with the Macintosh, that contains utilities used to maintain your computer system. Examples of utility programs contained on this disk are the Font/DA Mover and the Installer.

Video card. A circuit board containing the video controller and related components that connects or plugs into a computer to control the video display. See also *Video controller circuit.*

Video controller circuit. A circuit that modifies digital information to create the signal necessary for display on a computer screen. See also *Cathode ray tube (CRT).*

Video RAM. A section of RAM devoted to screen information. In the Macintosh, the video RAM stores a bit-mapped image of the screen display. See also *Random-access memory (RAM).*

Virus. A computer program that is designed to alter the normal functioning of a computer by destroying data, corrupting system files, or locking users out of the computer. In many cases, the user may be unaware that a virus exists in the system until it is too late to protect the existing data. A virus is generally passed from disk to disk and from computer to computer through disk sharing or telecommunication file transfers.

Virus-protection software. A utility software program that is designed to check existing files and applications for the presence of a virus. Some protection software identifies the strain of virus and attempts to eradicate it. Other software just informs the user that a virus exists.

Visual interface. The system of representing files, folders, and commands in symbols, such as icons, that can be easily recognized.

Volatile memory. Memory that loses its contents when the power is removed.

Window. The area on the desktop that displays information. To view a document, the user uses a window. Windows can be opened or closed as well as moved around on the desktop, resized, and scrolled through.

Word processor. An application that allows the user to enter characters, such as text, to create documents like letters, newsletters, and memos. Examples include MacWrite II, Microsoft Word, and WordPerfect.

Wordwrap. In word processing, a text-entry feature that automatically advances to the next line at the end of the line.

Wristwatch cursor. The wristwatch cursor appears on the screen when the Macintosh is busy performing some activity. During the time that the wristwatch is on the screen, the user cannot access additional commands. The wristwatch's hands turn indicating that the Macintosh is working.

Write-protect tab. A small tab or box built into a 3.5-inch disk casing to prevent accidentally erasing or overwriting disk contents. See also *Copy protected*.

Zone. An AppleTalk network in a series of interconnected networks joined by bridges.

Zoom box. The zoom box is located on the right side of the title bar. The zoom box allows the user to expand the active window to its maximum size. When the zoom box is clicked again, the window returns to its previous size.

Index

D

T

X–Z

Add a Tip to Big Mac

The Big Mac Book has tried to be all things to all Mac users, and to cover every issue of interest to anyone who uses a Macintosh. But we know that we must have missed something that you know and that you are sure should have been in this book. Well, here's your chance. You can improve this book, help your fellow Mac users, and get a little bit of fame as well. Just write out your idea, either on this page or on another sheet, and send it to

The BIG MAC Book
Que Corporation
c/o Karen Bluestein
11711 N. College Ave.
Carmel, IN 46032

If we use your idea (probably in edited or rewritten form) in the next edition of *The Big Mac Book*, we will list your name in the back of the book—along with names of other contributors. If you want, we will withhold your name or use only your initials, but we must have your name and address, or we cannot use your idea.

Thanks for helping *The Big Mac Book* get better—and maybe bigger.

YOUR NAME _____

ADDRESS _____

_____

May we credit your name? _____

Use your initials only? _____

More Computer Knowledge from Que

Lotus Software Titles

1-2-3 QueCards	21.95
1-2-3 for Business, 2nd Edition	22.95
1-2-3 QuickStart	21.95
1-2-3 Quick Reference	7.95
1-2-3 Release 2.2 Quick Reference	7.95
1-2-3 Release 2.2 QuickStart	19.95
1-2-3 Release 3 Business Applications	39.95
1-2-3 Release 3 Quick Reference	7.95
1-2-3 Release 3 QuickStart	19.95
1-2-3 Release 3 Workbook and Disk	29.95
1-2-3 Tips, Tricks, and Traps, 2nd Edition	21.95
Upgrading to 1-2-3 Release 3	14.95
Using 1-2-3, Special Edition	24.95
Using 1-2-3 Release 2.2, Special Edition	24.95
Using 1-2-3 Release 3	24.95
Using 1-2-3 Workbook and Disk, 2nd Edition	29.95
Using Lotus Magellan	21.95
Using Symphony, 2nd Edition	26.95

Database Titles

dBASE III Plus Applications Library	21.95
dBASE III Plus Handbook, 2nd Edition	22.95
dBASE III Plus Tips, Tricks, and Traps	21.95
dBASE III Plus Workbook and Disk	29.95
dBASE IV Applications Library, 2nd Edition	39.95
dBASE IV Handbook, 3rd-Edition	23.95
dBASE IV Programming Techniques	24.95
dBASE IV QueCards	21.95
dBASE IV Quick Reference	7.95
dBASE IV QuickStart	19.95
dBASE IV Tips, Tricks, and Traps, 2nd Edition	21.95
dBASE IV Workbook and Disk	29.95
dBXL and Quicksilver Programming: Beyond dBASE	24.95
R:BASE User's Guide, 3rd Edition	22.95
Using Clipper	24.95
Using DataEase	22.95
Using Reflex	19.95
Using Paradox 3	22.95

Applications Software Titles

AutoCAD Advanced Techniques	34.95
AutoCAD Quick Reference	7.95
CAD and Desktop Publishing Guide	24.95
Introduction to Business Software	14.95
PC Tools Quick Reference	7.95
Smart Tips, Tricks, and Traps	24.95
Using AutoCAD	29.95
Using Computers in Business	24.95
Using DacEasy	21.95
Using Dollars and Sense: IBM Version, 2nd Edition	19.95

Using Enable/OA	23.95
Using Excel: IBM Version	24.95
Using Generic CADD	24.95
Using Managing Your Money, 2nd Edition	19.95
Using Q&A, 2nd Edition	21.95
Using Quattro	21.95
Using Quicken	19.95
Using Smart	22.95
Using SuperCalc5, 2nd Edition	22.95

Word Processing and Desktop Publishing Titles

DisplayWrite QuickStart	19.95
Microsoft Word 5 Quick Reference	7.95
Microsoft Word 5 Tips, Tricks, and Traps: IBM Version	19.95
Using DisplayWrite 4, 2nd Edition	19.95
Using Harvard Graphics	24.95
Using Microsoft Word 5: IBM Version	21.95
Using MultiMate Advantage, 2nd Edition	19.95
Using PageMaker: IBM Version, 2nd Edition	24.95
Using PFS: First Choice	22.95
Using PFS: First Publisher	22.95
Using Professional Write	19.95
Using Sprint	21.95
Using Ventura Publisher, 2nd Edition	24.95
Using WordPerfect, 3rd Edition	21.95
Using WordPerfect 5	24.95
Using WordStar, 2nd Edition	21.95
Ventura Publisher Techniques and Applications	22.95
Ventura Publisher Tips, Tricks, and Traps	24.95
WordPerfect Macro Library	21.95
WordPerfect Power Techniques	21.95
WordPerfect QueCards	21.95
WordPerfect Quick Reference	7.95
WordPerfect QuickStart	21.95
WordPerfect Tips, Tricks, and Traps, 2nd Edition	21.95
WordPerfect 5 Workbook and Disk	29.95

Macintosh and Apple II Titles

The Big Mac Book	27.95
Excel QuickStart	19.95
Excel Tips, Tricks, and Traps	22.95
HyperCard QuickStart	21.95
Using AppleWorks, 2nd Edition	21.95
Using dBASE Mac	19.95
Using Dollars and Sense	19.95
Using Excel: Macintosh Version	22.95
Using FullWrite Professional	21.95
Using HyperCard: From Home to HyperTalk	24.95

Using Microsoft Word 4: Macintosh Version	21.95
Using Microsoft Works: Macintosh Version, 2nd Edition	21.95
Using PageMaker: Macintosh Version	24.95
Using WordPerfect: Macintosh Version	19.95

Hardware and Systems Titles

DOS QueCards	21.95
DOS Tips, Tricks, and Traps	22.95
DOS Workbook and Disk	29.95
Hard Disk Quick Reference	7.95
IBM PS/2 Handbook	21.95
Managing Your Hard Disk, 2nd Edition	22.95
MS-DOS Quick Reference	7.95
MS-DOS QuickStart	21.95
MS-DOS User's Guide, Special Edition	29.95
Networking Personal Computers, 3rd Edition	22.95
Understanding UNIX: A Conceptual Guide, 2nd Edition	21.95
Upgrading and Repairing PCs	27.95
Using Microsoft Windows	19.95
Using Novell NetWare	24.95
Using OS/2	23.95
Using PC DOS, 3rd Edition	22.95

Programming and Technical Titles

Assembly Language Quick Reference	7.95
C Programmer's Toolkit	39.95
C Programming Guide, 3rd Edition	24.95
C Quick Reference	7.95
DOS and BIOS Functions Quick Reference	7.95
DOS Programmer's Reference, 2nd Edition	27.95
Power Graphics Programming	24.95
QuickBASIC Advanced Techniques	21.95
QuickBASIC Programmer's Toolkit	39.95
QuickBASIC Quick Reference	7.95
SQL Programmer's Guide	29.95
Turbo C Programming	22.95
Turbo Pascal Advanced Techniques	22.95
Turbo Pascal Programmer's Toolkit	39.95
Turbo Pascal Quick Reference	7.95
Using Assembly Language	24.95
Using QuickBASIC 4	19.95
Using Turbo Pascal	21.95

For more information, call

1-800-428-5331

All prices subject to change without notice. Prices and charges are for domestic orders only. Non-U.S. prices might be higher.

Excel QuickStart
Developed by Que Corporation

Excel QuickStart takes readers step-by-step through basic Excel operations—including spreadsheets, databases, and graphs—with more than 100 two-page illustrations. Covers both IBM and Macintosh.

Order #957
$19.95 USA
0-88022-423-1, 400 pp.

Using Microsoft Word 4: Macintosh Version
by Bryan Pfaffenberger

Word processing expert Bryan Pfaffenberger leads users step-by-step from Word basics to the program's advanced features. Ideal for beginning and intermediate users of the Macintosh version of Microsoft Word.

Order #987
$21.95 USA
0-88022-451-7, 500 pp.

Using Microsoft Works: Macintosh Version, 2nd Edition
by Ronald Mansfield

Updated for Version 2! Covers both basic and advanced features of all four Works' applications: word processing, database, spreadsheet, and communications. Also includes expanded coverage on desktop publishing and a new section on recording and using macros.

Order #1009
$21.95 USA
0-88022-461-4, 500 pp.

Using PageMaker: Macintosh Version
by C. J. Weigand

Covering both program fundamentals and basic design principles, this informative text helps users produce professional-quality documents. Includes numerous applications and examples.

Order #949
$24.95 USA
0-88022-411-8, 600 pp.

Que Order Line: **1-800-428-5331**

Free Catalog!

Mail us this registration form today, and we'll send you a free catalog featuring Que's complete line of best-selling books.

Name of Book _____

Name _____

Title _____

Phone (____) _____

Company _____

Address _____

City _____

State _____ ZIP _____

Please check the appropriate answers:

1. Where did you buy your Que book?
   - ☐ Bookstore (name: _____)
   - ☐ Computer store (name: _____)
   - ☐ Catalog (name: _____)
   - ☐ Direct from Que
   - ☐ Other: _____

2. How many computer books do you buy a year?
   - ☐ 1 or less
   - ☐ 2-5
   - ☐ 6-10
   - ☐ More than 10

3. How many Que books do you own?
   - ☐ 1
   - ☐ 2-5
   - ☐ 6-10
   - ☐ More than 10

4. How long have you been using this software?
   - ☐ Less than 6 months
   - ☐ 6 months to 1 year
   - ☐ 1-3 years
   - ☐ More than 3 years

5. What influenced your purchase of this Que book?
   - ☐ Personal recommendation
   - ☐ Advertisement
   - ☐ In-store display
   - ☐ Price
   - ☐ Que catalog
   - ☐ Que mailing
   - ☐ Que's reputation
   - ☐ Other: _____

6. How would you rate the overall content of the book?
   - ☐ Very good
   - ☐ Good
   - ☐ Satisfactory
   - ☐ Poor

7. What do you like *best* about this Que book?

   _____

   _____

8. What do you like *least* about this Que book?

   _____

   _____

9. Did you buy this book with your personal funds?
   - ☐ Yes   ☐ No

10. Please feel free to list any other comments you may have about this Que book.

    _____

    _____

    _____

Que

Order Your Que Books Today!

Name _____

Title _____

Company _____

City _____

State _____ ZIP _____

Phone No. (____) _____

Method of Payment:

Check ☐   (Please enclose in envelope.)

Charge My: VISA ☐   MasterCard ☐

American Express ☐

Charge # _____

Expiration Date _____

Order No.	Title	Qty.	Price	Total

You can **FAX** your order to **1-317-573-2583**. Or call **1-800-428-5331, ext. ORDR** to order direct.

Please add $2.50 per title for shipping and handling.

Subtotal _____

Shipping & Handling _____

Total _____

Que

NO POSTAGE
NECESSARY
IF MAILED
IN THE
UNITED STATES

BUSINESS REPLY MAIL
First Class Permit No. 9918   Indianapolis, IN

Postage will be paid by addressee

11711 N. College
Carmel, IN 46032

NO POSTAGE
NECESSARY
IF MAILED
IN THE
UNITED STATES

BUSINESS REPLY MAIL
First Class Permit No. 9918   Indianapolis, IN

Postage will be paid by addressee

11711 N. College
Carmel, IN 46032